The World
around the
Old Testament

The World around the Old Testament

THE PEOPLE AND PLACES OF THE ANCIENT NEAR EAST

Edited by
Bill T. Arnold
AND Brent A. Strawn

Baker Academic
a division of Baker Publishing Group
Grand Rapids, Michigan

© 2016 by Bill T. Arnold and Brent A. Strawn

Published by Baker Academic
a division of Baker Publishing Group
P.O. Box 6287, Grand Rapids, MI 49516-6287
www.bakeracademic.com

Paperback edition published 2019
ISBN 978-1-5409-6231-7

Printed in the United States of America

All rights reserved. No part of this publication may be reproduced, stored in a retrieval system, or transmitted in any form or by any means—for example, electronic, photocopy, recording—without the prior written permission of the publisher. The only exception is brief quotations in printed reviews.

The Library of Congress has cataloged the hardcover edition as follows:
Names: Arnold, Bill T., editor. | Strawn, Brent A., editor.
Title: The world around the Old Testament : the people and places of the ancient Near East / edited by Bill T. Arnold and Brent A. Strawn.
Description: Grand Rapids : Baker Academic, 2016. | Includes bibliographical references and index.
Identifiers: LCCN 2016025103 | ISBN 9780801039188 (cloth)
Subjects: LCSH: Middle East—History—To 622. | Middle East—History, Local. | Bible. Old Testament—History of contemporary events.
Classification: LCC DS62.2 .W67 2016 | DDC 221.9/1—dc23
LC record available at https://lccn.loc.gov/2016025103

Unless indicated otherwise, Scripture quotations are from the New Revised Standard Version of the Bible, copyright © 1989 National Council of the Churches of Christ in the United States of America. Used by permission. All rights reserved.

Scripture translations labeled AT are those of the author.

In keeping with biblical principles of creation stewardship, Baker Publishing Group advocates the responsible use of our natural resources. As a member of the Green Press Initiative, our company uses recycled paper when possible. The text paper of this book is composed in part of post-consumer waste.

Walter Burkert (1931–2015)
in memoriam

Contents

List of Illustrations   ix

Preface   xiii

Introduction   xv
Bill T. Arnold and Brent A. Strawn

List of Contributors   xix

Abbreviations   xxi

1. The Amorites   1
   Daniel E. Fleming

2. Assyria and the Assyrians   31
   Christopher B. Hays with Peter Machinist

3. Babylonia and the Babylonians   107
   David S. Vanderhooft

4. Ugarit and the Ugaritians   139
   Mark S. Smith

5. Egypt and the Egyptians   169
   Joel M. LeMon

6. The Hittites and the Hurrians   197
   Billie Jean Collins

7. Aram and the Arameans   229
   K. Lawson Younger Jr.

8. Phoenicia and the Phoenicians   267
   Christopher A. Rollston

9. Transjordan: The Ammonites, Moabites, and Edomites   309
   Joel S. Burnett

10. Philistia and the Philistines   353
    Carl S. Ehrlich

11. Persia and the Persians   379
    Pierre Briant

12. Arabia and the Arabians   417
    David F. Graf

13. Greece and the Greeks   467
    Walter Burkert†

Index of Authors   501

Index of Scripture and Other Ancient Sources   511

Index of Subjects   519

Illustrations

Map: The Ancient Near East   xxvii

2.1 Map: The Assyrian Empire   38

2.2 Black Obelisk of Shalmaneser III   46

2.3 Statue of Assurnasirpal II   78

2.4 Relief of a dying lion   79

2.5 The Balawat Gates   80

2.6 Judean archer on black stone seal   81

2.7 Assyrian archers on Lachish relief   81

3.1 Map: Babylonia   108

3.2 Shitti-Marduk *kudurru* image   116

3.3 Sun-God Tablet   123

3.4 Mushhushu dragon on the Ishtar Gate   129

3.5 Site map of Babylon   130

4.1 Site map of Ugarit   140

4.2 Merenptah Stela   142

4.3 Ruins of ancient Ugarit   144

4.4 Bronze figurine of Baal found at Ras Shamra   152

4.5 Baal with thunderbolt   158

5.1 Map: Egypt   170

5.2 Table: Periods of Egyptian History   171

5.3 Akhenaten, Nefertiti, and three daughters beneath the Aten   176

5.4 Relief from the Mortuary Temple of Ramesses III   181

5.5 Bronze statuette of Taharqo   186

5.6 Ivory plaque from Megiddo   192

5.7 Ivory inlay of Isis and Nephthys   193

5.8 Tomb painting from Abd el-Qurna   194

5.9 Judean *lmlk* seals   195

6.1 Map: Anatolia   198

6.2 Plan of the Hittite capital at Hattusa   199

6.3 Table: The Kings of the Hittites   200–201

6.4 Relief of Tudhaliya IV   212

6.5 Section of Suppiluliuma II's Südburg inscription   214

6.6 Reliefs on the rock outcropping at Yazılıkaya   219

7.1 Map: The Aramean kingdoms   237

7.2 Relief of Assurnasirpal II   247

7.3 Tell Dan Stela   250

7.4 Katumuwa Inscription   258

7.5 Hadad Statue   260

8.1 Map: Phoenicia   269

8.2 Table: Correspondence of West Semitic Consonants   281

8.3 Table: *Qal* Perfect and Imperfect   284

8.4 Azarbaʻal Inscription   285

8.5 Ahiram Sarcophagus Inscription   286

8.6 Yehimilk Inscription   287

Illustrations

8.7 Shipitba'al Inscription 289

8.8 Nora Inscription 293

8.9 The Kition Bowl 294

9.1 Map: Transjordan 310

9.2 Excavation of Iron I compound at Tall Abu Kharaz 314

9.3 Table: Kings of Iron Age Transjordan Appearing in Epigraphic Texts 321

9.4 Remains of Iron II fortress at Lahun 324

9.5 Fortification wall of copper-processing center at Khirbat en-Nahas 332

9.6 Iron II remains at Umm al-Biyara 334

9.7 Karak Inscription fragment 341

9.8 Basalt statue of an Ammonite king 344

9.9 Terra-cotta bull statue from Khirbat Ataruz 349

10.1 Map: The Philistine plain 354

10.2 Ekron Inscription 372

10.3 Tell eṣ-Ṣafi 374

11.1 Map: The Achaemenid Empire 380

11.2 Audience relief at Persepolis 384

11.3 Behistun relief 385

11.4 Cyrus's tomb 386

11.5 Irrigation canal in the gardens of Pasargadae 388

11.6 Plan of Susa 389

11.7 Plan of Persepolis 390

11.8 Elamite delegation on the "tribute" reliefs at Persepolis 391

11.9 Ostracon of the hunt 396

11.10 Two subject peoples on the statue of Darius 400

11.11 Saqqara stela 404

11.12 Audience scene from Daskyleion   406
11.13 Persian king on painted beam from Tatarlı   408
11.14 Meydancıkkale reliefs   409
11.15 Taymā' rider   410
12.1 Map: Arabia   418
12.2 Al-Jawf, the fortress of Qasr Mārid at Dumah   435
12.3 Palace of Qasr al-Hamra at Taymā'   440
12.4 Taymanite text from the Mahaijah region   443
12.5 Mantar Bani 'Atiya   445
12.6 Close-up of Mantar Bani 'Atiya   446
12.7 Dedan   448
12.8 The necropolis at Khurayba in Dedan   449
13.1 Map: Greece   468
13.2 Bronze tympanon from Ida   480
13.3 *Piraeus Apollo* bronze   485
13.4 Alexander the Great   494

Preface

We wish to express our gratuide to our academic institutions, Asbury Theological Seminary and the Candler School of Theology of Emory University, for being places that make time for scholarly work, including the important but often behind-the-scenes work of editing. We lift up for special recognition the gifted assistance of Henry Huberty, who did preliminary screening of each essay and offered invaluable comments, and also thank T. Collin Cornell, who was instrumental in getting the project finished.

Jim Kinney and the good people of Baker Academic have been helpful throughout the project. As anyone who has edited knows, editorial work, especially on a complicated project like this one, can be a protracted affair, and not without its fair share of difficulties. Our labors have been gratifying nevertheless, not least because we have long schemed about a joint project that would allow us to work together more regularly. Jim and his team at Baker provided us with exactly such a project and eased our labor in key ways, making the entire venture that much better. Among many other things, we thank Baker for funding the work of Stephen Germany, who translated Professor Briant's essay on Persia and the Persians.

Our deepest gratitude goes to our stellar roster of contributors. It is not always easy to get a project like this off the ground; it is even harder to bring it to completion. We thank the contributors who were on time with their contributions for their punctuality and for their extreme patience while we waited for those that arrived later. We are also thankful to colleagues who stepped in at later stages to fill in some missing pieces or even to pen essays that were originally assigned to someone else but, for whatever reason, could not be completed. We thank each of our contributors for their patience (often strained), good humor, and most of all for their excellent work. The volume's delays are no doubt due in part to the fact that the contributors are world-class scholars, each with multiple projects and very busy professional lives. Despite a few unfortunate interruptions in the production schedule, we believe the volume is much better for the wait—we hope that the authors themselves and all who read their work will agree.

A final word: one of our contributors, the eminent classicist Walter Burkert, died as the volume was about to go to press. It seemed only right to dedicate the volume to his memory given all that he did to help us better understand the ancient world, including that around the Old Testament.

Bill T. Arnold
Lexington, KY

Brent A. Strawn
Atlanta, GA

Introduction

Bill T. Arnold and Brent A. Strawn

Perhaps second only to "What do you do (for a living)?," the question "Where are you from?" must be the most frequent inquiry when people meet for the first time. When two people are becoming acquainted, the request to learn someone's hometown or homeland reflects the belief that such knowledge is not only *interesting* information—a conversation starter, for instance—but also somehow *fundamental*. The point of origin is reckoned to be determinative, illustrative, even explanatory for who a person is now, in this particular moment of social exchange. Most of us assume as much, even if, and quite apart from the fact that, the person in question may be *from* a very different place presently or at least *be* a quite different person than the one they were whenever they hailed from wherever they hailed from originally.

This question of origin—where one is from—can be asked not only of people, of course, but of other subjects, including texts and, in the case of the book before you, even the Bible itself, or, still more specifically for present purposes, the Old Testament. In no small way the thirteen essays gathered here tell the story of where the Old Testament is from. They do that, however, in an oblique way. The essays deal with the world *surrounding* the Old Testament, whence comes the volume's name: *The World around the Old Testament* (*WAOT*). Included here, then, are essays on the main regions and cultural groups that lived around ancient Israel, which gave us the Old Testament. Such books have been produced before, with volumes like *Peoples of Old Testament Times* and *Peoples of the Old Testament World* serving in their day as classic textbooks.[1] Like those books, the present volume has essays on regions and groups from parts north, south, east, and west of ancient Israel/Palestine. If anything, we hope that WAOT is even more helpful in including some topics that have not always been included in works of this kind—specifically Arabia and Greece. The contributors and editors have done their best to make WAOT as up-to-date as possible and at the same time user-friendly so as to maximize its utility whether in a classroom or a reading room.

Two further brief points of introduction are in order—one concerns the structure of what is found in WAOT, and the other concerns what will not be found here.

1. As indicated already by its title, WAOT is not primarily about ancient Israel/Palestine or the Old Testament proper, so the essays are not overly oriented toward possible contacts with either. This caveat duly entered, each essay pays particular attention to that period (or those periods) that are most important for or pertinent to biblical studies. Within each essay, the reader may expect to find information on four important foci: (1) a general overview of the history and culture of the region or people group in view in that chapter; (2) special attention to ancient Near Eastern history from the Late Bronze Age to the end of the Persian Period (ca. 1550–332 BCE) as the time frame most apposite to Israelite literature and history; (3) a discussion of important items beyond political history proper, including religion, the arts, literature, and the like; and (4) remarks about the relevance of the region or people group for ancient Israel and/or the Old Testament. To be sure, these four foci are not always laid out by number in precisely this order, but we have been at pains to make sure that each focus is addressed in a way suitable to the topic of each essay included in WAOT. In this way, each chapter is a study of its primary subject matter—first and foremost in its own right—but is also not naïve about the importance of these areas and groups for the study of the Old Testament proper.

2. What the reader will *not* find in WAOT is a separate chapter on Canaan and the Canaanites. Although it is possible to make a case that such an essay should be included here, we believe that WAOT can proceed without it if only because—quite apart from the deeply vexed question of the Canaanite origins of ancient Israel—the land of Canaan is where the Israelites lived and so, technically, is not *around* the Old Testament but the place where Israel was *from*, though the essays gathered here show how it is not only

---

1. D. J. Wiseman, ed., *Peoples of Old Testament Times* (Oxford: Oxford University Press, 1973); Alfred J. Hoerth, Gerald L. Mattingly, and Edwin M. Yamauchi, eds., *Peoples of the Old Testament World* (Grand Rapids: Baker, 1994).

from Canaan; it is also, if not equally, from other parts—those parts around the Old Testament.

This brings us full circle to where we started. "Where are you from?" is the question we often ask of new acquaintances. "Well, I'm originally from such-and-such," they reply, "but I now live in such-and-such." Where a person begins, initially, originally—where they are *from*—may be important, but it is rarely the last word. So also with the Old Testament. It is "from" somewhere—or rather, "somewhere*s*" (plural)—the places and regions that surround(ed) it and that are discussed in *WAOT*, but it is equally true that the Old Testament now lives most of its days elsewhere and so it may "be" a different thing than it once was. Indeed, it does not seem to be stretching things too far to say that the history of biblical interpretation is in many ways the story of the Old Testament (and the New) moving to different places—many of which are far removed from the ancient Near East and the ancient Mediterranean. As the Bible traveled these miles and millennia, it has come to mean and come to be many different things. This is a crucial point and quite true, but it is equally true that points of origin remain seminal. Our standard, go-to question with new acquaintances reveals that origins are not only important, they are also, sometimes at least, definitive, determinative, or otherwise explanatory. And so, despite the many different places where the Old Testament now resides, and despite what it has come to be and to mean as a result, we still think that where it originally hailed from is of vital importance, not only for back then, initially or formerly, but also for here and now. In the end, then, we hope the essays in this volume shed significant light on where the Old Testament is "from" and also (and as a result) what it "is," even for today.

Contributors

Pierre Briant
Collège de France

Walter Burkert†
University of Zurich

Joel S. Burnett
Baylor University

Billie Jean Collins
Emory University

Carl S. Ehrlich
York University

Daniel E. Fleming
New York University

David F. Graf
University of Miami

Christopher B. Hays
Fuller Theological Seminary

Joel M. LeMon
Emory University

Peter Machinist
Harvard University

Christopher A. Rollston
George Washington University

Mark S. Smith
Princeton Theological Seminary

David S. Vanderhooft
Boston College

K. Lawson Younger Jr.
Trinity Evangelical Divinity School

Abbreviations

General

Akk.	Akkadian	Heb.	Hebrew
Ann.	*Annal/Annalen* (German); annal/annals	KAJ	Khirbet al-Jariyeh
		KEN	Khirbet en-Nahas
Aram.	Aramaic	km.	kilometers
BCE	Before the Common Era	lih.	Lihyanite texts
c.	century	lit.	literally
ca.	*circa*, about, approximately	m.	meter(s)
CE	Common Era	masc.	masculine
col(s).	column(s)	mi.	mile(s)
d.	died	n.	note
ed.	edition; edited by; editor	obv.	obverse (front) of a tablet
Eng.	English	OP	Old Persian
esp.	especially	pt.	part
fem.	feminine	r.	reigned
fig(s).	figure(s)	repr.	reprint(ed)
fl.	*floruit*, flourished	rev.	reverse of a tablet; revised, revised by
Fr.	Fragment		
ft.	feet	s.v.	*sub verbo*, under the word
Gk.	Greek	trans.	translated by; translator
ha.	hectare(s)	vol.	volume

Sigla of Texts, Tablets, and Other Objects

A	Objects in the Louvre Museum, Paris
ÄM	Objects in the Ägyptisches Museum, Berlin
BM	Objects in the British Museum, London

EA	El-Amarna tablets. According to the edition of Jørgen A. Knudtzon. *Die el-Amarna-Tafeln*. Leipzig: Hinrichs, 1908–15. Repr., Aalen: Zeller, 1964. Continued in Anson F. Rainey, *El-Amarna Tablets, 359–379*. 2nd rev. ed. Kevelaer: Butzon & Bercker, 1978.
LXX	Septuagint (the Greek Old Testament)
M.	Tablets from Mari
MI	Mesha Stela Inscription
MT	Masoretic Text (of the Hebrew Bible)
ND	Tablets from the British excavations at Nimrud (Kalah)
PF	Texts published in: Hallock, Richard T. *Persepolis Fortification Tablets*. OIP 92. Chicago: University of Chicago Press, 1969.
PFa	Texts published in: Hallock, Richard T. "Selected Fortification Texts." *CDAFI* 8 (1978): 109–36.
PT	Texts published in: Cameron, George G. *Persepolis Treasury Tablets*. OIP 65. Chicago: University of Chicago Press, 1948.
RIH	Ras Ibn Hani
RS	Ras Shamra

Books, Journals, and Series

AAE	*Arabian Archaeology and Epigraphy*
AASOR	Annual of the American Schools of Oriental Research
ÄAT	Ägypten und Altes Testament
AB	Anchor Bible
ABD	*Anchor Bible Dictionary*. Edited by David Noel Freedman. 6 vols. New York: Doubleday, 1992.
ABL	*Assyrian and Babylonian Letters Belonging to the Kouyunjik Collections of the British Museum*. Edited by Robert F. Harper. 14 vols. Chicago: University of Chicago Press, 1892–1914.
ABRL	Anchor Bible Reference Library
ABS	Archaeology and Biblical Studies
AchHist	Achaemenid History
ADAJ	*Annual of the Department of Antiquities of Jordan*
ADPV	Abhandlungen des Deutschen Palästina-Vereins
AfO	*Archiv für Orientforschung*
AfOB	Archiv für Orientforschung: Beiheft
AHw	*Akkadisches Handwörterbuch*. Wolfram von Soden. 3 vols. Wiesbaden, 1965–81.
AJP	*American Journal of Philology*
ALASP	Abhandlungen zur Literatur Alt-Syrien-Palästinas und Mesopotamiens
ANEM	Ancient Near East Monographs / Monografías sobre el Antiguo Cercano Oriente
ANESSup	Ancient Near Eastern Studies Supplement Series
ANET	*Ancient Near Eastern Texts Relating to the Old Testament*. Edited by James B. Pritchard. 3rd ed. Princeton: Princeton University Press, 1969.
AnOr	Analecta Orientalia

AnSt	*Anatolian Studies*
AOAT	Alter Orient und Altes Testament
AoF	Altorientalische Forschungen
AOS	American Oriental Series
ARAB	*Ancient Records of Assyria and Babylonia.* Daniel David Luckenbill. 2 vols. Chicago: University of Chicago Press, 1926–27. Repr., New York: Greenwood, 1968.
ARM	Archives Royales de Mari
ARTA	*Achaemenid Research on Texts and Archaeology*
AS	Assyriological Studies
AuOr	*Aula Orientalis*
AUSS	*Andrews University Seminary Studies*
BA	*Biblical Archaeologist*
BAR	*Biblical Archaeology Review*
BARIS	BAR (British Archaeological Reports) International Series
BASOR	*Bulletin of the American Schools of Oriental Research*
BASORSup	Bulletin of the American Schools of Oriental Research Supplements
BHAch 1	"Bulletin d'histoire achéménide (*BHAch*) I." Pierre Briant. In *Recherches récentes sur l'empire achéménide*, Topoi: Orient-Occident Supplément 1, edited by J. Andreau, M.-F. Boussac, et al., 5–125. Lyon: Topoi; Paris: de Boccard, 1997.
BHAch 2	*Bulletin d'histoire achéménide II.* Pierre Briant. Persika 1. Paris: Thotm éditions, 2001.
BIAUL	*Bulletin of the Institute of Archaeology of the University of London*
BJRL	*Bulletin of the John Rylands University Library of Manchester*
BN	*Biblische Notizen*
BO	*Bibliotheca Orientalis*
BZAW	Beihefte zur Zeitschrift für die alttestamentliche Wissenschaft
CAD	*The Assyrian Dictionary of the Oriental Institute of the University of Chicago.* Chicago: Oriental Institute of the University of Chicago, 1956–2006.
CAI	*A Corpus of Ammonite Inscriptions.* Walter E. Aufrecht. 2nd ed. Lewiston, NY: Edwin Mellen, forthcoming.
CANE	*Civilizations of the Ancient Near East.* Edited by Jack M. Sasson. 4 vols. New York, 1995. Repr. in 2 vols. Peabody, MA: Hendrickson, 2006.
CBQMS	Catholic Biblical Quarterly Monograph Series
CDAFI	*Cahiers de la Délégation Archéologique Française en Iran*
CDOG	Colloquien der Deutschen Orient-Gesellschaft
CHANE	Culture and History of the Ancient Near East
CIS	*Corpus Inscriptionum Semiticarum.* Paris, 1881–.
CM	Cuneiform Monographs
COS	*The Context of Scripture.* Edited by William W. Hallo. 3 vols. Leiden: Brill, 1997–2002.
CRAI	Comptes rendus de l'Académie des inscriptions et belles-lettres
CT	*Cuneiform Texts from Babylonian Tablets in the British Museum*
CTH	*Catalogue des textes hittites.* Emmanuel Laroche. Paris: Klincksieck, 1971.
CUSAS	Cornell University Studies in Assyriology and Sumerology

DBH	Dresdner Beiträge zur Hethitologie
DBSup	*Dictionnaire de la Bible: Supplément.* Edited by Louis Pirot and André Robert. Paris: Letouzey et Ané, 1928–.
DDD	*Dictionary of Deities and Demons in the Bible.* Edited by Karel van der Toorn, Bob Becking, and Pieter W. van der Horst. Leiden: Brill, 1995. 2nd rev. ed. Grand Rapids: Eerdmans, 1999.
DJD	Discoveries in the Judaean Desert
EAEHL	*Encyclopedia of Archaeological Excavations in the Holy Land.* Edited by Michael Avi-Yonah. 4 vols. Jerusalem: Israel Exploration Society and Massada Press, 1975.
EFAH	Epigraphische Forschungen auf der Arabischen Halbinsel
EI	*Encyclopedia of Islam.* Edited by Clifford E. Bosworth et al. 2nd ed. 12 vols. Leiden: Brill, 1954–2005.
ErIsr	*Eretz-Israel*
FAT	Forschungen zum Alten Testament
FM	*Florilegium marianum*
FRLANT	Forschungen zur Religion und Literatur des Alten und Neuen Testaments
GAT	Grundrisse zum Alten Testament
GMTR	Guides to the Mesopotamian Textual Record
HBS	Herders Biblische Studien
HdO	Handbuch der Orientalistik
HDT	*Hittite Diplomatic Texts.* Edited by Gary Beckman. 2nd ed. WAW 7. Atlanta: Scholars Press, 1999.
HSAO	Heidelberger Studien zum Alten Orient
HSM	Harvard Semitic Monographs
HSS	Harvard Semitic Studies
HTAT	*Historisches Textbuch zum Alten Testament.* Manfred Weippert. GAT 10. Göttingen: Vandenhoeck & Ruprecht, 2010.
HTR	*Harvard Theological Review*
HTS	Harvard Theological Studies
HUCA	*Hebrew Union College Annual*
HUS	*Handbook of Ugaritic Studies.* Edited by Wilfred G. E. Watson and Nicholas Wyatt. HdO I/39. Leiden: Brill, 1999.
ICS	*Illinois Classical Studies*
IEJ	*Israel Exploration Journal*
IOS	*Israel Oriental Studies*
IstMitt	*Istanbuler Mitteilungen*
JAEI	*Journal of Ancient Egyptian Interconnections*
JANER	*Journal of Ancient Near Eastern Religions*
JANES	*Journal of the Ancient Near Eastern Society*
JAOS	*Journal of the American Oriental Society*
JAS	*Journal of Archaeological Science*
JASP	*Jutland Archaeological Society Publications*
JCS	*Journal of Cuneiform Studies*
JCSMS	*Journal of the Canadian Society of Mesopotamian Studies*
JEA	*Journal of Egyptian Archaeology*

JNES	Journal of Near Eastern Studies
JNSL	Journal of Northwest Semitic Languages
JS	Jaussen, Antonin, and R. Savigniac. *Mission archéologique en Arabie*. 3 vols. Paris: Leroux, 1909–11.
JSOT	Journal for the Study of the Old Testament
JSOTSup	Journal for the Study of the Old Testament Supplement Series
JSS	Journal of Semitic Studies
JSSSup	Journal of Semitic Studies Supplements
KAI	*Kanaanäische und aramäische Inschriften*. Herbert Donner and Wolfgang Röllig. 2nd ed. Wiesbaden: Harrassowitz, 1966–69.
KBo	*Keilschrifttexte aus Boghazköi*. Leipzig: Hinrichs, 1916–23; Berlin: Gebr. Mann, 1954–.
KTU	*Die keilalphabetischen Texte aus Ugarit*. Edited by Manfred Dietrich, Oswald Loretz, and Joaquín Sanmartín. Münster: Ugarit-Verlag, 2013. 3rd enl. ed. of *KTU: The Cuneiform Alphabetic Texts from Ugarit, Ras Ibn Hani, and Other Places*. Edited by Manfred Dietrich, Oswald Loretz, and Joaquín Sanmartín. Münster: Ugarit-Verlag, 1995 (= *CTU*).
KUB	*Keilschrifturkunden aus Boghazköi*. Berlin: Akademie, 1921–.
LAOS	Leipziger altorientalistische Studien
LAPO	Littératures anciennes du Proche-Orient
LCL	Loeb Classical Library
LHBOTS	The Library of Hebrew Bible/Old Testament Studies
MARI	*Mari: Annales de recherches interdisciplinaires*
MDAI	*Mitteilungen des Deutschen archäologischen Instituts*
NABU	*Nouvelles assyriologiques brèves et utilitaires*
NCBC	New Cambridge Bible Commentary
NEA	Near Eastern Archaeology
NEAEHL	*The New Encyclopedia of Archaeological Excavations in the Holy Land*. Edited by Ephraim Stern. 4 vols. Jerusalem: Israel Exploration Society & Carta; New York: Simon & Schuster, 1993.
NEASB	Near East Archaeological Society Bulletin
OBO	Orbis Biblicus et Orientalis
OBO.SA	Orbis Biblicus et Orientalis, Series Archaeologica
OeO	Oriens et Occidens
OIP	Oriental Institute Publications
OIS	Oriental Institute Seminars
OLA	Orientalia Lovaniensia Analecta
Or	*Orientalia*
PEQ	Palestine Exploration Quarterly
PIHANS	Publications de l'Institut historique-archéologique néerlandais de Stamboul
PJBR	Polish Journal of Biblical Research
PNA	*The Prosopography of the Neo-Assyrian Empire*. Edited by Karen Radner and Heather Baker. Helsinki: Neo-Assyrian Text Corpus Project, 1998–2011.
PRU	*Le palais royal d'Ugarit*
PSAS	Proceedings of the Seminar for Arabian Studies

RA	*Revue d'assyriologie et d'archéologie orientale*
RB	*Revue biblique*
RBS	Resources for Biblical Study
RES	*Répertoire d'épigraphie sémitique*
RevQ	*Revue de Qumran*
RGRW	Religions in the Graeco-Roman World
RGTC	Répertoire géographique des textes cunéiformes
RIMA	The Royal Inscriptions of Mesopotamia, Assyrian Periods
RIMB	The Royal Inscriptions of Mesopotamia, Babylonian Periods
RINAP	Royal Inscriptions of the Neo-Assyrian Period
R*l*A	*Reallexikon der Assyriologie*. Edited by Erich Ebeling et al. Berlin: de Gruyter, 1928–.
RO	*Rocznik Orientalistyczny*
RSO	Ras Shamra-Ougarit
SAA	State Archives of Assyria
SAAB	*State Archives of Assyria Bulletin*
SAAS	State Archives of Assyria Studies
SAOC	Studies in Ancient Oriental Civilizations
SBLDS	Society of Biblical Literature Dissertation Series
SBLMS	Society of Biblical Literature Monograph Series
SEG	Supplementum epigraphicum graecum
Sem	*Semitica*
SHAJ	Studies in the History and Archaeology of Jordan
SHCANE	Studies in the History and Culture of the Ancient Near East
SMEA	*Studi Micenei ed Egeo-Anatolici*
StBoT	Studien zu den Boğazköy-Texten
TA	*Tel Aviv*
TCRPOGA	Travaux du Centre de Recherche sur le Proche-Orient et la Grèce Antiques
TMOM	Travaux de la Maison de l'Orient et de la Méditerranée
TMRG	Travaux de la Maison René-Ginouvès
Transeu	*Transeuphratène*
TZ	*Theologische Zeitschrift*
UF	*Ugarit-Forschungen*
VAB	Vorderasiatische Bibliothek
VDI	*Vestnik drevnej istorii*
VT	*Vetus Testamentum*
VTSup	Supplements to Vetus Testamentum
WAW	Writings from the Ancient World
WMANT	Wissenschaftliche Monographien zum Alten und Neuen Testament
WO	*Die Welt des Orients*
YOS	Yale Oriental Series, Texts
ZA	*Zeitschrift für Assyriologie*
ZAVA	*Zeitschrift für Assyriologie und Vorderasiatische Archäologie*
ZAW	*Zeitschrift für die alttestamentliche Wissenschaft*
ZDMG	*Zeitschrift der deutschen morgenländischen Gesellschaft*
ZDPV	*Zeitschrift des deutschen Palästina-Vereins*

The Ancient Near East

1

The Amorites

Daniel E. Fleming

According to the Bible, Israel's origins had to be explained at two different levels: as a people established in their own land by Moses and Joshua, and as a family reaching back to Abraham, Isaac, and Jacob. In both cases, the Bible presents Israel as outsiders. Their forebears were not among the original inhabitants of the southern Levant, where they would later be established as ancient Israel. Abraham and company had to move south from Haran and before that from Babylonian Ur. Israel as a mass entered the land from the desert after living in Egypt for generations.

A tradition fixed on the notion of Israel's foreignness to their own land naturally raises questions of who was replaced and how. The land as a whole would come to be called Canaan (e.g., Gen. 12:5), but the various stories of origin make reference to the prior inhabitants by various names. Israel is not portrayed as displacing a single entity, whether as a kingdom or as a people with one identity. Rather, the landscape consisted of many freestanding domains, often associated with town centers, as in the list of defeated kings in Joshua 12. For the biblical writers, these local political identities were embedded in larger group identities that were not in themselves political. Yahweh's promise to Moses of a land flowing with milk and honey is defined by a list of such populations: Canaanites, Hittites, Amorites, Perizzites, Hivites, and Jebusites (Exod. 3:8). Even the Philistines, whom Israel encounters as a perennial enemy in the time of Saul and David, are regarded as another such population, ruled by five lords from separate town centers (1 Sam. 6:17).

These prior populations of Israel's land represent a fascinating collection of disparate names, some completely unknown outside the Bible and others familiar but with ancient associations that leave them seeming out of place in the Bible. For example, the Hittites are known first of all from their late second-millennium kingdom based in Anatolia, and even their early first-millennium namesakes are found in the northern reaches of Syria once controlled by the older kingdom.[1] Canaan and the Canaanites at least belong to the lands that the Bible defines as Israelite, though the terminology comes likewise from the late second millennium.[2] Among the names from lists such as the one in Exodus 3, the Amorites more resemble the Hittites—familiar yet out of place. Like the Canaanites and the Hittites, the Amorites belong first of all to the Bronze Age of the third and second millennia BCE, and their presence in the Bible represents some kind of survival from a much older identity. Also like the Hittites, the Amorites belonged first of all to lands far north of Israel in Syria and beyond, so that the presence of the name so far south is surprising and intriguing.

The significance of the Amorites for readers of the Bible, however, goes beyond their inclusion among the peoples supplanted by Israel. Historians of the larger Near East have grappled for generations with this category from early Mesopotamian cuneiform, where the rulers of the last Sumerian kingdom, which was based at Ur, somehow identified them as a key enemy.[3]

1. For recent discussion of the second-millennium Hittite kingdom, see Trevor Bryce, *The Kingdom of the Hittites* (Oxford: Oxford University Press, 2005); and for the first-millennium Syrian realms that continued this cultural stream, see Bryce, *The World of the Neo-Hittite Kingdoms: A Political and Military History* (Oxford: Oxford University Press, 2012).

2. The extended treatment by Niels Peter Lemche proposes a controversial interpretation that limits application of the term in a way that is not broadly accepted, yet it nevertheless provides a basic idea of the sources (*The Canaanites and Their Land: The Tradition of the Canaanites* [Sheffield, UK: Sheffield Academic, 1991]).

3. The essential study was long that of Giorgio Buccellati, *The Amorites of the Ur III Period* (Naples: Istituto Orientale di Napoli, 1966). This is now dated, as interpretation of ancient social and political structures has evolved. Now the essential recent discussions are found in Anne Porter, "You Say Potato, I Say . . : Typology, Chronology, and the Origin of the Amorites," in *Sociétés humaines et changement climatique à la fin du troisième millénaire: Une crise a-t-elle eu lieu en Haute-Mésopotamie?*, ed. C. Marro and C. Kuzucuoglu (Paris: de Boccard, 2007), 69–115; Porter, "Tax and Tribulation, or Who Were the Amorrites?," in *Mobile Pastoralism and the Formation of Near Eastern Civilizations: Weaving Together Society* (Cambridge: Cambridge University Press, 2012), 251–325; and Piotr Michalowski, "The Amorites in Ur III Times," in *The Correspondence of the Kings of Ur: An Epistolary History of an Ancient Mesopotamian*

In downstream Mesopotamia, now southeastern Iraq, this Sumerian fear of Amorite attack was followed by the actual defeat of Ur (ca. 2000 BCE) and the realignment of regional power in less centralized terms. Most local rulers in the succeeding period bore names from a Semitic type not familiar to the region's own Akkadian language, and these names suggested continuity with western Semitic dialects. If the Amorites were "western" from a Sumerian perspective, the non-Akkadian names could be considered "Amorite" and regarded as evidence of a major social shift, reflecting a new Amorite age. Archives from the early second millennium could be treated as evidence for this Amorite world, whether in Babylon's domain in south-central Iraq or in the rich royal correspondence from Mari, upstream.[4]

Meanwhile, the transformations of the social landscape across Syria and Mesopotamia coincided roughly with changes in the Levant, including the southern regions later occupied by Israel and Judah. As biblical scholars sought a background for Genesis and historians weighed the possible usefulness of biblical lore for understanding Israelite origins, the Amorites of the north offered a potential framework. If large-scale migrations of Amorites led to a complete recasting of power in Syria and Mesopotamia, the same populations and pattern could account for the rise of new cities and societies in the Middle Bronze Age Levant. Abraham's journey from Ur to Haran to "the land of Canaan" (Gen. 11:31) could be understood as a narrative reflection of this historical reality. This application of a northern and Mesopotamian phenomenon to the Levant would also explain how the Amorite name came to be included in the biblical lists of prior peoples. The whole package placed the Amorites on the map of essential peoples of interest for the world around the Bible.[5]

Today, almost every component of the above reconstruction has been challenged or reinterpreted. The fall of Ur and the establishment of new powers

---

Kingdom (Winona Lake, IN: Eisenbrauns, 2011), 82–121. Porter is an archaeologist, and Michalowski is a Sumerologist specializing in texts, though each undertakes a historical reconstruction that takes account of broader evidence.

4. One expression of this application of Amorite identity to Mesopotamia after the fall of Ur is found in the treatment of early second-millennium history by Dominique Charpin, a key player in the past generation of publication of and research based on the Mari archives: "Histoire politique du Proche-Orient amorrite (2002–1595)," in *Mesopotamien: Die altbabylonische Zeit*, ed. Pascal Attinger, Walther Sallaberger, and Markus Wäfler (Göttingen: Vandenhoeck & Ruprecht, 2004).

5. One influential expression of this historical reconstruction is found in John Bright, *A History of Israel*, 3rd ed. (Philadelphia: Westminster, 1983), 48–56. On the specific question of Amorites in the southern Levant, Bright concludes a review of evidence that might indicate new populations in the early second millennium: "That these newcomers were 'Amorites,' of the same Northwest-Semitic stock as those whom we met in Mesopotamia, seems highly probable. Their names, so far as these are known, point unanimously in that direction" (p. 55).

in the next period indeed represented a shift toward regions upstream, but the peoples called Amorites were no western intruders and had long contributed to the Near Eastern landscape of peoples, east and west. Both Mesopotamian and Levantine social shifts involved many factors, with local changes as important as factors of distance and little evidence for migratory waves of true outsiders in either region. The biblical texts and traditions involving Amorites are often dated much later than once imagined, sometimes after the demise of Judah in 586 BCE, so that the biblical name stands at an even greater distance from the Mesopotamian groups.[6]

In spite of all these obstacles, there is still an argument to be made for the relevance of Mesopotamia's Amorites for the emergence of Israel in lands far to the south. Mesopotamia's Amorites were mobile pastoralists, not best understood as nomads but as communities identified by their reliance on herds of sheep and goats that were pastured over great distances. These herding populations were deeply integrated with settled people as part of a single social fabric that was maintained especially with bonds defined by kinship rather than by place. Whether or not any of the particular groups linked to Mesopotamia and Syria in the early second millennium were involved with changes in the Levant, the Bible's portrait of Israel's tribal organization and mobile herding background suggests continuity with the same social patterns. In order to understand the deeper origins of Israel, so far as they involve more than just the reordering of settled populations in the southern Levant, as well as the origins of the Arameans in Syria, we do well to look behind both groups to this older phenomenon. Between the term "Amorite" (Sumerian mar-tu), which goes back to the third millennium, and the peoples of Israel and Aram stand the *'apiru*, another type that reflects the same broader pattern of mobile and settled populations integrated into whole social fabrics. It seems that the biblical Amorites must derive their name ultimately from the ancient northern category, and however this label was carried across time and space, it is likely that it was borne by people who shared this pattern of mobile herding community joined to permanent settlement.[7]

---

6. For a recent history that reflects the current state of affairs and takes into account European, Israeli, and American scholarship, see Lester L. Grabbe, *Ancient Israel: What Do We Know and How Do We Know It?* (London: T&T Clark, 2007). The first broad historical challenge was issued by Thomas L. Thompson, *The Historicity of the Patriarchal Narratives: The Quest for the Historical Abraham* (Berlin: de Gruyter, 1974). There remains enormous room for debate, but the foundations for discussion have shifted massively since the mid-twentieth century.

7. I undertook two extended efforts to reconsider how early second-millennium settings could have produced echoes that still resound in elements of the biblical account of Israelite origins: "Mari and the Possibilities of Biblical Memory," *RA* 92 (1998): 41–78; and "Genesis in History and Tradition: The Syrian Background of Israel's Ancestors," in *The Future of Biblical*

1. Who Were the Amorites?

Who were the Amorites? There is no single answer to this question. At the same time, the diversity of possible answers shows that the category cannot be constrained to a single historical moment—that is, the disruption of Sumerian dominance in southeastern Mesopotamia under the rulers of Ur, and the concurrent social changes in regions far to the west that accompanied the transition between the Early and Middle Bronze Ages. The Amorites appear to have been a class of people defined by mode of life, not by regional origin, and any application of the term to geography, politics, or language would have been secondary to this social usage. In particular, they were shepherds, or communities identified with the herding of flocks over distance.

The Amorites of Third-Millennium Mesopotamia

The starting point for understanding the Amorites in Mesopotamia has been their identification in texts from the Third Dynasty of Ur during the last century and more of the third millennium.[8] For the rulers of Ur, the last bastion of Sumerian power and cultural dominance, the Amorites were outsiders twice over: their name was associated with highlands apart from the Mesopotamian valleys, and they could be denigrated as primitives.[9] The western orientation of some Amorite references was often taken as universal, so that the term's primary meaning could be considered as the direction, as "west." At least this is how the evidence looked in early analysis. Moreover, Ur fought people whom it identified as Amorite during the later stages of its hegemony, and an "Amorite wall" was built to stave off attacks from the north. When the succeeding period saw the emergence of new centers at Isin and Larsa in the old Sumerian territory but under leaders with non-Akkadian Semitic names and novel, perhaps tribal, backgrounds, an Amorite conquest was the logical explanation.

With the accumulation of further evidence and ongoing reevaluation, however, the picture of the Amorites has shifted and remains open to discussion. One Amorite land may be found south of the Euphrates in central Syria,

---

Archaeology: Reassessing Methodologies and Assumptions, ed. James Hoffmeier and Alan Millard (Grand Rapids: Eerdmans, 2004), 193–232. In *The Legacy of Israel in Judah's Bible: History, Politics, and the Reinscribing of Tradition* (Cambridge: Cambridge University Press, 2012), I reevaluate the relationship of the Bible to the history of Israel in more sweeping terms.

8. See Buccellati, *Amorites*, and Michalowski, "Amorites," above.

9. The term "Amorite" is written with cuneiform signs that are generally read mar-tu, and readers will often encounter the name "Martu" or "Mardu" in discussions of Amorites in Sumerian texts. Michalowski ("Amorites," 105–7) now concludes that there was no such Sumerian word, and these signs were in fact simply read amurrum or "Amorite."

possibly including the Jebel Bishri.[10] Yet the principal Amorite enemies of Shu-Sin, the second to last king of Ur, were the Tidnum, who came from the country east of the Tigris. Further, the repeated references to livestock from an "Amorite land" in the records from Puzrish-Dagan (Drehem) have likewise been linked to origins at least partly on the Iranian flank of Mesopotamia. For all the likelihood that the "royal correspondence of Ur" does not represent actual letters involving its kings, these literary works also envision an eastern highland home for the Amorites.[11] Even if some Amorites could be connected with the Jebel Bishri and the west, substantial elements had nothing to do with this geographical limitation, and the pattern suggests a different primary meaning for the category. The notion of Amorites as outsiders to Ur and their characterization as uncivilized seem to reflect particular conditions from that realm, during which some circles clung to a narrowly defined Sumerian cultural heritage, with the alternative depicted in starkly unattractive terms. Sumerian identity was idealized by celebrating the city-based achievements of the region at the expense of long-standing social traditions of integration between urban and rural sectors, settled and mobile modes of life, and agricultural and pastoralist subsistence. One factor in this opposition of Sumerian and Amorite identities may have been the attempt by Shulgi of Ur (2094–2047 BCE) to dominate the pastoralist populations and economy of the highlands between the Tigris River and the Zagros Mountains, northeast of Sumer.[12]

The oldest references to Amorites come from Shuruppak (Fara) in the Sumerian heartland, where they were not isolated as foreigners. In lists that generally identify individuals by town, "Amorite" seems to offer a provenance for people who cannot be labeled by fixed residence.[13] While the precise intent may elude us, it is likely that the early term represents a type, not a named

---

10. See Walther Sallaberger, "From Urban Culture to Nomadism: A History," in Marro and Kuzucuoglu, *Sociétés humaines et changement climatique*, 445, for one identification of this western site as the original Amorite land.

11. Both Michalowski ("Amorites," 93–105) and Porter ("Tax and Tribulation," 296–310) argue vigorously that Amorites are as much associated with lands east of Sumer as west.

12. In this analysis I align myself with the interpretation of Porter, who understands Amorite identity to be rooted in the pastoralist communities who were completely integrated into settled and urban life, even as elements from these communities moved across long distances with the flocks. Sallaberger ("From Urban Culture to Nomadism," 417–56) likewise considers the Amorite category to indicate herdsmen, but in confining pastoralism to separate "nomadic" groups he gives too little weight to the abundant evidence for Amorites in urban settings. In an argument that in some ways parallels that of Porter, Michalowski likewise points out the interplay of settled and mobile life in ancient pastoralism, though he then minimizes the identification of Amorites in Sumerian texts with herding groups ("Amorites," 88–93).

13. See Porter, "Tax and Tribulation," 314–15, including table 5, for the general chronological and geographical range of third-millennium evidence.

people. Given the consistent association of Amorites with herding livestock and the products derived from them, the primary identity appears to assume participation in mobile pastoralism, which does not exclude settled residence. For those who understand "Martu" to mean "Western," perhaps with a specific western region of origin somewhere in Syria, even these earliest references to the Amorites in Sumer must derive from the geographical sense of the word. The reverse offers a more plausible scenario, however, especially since the Amorites persist in inhabiting lands both east and west of the Sumerian center. Because the Syrian steppe provided a major setting for grazing sheep and goats during the third millennium, this region "west" (or northwest) of Sumer would have been one home for people of Amorite type. Just as the far-western land of Amurrum took its name in the early second millennium from the Amorite category and cannot provide an origin for all the Amorites of eastern Mesopotamia, other such "Amorite" lands would have been named for the mobile herdsmen found there.[14]

The implications of this conclusion are straightforward. The Amorites were not a "people" in any ethnic or political sense. They lived throughout Syria and Mesopotamia, and their relationship to cities and farmers must be deduced from the details of written evidence, from a sense of regional society grounded in excavation and survey, and from consideration of the social and political frameworks most compelling for the mix of settled agriculture and long-distance pastoralism attested for the ancient Near East. Especially in this last regard, Anne Porter proposes a social integration that challenges the common idea that nomads were outsiders to all society defined by settlement, so that, however these groups interacted, nomads could always be isolated as socially distinct. Instead, by social ties that transcended distance through kinship, mobile herding communities belong to the same "peoples" as their settled relations. As early participants in such a social fabric, the Amorites were not a separate people but one dimension of its mixed makeup—whether warp or weft.[15]

Use of **Amurrû** *in the Mari Archives*

Just as the term mar-tu has had to be reevaluated for its application to people who lived at the same time as the Sumerians of Ur and earlier, the Amorites of the early second millennium must be reconsidered. Even if the Amorites were

---

14. On the western land of Amurrum, see the next section. Michalowski ("Amorites," 104) observes with regard to specific references to an Amorite "land," "The term kur MAR.TU is not, properly speaking, a specific location, which is why it never has a place-name classifier /ki/ but is a descriptive term that refers to the highlands in which certain Amorites were thought to live. As such, it has no borders and could possibly be used of more than one area."

15. This is the burden of her entire discussion in *Mobile Pastoralism*.

first of all herding communities and the Sumerians of Ur were particularly concerned about Amorites in the lands upstream and thus to the "west," the old Mesopotamian word cannot be universalized to describe all such herding peoples in every age and in every place. If it is the Amorites specifically whom we wish to understand, then we must discipline our study by the use of the word *amurrû* and acknowledge the ever-evolving social landscape and social terminology that came to identify similar populations by different words and logic.

Just as the Amorites of the late third millennium could be found across Mesopotamia and Syria, not confined to lands west of Sumer, the tribal peoples who came to new prominence in the period after Ur were also present throughout the region. It is often observed that the new centers of power in downstream Mesopotamia display both non-Akkadian Semitic royal names and hints of tribal backgrounds not defined by the cities ruled by these new kings. This is true of Isin, Larsa, Uruk, Eshnunna, and Babylon, as well as of cities further north and west.[16] All of these southeastern domains, however, fell within the immediate sphere of the prior kingdom of Ur, and they were influenced powerfully by Sumerian ideals and their written expressions, especially as developed under Ur's hegemony. For a sense of the world outside this Ur-focused realm, it is useful to consider evidence from other lands. During this period, cuneiform was used broadly by scribes trained in the downstream Mesopotamian tradition, and archives have been found as far away as Kanesh in central Anatolia, where the city of Ashur had established a trading colony.[17] Perhaps more than any other written evidence, the massive archives of Mari provide a picture of society and politics that spans east and west.[18] Mari itself stands just inside the modern Syrian border with Iraq, on the north side of the Euphrates River below where the Habur River empties

---

16. This commonplace is taken up, for example, in the overview of Amélie Kuhrt, *The Ancient Near East, c. 3000–330 BC* (London: Routledge, 1995), 1:74–75.

17. The archives found at Kanesh (Kültepe) in central Turkey generated even more tablets than the huge finds for ancient Mari, and the bibliography is naturally enormous. For a sampling, consider Mogens Trolle Larson, *The Old Assyrian City-State and Its Colonies* (Copenhagen: Akademisk, 1976); Cécile Michel, ed., *Old Assyrian Studies in Memory of Paul Garelli* (Leiden: Nederlands Instituut voor het Nabije Oosten, 2008); Gojko Barjamovic, *Ups and Downs at Kanesh: Chronology, History and Society in the Old Assyrian Period* (Leiden: Nederlands Instituut voor het Nabije Oosten, 2012).

18. The bibliography for Mari is equally overwhelming. For fairly recent treatments in English, see Wolfgang Heimpel, *Letters to the King of Mari: A New Translation, with Historical Introduction, Notes, and Commentary* (Winona Lake, IN: Eisenbrauns, 2003); and Daniel E. Fleming, *Democracy's Ancient Ancestors: Mari and Early Collective Governance* (Cambridge: Cambridge University Press, 2004). In fact, primary expertise in this material is found in France, based on responsibility for publishing the finds for Mari. Beginning in 1982, this project was led by Jean-Marie Durand, and his collection of French translations with commentary remains an important resource: *Documents épistolaires du palais de Mari, Tomes I, II, III, LAPO 16–18*

into it. From this vantage, the kings of Mari kept contacts with and negotiated their political survival among other powers from Babylon and Eshnunna in the east to Yamhad and Qatna in the west.

A number of Mari specialists have undertaken to explain the varied use of the word *amurrû* in this material. There is a polity called Amurrum, just as mid-third-millennium Ebla identified a land near the Jebel Bishri with the Martu label, yet the two locations are not the same: Amurrum in the Mari archives seems to have been further west. Dominique Charpin links the whole origin of the Amorites to this land, which he considers to have extended from the mountains east of Ugarit all the way to the Jebel Bishri.[19] Jean-Marie Durand likewise associates the name itself with the far west, as derived from the root *mrr*, "to be bitter," with reference to the salt water of the Mediterranean.[20] Beyond the western land, the word *amurrû* can also describe an "Amorite" language, and it can identify people in the realm of Mari's own kings, in a sweeping generalization that somehow indicates a population type that crosses the lines of kingdoms or tribes. The uses for language and population are most simply understood as related, with the one defined in terms of the other.

First of all, the western polity of Amurrum takes its name from the older population type; this is surely not the homeland of a migratory wave that overturned the power of Ur. One letter associates the Binu Yamina tribal coalition with three western realms, each defined by the term *mātum*, which is reserved for polities ruled by one or more kings (*šarrum*). These are the lands of Yamhad, Qatna, and Amurrum, the first two dominating the lowlands that flank the inland slopes of the Lebanese and western Syrian mountains:

> While the land of Yamhad, the land of Qatna, and the land of Amurrum are the range(?) of the Binu Yamina—and in each of those lands the Binu Yamina have their fill of barley and pasture their flocks—from the start(?), the range(?) of the Hana has been Ida-Maraṣ.[21]

One clue to the location of Amurrum may be found in a new reading for an early second-millennium (Old Babylonian) extract of the Gilgamesh Epic,

---

(Paris: Cerf, 1997, 1998, 2000). For broader reference to the literature of those involved with Mari publication, see the notes for any of these works.

19. Charpin, "Histoire politique," 57–58.

20. Durand, "Le mythologème du combat entre le dieu de l'Orage et la Mer en Mésopotamie," *MARI* 7 (1993): 46–47.

21. For publication of the text (A.2730) see Jean-Marie Durand, "Peuplement et société à l'époque amorrite (I): Les clans Bensim'alites," *Amurru* 3 (2004): 120–21; Durand kindly allowed me to cite the relevant part of this text before his publication, with my translation, in Fleming, "Possibilities of Biblical Memory," 61n91.

where Andrew George identifies the home of Huwawa as "where the Amurrû lives," west of Ebla.²² Other evidence from Mari confirms the far-western location of this realm. One brief missive confirms the writer has accounted for "messengers from Hazor and messengers from four Amurrû kings." This group is to join the king of Qatna's own messenger, who will escort them to that city.²³ Another letter reports that various men have arrived at Mari from points far west: two from Hazor, two from Qatna, and three "Amurrû singers." Such terminology may indicate their language, yet the geography matches the previous example.²⁴

The most obvious location for the land of Amurrum is that known for Amurru in the Late Bronze Age, during the second half of the second millennium. According to evidence from el-Amarna, Ugarit, and Hatti, Amurru was based in the mountains between the Mediterranean coast and the Orontes River valley.²⁵ In the Amarna letters dispatched by Rib-Hadda, ruler of Gubla (or, Byblos), the ruler of the Amurru peoples alternately importunes and assaults the coastal cities one by one until Gubla itself is in play. This attack on the coast presumes a highland center for Amurru as such. When Amurru passes from the domination of Abdi-Ashirta to Aziru, this later leader writes repeatedly about the opposite frontier, to the north and east. Amurru faces threats from Hatti through the Orontes realm of Nuhashhe. Later, after Aziru definitively abandons Egypt for alliance with Hatti, Amurru makes a treaty with Ugarit, as a separate coastal power to its northwest. Some portion of the Mari texts that have been associated with generic or ethnic Amorites may in fact pertain to the specific land of Amurrum. When Nur-Sin writes to his master Zimri-Lim, the last king of Mari in the mid-eighteenth century, about "Amurrû figs" in a delivery from the region of Yamhad, these may come from the western mountain land.²⁶ Such labels are also applied, however, to wool, to livestock, and even to a woman included in a delivery to the Mari palace, and we must be prepared for different points of reference in different contexts.

As a whole, the Amurrû identity is not common in texts from Mari. The land of Amurrum was far away and contacts were rare. The word could be applied

---

22. See the revised edition of this text in Andrew George, *Babylonian Literary Texts in the Schøyen Collection* (Bethesda, MD: CDL Press, 2009), 32–33.

23. A.2760; Marco Bonechi, "Relations amicales syro-palestiniennes: Mari et Haṣor au XVIIIᵉ siècle av. J.C." *FM* 1 (1992): 10.

24. *FM* 3 143; Grégoire Ozan, "Les lettres de Manatân," *FM* 3 (1997): 296–97.

25. For extended historical discussion, see Itamar Singer, "A Concise History of Amurru," appendix in *Amurru Akkadian: A Linguistic Study*, by Shlomo Izre'el (Atlanta: Scholars Press, 1991), 2:135–95.

26. *FM* 7 26:49, 52; Jean-Marie Durand, "Le culte d'Addu d'Alep et l'affaire d'Alahtum," *FM* 7 (2007): 99–102.

with more local considerations, but this did not occur often. This pattern in itself means something. So far as the word "Amurrû" defined some category of interest to the circle of Zimri-Lim and his people, it was not relevant to the everyday experience of the supporters and servants who constantly reported back to the palace. What then is the basis for Amurrû identity?

One significant factor appears to be language, involving both the consciousness of a linguistic distinction capable of separate classification and the choice to identify that distinct language category as "Amorite." One remarkable text boasts a scribe who is said to understand Akkadian and Subarian—evidently Hurrian—along with Amorite.[27] In another letter, Samsi-Addu, king of upper Mesopotamia, complains that his son Yasmah-Addu has requested a capable Sumerian scribe who can speak Amorite. Jack Sasson translates:

> You have written me about sending you a man competent in Sumerian, "Take for me [. . .] a man competent in Sumerian but speaks Amorite." Who is the person competent in Sumerian and lives here? Please, am I to send you Šu-Ea who is competent in Sumerian? Šu-Ea and [. . .]; Iškur-zikalama is competent in Sumerian; but he holds an administrative post. Must he leave his post and run to you? Nanna-palil is competent in Sumerian; but I have to send him to Qabra. You have written me, "[My father] should send me a man from Rapiqum who is competent in Sumerian. There is no one here competent in Sumerian in [. . .]!"[28]

Such exists but is a valuable commodity, not available for posting to Mari at the drop of a hat. These references to language involve a self-conscious classification that does not follow simple political lines, and the speaking populations cannot be assumed isolated to fully separate living groups. By this date, and in this context, Sumerian was essential to scribal practice, and while it may still have been associated with the region downstream from Babylon, it reflected no particular political body. "Subarian" evokes the allied kings of Shubartum, probably east of the Tigris, but the separate language must be distinct from the other broad types, perhaps as Hurrian, another category that crosses political lines. This leaves two clearly Semitic types, Akkadû and Amurrû. From a scribal point of view, these need not have represented

---

27. The text is A.109, cited in isolation in Jean-Marie Durand, "Unité et diversités au Proche-Orient à l'époque amorrite," in *La circulation des biens, des personnes et des idées dans le Proche-Orient ancien*, ed. Dominique Charpin and Francis Joannès (Paris: Éditions Recherche sur les Civilisations, 1992), 125.

28. M.7950+, published by Dominique Charpin, "Les malheurs d'un scribe ou de l'inutilité du sumérien loin de Nippur," in *Nippur at the Centennial*, ed. Maria de Jong Ellis (Philadelphia: University Museum, 1992), 24–25. This translation is that of Jack Sasson, "About Mari and the Bible," *RA* 92 (1998): 121–22.

comparable categories, in that Amorite seems not to have been written with cuneiform, so that from a modern view, we have no way to identify it securely. Nevertheless, Akkadian and Amorite are identified as distinguishable types, each with a coherent if overlapping speaking community.

At this point, the identification of language returns us to the issue of populations. During the centuries after Ur's end, none of these language names followed political lines. Sumer was recalled as the fountainhead of Mesopotamian civilization, but the language was no longer in common use, and there was no single polity called Sumer.[29] Akkad was once the urban center of a major kingdom launched by Sargon and associated with Naram-Sin, before the rise of Ur. This city gave its name to the language, and Sumer and Akkad together could be regarded as a merism for the territory of southern Iraq later ruled by Hammurabi and his descendants. Sumerian represents a totally different language class from the eastern Semitic Akkadian, and the two languages had clearly defined uses among scribes of the early second millennium, regardless of the political implications in the territorial claim. The question is what was meant by the distinction of Akkadian from Amorite, which was not part of scribal use with cuneiform.

Like Sumer and Akkad in royal inscriptions from the early second millennium, Amorite also defined people and speech by a category from the distant past. Across both Babylonia and the Mari region, where both Semitic language types would have been in use, Akkadian and Amorite also labeled masses of people in broad terms that transcended political bounds. One Mari letter reports a treaty between several groups in the Jebel Sinjar and eastern Habur regions and an Akkadian power, which the sender admits could be either Eshnunna, a major power east of the Tigris River, or Babylon.[30] In his treaty with the king of Eshnunna, a copy of which was found at Mari, Zimri-Lim guarantees the loyalty to Eshnunna of any force he sends in support, whether it is identified with Mari, with its Hana people, with the Suhûm land long disputed between the two kingdoms, with any individual leader, or with any Amorite or Akkadian group.[31] We know from a badly damaged Mari letter that Zimri-Lim is once said

29. For contrasting perspectives on the situation of Sumerian after the fall of Ur, see two articles in Seth L. Sanders, ed., *Margins of Writing, Origins of Culture* (Chicago: Oriental Institute of the University of Chicago, 2007): Christopher Woods, "Bilingualism, Scribal Learning, and the Death of Sumerian," 95–124; and Piotr Michalowski, "The Lives of the Sumerian Language," 163–90.

30. ARM XXVII 135, letter to Zimri-Lim of Mari from Zimri-Addu, governor of the Qaṭṭunân district.

31. A.361, in Dominique Charpin, "Un traité entre Zimri-Lim de Mari et Ibâl-pî-El II d'Ešnunna," in *Marchands, diplomats et empéreurs: Études sur la civilisation mésopotamienne offertes à Paul Garelli*, ed. Dominique Charpin and Francis Joannès (Paris: Éditions Recherche

to be "king of the Akkadian and the Amorite" equally.³² Similarly, the Edict of Ammi-ṣaduqa, a slightly later ruler of Babylon, assumes the same breakdown of population types within his domain as defining the full range of citizens who merit equal treatment under the king's declaration of debt cancellation.³³

Given that the earlier Amorites were herding peoples, this population offers a natural point of reference for the usage after the fall of Ur. With their intense interest in herding groups and their tribal organizations, the Mari archives present a wealth of evidence for just the people in question. In general, Mari suggests that the Amorite category had gone out of common use by this date. It could be applied to the language and to sweeping distinctions between peoples or even cultures associated with language, but specific herding groups were identified most often by their mobility through the term "Hana" or "nomad," possibly as people who camp in tents. Zimri-Lim, the king under whom most of these archives were collected, even calls himself "king of Mari and the Hana people (*māt* Hana)."³⁴ Most of the ubiquitous uses of the word "Hana" in the Mari correspondence take for granted that these are Zimri-Lim's own tribespeople, the Binu Sim'al, who are thus identified by their mobile herding component.

One letter to Zimri-Lim from the district governor based at the Mari center sets up a duality that resembles the Akkadian/Amorite pair. Bahdi-Lim exhorts the king to respond carefully after consolidation of his rule over a part of his realm that includes an "Akkadian" population:

> [My lord] must honor the head of his kingship. [Just as] you are the king of the Hana, [so] you are secondly the king of the Akkadian. [My lord] must not (therefore) ride a horse. My lord must (rather) ride [on] a litter and mules, if he is to honor the head of his kingship.³⁵

---

sur les Civilisations, 1991), 141–45. The key list appears in two places, II 2′–4′ and III 13′–15′, more complete in the latter.

32. A.489, in Dominique Charpin and Jean-Marie Durand, "La prise du pouvoir par Zimri-Lim," *MARI* 4 (1985): 323n131; the letter is from an official named Rip'i-Dagan to Zimri-Lim and addresses the defeat of Ishme-Addu and Yasmah-Addu, the two sons of Samsi-Addu. Rip'i-Dagan reproaches some group that has not been adequately enthusiastic in its support for Zimri-Lim in the past. The reference to the population ruled by the Mari king seems to occur after this main preserved section, in the last visible lines, cited in Durand, "Unité et diversités," 113n137.

33. F. R. Kraus, *Ein Edikt des Königs Ammi-ṣaduqa von Babylon* (Leiden: Brill, 1958), e.g., p. 30, paragraphs 2′:9′; 4′:24; 6′:1.

34. Durand, "Unité et diversités," 13–14; with extended discussion of Zimri-Lim's Hana kingdom in Fleming, *Democracy's Ancient Ancestors*, 142–69; reinterpreted in Fleming, "Kingship of City and Tribe Conjoined: Zimri-Lim at Mari," in *Nomads, Tribes, and the State in the Ancient Near East: Cross-Disciplinary Perspectives*, ed. Jeffrey Szuchman (Chicago: Oriental Institute of the University of Chicago, 2009), 227–40.

35. ARM VI 76, letter to Zimri-Lim from Bahdi-Lim, governor of the Mari district, discussed in Fleming, *Democracy's Ancient Ancestors*, 156–59.

In spite of efforts to isolate which of these modes of transportation is specifically "Akkadian" or "Hana," the main point seems to be that the horse is not an appropriate royal mount for ceremonial occasions. What is striking for this discussion is the definition of Zimri-Lim as king of two broad populations, identified by "Akkadian" and a second term. In both this text and the reference to the "king of the Akkadian and the Amorite" (above), Zimri-Lim is characterized as ruling two broad groups, one of which is Akkadian. This is the only such identification of what Zimri-Lim rules by "Akkadian" and "Hana." Based on the occurrence of the Akkadian/Amorite combination in the Eshnunna treaty and the Babylonian royal edict, the Amorite element appears to be standard to such pairing. Bahdi-Lim's use of "Hana" seems then to take the place of "Amorite" for Zimri-Lim's particular kingdom based at Mari.

If the pairing of Akkadian and Hana does indeed match that of Akkadian and Amorite, this may strengthen the association of the word *amurrû* with mobile pastoralists in the post-Ur period. As Hana, these are not isolated from the core settled population, whether as a distinct "ethnic" group or as separate "nomads." Most often, Zimri-Lim's Hana are his tribal kinsmen of the Binu Sim'al, fully integrated into the leadership of the kingdom, and the primary military force on which he relies. The Binu Sim'al occupy many towns and villages in the Mari kingdom, and it is impossible to disentangle the nomadic population from the social fabric of the settled tribespeople. While the Hana of Bahdi-Lim's schema represent Zimri-Lim's own people by name, the Amorites— ruled as one element of the "Akkadian and Amorite" pair in the Eshnunna treaty—would identify the same pastoralist type by a category in wider use. As with Zimri-Lim's Hana, the Amurrû need not be restricted to mobile herdsmen only, for they could equally include whole populations that incorporate a significant mobile herding component.

As a language designation, then, the Amurrû category is particularly intriguing. In the eyes of certain scribes, at least, groups with such a mobile component are characterized by use of a language or set of dialects that could be considered separate from Akkadian. In the kingdom of Zimri-Lim, not only was Akkadian the language of formal correspondence, but the name could also identify distinct communities that could supply a coherent fighting force. Both these and the "Amorite" groups somehow represented definable speaking groups, if the treaty labels align with the language types.

As I understand the evidence, the identification of certain speakers with an "Amorite" language is bound up with the distinction of an "Amorite" component to the population, both set against what is "Akkadian." I prefer not to treat this distinction as "ethnic," a term laden with overtones of separation amidst inequalities of power that will only confuse our interpretation of early

Mesopotamia. By my approach, both Ebla's Martu-land and the later land of Amurrum take their names from the identification of Amurrû populations, and neither provides a geographical origin for "the Amorites," as if these were a single group migrating from the west. If the Amorite category in Old Babylonian evidence indicates peoples with a mobile pastoralist component, this use may preserve the original intent of the word "Martu" from the third millennium, before the distractions of Ur and its famous collapse.

The Bible's Amorites

One way to divide the biblical geography of Israel's neighborhood is between the landscape of kingdoms and the world before Israel. During the era of the two kingdoms, Israel and Judah were situated among a clearly delineated map of neighbors. One version of this map is on display in the opening salvo of the book of Amos: Ammon, Moab, and Edom in the east; Damascus representing Aram to the northeast; the Philistines on the southern coast, with Gaza, Ashdod, Ashkelon, and Ekron; and Tyre for the Phoenicians on the northern coast. According to this political geography, the territories of Israel and Judah are fixed and inviolate, lacking any overlap with the lands of their rivals. The Amorites are nowhere to be found in this landscape—nor are the Canaanites and the Hittites, known from early written evidence outside of the Bible; nor are the Jebusites, Perizzites, and so on, who belong more particularly to the Bible's picture of populations that preceded Israel in the land.

According to the Bible, the world before Israel likewise had external neighbors, though some of these are also recognized as new, sharing ancestry with Israel through the family of Abraham. In the land itself, however, were found a jumble of town centers and populations that formed no single political entity. Recurrent lists of peoples define the specific targets for acquisition of the promised land, first announced to Abraham as a long list of ten in Genesis 15:19–21, given a shorter, classic form to Moses from the burning bush in Exodus 3:8: the Canaanites, the Hittites, the Amorites, the Perizzites, the Hivites, and the Jebusites. The same list of six peoples describes the successful conquest in Joshua 12:8, and these texts represent just a selection from an oft-repeated trope.

In the finished biblical schema, the Amorites, the Canaanites, and others from these lists remained part of Israel's population landscape through the initiation of monarchy, when David is credited with completing the conquest begun under Moses and Joshua. Judges 1 recounts a series of failures, individual settlements, and territories still held by the Canaanites (vv. 27–33) or the Amorites (vv. 34–36). After the establishment of the kingdom and its consolidation under David and Solomon, David's son is said to have made slaves of all the remaining people identified by such listed names, in this case the Amorites, Hittites, Perizzites, Hivites, and Jebusites (1 Kings 9:20; cf. 2 Chron. 8:7). This reference under Solomon is the last time that the biblical narratives bother with such a list of prior inhabitants. Once we reach the period of two kingdoms, the issue of such peoples is relegated to the distant past, the time when the ancestors of Israel and Judah still had to prove their ability to take and hold this land.

Within this tradition of displaced populations, the Amorites have more than one particular role, reflecting interest in their specific place among these disparate groups. One set of texts linked the land east of the Jordan with the Amorites, and especially the territory available for Israelite possession. In Deuteronomy 2–3 the kingdoms of Edom, Moab, and Ammon are treated as belonging to these peoples (though not yet ruled by kings) before Israel's arrival, and only the land belonging to Sihon the Amorite and Og of Bashan (e.g., 2:24; 3:1) can be seized and occupied by Israel. Elsewhere, both Sihon and Og are treated as Amorite kings (Deut. 3:8; 4:47; 31:4; Josh. 2:10; 9:10; 24:12), and this eastern land is identified with Sihon and the Amorites (e.g., Num. 21:31; Josh. 24:8; Judg. 10:8; 11:21). It is also possible for the western highlands to be considered generically Amorite; Joshua undertakes his first regional campaign against five "Amorite" kings who rule cities that define the south: Jerusalem, Hebron, Jarmuth, Lachish, and Eglon (Josh. 10:5, 12). Also in the book of Amos, the writer recounts how Yahweh brought the people out of "the land of Egypt" so that Israel could take possession of "the land of the Amorite," which in this context must at least include the west (Amos 2:9–10).

Rarely, the Bible includes the Amorites in schemes that propose regional distinctions between pre-Israelite peoples. Numbers 13:29 locates the Amalekites in the southern Negev wilderness, the Hittites, Jebusites, and Amorites in the (western) highlands, and the Canaanites by the sea and in the Jordan River valley. Yahweh's first instructions to enter the land in Deuteronomy 1:6–8 separate "the Amorite highlands" from various other regions, including "the shore of the sea, the Canaanite land," which suggests a similar division. When these two texts are set beside the tradition of the Amorite east and Joshua's southern highland victory, it appears that the Bible's Amorites are specifically linked to high country once frequented by pastoralists, like the land of Amurru in northern Syria and other "Amorite" lands in Mesopotamia. Without reference to the biblical pattern, Porter suggests that the apparently contradictory locations of "Amorite lands" in cuneiform evidence reflect the fact that these were not originally political entities at all, even if they came to be such.³⁶ They were simply local manifestations of pastoralist territory that could be found in various highland and steppe settings. Remarkably, the biblical inclination to associate Amorites with high country would align with the same pattern, even if the logic of such naming was long forgotten. Nevertheless, it seems that the identification of Amorites with highlands and Canaanites with lowlands is no coincidence, and this is best explained by some actual survival of the term's usage in connection with highland populations rather than lowland ones, most simply in such regions or among such peoples themselves.

2. Amorite Culture?

Inspired by modern ideas of nationality or ethnicity, we may seek a "culture" to accompany any "people" capable of identification as such. This search for distinguishable culture is problematic because of its expectation that peoples and their ways of life will align according to these social boundaries. Israelites would have had a different culture from Moabites or from Phoenicians. Where it is possible to define an ethnicity, a self-conscious identity based on shared sense of difference that is often tied to the domination of one group over another, such cultural distinctions are meaningful.³⁷ In the world of Israel and its predecessors, however, the political and social lines by which people organized themselves did not line up neatly with contrasts of language, of religion, of visual arts and craftsmanship, or of literature. All of these varied through time and place, and political lines became one factor governing their development and distribution. We should be cautious about identifying specific cultural features for each named group, as though these features could be isolated for that group alone. Of course, any given object of our study will have evidence for religion, art, craftsmanship, or literature, all well worth our attention.

The Case of Religion

In the case of the Amorites, the search for culture may be particularly misleading if it treats a social type as a "people" separate from the populations of Mesopotamian cities. One example of this misconception is the notion of a distinct "Amorite" religion. Given the range of Amorite populations across

---

36. Porter, *Mobile Pastoralism*, 309–10.
37. For an orientation to recent discussion of ethnicity as a category in archaeological research, see Siân Jones, "Ethnicity: Theoretical Approaches, Methodological Implications," in *Handbook of Archaeological Theories*, ed. R. Alexander Bentley, Herbert D. G. Maschner, and Christopher Chippindale (Plymouth, UK: Altamira, 2008), 321–34.

Syria and Mesopotamia, it is natural that they participated in varied religious practices with diverse gods. The mobility of their active herding population would have made them natural carriers of religious customs to new regions, though ancient practice tended to adapt to the local landscape with its traditional attention to local powers and needs. We can see this inclination in Mari evidence for the Binu Yamina, the large tribal coalition that rivaled the Binu Sim'al based at Mari under Kings Yahdun-Lim and Zimri-Lim. The Binu Yamina consisted of five tribes with no combined center or single ruler. Their populations and settlements associated with them were spread from Babylonia to the western Syrian mountains.

One letter found at Mari reports a meeting of all the Binu Yamina leadership at Harran, the same north Syrian city associated with Abraham and Jacob (biblical Haran). The chiefs of these gathered groups have decided to go to war against an ally of Mari, and in order to enter a formal agreement they must swear an oath and slaughter a donkey, the rite linked to confirming political alliance. All this is carried out at the temple of the moon god.[38] One might conclude from this that the moon god had a special role in "Amorite" religion, but this would be a mistake. Indeed there is a particular connection with the Binu Yamina, yet there is nothing specific to Amorite peoples about this god and his temple. Harran had a lasting association with the moon god that persisted into the first millennium. The Binu Yamina peoples maintained close relations with a land called Zalmaqum that was defined by four associated towns, one of which was Harran. This influential sacred site and its god thus offered a natural choice for ratifying a commitment to joint action—without any specifically Amorite use or significance.

Likewise, the Binu Sim'al were compelled by Yahdun-Lim to accept his individual leadership, with Mari as capital. Mari itself was not a Binu Sim'al town; Yahdun-Lim took it and made it such. With this base in the Euphrates River valley, Dagan became a key figure in the religious life of the kingdom, especially through his established shrine at Terqa. Dagan was the dominant deity of the middle Euphrates region, and a polity that incorporated Terqa and Mari could not avoid giving him a major religious role.[39] This did not make Dagan an Amorite god, however, nor even a favorite of the Binu Sim'al. In fact, the Terqa district was populated almost entirely by the Binu Yamina during this period.[40] The Amorite identity of the third millennium distinguished the

---

38. ARM XXVI 24; on this letter, see Fleming, "Possibilities of Biblical Memory," 69–70.
39. On the importance of this god to the region, see Lluís Feliu, *The God Dagan in Bronze Age Syria* (Leiden: Brill, 2003).
40. Adelina Millet Albà, "La localisation des terroirs benjaminites du royaume de Mari," in *Amurru* 3 (2004): 225–34.

herding component of an integrated society that included both settled and mobile segments of the population as a whole. The tribal groups in the Mari archives reflect the same combination, and we have repeated opportunity to see the mobile herdsmen. Their pattern of social and cultural integration follows the ancient structure of life in the Near East.

The Marriage of Martu

Aside from the patterns of religious practice observed for the tribal peoples of the Mari archives, the Amorites have been supposed to have their own "eponymous" god, named Amurru and written in Sumerian as ^{d}Mar-tu.[41] Because this god bears the name "Amorite," many have considered him an "Amorite" god, as if distinct to such a named people. Amurru first appears just before the Ur III period in the late third millennium, and it is not clear who initiated his cult. In the context of the social landscape suggested here, there is no reason to imagine that the "Pastoralist" god had to be worshiped only or first of all by pastoralists. The deity represented this portion of the community and would have specialized in the needs of long-distance shepherds and their flocks. Amurru need not have been an Amorite god but rather a divine representative of the Amorite contribution to Mesopotamian life, taking his place in a pantheon shared by the general populace. The literary narrative commonly called the Marriage of Martu (or Amurru) reflects this background, even as it grapples with conflicting attitudes toward this traditional component of Mesopotamian society.

The old scholarly hypothesis of an Amorite migration was made possible in large part by the attitudes of scribes from Ur who denigrated the herding class and isolated them as a foreign threat. From this point of view, which was reproduced in the work of scribes trained in the Sumerian tradition during the early second millennium, Amorites had no culture in the modern sneering sense: they were uncivilized.[42] One Sumerian text that superficially shares this indictment supplies some of the strongest evidence that it was groundless and easily shown to be so. Anne Porter points out that the title character, who personifies the Amorites in his name "Martu," is presented as the object of unreasoning prejudice, which rational city dwellers set aside.[43] The details of Martu's story display a man completely at home in the city, even as his wealth—which is formidable and alluring—comes from the backcountry.

41. Karel van der Toorn, "Amurru," *DDD* 32–34.
42. On the theme of uncivilized Amorites in early second-millennium literature, see Jerrold S. Cooper, *The Curse of Agade* (Baltimore: Johns Hopkins University Press, 1983), 30–33.
43. Porter, *Mobile Pastoralism*, 293–95, treats the Marriage of Martu at some length. The text itself is available, with English translation, on the site of the Electronic Text Corpus of Sumerian Literature (http://etcsl.orinst.ox.ac.uk/section1/tr171.htm).

The Marriage of Martu is set in a time gone by, in a town not belonging to the known political landscape of Sumer. Inab is "a land of magnificence" as measured by all other cities, introduced as existing from a time when certain sacred innovations had not yet been invented: a type of crown, cedar, and cleaning powder. For all its antiquity and mystery, outside the grid of known Sumerian cities, Inab is a classic urban center, with an "ensi" as city-based ruler on behalf of the city's resident god. Martu is introduced as a man of Inab, identified by the city, participating in a city-based administration of imposed payments into a common fund, for which married men provide for two, and those with a child provide for three. The problem is that Martu is treated differently, made to pay double while still being unmarried, and this is his motivation for finding a bride. He solves the problem in unsettling fashion, choosing for himself Adgarkidug, the daughter of a character named Numushda, who attend a city-wide festival as a family. The standing of Numushda at Inab is not clear, although Martu wins the right to marry Adgarkidug by defeating every opponent in single combat at the festival. All three named characters, including Martu himself, are marked with the divine category in the cuneiform, and both Martu (Amurru) and Numushda are treated as gods in other settings.[44] In this story, Numushda is no more than a wealthy figure in Inab, so that all of these figures' deity derives from their roles as part of a prototypical society in hoary antiquity.

For all that Martu takes part in every aspect of city life at Inab, his double payment indicates separate treatment, and Numushda is not happy about the prospect of his daughter marrying Martu. Numushda offers him generous financial compensation, but Martu insists. Moreover, Martu challenges Numushda to account for the source of his silver and gems, seeming to imply that it may have been generated by herdsmen like himself. The text that follows this exchange is damaged, but Numushda demands a marriage gift that involves a guarantee that all his livestock will thrive and multiply—just the domain of a herdsman—and the narrative lingers over the account of the cattle, sheep, and goats in question. Martu responds with massive gifts of precious goods to all the households of Inab, fathers and mothers, male and female servants. The entire city benefits overwhelmingly from the wealth and generosity of the figure who represents the pastoralist segment of the economy.

In spite of the obvious attraction of this alliance between the herdsman and the rest of the city, one more obstacle remains. Adgarkidug's own friend voices a prejudice that stands at odds with the character of Martu as presented

---

44. For Numushda, see "A Hymn to Numushda for Sîn-iqisham (Sîn-iqisham A)" in the collection of the online Electronic Text Corpus (http://etcsl.orinst.ox.ac.uk/section2/tr2671.htm).

in the preceding narrative. It is a caricature of bias against herdsmen. First of all, they eat what the moon god Nanna forbids, an objection defined by the leading god of Ur, as if the great kingdom lies at the root of the prejudice. Further, they are "always roaming," as if their very mobility is inappropriate. They supposedly wear skins rather than wool cloth, and they live in tents, exposed to wind and rain, as if from failure to realize the advantages of settled life. They live in the highlands, which cannot be imagined a proper human home, and the friend imagines them grubbing for mushrooms and gnawing raw meat. She claims that they have no houses and receive no burial. Step by step, the friend makes her accusations ever more ridiculous, threading together bits of fact with preposterous assumption. Adgarkidug finally gives her friend the answer she deserves, which concludes the tale. Echoing Martu's earlier declaration to her father that he would nevertheless marry his daughter, refusing his payoff, she tells her friend that she shall nevertheless marry Martu, likewise refusing this final distraction.[45]

It is obvious from the story that herding populations are to be included in larger society through Martu as their representative. It may be less obvious how thoroughly the text rejects the characterization of the Amorite population presented at the end. Adgarkidug's friend portrays a mass of wild-eyed primitives, isolated from urban civilization with its benefits and norms. The preceding narrative offers us Martu, a full participant in the life of Inab, identified by his residence there, along with his mother, and suffering only from the double financial burden that he intends to settle by marrying one of his fellow citizens. Martu is enormously wealthy, evidently as a result of his herding gains, and he is without equal in fighting prowess, defeating the best of Inab on their own turf at their own game. This text not only includes the Amorites in Mesopotamian society but also scoffs at any notion that they partake of a separate culture. In some circles, the integration of Amorite herding communities into city centers may have been doubted or disapproved, but it represented a centuries-old tradition in Mesopotamian life.

3. Amorites, ʿApiru, and Arameans

By the time of Hammurabi's Babylon and Mari of the tribal peoples, the term "Amorite" had begun to be fossilized in a variety of uses that derived from the original application to communities defined by long-distance herding even as they were removed to varying degrees from that definition. Amorites came to be identified with peoples of this type from lands west of Babylonia, no longer

---

45. See lines 82–83, 139–41.

as a population indigenous to Mesopotamia and active in the highlands and steppe in every direction from the urban centers of Sumer. The association with the west outlasted the existence of distinct Amorite people. A particular polity in the Syrian mountains acquired the lasting name Amurru, which survived until the end of the Bronze Age and the shift of social and political alignments as the Iron Age began. The Bible's Amorites and Hittites were two archaic names attached to groups whom Israel replaced, peoples who would cease to exist in the new order of kingdoms in the first millennium, both of which had roots in real groups from the north. By the time these found their way into the Bible, they referred only to those who by the very pattern of usage had ceased to exist, so it is difficult to have confidence in the precision of their territorial associations. Nonetheless, these Amorites could be placed particularly in the high country east and west of the Jordan River, in contrast to the lowland Canaanites and in terrain generally suited to grazing flocks. A hint of their older associations seems to have followed their attribution to the Bible's pre-Israelite landscape.

It is a mistake, however, to track the Amorite category across time exclusively by the word itself. So far as the Amorites were first of all mobile herdsmen who were fully integrated into the fabric of regional societies with their urban centers, such people were identified by other terms with their own conceptual histories in later settings. The Mari archives offer a relatively early example in Zimri-Lim's rule over "Mari and the land of the Hana." In this title, the word "Hana" names the primary people by which Zimri-Lim derived his power, and these were his tribal kinsmen, the Binu Sim'al, who were most often identified by their mobile component. "Hana" were literally long-distance pastoralists, so "nomads"; yet as a designation for the Binu Sim'al tribe, they incorporated many settlements and Mari itself became a Binu Sim'al city under Zimri-Lim's kingship. The social structures involved in this configuration would have been familiar to the Amorites of the third millennium, and these structures were the direct descendants of the earlier Amorite peoples. The word "Amorite" was rarely applied to them, however, and then perhaps only to describe a broad type.

The key link between the early Amorites and Israel lies therefore less in the name than in the social type. Israel itself is difficult to define for the period before the two kingdoms, when excavation has yielded no written finds to identify this people, its land, or its character. Only the late thirteenth-century reference in the stela of Egypt's pharaoh Merenptah confirms Israel's existence, with little elaboration.[46] The Bible's tradition that Israel consisted of associated

---

46. The bibliography on Merenptah's reference to Israel is extensive and the points of view vary greatly. See among these William G. Dever, "Merenptah's 'Israel,' the Bible's, and Ours,"

tribes and had mobile pastoralist ancestors suggests a possible background in such a blended society, although that hypothesis requires extended discussion on its own terms.[47] Outside the Bible, two prominent categories may be understood best in light of the same structures: the 'apiru of the Amarna letters and the Late Bronze Age, and the Arameans of the Iron Age. Both of these represent unique terms with particular conceptions and histories of use, yet they both reflect efforts to characterize mobile populations that probably maintained social bonds through kinship. Like the Amorites, neither the 'apiru nor the Arameans were first of all a "people" in some kind of ethnic or national sense; the terms identified people of a certain social type.

The 'Apiru[48]

The 'apiru category is Semitic and appears in cuneiform writing from the early second millennium, describing displaced individuals or groups in regions far north of Israel, as with the Amorites. Unlike the Amorites, the 'apiru are found in the exact range of Israel's territory in the Late Bronze letters found at el-Amarna in Egypt. A local ruler named Lab'ayu kept close connections with the 'apiru, and the term became an epithet for groups accused of disloyalty to Egypt in communications from the empire's vassals in the Levant. In this pejorative use, the 'apiru are defined by their refusal of social frameworks amenable to Egyptian administration, as outcasts and gangs of bandits. Yet they are identified with cities and can cause problems by their mobility. This combination is familiar to the integrated structure to which the Amorites belonged.

The numerous Amarna references to the 'apiru have greatly influenced definitions of the type as renegade outsiders.[49] Based on this material, they have been called landless, impoverished, socially marginalized, and social

---

in *Exploring the Longue Durée: Essays in Honor of Laurence E. Stager*, ed. J. David Schloen (Winona Lake, IN: Eisenbrauns, 2009), 89–96; and Kenneth Kitchen, "The Victories of Merenptah, and the Nature of Their Record," *JSOT* 28 (2004): 259–72.

47. By this characterization, I do not refer to origin by migration or by the sedentarization of nomadic pastoralists. In my *The Legacy of Israel in Judah's Bible*, I treat several dimensions of this historical problem as the Bible relates to it, without attempting to reconstruct Israel's origin in itself, which remains especially a project for historians working above all from archaeological evidence. On the herding tradition in writing from the Israelite kingdom, see *Legacy*, 163–71; and on pastoralism and the origins of Israel, see *Legacy*, 271–75.

48. This section parallels the more developed treatment found in my *Legacy*, "The 'Apiru in the Pre-Israelite Landscape," 258–69. More complete references are found with that discussion.

49. For extended discussion of the social landscape reflected in the Amarna archives, including the 'apiru, see Brendon C. Benz, *The Land before the Kingdom of Israel: A History of the Southern Levant and the People Who Populated It* (Winona Lake, IN: Eisenbrauns, 2016).

bandits. More neutrally, they have been considered refugees or migrants, populations that could represent a threat to the long-standing locals. All of these interpretations treat the ʿapiru as not fully integrated into the society of town dwellers. In the Amarna letters, the ʿapiru generally appear as powerful groups with effective political leadership on a scale that could be seen to threaten every city-based vassal in the Egyptian Levant. Peoples identified as ʿapiru, especially as followers of Abdi-Ashirta in the north or Lab'ayu in the southern highlands, defeated or won the support of major towns and would have incorporated large populations that were indistinguishable from those of the kingdoms they overwhelmed. The ʿapiru peoples were never identified by a city center, however, and some of Egypt's vassals regarded them as intrinsically resistant to Egyptian authority.[50]

One of the rare letters from Lab'ayu himself offers a closer view of the ʿapiru that should not be pejorative. In EA 254, Lab'ayu responds to Pharaoh's request that he hand over his son for a visit to Egypt, an invitation that forced submission to the suzerain. Lab'ayu insists that he would give anything the king requests, including his own wife if so ordered. Unfortunately, his son has been frustratingly out of contact. William Moran translates the excuse, "I did not know that my son was consorting with the Apiru. I herewith hand him over to Addaya."[51] Without the assumption that the ʿapiru category is necessarily negative in this case, the key lines may be rendered differently: "I did not know that my son was going around with the ʿapiru, and I hereby entrust him to Addaya." For Lab'ayu, if his son is not currently with him, he is naturally with the ʿapiru, who are understood to live or move at a distance from their king, rather like the Hana of Zimri-Lim. As addressed by Lab'ayu, the ʿapiru are a coherent population with an established relationship to himself, yet whose movements cannot be managed by the ruler they acknowledge. Such independence may reflect a life in more remote areas, especially in highlands and inland regions that were less accessible to Egyptian power.

Texts from the early second millennium attest a verb that defines the ʿapiru as individuals who have had to leave home while maintaining that identity

---

50. Rib-Hadda of Byblos and others speak of "the war of the ʿapiru" (EA 68, 71, 75, 185, 243, 313, 366). Peoples who might join the ʿapiru are often identified by their towns, either generically (EA 74, 116, 117, 144, 189) or with specific names, including Ṣumur (EA 76), Byblos/Gubla (EA 104), and Hazor (EA 148). Whole "lands" (*mātu*) are sometimes at stake (EA 77, 79, 85, 88, 272, 273, 290). None of these references can be taken as attempts to describe an ʿapiru community or way of life, but they warn against treating them as disconnected from settlements and their structure.

51. William L. Moran, *The Amarna Letters* (Baltimore: Johns Hopkins University Press, 1992), with EA 254.

and affiliation from a distance.[52] The question, then, is how such displaced people came to be identified by large groups. The notion of their gathering in "bands" does not explain the scale and integration of the Amarna evidence and is not required by the ʿapiru evidence as a whole. One answer may be found in the model of the 438 fighters counted by Tunip-Tesshup as ʿapiru in a text from the upper Tigris region during the late seventeenth century.[53] This mass of men appears to reside in the king's domain but will not fight according to town and village units, which are based on long-term solidarity and serve together. Wherever and however they live, they are joined for military service under a separate census category, and this is what unites them for classificatory purposes. In actual combat, such groups would probably have moved and camped and fought together, as they were organized under this heading.

When the ʿapiru are compared to the Hana in the Mari letters, we find two groups defined by different dimensions of their mobility. If the word ḫana derives from the root ḫny, "to camp," then the category focuses on the mode of residence, which depends on movable tents rather than fixed houses.[54] In contrast, the verb ʿab/pāru has to do with the movement itself, leaving one residence to take up another. Only the word "Hana" envisions life with movement as a habit, whereas the ʿapiru category is rooted in the notion of a single disruption. They share, however, the picture of people who continue to be defined by the fact that they cannot be identified by a town of current and permanent residence. The question is who such people can be when they represent a large social class, and here again Mari offers a useful point of reference, because this archive gives us an unusually detailed view of the world away from settlements.

In the social landscape offered by the Mari archives, there are no appreciable numbers of migrant bandits or gangs of dislocated people who live outside of urban boundaries. Equally, there is no special concern to define "resident aliens," a class of permanent outsiders who may reside in a town long-term and yet who are always foreign. Where groups of significant scale are considered as peoples identified by names, these are of the sort commonly called "tribal": the Binu Sim'al and the Binu Yamina, the

---

52. The cognate verb is found especially in the Mari archives, with one attestation from older Kanesh (Kültepe) in Anatolia; the most systematic work on the cuneiform evidence is that of Jean Bottéro, first of all in *Le problème des Ḫabiru à la 4e Rencontre Assyriologique Internationale* (Paris: Imprimerie Nationale, 1954). For further bibliography, see my *Legacy*, 264–65.

53. Mirjo Salvini, *The Ḫabiru Prism of King Tunip-Teššup of Tikunani* (Rome: Istituti editoriali e poligrafici internazionali, 1996).

54. This is the interpretation of Durand, "Unité et diversités," 113.

Numhâ, the Yamutbal, and others.⁵⁵ The question is what such groups may be when identified as a class by those who have no interest in their named associations. By the time of the Amarna letters, the answer may be ʿapiru. The earliest treatment of ʿapiru as massed groups appears to have been for military enlistment, when such people lived in the domain served and yet could not be said to originate there. We know neither the backgrounds of these people nor their current affiliations—only that the government did not know how to count them by towns. In the Amarna correspondence, however, the ʿapiru are coherent, connected, and the primary political base for the kingdom of Lab'ayu, as seen from outside. The same may be said for the kingdom of Amurru under Abdi-Ashirta, to the north. If we set aside the assumption that the backcountry of the southern Levant was populated by disaffiliated bands with no durable identity, it is more likely that the population not defined by towns would have maintained identities that could transcend settled space. Such identities would look like those of the Binu Sim'al and the Binu Yamina at Mari, where they are called "tribal." One Mari text (A.2939:13–14) identifies a fighting force of ʿapiru as explicitly belonging to one such group, the Yamutbal, serving under a Yamutbal leader who has offered to help Mari capture a recalcitrant city.⁵⁶ These are not people who are displaced from their proper places in a social system; they are merely classed as a group traveling from what they might consider a fixed home base, or without one—yet identified adequately as Yamutbal on the move.

The ʿapiru of Amarna would not be "tribes" in any direct sense, especially as viewed from inside. Rather, they would include so-called tribal peoples as viewed from outside by the rulers of towns not invested in this social framework, undifferentiated from others who lack town-based identity. This would explain why the Egyptians did not fight against the ʿapiru or consider them enemies; the ʿapiru who fought for Egypt were simply people from such tribe-like groups—not nomads, not necessarily herdsmen, but listed this way as the most convenient way to take their census for military purposes. Viewed this way, the ʿapiru need not be detached from the social order, and we need not even assume that they had cut ties to settled homes and kin. They were identified as lacking a fixed town of residence, like Mari's Hana, but this may often have reflected an integrated society of farmers and herdsmen.

55. See Fleming, *Democracy's Ancient Ancestors*, chap. 2, "The Tribal World of Zimri-Lim"; and Durand, "Peuplement."

56. "Thirty Yamutbalite ʿapiru are under his command"; in Dominique Charpin, "Un souverain éphémère en Ida-Maraṣ: Išme-Addu d'Ašnakkum," *MARI* 7 (1993): 188.

The Arameans[57]

It is striking that the first clear definition of Arameans as a distinguishable population by Tiglath-pileser I treats them as a single mass and fails to identify them with any focused political domain. No leadership, whether royal or otherwise, is mentioned in connection with the Assyrian king's western campaigns, as opposed to the "houses" that come into view when Aramean groups attack the Tigris River region of Assyria itself. Tiglath-pileser I does not claim to have defeated a kingdom or a coalition but rather to have pushed back a population of a certain type.[58] Based only on this evidence, it would be presumptuous to interpret "Aramean" as a "tribal" label, as if any single group identified itself that way as "the Arameans," and equally incautious to pronounce the term "ethnic," any more than Amorites, Hana, or Sutû could be called this.

Returning to the initial geography of Tiglath-pileser I's encounter, the broad range and undifferentiated characterization of these first Arameans indeed recalls the Amorites, who most likely took their name from a population type that was identified with mobile herding communities. The Assyrian king understands the Arameans to have occupied the Euphrates valley across all of modern Syria, with interests that reached south and west to Palmyra in the desert and to the base of the Lebanon Mountains. In spatial terms alone, this was the core domain of long-distance mobile herding, an area associated for millennia with "tribal" peoples that organized themselves in ways that maintained social bonds beyond the limits of easy face-to-face contact, as was possible in concentrated areas of settlement. As evident from the social landscape of the Mari archives, which reflect much of the same space, this interplay of herding, mobility, and kinship is not to be explained as "nomadism" and relegated to the "periphery" of land dominated by city-centered states.

It appears that the middle Euphrates valley and significant sections of Syria retained the use of West Semitic dialects in spite of domination by outside powers associated with other languages: the Hurrian kingdom of Mittani based in northeastern Syria and northern Iraq; and the Hittites of Anatolia. Both the modest Hana kingdom based at Terqa and the late second-millennium evidence

---

57. This brief section reflects the direction of interpretation undertaken in my *Legacy*, chap. 14, "Israel's Aramean Contemporaries," 220–35. For general treatments of the Arameans, see Hélène Sader, *Les états araméens de Syrie: Depuis leur fondation jusqu'à leur transformation en provinces assyriennes* (Wiesbaden: Franz Steiner, 1987); Paul-Eugène Dion, *Les Araméens à l'âge du fer: Histoire politique et structures sociales* (Paris: J. Gabalda, 1997); and Edward Lipiński, *The Aramaeans: Their Ancient History, Culture, Religion* (Leuven: Peeters, 2000).

58. For the earliest reference to the Arameans in the annals of Tiglath-pileser I (1114–1076 BCE), see A. Kirk Grayson, *Assyrian Rulers of the Early First Millennium BC*, vol. 1, *1114–859 BC* (Toronto: University of Toronto Press, 1991), 23; text A.0.87.1:46–47; etc.

from Emar further upstream show the predominance of Semitic language across large parts of Syria, which thus maintained continuity with patterns displayed at Mari for centuries earlier.[59] The potential implication of this comparison is striking and contrasts with common conceptions. It is increasingly plausible that the Amorites did not invade eastern Mesopotamia, in spite of the characterization of Amorites as western outsiders in writing from the land of Sumer. They were always there, involved with their herds and flocks in the steppe regions across Mesopotamia and Syria together. Whether by a West Semitic "Amorite" language family, which remains a delicate construction in any case, or by use of Akkadian in contrast to Sumerian, these peoples mingled and merged with the peoples of the southeastern river valleys. What then of the Arameans? As specific impediments to Assyrian expansion, groups by this name are linked to the whole pastoralist range of Syria. By the early first millennium, their non-Akkadian, West Semitic language exerted a powerful influence on populations in the east.[60] As with the Amorites, it is generally imagined that the Arameans migrated eastward. Could it be instead that such people were always nearby? Just as there were constant shifts in power and movements of people in earlier times, the same could apply later, yet in neither case would it be necessary to cast this as east against west, urban civilization against marauding nomads. The people whom the Assyrians finally identified as Aramean belonged to, and may even have been understood by name to represent, an old heritage of peoples with strong ties to the backcountry, who tended to organize themselves by lines of kinship that yielded associations that we naturally call "tribal." If such is the case, then the juxtaposition of Aramaic evidence with material from Mari is historically appropriate, even across several centuries. Both represent a persisting population across a swath of Syria and Mesopotamia, the influence of which derives not from a habit of marauding, followed by sedentarization, but rather from the inability of city-based eastern Mesopotamians to define a world that excluded them.

The Heritage of the Amorites

The picture of pastoralism offered here is not intended to present a static conception of ancient society, with a single mode of engagement between farmers

---

59. For Hana, see Amanda Podany, *The Land of Hana: Kings, Chronology, and Scribal Tradition* (Bethesda, MD: CDL Press, 2002); and for Semitic dialects at Emar, see Eugen Pentiuc, *West Semitic Vocabulary in the Akkadian Texts from Emar* (Winona Lake, IN: Eisenbrauns, 2001); and Regine Pruzsinszky, *Die Personennamen der Texte aus Emar* (Bethesda, MD: CDL Press, 2003).

60. Paul-Alain Beaulieu, "Official and Vernacular Languages: The Shifting Sands of Imperial and Cultural Identities in First-Millennium B.C. Mesopotamia," in Sanders, *Margins of Writing*, 191–220.

and herders, settled and mobile communities, as populations related by residence and by kinship. Each historical period brought innovations and extinctions, and the social landscape varied from place to place, interacting with the particular conditions of each one. Nevertheless, it appears that the integration of long-distance pastoralism with agricultural communities has been underestimated across wide swaths of time and place through the early history of the Near East. Where we encounter social bonds based on kinship, especially in larger constellations that may be called "tribal," these may often serve just the kind of integration represented by the Amorites of third-millennium Mesopotamia.

In the Iron Age, both Israel and the Arameans preserve evidence of tribal organization as one dimension of their social traditions. These peoples took political form in similar lands at the margins of settlement and steppe, and herding groups appear to have contributed at some level to both Israelites and individual Aramean peoples. As such, these were to some degree the social descendants of the Amorites—the only kind of descent possible from Amorites, who do not define an ethnic or political category. According to the Bible, Israel was originally an association of tribes, but in the scheme of Samuel and Kings, inherited by Chronicles, the tribal lines faded in significance before the unifying force of monarchy. Given this attention to kings and their influence, it is difficult to measure the perseverance and strength of tribal bonds under the new institution. One hint of their survival may be found in the blessings of Jacob, where the people of Asher are praised for their provision of the king (Gen. 49:20), suggesting a monarchic setting for this tribal text.[61] By this time, however, the role of mobile pastoralism may have faded in Israel, leaving only the shells of forgotten forms and customs. The nomads known to monarchic Israel and Judah, especially in the west, may have been true outsiders to Israelite society in a way that had been the case for the Amorites or those who followed them in the early Iron Age.

For Further Reading

Buccellati, Giorgio. *The Amorites of the Ur III Period*. Naples: Istituto Orientale di Napoli, 1966.

Charpin, Dominique. "Histoire politique du Proche-Orient amorrite (2002–1595)." In *Mesopotamien: Die altbabylonische Zeit*, edited by Pascal Attinger, Walther Sallaberger, and Markus Wäfler, 25–480. Göttingen: Vandenhoeck & Ruprecht, 2004.

---

61. This is the conclusion of Jean-Daniel Macchi, *Israël et ses tribus selon Genèse 49* (Göttingen: Vandenhoeck & Ruprecht, 1999).

Durand, Jean-Marie. *Documents épistolaires du palais de Mari, Tomes I, II, III.* LAPO 16–18. Paris: Cerf, 1997, 1998, 2000.

Fleming, Daniel E. *Democracy's Ancient Ancestors: Mari and Early Collective Governance.* Cambridge: Cambridge University Press, 2004.

———. *The Legacy of Israel in Judah's Bible: History, Politics, and the Reinscribing of Tradition.* Cambridge: Cambridge University Press, 2012.

Heimpel, Wolfgang. *Letters to the King of Mari: A New Translation, with Historical Introduction, Notes, and Commentary.* Winona Lake, IN: Eisenbrauns, 2003.

Michalowski, Piotr. *The Correspondence of the Kings of Ur: An Epistolary History of an Ancient Mesopotamian Kingdom.* Winona Lake, IN: Eisenbrauns, 2011.

Porter, Anne. *Mobile Pastoralism and the Formation of Near Eastern Civilizations: Weaving Together Society.* Cambridge: Cambridge University Press, 2012.

———. "You Say Potato, I Say . . .: Typology, Chronology and the Origin of the Amorites." In *Sociétés humaines et changement climatique à la fin du troisième millénaire: Une crise a-t-elle eu lieu en Haute-Mésopotamie?*, edited by C. Marro and C. Kuzucuoglu, 69–115. Paris: de Boccard, 2007.

Sallaberger, Walther. "From Urban Culture to Nomadism: A History." In *Sociétés humaines et changement climatique à la fin du troisième millénaire: Une crise a-t-elle eu lieu en Haute-Mésopotamie?*, edited by C. Marro and C. Kuzucuoglu, 417–56. Paris: de Boccard, 2007.

Toorn, Karel van der. "Amurru." *DDD* 32–34.

2

Assyria and the Assyrians

Christopher B. Hays with Peter Machinist

1. Introduction

The Assyrians loom large in any discussion of the world around the Old Testament. They controlled by far the most extensive empire the ancient Near East had seen up to that point, they had an enormous impact on both Israel and Judah, and their culture is better documented than any other from the period. For all that, they have often received a bad press in modern times; they have come down to us, over the centuries through various traditions, as a brutal, overwhelming military force, destroying everything in their path. However, once excavations in the Assyrian heartland began, starting just before the middle of the nineteenth century, they appeared no longer, or not merely, as brutal barbarians, but as creators and transmitters of great achievements in architecture and art, in literature and religion, and, especially through the written evidence unearthed, in the sophistication and elaboration of their statecraft.

In this chapter we shall take the measure of the Assyria given to us by the long-known sources and the ones discovered through excavations and studies of the last two centuries, trying to balance the picture of its military ferocity with that of its political and cultural achievements. Our discussion begins with the memory Assyria left after its demise and how its history was recovered. There follows a description of its geographical setting and of the sources and chronological periodization of its history. This history, then, will claim the bulk of our attention, chronicling Assyria's development from city-state to world empire and then collapse. Finally, we shall consider selected elements of Assyrian polity, society, and culture, including administration, social structure, ruling ideology, economy, and religion.

2. The Recovery of Assyria

The memory of Assyria and its imperial achievements never completely disappeared. The last indication of Assyria as a polity—albeit just of its army far west of the Assyrian heartland in Harran—is dated to 609 BCE, and the text in which it is found, the Babylonian Chronicle, itself represents an accumulation of data about Babylonian history of the first millennium BCE that in its latest version comes from the following decades of the sixth century BCE. Other Babylonian references from this century, and those from the succeeding Achaemenid Persian Empire of the sixth through the fourth centuries BCE, constitute one source of the memory of Assyria. To them may be added three other sources: (1) the Hebrew Bible and the subsequent texts, art, and oral traditions based on it, such as the book of Tobit, early histories like Josephus's *Jewish Antiquities*, and the classical Jewish and Christian commentary literature; (2) classical pagan Greek and Latin authors; and (3) Arab and Islamic traditions, as expressed in texts and oral recollections associated, for example, with particular place-names—the latter based on the biblical traditions just mentioned and on other, more direct connections with Assyrian history. The oral traditions that underlie some of these sources of memory were in part gathered by travelers to the Near/Middle East starting already in pre-Christian antiquity and continuing through the present—for example, in the writing of the medieval Jew Benjamin of Tudela.

All the sources just described focus their attention, explicitly or implicitly, on the last phase of Assyrian history, that of the Neo-Assyrian Empire from the late ninth through the late seventh centuries BCE. This was the period of the greatest power and territory of Assyria, which made it the first world empire in the Near East, and even after its collapse at the end of the seventh century BCE, a part of its architectural and sociocultural legacy continued in what had been its main center in the upper Tigris River basin through at least the Parthian period of late Hellenistic/Roman times. The picture of Neo-Assyria that our four memory sources have provided has two principal features. On the one hand, it sometimes elides—this especially in the Greek and, behind the Greek, the Achaemenid Persian sources—Assyria with Babylonia to the south and/or Syria to the west; indeed, the very name "Syria" appears to have been a shortened form of "Assyria." The elision reflects a post-Neo-Assyrian reconfiguration of administrative boundaries instituted by the Achaemenid Persians who took over Babylonia, Assyria, Syria, and the rest of the Near East—a reconfiguration that ate away at the memory of Assyria as a political entity in its own right. On the other hand, something of that memory did survive through Babylonian, Achaemenid Persian, and then Greek and biblical traditions, and there is the image of Neo-Assyria as the Oriental despot, the world empire par excellence, which collapsed as thoroughly as it had prevailed. Compare, on the one hand, the picture of the Assyrian army marching inexorably against its enemies in the biblical book of Isaiah (5:26–30) and Lord Byron's poem "The Destruction of Sennacherib," with its famous lines "The Assyrian came down like a wolf on the fold / And his cohorts were gleaming in purple and gold." And, at the other end, we have the same poem of Byron going on to limn the death and devastation of the Assyrian forces; the biblical Nahum exclaiming in righteous triumph over the destruction of the last Assyrian capital city, Nineveh; and the Greeks depicting the death of the last Assyrian king, whom they named Sardanapalus and described as dissipated and effeminate, by self-immolation with his attendants as they faced the onslaught of their enemies—a portrait sensuously captured in the painting of Eugène Delacroix in the early nineteenth century.

These images, while they had some ultimate connection with the historical Assyria, were connected at most only partially and often in a distorted way. It remained for actual exploration of Assyria to fill in the gaps and change the configuration. The effort began in earnest in the 1840s with exploration of several of the Assyrian capital cities, Dur-Sharrukin (Khorsabad), Nineveh (Kuyunjik), and Kalah (Nimrud), by the French Paul-Émile Botta, Eugène Flandin, and later Victor Place, and the British Austen Henry Layard and later Hormuzd Rassam. The competition between them yielded the discovery of several palace and temple structures, from which came an abundance of monumental sculptures and reliefs portraying the Assyrian king and his court in scenes of warfare, hunting, and piety. In addition, thousands of cuneiform tablets were found, especially by Layard and Rassam in the Kuyunjik mound of Nineveh—the latter comprising the so-called library of Assurbanipal, the last major Assyrian king, which represented the cream of the Mesopotamian literary and scholastic traditions. Much of this material, artistic and textual, was taken back, with the allowance of the ruling Ottoman authority, to the British Museum (which obtained the bulk of the Assurbanipal tablets) and the Louvre, as well as to other museums and private collections in Europe and America. The Western publics responded with enthusiasm and amazement at the discoveries, and scholars who had already been working, though desultorily, on the decipherment of the cuneiform script and its languages now redoubled their efforts.

Over the next several decades, through the 1870s, it was the study of this Assyrian material, and especially the tablets from the Assurbanipal library, that crystallized the study of Mesopotamia as a whole into an academic field, and because this material dominated the work—though there was some more modest exploration of Assyria's southern neighbor, Babylonia—the new field became known as Assyriology, a name that remains.

Several moments in the evolution of the academic study of Assyria may be noted. The first came in 1857 and involved an experiment, organized by the British Royal Asiatic Society, to test whether the cuneiform script had really been deciphered and whether the major language in it then identified, the Semitic Akkadian (or as it was known at that time, Assyrian, after the finds in the Assyrian heartland), could be understood. Four of the outstanding scholars of the day were each given the same Assyrian text, the prism annals of the Middle Assyrian king Tiglath-pileser I (1114–1076 BCE), newly acquired by the British Museum, and asked independently to decipher it. The results were close enough to convince most onlookers that the decipherment of the script and its Akkadian language, while not yet complete, was on the right track. In the following two decades, the major European museums began to publish copies of their cuneiform tablet holdings, principally those from the Assurbanipal library, and the first grammars, glossaries, and sign lists appeared. Then in 1872 came another public moment: the lecture of a British Museum Assyriologist, George Smith—already becoming known to the scholarly world for his exemplary editions of Assyrian royal historical texts—which announced to a wider audience the discovery and decipherment of another Assurbanipal library tablet, this one with an account of the primeval flood too close in detail to the biblical account in Genesis to be an accident. Smith's announcement sparked a wave of new enthusiasm for Assyriology and for its importance as a legitimate field of study, not least because of its value for the understanding of the Hebrew Bible and ancient Israel. Academic positions for its study began to appear in Europe, and in the 1880s spread to America, where they were initially held by those who had trained in Europe, especially in Germany.

But by the 1880s the study of Assyria was not the only branch of Mesopotamian studies that drew attention. Increasingly, the focus turned to Babylonia, as it became clear that here was the older center of Mesopotamian culture and religion, which affected also Assyria and beyond. Many of the literary and scholastic texts in the Assurbanipal library—for example, George Smith's flood narrative—were texts that originated in Babylonia. Thus, from the 1880s, exploration of Babylonian sites like Nippur and Ur began, along with a more concerted study of all variety of Babylonian texts, literary and those from daily life, and the investigation and debate over the other major Mesopotamian cuneiform language, Sumerian, whose base lay in Babylonia.

This concern for Babylonia, once established, has remained to the present, and during the first half of the twentieth century, until World War II, arguably dominated Mesopotamian scholarship and the wider public's understanding of Mesopotamia. Yet if so, it was not the dominance that Assyrian studies had had in the middle decades of the nineteenth century when the whole field was just getting started. Indeed, research on Assyria, in this same pre–World War II period, continued in a substantial way. Thus, at the turn of the century, the British came back briefly to Kuyunjik at Nineveh, focusing on its temple to the god Nabû. More elaborately, the German Oriental Society, with the support of Kaiser Wilhelm II, sought to balance its excavations at Babylon (1899–1917) with a project at Assur (Qa'alat Sherqat) (1903–14), the oldest of the Assyrian capital cities, which had been virtually untouched by archaeologists hitherto. The results not only enriched the understanding of the last, Neo-Assyrian period of Assyrian history but also extended that history back to the third millennium BCE. Particularly noteworthy was the exposure of the Middle Assyrian period, of the second half of the second millennium BCE, both at Assur and at the adjacent royal city of Kar-Tukulti-Ninurta (Tulul al-Aqar); that period had barely been known before. The Assur excavations did not continue after 1914, being resumed only much later, in the last decades of the twentieth century. But between the two world wars other, albeit shorter and less extensive, Assyrian excavations took their place. For the Neo-Assyrian period, there was the renewal of work on the capital city of Dur-Sharrukin (Khorsabad) by the University of Chicago Oriental Institute, which also explored the aqueduct of Sennacherib around Nineveh. Nineveh itself was again the object of a British excavation working at the mound of Kuyunjik but also more briefly at the other mound, Nebi Yunus; while the Neo-Assyrian period was emphasized, a sounding at Kuyunjik brought the history of the site back deep into prehistory. Both Middle and Neo-Assyrian in date were two small sites, Shibaniba (Tell Billa), northeast of Nineveh, and the provincial outpost, Tell Fekheriye, west of the upper Tigris heartland on the Habur River tributary of the Euphrates. And for the Old Assyrian period, of the first part of the second millennium BCE, there was the Czech excavation (1925) of the Assyrian settlement that was part of the site of Kanesh (Kültepe) in Turkey. Accompanying this diverse archaeological activity up to World War II were several lines of textual research. Newly discovered Middle and Neo-Assyrian royal inscriptions and other historical texts especially from Assur were published, as was the correspondence between various Neo-Assyrian kings and their advisors (the "Harper Letters"), which had been found earlier in the Assurbanipal library and deposited in the British Museum. Both historical texts and correspondence sparked a number of studies of the Assyrian dialect of Akkadian, of Assyrian historiographic techniques, and of the activities of the Middle and Neo-Assyrian imperial court. Finally, the tablets from the Czech Kültepe expedition, joined to several published before World War I, opened up the period of Old Assyrian history and its complex economic system.

Scholarly work on Assyria after World War II built on these earlier undertakings and considerably added to them. It is in this period, continuing to the present, that Assyrian studies have become the full and equal partners to work on Babylonia. Archaeological excavation has not only dealt with the capital cities on the upper Tigris but also extended into Assyrian settlements or Assyrian artifacts in the wider territories of the Middle and Neo-Assyrian Empires, especially to the west in Syria and Palestine and northwest in Turkey, where the earlier excavation of Kültepe was resumed on a larger and longer scale along with other sites of Old Assyrian settlement. For the capital cities, preeminent has been the decades-long excavation at Kalah (Nimrud), picked up by the British in 1949, after the first efforts in the nineteenth century, and continued by others. For the outlying settlements the equally long German work at Dur-katlimmu (Tell Sheikh Ḥamad), and minor sites on the Habur River, a tributary of the upper Euphrates, stands out. Textual studies of the new tablets from these excavations and the older collections in museums and private hands have been just as energetic, and among the major multivolume projects three may here claim notice: the Assur Project (Berlin and Heidelberg), resuming the interwar publication of tablets found at Assur, which bear on the administrative and cultural life of the Middle and Neo-Assyrian periods; the Royal Inscriptions of Mesopotamia (Toronto and now Philadelphia), producing critical editions and English translations of all such texts from Assyria and, in part, from Babylonia; and the State Archives of Assyria (Helsinki), offering the same for all other texts relating to the Neo-Assyrian Empire. The last two series, which are now approaching completion and exist in part electronically, mark a new stage in the study of Assyrian history, opening it up to a wide range of scholars beyond Assyriology and presenting thrilling possibilities for detailed and comparative analysis of politics, the military, society, economy, and culture.

3. Geography, Sources, and Chronology

The core of Assyrian settlement, as already indicated, lay on the banks of the upper Tigris River, starting just above its eastern tributary, the Upper or Greater Zab, and extending south to its parallel, also on the east, the Lower or Lesser Zab. It was here that the capital cities of the state were located: Assur, Kar-Tukulti-Ninurta, Nineveh, Kalah, and Dur-Sharrukin. These cities themselves can be divided into two groups: Assur and, about three kilometers north, Kar-Tukulti-Ninurta, both downstream on the Tigris, just above the Lower Zab; and Nineveh, Kalah, and Dur-Sharrukin farther upstream, around or above the Upper Zab. This whole area is partly flat and partly hilly and moves out to the west, between the Tigris and Euphrates Rivers, into a flat, steppe area known as the Jazirah ("island") in Arabic. That steppe, which already in the earlier second millennium BCE became the object of Assyrian territorial expansion, marked, thus, the western border of the Assyrian heartland.

As for the northern and eastern borders, these were the mountains: the Taurus, in the northwest above the Jazirah in eastern Turkey, connecting as one moved northeast with the Zagros, which ran down the eastern side of the Assyrian heartland and of Babylonia to its south, and divided them both from the Iranian highlands further to the east, though this dividing line became less sharp and more porous as the Zagros moved south along Babylonia. The southern border of this Assyrian heartland, then, was the Babylonian south. It began in earnest where the Tigris and Euphrates come closest together, roughly at the location of modern Baghdad and at the junction of the Diyala River with the Tigris—the Diyala being another Tigris tributary to the east, parallel with the Lower and Upper Zabs north of it. The area between the Diyala and the Lower Zab, stretching across the Tigris and the Euphrates, formed an intermediate zone between Assyria and Babylonia, which at various times was claimed by both.

The Assyrian heartland just defined displayed a rather different ecology from the Babylonian south. The south formed a plain between the Tigris and Euphrates, reaching down through a marshy area to the Persian Gulf. The region was generally dry, except for this marsh, and at times extremely hot, with no real rainfall. Agriculture, however, flourished with the rich alluvium brought down by the Tigris and Euphrates and distributed across the plain through a complex of human-made irrigation canals, which came to be controlled, and occasionally fought over, by the different Babylonian cities. In Assyria, however, irrigation was to be found only modestly; the region, particularly its upper and eastern parts being well watered by rivers and streams and adequate rainfall, allowed natural agriculture without the

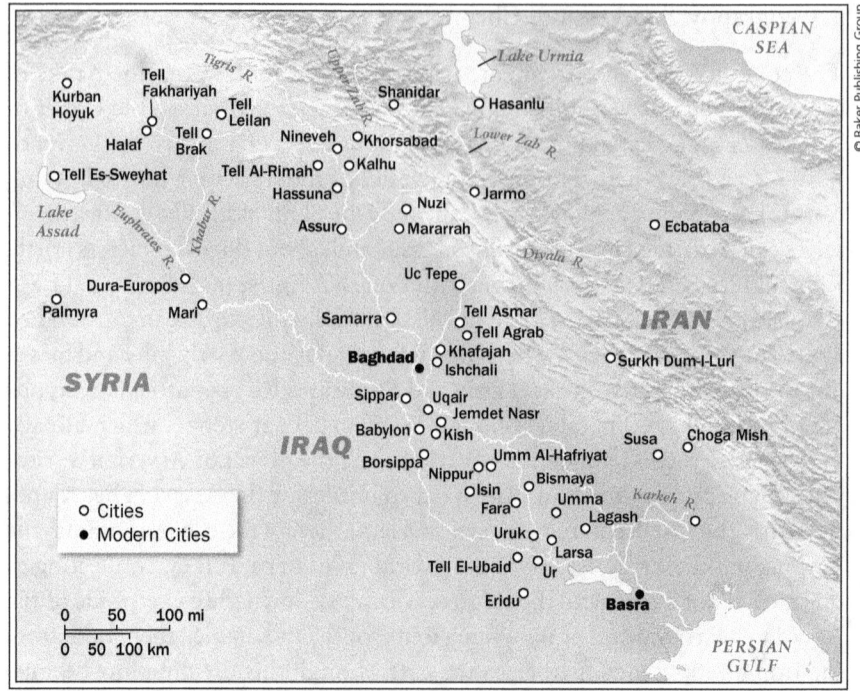

Figure 2.1. The Assyrian Empire

need for large artificial installations and the kinds of societal tensions over water that the south experienced.

This ecological difference, in conjunction with differences in the natural boundaries, provided a platform for differing societal profiles in Assyria and Babylonia. To be sure, the south, as the older high culture, supplied much of the world of religious belief and practice to the north as well, particularly at the level of state religion (see below). But this was not enough to overcome all of the differences in social, cultural, and political traditions. It is thus not surprising that there never really developed a single term for the whole area in antiquity. "Mesopotamia" is the term used in modern times for the whole, but this is a Greek term, albeit based on an Akkadian phrase, and in Akkadian/Greek it originally referred only to the land around the bend of the western Euphrates, not to the Assyrian heartland or Babylonia. Otherwise, in pre-Hellenistic times separate terms were used for the Babylonian south and the Assyrian north. In the case of the latter, one word continued through most of its history: "Aššur" (in which š represents sh). This refers to the city Aššur, the national god Aššur, and the state and empire as the land of Aššur. Today it is customary to distinguish these usages by labeling the city, Assur;

the god, Ashur or Aššur; and the land of Aššur, Assyria. In the Assyrian writing system (cuneiform) they could be distinguished by the juxtaposition of different determinative signs or words, but this should not obscure the fact that the ancient Assyrians saw an intimate connection among them all, with the city and the god understood to be the origin of the state.

The sources for the history of Assyria are, as for many other human groups, both written and nonwritten, the latter comprising artistic works, other artifacts, architectural structures, and human settlements—that is, houses, villages, towns, and cities and their forms and distribution. On this nonwritten side, Assyria certainly did create monumentally, its monuments growing in individual size and refinement, in quantity, and in distribution as the state turned into an empire, and then, in the Neo-Assyrian period, into a world empire—the largest that the Near East had experienced up to that time. Indeed, it is in this monumentality that the size, power, and complexity of the Assyrian imperial achievement become most readily tangible to us as modern interpreters. Neo-Assyrian Nineveh, for example, comprised 750 hectares (1875 acres) by the seventh century BCE when it became the principal Assyrian capital. This made it the largest city in the Near East up to that point; it was only exceeded, and then slightly, by Babylon in the south in the following Neo-Babylonian period, and one suspects that the design for Babylon had Nineveh as a standard to exceed. Moreover, within such cities as Nineveh but also beyond, the Assyrian elites created a monumental art in the Middle and Neo-Assyrian periods, which, drawing as it did from earlier traditions, yet achieved a distinctive profile of its own. The huge human-headed bulls guarding the entrances to palaces and temples, the standing statues of the emperors, copied by certain of their vassal-kings for themselves, and especially the reliefs of the emperors in battle, hunting, and worship—all made an imposing impression. It impressed, as already noted, the European audiences who saw them in the nineteenth century, but it was also something that overwhelmed the ancient subjects of the emperors who were made to gaze on these monuments either as erected in their own lands or as arranged in procession on the walls of the palace complexes at Nineveh or one of the other capital cities, to which the subjects came with tribute.

It is this physical monumentality that is so striking. Yet the history of Assyria could not be substantially investigated without the multitude and variety of the written records that have survived. While these will be referred to at various points later in this chapter, we may observe here that the records divide, broadly, into three categories: official statements of state policy and activities, embodied in such texts as royal inscriptions, the Assyrian King List, and chronicles; texts in the so-called stream of tradition—here slightly modifying the use of a term introduced and made famous by A. Leo Oppenheim[1]—that is, concerned with religious activities like rituals and divination, the sciences like medicine, astronomy, and mathematics, and literature like mythology; and everyday texts like letters and administrative documents. In the early stages of Assyriology, it was the official statements that were the center of the study of Assyrian political and military history, and editions of these texts were among the first Assyrian source publications, for example, by George Smith in the 1870s. The bombastic proclamations of these sources, to be sure, did not go unnoticed, but how to deal with them so that these texts could be used as historical sources proved—and has remained—a persistent problem. Important advances, however, were made by such scholars as A. T. Olmstead, Hayim Tadmor, and Mario Liverani dealing with the structure, compositional history, and rhetorical conventions of the inscriptions and offering an expanded and more varied sense of the kind of history they could convey: not only about the events they purported to record but about the worldviews and circumstances of their authors and the kings they celebrated. In the process, scholars have become ever more sensitive to the ways in which these inscriptions fit and do not fit within a larger web of evidence, embracing the other two categories of written sources and the artistic and archaeological remains.

4. Assyrian History

The history of Assyria is conventionally divided into Old Assyrian, Middle Assyrian, and Neo-Assyrian periods. This tripartite division reflects the periods for which texts are most available and the linguistic dialects of Akkadian that were used in those periods. However, like similar periodizations of history for Egypt, Babylonia, or Hatti, these must be regarded as somewhat heuristic.

The present historical survey focuses on the Neo-Assyrian period because that is the only period in which Assyria overlapped with the histories of Israel and Judah. It will become clear that the Neo-Assyrian period was in fact essentially continuous with the Middle Assyrian period.[2] By contrast, the connections between these later Assyrian rulers and the rulers of the Old Assyrian period are far less clear.

---

1. Oppenheim, "Assyriology—Why and How?," reprinted in his *Ancient Mesopotamia: Portrait of a Dead Civilization*, rev. ed., completed by Erica Reiner (1964; Chicago: University of Chicago Press, 1977), 13; original essay in *Current Anthropology* 1 (1960): 412.

2. David Kertai, "The History of the Middle-Assyrian Empire," *Talanta: Proceedings of the Dutch Archaeological and Historical Society* 40–41 (2008–9): 25–51. On the period in general, see also Brian Brown, "The Structure and Decline of the Middle Assyrian State: The Role of Autonomous and Nonstate Actors," *JCS* 65 (2013): 97–126.

The Old Akkadian and Old Assyrian Periods

The imperial rulers of the Neo-Assyrian period sought to connect themselves with legendary Mesopotamian kings of the distant past, even into the third millennium BCE. In the Old Akkadian period that preceded the Old Assyrian period, great kings such as Sargon (r. 2334–2279) and Naram-Sin (r. 2254–2218) won fame that lasted for thousands of years after their reigns. As the most powerful rulers of their times, they campaigned eastward into Iran, and westward at least as far as Syria. Naram-Sin suppressed a great revolt of multiple cities in southern Mesopotamia, after which he declared himself a god; some of his successors seem to have followed him in this conceit. As the first Semitic speakers to dominate Mesopotamia, the Old Akkadian kings were the propagators of the Akkadian language, which eventually became the lingua franca for the entire Near East. Therefore, it is natural that later Assyrian rulers would want to associate themselves with these famous figures by inserting them into the stylized history of the Assyrian King List or by adopting their names, as did Sargon II (r. 722–705). However, the Old Akkadian kings' capital city, Akkad, was probably in central Mesopotamia, at the confluence of the Tigris and Adheim Rivers, south of the heartland of the later Assyrian Empire.[3] Under Naram-Sin's son, Shar-kali-sharri, the empire collapsed as Amorites, Elamites, and Gutians all rebelled. A later text reports that Shar-kali-sharri was killed by his fellow Akkadians in a coup. The territory of the post-Sargonic kings was limited to parts of central and northern Mesopotamia.

Four centuries later Shamshi-Adad I (r. 1807–1775)[4] briefly established a "Kingdom of Upper Mesopotamia." Although this has been dubbed the Old Assyrian period, and Shamshi-Adad's kingdom included later Assyrian imperial centers such as Assur and Nineveh, the term "Assyria" (Aššur) was not used for it. Shamshi-Adad himself appears to have been an Amorite usurper with a base in Babylonia. He moved north and established a centralized government with a capital well outside of the traditional Assyrian heartland, in Shubat Enlil (Tell Leilan) to the northwest. He jockeyed for power among the city-states of Syria and Mesopotamia, but his dominance was short-lived, as his kingdom was overrun by other regionally powerful city-states.[5] Still, at least four Middle and Neo-Assyrian kings later adopted his name.

3. The site of Akkad has never been conclusively identified.
4. These dates are somewhat different from the Old Babylonian chronology used elsewhere in this volume.
5. On the period's history, see Klaas R. Veenhof and Jesper Eidem, *Mesopotamia: The Old Assyrian Period*, OBO 160/5 (Fribourg: Academic Press; Göttingen: Vandenhoeck & Ruprecht, 2008).

One outstanding feature of the Old Assyrian period was the wide range of trading contacts that Assyrians built, and far-flung outposts sprang up. A larger one was called a *kārum* (roughly equivalent to "port" for those along major waterways, or "entrepôt" for those that were not). One of the best excavated, known as Karum Kanesh, was found in a tell near Kültepe, in central Anatolia; the *kārum* was not an independent Assyrian town but was contained in a quarter of an Anatolian city. These outposts were usually run by Assyrian families who would send a representative to the outlying areas, where he would oversee trade and send home profits and goods. For areas beyond the reach of a *kārum*, there were extended caravan stops (called a *wabartum*) where land-traveling merchants might stop over. Most trade in Mesopotamia involved some transport over water, but after arriving at ports, goods might be transported for weeks by donkey. The network gave the Assyrians wide economic reach.

The Middle Assyrian Period

After the Old Assyrian period, there is a lengthy gap for which sources are spotty, but they resume in the Late Bronze Age, a time when international connections flourished and large empires vied for power. Assur-uballiṭ I (r. 1363–1328) came to the throne at a time when Assyria was overshadowed by Mittani, but he was able to capitalize on Hittite incursions by simultaneously attacking the Mittanians from the east. He eventually annexed their eastern side, and these gains were solidified in the thirteenth century under Adad-nirari I (r. 1305–1274), Shalmaneser I (r. 1273–1244), and Tukulti-Ninurta I (r. 1243–1207). The last founded a new capital city in Kar-Tukulti-Ninurta, and Assyria gradually extended its control into Babylonia and eastern Syria and Anatolia.

This Middle Assyrian Empire thus had international reach, and it was able to place its officials at outposts along canal routes and roads in a far-reaching network. These were primarily for the purpose of controlling and protecting trade routes in outlying regions; there is little indication that the Assyrians were interested in influencing all aspects of life in distant lands. Government and business activities were tracked by well-developed bureaucracies in Assur and in provincial cities, which kept extensive written records. The picture of Middle Assyrian administrative practices rendered by these archives is the most complete available for any of the Late Bronze Age states.[6]

Despite the Assyrians' military and economic successes during this period, they struggled more than some other nations to win political recognition from

---

6. J. N. Postgate, *Bronze Age Bureaucracy: Writing and the Practice of Government in Assyria* (Cambridge: Cambridge University Press, 2013), 4.

other large powers. The Late Bronze Age was characterized by the dominance of several major states with imperial ambitions, including Egypt, Hatti, Mittani, and Babylonia, whose rulers styled themselves "great kings." This group has been called "the club of great powers."[7] A group of smaller states sought protection under the aegis of one of the major states. The status that the Middle Assyrian rulers had achieved brought them into constant tension with their neighbors as they sought recognition as one of the great powers.

The Amarna letters from this period shed light on international politics at a very personal level. In them one sees Assur-uballiṭ I become the first ruler of the time to call himself "king of Assyria." As such, he sought to claim status as a "brother" to Egypt (EA 15–16), which was a common gesture of equality among the "Great Kings" of the Late Bronze Age. However, the ruler of Babylonia, Burnaburiaš II, was simultaneously writing to the pharaoh telling him Assur-uballiṭ was his vassal and had no right to go to Egypt without his permission (EA 9).[8] Later, when Adad-nirari I had conquered Mittani, he wrote to his new neighbor, the Hittite king who was probably Mursili III (= Urhi-Teshshup), and addressed him as "brother." Mursili III, however, retorted: "Why should I write to you about brotherhood? . . . Were you and I born from one mother?" (*HDT* 24A). In sum, it appears that the Middle Assyrian kings rose to power rather quickly, but they did eventually achieve status among their peers: Egypt sent a gift of gold to Assur-uballiṭ (albeit not enough to make him happy); Burnaburiaš married a daughter of Adad-nirari; and even Mursili III grudgingly allowed that "by force of arms . . . you have become a Great King" (*HDT* 24A).

The Middle Assyrian efflorescence, however, came to an equally abrupt end with the assassination of Tukulti-Ninurta I in 1207. Assyria struggled for most of the next two and a half centuries against Aramean kingdoms in Syria and Mesopotamia, and also against Babylonia. David Kertai points out that Assyria's regional empire did not suddenly disappear: "What changed was the *way* these territories belonged to the king. . . . During the 12th century the territories belonging to the Assyrian king became more indirectly governed,"[9] for example through client kings. However, it appears that Assyria even became a vassal of Babylonia for a time, so the power of the former was much reduced.

---

7. Hayim Tadmor, "The Decline of Empires in Western Asia ca. 1200 BCE," in *Symposia Celebrating the Seventy-Fifth Anniversary of the Founding of the American Schools of Oriental Research*, ed. F. M. Cross (Cambridge, MA: American Schools of Oriental Research, 1979), 3.

8. See further Raymond Westbrook, "Babylonian Diplomacy in the Amarna Letters," *JAOS* 120 (2000): 377–82; Raymond Cohen and Raymond Westbrook, eds., *Amarna Diplomacy: The Beginnings of International Relations* (Baltimore: Johns Hopkins University Press, 2000).

9. Kertai, "History of the Middle-Assyrian Empire," 27 (emphasis added).

Under Tiglath-pileser I (r. 1115–1077), Assyria restored its hegemony over Babylonia and saw a brief period of expansion and flourishing. He campaigned as far as the Mediterranean and reconquered Babylon, but by the middle of the eleventh century, Assyria had shrunk back again to its northern Mesopotamian homeland.

Some further light is shed on Assyrian culture in this period by the Middle Assyrian Laws and Palace Decrees.[10] While the collection as a whole shows some continuity with the cuneiform legal tradition that also includes the Code of Hammurabi and other law collections, the Palace Decrees evince a particular concern with controlling access to court women, prescribing that visitors stand seven paces back at all times, not visit unless the women are fully dressed, and not listen in on their conversations. For this reason they are also known as the Harem Edicts. The decrees dictate draconian punishments for any person who violates its rules, such as cutting off the ears or nose, or pouring hot pitch over the lawbreaker. The militarism of the culture is reflected by the detailed laws about women whose husbands had been captured in battle (they were to wait two years before they could remarry). Royal inscriptions, beginning in the Middle Assyrian period even before Tiglath-pileser I, increasingly emphasized military campaigns and epic poems about these campaigns, and the Middle Assyrian coronation ritual specifies that one of the duties of the Assyrian king was "to expand the land."

The Neo-Assyrian Period

With the decline after Tiglath-pileser I, a "dark age" of more than a century followed, for which there are few sources. Estimates vary regarding the degree of continuity between the Middle and Neo-Assyrian Empires; the Assyrians themselves viewed the kingdom as existing continuously, but sources such as their king lists are partially literary constructs.

Eventually, Assur-dan II (r. 934–912) and his successors rebuilt Assyria's economic power and reconsolidated its hold on its immediate environs. This involved regular military campaigns to drive out Arameans from the countryside surrounding Assyrian cities, rebuilding the city of Assur as well as canals and roads, and establishing more permanent rule. His successors, Adad-nirari II (r. 911–891) and Tukulti-Ninurta II (r. 890–884), campaigned even farther afield against the Arameans, and they claim to have eventually reached the point where the western tribal leaders voluntarily submitted to

---

10. G. R. Driver and J. C. Miles, *The Assyrian Laws: A Translation and Commentary* (New York: Oxford University Press, 1935); Martha T. Roth, *Law Collections from Mesopotamia and Asia Minor*, 2nd ed., WAW 6 (Atlanta: Scholars Press, 2003), 153–209.

them and brought tribute without a fight. They also continued construction projects at Assur and Nineveh.

However, it was Assurnasirpal II (r. 883–859) who was dubbed "the real founder of the final Neo-Assyrian empire" by H.W. F. Saggs.[11] Assurnasirpal extended the kingdom to the Taurus Mountains in the north and to the Euphrates in the west; he became the first Assyrian in two centuries to control the routes to the Mediterranean and received tribute from as far south as Tyre. He set up for the first time a provincial administration in outlying territories, with garrison troops and supplies for them. In 879 Assurnasirpal also moved the capital of the empire to Kalhu (biblical Calah/modern Nimrud), a city that had been a provincial capital and was located in the center of the Assyrian homeland, between Assur, Nineveh, and Arbela. This move consolidated royal power at the expense of those major cities.[12] Kalhu was raised to new glory by his ambitious construction of palaces and temples, which were in some cases completed and extended by his son Shalmaneser III.

"Tribute" is a somewhat euphemistic name given to the payments that ancient empires required of their vassals. Generally, the goal of the Assyrian Empire was not merely to maximize its territory, but to extract as much wealth as possible from outlying areas. (Keeping states that bordered other major powers as nominally independent also created a buffer that lessened Assyria's need to fight major wars.) So although the empire continued to benefit from trade as had its Middle Assyrian forebears, it depended for its flourishing on extracting these very heavy taxes. It worked very much like a mafia protection racket: kings of smaller nations had to pay the tribute or be deposed, and likely killed. As an inscription of Sennacherib says, this tax was payable "yearly (and) *without interruption.*"[13] This "yoke of Aššur" weighed heavily on the smaller client states.

Shalmaneser III (r. 858–824) continued Assyria's ambitious campaigning. In the north, he won a major victory against Urartu in 856. Starting in 853 he faced a federation of twelve western kings who had banded together to attempt to throw off Assyrian control. As recounted on Shalmaneser's Kurkh Monolith, the coalition brought more than 50,000 footsoldiers, plus almost 4,000 chariots and 2,000 cavalry.[14] The group was largely composed

---

11. H. W. F. Saggs, *The Might That Was Assyria* (London: Sidgwick & Jackson, 1984), 72.

12. Karen Radner, "Economy, Society, and Daily Life in the Neo-Assyrian Period," in *A Companion to Assyria*, ed. Eckart Frahm, Blackwell Companions to the Ancient World (Oxford: Wiley-Blackwell, forthcoming).

13. A. Kirk Grayson and Jamie R. Novotny, *The Royal Inscriptions of Sennacherib, King of Assyria (704–681 BCE), Part 1*, RINAP 3/1 (Winona Lake, IN: Eisenbrauns, 2012), 64 (emphasis added).

14. A. Kirk Grayson, *Assyrian Rulers of the Early First Millennium BC*, vol. 2, 858–745 BC, RIMA 3 (Toronto: University of Toronto Press, 1991), 23–24. See also COS 2.113A.

Figure 2.2. Black Obelisk of Shalmaneser III

of Syrian city-states, but notably it included a force led by Ahab of Israel, said to comprise 10,000 soldiers and 2,000 chariots. Shalmaneser had to wage four campaigns against the coalition between 853 and 845; he claimed victory each time but probably actually suffered serious setbacks. It appears that he eventually wore down the western city-states, however, since his famous Black Obelisk includes a record of receiving tribute from Jehu of Israel a few years later (841); the obelisk even seems to depict Jehu, which would be the only contemporaneous artistic depiction of an Israelite or Judean king that has survived (fig. 2.2).

Assyria suffered a bit under its subsequent rulers. To the north, Urartu emerged again as a major rival to Assyria that required multiple military campaigns. Babylonia remained a political and military challenge, demanding a delicate balance between diplomacy and force. There was also internal strife at the end of Shalmaneser's reign; the principal military commander, Shamshi-ilu, began leading his own campaigns, and Shalmaneser's heir, Shamshi-Adad V (r. 823–811), had to fight for six years, especially against his brother, for the throne. This was also the period of the queen Šammuramat, source of the later Greek legends about Semiramis. A wife of Shamshi-Adad, she wielded significant influence. She bore his heir, Adad-nirari III (r. 810–783), and is described as a virtual coregent with her son in certain inscriptions. During Adad-nirari's reign some territorial expansion occurred to the north and west, but the issue of internal stability continued unsettled. Its major manifestation was the growth of a certain independence among the imperial magnates. Governorships had been established over the provinces and could be passed hereditarily from father to son. These governors—the most powerful of whom was the commander in chief of the army, Shamshi-ilu—could become kinglets, having their own inscriptions written and ruling on conflicts among smaller, local powers. Also during this time, Urartu's territory and power in the north expanded greatly, to the point that it threatened the Assyrian heartland. Not coincidentally, this period of Assyrian disarray and attention to the north coincides with the long and apparently successful reign of Jeroboam II in Israel (r. 788–748).

With the ascension of Tiglath-pileser III (r. 744–727) through a revolt in the capital city of Kalhu (Nimrud), Assyria regained its teeth and its interest in the west. By comparison with Assyria's deliberate and partly defensive expansion up to the second half of the eighth century, its explosion southward to Egypt over the ensuing seventy-five years is almost startling, and with the expanded territory came an expanded administration. Within five years of taking power, Tiglath-pileser had reestablished Assyria's security against Babylon and Urartu. After putting down a Chaldean revolt in Babylonia, he became the first Neo-Assyrian king formally to take the Babylonian throne.

He pushed into Syria-Palestine again in 738, coercing tribute from King Menahem of Israel (r. 746–737), among others. A biblical text such as 2 Kings 15:19–20 gives an idea of how a vassal-king had to maintain his rule:

> King Pul of Assyria [Tiglath-pileser III] came against the land; Menahem gave Pul a thousand talents of silver, so that he might help him confirm his hold on the royal power. Menahem exacted the money from Israel, that is, from all the wealthy, fifty shekels of silver from each one, to give to the king of Assyria. So the king of Assyria turned back, and did not stay there in the land.

The translation "all the wealthy" is probably misleading: at 3,000 shekels to the talent, Menahem would have had to impose his tax on 60,000 people in the kingdom, and it is highly unlikely that there were that many "wealthy" people at the time. This may thus have been a tax on all the landowners, and for many it would have been a staggering burden. Although this tax may have satisfied the Assyrians, it was not a way to become popular among one's own people.

The renewed Assyrian aggression had a polarizing effect on the politics of the Levant; there was no middle ground for the smaller states. Tiring of Assyrian domination, Israel joined forces with what John H. Hayes has called a "Syro-Palestinian anti-Assyrian coalition,"[15] surely hoping to replicate the relative successes that similar coalitions had had in the ninth century. Judah, however, declined to oppose the empire. This set the stage for the greatest historical conflict between the northern and southern kingdoms, for Israel's coalition attacked Judah in the Syro-Ephraimite War in 734, intending to replace Ahaz with a ruler more sympathetic to their goals. Judah weathered the assault, however,

---

15. J. Maxwell Miller and John H. Hayes, *A History of Ancient Israel and Judah*, 2nd ed. (Louisville: Westminster John Knox, 2006), 374.

and Tiglath-pileser wiped out the anti-Assyrian movement in his western campaign of 734–731 (2 Kings 16:5–9; Cogan, *Raging Torrent*, 60–79). Israel's king, Pekah (r. 734–731), was killed and replaced with Hoshea (r. 730–722), whom Assyria supposed to be its puppet, with Israel its client state. Tiglath-pileser also removed some of Israel's territory and made it into Assyrian provinces, leaving just the area of and around the capital city of Samaria as a vassal state.

However, Hoshea himself withheld tribute in 725—a move that constituted rebellion in the eyes of the Assyrians. Israel instead called on the support of Egypt (2 Kings 17:4); unfortunately, it became clear that Egypt was in no position to resist Assyria either. Although it took a few years for Assyria to return westward, when it did it crushed the rebellion without much trouble. Israel's capital city, Samaria, was besieged and sacked in 722–721, and its population largely fled or was deported. It is likely that this led to an influx of northern refugees into Judah. Both Shalmaneser V (r. 726–722) and Sargon II (r. 722–705) are said to have overthrown Samaria in inscriptions, and it is possible that one started a siege and the other finished it. Even if the historical details are in dispute, the larger outcomes are clear: Samaria became the Assyrian province of Samerina, while the political expediency of Judah's consistent submission to Assyria was confirmed. Sargon reported that he deported more than 27,000 Israelites,[16] and surely many others fled southward as refugees and were incorporated into Judean society.[17] It was the practice of the Assyrians to exile peoples from lands that became provinces and to settle others there; the practice is discussed in more detail below.

Sargon was another usurper; his name in Akkadian (*Šarru-kēnu*) means "true king," which protests a bit too much. His taking of the throne was met with immediate uprisings in Mesopotamia and to the west. Although he was able to consolidate his rule in Assyria, he lost control of Babylonia to an uprising led by Marduk-apla-iddina II (called Merodach-baladan by the biblical authors in 2 Kings 20:12 and its parallel in Isa. 39:1).

Eventually, however, Sargon conquered some wealthy cities—Carchemish in the west (717) and Muṣaṣir in the north in Urartu (714). The riches from these campaigns allowed him to begin construction on a new capital city, Dur-Sharrukin (Sargon's Fortress), apparently as early as 717 BCE. Sargon's

---

16. Mordechai Cogan, *The Raging Torrent: Historical Inscriptions from Assyria and Babylonia Relating to Ancient Israel* (Jerusalem: Carta, 2008), 82.

17. Recently, Nadav Na'aman has challenged the idea that Jerusalem's growth in the eighth and seventh centuries was due to refugees from the north; see Na'aman, "Dismissing the Myth of a Flood of Israelite Refugees in the Late Eighth Century BCE," *ZAW* 126 (2014): 1–14. He made this case in other, earlier articles, which have been refuted by Israel Finkelstein, "The Settlement History of Jerusalem in the Eighth and Seventh Centuries BC," *RB* 115 (2008): 499–515.

attempts to create provinces at the edges of the empire, in the Zagros Mountains and central Anatolia, met with continuing strife, but he also had successes. One event referred to in the Bible (Isa. 20) was the so-called Ashdod Affair (Cogan, *Raging Torrent*, 83). In 716 Yamani, ruler of Ashdod, led other small Syro-Palestinian city-states against the Assyrians and sought support from Egypt. From 713 to 711 the Assyrians campaigned in the west to put down the rebellion. Yamani fled to Egypt, expecting to find allies there. However, the Kushite ruler Shebitku extradited Yamani back to Sargon and the Assyrians rather than create a diplomatic incident. Sargon also finally reconquered Babylon in 710; he lived there for the next three years.

Throughout this period of expansion, the Assyrians built a number of outposts and provincial cities around the Levant, including in Samaria, where they installed Assyrian governors and officials. Identified archaeologically by architecture and pottery that mimic the styles of the heartland, these allowed them to keep tabs on the affairs of the Levant and the Egyptian border.[18]

In Judah, despite the burdens of vassalship to the Assyrians, it appears that the royalty and trading classes profited to some extent from the increased trade brought by the Assyrian Empire.[19] Judah was known even in central Assyria as a major grain producer,[20] and its upper classes seem to have seen an upswing in wealth during the time of King Hezekiah.[21] The same geography that made Judah a battleground also positioned it to benefit from commerce. The oracle in Isaiah 19:23–24 envisions that "there will be a highway from Egypt to Assyria, and the Assyrian will come into Egypt, and the Egyptian into Assyria. . . . On that day Israel will be the third with Egypt and Assyria, a blessing in the midst of the earth."[22] The wealth of the Judean elite also would have led to intrasocietal tensions in Judah between the palace and landowners, who may have felt the pinch of taxation acutely.[23]

---

18. Jeffrey A. Blakely and James W. Hardin, "Southwestern Judah in the Late Eighth Century B.C.E.," *BASOR* 326 (2002): 11–64, esp. 44.

19. Stephanie Dalley sees Hezekiah's Judah as "a wealthy [nation] which had found ingenious ways to enrich itself" (Dalley, "Recent Evidence from Assyrian Sources for Judaean History from Uzziah to Manasseh," *JSOT* 28 [2004]: 393).

20. Avraham Faust and Ehud Weiss, "Judah, Philistia, and the Mediterranean World: Reconstructing the Economic System of the Seventh Century BCE," *BASOR* 338 (2005): 71–92.

21. John S. Holladay Jr., "Hezekiah's Tribute, Long-Distance Trade, and the Wealth of Nations ca. 1000–600 BCE: A New Perspective," in *Confronting the Past: Archaeological and Historical Essays on Ancient Israel in Honor of William G. Dever*, ed. Seymour Gitin et al. (Winona Lake, IN: Eisenbrauns, 2006), 309–31.

22. Although this passage has often been dated to a later period, its earliest form is quite plausibly rooted in the geopolitics of the eighth century.

23. These same tensions seem to have flared up in the time of Josiah (r. 640–609), who came to power as a puppet king after a revolt by the *'am hā'āreṣ* ("the people of the land"; 2 Kings

In 705 Sargon met his end on the battlefield while campaigning in the western mountains. Worse, he was not buried in his palace, which seems to have been the custom for Assyrian kings; the royal ancestor cult likely put a premium on the proximity of the corpse. (Sargon's unusual death may be reflected in Isa. 14:18–20, which taunts a king who does not enjoy a proper burial like other kings: "You are cast out, away from your grave, like loathsome carrion, clothed with the dead, those pierced by the sword.") In an exceptional text known colloquially as "The Sin of Sargon," his son Sennacherib seeks divinatory knowledge about why his father was cursed to suffer such a fate. The text reads, "[Let me examine] by means of extispicy the sin of Sargon, my father, let me then determine [the circumstances] and le[arn the . . . ; let me make] the sin he committed against the god an abom[ination to myself], and with the god's help let me save myself."[24] Sennacherib also moved the capital away from Dur-Sharrukin to Nineveh. Since the royal court had only moved to Dur-Sharrukin a year before Sargon's death, it is frequently assumed that Sennacherib concluded that the gods must not have approved of the new city.[25] Sargon's boasts about his new city might have been interpreted as hubris.[26]

With Sennacherib's accession, a common pattern repeated itself, and Judah decided to withhold tribute from Assyria. They were joined in resistance by other cities and states, including Sidon, Byblos, Ashdod, Ashkelon, Edom, and Moab. It took Sennacherib a few years to take charge of his affairs closer to home, but in 701 he mounted a major western campaign. He recounts that most of the kings submitted immediately and paid not only tribute but a penalty as well (probably a kind of "back taxes" for the missed years). Luli of Sidon is said to have fled, while Sidqa of Ashkelon and his family were deposed and deported; both were replaced with puppet rulers.

Sennacherib's account of his 701 campaign reaches its crescendo with his campaign against Judah, which was violent and mostly successful. Sennacherib counted forty-six cities pillaged; his inscriptions boast that from those

---

21:24). See Christopher R. Seitz, *Theology in Conflict: Reactions to the Exile in the Book of Jeremiah*, BZAW 176 (New York: de Gruyter, 1989), 42–51.

24. Hayim Tadmor, Benno Landsberger, and Simo Parpola, "The Sin of Sargon and Sennacherib's Last Will," *SAAB* 3 (1989): 3–51. The text actually seems to have been written in Esarhaddon's time. It would fit well with Esarhaddon's Babylonian policy, described below.

25. Karen Radner, however, points out other reasons for the move. Nineveh was naturally positioned to control the routes to the increasingly important western regions, and Sennacherib, unlike Sargon, came to power without controversy and had less need to distance himself from traditional cities and their powerful elites (Radner, "Economy, Society, and Daily Life").

26. Marc Van De Mieroop, *The Ancient Mesopotamian City* (New York: Oxford University Press, 1997), 54–61; Van De Mieroop, *Cuneiform Texts and the Writing of History* (New York: Routledge, 1999), 73–76.

cities, he took "200,150 people, young (and) old, male and female, horses, mules, donkeys, camels, oxen, and sheep, which were without number, and counted (them) as booty."[27] Jerusalem, however, survived. Isaiah compared it to "a shelter in a cucumber field" (1:8)—in other words, the only thing still standing. Hezekiah paid a heavy tribute but even managed, surprisingly, to retain his throne. The events at Jerusalem and the reasons for the outcomes are disputed because of the complex and conflicting assortment of sources. The issues and questions are reviewed in section 6 below.

Although Sennacherib did not take Jerusalem, he took great pride in that campaign to Judah. The most heavily fortified city that he actually overthrew was apparently Lachish, a significant fortress on a large tel to the south of Jerusalem. Sennacherib had the conquest of Lachish featured prominently in the wall reliefs in his "Palace without Rival" (see below, under "Arts, Crafts, and Architecture"). In general, the new palace broke new artistic ground and involved an incredible amount of labor and materials. Though it has never been fully excavated, it had at least 70 rooms, and the colossi that flanked his throne room were each 20 feet tall and weighed 40–50 tons.[28] The new palace was begun shortly after the 701 campaign and finished by 691. The move established Nineveh as the center of the greatly expanded empire.

Sennacherib struggled with Babylonia as well. Although he took the title "king of Babylon" like his successors, he did not rule it directly. The Assyrians seem to have held Babylonia in high esteem for its venerable cultural and religious traditions, and so accorded it special status and relative independence among the regions it ruled. The relationship was frequently an uneasy one, however. Sennacherib tried numerous strategies to pacify the region, including puppet kings and even installing his own son (whom the Babylonians handed over to raiding Elamites after just a few years). In 691 a coalition that included Babylonians, Arameans, and Elamites formed against Sennacherib. After fighting them off, he returned in 690 and besieged Babylon. After more than a year, he captured the city and destroyed it. He claimed that after tearing down the city and burning it, he dug a canal through it to level it completely, so that in the future "the site of that city . . . will be unrecognizable."[29]

Sennacherib had serious domestic problems as well. He named Esarhaddon as his heir, and in response the brothers apparently later murdered Sennacherib while Esarhaddon was on a military campaign, intending to usurp

27. Grayson and Novotny, *Royal Inscriptions of Sennacherib*, 65. See also COS 2.119B.
28. John Malcolm Russell, *Sennacherib's Palace without Rival at Nineveh* (Chicago: University of Chicago Press, 1991), 96.
29. Grayson and Novotny, *Royal Inscriptions of Sennacherib*, 206.

power. Simo Parpola has shown that the leader of the coup was Esarhaddon's older brother Arda-Mulissi, who had been passed over in the line of succession.[30] Esarhaddon, however, was able to return quickly and successfully fight the coup. These events are referred to very briefly in 2 Kings 19:36–37 and Isaiah 37:37–38, which report that the murderers fled to "Ararat"—that is, Urartu—a plausible destination for those who had murdered the Assyrian king.[31]

Esarhaddon was a skilled statesman. After Sennacherib's devastation and looting of Babylon, Esarhaddon restored its civic and religious functioning, along with special privileges and tax exemptions benefiting its citizens. He also fostered good relations with the ascendant Medes to the east and enforced order in the west, where he seems to have faced only a single uprising during his reign. This smooth handling of national affairs allowed Esarhaddon to push south and conquer a part of Egypt between 675 and 671, although he died while returning to Egypt in 669. The cause of death seems to have been a disease akin to lupus, from which Esarhaddon suffered throughout his reign. In part because of concerns about his health, he also is known to have relied on oracles from diviners more than any other Assyrian king, earning him a reputation for superstition.

The biblical narrative seems to lose interest in Assyrian events after Sennacherib's death, perhaps because of Esarhaddon's relatively uneventful relations with the Levant. It appears that he continued the policy of his grandfather, Sargon II, of moving populations to and from the province of Samerina: Ezra 4:2 tells of the returnees from exile rebuffing an offer of help in rebuilding the Jerusalem temple from people who claimed that their families had been in the land and worshiping Yahweh "ever since the days of King Esarhaddon of Assyria who brought us here." An inscription of Esarhaddon reveals that Manasseh of Judah was among the foreign kings summoned by him to

---

30. Simo Parpola, "The Murderer of Sennacherib," in *Death in Mesopotamia, XXVIeme Rencontre Assyriologique Internationale*, ed. Bendt Alster (Copenhagen: Akademisk Forlag, 1980), 171–82.

31. It has also been suggested that Šubria/Kullimeri, another northern border state, was their destination. See Tamás Dezső, "Šubria and the Assyrian Empire," *Acta Antiqua* 46 (2006): 33–38. See also Karen Radner, "Šubria, a Safe Haven in the Mountains," in *Assyrian Empire Builders*, University College London, 2012, http://www.ucl.ac.uk/sargon/essentials/countries/ubria/. The argument here was made earlier by A. L. Oppenheim, "Neo-Assyrian and Neo-Babylonian Empires," in *Propaganda and Communication in World History, 1: The Symbolic Instrument in Early Times*, ed. Harold D. Lasswell et al. (Honolulu: University Press of Hawaii, 1979), 111–44; and, building on Oppenheim, by Erle Leichty, "Esarhaddon's 'Letter to the Gods,'" in *Ah, Assyria . . . : Studies in Assyrian History and Ancient Near Eastern Historiography Presented to Hayim Tadmor*, ed. Mordechai Cogan and Israel Eph'al, Scripta Hierosolymitana 33 (Jerusalem: Magnes and the University of Jerusalem, 1991), 52–57.

bring building supplies to Nineveh for a palace building.[32] A long reign such as Manasseh's (r. 698–644) would not have been possible without the Assyrians' tolerance. It is also clear that Judah resumed its vassal status to Assyria because the latter continued its southward expansion. It is hard to imagine that Assyria could have pressed so far south had they not been in firm control of Judah and its environs. So whereas Judah was not turned into a province as Israel had been, it was returned to vassalship.

Since Esarhaddon suffered through such a rocky accession himself, it is not surprising that he took exceptional pains to ensure that his own son would accede to the throne more smoothly. The primary evidence of that effort is the Vassal Treaties of Esarhaddon, in which the king swore both client states and his own people to remain loyal to his son Assurbanipal after his death. These loyalty oaths are often compared to biblical covenants (see below). After Esarhaddon's untimely death, the succession to the Assyrian throne went smoothly, but Esarhaddon had tried to placate his older son Shamash-shum-ukin by giving him a lesser, regional throne in Babylonia. Assurbanipal (r. 668–631), the younger son whom Esarhaddon chose as Assyrian king, seems to have viewed Shamash-shum-ukin as a vassal, and this led to tensions.

Assurbanipal also was left to complete his father's conquest of Egypt. Because of its large size and great distance from Assyria, Egypt was never completely dominated by the Assyrians. Esarhaddon's administration there, such as it was, included many native Egyptians and was primarily oriented to extracting wealth. By the time he died, the Assyrian presence had already been forced out by a Nubian force led by Taharqa. Thus, one of Assurbanipal's first projects was an Egyptian campaign. In 667 he drove out the Nubians as he traveled up the Nile, and he installed Neco as a puppet ruler in Sais. However, just a few years later the Nubians returned under a new king, Tantamani. Assurbanipal thus campaigned there again in 664 and 663. This time, he was even more ambitious, making it all the way to Thebes, which he conquered and plundered (cf. Nah. 3:8–9).

By the middle of the seventh century BCE, Assyria was by far the largest empire that the Near East had ever seen. However, it also seems to have been overextended and unable to wage war on many fronts simultaneously. Even as Assurbanipal was fighting in Egypt, far to the south, Elam was causing trouble to Assyria's east, at the other end of the empire. Assurbanipal seems to have tried various sorts of interventions with the Elamites, including economic aid and interfering with the succession of their kings. The Assyrians fought off

---

32. Erle Leichty, *The Royal Inscriptions of Esarhaddon, King of Assyria (680–669 BC)*, RINAP 4 (Winona Lake, IN: Eisenbrauns, 2011), 23.

an Elamite advance in 665, but this only gave them a few years' rest on that front. It seems that the Elamite king who took the throne in 664, Te'umman, had participated in the earlier anti-Assyrian hostilities and maintained his opposition.[33] Assurbanipal clearly hated him and described him as demonic. By 653 Assurbanipal felt compelled to mount a major offensive against Elam, with which he sought to wipe out this rival kingdom once and for all and turn it into an unoccupied wilderness. (As part of that effort, Assurbanipal is said to have deported Elamites to Samaria; see Ezra 4:10, which refers to him as Osnappar.) He destroyed Elam's cities, sowed salt in its fields, plundered its temples, and even exhumed its royal tombs:

> The burial places of their early (and) later kings, who had not feared Ashur and Ishtar, my lords, (and) who had made my royal predecessors tremble, I devastated, I destroyed (and) let them see the sun; their bones I removed to Assyria. I laid restlessness on their spirits. Food-offerings (to the dead) and water-libations I denied them.[34]

In the same spirit, he killed and beheaded Te'umman, then slashed the head and hung it up on a tree while he had a picnic—a scene depicted in one of his reliefs. Saggs concludes that Assurbanipal was hotheaded and vindictive rather than strategic in his decisions, since the destruction of Elam allowed the Persians and Medes to expand there.[35] Combined with the well-known image of Assurbanipal as a patron of scholarship, this would create the picture of a complicated personality.

As Assyria moved against Elam, its victories in Egypt proved short-lived. By the mid-650s, Egypt was again asserting its independence, and this time Assyria could not respond because of problems much closer to home: the tension between Esarhaddon's sons flared up into civil war between Assyria and Babylonia. Assyria was able to quell what was essentially an internal uprising, but it took four years. By that time, Egypt had again thrown off Assyrian rule, this time for good.

Given Assyria's power and prominence at the middle of the seventh century, the relative suddenness of its fall is somewhat shocking, and the historian has relatively little information to work with: the few Assyrian royal inscriptions from later than 639, from the reigns of Assur-etel-ilāni and Sin-shar-ishkun,

---

33. Matthew W. Waters, "Te'umman in the Neo-Assyrian Correspondence," *JAOS* 119 (1999): 473–77.

34. Annals, col. 6, lines 70–76, in Amélie Kuhrt, *The Ancient Near East, c. 3000–330 BC* (London: Routledge, 1995), 2:500. See Maximilian Streck, *Assurbanipal und die letzten assyrischen Könige bis zum Untergange Niniveh's* (1916; repr., Leipzig: Zentralantiquariat, 1975), 54–57.

35. Saggs, *Might That Was Assyria*, 115–17.

are not very helpful for reconstructing the political and military events of those years; and administrative documents give very little indication of trouble. One must rely primarily on notices from Babylonian sources, especially the Babylonian Chronicle series.

Assurbanipal had an extraordinarily long reign, which led to succession problems; but those were nothing new. He died in 631[36] and was succeeded by his son, Assur-etel-ilāni, a minor who was overshadowed by others, especially the powerful eunuch, Sin-shum-lishir, who took over the kingship in 627. He, in turn, was overthrown by another son of Assurbanipal, Sin-shar-ishkun. But that did not put an end to the instability; revolt was everywhere.

The crumbling of Assyrian power was felt in Judah, even though the vacuum was quickly filled by Egyptian influence. There are no records of Assyrian presence in Palestine after 645,[37] and Assyrian control was certainly gone by 630. Judah began to reassert its political independence, but not immediately. Josiah made no moves regarding Assyria at all until his twelfth or eighteenth regnal year—that is, 628 or 622.[38] His reforms—based on his propagation of some version of the Deuteronomic laws—have often been thought to be a program meant to subvert Assyrian hegemony. That is because Deuteronomy's demands for love of and faithfulness to God are in some ways closely modeled on Neo-Assyrian loyalty oaths that demand love of and loyalty to the emperor (see discussion below).

The period of Assyria's decline also saw an upswing of Babylonian power. In short, Babylonia returned to international power under the leadership of a Chaldean prince named Nabopolassar.[39] He claimed the title "king of Babylon" already in 626, but it took until 616 for Babylon to muster itself sufficiently to attack Assyria in earnest. Leading a coalition that also consisted of Medes

---

36. The year of Assurbanipal's death is unclear. One commonly sees it dated to 627 (including elsewhere in this volume) on the basis of later sources that assigned him a 42-year reign, but there are no contemporaneous records mentioning him after 631. It has sometimes been theorized that he abdicated power to his sons, and retired to live elsewhere. Another theory relates to the Assyrian regent of Babylonia, Kandalanu, who died in 627; it has been hypothesized that Kandalanu was simply a Babylonian throne name for Assurbanipal (as Tiglath-pileser III and Shalmaneser V had earlier taken distinct Babylonian throne names), but that theory is not accepted here. For an accessible presentation and discussion of the sources, see John Boardman et al., eds., *The Cambridge Ancient History*, vol. 3, pt. 2, *The Assyrian and Babylonian Empires and Other States of the Near East, from the Eighth to the Sixth Centuries B.C.* (Cambridge: Cambridge University Press, 1991), 167–69.

37. Ephraim Stern, *Archaeology of the Land of the Bible*, vol. 2, *The Assyrian, Babylonian and Persian Periods, 732–332 BCE*, ABRL (New York: Doubleday, 2001), 4.

38. Chronicles records that Josiah began his reform in the twelfth year of his reign (2 Chron. 34:3), while Kings has it in the eighteenth (2 Kings 22:3).

39. For more information, see David S. Vanderhooft's chapter in this volume, and Bill T. Arnold, *Who Were the Babylonians?*, ABS 10 (Atlanta: Society of Biblical Literature, 2004), 87–93.

and Scythians, Babylonia began to attack Assyrian cities in 615. This process moved slowly but inexorably, as Nabopolassar pushed the Assyrians back to their core cities, starting in the late 620s. The arrival of the Medes as allies of the Babylonians in 614, under their leader, Cyaxares, was decisive.

It appears that the Assyrians were taken by surprise in various ways—most significantly, by the sudden need to defend their heartland. Sarah Melville argues that key central cities such as Kalhu and Nineveh had been built with an eye to concerns such as display, access, and water use, rather than defense, since the Assyrian philosophy of warfare was to attack preemptively. To them, the best defense was a good offense, so when they actually needed a defense, the cities were architecturally unprepared. Furthermore, the empire had by this time suffered some economic setbacks, and "it would have been unconscionable to invest in enhancing defenses that had not been needed since time immemorial."[40] Thus in 612 the capital city of Nineveh fell after a siege of only three months. It may be that Nahum 2:6—"The gates of the rivers are opened; the palace melts" (AT)—reflects the actual use of a limited inundation to certify, in symbolic fashion, the capture of the city.[41] That would mirror what Sennacherib had done to Babylon. The theory receives some support from possible muddled references in Ctesias and Xenophon.[42]

The Assyrians may also have been surprised by the ferocity of the Medes, who did not share common Mesopotamian cultural assumptions. Even the Babylonians sought to wash their hands of the destruction of Assyrian cities and temples, after the fact. They described their allies the Medes as impious and out of control, pillaging Assyria while the Babylonian king mourned.[43]

Some portions of the Assyrian court and military seem to have survived the fall of the major cities and fled westward into what is now Syria, where they held out for a time—with Egyptian support, remarkably. The Babylonian Chronicle records Assyrian holdouts still fighting in the west in 609. Thereafter they disappear into the mists of history. Remarkably, no account of their final extinction

---

40. Sarah C. Melville, "A New Look at the End of the Assyrian Empire," in *Homeland and Exile: Biblical and Ancient Near Eastern Studies in Honour of Bustenay Oded*, ed. G. Galil et al., VTSup 130 (Leiden: Brill, 2009), 194.

41. For discussion and citations, see David S. Vanderhooft, "Biblical Perspectives on Nineveh and Babylon: Views from the Endangered Periphery," *JCSMS* 3 (2008): 86.

42. Peter Machinist, "The Fall of Assyria in Comparative Ancient Perspective," in *Assyria 1995: Proceedings of the 10th Anniversary Symposium of the Neo-Assyrian Text Corpus Project, Helsinki, September 7–11, 1995*, ed. S. Parpola and R. M. Whiting (Helsinki: Neo-Assyrian Text Corpus Project, 1997), 179–95. See also J. D. A. MacGinnis, "Ctesias and the Fall of Nineveh," *ICS* 13 (1988): 37–42.

43. Mario Liverani, "The Fall of the Assyrian Empire: Ancient and Modern Interpretations," in *Empires: Perspectives from Archaeology and History*, ed. S. E. Alcock et al. (Cambridge: Cambridge University Press, 2001), 374–91, esp. 390.

has yet come to light in surviving documents, even by the Babylonians who vanquished them. Nebuchadnezzar II (604–562) appears to have employed an Assyrian scribe or two at his court, as Babylonian documents from 603 and 600 have been found in the Neo-Assyrian dialect.[44] But overall, Assyria was simply swallowed up by the Neo-Babylonians, not to reemerge. Liverani captures the upheaval well: "What had once been the center of the world became a border area between conflicting empires; what had once been the most intensively cultivated countryside reverted to tribal pastoralism; what had once been the core of international trade was bypassed as a dangerous crossing-point."[45]

The Babylonians, on the other hand, framed Assyria's fall as a rightful reestablishment of Babylonia's supremacy, continuous with previous periods in which it had been dominant. In practical terms, the shift in Mesopotamian powers would have been received in outlying areas little differently from the accession of any new king. However, the fall of Assyria was noted by the Hebrew prophets, who took up Isaiah's tradition of the taunt-song of false mourning, crying over Nineveh: "Alas, O city of bloodshed, completely deceitful, full of plunder—there was no end to (your) depredations! . . . There is no relief for your wound, your injury is mortal. All who hear the report about you clap their hands over you. For over whom did your relentless evil not sweep?" (Nah. 3:1, 19 [AT]; see also Zeph. 2:13–15).

5. Aspects of Assyrian Culture

What were the most salient aspects of Assyrian culture? To put it another way, what was distinctive about the Assyrians? They have often been subordinated to the Babylonians in discussions of Mesopotamian culture; despite all their overlap and reciprocal influence, the two cultures were not identical.

One necessary caveat in such a discussion is that it focuses largely on elite culture. Less is known about the cultures and lives of common people in the Assyrian Empire, because the excavations at major Assyrian cities have focused on the royal citadels while expending less effort to explore the parts of the cities where most of the people would have lived.

Military

Assyria's military was arguably its most distinctive cultural achievement. The Assyrians were adept with diverse weaponry, incorporated mercenaries

---

44. John A. Brinkman, "Unfolding the Drama of the Assyrian Empire," in Parpola and Whiting, *Assyria 1995*, 5.
45. Liverani, "Fall of the Assyrian Empire," 383.

from conquered nations, and had an array of siege tactics at their disposal, as the remains of a huge Assyrian ramp built at Lachish show. The Neo-Assyrian kings also boasted more often and at greater length about their conquests than did the rulers of any of the surrounding nations. This pride was not baseless: the army became the engine of Assyrian expansion and wealth.

How large was the Assyrian army? H. W. F. Saggs has opined that at its apex in the Neo-Assyrian period, Assyria theoretically could have raised an army of several hundred thousand troops,[46] but this was almost surely never done in practice.[47] Shalmaneser III (r. 858–824) claimed to have crossed the Euphrates with 120,000 soldiers, and that was not the peak of the empire. The Kurkh Monolith of Shalmaneser III reports that the coalition of Syro-Palestinian kings mustered about 65,000 men to fight the battle of Qarqar, which would make a somewhat larger number for the Assyrian army seem possible. Such numerical claims are notoriously untrustworthy,[48] but administrative documents from later in the imperial period show that the Assyrian kings were indeed supporting tens of thousands in their standing armies. In any case, in most conflicts the Assyrians were able to bring overwhelming forces to bear. The scale of the Assyrian military is also suggested by the incredible 160,000 kilograms (352,740 pounds) of iron found in a single room at Sargon II's palace at Khorsabad.

The composition of the Assyrian military was complex; a great variety of terms for various types of soldiers appear over the centuries in Assyrian inscriptions. The most recent and comprehensive analysis, incorporating textual and iconographic data, groups the servicemen into three categories: light, regular, and heavy.[49] The light troops were made up of conquered peoples; the regular troops were generally conscripted Assyrians; the heavy troops seem to have been professional full-time soldiers. The light troops were primarily infantry, while the regular and heavy troops included infantry, cavalry, and chariotry. Within these categories were specialists with various weapons, such as archers, spearmen, slingers, and lancers. At the pinnacle of the forces were elite bodyguard corps of armored spearmen. There were, in fact, two distinct armies, one directly commanded by the king (*kiṣir šarrūti*, "the royal corps"), the other covering all the soldiers (*ṣāb šarri*, "the troops of the king").

---

46. H. W. F. Saggs, "Assyrian Warfare in the Sargonid Period," *Iraq* 25 (1963): 165–70.

47. Michael Mann, *The Sources of Social Power*, vol. 1, *A History of Power from the Beginning to AD 1760* (Cambridge: Cambridge University Press, 1986), 232–33.

48. Marco De Odorico, *The Use of Numbers and Quantifications in the Assyrian Royal Inscriptions*, SAAS 3 (Helsinki: Neo-Assyrian Text Corpus Project, 1995).

49. Tamás Dezső, *The Assyrian Army I: The Structure of the Neo-Assyrian Army, as Reconstructed from the Assyrian Palace Reliefs and Cuneiform Sources* (Budapest: Eötvös University, 2012).

Just as the Assyrian Empire was the largest the Near East had seen, so too its military was the most multiethnic, and the conquered peoples who served alongside the Assyrians are shown in reliefs to have kept their ethnic markers and dress. (Herodotus's portrayal of the diverse Persian army in *Histories* 7 is probably more familiar and may give some idea of the impression the Assyrians had earlier made.) Certain subject nations were known for specialities: for example, the Samarians, Urartians, and Nubians were expert horsemen and charioteers; the Ituaeans and the Qurraeans were archers and spearmen; and it has been claimed that the Syrians and Palestinians were employed as slingers.[50] In any case, after Sennacherib campaigned to Jerusalem in 701, he claimed that King Hezekiah of Judah handed over "his elite troops (and) his best soldiers" along with the tribute. The author of Isaiah 29:7 refers to "the multitude of all the nations that fight against" Jerusalem, which may be a reflection of the impression created by such a diverse fighting force.

The Assyrian military was not made up only of soldiers; the staff required to support the troops would also have comprised a significant portion of the numbers. At the elite end of the spectrum, there would have been *ummânū*—"masters," or experts in various fields. The best-known examples are the diviners whose job it was to test the will of the gods before campaigns and battles, and the scribes and artisans whose job it was to record and represent them. But most of the workers would have been the *niš bīti*, the household staff: craftsmen, domestic workers, cooks, butchers, cleaners, and caretakers for the livestock. These were seemingly "civilians," since they have no markers of military rank or religious status on their clothing in iconographic portrayals. These staff are not often portrayed in reliefs or royal inscriptions and so are documented mostly in administrative letters.

The Assyrian army was fast moving, thanks to a system of highways connecting major points on the imperial grid. Nevertheless, war chariots, which had been a very important military technology in the Late Bronze Age, gradually decreased in importance in the first millennium as fewer battles were fought on open plains.

Siege warfare became a specialty of the Assyrians.[51] In his campaign against Judah in 701, Sennacherib boasted of besieging numerous walled cities and towns, "using packed-down ramps and battering rams, the assault of foot-soldiers, mines, breeches, and siege engines."[52] He claimed to have surrounded Jerusalem with blockades so as to make entry and exit impossible. This one

---

50. Rassam Cylinder, lines 55–56.
51. F. M. Fales, *Guerre et paix en Assyrie: Religion et imperialism* (Paris: Cerf, 2010), 126–27.
52. Grayson and Novotny, *Royal Inscriptions of Sennacherib*, 65 (text 4, lines 49–51).

passage indicates the variety of available siege tactics. The Assyrians built temporary encampments to facilitate sieges, but also more permanent forts that were well constructed and maintained. Ramat Raḥel, just outside Jerusalem, seems to have been one such Assyrian administrative fort. Wealthy and associated with the imperial power, these miniature Assyrian cities seem to have been viewed as unwelcome intrusions by the natives (cf. Isa. 14:21: "Let [the Mesopotamian king's sons] never rise to possess the earth or cover the face of the world with cities").

The Assyrian military was almost exclusively a land force. On the rare occasions that they took to the sea, it was usually with the support of vassals with seafaring expertise, primarily the Phoenicians. The Assyrians might employ boats to transport the military over seas or rivers but did not engage in naval warfare. One possible exception is the repeated boast of Sargon II about defeating pirates from the Greek islands:

> In order to [conquer the Ionians, who live] in the midst of the sea, who since long [in the past] used to kill the inhabitants [of the city] of Tyre (and) [of the land] of Que and to interrupt commercial traffic, I attacked them at sea [with ships from the land of] Hatti and destroyed them all.[53]

In sum, the technological and ideological apparatus of the military was the primary force that allowed Assyria to rise from among the regional powers left standing by the great disruptions at the end of the Late Bronze Age. Ahead of their time, they introduced some of the military techniques that were later honed in Babylonia, Persia, Greece, and Rome. The impression the Assyrian military made on smaller nations is captured well by an unforgettable passage from Isaiah:

> Here they come, swiftly, speedily!
> None of them is weary, none stumbles,
>   none slumbers or sleeps,
> not a loincloth is loose,
>   not a sandal-thong broken;
> their arrows are sharp,
>   all their bows bent,
> their horses' hoofs seem like flint,
>   and their wheels like the whirlwind.

---

53. The term "Hatti" refers to the western region, not to the former Hittite territory specifically. The ships probably were supplied by Tyre itself. For discussion of the inscription, see Nino Luraghi, "Traders, Pirates, Warriors: The Proto-History of Greek Mercenary Soldiers in the Eastern Mediterranean," *Phoenix* 60 (2006): 31.

> Their roaring is like a lion,
> > like young lions they roar;
> > they growl and seize their prey,
> > > they carry it off, and no one can rescue.
> > They will roar over it on that day,
> > > like the roaring of the sea.
> > And if one look to the land—
> > > only darkness and distress;
> > and the light grows dark with clouds. (Isa. 5:26b–30)

Use of Propaganda

Because of the Assyrians' emphasis on military might, they are often portrayed in simplistic terms. For example, in Byron's poem "The Destruction of Sennacherib," the Assyrian king descends on Jerusalem "like a wolf on the fold," and many interpreters have emphasized the Assyrians' aggressiveness and violence. However, others (especially in recent years) have perceived administrative practicality, a willingness to allow independence, and the benevolent imposition of a *pax Assyriaca* over the region.[54] Parpola is probably correct that the Assyrians' success was due to the tension between the "chilling fear" that they inspired and the "numerous benefits" that allegiance to them could bring.[55]

If history has generally held a negative view of the Assyrians, they themselves bear much of the guilt—not only for their real depredations of other nations but also because violence did in fact figure prominently in their iconography and propaganda. Their own inscriptions tell the story: Assurnasirpal II bragged, "I captured many troops alive: I cut off of some their arms and hands; I cut off of others their noses, ears, [and] extremities. I gouged out the eyes of many troops. I made one pile of the living and one of their heads. I hung the heads on trees around the city."[56] Tiglath-pileser III said of a rebel king: "I impaled [him] before the gate of his city and exposed him

---

54. Among Assyria's defenders is Saggs, who wrote, "[The Assyrians] have been maligned. Certainly they could be rough and tough to maintain order, but they were defenders of civilization, not barbarian destroyers" (*Might That Was Assyria*, 2). F. M. Fales wrote: "Le temps est . . . venu d'abandonner les interprétations moralisantes insistant sur le caractère belliqueux des Assyriens" (*Guerre et paix en Assyrie*, 229).

55. Simo Parpola, "Assyria's Expansion in the 8th and 7th Centuries and Its Long-Term Repercussions in the West," in *Symbiosis, Symbolism and Power of the Past: Canaan, Ancient Israel, and Their Neighbors from the Late Bronze Age through Roman Palaestina*, ed. William G. Dever and Seymour Gitin (Winona Lake, IN: Eisenbrauns, 2003), 102.

56. A. Kirk Grayson, *Assyrian Royal Inscriptions*, pt. 2, *From Tiglath-pileser I to Ashurnasir-apli II* (Wiesbaden: Harrassowitz, 1976), 126.

to the gaze of his countrymen. His wife, his sons, his daughters, his possessions, the treasure of his palaces I despoiled."[57] Neo-Assyrian treaties also contain graphic depictions of the violence and death that were to befall those who rebelled. Texts such as these were certainly propagandistic—they were intended to terrify anyone who would think of resisting Assyria—but there is little doubt that they also reflect real practices.

Nevertheless, cartoonish images of Assyria as *merely* rapacious and bloodthirsty risk missing its similarities to modern empires. It was not through sheer aggression that Assyria built its massive empire. Instead, the portrait that has emerged in the past fifty years is of a nuanced and savvy administration that was bent on maximizing wealth and consolidating power more than wreaking havoc. If every nation had been content to bow at the emperor's feet and send the heavy tribute every year (which was Assyria's primary source of wealth from its empire),[58] Assyria might never have fought a battle.[59]

Of course, the Assyrians *did* fight many battles and shed a lot of blood—not only because of the smaller nations' sense of pride or independence but also because the tribute was a serious economic hardship that degraded their quality of life and led to suffering in vassal nations by sapping their resources. That is likely the primary reason that nations "rebelled." Thus, it was Assyrian military might that largely built the empire later bequeathed to the Babylonians and Persians.

Mass Deportation

The frequent Neo-Assyrian practice of mass deportation goes by other names, including population resettlement and forced migration, but readers of the Bible may know it best as exile. Although the most often mentioned biblical exile was carried out by the Babylonians, and although the phenomenon was attested in earlier periods of Mesopotamian history,[60] it was the Assyrians

---

57. Hayim Tadmor, *The Inscriptions of Tiglath-pileser III, King of Assyria: Critical Edition, with Introductions, Translations, and Commentary* (Jerusalem: Israel Academy of Sciences and Humanities, 1994), 122–23.

58. Susan Sherratt and Andrew Sherratt, "The Growth of the Mediterranean Economy in the Early First Millennium BC," *World Archaeology* 24 (1993): 361–78.

59. A. Kirk Grayson, "Assyrian Rule of Conquered Territory in Ancient Western Asia," *CANE* 2:961: "The Assyrians came to prefer psychological warfare whenever it was feasible"; Simo Parpola and Kazuko Watanabe, *Neo-Assyrian Treaties and Loyalty Oaths*, SAA 2 (Helsinki: Helsinki University, 1988), xxiii: "No doubt the Assyrian kings preferred 'expansion by treaties' to expansion by aggression. Waging war was costly and time-consuming, and wasted resources."

60. For recent discussions, see Davide Nadali and Jordi Vidal, eds., *The Other Face of the Battle: The Impact of War on Civilians in the Ancient Near East*, AOAT 413 (Münster: Ugarit-Verlag, 2014), esp. 7–78.

who developed the practice. It was not simply one feature of Assyrian rule, but one of the central ones, crucial to the economy and the imperial mission. They inflicted mass deportations on the Babylonians (and the Israelites) before the Babylonians inflicted them on the Judeans.

In his foundational study, Bustenay Oded counted 157 mass deportations mentioned in Assyrian texts—often royal inscriptions but also letters and administrative documents. The practice was attested as early as Assur-dan II but became much more frequent with the reign of Tiglath-pileser III, who carried out at least 37 such population movements. (Sargon II had the largest number, 38.)[61] The exact scale of deportations is somewhat difficult to assess, since Assyrian kings and scribes clearly inflated the numbers of captives.[62] One example of this is Sennacherib's claim to have taken 200,150 people from Judah in 701—which would have far exceeded the entire population of the land.

The most common sort of population movement was into Assyria itself, but populations could also be moved into outlying regions. One letter describes a single population of 6,000 being distributed to 105 different settlements.[63] Sometimes "two-way" deportations were carried out—a city's people were uprooted, and the city was resettled with people from elsewhere. This diversity of practice reflects the various purposes of population movements. These included: punishment for rebellion; liquidation of rival powers and weakening resistance; provision of manpower (both military and civilian); and populating other areas of the empire, including conquered cities and undeveloped arable land.[64]

Families were moved together, presumably in the hope that it would encourage them to put down roots in the new area. In general, captives were not bound or shackled for the journey, and there seems to have been some concern that they reach their destination in good condition. However, elite captives might be shackled, perhaps to shame them.

The outcomes for resettled peoples were quite diverse. Throughout much of the imperial period the inscriptions say that the exiles were "counted as Assyrians," and they seem to have had the same rights (and duties) as other people who lived in the same land. Some of them came to own land in their new area; others continued their craft or trade, conducted business activities, or served as officials of the royal court. Finally, some became slaves. With the

---

61. Bustenay Oded, *Mass Deportations and Deportees in the Neo-Assyrian Empire* (Wiesbaden: Reichert, 1979), 20. Note also the newer studies in Oded's Festschrift: Galil et al., *Homeland and Exile*.
62. De Odorico, *Use of Numbers and Quantifications*, passim.
63. Oded, *Mass Deportations*, 30.
64. Ibid., 41–74.

reign of Sennacherib the formulation "counted as Assyrians" disappears, and Oded surmises that this was not accidental but reflects that the expanded empire increasingly treated exiles more like slave labor and less like citizens.[65] J. N. Postgate considers this later distribution of conquered people as an economically motivated practice distinct from the politically motivated mass deportations.[66]

Whether resettling people for political or economic reasons, the empire's goal was simply to create more productive and pacified Assyrians. For the king and the state, "ordering the disorder of the non-Assyrian world" meant imposing "obedience to the dictates of the Assyrian king as agent for the Assyrian pantheon headed by Assur."[67] Sargon famously ordered not only resettlement but reeducation for conquered people, writing:

> The population of the four (quarters), of foreign tongue and divergent speech, inhabitants of mountain and plain, all whom the Light of the gods, the lord of all, shepherded, whom I had carried off with my powerful scepter by the command of Aššur, my lord—I made them of one mouth and put them in its [= Dur-Šarrukin's] midst. And I ordered Assyrians, versed in all the proper culture, as overseers and supervisors to give them instruction in fearing god and king.[68]

Thus, to be an Assyrian meant to be obedient to Assyria and its values. It was a political and ideological term rather than an ethnic one.[69]

Like other aspects of Assyrian imperial practice, mass deportations have been variously assessed. It is not uncommon for historians to emphasize the Assyrians' desire to see the exiles arrive in good physical condition, which perhaps minimizes the exiles' suffering. Often cited is the speech of the *rab šāqēh* in 2 Kings 18, where he promises the Judeans that the Assyrians only want to "take [them] away to a land like [their] own land, a land of grain and wine, a land of bread and vineyards, a land of olive oil and honey" (18:32).

---

65. Ibid., 89–91. Peter Machinist has pointed out that a hardening of attitudes is more apparent than hardening of practices: "Assyrians on Assyria in the First Millennium BC," in *Anfänge politischen Denkens in der Antike*, ed. K. A. Raaflaub, Schriften des Historischen Kollegs: Kolloquien 24 (Munich: Oldenbourg, 1993), 60–61.

66. J. N. Postgate, "The Economic Structure of the Assyrian Empire," in *Power and Propaganda: A Symposium on Ancient Empires*, ed. Mogens Trolle Larsen, Mesopotamia 7 (Copenhagen: Akademisk Forlag, 1979), 210.

67. Machinist, "Assyrians on Assyria," 89.

68. David G. Lyon, *Keilschrifttexte Sargons, Königs von Assyrien (722–705 v. Chr.)*, Assyriologische Bibliothek 5 (Leipzig, 1883), 11–12, 38–39, lines 72–74 (Cylinder); 18, 46–47, lines 92–96 (Bull); translation in Machinist, "Assyrians on Assyria," 95.

69. Machinist, "Assyrians on Assyria," 89.

Good times awaited! But as the summation of that same speech indicates, the positive promise was not enough. To give the rhetoric some teeth, he added: "... that you may live and not die!" (18:32). There can be no doubt that the deportees viewed the prospect of resettlement negatively, so that the practice was coercive and abusive. The victims saw "their lives entirely reprogrammed and reinvented according to the necessities of the victor."[70] This is to say nothing of the disastrous effects that depopulation could have on areas that were not resettled.[71]

Economy

There has been less scholarship on the economy of the Neo-Assyrian Empire than, for example, on the Ur III or even the Old Babylonian economies. This is partly due to limitations of the sources, which demonstrate a strong bias toward royal affairs rather than private[72] or temple[73] economics. The broad analyses that exist have also focused on the latest period of the Assyrian imperial period, when "the main tracts of the empire had been under Assyrian rule long enough to have acquired a certain stability and to have adjusted their economic and civil life to the new conditions."[74] Prior to that, J. N. Postgate notes, Assyria was "consolidating its conquests with an essentially military administration."[75] Before moving on to the conditions in the late period, it should be briefly noted that the phenomenon of mass deportation, discussed above, was an integral aspect of the economy. It was crucial to the populating of Assyrian cities and to the supply of skilled artisans and tradespeople. It continued well into the reign of Assurbanipal, as Egyptians conquered in the seventh century were settled in Assyrian cities.

Farming was foundational to the Assyrian economy. As noted above, the Assyrian heartland in northern Mesopotamia enjoyed rain-fed agriculture, although the state also undertook large irrigation projects as a buffer against drought. These fields yielded barley, corn, and wheat. The king occasionally took the title "farmer," which Karen Radner argues reflected a key royal role

---

70. Davide Nadali, "The Impact of War on Civilians in the Neo-Assyrian Period," in Nadali and Vidal, *Other Face of the Battle*, 101–11.
71. For a brief look at the socioeconomic side effects of war, see Van De Mieroop, *Cuneiform Texts*, 97–103.
72. Karen Radner, *Ancient Assyria: A Very Short Introduction* (Oxford: Oxford University Press, 2015).
73. Postgate does not discuss the temples' function in the economy, saying only that it was "very similar to that of the palaces, although quantitatively less important" ("Economic Structure," 202).
74. Ibid., 194.
75. Ibid.

in converting unused land into productive farmland. Sargon II, for example, seems to have ordered a governor in northern Babylonia to "survey in detail the surroundings of the fort in regard to cultivating the steppe."[76]

Also important to the Assyrian economy were the flocks that were herded in the meadows on the edges of settled areas. The most significant herd animal was the sheep, which supplied wool, a mainstay of the textile industry, and mutton, the most frequently consumed meat.[77] Kings took an interest in ensuring that the flocks had adequate pasture land, partly because when they did not, and subsistence became challenging, the herdsmen were prone to raid towns instead.

In addition to grains and animal products, villages provided straw, timber, and certain textiles and household products. Some regions provided more specialized resources—metals came from the mining towns in the Taurus Mountains, and the harbor dues were paid to the empire once it controlled Levantine coastal cities such as Tyre and Sidon.

For much of the empire, the basis of the economy was this village industry, which the government sector used to supply resources for military and civil projects. Provincial governors were responsible for ensuring the flow of resources from their regions—not only goods but also soldiers and laborers. In the Neo-Assyrian period, an increasingly complex bureaucracy or civil service was instituted to supervise these processes. At the individual level, Assyrian citizens owed the nation an *ilku*, a service or payment in lieu of the service. There was also direct taxation of traded goods, normally paid in kind. There is not much evidence for tax rates, but rates of 10 percent for corn and 25 percent for straw are attested.[78]

The palace sector was closely related to the government sector, but the two were not equivalent. Some sources of income were closely linked to the military and the provincial system, including war spoils, tribute from client states, and gifts to the king. The palace sector generated income through owning land, as it controlled large estates in various parts of the empire. It also profited by making loans and selling slaves.[79] These income sources were balanced by significant expenses for the upkeep of palaces, support of royal families and their staffs, and gifts to officials.

---

76. Karen Radner, "How Did the Neo-Assyrian King Perceive His Land and Its Resources?," in *Rainfall and Agriculture in Northern Mesopotamia: Proceedings of the 3rd MOS Symposium, Leiden, 21–22 May, 1999*, ed. R. M. Jas, MOS Studies 3 (Istanbul: Nederlands Historisch-Archaeologisch Instituut te Istanbul, 2000), 233–46; here 238. The title was assumed by the king when he abdicated temporarily for the substitute king ritual.

77. Radner, "Economy, Society, and Daily Life."

78. Postgate, "Economic Structure," 205.

79. Ibid., 201.

The private sector of the economy in the Neo-Assyrian period is less well understood because of the lack of records. The very existence of private trade has been doubted; it has been argued that the crown controlled all trade. It is difficult to ascertain the reality, since trade documents do not typically specify on whose behalf traders were acting. However, Postgate thinks it unlikely that there was a government monopoly on trade; instead, the government would have profited by taxing traders.[80] Currency appears to have been increasingly used, since there are records of payments in copper and silver, with the latter becoming more abundant in the seventh century.

Long-distance international trade was a special case. Where it was impossible or impractical to control foreign cities and industries directly, Assyrians established ports or way stations called *bīt kāri* where they had special trading privileges. Unlike the trading outposts (*kāru*) of the Old Assyrian period, however, these were less dependent on agreements with local governments; they were imposed by imperial power.[81] Sargon II, for example, boasted after defeating an Egyptian army on the border of Egypt that he had opened the trade stations of Egypt, "mingled together" Assyrians and Egyptians, and "made them trade."[82] The Assyrians were very interested in Egyptian goods such as gold, linen garments, minerals, and papyrus, but they had to rely on Phoenician coastal cities for sea trade and Arab desert tribes for overland trade. Despite the fact that records of international trade are scarce, it may be possible to infer the goods that were traded from records of tribute or from later trade documents, such as a Neo-Babylonian report that names "metals (copper, iron and tin), chemicals (dyes and alum), foodstuffs (wine, honey and other unidentified), fibres (dyed wool and linen), juniper resin and lapis lazuli."[83]

Common Neo-Assyrian families were patriarchal, monogamous, and not overly large—averaging about four people in a household—although this changed over time and depended on social status. (Wealthier families typically had more children.) How many of the lower classes were slaves? One recent survey of the data estimates that only about 30 percent of lower-class families lived in slavery, though others who were not technically slaves were named in documents of sale for land that they worked, presumably because they had nowhere else to go.[84] Some of this would have been debt slavery,

80. Ibid., 205–7.
81. Moshe Elat, "The Economic Relations of the Neo-Assyrian Empire with Egypt," *JAOS* 98 (1978): 26–27.
82. Hayim Tadmor, "The Campaigns of Sargon II," *JCS* 12 (1958): 34. See *COS* 2.118A, D.
83. Postgate, "Economic Structure," 207.
84. Gershon Galil, *The Lower Stratum Families in the Neo-Assyrian Period*, CHANE 27 (Leiden: Brill, 2007), 342–43.

and Neo-Assyrian kings are known to have carried on an old Mesopotamian tradition by issuing *andurāru* edicts, which freed slaves and canceled debts.

Religion

Describing Assyrian religion entails challenges: its long history, over which it changed significantly; large gaps in the sources; and the lack of philosophical systematization or dogmatic summaries. Because of the difficulties, the eminent Assyriologist A. Leo Oppenheim famously titled a section of his *Ancient Mesopotamia*, "Why a 'Mesopotamian Religion' Should Not Be Written."[85] A different sort of challenge is posed by the overwhelming amounts of data for certain periods. Many of the texts that have survived are relevant to the reconstruction of Assyrian religion. In addition to large numbers of texts directly related to the service and worship of the gods, theological rhetoric is pervasive in numerous genres from royal inscriptions to law codes. Even personal names often bear witness to theological proclivities.[86]

Scholars have nevertheless risen to the challenge of writing an account of Mesopotamian religion,[87] although most of them subordinate Assyrian religion to its Babylonian counterpart in various ways. That is an understandable decision for an overview—not so much because of the relative prevalence of data for Babylonian religion but because of the ways in which Assyrian religion seems to have been conditioned (and sometimes overshadowed) by the influence of its southern neighbor. Babylon's status as a site of great religious significance for the whole region was reflected in a special tax status that it was usually granted even when Assyrian kings ruled it. Assyrian kings invoked the gifts of Marduk and Nabû (see below) and suffered from anxiety about their treatment of Babylon and its temples (as reflected, for example, by the policies of Esarhaddon described above). Nevertheless, Assyria had its own religious climate and features and deserves to be discussed for itself as much as possible.

A discussion of Assyrian religion finds better focus by limiting itself largely to the Neo-Assyrian period. It is not coincidental that this period of dominant Assyrian power also saw the increasing prominence of the Assyrian national god, Aššur. Aššur was above all else the apotheosis of Assyria's sense of

---

85. Oppenheim, *Ancient Mesopotamia*, 172–83.
86. The majority of ancient Mesopotamian names include theophoric elements, i.e., the names of gods.
87. E.g., Manfred Hutter, *Religionen in der Umwelt des Alten Testaments*, vol. 1, *Babylonier, Syrer, Perser*, Studienbücher Theologie 4.1 (Stuttgart: Kohlhammer, 1996); Jean Bottéro, *Religion in Ancient Mesopotamia*, trans. Teresa Lavender Fagan (Chicago: University of Chicago Press, 2001); Tammi J. Schneider, *Ancient Mesopotamian Religion* (Grand Rapids: Eerdmans, 2011).

"Manifest Destiny." Assyrian kings regularly portrayed their military conquests as instigated and blessed by Aššur. For example, Tiglath-pileser III says it was "with the help of Aššur, his lord" that he "smashed like pots all who were unsubmissive to him," and that he marched "at the command of Aššur."[88] The deity's origins are rather obscure, but he seems to have been a minor city deity until he was allied to the power of empire. It has been suggested Aššur might be the "deified city of Aššur,"[89] since the city was occupied even prior to the Old Akkadian period, but W. G. Lambert modified that theory, arguing that cities were never deified in Mesopotamia, so that Aššur must rather have been a deified mountain.[90]

With a lack of known original characteristics, Aššur assimilated those of other major deities in the pantheon. He was sometimes described as the "Assyrian Enlil"—as a god of the heavens—and in that role he could take Ninlil as his wife and Ninurta as his son (as in the Sumerian pantheon). In fact, many of the Assyrian ideas that developed about Aššur were recycled traditions from southern Mesopotamia.

As Assyrian power grew, Assyrian theologians found ways to integrate Aššur into foundational Mesopotamian myths such as the Babylonian Epic of Creation. Under Sargon II he was identified with Anshar, Marduk's ancestor in the myth's theogonic order. Eventually Aššur took on the role of Marduk himself, as the champion of the gods and presumably as the bearer of the "50 names," although details are unclear because many of our sources are incompletely preserved.[91] Aššur came to be considered in some sense the true foundation of all the divinities, just as Marduk was in the Babylonian version of the myth. This variety of theological rhetoric was described by Saggs as "incipient monotheism,"[92] and Simo Parpola has gone so far as to reconstruct an Assyrian Trinity, with Aššur as the Father, Anu as the Son (he was Anshar's son in the creation myth), and Ishtar as the Holy Spirit.[93] Few have followed Parpola in that vein, and the tendency

88. H. Tadmor and S. Yamada, *The Royal Inscriptions of Tiglath-pileser III (744–727 BC) and Shalmaneser V (726–722 BC), Kings of Assyria*, RINAP 1 (Winona Lake, IN: Eisenbrauns, 2011), 117–18 (text 47, lines 1–3).

89. Benno Landsberger and Kemal Balkan, "Die Inschrift des assyrischen Königs Irisum," *Belleten* 14 (1950): 231.

90. W. G. Lambert, "The God Assur," *Iraq* 45 (1983): 82–86. However, Lambert may have overstated the case against deification of cities; see William W. Hallo, "Antediluvian Cities," *JCS* 23 (1970): 57–67.

91. Jeremy Black and Anthony Green, *Gods, Demons, and Symbols of Ancient Mesopotamia* (Austin: University of Texas Press, 1992), 38.

92. Saggs, *Might That Was Assyria*, 203.

93. Simo Parpola, *Assyrian Prophecies*, SAA 9 (Helsinki: Helsinki University Press, 1997), xxi–xxxi. Note perhaps the germ of the idea in Saggs, *Might That Was Assyria*, 202.

is better described in more nuanced terms as "summodeism," since there is no disavowal of the existence of many gods. Summodeism allows worshipers to call on the names of various gods, but "the deities are regarded as aspects or functions of a chief god, with political power often key to its expression."[94]

Even Aššur's iconography was adapted from that of other gods: his horned cap from Anu and his snake-dragon animal from Marduk. It has sometimes been argued that another common symbol, the winged disk, also represented Aššur, but it usually represented the sun god Shamash instead.

The most prominent goddess of the Mesopotamian pantheon, Ishtar (Inana in Sumerian), was very significant in Neo-Assyrian culture. She was a goddess of war, and her primary cult centers were in Nineveh and in Arbela, where she was said to speak through a cadre of prophets, which was majority female but also included men. (See further below on Neo-Assyrian prophecy.)

Ishtar was also a goddess of love, and particularly extramarital sex—as reflected by Gilgamesh's long diatribe about her exploits with a series of lovers in tablet 6 of that eponymous epic (he declines to join the list). She was sometimes considered a daughter of Anu (sky) and was symbolized by a star, or in animal form as a lion.

Shamash, the sun god associated with law and justice, continued to be venerated throughout Assyrian history, as did other celestial deities—for example, Sîn the moon god and Adad the storm god. Other gods were worshiped in association with various roles or functions: Ea as a god of wisdom, Nabû as a god of scribes, Nergal as the underworld god, Ninurta as a god of war and hunting. In addition to these major gods of the pantheon, there were many others. Patron deities of various towns and cities were also worshiped, while still other divinities simply made up the supporting cast of the heavenly court.

Assyrian piety took various forms depending on the social location. Official religion was conducted in the temples, and major cities could have temples (or shrines) to numerous gods. Temples were commonly viewed as the house of the god who was worshiped there, and the god was usually represented by a statue or by some other symbol. The most prominent Assyrian example of a nonanthropomorphic divine symbol was the "weapon of Aššur," which Assyrian kings sometimes placed in the shrines of conquered peoples as a reminder of Assyrian hegemony. In keeping with the view of a temple as a house, the god was said to require care and sustenance much

---

94. Mark S. Smith, *God in Translation: Deities in Cross-Cultural Discourse in the Biblical World*, FAT 57 (Tübingen: Mohr Siebeck, 2008), 169.

like any human ruler. Food and drink offerings were made regularly, and temple functionaries took care of the cleaning and other activities that an estate requires. Where statues were used, they were not believed to be gods as such but rather were imbued with the god's presence through ritual activities.[95]

The Assyrians built temples in various styles. Some temples incorporated apparently original architectural features, such as the "double temples" with paired sanctuaries,[96] but the Assyrians also emulated the ziggurats of southern Mesopotamia—stepped buildings that perhaps originally symbolized gods' mountain homes. The most impressive surviving ruin of an Assyrian ziggurat is found in Nimrud (ancient Kalhu; biblical Calah). Neo-Assyrian temples could be quite wealthy and ornate, but due to the rise of centralized imperial power, it seems that they did not control large areas of land as Mesopotamian temples had in some earlier periods, especially in the south.

Space does not permit a detailed discussion of temple personnel or festivals and cultic calendars—both complex realities.[97] Many of the rituals that are known centered on the king as a participant or officiant (see further on royal ideology below). For example, the Assyrians had their own versions of the *Akītu* ritual (often called a "New Year's festival") in which the king was a primary player, but the schedule was different in Assur than in Babylon, and the structure and meaning may have differed as well.

Beyond the central temples and sanctuaries where official religion found its place, there were myriad manifestations of popular and family religions. Because most of the texts that have survived are from very elite libraries, it is difficult to know as much about religious practice at the common levels of society. However, nonroyal individuals are likely to have thought of themselves as having a god or goddess who was specifically concerned with them. Sometimes such personal gods were cited as protective and comforting presences; for example, there are references to the personal god as the speaker's creator and the protector of his or her family line. At other times, however, personal gods were thought to cause misfortune or suffering. The "prayers for appeasing the heart of an angry god"—copies of which have been found

---

95. M. B. Dick, *Born in Heaven, Made on Earth: The Making of the Cult Image in the Ancient Near East* (Winona Lake, IN: Eisenbrauns, 1999). The presence of the god may thus be compared to the Catholic doctrine of the Eucharist, in which the elements become the body and blood of Christ (i.e., transubstantiation).

96. Seton Lloyd, *The Archaeology of Mesopotamia: From the Old Stone Age to the Persian Conquest* (London: Thames & Hudson, 1978), 181.

97. For cultic personnel, see Saggs, *Might That Was Assyria*, 209–20; and Schneider, *Ancient Mesopotamian Religion*, 79–90. For cultic calendars, see Mark E. Cohen, *The Cultic Calendars of the Ancient Near East* (Bethesda, MD: CDL Press, 1993).

in Assyrian cities such as Nineveh and Assur, dating to the seventh century BCE—sought to assuage a god who had been provoked to anger. A representative section reads:

> My god, my lord, who created my "name,"
> Who guards my life, who brings my progeny into existence,
> My fierce god, may your heart rest,
> My angry goddess, be reconciled to me. . . .
> I am constantly in grief; my god, where are you?[98]

Understandably, such prayers are often compared to the Psalms (e.g., Ps. 22).

There are a great many possibilities for what the supplicant's suffering might have entailed. A "medical" text lists some of the problems that could be attributed to the wrath of a personal god:

> If a man has experienced something untoward and he does not know how it happened to him; he has continually suffered losses: losses of barley and silver, losses of male and female slaves, cattle, horses, and sheep; dogs, pigs, and servants dying off altogether; he has heart-break time and again; he constantly gives orders but no (one) complies, calls but no (one) answers; the curse of numerous people; when lying (in his bed) he is repeatedly apprehensive, he contracts paresis,[99] he is filled with anger against god and king . . . his limbs are hanging down, from time to time he is apprehensive, he does not sleep day or night, he often sees terrifying dreams, he often gets paresis, his appetite for bread and beer is diminished, he forgets the word he spoke: *that man has the wrath of the god and/or the goddess on him; his god and his goddess are angry with him.*[100]

In keeping with this wide variety of possibilities, catalogues of rather diverse forms of suffering can be seen in the aforementioned Mesopotamian prayers. Those prayers, therefore, hunt about for a cause of the suffering and cover more ground than any individual sufferer was likely to experience at one moment. The Psalms, too, often combine a dizzying array of physical, social, and even military problems (e.g., Ps. 38).

Dead ancestors represented another set of supernatural powers thought to be significant to the living. Mesopotamians seem to have been the primary practitioners of the *kispu* rite, a form of libation and sacrifice for (or cultic

---

98. W. G. Lambert, "DINGIR.ŠÀ.DIB.BA Incantations," *JNES* 33 (1974): 277.
99. A nerve disease that is often an aftereffect of syphilis.
100. Tzvi Abusch, "Witchcraft and the Anger of the Personal God," in *Mesopotamian Magic: Textual, Historical, and Interpretative Perspectives*, ed. Tzvi Abusch and Karel van der Toorn (Groningen: Styx Publications, 1999), 85 (emphasis added).

feeding of) the dead.¹⁰¹ Texts from a range of times and places throughout Mesopotamian history attest to food and drink being set aside for this purpose, and it is attested architecturally and textually in clay libation pipes known as *arūtu*. The *kispu* was performed by an heir for the deceased paterfamilias, both when the spirit first entered the underworld and perhaps later at regular intervals. Mortuary care was perceived as the single greatest factor in one's happiness in the afterlife. This is apparent in Gilgamesh Tablet XII, in which Enkidu returns from the underworld to tell Gilgamesh about it and recounts that the more sons a man had, the more he would flourish in the afterlife.

The *kispu* was also used in various rituals intended to dispel evil or appease harmful spirits, and could be employed to conjure a spirit for help, sometimes of a necromantic nature. In one typical *kispu* text, the offerer invokes the "ghosts of my family . . . my father, my grandfather, my mother, my grandmother, my brother, my sister, my family, kith and kin, as many as are asleep in the netherworld."¹⁰² A *kispu* could also be performed for the Annunaki, the gods of the underworld.

One of the best-attested uses of the *kispu* is among royal families. In such cases it affirmed the continuity and authority of the royal family, and could even be used by a usurper to assert his legitimacy.¹⁰³ In the Neo-Assyrian period, Assurbanipal claimed in an inscription that he had reinstated the *kispu*; but this was a common sort of boast among kings—reinstituting traditions, whether or not they had ever been discontinued.¹⁰⁴ In the Neo-Assyrian period, the king also brought *kispu* offerings on some feast days—as if to allow the dead to participate in the festivities.¹⁰⁵

It was long assumed that burial near the living was crucial for the care of the dead in case one needed to summon them for various sorts of help, and this was likely the preference.¹⁰⁶ However, a recent study argues that in fact a king might rule from one city while the cult of dead ancestors was maintained in another.¹⁰⁷ This is only logical since the Assyrian capital city was

101. The foundational study is Akio Tsukimoto, *Untersuchungen zur Totenpflege (kispum) im alten Mesopotamien*, AOAT 216 (Neukirchen-Vluyn: Neukirchener Verlag, 1985).

102. Benjamin R. Foster, *Before the Muses: An Anthology of Akkadian Literature*, 3rd ed. (Bethesda, MD: CDL Press, 2005), 658.

103. E.g., Nabonidus; *ANET*, 561. See discussion in J. C. Greenfield, "Un rite religieux araméen et ses parallèles," *RB* 80 (1973): 49.

104. There are records of provisioning the *kispum* during the reign of Esarhaddon, Assurbanipal's father (Tsukimoto, *Untersuchungen zur Totenpflege*, 111).

105. Ibid., 223–27.

106. In the Neo-Assyrian period, "bei der 'Totenpflege' damals das Vorhandensein des wirklichen Grabes oder der Leiche wichtig und notwendig war" (ibid., 115).

107. Brian Brown, "Kingship and Ancestral Cult in the Northwest Palace at Nimrud," *JANER* 10 (2010): 1–53. Brown shows that Tsukimoto's textual case for the necessity of the corpse's proximity is based on spotty data.

moved on more than one occasion, and tombs were not very portable. When Assurnasirpal II moved the capital from Assur to Kalhu in the early ninth century, he constructed a wing of the new palace for the maintenance of a royal mortuary cult, complete with pipes for libation offerings to the dead (see below).[108] It has also been argued that Assurnasirpal built a large-scale "garden of ancestors" at the new capital for the royal mortuary cult.[109]

With so many powers and forces believed to be at work in the world, it was crucial for a king to have access to diviners who could accurately discern the will of the gods. Prophets took on larger importance for late Neo-Assyrian rulers than in earlier periods, but there were also numerous other means of divination available. Many of the other types were inductive—that is, based on the observation of concrete phenomena. The most important of these were extispicy, the examination of animal entrails, and hepatoscopy, the examination of (usually sheep) livers. Extispicy was often considered more reliable than prophecy. Other forms of divination included astrology, oneiromancy (revelation through dreams), augury (interpretation of the flight of birds), and lecanomancy (from the shape and behavior of oil on water).

The diviner moved from observation to interpretation on the basis of accepted canons. The results were collected into extensive "omen series" that attempted to cover as many cases as possible, and there were even clay models made that functioned as "maps" of the liver, as resources that others could read and check, and as a means to teach hepatoscopy. A divinatory professional (*barû*, in Akkadian) had to know how to identify the signs and where to find the correct entry in the written omen series, but ideally the process was otherwise impersonal; theoretically, any trained interpreter could be expected to arrive at the same interpretation.

Omen series were taken seriously enough that when an omen arose against the king, especially an eclipse, he might temporarily abdicate the throne and place another man on it to suffer the bad omen. This practice of the "substitute king ritual" stretches back to the early second millennium BCE in Mesopotamia, but it is best attested in the late Neo-Assyrian period, during the reigns of Esarhaddon and Assurbanipal.[110] After a certain number of days—as many as one hundred, but often less—the substitute king was killed to ensure that the evil was done with.

---

108. Ibid., 16.
109. Seth Richardson, "An Assyrian Garden of Ancestors: Room I, Northwest Palace, Kalḫu," *SAAB* 13 (1999–2001): 145–216.
110. Jean Bottéro, "The Substitute King and His Fate," in *Mesopotamia: Writing, Reasoning, and the Gods*, trans. Zainab Bahrani and Marc Van De Mieroop (Chicago: University of Chicago Press, 1992), 138–55. See also Simo Parpola, *Letters from Assyrian and Babylonian Scholars*, SAA 10 (Helsinki: Helsinki University Press, 1993).

The Assyrians' belief in omens may seem foreign today, but in its own way it reflects faith in divine power and initiative toward humankind—it indicates a belief that the gods had inscribed their will in myriad ways in the natural world.

Ideology of Kingship

The Assyrian ideology of kingship shared much with those of other Mesopotamian states, but had certain distinctive historical manifestations and resonances with Israelite/Judean kingship. H. W. F. Saggs has noted that the French monarchic saying "L'état, c'est moi" ("I am the state") could rightfully be applied to Assyrian kings,[111] and indeed the willingness to slaughter an innocent citizen to "save the king" in the substitute king ritual just described emphasizes the degree to which the king's perceived value was greater than other citizens'. However, the Assyrian kings' status was not the same in all periods, and so a more nuanced discussion is necessary.

Prior to the Assyrians in the third millennium BCE (i.e., in the Old Akkadian period), many facets of the state's functioning revolved around the royal throne. The king was military general, priest, and supreme judge. As noted above, Sargon's grandson Naram-Sin claimed to be divine, calling himself "the god of Agade" and asserting his rule over "the four corners of the earth." According to one of his inscriptions, after he withstood one particularly epic uprising, his relieved subjects "begged to worship him publicly as a god," and there was indeed a cult dedicated to him during his life, which continued after his death.[112] Claims to divine status continued sporadically into the second millennium, but they were not the norm. Instead, the formal title was "viceregent of Aššur"—that is, the national god's representative on earth. More commonly, the king was called "prince" (*rubā'um*) or "lord" (*bēlum*). Only with the conquest of Shamshi-Adad I did an Assyrian ruler take the title of "king" (*šarru*), and Assur-uballiṭ I was the first to claim the title "king of Assyria."

The power of Assyrian kings had counterbalances, especially in certain periods. Through the Old Assyrian and Middle Assyrian periods, a group of nobility also had large political significance, though by the latter part of the Middle Assyrian period their power appears to have been limited by the emergence of a more centralized monarchy. Some of these elites were given the title *līmu*; years were named for them, and stelae were erected in Assur

---

111. Saggs, *Might That Was Assyria*, 147.
112. The key text testifying to this is from the base of the Bassetki Statue. See Walter Farber, "Die Vergöttlichung Narām-Sins," *Or* 52 (1983): 67–72.

for each one. At about the same time, the capital city of Assur seems to have been governed as an oligarchy by a group of wealthy men who looked after the interests of their powerful families. Furthermore, provincial governors often gained power in times when the central government was less active. Boastful inscriptions by the governors that ignored the king entirely show that this took place even in the eighth century, seemingly the height of Neo-Assyrian imperial power.

Even when the nation's power was somewhat reduced, its kings did not necessarily shy away from self-aggrandizing rhetoric. When Assur-uballiṭ I (r. 1365–1330) merely annexed part of eastern Mittani, he gave himself the title "king of the universe." But as noted above, letters from the Late Bronze Age show that Assyrian rulers were not always highly regarded by the "great kings" of other major nations.

The Neo-Assyrians had not only a practical challenge in building the largest empire yet seen but also an ideological one; their ideology had to impel and legitimate a very large imperial apparatus.[113] The Old Akkadian and Middle Assyrian kings' rhetoric about the extent of their rule (e.g., "the four corners of the earth") was reused and became slightly less exaggerated. As noted above, this included the claim that the king was the viceroy of the god Aššur and thus the one to carry out the manifest destiny of national expansion. Similarly, there was an increase in "sovereignty idioms" (both royal titles and boasts about imperial activities) in the Neo-Assyrian period in general, and especially from the reign of Tiglath-pileser III on, when Assyrian expansion was most aggressive.[114] Other titles were also used—for example, Sennacherib called himself "the maker of Assyria" (*epiš māt Aššur*) on the basis of his military success and civic works projects.[115]

Finally, the Assyrians took part in a long Mesopotamian tradition that emphasized the wisdom and education of the king.[116] Names from the early Sargonic period such as Sharru-mūda (The King Is Wise) show that the tradition was of great antiquity, and it was enthusiastically propagated by famous Babylonian kings such as Hammurabi, who in the prologue to his law collection called himself "wise one . . . he who has mastered all wisdom" and claimed to be "steeped in wisdom."[117] First-millennium inscriptions by Assyrian kings

---

113. Machinist, "Assyrians on Assyria," 78, 104.
114. Ibid., 92.
115. Ibid., 84.
116. R. F. G. Sweet, "The Sage in Akkadian Literature: A Philological Study," in *The Sage in Israel and the Ancient Near East*, ed. John G. Gammie and Leo G. Perdue (Winona Lake, IN: Eisenbrauns, 1990), 31–44.
117. Roth, *Law Collections from Mesopotamia and Asia Minor*, 79, 78, respectively.

boast of their wisdom in the performance of a wide range of activities: the arts of war, the building of palaces and temples, and domestic projects such as founding new cities, planting, and irrigating. Sennacherib (r. 704–681) called himself "wise shepherd," a title that also echoed Hammurabi.

It was Assurbanipal, however, who insisted most specially on his wisdom and learning, even to the point of claiming to be "the most able of all the experts" at his royal court:

> Marduk, the sage of the gods, gave me wide understanding and broad perceptions as a gift. Nabû, the scribe of the universe, bestowed on me the acquisition of all his wisdom as a present. Ninurta and Nergal gave me physical fitness, manhood and unparalleled strength. I learnt the lore of the wise sage Adapa, the hidden secret, the whole of the scribal craft. I can discern celestial and terrestrial portents and deliberate in the assembly of the experts. I am able to discuss the series "If the liver is a mirror image of the sky" with capable scholars. I can solve convoluted reciprocals and calculations that do not come out evenly. I have read cunningly written text in Sumerian, dark Akkadian, the interpretation of which is difficult. I have examined stone inscriptions from before the flood, which are sealed, stopped up, mixed up.[118]

It would be easy to dismiss these claims as inflated boasts, but Alasdair Livingstone has recently argued that it is possible to identify tablets written by Assurbanipal himself, as well as by some of the young royal women of Esarhaddon's court, in Assyrian archives.[119] The fact that Assurbanipal built one of the great libraries of antiquity—a collection of more than 30,000 tablets in Nineveh—also lends a certain credibility to his claims to scholarship.

These claims about the wisdom of Mesopotamian kings find an echo in the biblical stories of Solomon. A representative passage is found in 1 Kings 4:29–33:

> God gave Solomon very great wisdom, discernment, and breadth of understanding as vast as the sand on the seashore, so that Solomon's wisdom surpassed the wisdom of all the people of the east, and all the wisdom of Egypt. . . . He composed three thousand proverbs, and his songs numbered a thousand and five. He would speak of trees, from the cedar that is in the Lebanon to the hyssop that grows in the wall; he would speak of animals, and birds, and reptiles, and fish.

Solomon's ability to build the Jerusalem temple is also attributed to his wisdom in 1 Kings 5:7, 12—another close analogue to Assyrian kings' wisdom in temple building.

---

118. Translation in Alasdair Livingstone, "Ashurbanipal: Literate or Not?," *ZAVA* 97 (2007): 100.
119. Ibid., 103–15.

Arts, Crafts, and Architecture

Assyrian art is some of the most famous from the ancient Near East. The best-known Assyrian works of art are the sculptures and reliefs. The colossal sculptures of supernatural composite beings (e.g., human-headed winged bulls) that guarded entryways in Neo-Assyrian palaces such as Nimrud and Khorsabad tower over their viewers and were a sensation with the viewing public when they were first discovered and brought to the West. Today they stand in some of the world's great museums: the British Museum, the Louvre, the Metropolitan Museum of Art, and the Oriental Institute of the University of Chicago. These figures, called *lamassū* or *šēdū* (both referring to a "protective spirit"), are not fully carved statues in the round but high-relief images. Viewed from the front, they generally appear to be standing still, and viewed from the side they appear to be striding; therefore, when viewed from a three-quarters perspective early examples appear to have five legs. (Sennacherib's artisans deleted the fifth leg for the examples in his palace at Nineveh.)

Relatively few Assyrian sculptures in the round have survived; the royal statue of Assurnasirpal II from the Ishtar temple in Nimrud shows the king striking a dignified and serene pose (fig. 2.3). At a more common level, there are many small figurines in stone, metals, and clay, representing gods, goddesses, and other supernatural figures. Some of these were worn as amulets, while others served as foundation deposits.

The wall reliefs from royal palaces are both aesthetically impressive and historically and culturally significant. In their original architectural contexts, they lined the mud-brick walls of Neo-Assyrian palaces. They were also painted, although the pigments have almost completely worn off and faded away. Above all, the reliefs portrayed the king as heroic in light of his feats in battle and the hunt, but they are full of incidental detail—about the weapons, tactics, and personnel of

Figure 2.3. Statue of Assurnasirpal II

the military; about the way sieges were carried out; about how the Assyrians viewed different ethnicities; about architecture, livestock, and scribal culture; and even about the way different classes of people dressed and the chores of daily life. All of this means that the reliefs are "texts" that can be read and interpreted alongside the inscriptions.

Pope Gregory the Great (sixth–seventh centuries CE) famously said that "the picture is for simple men what writing is for those who can read," and that is how the reliefs functioned in an era when few in the ancient Near East could read the Assyrians' language.[120] Some of the reliefs portray the awful fates of those who opposed the Assyrian Empire: exile, death, and torture. These were prominently placed, for example, at the entry to Sennacherib's throne room to send a message to the emissaries of foreign cultures who visited his court. Those same reliefs have great significance for biblical interpreters because they portray Sennacherib's 701 conquest of Lachish, a fortified city to the south of Jerusalem. On this same campaign, the king besieged Jerusalem, an event remembered in 2 Kings 18–19 (see below). The viewer therefore is able to get a better idea of the military that threatened Judah's existence in the time of the prophet Isaiah ben Amoz.

Figure 2.4. Relief of a dying lion

Some of the finest Assyrian reliefs come from slightly later, in the reign of Assurbanipal. While his palace reliefs still exhibited much of the style of earlier ones, some of the carvings are remarkably lifelike and supple. One set of reliefs shows a royal lion hunt in which the lion is released from a cage and springs at the king in a set of sequential images like still frames from a video. The image of the "dying lion," not a common one, exhibits skill and evokes pathos (fig. 2.4). In general, the level of detail in Assyrian reliefs is often breathtaking; they should be seen in person to be fully appreciated.

A similar motif of the king slaying a lion was used, in much smaller form, as the image on Neo-Assyrian royal seals that were used to stamp official

---

120. David M. Carr, *Writing on the Tablet of the Heart: Origins of Scripture and Literature* (Oxford: Oxford University Press, 2005), 20.

clay tablets for centuries. These stamp seals coexisted in Assyria with cylinder seals, which often contained mythological images. From 1200 to 900 BCE, many of the cylinder seals were of a relatively low artistic quality, composed of stylized figures made up of linear cuts and circular drill marks, but later a more finely carved style evolved, perhaps under Babylonian influence.

Assyrian architecture was characterized by mud-brick structures supported by wooden pillars, but palaces were highly decorated—not only with the wall reliefs mentioned above but also with carved stone column bases, glazed bricks, metal overlays, painted plaster, and inset plaques of various materials. In certain high-traffic areas, "carpets" were carved into stone floors, probably imitating real carpets used elsewhere in the building. Assyrian palaces would have been brilliantly colorful.

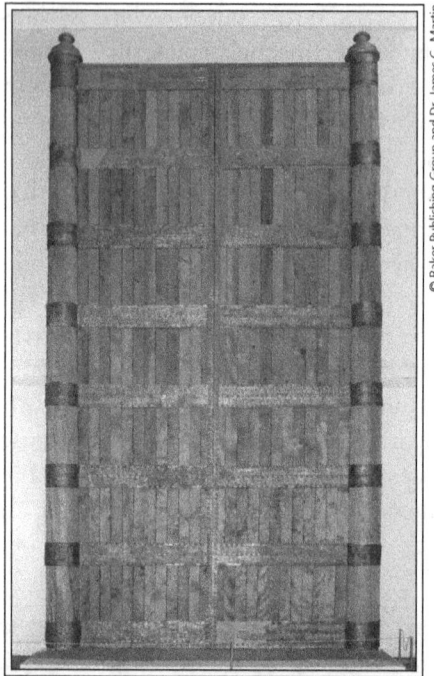

Figure 2.5. The Balawat Gates

Among the most impressive examples of Assyrian royal architecture were the Balawat Gates, built by Assurnasirpal II and Shalmaneser III in the mid-ninth century (fig. 2.5). Intricately decorated bands of bronze bound massive timbers in gates that are believed to have been almost seven meters tall. Each of the bands has two registers that portray the kings' campaigns. The images are chased and embossed in the bronze, and they resemble smaller versions of the wall reliefs. The bands, commissioned by Shalmaneser III, portray his campaigns to western cities such as Tyre and Sidon.

There is no doubt that Neo-Assyrian palaces were architectural marvels of their times, and Stephanie Dalley has recently proposed that one of the seven wonders of the ancient world, the so-called hanging gardens of Babylon, were not in Babylon at all but rather in Sennacherib's "Palace without Rival" at Nineveh.[121] She refers to the massive system of canals and aqueducts ordered

---

121. Stephanie Dalley, *The Mystery of the Hanging Garden of Babylon: An Elusive World Wonder Traced* (Oxford: Oxford University Press, 2013).

by Sennacherib that brought water from the northern mountains, and believes that the king engineered an "Archimedes screw" pump (centuries before Archimedes himself) that raised the water to an elevated garden platform using the power of the water itself. The theory is impressively argued, despite the fact that political conditions in Iraq have made it nearly impossible to test archaeologically.

Common necessities were also artistically elevated for elite Assyrians—vases and vessels were made from precious metals and glass, while horse tack and chariot equipment were ornamented with carved ivory, stone, and shells. Furniture was made luxurious with the addition of artistic flourishes. Ornate royal furniture is depicted in the reliefs, and fragments of furniture pieces have survived. Various materials were used by craftsmen, including wood, bronze, and stone, and (as with surviving complete examples from Egypt) it is clear that animals' heads and feet were a popular decorative motif. Parts of the furniture included carved ivory inlays, and these show styles and motifs borrowed from other regions, primarily Phoenicia and Syria. It is not clear in all cases whether the ivories were made in the west and imported or whether the Assyrians had foreign craftspeople working at their courts. Some ivories with Assyrian motifs indicate that a native school probably eventually sprung up, but the more common westernized examples demonstrate how international the world of art and culture was at that time.

Figure 2.6. Judean archer on black stone seal

Figure 2.7. Assyrian archers on Lachish relief

The Assyrians were great "collectors," and luxury goods from all over the Near East flowed to their royal courts, but in fact cultural influence ran in all directions. The question of Assyrian influence on Israel and Judah is discussed in the next section, but one striking example can be mentioned here: the stamp seal of Hagab, in which this Judean owner depicts himself in native garb, but in a pose that is precisely that of Assyrian archers on various reliefs (see figs. 2.6 and 2.7).

In fact, the rise of Assyrian power in the Levant brought major, unmistakable changes to almost all aspects of the region's material culture, from architecture and city planning to styles of pottery and other arts and crafts.[122] Insofar as they dominated and colonized an area, the Assyrians also brought new styles of temples, cultic objects, and burial practices. This recognition of the cultural exchange among ancient Near Eastern cultures provides background for a consideration of literary connections between Assyria and the Hebrew Bible/Old Testament.

6. Comparisons with Ancient Israel and Biblical Texts

At the peak of their power, the Assyrians dominated the ancient Near East in a way that no other nation had done up to that point. Along with their political and economic power, their cultural hegemony and influence were also broad, and often deep. The archaeologist Ephraim Stern has remarked that "the Assyrians' impact on every aspect of Palestine's [material] culture may be regarded as revolutionary."[123] Not surprisingly, one can also identify a number of significant instances in which Assyrian texts are specifically relevant for comparison with biblical texts.

Mechanisms of Assyrian Influence

Before turning to specific instances of Assyrian influence on the authors of the Hebrew Bible, it is worth reflecting on how that influence worked. Influence on Judah (specifically the Jerusalem court and its attendant elites) could have come through multiple means:[124]

- Assyria has been called "an empire of communications."[125] Diplomatic and economic contacts were inevitable between an ancient Near Eastern state and its clients. Ambassadors and correspondence shuttled between cities, and Jerusalem was one node in this network of information.

---

122. Stern, *Archaeology of the Land of the Bible*, 14–41.
123. Ibid., 19.
124. The influence of Assyria on the northern kingdom of Israel is somewhat less traceable, and in any case, less pertinent for the development of the biblical texts.
125. Mario Liverani, "The Growth of the Assyrian Empire in the Habur/Middle Euphrates Area: A New Paradigm," *SAAB* 2, no. 2 (1988): 91.

- Another conduit of cultural contact was trade, and Judah is known to have exported its grain as far away as Assyrian provincial cities. The Judahite *sĕ'āh* was used as a measure even in Nineveh itself, and Judean weights have been found in various neighboring countries, suggesting that they served as one of the basic units of measure for trade in the region.[126]
- Even the despised Assyrian system of mass deportations (i.e., exiles) would have played a role in allowing cultural ideas and motifs to be exchanged more extensively than through ordinary trading contacts.[127]

The precise manner in which Assyrian *literature* influenced biblical authors is not clear, however, partly because the influence of Mesopotamia might have been felt in the Levant in a number of periods. For example:

- There might have been survivals of cuneiform culture from the Late Bronze Age, during which time the numerous Amarna letters and other documents testify to a relatively widespread cuneiform scribal activity in the Levant; however, it is often thought that this scribal culture did not survive the political and cultural upheavals of the transition to the Iron Age.[128]
- Scholars often see Mesopotamian influence primarily in the period of the Babylonian exile, when the Judean elites taken to Babylon could have been heavily exposed to cuneiform literature. However, certain aspects of biblical texts do suggest specifically Assyrian influence (as discussed below).

If there was literary influence in the Neo-Assyrian period, how did it take place, from a linguistic standpoint? At one extreme, some scholars think that Judean scribes could read Akkadian cuneiform texts. Sargon II famously boasted that he made "populations of the four quarters of the world with strange tongues and incompatible speech . . . accept a single voice."[129]

126. Faust and Weiss, "Judah, Philistia, and the Mediterranean World," 82–83.
127. W. S. Smith, *Interconnections in the Ancient Near East: A Study of the Relationships between the Arts of Egypt, the Aegean, and Western Asia* (New Haven: Yale University Press, 1965), 55.
128. William Morrow, "Resistance and Hybridity in Late Bronze Age Canaan," *RB* 115 (2008): 321–39; Wayne Horowitz, Takayoshi Oshima, and Seth Sanders, *Cuneiform in Canaan: Cuneiform Sources from the Land of Israel in Ancient Times* (Jerusalem: Israel Exploration Society and The Hebrew University of Jerusalem, 2006), 19.
129. Translation from Stephanie Dalley, *The Legacy of Mesopotamia* (Oxford: Oxford University Press, 1998), 27. See also Andreas Fuchs, *Die Inschriften Sargons II. aus Khorsabad*

However, there is almost no evidence of native competence in Mesopotamian cuneiform from Iron Age Israel or Judah. At the other extreme, some scholars think that Judeans would have no knowledge of Akkadian, even in spoken form, and could only have absorbed Mesopotamian literature if it was translated into Aramaic, the administrative language of the Neo-Assyrian Empire in the west by the seventh century.[130] The third theory is that Judeans could understand and even speak some Akkadian, but without reading cuneiform.[131]

Akkadian loanwords (or whole phrases) in biblical texts lend support to the idea that Judeans knew some Akkadian. Paul Mankowski has identified eighty likely loanwords from Akkadian to Hebrew.[132] It would have put the Jerusalem court at an enormous diplomatic disadvantage to have no resident knowledge of Akkadian, and insofar as Assyrian administration of the area employed cuneiform, it certainly would have been desirable to have scribes who could read it.[133]

Another debated issue in the analysis of Assyrian influence is whether the Assyrians actively imposed religious burdens on their subject peoples. For a long time it was the leading scholarly position that Assyria did impose its religion. A. T. Olmstead said that the "whole organization" of the Assyrian provincial system "centered around the worship of Ashur, the deified state and reigning king."[134] Morton (Mordechai) Cogan modified this theory by pointing out the distinction between provinces and vassal states. In the provinces that were formally incorporated into Assyria, "Ashur became the

---

(Göttingen: Cuvillier, 1994), 43. For discussion, see Bernard Levinson, "Is the Covenant Code an Exilic Composition? A Response to John Van Seters," in *In Search of Pre-Exilic Israel: Proceedings of the Oxford Old Testament Seminar*, ed. John Day (London: T&T Clark, 2004), 295–96.

130. In a lengthy analysis, Shawn Zelig Aster emphasized this theory while leaving open the third theory as a possibility as well: "Transmission of Neo-Assyrian Claims of Empire to Judah in the Late Eighth Century B.C.E.," *HUCA* 78 (2007): 1–44; see also William M. Schniedewind, "Aramaic, the Death of Written Hebrew, and Language Shift in the Persian Period," in *Margins of Writing, Origins of Culture*, ed. Seth L. Sanders (Chicago: Oriental Institute of the University of Chicago, 2006), 139.

131. Sargon II's eighth campaign was addressed to the whole city, as if for public reading; such reading may reflect a more general practice of propaganda by means of the spoken word. For discussion, see Machinist, "Assyrians on Assyria," 98–102. See also, with a critique of Machinist, Louis D. Levine, "Observations on 'Sargon's Letter to the Gods,'" *ErIsr* 27 (2003): 111*–19*. See also Zelig Aster, "Transmission of Neo-Assyrian Claims of Empire."

132. Paul V. Mankowski, *Akkadian Loanwords in Biblical Hebrew* (Winona Lake, IN: Eisenbrauns, 2000), 168–70.

133. As William Morrow remarks elsewhere, scribes certainly had enough motivation to become familiar with Akkadian—it was a matter of national security, if nothing else. See Morrow, "Cuneiform Literacy and Deuteronomic Composition," *BO* 62 (2005): 210.

134. Cited in Morton [Mordechai] Cogan, *Imperialism and Religion: Assyria, Judah and Israel in the Eighth and Seventh Centuries B.C.E.*, SBLMS 19 (Missoula, MT: Scholars Press, 1974), 3.

recognized head of a pantheon that now encompassed new foreign gods."[135] Furthermore, the provinces owed support specifically for the provisioning of the Aššur temple, although there was no direct abrogation of previous cults. Vassal states fared better still; they "bore no cultic obligations whatsoever."[136] Cogan's analysis was challenged by Hermann Spieckermann, who argued that not only was Assyrian religion imposed by the empire in some ways, it was also sometimes adopted voluntarily by vassal rulers because of its prestige.[137] Nor did Spieckermann find any clear distinction between provinces and vassals with respect to religious imposition.

The latest and most extensive survey of the data is by Steven W. Holloway, who concluded that a cult of Aššur was not "established on foreign soil."[138] He agreed with Cogan that dues for the cult of Aššur were characteristic of provinces but not client states.[139] However, Holloway perceived that the Assyrian Empire did not adhere to fixed policies; instead, it responded to problems in an ad hoc manner and "followed the dictates of situational military and political expediency."[140]

It is important to bear in mind that, in ancient times as well as modern, the nature of colonial hegemony is to function not only by force but also by prestige. That is, the vassal may admire and embrace foreign ways. J. N. Postgate described the process as "one of active emulation: we should not see the client rulers as cowering in their citadels waiting to be irradiated with Assyrian influence, but absorbing the scene in Nineveh, fingering the tapestries and envying the silverware."[141] It appears that in many cases the Assyrians were able to persuade foreign rulers and elites to think of the benefits

---

135. Ibid., 112.
136. Ibid.
137. Hermann Spieckermann, *Juda unter Assur in der Sargonidenzeit*, FRLANT 129 (Göttingen: Vandenhoeck & Ruprecht, 1982); Simo Parpola has recently asserted his support of the idea of Assyrian religious imposition as well ("Assyria's Expansion," 100–101n4).
138. Steven W. Holloway, *Aššur Is King! Aššur Is King! Religion in the Exercise of Power in the Neo-Assyrian Empire*, CHANE 10 (Leiden: Brill, 2002), 200.
139. Postgate concurs: "Correspondence from the royal archives reveals an obligation on provincial governors to supply sheep offerings to the Assur Temple (and a failure of some governors to meet those obligations on time). . . . This is not tribute from a client state, but offerings from one part of the land to its central shrine" ("Royal Ideology in Sumer and Akkad," CANE 1:409–10).
140. Holloway, *Aššur Is King!*, 214. See also Bradley J. Parker, *The Mechanics of Empire: The Northern Frontier of Assyria as a Case Study in Imperial Dynamics* (Helsinki: Neo-Assyrian Text Corpus Project, 2001), 252.
141. J. N. Postgate, "The Land of Assur and the Yoke of Assur," *World Archaeology* 23 (1992): 259–60. As an example Postgate cites the "sheik's hall" at Tell Halaf. Of course, the elite structures of Jerusalem have long since been destroyed, but the changes mentioned in 2 Kings 16:17–18 suggest similar mechanisms of influence even in more distant Judah.

of "supranational structures" rather than about "local independence and autonomy."¹⁴²

In ancient Palestine, imitation of Assyrian models can be seen in numerous aspects of material culture, from art to architecture. Second Kings 16:10–11 provides a narrative example of this sort of influence:

> When King Ahaz went to Damascus to meet King Tiglath-pileser of Assyria, he saw the altar that was at Damascus. King Ahaz sent to the priest Uriah a model of the altar, and its pattern, exact in all its details. The priest Uriah built the altar . . .

There is no suggestion here that Ahaz was compelled by the Assyrian king to emulate the altar he saw, but apparently he was impressed by it. Perhaps he thought it expedient to conform his altar to those of his cosmopolitan neighbors. R. H. Lowery offered a useful perspective on these subtle distinctions: "In lopsided social-political relationships, the line between force and persuasion is very thin. In such cases, 'imitation' is very difficult to distinguish from 'imposition.'"¹⁴³

The next section takes up five different case studies.¹⁴⁴

Prophecy

The Neo-Assyrian prophetic texts constitute the most significant corpus for comparison with the Hebrew prophets, rivaled only by the reports from the Bronze Age Syrian city of Mari. The behavior of prophets, the form and content of oracles, and the compilation of those oracles into collections all bear comparison with the prophets of Israel and Judah, some of whom were contemporaries.¹⁴⁵

In Neo-Assyrian sources, the usual term for a prophet was *rāgintu* (fem.; masc. *rāgimu*), a nominal form of the verb *ragāmu*, "to shout, proclaim." Prophets proclaimed the words of the goddess or god (most commonly Ishtar

---

142. Giovanni B. Lanfranchi, "Consensus to Empire: Some Aspects of Sargon II's Foreign Policy," in *Assyrien im Wandel der Zeiten*, ed. H. Waetzoldt and H. Hauptmann, HSAO 6 (Heidelberg: Heidelberger Orientverlag, 1997), 87.

143. R. H. Lowery, *The Reforming Kings: Cults and Society in First Temple Judah*, JSOTSup 120 (Sheffield, UK: JSOT Press, 1991), 140.

144. Primary texts and more extensive discussions of some of these comparisons may be found in Christopher B. Hays, *Hidden Riches: A Sourcebook for the Comparative Study of the Old Testament and the Ancient Near East* (Louisville: Westminster John Knox, 2014).

145. Simo Parpola, *Assyrian Prophecies*, SAA 9 (Helsinki: Helsinki University Press, 1997); Martti Nissinen et al., *Prophets and Prophecy in the Ancient Near East*, ed. Peter Machinist, WAW 12 (Atlanta: Society of Biblical Literature, 2003).

in the preserved texts), as Hebrew prophets proclaimed the words of Yhwh. Neo-Assyrian prophets seem to have enjoyed relatively high status and were believed to have the ability to become "possessed by the god(dess)." Unlike scholars, who were predominantly male, the majority of prophets seem to have been female (eight of thirteen in preserved oracles). Reports usually mention the name, gender, and home city of the prophet, so certain prophets probably attained personal authority.

Another Neo-Assyrian term for prophets is attested in administrative lists: *zabbu/zabbatu* (frenzied one), reflecting the ecstatic state that was thought to characterize close contact with the divine. Similarly, biblical prophets were said to behave oddly; examples include Isaiah's walking around naked for three years (Isa. 20:2–3), Jeremiah's shattering a jug (Jer. 19), or Ezekiel's lying on his side for more than a year and eating barley cakes cooked over dung (Ezek. 4:1–15).

The Neo-Assyrian term for an oracle was *šipir maḫḫe* (message of prophets). The addressee of the message was usually the king. Oracles may have been produced in large numbers, but only twenty-nine have survived on their original tablets—preservation seems not to have been standard procedure. Esarhaddon and Assurbanipal were the only Assyrian kings who seem to have had prophecies archived, and the only ones who mention prophets in their inscriptions.

Most of the messages were "oracles of well-being." One begins:

[Esarh]addon, king of the lands, fear [not]! What wind has risen against you, whose wing have I not broken? Your enemies will roll before your feet like ripe apples. I am the Great Lady; I am Ištar of Arbela, who cast your enemies before your feet. What words have I spoken to you that you could not rely upon? I am Ištar of Arbela. I will flay your enemies and give them to you. I am Ištar of Arbela. I will go before you and behind you. Fear not![146]

The Akkadian term for oracles of well-being is *šulmu*, etymologically related to the Hebrew *šālôm*, "peace"—so when Jeremiah fumes that he hears "'Peace, peace,' but there is no peace" (Jer. 6:14; 8:11 [AT]), he may be referring specifically to the oracles of false prophets promising that Jerusalem will survive a Babylonian assault. Ishtar's reassuring words "Fear not!" recall the same sentiment expressed numerous times by the biblical prophets (e.g., Isa. 7:4; 40:9; Jer. 1:8; Ezek. 2:6; Joel 2:21–22; Zech. 8:13–15).

The image of the warlike Ishtar fighting alongside the king also resonates with the image of Yhwh the Divine Warrior. Certain specific imagery from the Neo-Assyrian oracles finds close analogues in biblical prophecy. For example,

---

146. Parpola, *Assyrian Prophecies*, 1.1, lines 4–24.

SAA 9 2.3 bears a resemblance to Isaiah 31:4–5. In the Assyrian text, Ishtar says: "Like a winged bird ov[er its young] I will twitter over you and go in circles around you. Like a beautiful (lion) cub I will run about in your palace and sniff out your enemies." In the Isaianic prophecy Yhwh says:

> When the lion growls,
>   the young lion, over its prey,
> though a band of shepherds is summoned against it,
>   it isn't scared off by their noise
>   or frightened by their roar.
> So Yhwh of heavenly forces will go down
>   to fight on Mount Zion and on her hill.
> Like birds flying aloft,
>   so Yhwh of heavenly forces will shield Jerusalem:
> shielding and saving,
>   sparing and rescuing. (AT)

This similarity probably does not indicate that one prophet knew of the other's work, but that they may have both shared in a common tradition that included similar rhetorical tropes. Finally, it should be noted that Neo-Assyrian oracles were not *always* in support of the reigning king. They could also be used against him—for example, in support of a coup attempt.

The compilation and reediting of Neo-Assyrian oracles may also provide an empirical model for understanding the formation of the earliest versions of biblical prophetic books.[147] Neo-Assyrian oracles are preserved on two different types of tablets: individual oracles have survived on horizontal cuneiform tablets (used for daily record keeping and only occasionally archived); and multioracle compilations are attested on vertical tablets, which were meant for longer-term preservation.

Most individual Assyrian oracles are easily datable and can be more or less firmly associated with historical events. These were records of words spoken on particular historical occasions. The compilations, however, were produced at some temporal remove from their original utterance, sometimes as much as seven years. Oracles might be altered and stylized for reuse. Compilations were created for major events, and the individual oracles they comprised might be repurposed for this new situation. One collection was created to support the succession of Esarhaddon after the death of his father, Sennacherib. Another endorsed Assurbanipal's campaign against the Elamites.

---

147. See esp. Matthijs J. de Jong, *Isaiah among the Ancient Near Eastern Prophets: A Comparative Study of the Earliest Stages of the Isaiah Tradition and the Neo-Assyrian Prophecies*, VTSup 117 (Leiden: Brill, 2007).

Historiography

Assyrian texts inform our understanding of biblical history in at least two major ways: (1) the *genres* of Assyrian historiography may give us clues about the nature of the sources for biblical histories; and (2) numerous specific events are recounted in both Assyrian and biblical texts, giving researchers a binocular perspective on those events.

CASE STUDY: ANNALS AND KING LISTS

Assyrian annals and king lists were among the types of chronological records kept in ancient Mesopotamia. These raise questions about the existence and nature of possible sources that lay behind the biblical histories.

Assyrian scribes marked the years with eponym lists, also called *līmu* lists after the native Akkadian word. *Līmu* was an honorary title given to a high-ranking person, and the year was then named after that person. These lists occur in two forms: one with only a list of officials after which each year is "named," and another that adds a major event for each year. Here is an excerpt from the latter type, with the years numbered according to the modern system in parentheses:

- (745 BCE) In the eponymate of Nabû-belu-usur, of Arrapha, in Ayar on the 13th day, Tiglath-pileser (III) sat himself on the throne; in Teshrit he went to the land at the river's bend.
- (744 BCE) In the eponymate of Bel-dan, of Kalah, [the army campaigned] to Namri.[148]
    10 years [Ashur-nerari] king of Assyria
- (743 BCE) In the eponymate of Tiglath-pileser, king of Assyria, against Arpad, defeat inflicted on Urartu.
- (742 BCE) In the eponymate of Nabû-da"inanni, commander in chief, [the army campaigned] against Arpad.
- (741 BCE) In the eponymate of Bel-Harran-belu-usur, palace herald, [the army campaigned] against Arpad, conquered after three years.[149]

The form is not unique to Assyria. Examples go back as far as the early second millennium and have been found in multiple locations. By the Neo-Assyrian period, the title *līmu* was rotated in a relatively regular way: a new

---

148. Here and below, the words "the army campaigned" are not present in the text, which is written as tersely as possible.

149. Translation adapted from A. R. Millard, *The Eponyms of the Assyrian Empire 910–612 B.C.*, SAAS 2 (Helsinki: Neo-Assyrian Text Corpus Project, 1994).

king served as eponym in his second year, followed by his commander in chief (*turtanu*; cf. 2 Kings 18:17), and then usually by the "chief cupbearer" (*rab šāqēh*; cf. 2 Kings 18–19), the palace herald, the chamberlain, and then various provincial governors.

The duties of one who held the title *līmu* are not thoroughly understood, but he had the power to enforce the payment of taxes by confiscating property. Nearly a hundred stone stelae bearing the names of eponyms have been recovered from a single location in the city of Assur, and it may be that they were moved there after they stood in a temple during their eponymates. The practice may also have commemorated the eponyms after their deaths.

Another chronological document that finds echoes in the Bible is the Assyrian King List, which sought to record the reigns of Assyrian kings back to the start of the second millennium. It includes the king's name, father, and the length of his reign. Here is a representative excerpt:

> Adad-nirari (III), son of Shamshi-Adad, ruled for 28 years.
> Shalmaneser (IV), son of Adad-nirari, ruled for 10 years.
> Assur-dan (III), brother of Shalmaneser, ruled for 18 years.
> Assur-nirari (V), son of Adad-nirari, ruled for 10 years.
> Tiglath-pileser (III), son of Assur-nirari, ruled for 18 years.
> Shalmaneser (V), son of Tiglath-pileser, ruled for 5 years.[150]

Occasionally it will add a few more details about events in the reign, but such additions are exceptions to the rule.

Similar regnal records were also kept at Ugarit and in Egypt, and so they seem to reflect a widespread practice. If Judah and Israel also kept king lists of some sort, they could have served as the framework for the biblical histories of the monarchies in 1–2 Kings. The year notices that punctuate the biblical history are quite reminiscent of the Babylonian Chronicle. For example, 2 Kings 15:27 says: "In the fifty-second year of King Azariah of Judah, Pekah son of Remaliah began to reign over Israel in Samaria; he reigned twenty years." There are numerous references in the Bible to various textual records, but no copies of them are known to exist. A partial list would include the Book of the Wars of Yhwh (Num. 21:14), the Book of Jashar (Josh. 10:13), the Book of the Acts of Solomon (1 Kings 11:41), the Book of the Annals of the Kings of Israel (1 Kings 14:19), and the Book of the Annals of the Kings of Judah (1 Kings 14:29).

It must be noted that even if sources akin to the Assyrian annals and lists lay behind the biblical histories, in the form that we have those histories today

---

150. Adapted from Jean-Jacques Glassner, *Mesopotamian Chronicles*, ed. Benjamin R. Foster, WAW 19 (Atlanta: Society of Biblical Literature, 2004), 145.

they are of a very different genre, having been extensively expanded by later historians and heavily overlaid with their perspectives.

Case Study: The Siege of Sennacherib

Assyrian kings reveled in their military exploits, recounting them in their inscriptions even more than their southern counterparts in Babylonia. Because Assyria, at the height of its power, repeatedly fought against and eventually overran Israel and Judah, the royal inscriptions also offer the interpreter an unusually direct set of extrabiblical witnesses to specific events that were also recounted in the Bible. Some of the references to campaigns against the west are terse and/or fragmentary, but not all. Because Sennacherib's western campaign of 701 was undertaken specifically to punish Hezekiah for his role in a regional attempt to throw off the yoke of Assyrian rule, the Assyrian accounts of that part of the campaign are quite extensive. Dozens of copies of the text exist, and the oldest one (called the Rassam Cylinder after its discoverer, Hormuzd Rassam) dates to 700 BCE, roughly six months after the campaign.

In Sennacherib's account, the battle against Hezekiah and Judah is the climax of the campaign, and it is a rout: "I surrounded (and) conquered forty-six of [Hezekiah's] fortified walled cities and smal(ler) settlements in their environs. . . . I brought out of them 200,150 people, young (and) old, male and female, horses, mules, donkeys, camels, oxen, and sheep and goats, which were without number, and counted (them) as booty."[151] The violence of the campaign is confirmed by destruction layers, attributed to Assyrians, in many Judean cities.[152] Sennacherib goes on to say, "[Hezekiah] himself, I locked up within Jerusalem, his royal city, like a bird in a cage." Significantly, he does not claim to have taken Jerusalem, but he does say that Hezekiah, "overwhelmed by the awesome splendor of my lordship," relented and sent massive tribute that included 30 talents of gold, 800 talents of silver, large numbers of people, and many kinds of luxury products.[153]

The Bible's account is more complicated. A brief notice in 2 Kings 18:13–16 has much in common with the Assyrian version: Sennacherib is said to have captured "all the fortified cities of Judah" and then come up against Jerusalem. Hezekiah grovels before him and gives him 300 talents of silver and 30 talents of gold, a figure strikingly similar to the Assyrian account. To do this, he is said even to have stripped the gold from the Jerusalem temple.

---

151. Grayson and Novotny, *Royal Inscriptions of Sennacherib*, 65. (See also COS 2.119B.)
152. Stern, *Archaeology of the Land of the Bible*, 10.
153. Grayson and Novotny, *Royal Inscriptions of Sennacherib*, 65. (See also COS 2.119B.)

However, 2 Kings 18 seems to indicate that Hezekiah paid in advance, whereas Sennacherib recounted that he received his tribute after blockading the city.

These differences are comparatively minor, but the biblical passage goes on to tell a very different version of the events in 2 Kings 18:17–19:37 (paralleled in Isa. 36–37). This time, instead of terse notes, one gets a sequence of dramatic scenes. In 2 Kings 18:17–19:9a, an Assyrian detachment comes to the walls of Jerusalem and the *rab šāqēh*, a high official, gives a lengthy speech (in Hebrew, no less) intended to demoralize the Jerusalemites and secure their surrender without a fight. The *rab šāqēh* is remarkably well-informed for an Assyrian. He knows not only that the Judeans are hoping for help from Egypt (which he scoffs at) but also that Hezekiah has taken steps to shut down the worship of Yhwh outside of Jerusalem, and he suggests that Yhwh is angry with Hezekiah and will not protect the city. When Hezekiah receives the message, he is deeply distressed, but he also receives a word from the prophet Isaiah that Sennacherib will hear a rumor and retreat. Immediately afterward, another message arrives that the Kushite military is coming up from the south.

In a kind of doublet (2 Kings 19:9b–37), the Assyrian contingent returns to the walls of Jerusalem and delivers a second, similar speech demanding submission. This time Hezekiah is slightly less distressed, and Isaiah delivers an even more forceful word of protection from Yhwh. That night, the story goes, an angel of the Lord strikes down 185,000 Assyrian soldiers, and the king is forced to retreat.

Sennacherib's siege of Jerusalem is recounted yet again in 2 Chronicles 32:1–23, where Hezekiah is truly heroic instead of distressed, in keeping with the pro-Davidic-monarchy ideology of the Chronicler. Thus there are as many as four retellings of the story in the Bible. In general, it has seemed clear to most critical scholars that the story of Sennacherib's siege was repeated and built up into increasingly legendary forms over a long period of time. The final version of the Kings account is usually thought to be no earlier than the Babylonian exile, and the Chronicles account even later: the fifth or fourth century.

Since many aspects of the biblical accounts cannot be correlated with the Assyrian version, some have dismissed them as historical sources. That is not due to antibiblical bias; rather, it is one of the principles of historiography that an account that is closer in time to the events it describes is to be preferred, all else being equal. Since the Assyrian account of the campaign is far closer in time to 701 than the final forms of the biblical histories, the former is often assumed to be a priori more accurate.

That approach to the conflict of sources is probably insufficiently nuanced, however. In the first place, it has been shown that numerous aspects of the *rab šāqēh*'s speeches in 2 Kings 18–19 do in fact mirror Neo-Assyrian rhetoric in numerous details, which may suggest firsthand knowledge.[154]

Furthermore, suspicions about the biblical sources must be balanced against a recognition of the ideological and literary shaping of the Assyrian accounts. For example, A. Kirk Grayson has pointed out that there are more than a few cases in which the Assyrian royal inscriptions falsely claimed victory over Babylon; the Assyrian versions of events are contradicted both by other sources and by the broader reconstructions of the history of their periods.[155] K. Lawson Younger has further shown that Assyrian campaign accounts were not constructed according to modern ideals of journalistic accuracy, but according to literary conventions.[156] Putting these insights together, one finds that (not surprisingly) Assyrian authors in the royal court wanted to tell a good story, and one that made the king look good.

There are details of Sennacherib's own account that are unusual and prompt reflection: Why did he only surround Jerusalem? Why did he not capture it and even destroy it? Why did he not punish or depose Hezekiah, since that was the apparent goal of the campaign? Why did he leave before the tribute was even sent?

As has often been noted, Sennacherib claimed only to have "shut [Hezekiah] up like a bird in a cage," which was not only a modest claim by Assyrian standards but one that was borrowed from an earlier inscription of Tiglath-pileser III.[157] It is not entirely clear whether Hezekiah was simply spared by Sennacherib because of a change of heart or whether some combination of Egyptian military aid (2 Kings 19:7–9), sickness among the Assyrian troops,[158]

---

154. Peter Machinist, "Assyria and Its Image in First Isaiah," *JAOS* 103 (1983): 719–37; Chaim Cohen, "Neo-Assyrian Elements in the First Speech of the Biblical Rab-Šāqê," *IOS* 9 (1979): 32–48.

155. Grayson, "Problematical Battles in Mesopotamian History," in *Studies in Honor of Benno Landsberger on His Seventy-Fifth Birthday, April 21, 1963*, ed. Hans G. Güterbock and Thorkild Jacobsen, AS 16 (Chicago: University of Chicago Press, 1965), 337–42.

156. K. Lawson Younger Jr., *Ancient Conquest Accounts: A Study in Ancient Near Eastern and Biblical History Writing*, JSOTSup 98 (Sheffield, UK: JSOT Press, 1990).

157. W. W. Hallo, "Jerusalem under Hezekiah: An Assyriological Perspective," in *Jerusalem: Its Sanctity and Centrality to Judaism, Christianity, and Islam*, ed. Lee I. Levine (New York: Continuum, 1999), 39–40; Hayim Tadmor, "Sennacherib's Campaign to Judah," *Zion* 50 (1985): 65–80.

158. It has sometimes been thought that Herodotus's account in *Histories* 2.141 of mice that ate the gear of Sennacherib's soldiers while they were on campaign in Egypt is a (loose) reimagination of a story in which mice caused disease in his camp at Jerusalem. For discussion, see Brent A. Strawn, "Herodotus' *Histories* 2.141 and the Deliverance of Jerusalem: On Parallels, Sources, and Histories of Ancient Israel," in *Israel's Prophets and Israel's Past: Essays on the Relationship of Prophetic Texts and Israelite History in Honor of John H. Hayes*, ed. B. E. Kelle and M. B. Moore, LHBOTS 446 (New York: T&T Clark, 2006), 210–38.

or something else caused the Assyrian king to return home in a hurry. It is certainly most surprising that Sennacherib would allow a king who led an international rebellion to remain on the throne—so surprising that some scholars have argued it can only be attributed to divine intervention.[159]

Recently, Stephanie Dalley has made the controversial suggestion that Judah had a friendly history with Assyria, which helped to spare Jerusalem in 701. She claims that relations between Assyria and Judah were very warm during Hezekiah's reign—indeed familial, in that she believes Judean princesses were married to Tiglath-pileser III and Sargon II. Among other supporting data, Judeans seem to have served as bodyguards for Sennacherib,[160] who also praised Hezekiah as "tough and strong" in an inscription, which is an exceptional literary treatment for a foreign, rebel king.[161]

Other scholars, looking at the events of 701 from the standpoint of Assyrian economic interests, see no need to posit special circumstances. It is likely that Assyria did not deem Judah a highly profitable area to control and so did not expend the energy to conquer it completely and turn it into a province.[162] Hezekiah's survival is reminiscent of another rebel king who was also anomalously left on his throne, Hanunu of Gaza. The Sargonid monarch in that instance, Tiglath-pileser III, installed a gold image of himself in Hanunu's palace, "perhaps cast from Hanunu's own trade-gotten wealth."[163] It may be the case for both Hezekiah and Hanunu that "the economic networks they dominated rendered them more useful alive than flayed," but in both cases "the lenient treatment . . . may have come with a variety of unsubtle 'reminders' of Assyrian sovereignty . . . intended to remind the wayward ruler that a sizable cut of his annual profits was earmarked for the Great King."[164] It was one thing to survive an Assyrian military campaign, but it is unthinkable that Sennacherib would have left Jerusalem without sending a strong message about imperial authority.

In sum, it is manifest that both the Assyrian and the biblical texts serve ideological interests in this instance. Although both supply useful information,

---

159. Robert D. Bates, "Assyria and Rebellion in the Annals of Sennacherib: An Analysis of Sennacherib's Treatment of Hezekiah," *NEASB* 44 (1999): 57; H. H. Rowley, "Hezekiah's Reform and Rebellion," *BJRL* 44 (1962): 431; Baruch Halpern, *The First Historians: The Hebrew Bible and History* (San Francisco: Harper & Row, 1988), 247.

160. This is based on her interpretation of one of Sennacherib's reliefs from Nineveh (Dalley, "Recent Evidence," 391–92). Dalley does not explain, however, how a Judean could be distinguished iconographically from a Semite from the former kingdom of Israel or another state.

161. Ibid., 392.

162. Parker, *Mechanics of Empire*, 25.

163. Holloway, *Aššur Is King!*, 192.

164. Ibid., 192–93; Holloway is speaking of Hanunu.

neither reveals the whole, complex reality, and one is not likely to get any closer to the precise historical truth of the incident without further information coming to light.

TREATY, OATH, AND COVENANT

Another highly significant Assyrian genre that is compared to biblical texts is the treaty-oath, which shares many features with biblical covenants. The most famous example is the Vassal Treaties of Esarhaddon (VTE), which are focused on the succession of Esarhaddon's son, Assurbanipal. Esarhaddon wanted to ensure that Assurbanipal would take the throne smoothly when the time came.

The goal of this treaty-oath was to protect Assurbanipal from threats—both from foreign nations and from within Assyria. The oath adjures those who swear it to be faithful and loyal to Assurbanipal. For example, foreign nations are required to supply military aid and to take action against traitors of various kinds. Nine copies of Esarhaddon's treaty have been recovered, and a different ruler of a peripheral city-state is named on each one: eight of them found at the imperial capital city of Kalhu (Nimrud) concerning Median vassals from western Iran and one from the west, found at the Syrian city of Unqi (Tell Ta'yinat), capital of the Assyrian province of Kullania.

The structure of the Assyrian oaths seems to have been flexible, but usually it included these basic elements:

1. Preamble, identifying the Assyrian king and the vassal who was placed under oath
2. Designation of the Assyrian ruler or successor to whom loyalty was due
3. Divine witnesses/adjuration
4. Historical introduction
5. Stipulations
6. Curses for failing to carry out the stipulations
7. Vow[165]

Rubrics calling for vows to be taken could also be inserted in various places.

The biblical covenants can be seen as *adaptations* of the treaty form rather than as examples of it. The order and weight of the various elements are not the same. However, the similarities of the rhetoric are undeniable and

---

165. This list is a hybrid of those found in George E. Mendenhall and Gary A. Herion, "Covenant," *ABD* 1:1179–202; and Parpola and Watanabe, *Neo-Assyrian Treaties and Loyalty Oaths*, xxxv–xlvii.

striking. Most of the same elements are present, especially as given in the book of Deuteronomy:

1. Identification of the covenant giver (Deut. 5:6)
2. Historical prologue (1:1–4:14)
3. Divine witnesses (4:26)
4. Stipulations (4:44–27:8)
5. Blessings (28:1–14)
6. Curses (28:15–68)
7. Oath taking (27:9–26)

Perhaps the largest single distinguishing aspect of the biblical covenants is that Yhwh takes on the role of the human emperor. The casting of Yhwh as a king whose claims mirror those of foreign kings can be observed fairly widely in the Bible and has been called "replacement theology."[166]

One of the most famous aspects of Deuteronomy's theological message—its call to "love Yhwh your God with all your heart, and with all your soul, and with all your might" (6:5)—can be seen to mirror Assyrian rhetoric about faithfulness to the royal line.[167] Esarhaddon issues a similar call for the vassals to love his heir: "You shall love Assurbanipal . . . your lord, like yourselves" (see also Lev. 19:18; Matt. 22:39, etc.). Indeed, the language of "love" was used to express political faithfulness in diplomatic texts and letters reaching back into the Bronze Age; they speak of the brotherly love between allied kings. Not surprisingly, Deuteronomy frames the call to love in an explicitly covenantal framework:

> Know therefore that Yhwh your God is God, the faithful God who maintains covenant loyalty with those who love him and keep his commandments, to a thousand generations, and who repays in their own person those who reject him. He does not delay but repays in their own person those who reject him. (Deut. 7:9–10; cf. 5:9–10; Exod. 20:5–6; 34:6–7)

The prophets adapted the language of love to describe the nation as the bride of Yhwh (e.g., Hosea 1–3; 6:4–5; 12:6; Jer. 2:2; 33:11; Ezek. 16:8).

Various differences follow from Yhwh's replacement of the Assyrian king. For example, Yhwh takes on a speaking role, whereas the Assyrian gods do not. The fact that loyalty in Deuteronomy was pledged to God also seems to have

---

166. See, e.g., Shawn Zelig Aster, "The Image of Assyria in Isaiah 2:5–22: The Campaign Motif Revisited," *JAOS* 127 (2007): 257.

167. William L. Moran, "The Ancient Near Eastern Background of the Love of God in Deuteronomy," *CBQ* 25 (1963): 77–87; Bill T. Arnold, "The Love-Fear Antinomy in Deuteronomy 5–11," *VT* 61, no. 4 (2011): 551–69.

affected the content of the stipulations. If the laws of the Deuteronomic Code (4:44–27:8) are the stipulations of the covenant, then they cover many topics that are never broached in the ancient Near Eastern treaties. However, the stipulations are not entirely different. There are resonances between the prohibition of speaking treason in VTE §§10, 12 and the prohibition of false prophetic speech in Deuteronomy 18:20–22, and especially the apostasy laws of Deuteronomy 13:2–19 (Eng. 13:1–18). Furthermore, in Deuteronomy 2:4–19 Yhwh acts like an ancient Near Eastern emperor commanding peace among his vassal nations when he orders the Israelites not to make war with Edom, Moab, or Ammon.

Some features of biblical covenants, including the Deuteronomic one, are more similar to Hittite treaties of the Late Bronze Age, which suggests that they are adaptations of a widely known form rather than just an Assyrian one. For example, their historical prologues are lengthy and focused on divine grace. Neo-Assyrian kings were far less interested in portraying themselves sympathetically; they may have deemed it beneath them to justify their demands for loyalty. Furthermore, Deuteronomy includes clauses calling for the storage and regular recital of the text (10:1–2; 31:10–13, 24–29), as do Hittite treaties.

Then again, Deuteronomy looks more like an Assyrian treaty in some of its specific rhetoric, and especially in its lengthy curse sections (27:15–26; 28:15–68), which are about four times as long as its blessings (28:1–14).

It is clear that these competing demands for absolute allegiance—to Assurbanipal and to Yhwh—would have come into conflict with one another. The adaptation of the Assyrian covenant form to Yahwistic use was meant to subvert the claims of the empire. That is, the demand of faithfulness to Yhwh necessarily precluded complete faithfulness to a foreign emperor, and to frame that demand in the very literary form that the empire used makes the contrast especially stark. It is generally thought that Josiah propagated the Deuteronomic Code as part of the process of throwing off the Assyrian yoke as the empire was growing weaker.[168] Second Kings 22–23 says that in the eighteenth year of Josiah (622 BCE), a "book of the law" was found in the temple (22:8) and was newly propagated by the king at that time. Most scholars conclude that some form of Deuteronomy was Josiah's law book, since Deuteronomy also refers to itself as a "book of the law" (29:21; 30:10; 31:26), and some of Josiah's reforms correspond with Deuteronomic laws.[169]

---

168. The seventh-century kings of Judah likely were aware of loyalty oaths whether or not they took them. See Hayim Tadmor, "Treaty and Oath in the Ancient Near East: An Historian's Approach," in *Humanizing America's Iconic Book*, ed. G. M. Tucker and D. A. Knight (Chico, CA: Scholars Press, 1982), 148–52.

169. A negative assessment of the theory that Deuteronomy was a reaction to Assyrian hegemony specifically has been offered by Carly Crouch, *Israel and the Assyrians: Deuteronomy,*

In addition to the VTE, Deuteronomy has also been compared to the Middle Assyrian Laws (MAL). In particular, Eckart Otto has sought to identify numerous terminological parallels between the two texts, and on that basis has argued that both were reform documents advancing the causes of centralization and nationalization, and that a primary feature of both reform efforts was the professionalization of legal procedures and the appointment of judges.[170] In this view, Deuteronomy's adoption of the MAL's ideas and phrasings was part of its larger reaction to Assyrian hegemony. One problem with this theory is that the MAL were composed in the Late Bronze Age and were not copied with any regularity in the Neo-Assyrian period, so it is not clear that they were influential in Assyria at that time, let alone in Judah.

Birth Accounts of Sargon and Moses

The birth legend of Sargon purports to recount the birth, childhood, and reign of the great king Sargon of Akkad (r. ca. 2340–2284 BCE; see further above). However, since no copy of the text from anywhere close to the period of Sargon himself has survived, it is now accepted that it must be a much later composition, produced, quite probably, by the scribes of Sargon II (r. 722–705), who adopted Sargon's name and thus had an interest in propagating legends about him. As noted in section 4, Sargon II was a usurper who initiated a new royal line, so he had to assert his legitimacy as a ruler.

The Sargon account belongs to a Mesopotamian genre called pseudoautobiography (or simply fictional autobiography). It is based on inscriptions by Mesopotamian kings that included three parts: an opening self-introduction, a first-person narrative of the king's accomplishments, and an epilogue with a blessing for those who preserve his words or a curse for anyone who would efface them.

The text begins by stating that the king did not know his father, and that his mother was a priestess who hid the pregnancy and sent him away. While this mystery might indicate that something was socially inappropriate about the pregnancy,[171] it also leaves open the interpretation that he was fathered by a god, a claim that was made by other Mesopotamian kings. The detail that

---

the Succession Treaty of Esarhaddon, and the Nature of Subversion, ANEM 8 (Atlanta: Society of Biblical Literature, 2014).

170. Eckart Otto, *Das Deuteronomium: Politische Theologie und Rechtsreform in Juda und Assyrien*, BZAW 284 (Berlin: Walter de Gruyter, 1999).

171. Priestesses like Sargon's mother in the story would have been associated with temples in many major cities, and are thought to have been sworn to chastity except for participation in the ritual of "sacred marriage," in which she might portray a goddess, having intercourse with a king portraying the god. But if Sargon's father was a king, why would a legend glorifying him not say so?

Sargon was the child of a priestess already points to a comparison with Moses, who was descended from Levites (Exod. 2:1), who were temple functionaries.

It is the distinctive opening of Sargon's narrative, however, that is the primary reason this text has fascinated biblical scholars and students. Like Moses, Sargon is said to have been laid by his mother in a basket of reeds sealed with pitch and placed in a river. However, the similarity of the act of placing the child in a river may mask different motivations. In the case of Moses, it is an act of desperation; in the case of Sargon, the motive is less clear. It might be that Sargon's fate is being put in the hands of the river god, a practice known in Mesopotamia under other circumstances.

Sargon is drawn out by a water bearer called Aqqi. That name can be understood as a verb meaning, "I poured," essentially identifying him by his profession. Similarly, Moses's name was given a folk etymology that connected it with being drawn from water: the Hebrew verb *māšâ* means "to draw water" and sounds very much like the Hebrew form of Moses's name, *Mōšeh*; thus Exod. 2:10 recounts that the pharaoh's daughter "named him Moses, 'because,' she said, 'I drew him out of the water.'"[172]

Aqqi lifts Sargon up out of the water and then raises him up, putting him to work in his garden. This is by no means a typical upbringing for an Assyrian king. The work in the garden, carrying with it overtones of fertility, may suggest something like a sacred marriage and thus be appropriate for a future king. After that, however, Ishtar bestows her blessing on Sargon, which was a more typical qualification to rule; as noted above, Ishtar was frequently invoked by Assyrian rulers for blessings and support. Moses is similarly called by God from humble circumstances (herding flocks) to his lofty mission.

There are, of course, notable differences between the Sargon and Moses stories. Moses is abandoned not for some individual reason (such as scandal or economic hardship) but because of a more general threat of genocide. The agency of Moses's sister and mother in protecting and watching over him finds no parallel in the Sargon account. And perhaps most significantly, Moses begins life as a slave, is found and raised by a princess, and then returns to his common roots; Sargon is born to a high priestess, saved by a workman, and then elevated again by a goddess. The patterns of their ascents and descents are thus mirror images of each other.

There are many stories, from the ancient Near East and elsewhere, of an exposed child who is saved and rises to prominence. In the Bible alone, one

---

172. Typically scholars identify the real etymology of Moses's name as an Egyptian one, arguing that "Moses" is derived from the common element in names such as "Ramesses" (Ra created him).

can point to Genesis 21 (Ishmael), Ezekiel 16 (a personified Jerusalem), and, in a more attenuated form, Genesis 37 and 39 (Joseph). Therefore, one is probably dealing in these two stories with individual adaptations of a traditional fable or story type.

Temple-Building Accounts

Ancient Near Eastern kings loved to boast of their building exploits in their own inscriptions. Particularly when these accounts involved temple building, they presented the ruler as pious and divinely elected to carry out the work. As a significant additional benefit, they would have reminded the temple's priests who their benefactor was.

Despite significant variations among such accounts, it is possible to identify an archetypal form. A passage from the annals of Tiglath-pileser I (r. 1114–1076)[173] turns out to have very close similarities with the account of Solomon's building of the Jerusalem temple in 1 Kings, even down to the ordering of the elements (the tablet and line numbers from the Assyrian inscription are followed by the corresponding biblical passage):

1. Circumstances of the project and the decision to build (vii 60–70; 1 Kings 5:1–5)
2. Preparations—for example, gathering materials (vii 71–84; 1 Kings 5:6–18)
3. Description of the building (vii 85–107; 1 Kings 6:1–38; 7:13–51)
4. Dedication rites and festivities (vii 107–14; 1 Kings 8:1–11, 62–66)
5. Blessing and/or prayer of the king (viii 17–49; 1 Kings 8:12–61)
6. Blessings and curses of future generations (viii 50–88; 1 Kings 9:3–9)

Both building accounts were embedded in historical narratives, and in each case the concern to memorialize the king is quite clear. The Assyrian temple-building account takes up only about one and a half columns excerpted from an eight-column text containing annals of Tiglath-pileser I's reign. After introducing himself and touting his greatness and favor with the gods, Tiglath-pileser spends about five columns—the great majority of the tablet—discussing his military campaigns and victories. Even though the temple-building account is not the bulk of the annals, it might be said that the text builds to it and culminates in it, since it is the last event recounted, and it comprises the longest single section. Tiglath-pileser's temple-building account expresses

---

173. A. Kirk Grayson, *Assyrian Rulers of the Early First Millennium BC*, vol. 1, 1114–859 BC, RIMA 2 (Toronto: University of Toronto Press, 1991), 28–31.

thanks for the grace of the gods during his reign and seeks to affirm his close relationship with them. These annals glorifying the king seem to have achieved their purpose. In the case of 1 Kings, the temple-building account is certainly intended to help portray Solomon as one who "excelled all the kings of the earth in riches and in wisdom" (1 Kings 10:23)—and as with Tiglath-pileser, his fame endured through the centuries.

There are other building accounts in the Bible, including Exodus 25–31, 35–40 (the construction of the tabernacle); 2 Chronicles 2–7 (the Chronicler's version of Solomon's temple building); and Ezekiel 40–48 (Ezekiel's vision of a restored temple), but 1 Kings 5–9 is the most clearly influenced by a Neo-Assyrian milieu. The extensive dedication ceremony in the 1 Kings passage, especially its lengthy blessings and curses, is more akin to Assyrian building accounts than those of other periods and locations in the ancient Near East.[174]

A theological aspect of the 1 Kings account may also point to a Neo-Assyrian-period provenance: its insistence on exclusive worship of Yhwh. For example, 1 Kings 9:6–9 forbids hearers from worshiping any other god along with Yhwh. This is of course a radical departure from other ancient Near Eastern building accounts, in which numerous gods are commonly invoked to enforce the blessings and curses. It also suggests a composition in the reign of Josiah, when the exclusive worship of Yhwh was advocated (and seemingly enforced) more energetically than in any other period of the monarchy. As an example, phrases in 1 Kings 9:6 such as "turning aside," "keeping commandments and statutes," and "serving other gods" are all quintessentially characteristic of the Deuteronomistic Historians, who are thought to have been working in Josiah's time.

Summary

The foregoing discussion indicates the interconnectedness between the literary cultures of Israel/Judah and Assyria, and the relevance of each to the study of the other. If space allowed, many more comparisons with biblical literature could be discussed—not surprisingly, since the Assyrian textual corpus is very large. Neo-Assyrian mantic texts such as the Underworld Vision of an Assyrian Prince shed light on biblical apocalyptic.[175] Ezekiel's supernatural imagery is often compared with Assyrian (as well as Babylonian) iconography.[176]

---

174. See, further, Victor Avigdor Hurowitz, *I Have Built You an Exalted House: Temple Building in the Bible in Light of Mesopotamian and North-West Semitic Writings*, JSOTSup 115 (Sheffield, UK: Sheffield Academic, 1992).

175. Helge S. Kvanvig, *Roots of Apocalyptic*, WMANT 61 (Neukirchen-Vluyn: Neukirchener Verlag, 1988).

176. Christoph Uehlinger and Susanne Müller Trufaut, "Ezekiel 1, Babylonian Cosmological Scholarship and Iconography: Attempts at Further Refinement," *TZ* 57 (2001): 140–71.

Middle and Neo-Assyrian love songs, especially the Love Lyrics of Nabû and Tašmētu, offer some close parallels with the Song of Songs,[177] and Martti Nissinen has suggested that the "wisdom literature of the Hebrew Bible has plenty of largely still unexplored cognates in Mesopotamian wisdom."[178]

7. Assyria in Biblical Tradition

In its own time and long after, the Assyrian Empire figured prominently in the imaginations of biblical authors.

In the primeval history, Genesis 10:8–12 remembers Nimrod as the founder of Mesopotamia. "The land of Nimrod" appears in parallel with "the land of Assyria" in Micah 5:5 (Eng. 5:6), so it appears the two could be treated as roughly synonymous. It is likely that the name Nimrod, rather than belonging to any historical individual, reflects an adaptation of a Mesopotamian divine name such as Ninurta or Marduk; it is also possible that it was intended as a denigrative reinterpretation meaning "we will rebel," from the Hebrew verb *mārad*.[179] Genesis 10:10–12 goes on to name some of the major cities of Mesopotamia: "The beginning of his kingdom was Babylon, Erech [= Uruk], and Akkad, all of them[180] in the land of Shinar. From that land Aššur went forth and built Nineveh, a most wide city,[181] Calah, and Resen between Nineveh and Calah; that is the great city" (AT). Of the cities named, the most difficult to identify has been Resen; possibly it refers to Dur-Sharrukin by the name of one of its satellite towns.[182] If so, then the latter part of the list of towns would reflect the state of affairs in Assyria in the late eighth century. In any case, it is notable that the city of Assur is mentioned nowhere in the Bible, reflecting that the biblical traditions coalesced after the capital had moved elsewhere.[183]

---

177. For a thorough discussion and citations of other literature, see Martti Nissinen, "Akkadian Rituals and Poetry of Divine Love," in *Mythology and Mythologies*, ed. R. M. Whiting, Melammu Symposia 2 (Helsinki: Neo-Assyrian Text Corpus Project, 2001), 93–136.

178. Martti Nissinen, "Assyria," *Encyclopedia of the Bible and Its Reception*, vol. 2, *Anim–Atheism*, ed. Christine Helmer et al. (Berlin: de Gruyter, 2009), 1090.

179. See further Peter Machinist, "Nimrod," *ABD* 4:1116–18; Christoph Uehlinger, "Nimrod," *DDD* 627–30.

180. Emending from *kalnēh* to *kullānâ*. See William F. Albright, "The End of 'Calneh in Shinar,'" *JNES* 3 (1944): 254–55.

181. Most translations transliterate this phrase as Rehoboth-ir, but (1) no such city is known in Mesopotamia; (2) Nineveh is frequently described in terms of its great size (so Jon. 3:3); and (3) to remove "Rehoboth-ir" as a city name creates paired lists of three cities in southern and northern Mesopotamia, respectively. See Jack M. Sasson, "Reḥōvōt 'îr," *RB* 90 (1983): 94–96.

182. For discussion and citations, see Vanderhooft, "Biblical Perspectives on Nineveh and Babylon," 84.

183. Ibid., 85.

Nimrod, who was treated as a historical figure by most interpreters, enjoyed a rich and complex reception history in Judaism, Christianity, and Islam; he was frequently associated with the building of the Tower of Babel and came to be envisioned as an evil counterpart to the righteous Abraham. For example, in various Jewish writings Nimrod is said to have thrown Abraham into a fiery furnace for refusing to worship idols.[184]

The biblical prophets of the Neo-Assyrian and Neo-Babylonian periods often condemned the leaders of Israel and Judah for reliance on foreign empires, and frequently Assyria is one of the nations named (Hosea 5:13; 7:11; 8:9, etc.; Jer. 2:18, 36; Ezek. 23; cf. Lam. 5:6). Ezekiel 31 portrays Assyria as a "world tree" that once flourished as the envy of the earth but was then cut down; and Ezekiel 32:22–23 enumerates the Assyrians among the empires that have "gone down to the Pit," as precursors to the Egyptians.

Assyria took on a literary and ideological role as the second nation, alongside Egypt, to represent the prototypical foreign imperial power that is judged by God. So it is that the oracle of Zephaniah 2:11–13 proclaimed cosmic judgment by the Divine Warrior, beginning with the coastlands and islands and mentioning Ethiopia, but culminating with the proclamation that the Lord will "stretch out his hand against the north, and destroy Assyria; and he will make Nineveh a desolation, a dry waste like the desert" (Zeph. 2:13). Assyria and Egypt are also repeatedly mentioned as places from which the Lord will recover his scattered people (Isa. 11:11, 16; 27:13; Hosea 11:11; Mic. 7:12). Because deportations to Assyria began in the eighth century, it can be difficult to determine whether such references are original to preexilic prophets or later additions.

Assyria continued to be seen as one of the ends of the earth after its time, so that it was paired with Egypt again in Zechariah 10:10–12. Such oracles of "cosmic" judgment reflect a nascent reaction to the might of empires that seemed too great for historical redress, so that only God can overcome it. In these mythologized passages, Assyria loses its historical specificity; it is merely a hypostasis of the cosmic chaos that opposed Yahweh's order.

Assyria was "dehistoricized" in a different way in late biblical narratives such as the books of Ezra and Jonah. The Persian king who "aided [the Judeans] in the work on the house of God" is called "the king of Assyria" (Ezra 6:22; cf. 1 Esd. 7:15), as if "Assyria" has become a catch-all term for the East, just as "Hatti" was a term Mesopotamians used for all of the West. (As noted above, the Assyrians were correctly identified in Ezra 4:2, 10; Neh. 9:32.) Jonah has little to do with the historical Assyria, either, even though it

---

184. Karel van der Toorn and P. W. van der Horst, "Nimrod before and after the Bible," *HTR* 83 (1990): 1–29.

hyperbolically remembers Nineveh's fame as a large city.[185] Rather, it is about prophetic calling and the relationship of the Lord to the nations.

In the deuterocanonical/apocryphal literature, Assyria continued to be employed as a literary trope in similar ways. In Judith, Nebuchadnezzar is remembered as a king "who ruled over the Assyrians in the great city of Nineveh" (1:1), and the eponymous heroine establishes herself by making her way into the imperial camp and cutting off the head of an Assyrian general—equal parts Jael (Judg. 4:17–22) and David (1 Sam. 17:51). In Tobit the eponymous hero establishes himself as a noble, wise figure among the Jewish exiles in Nineveh, exemplifying survival in the diaspora. However, in the end, Tobit says, "I believe the word of God that Nahum[186] spoke about Nineveh" (14:4), and his son Tobias "before he died . . . heard of the destruction of Nineveh" (14:15). In Maccabees the deliverance of Jerusalem from the Assyrians' onslaught in 701 was remembered in prayers for similar miraculous victories in later times (1 Macc. 7:41; 3 Macc. 6:5).

The New Testament provides an exception to the image of Assyria as the evil empire: the repentance of the people of Nineveh upon Jonah's mission is remembered as a paradigm for the appropriate repentance in response to Jesus (Matt. 12:41; Luke 11:30–32).

Assyria's role as the paradigmatic and cartoonish imperial power was partly usurped by Babylon—e.g., in Revelation and Daniel (although 4 Macc. 13:9 puts the fiery-furnace episode in Assyria).[187] Nevertheless, the fame of Assyria and Nineveh, "that great city" (Jon. 1:2), lived on in cultural history in numerous ways. A full history of its reception is thus beyond the scope of this chapter, but it points again to the benefits of recovering the historical Assyria in all its specificity.

For Further Reading

Note: Those interested in Assyria will want access to the many State Archives of Assyria (SAA) volumes produced in Helsinki and published by Eisenbrauns, as well as the series The Royal Inscriptions of Mesopotamia: Assyrian Periods (RIMA; University of Toronto) and The Royal Inscriptions of the Neo-Assyrian Period (RINAP; Eisenbrauns).

---

185. On the scale of Nineveh, see D. Stronach, "Notes on the Topography of Nineveh," in *Neo-Assyrian Geography*, ed. M. Liverani (Rome: Università di Roma "La Sapienza," 1995), 161–70.
186. Other manuscripts read "Jonah." See Machinist, "Fall of Assyria," 185–86.
187. See further, Machinist, "Fall of Assyria," 184–85.

Cancik-Kirschbaum, Eva. *Die Assyrer: Geschichte, Gesellschaft, Kultur.* Munich: Beck, 2003.

Fales, Frederick Mario. *Guerre et paix en Assyrie: Religion et impérialisme.* Paris: Cerf, 2010.

Fuchs, Andreas. "Assyria at War: Strategy and Conduct." In *The Oxford Handbook of Cuneiform Culture*, edited by Karen Radner and Eleanor Robson, 380–401. Oxford: Oxford University Press, 2011.

Holloway, Steven W. *Aššur Is King! Aššur Is King! Religion in the Exercise of Power in the Neo-Assyrian Empire.* CHANE 10. Leiden: Brill, 2002.

Liverani, Mario. "The Ideology of the Assyrian Empire." In *Power and Propaganda: A Symposium on Ancient Empires*, edited by Mogens Trolle Larsen, 297–317. Mesopotamia 7. Copenhagen: Akademisk Forlag, 1979.

Macgregor, Sherry Lou. *Beyond Hearth and Home: Women in the Public Sphere in Neo-Assyrian Society.* SAAS 21. The Neo-Assyrian Text Corpus Project. Winona Lake, IN: Eisenbrauns, 2012.

Machinist, Peter. "Assyria and Its Image in the First Isaiah." *JAOS* 103 (1983): 719–37.

Mattila, Raija. *The King's Magnates: A Study of the Highest Officials of the Neo-Assyrian Empire.* SAAS 11. The Neo-Assyrian Text Corpus Project. Winona Lake, IN: Eisenbrauns, 2000.

Parker, Bradley J. "The Construction and Performance of Kingship in the Neo-Assyrian Empire." *Journal of Anthropological Research* 67 (2011): 357–86.

Parpola, Simo. *Assyrian Prophecies.* SAA 9. Helsinki: Helsinki University Press, 1997.

Parpola, Simo, and Kazuko Watanabe. *Neo-Assyrian Treaties and Loyalty Oaths.* SAA 2. Helsinki: Helsinki University Press, 1988.

Radner, Karen. *Ancient Assyria: A Very Short Introduction.* Oxford: Oxford University Press, 2015.

Saggs, H. W. F. *The Might That Was Assyria.* London: Sidgwick & Jackson, 1984.

Svärd, Saana. *Women and Power in Neo-Assyrian Palaces.* SAAS 23. The Neo-Assyrian Text Corpus Project. Winona Lake, IN: Eisenbrauns, 2015.

Tadmor, Hayim. "World Dominion: The Expanding Horizon of the Assyrian Empire." In *"With My Many Chariots I Have Gone Up the Heights of Mountains": Historical and Literary Studies on Ancient Mesopotamia and Israel*, 87–102. Jerusalem: Israel Exploration Society, 2011.

Younger, K. Lawson, Jr. "The Assyrian Economic Impact on the Southern Levant in the Light of Recent Study." *IEJ* 65 (2015): 179–204.

3

Babylonia and the Babylonians

David S. Vanderhooft

"Babylonia" refers to the region of the lower Mesopotamian alluvium from roughly ancient Sippar in the north to the head of the Persian Gulf in the south, from the desert areas west of the Euphrates to the Zagros foothills east of the Tigris.[1] A variety of ancient designations described this region in antiquity, the most common of which was, in Akkadian, *māt šumeri u akkadi*, "the land of Sumer and Akkad," with Sumer in the south and Akkad in the north. The region farther north, in the zone of the upper Tigris, was the Assyrian heartland. The term "Babylonia" itself seldom appeared in ancient sources. During the period when the Kassite kings dominated the region (1596–1158 BCE), they preferred the geographical name Karduniash. Meanwhile, "Babylon," the name of a particular city, and "Babylonians," denizens of that city (and sometimes the wider region over which it held sway), appear widely in ancient sources from Mesopotamia and beyond. The Sumerian name for Babylon was KÁ.DINGIR.RA, the Akkadian *bāb ilim*, "gate of the god," a learned etymology, one that signals the ancient cultic associations of the city.

  1. For an insightful spatial overview of Babylonian history and of the role of "countrysides" in Babylonian political thought and organization, see S. Richardson, "The World of Babylonian Countrysides," in *The Babylonian World*, ed. G. Leick (New York: Routledge, 2007), 13–38.

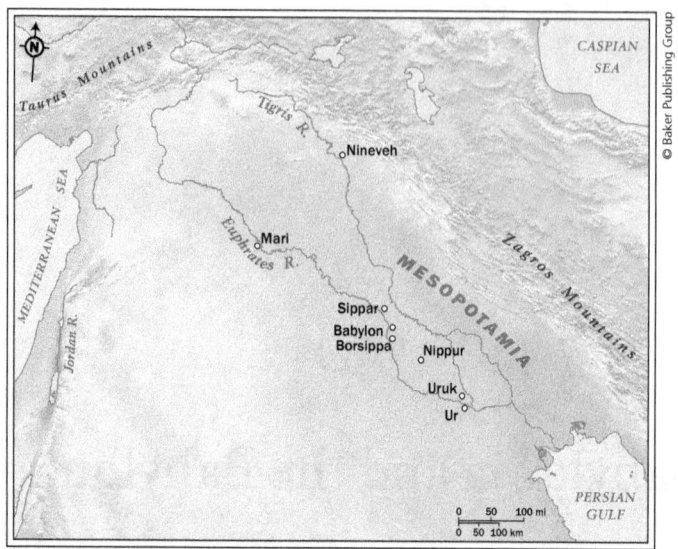

Figure 3.1. Babylonia

The Hebrew name for the city was a calque of the Akkadian, *bābel*, while the Greek transcription, *babylōn*, probably a vocalization of the Akkadian plural (*bāb ilāni*), was retained after the historical demise of the city. Many other more technical designations and spellings for the city, its temples, districts, and the surrounding region existed, most of which are elaborately preserved and commented on in the important cuneiform compilation TIN.TIR = Babylon, edited by A. R. George.[2] This text offers a sort of ancient scholarly compendium about the significance of Babylon's sacred geography. Its arcane and learned insights possess a wealth of information about scribal perceptions of sacred space, and A. R. George's masterful treatment deserves special regard.

The great antiquity of the city Babylon and its widely recognized status as the seat of deities and kings would shape Babylonian religious and political conceptions for centuries, even millennia. No city retained such a revered status for such a lengthy period, and even its afterlife has continued to shape artistic and cultural production since antiquity. Outside of Mesopotamia, Babylon's greatness and antiquity already receive emphasis in the Hebrew Bible. The so-called Table of Nations in Genesis 10 associates the origins of civilization in the East with the city of Babylon:

> Kush begot Nimrod; he was the first on earth to become a warrior. He was a warrior-hunter before YHWH; thus it is said: "like Nimrod, a warrior-hunter

---

2. A. R. George, *Babylonian Topographical Texts*, OLA 40 (Leuven: Peeters, 1992).

before YHWH." The capital[3] of his kingdom was Babel, with Erech and Akkad; all of them[4] in the land of Shinar. (Gen. 10:8–10 [AT])

The famous narrative of humanity's effort to build a city and tower—the city of course called Babel (Gen. 11:1–9)—reinforces the received tradition about Babylon's antiquity and its centrality within the Mesopotamian political and cultural realms. The tower story imagines Babel's original builders to have shared a common language, which God "jumbled," *bālal*, to effect their dispersion. Later, in Genesis 11, Abram and his kin depart the city "Ur of the Chaldeans," in the southern part of Sumer, and journey via Haran, in Syria, to the land of Canaan (Gen. 11:28, 31). Thus, from a biblical point of view, culture proper and Israel's ancestors in particular originated in Babylonia and moved from east to west. Other biblical texts occasionally reflect the assumption that Babylon was the capital of an ancient and prominent kingdom. Jeremiah, in the sixth century, warns that God will punish his apostate people of Judah by bringing a foe from the "north," almost certainly a reference to the Neo-Babylonian kingdom under Nebuchadnezzar II (605–562 BCE). The foe from the north is described as follows: "It is an enduring nation [*gôy*], it is a primeval nation; it is a nation whose language you do not know" (Jer. 5:15 [AT]).

While Babylon's antiquity was assumed in ancient Israel and Judah, the dominant concern of the Hebrew Bible is with Babylon as the seat of hostile kings or as a real or threatened place of deportation for Judeans. Of the 289 occurrences of the name Babylon in the Hebrew Bible, 134 refer to the king of Babylon, most often Nebuchadnezzar II (118 of 134). Three biblical books that treat the last decades of the history of the Judean kingdom—Jeremiah, Ezekiel, and 2 Kings (along with parallels to the latter in 2 Chronicles)—account for 224 of the 289 occurrences of the toponym. Quite obviously, then, texts of the Hebrew Bible are much less concerned with Babylon's origins and early history than they are with the dangers posed by the Babylonian kingdom under Nebuchadnezzar and his successors and the consequences of Babylonian depredations in the Mediterranean littoral.

Yet the early history of the city of Babylon, and of the lands of Sumer and Akkad—which scholars refer to as Babylonia for convenience—have relevance not only for Israelite and Judean history but also for human history,

---

3. For ראשית ממלכתו as "capital of his kingdom," compare other examples where the term ראשית may refer to "first city," i.e., "capital": Jer. 49:35; Amos 6:1. For a comparable Akkadian usage, see *CAD* R, s.v. *rēštû* 2.a).

4. Reading "all of them" for the unknown toponym "Calneh"; see William F. Albright, "The End of 'Calneh in Shinar,'" *JNES* 3 (1944): 254–55.

inasmuch as seminal political, juridical, literary, religious, and other influences emerged in the East and were carried west in the second and first millennia. The extent to which such influences came directly or indirectly to the West will be discussed throughout.

1. Babylonia in the First Half of the Second Millennium: An Overview of the Old Babylonian Period

The recovery of primary evidence pertaining to the history and culture of ancient Babylonia has proliferated so dramatically since the nineteenth century that it is now quite impossible for any scholar to control all of the data. In addition, both the exact chronological dating of events and the general historical framework of the second millennium have become more complex as a consequence of this proliferation of data. Despite this, the following section will outline in broad terms the emergence and history of Babylon and Babylonia as political and cultural forces in the first half of the second millennium, the so-called Old Babylonian period, for this period also held a pivotal role in the cultural memory of subsequent Mesopotamian polities.[5]

During approximately the last century of the third millennium, the regions of Sumer and Akkad flourished under the so-called Third Dynasty of Ur. It reached its apogee, culturally and geographically, under the rule of Shulgi (2094–2047), the successor of Ur-Nammu (2112–2095), when Ur exercised control as far as Mari on the upper Euphrates.[6] The cultural, military, and administrative innovations of Shulgi, reflected in a rich deposit of Sumerian royal hymns, letters, juridical collections, and many thousands of administrative texts, exerted a strong influence on Babylonian thought and practice for centuries. The Ur III dynasty collapsed during the reign of

---

5. For a survey of the third-millennium history of Sumer and Akkad, consult Piotr Steinkeller, "Mesopotamia, History of (Third Millennium)," *ABD* 4:724–32.

6. The relative chronology of Babylonia in the late third millennium and in the first half of the second millennium is quite well established on the basis of occasional notices in royal inscriptions, year names, administrative texts, and letters. Absolute chronology, however, is more problematic and rests on interpretation of astronomical observations. Several systems have emerged as a result, often categorized "High," "Middle," and "Low." Recently, scholars have increasingly argued in favor of the Low Chronology, which would place the fall of Babylon to the Hittites and the end of the Old Babylonian period in the years immediately after 1500. See Hermann Gasche et al., *Dating the Fall of Babylon: A Reappraisal of Second-Millennium Chronology* (Chicago: University of Ghent and the Oriental Institute of the University of Chicago, 1998); Regine Pruzsinszky, *Mesopotamian Chronology of the 2nd Millennium B.C.* (Vienna: Austrian Academy of Sciences Press, 2009); and Joachim Mebert, *Die Venustafeln des Ammī-ṣaduqa und ihre Bedeutung für die astronomische Datierung der altbabylonischen Zeit*, AfOB 31 (Vienna: Institut für Orientalistik der Universität, 2010).

Ibbi-Sin (2028–2004) with the encroachment of the so-called MAR.TU or Amorite peoples of the west along with Elamites from the east. This collapse was memorialized in the Sumerian composition known as the Lamentation over the Destruction of Sumer and Ur, which describes how the fate of Ur was decreed in the divine assembly, permitting enemies to overrun it. This episode would reverberate in later Mesopotamian thought, and the idea that the gods could punish their devotees' infidelity by permitting the invasion of foreign enemies would become a widely accepted principle, including among biblical writers.[7] The principle was so fundamental that it shaped theoretical and practical approaches to governance and to religious practice in myriad ways, and not only in Babylonia.[8]

The city of Babylon, although settled in the third millennium and attested in economic texts at least by the time of Shar-kalli-Sharri (2219–2193), receives mention during the reign of Shulgi of the Ur III dyansty, when it was a provincial city under the control of an *énsi*-official ("governor") appointed by Ur. During that period Babylon delivered offerings to the temple of Enlil in Nippur, the principal sanctuary of the Ur dynasty. Yet Babylon would not become a dominant cultural or cultic center until well after the Ur III period.

The collapse of the Sumerian cultural floruit of the Ur III period was followed by the emergence of western, Amorite royal authority over Sumer and Akkad in the previously minor city of Isin under its ruler, Ishbi-Erra, who came from Mari on the upper Euphrates. Larsa soon emerged as another powerful city in the region, also under Amorite rule. The so-called Isin-Larsa era marked the beginning of the Old Babylonian period in Babylonia, when the Semitic language of Akkadian came to the fore and Amorite tribal groups consolidated power in a number of cities throughout the alluvium, often competing with each other for regional authority. Sumerian language and traditions, as well as bureaucratic procedures, retained considerable prominence in this period, but new patterns emerged too. The tight administrative control of the royal and temple economies of the Ur III period loosened somewhat. Competition between local dynasties generated conflict and a concern for stability; in part to facilitate record keeping, years were reckoned by assigning them names during the period, and the names pertain to such matters as rebuilding of cities, fortifications, and sometimes temples. In this, then, we see a historiographical innovation that would help shape royal record keeping for centuries.

---

7. Piotr Michalowski, *Lamentation over the Destruction of Sumer and Ur*, Mesopotamian Civilizations 1 (Winona Lake, IN: Eisenbrauns, 1989); also *COS* 1.166:535–39.

8. See the trenchant analysis of Hanspeter Schaudig, "Erklärungsmuster von Katastrophen im Alten Orient," in *Disaster and Relief Management: Katastrophen und ihre Bewältigung*, ed. A. Berlejung, FAT 81 (Tübingen: Mohr Siebeck, 2012), 425–43.

Some one hundred years after the collapse of the Ur III state, an Amorite named Sumu-abum founded the so-called First Dynasty of Babylon. He and his four successors occupied the throne of Babylon throughout the nineteenth century, exerting their efforts in rebuilding the city's fortifications and consolidating its canal system for irrigation, which was crucial for agricultural success in the Mesopotamian plain. Still, Babylon exerted little influence beyond its hinterland during this time, forging alliances with other local kings, occasionally through royal marriages. During the reign of Sin-Muballit of Babylon, a powerful force emerged to the north and west of Babylon under the rule of Shamshi-Adad I, who also controlled the city of Mari, while Rim-Sin of Larsa ruled in the south. It was into this context that Babylon's most famous king stepped: Hammurabi.

Hammurabi's career has received massive attention, in part because of his promulgation of a famous collection of laws, colloquially referred to as the Code of Hammurabi, and in part because his legacy of military expansion and exertion of Babylonian influence beyond Babylonia was identified by later kings as Babylon's golden age. He ruled for forty-three years (1792–1750 [Middle]; 1719–1677 [Low]), and substantial written sources illuminate his career. The relative chronological framework and accomplishments of his reign are established by year names and references in such texts as the Chronicle of Early Kings,[9] the Babylonian King List, and his numerous royal inscriptions.[10] In the early part of his reign, he forged diplomatic relations with Shamshi-Adad and possibly also Rim-Sin of Larsa, while absorbing local cities, including Isin and Uruk, into his realm. He retained his alliance with Shamshi-Adad's successor at Mari, Zimri-Lim, but, as the chronicle claims, in his thirtieth year he "mustered his troops and marched on Rīm-Sîn, king of Ur. He conquered Ur and Larsa, [and] took away their possessions to Babylon."[11] Firmly in control of the whole of Sumer and Akkad, Hammurabi eventually also conquered Mari and, by his thirty-second year, forged the largest territorial kingdom centered at Babylon in history, to be exceeded only by Nebuchadnezzar II in the late seventh and sixth centuries, a millennium later.

Archaeology has revealed little about the city of Babylon during the Old Babylonian period because of its massive reconstruction in the sixth century

---

9. Albert Kirk Grayson, *Assyrian and Babylonian Chronicles*, Texts from Cuneiform Sources 5 (Winona Lake, IN: Eisenbrauns, 2000), no. 20B, obv. 8–12; Jean-Jacques Glassner, *Mesopotamian Chronicles*, ed. Benjamin R. Foster, WAW 19 (Atlanta: Society of Biblical Literature, 2004), 273, no. 40, lines 8–12.

10. For a selection, see COS 2.107A–D; Frans van Koppen, "Old Babylonian Period Inscriptions," in *The Ancient Near East: Historical Sources in Translation*, ed. Mark W. Chavalas (Oxford: Blackwell Publishing, 2006), 88–106, esp. 104.

11. Glassner, *Chronicles*, 273, no. 40, lines 8–12; see also Frans van Koppen, "Miscellaneous Old Babylonian Period Documents," in Chavalas, *Ancient Near East*, 107–33, esp. 107–11.

and because of the destructive agency of the high water table.[12] But the city achieved a prominence in the time of Hammurabi that it would retain for over a millennium, recognized ever after as the hub of Sumer and Akkad, which could now actually be called "Babylonia."

Perhaps the most evocative monument of Hammurabi's period is a large diorite stela from his reign that preserves his extensive collection of laws. The stela was excavated by a French team in the nineteenth century at Susa, in Iran (where it had been brought as spoil centuries after Hammurabi), and is now housed in the Louvre. The Laws of Hammurabi (a designation now preferred over "Code"), of which many copies are known, was not the first collection of laws in ancient Mesopotamia.[13] Yet the laws reflect the king's effort to consolidate some of the judicial principles on which the Babylonian conception of kingship and its relevance for social order both rest. The elaborate image of the king receiving juridical insignia from the enthroned sun god, Shamash, the guarantor of justice, aptly illustrates the presumption of divine legitimation of royal prerogatives, which the laws endorse. The prologue to the laws, similarly, announces a royal program indebted to archaic Mesopotamian models, one which would have enduring significance:

> When the august [gods] Anu... and Enlil... allotted power over all peoples to the god Marduk... named the city of Babylon with its august name and made it supreme within the regions of the world, and established for him within it eternal kingship... at that time, the gods Anu and Enlil, for the enhancement of the well-being of the people, named me by my name: Hammurabi, the pious prince, who venerates the gods, to make justice prevail in the land, to abolish the wicked and the evil, to prevent the strong from oppressing the weak, to rise like the sun-god Shamash over all humankind, to illuminate the land.[14]

The Laws of Hammurabi became a standard text of the Mesopotamian scribal curriculum, frequently copied, although evidently not undergoing as elaborate a history of commentary and interpretation as some other genres.[15] It seems unlikely that the legal stipulations contained in the collection were designed

---

12. Robert Koldewey, *Das wieder erstehende Babylon*, 5th ed., ed. Barthel Hrouda (Munich: C. H. Beck, 1990), 234; see also G. Bergamini, "Levels of Babylon Reconsidered," *Mesopotamia* 12 (1977): 111–52.

13. For a convenient collection of this and other legal corpora, see Martha T. Roth, *Law Collections from Mesopotamia and Asia Minor*, 2nd ed., WAW 6 (Atlanta: Scholars Press, 1997).

14. M. Roth, "Laws of Hammurabi," in *Law Collections*, 76–77, lines i 1–49; Roth, "The Laws of Hammurabi," COS 2.336, lines i 1–49.

15. See Eckart Frahm, *Babylonian and Assyrian Text Commentaries: Origins of Interpretation*, GMTR 5 (Münster: Ugarit-Verlag, 2011), 241–42 and passim, for discussion of Babylonian and Assyrian textual commentaries.

as a comprehensive law code, but were rather a kind of legal compendium that articulates a range of legal precedents and, thereby, the principles and the ideals that they reflect.

The influence of the laws was extensively felt in subsequent eras and regions, including centuries later in ancient Israel and Judah. Most scholars affirm that the so-called Covenant Code of Exodus 20:22–23:19 depends indirectly or directly on specific norms articulated in Hammurabi's Laws. Thus, for example, Hammurabi §209 states, "If a man strikes a woman of the *awīlu* [patrician] class and thereby causes her to miscarry her fetus, he shall weigh and deliver 10 shekels of silver for her fetus."[16] Exodus 21:22 reads, "When men fight, if they contact a pregnant woman and she miscarries, but there is no other damage, the responsible one shall be fined whatever the woman's husband imposes" (AT). Two recent scholarly opinions may be taken to reflect the range of options that might explain such similarities and numerous others between Hammurabi's Laws and the Covenant Code. In his extensive work on the legal traditions of the ancient Near East, Raymond Westbrook argues for what he calls a "common legal tradition." Diverse communities in diverse geographical and temporal contexts could articulate legal norms similar to one another because of this shared tradition.[17] According to Westbrook, the particular similarities between Hammurabi's Laws and the Covenant Code, which have long been recognized,[18] derive from the fact that the latter "is part of a widespread literary-legal tradition and can only be understood in terms of that tradition."[19] Mechanisms of direct genetic contact need not be presumed with Westbrook's model. By contrast, David Wright has argued for a much more direct influence of Hammurabi's Laws on the writers of the Covenant Code. Wright hypothesizes that whoever composed the Covenant Code of Exodus, perhaps during the era of Neo-Assyrian hegemony over Judah in the seventh century BCE, actually had access to a copy of Hammurabi's Laws in cuneiform, which the writer carefully scrutinized and which he then often followed in terms of both sequence and content. The purpose of this close dependence, in Wright's theory, was, in part, to incorporate the laws into a new Israelite framework and, by doing so, to offer "a symbolic counterstate-

---

16. COS 2.131 §209.

17. Westbrook's studies in this subject have been conveniently assembled in a two-volume collection, *Law from the Tigris to the Tiber: The Writings of Raymond Westbrook*, ed. Bruce Wells and Rachel Magdelene (Winona Lake, IN: Eisenbrauns, 2009). The first volume is subtitled *The Shared Tradition*. See also the important volume edited by Westbrook, *A History of Ancient Near Eastern Law*, HdO 72 (Leiden: Brill, 2003).

18. See, e.g., the presentation in COS 2.131 with running notations by the editor that list parallels.

19. Westbrook, "What Is the Covenant Code?," in *Law from the Tigris to the Tiber*, 1:118.

ment to the Assyrian hegemony" under which Judah chafed.[20] Whether one accepts one or another of these methodological approaches (or some third way) to explain the common legal materials, it is necessary to concede that Hammurabi's consolidation of legal traditions played a powerful role in the subsequent history of Near Eastern law. In this regard, Babylon may justly be considered the cradle of Western jurisprudence.

The Old Babylonian tradition bequeathed many other cultural treasures. Scholars of the era assiduously collected older Sumerian compositions and often translated them into their Semitic tongue, Akkadian. A notable example was the Gilgamesh Epic, which originated in Sumerian but is known in Akkadian from important Old Babylonian manuscripts. The authoritative scholarly edition of this text is by Andrew George. Many copies of the Gilgamesh Epic are known, including one Middle Babylonian exemplar from Late Bronze Age Megiddo, in northern Israel, which seems, however, to have been brought to Megiddo from elsewhere in the Levant.[21] The story, of course, revolves around the legendary hero, Gilgamesh, and his friendship with the strange figure of Enkidu. After adventures, great achievements, and terrible hardships, the two are eventually separated when Enkidu is killed. This prompts Gilgamesh to embark on a sublime effort to understand the limits of human mortality, to query gods and humans as he traverses the ends of the world in search of definitive answers to fundamental questions. Tablet 11 of the epic narrates Gilgamesh's lengthy audience with Uta-napishti, survivor of the primeval flood, on whom the great gods conferred immortality after his tragic journey in a vessel built to carry him and "the seed of every living thing" across the great divide, which the flood represents in human experience. The epic was clearly venerated in antiquity and has rightly been regarded since its rediscovery as a landmark in the evolution of human culture.

2. The Kassite Period

Scholars identify the end of the Old Babylonian period with the Hittite sack of Babylon in the sixteenth century by Mursili I.

20. David P. Wright, *Inventing God's Law: How the Covenant Code of the Bible Used and Revised the Laws of Hammurabi* (Oxford: Oxford University Press, 2009), 346.

21. A. R. George, *The Babylonian Gilgamesh Epic: Introduction, Critical Edition and Cuneiform Texts*, 2 vols. (Oxford: Oxford University Press, 2003); the Megiddo exemplar is treated by George on pp. 339–47; for the study of the origin of the clay used for the tablet, see Y. Goren, H. Mommsen, I. Finkelstein, and N. Na'aman, "A Provenance Study of the Gilgamesh Fragment from Megiddo," *Archaeometry* 51 (2009): 763–73.

During the following, Middle Babylonian period, a non-Semitic population known as the Kassites, *kaššū* in Akkadian, dominated the regions of Sumer and Akkad, which they called Karduniash. The origins and early history of the Kassites remain obscure; they may have originated in the Zagros Mountains of Iran, but began to arrive in southern Mesopotamia already during the First Dynasty of Babylon. The Kassites began integrating into Babylonia during the Old Babylonian period and adopted many of its cultural features before founding a dynasty, one of the earliest rulers of which was Agum-Kakrime, in the early sixteenth century. This dynasty, the longest lived in Mesopotamia, lasted until about 1158. Limited textual, artistic, adminstrative, and archaeological data from this era have been published and only indirect evidence exists for the Kassite language.²² Yet the broad outlines of Babylonian history in this period suggest that the Kassites achieved substantial political consolidation within the region and installed a ramified bureaucracy to administer an exceptionally long-lived state.²³ One distinctive type of cultural artifact that originated during this era is the so-called *kudurru*, or, better, "entitlement *narû*"—stone monuments that appear from the time of the Kassite Kurigalzu (probably Kurigalzu II, 1332–1308) onward (fig. 3.2). They describe royal benefactions, "the acquisition or affirmation of

Figure 3.2. Shitti-Marduk *kudurru* image

---

22. An important catalogue of texts is J. A. Brinkman, *Materials and Studies for Kassite History*, vol. 1, *A Catalogue of Cuneiform Sources Pertaining to Specific Monarchs of the Kassite Dynasty* (Chicago: Oriental Institute Press, 1976).

23. Excellent survey articles include W. Sommerfeld, "The Kassites of Ancient Mesopotamia: Origins, Politics, and Culture," *CANE* 2:917–30; and J. A. Brinkman, "Kassiten," *RlA* 5:464–73.

an entitlement to an ongoing source of income . . . that is hereditary."[24] These benefactions were evidently rewards for personal service to the crown. Early scholars thus saw in the Kassite administration a foreign, quasi-feudal system, but W. Sommerfeld challenged this view and argued that "granting lands is but an interesting manifestation in the conferral of royal favor, one that played a striking, but not decisive, role."[25] The "feudal" interpretation has therefore not won assent, and the extent of Kassite influence on native traditions remains under discussion. The inscriptions merge artistic, religious, and legal traditions in compact, three-dimensional form. The complex nexus between the gods, royal benefactions, and loyal service clearly served to reinforce the stability of regional political arrangements, to which these monuments eloquently attest.

During the Kassite period, Babylonia played a significant role in the international politics of western Asia, when the lingua franca was Akkadian. The Kassite kings, notably Kadashman-Enlil I (d. 1360) and Burna-buriash II (1359–1333), developed extensive diplomatic ties, including royal marriages, with an array of powers that included Egypt, Mittani, and Hatti. This can be seen in the extensive correspondence of the fourteenth century discovered at el-Amarna, in Egypt, in which the kings of the great powers designate each other as "brother."[26] Amanda Podany has well surveyed and described the diplomatic achievements of the period and Babylon's role in them.[27] The small kingdoms of the southeastern Mediterranean littoral were also clearly influenced by the converging interests of the great powers, including Babylonia, as the Amarna correspondence shows. Not only did local scribes use their own variation of Babylonian Akkadian, but they also knew of sophisticated Babylonian literary traditions such as the Gilgamesh Epic[28] and lexical word lists such as HUR.RA = ḫubullu, a fragment of which was discovered at the city of Ashkelon, on the southeastern Mediterannean coast.[29] Whether these types of scholarly texts were carried west by Babylonian scribes, or whether the traditions were mediated by more proximate sources, such as scribal circles

---

24. An excellent study of the corpus is Kathryn E. Slanski, *The Babylonian Entitlement* narûs *(kudurrus): A Study of Their Form and Function* (Boston: American Schools of Oriental Research, 2003), 180. The texts were not known as *kudurru*s in antiquity, and while they first appear in Kassite times, they continue in use in the first millennium.

25. Sommerfeld, "Kassites of Ancient Mesopotamia," 925; he is followed by Slanski, *Babylonian Entitlement* narûs, 287–89.

26. William L. Moran, *The Amarna Letters* (Baltimore: Johns Hopkins University Press, 1992).

27. Podany, *Brotherhood of Kings: How International Relations Shaped the Ancient Near East* (New York: Oxford University Press, 2010).

28. George, *Babylonian Gilgamesh Epic*, 339–47.

29. J. Huehnergard and W. van Soldt, "A Cuneiform Lexical Text from Ashkelon with a Canaanite Column," *IEJ* 49 (1999): 184–92.

at Ugarit, is less clear. In any case, even during the Late Bronze Age, a period of extensive Egyptian control in Canaan, Babylonian linguistic and cultural influences penetrated the region and must have informed local traditions.[30]

The demise of the Kassite Dynasty in the mid-twelfth century was effected by Assyrian and Elamite pressure on Babylonia. For several decades under Meli-Shipak (ca. 1186–1172) and his son, Marduk-apla-iddina I (ca. 1171–1159), Babylonia seems to have been relatively stable. After the death of the latter, however, raids first by Assur-dan I (1178–1133) of Assyria and then Shutruk-Nahhunte of Elam brought the long period of Kassite rule to an effective end. The symbolic emphasis of this point was Shutruk-Nahhunte's abduction of the statue of Marduk from his main temple, the Esagila of Babylon. The event would live in infamy, another example of the ancient principle that the angered deity could unleash his fury through the agency of an archetypal marauding foe.

3. The Late Middle and Early Neo-Babylonian Periods

The end of the thirteenth century and beginning of the twelfth witnessed an unparalleled collapse of previously robust polities throughout the Mediterranean and Near Eastern worlds. From Mycenae in the Greek west, to the Hittite kingdom of Asia Minor, to the city-state of Ugarit on the Syrian coast, to New Kingdom Egypt, formerly impressive bureaucratic polities rapidly faded in the regions to the north and west of Babylonia. Historians have debated the reasons for this systemic collapse. Recently, a group of scholars has analyzed pollen retrieved from a core drilled in the Sea of Galilee to support the hypothesis that a lengthy dry period corresponded precisely with this period of geopolitical turmoil and collapse.[31] Coupled with hints from textual and archaeological data, they suggest that "cold spells in the northern areas of the eastern Mediterranean and decrease in precipitation across the entire region had devastating effects on agriculture productivity and grazing."[32] In the wake of these "crisis years" and associated political collapses, new ethnic groups (e.g., the Sea Peoples) and a proliferation of minor polities emerged (including the territorial kingdoms of the Levant, like Israel). In Mesopotamia, Arameans from the west began to arrive in increasing numbers during the

---

30. For a convenient catalogue of the Late Bronze Age Babylonian cuneiform texts discovered in Canaan, see W. Horowitz and T. Oshima, *Cuneiform in Canaan* (Jerusalem: Israel Exploration Society, 2006).

31. D. Langgut, I. Finkelstein, and T. Litt, "Climate and the Late Bronze Age Collapse: New Evidence from the Southern Levant," *TA* 40 (2013): 149–75.

32. Ibid., 169.

same period. The significance of these upheavals for the political and cultural trajectories of the first millennium can scarcely be overemphasized. Babylonia would retain its place as a cultural lodestar in the ancient Near East, but even more than in the Amorite era of the Old Babylonian period, developments in the West would shape Mesopotamian aspirations and cultural developments.

Thus, although the climatological effects may have been different in Mesopotamia, it was also during this period that Kassite control of Babylonia ended. In its wake, a less coherent constellation of local rulers, coupled with an apparent influx of migrants—among them West Semitic Arameans and Chaldeans—ushered in a tumultuous period. Between the late twelfth century and the period of Neo-Assyrian dominance over Babylonia in the eighth century, a series of unstable dynasties governed Babylonia. The Babylonian Chronicles and related texts indicate that frequent turmoil existed between Babylonia, tribal Arameans, Assyrians in the north, and Elamites in the east. The history of the entire period was sketched in its most authoritative formulation by J. A. Brinkman in his monumental *A Political History of Post-Kassite Babylonia, 1158–722 B.C.*[33]

The most noteworthy Babylonian ruler from early in this period was undoubtedly Nebuchadnezzar I (1125–1104), the fourth ruler of the so-called Second Dynasty of Isin (1157–1026), the textual record for whom is fairly substantial.[34] A text labeled by scholars as the Synchronistic History indicates that Nebuchadnezzar fought on multiple occasions against the Assyrians along the northern border of Babylonia, apparently without much success.[35] On the other hand, Nebuchadnezzar campaigned successfully against the Elamites in the east. Several of his texts, including a lengthy bilingual (Sumerian-Akkadian) inscription, offer commentary on the vicissitudes of Babylonian history during the period; the bilingual text focuses especially on the behavior of the patron deity of Babylon, Marduk. The first part of the inscription narrates how Marduk had earlier become angered with his land and how this prompted him to permit Elamite depredations against it: "(Marduk) became angry and (full of) wrath. He commanded and the land was abandoned by its gods." Thereupon, "the wicked Elamite . . . laid waste the settlements (and) turned (the land) into a desert. He carried off the gods (and) turned the sanctuaries into ruins."[36] As noted above, the Elamites had even captured the cult statue of Marduk. Nebuchadnezzar I's entreaties to the

---

33. AnOr 43 (Rome: Pontifical Biblical Institute, 1968).
34. See Grant Frame, *Rulers of Babylonia: From the Second Dynasty of Isin to the End of Assyrian Domination (1157–612 BC)*, RIMB 2 (Toronto: University of Toronto Press, 1995), 11–35.
35. Glassner, *Chronicles*, 176–83; but the text is clearly biased toward Assyria.
36. Frame, *Rulers of Babylonia*, 26 (Nebuchadnezzar I B.2.4.8 lines 17–18 and 23–24).

god, however, proved effective according to the text: "In his generous heart [Marduk] had pity and turned back unto the holy city."[37] Nebuchadnezzar was able to humble the Elamites, and he made it possible for Marduk to journey home and take up residence in his shrine, to much rejoicing. Several of the king's inscriptions commemorate this dramatic event, yet another example of how the ancient religious principle of divine abandonment and return informed both political and theological speculation.[38]

W. Lambert argued that Nebuchadnezzar's repatriation of Marduk's cult statue to Babylon also provided the context in which the great literary composition known as Enuma Elish (sometimes dubbed the Babylonian Epic of Creation) was composed.[39] The text focuses in particular on Marduk's primordial defeat of the divine forces of chaos embodied by the goddess Tiamat, after which the other gods hail Marduk as king and he takes up residence in his temple, Esagila, in Babylon.[40] Indeed, Lambert and W. Sommerfeld have argued that it was during the Second Dynasty of Isin that Marduk was recognized in Babylon as the chief god of the Babylonian pantheon, a religious innovation that would shape first-millennium cultic history in Babylonia but also far beyond.[41] Lambert also argued that the text of Enuma Elish became, effectively, the libretto for the Babylonian version of the *Akītu* festival, an archaic ritual that celebrated the autumnal and vernal equinoxes. The seven-day-long Babylonian *Akītu* festival entailed reciting Enuma Elish on the evening of the fourth day, and thus celebrated Marduk's defeat of Tiamat and his reenthronement in his temple in Babylon at the midpoint of the festival.[42] The dramatic confirmation of Babylon's cultic supremacy and Marduk's primacy among the gods would remain durable elements of the Babylonian intellectual world for the next five hundred years. In its particular configuration, Enuma Elish has often been understood to have influenced Israelite conceptions of

---

37. Ibid., 29 (B.2.4.9 line 11).
38. Ibid.; see also the summary in J. A. Brinkman, "Nebukadnezar I," *RlA* 9:192–94.
39. W. G. Lambert, "The Reign of Nebuchadnezzar I: A Turning Point in the History of Ancient Mesopotamian Religion," in *The Seed of Wisdom: Essays in Honour of T. J. Meek*, ed. W. McCullough (Toronto: University of Toronto Press, 1964), 3–13.
40. Many English translations of the epic exist, including Benjamin R. Foster, "Epic of Creation," COS 1.111:390–402; Foster, *Before the Muses: An Anthology of Akkadian Literature*, 3rd ed. (Bethesda, MD: CDL Press, 2005), 436–86.
41. Lambert, "Reign of Nebuchadnezzar I"; and Sommerfeld, *Der Aufstieg Marduks: Die Stellung Marduks in der babylonischen Religion des zweiten Jahrtausends v. Chr.* AOAT 213 (Neukirchen-Vluyn: Neukirchener Verlag, 1982).
42. B. Pongratz-Leisten, *Ina Šulmi Īrub: Die kulttopographische und ideologische Programmatik der akītu-Prozession in Babylonien und Assyrien im 1. Jahrtausend v. Chr*, Baghdader Forschungen 16 (Mainz am Rhein: Philipp von Zabern, 1994); see also Pongratz-Leisten, "Neujahr(sfest). B.," *RlA* 9:296–98.

God's creation of the world and the celebration of his defeat of the forces of chaos. These events, in the influential reconstruction of Sigmund Mowinckel, were seen to have influenced Israel's cultus, including the Psalms, many of which, he argued, commemorate the annual ritual enthronement of God at an autumn New Year festival in Israel.[43]

Nebuchadnezzar I's reign also yielded several remarkable "entitlement *narû*" inscriptions (formerly called *kudurru*s), which detail benefactions to important courtiers.[44] One remarkable literary exemplar celebrates a local ruler called Shitti-Marduk and provides a heroic depiction of a Babylonian battle against the Elamites, detailing Shitti-Marduk's bravery and enumerating royal benefactions due him and his territory, particularly tax exemption.[45] The so-called Hinke Kudurru details land grants to the leader of Nippur.[46] The early Neo-Babylonian period likewise saw the composition or compilation of a number of other important texts, including Tintir, the great repository of topographical information about Babylon, and the sapiential text Ludlul bel nemeqi, or I Will Praise the Lord of Wisdom (also known as The Poem of the Righteous Sufferer).[47] The latter ostensibly contains the reflections of an individual beset by the gods—Marduk in particular—for reasons that escape him, since he has always been a faithful devotee. In a sense, this poem applies the historiographical principle of divine anger and abandonment, followed by reconciliation and well-being, to consideration of an individual's biography. It counts as one of the more influential psychological ruminations among Babylonian compositions, and was regarded by William Moran as having been composed after the individual in question recovered from a serious malady.[48] Its introspective component has intrigued scholars since its republication.

This apparent cultural boom came despite the fact that Babylon's regional power remained limited. The latter part of Nebuchadnezzar I's reign, moreover, coincided with a renewal of Assyrian power under Tiglath-pileser I (1114–1076),

43. The original analysis may be found in Mowinckel, *Psalmentudien* (Oslo, 1921–24; repr., Amsterdam: P. Schippers, 1961), trans. D. R. Ap-Thomas as *The Psalms in Israel's Worship* (New York: Abingdon, 1962).

44. For a thorough analysis of the form of these texts, see Slanski, *Babylonian Entitlement narûs*.

45. L. W. King, *Babylonian Boundary-Stones and Memorial-Tablets in the British Museum* (London: Trustees of the British Museum, 1912); Jeffrey L. Cooley, "The Shitti-Marduk Stele," in Chavalas, *Ancient Near East*, 160–64.

46. Slanski, *Babylonian Entitlement* narûs, 111–12, 158, 171.

47. For the text in translation, see B. Foster, "The Poem of the Righteous Sufferer," in COS 1.486–92.

48. W. L. Moran, "Notes on the Hymn to Marduk in Ludlu Bēl Nēmeqi," *JAOS* 103, no. 1 (1983): 255–60; see also the study of W. G. Lambert, *Babylonian Wisdom Literature* (Winona Lake, IN: Eisenbrauns, 1996), 21–62.

who was able to extend Assyrian influence relatively far to the west and also curtail Babylonian ambitions. When Nebuchadnezzar's younger brother, Marduk-nādin-ahhē, eventually came to the throne (1099–1082), he raided the Assyrian city of Ekallate and captured several Assyrian deities' statues. In retaliation, Tiglath-pileser I campaigned extensively through Babylonia, capturing important cities and devastating palaces in Babylon.[49] A Babylonian Chronicle entry for the reign of Marduk-shāpik-zēri (1081–1069), son of Marduk-nādin-ahhē, suggests that prosperity prevailed during his reign. Yet Assyrian pressure and then successive waves of Aramean migrations disrupted the internal stability of the Babylonian heartland. Few royal inscriptions from this period are known, and the Babylonian Chronicle texts emphasize that Aramean and Sutean tribal groups wreaked havoc. In the mid-eleventh century, under Adad-apla-iddina (1068–1047), the Babylonian Chronicle reads: "The Arameans and a usurper rebelled against Adad-apla-iddina . . . and [prof]aned the holy cities. . . . They destroyed Dēr, Nippur, Si[ppar, and Dūr]-Kurigalzu. The Suteans took the offensive and carried the booty of Sumer and Akkad into their country."[50]

It may also have been during this tumultuous era that another important text of the Babylonian literary tradition originated, although it is best known from an eighth-century version: the epic concerning Erra and Ishum (the Poem of Erra). The text, as Benjamin Foster writes, "is a portrayal of violence: its onset, course, and consequences. . . . Violence can eliminate even the order ordained by the gods and sweep away in its frenzy all the hopes and accomplishments of civilization."[51] The destructive god Erra threatens to rage against Babylonia, while the remote, apparently ineffective Marduk remains powerless to resist him. Only Erra's companion, Ishum, is able to dissuade Erra from his catastrophic course. The text seems to ruminate on Babylon's tumultuous recent past, and in its literary inventiveness and daring seems to question age-old pieties. Its influence on biblical thought, including the prophet Ezekiel, has been variously assessed,[52] but its novel formulations suggest the emergence of an iconoclastic intellectual tradition. Literary trends in the period, therefore, indicate that scribes sought self-consciously to move beyond preservation of, expansion of, and commentary on known genres and pushed the literary boundaries with somewhat more daring.

The end of the Second Dynasty of Isin is a little-known period in Babylonia, and the relative political weakness of the successive kings of the region in

---

49. Frame, *Rulers of Babylonia*, 38.
50. Glassner, *Chronicles*, 285, no. 47, lines 7–9; Grayson, *Chronicles*, 180–81, lines 7–9.
51. Foster, *Before the Muses*, 880.
52. For an overview, see D. Bodi, *The Poem of Erra and Ezekiel*, OBO 104 (Göttingen: Vandenhoeck & Ruprecht, 1991).

Figure 3.3. Sun-God Tablet

subsequent centuries makes the period rather unremarkable. Meanwhile, the Assyrian monarchs in the north solidified their political and military capacities. As a result, few Babylonian kings emerge into sharp focus, and their dynastic affiliations remain mostly unknown. The achievements of one king, Nabû-apla-iddina, who reigned for thirty-three years in the ninth century (roughly 887–855), do warrant attention, since he seems to have had some success stemming the tide of Sutean maurauders, and it is from his reign that we have one of the most remarkable documents ever recovered in ancient Babylonia, the so-called Sun-God Tablet (fig. 3.3).[53] The stone inscription, discovered at Sippar, was classified early on with other so-called *kudurru* texts of the late Kassite and early Neo-Babylonian eras.[54] The principal purpose of both the text and the elaborate image accompanying it—it is one of the most recognizable pieces of art from ancient Babylonia—was to celebrate the reestablishment of the cult of Shamash, the sun god, in the Ebabbar temple of Sippar, thanks

53. For a superb treatment of this text and its significance, see Christopher E. Woods, "The Sun-God Tablet of Nabû-apla-iddina Revisited," *JCS* 56 (2004): 23–103.
54. Slanski argues that this classification is correct, although she advocates for the term "entitlement-*narû*" (*Babylonian Entitlement*-narûs, 221).

to the solicitation of Nabû-apla-iddina, who authorized a priestly sinecure in the temple. "What is remarkable about this tablet, however, is the impressive marshalling of visual and literary devices in terms of archaic iconography and poetic, historical narrative to establish not only the great antiquity of the cult, but, more to the point, its ancient claim to these prerogatives and revenues."[55] The resuscitation of the Shamash cult in the ninth century rested in a remarkable antiquarian concern for re-creating and installing an image of the sun god, for which a model had miraculously been recovered. This intellectual interest would in turn become a kind of hallmark of the later Neo-Babylonian kings, in particular Nabonidus, who, some three hundred years later, may well have taken steps to preserve the famed tablet of Nabû-apla-iddina when the Ebabbar temple of Sippar was restored, if the reconstruction of Christopher Woods is correct.[56] This first-millennium Babylonian penchant for investigating the past and modeling present cultic realities on it has rightly been identified as an intellectual orientation of considerable influence.

It was also around the same period, the beginning of the ninth century, that we have our first attestation of Chaldeans, or *kaldū*, taking up residence in Babylonia. Some scholars argue that the *kaldū* may have had a relationship to the larger, undifferentiated Aramaic-speaking populations of western Asia around the early first millennium BCE. Others argue, more persuasively, that such an association between Chaldeans and Arameans was more indirect.[57] As Edzard notes, the *kaldū* settled almost entirely in Babylonia, both in the larger cities and in the far south. Arameans, by contrast, settled all over western Asia. A number of key *kaldū* leaders subsequently rose to positions of prominence or rulership in Babylonia, including Mukin-Zer and Merodach-baladan II in the eighth century. These prominent Chaldeans bore Babylonian names. What little we know of the *kaldū* onomasticon suggests that they were quite thoroughly acculturated into the Babylonian milieu by the ninth or eighth century, and, as Beaulieu emphasizes, were not considered "foreign" elements later in the first millennium.[58]

In Hebrew, the designation *kaśdîm*, "Chaldeans," appears only in the plural, and refers either to persons or to the "land of the Chaldeans." Likewise in

---

55. Woods, "Sun-God Tablet," 40.

56. Ibid., 35–39.

57. D. Edzard, "Kaldu," *RlA* 5:291–92; M. Fales, "Arameans and Chaldeans: Environment and Society," in Leick, *Babylonian World*, 288–98; see also, recently, P.-A. Beaulieu, "Arameans, Chaldeans, and Arabs in Cuneiform Sources from the Late Babylonian Period," in *Arameans, Chaldeans, and Arabs in Babylonia and Palestine in the First Millennium B.C.*, ed. A. Berlejung and M. P. Streck, LAOS 3 (Wiesbaden: Harrassowitz, 2013), 31–55; and Bill T. Arnold, "Aramean Origins: The Evidence from Babylonia," *AfO* 52 (2007): 179–85.

58. Beaulieu, "Arameans, Chaldeans, and Arabs," 52.

Babylonian the term *kaldu* may be defined either by the "people" determinative, LÚ, or the "country" determinative, KUR. Unlike in Hebrew, however, in Babylonian the noun often appears in the singular; an individual Chaldean would be referred to as LÚ *kaldu*, "*a* Chaldean."

The most prominent Chaldean king of eighth-century Babylonia was doubtless Marduk-apla-iddina II (721–710 and 703), biblical Merodach-baladan, a member of the Chaldean Bit-Iakin tribe, who ruled in Babylon during the period when the Assyrian Empire had begun to gain its footing. He is also the first king of Babylon mentioned in the Hebrew Bible, where it is said that the Babylonian sent a greeting gift—the traditional acknowledgment of a political relationship—to King Hezekiah of Judah when he was ill (2 Kings 20:12). However, a word of the prophet Isaiah to Hezekiah, set in this period during the last decade of the eighth century, warns the Judean king to forgo the relationship, and that, if he refuses, "Your sons . . . will be taken away and will serve as eunuchs in the palace of the king of Babylon" (2 Kings 20:18 [AT]). Even if, as some suggest, this is an *ex eventu* prophecy from the later period of Babylonian imperial hegemony, when Judeans certainly were deported to Babylon (605–539),[59] it is noteworthy. It suggests that biblical historiographers recalled that this Chaldean king was allied with western kings and opposed to the powerful Neo-Assyrian rulers, including Sargon II. As it happens, cuneiform sources repeatedly insist on the same point. Merodach-baladan seized control of Babylonia at the death of Shalmaneser V and ruled for about a decade before Sargon II sought to regain Assyrian control of the region in 710. Merodach-baladan fled Babylon for Dūr-Iakīn, the capital of his southern tribal home. The Assyrians exerted considerable efforts over the next several years to capture him, and brought massive destruction to the region.

For the duration of the seventh century, Babylonia found itself, like much of the rest of the Near East, chafing under direct Assyrian control. As the prophet Nahum would later rhetorically ask of Nineveh, the Assyrian capital: "Who indeed has not suffered from your interminable cruelty?" (Nah. 3:19 [AT]). Some of the Assyrian kings, such as Sennacherib, ruled Babylon with an iron fist. When Babylon's local leaders, especially the Chaldeans in the south, proved restive and resistant to Assyrian control, Sennacherib visited terrible destruction on the city in 689. The event would live long in the Babylonian consciousness. Sennacherib's own son, Esarhaddon, did seek to placate Babylon's cities and evidently worked to rebuild the capital and surrounding region, and even claimed many of the ancient titles and prerogatives

---

59. Mordechai Cogan and Hayim Tadmor, *II Kings: A New Translation with Introduction and Commentary*, AB 11 (Garden City, NY: Doubleday, 1988), 258–63.

of Babylonian kings. But it was left to native Babylonian kings of the later seventh and sixth centuries to unfold Babylon's greatest period of grandeur.

4. The Neo-Babylonian Empire

A new chapter, and perhaps the most remarkable period in the history of Babylon and Babylonia, began when a new king, Nabopolassar (625–605), claimed the throne of Babylon and cast off Assyrian control. Nabopolassar's reign marks the beginning of a dynasty that would become the first expansionist, even imperial, state centered in Babylonia since the time of Hammurabi in the Old Babylonian period. It would also have a definitive influence on many of the kingdoms and polities of ancient western Asia, including on Judah during the last decades of its existence as an independent kingdom. Indeed, it is this Neo-Babylonian era that would have an enduring legacy in the intellectual traditions of East and West for centuries, even to the present. In biblical tradition, of course, Babylon represents a hostile military force and the destination of Judean deportees. In the classical world, by contrast, the lore of Nebuchadnezzar II's hanging gardens and the contributions of "Chaldean" astronomers to understanding the heavens would typify Greek perspectives on the legacy of Babylon.

The origins of the Neo-Babylonian dynasty remain shrouded. Despite a common scholarly convention, the Babylonian dynasty founded by Nabopolassar, and which achieved its greatest status under his son, Nebuchadnezzar II (605–562), was not referred to as Chaldean in native Babylonian sources. It is not even clear from contemporary Mesopotamian sources that Nabopolassar himself was an ethnic *kaldu*.[60] The origin of the convention in modern Assyriological parlance, in fact, derives from biblical and Greek usage. Not only biblical texts but also the Babylonian priest Berossus in the later Hellenistic era sometimes refer to the Babylonians simply as Chaldeans. Although such associations may well be correct, evidence for it is still indirect, and it would be better to refer to the dynasty as Neo-Babylonian rather than Chaldean.

Whatever his exact ethnic origins, Nabopolassar's royal building inscriptions reveal a Babylonian king who did not understand himself as heir to

---

60. One Seleucid-era colophon on a cuneiform tablet describes Nabopolassar as *šar māt tâmtim*, "king of the Sealand." The Sealand was the traditional homeland of the Chaldeans, but the reference need not refer to the king's place of origin, let alone his ethnicity. See, for evaluations of the Akkadian evidence about the origin of the Neo-Babylonian dynasty, J. A. Brinkman, *Prelude to Empire: Babylonian Society and Politics, 747–626 B.C.* (Philadelphia: University Museum, 1984), 110n551; Brinkman, "Meerland," *RlA* 8:10; and Beaulieu, "Arameans, Chaldeans, and Arabs," 32–37.

Assyria's empire.[61] The war that Nabopolassar waged against Assyria clearly defined the king's reign and resulted in Babylonian independence, but during the last quarter of the seventh century, the Babylonians focused on reestablishing local rule, not on imperial ambitions. This does not mean that the Babylonians did not absorb any Assyrian habits or administrative concepts; Michael Jursa has proved that they did.[62] In fact, subsequent kings of the Neo-Babylonian period would each claim that they brought exotic foreign goods into Babylonia for beautifying its temples, including cedars of Lebanon from the west, and also foreign laborers for their construction programs. At least in this way, too, Babylonian kings resembled their Assyrian predecessors. Yet even though Babylonia was prosperous and secure by the last years of Nabopolassar's reign, he does not make such ambitious claims about Babylonian control of foreign lands. After decades of Assyrian control, the Babylonians were finally the dominant polity in of all southern Mesopotamia, much of former Assyria, and the middle Euphrates region. They enjoyed military successes as far west as Syria and as far north as Urartu, according to the Babylonian Chronicle. But their exercise of a full-throated imperialism would develop only during the reign of Nabopolassar's son, Nebuchadnezzar II.

The first step in this direction occurred in 605 BCE, when Babylonian forces led by Nebuchadnezzar, then the crown prince, defeated Pharaoh Neco of Egypt in battle at Carchemish.[63] The Babylonians thus curtailed Egyptian influence in Syria and became the dominant military force along the upper Euphrates and in the eastern Mediterranean—"Hatti" in Babylonian terminology—where Assyrian control had been defunct for some two decades. We thus read in the Babylonian Chronicle entry for Nebuchadnezzar's first full regnal year, 604/3, that "all the kings of Hatti" came before him and he received "their vast tribute."[64] Without mention of kings, the entries for 605 and 602 state that he carried the "heavy" or "vast" "tribute," *biltu*, of Hatti back to Babylon.[65] In the entries for 605, 604, 601, and probably 603, the

---

61. On the Neo-Babylonian royal inscriptions, see D. S. Vanderhooft, *The Neo-Babylonian Empire and Babylon in the Latter Prophets*, HSM 59 (Atlanta: Scholars Press, 1999), 13–32; and especially R. Da Riva, *The Neo-Babylonian Royal Inscriptions: An Introduction*, GMTR 4 (Münster: Ugarit-Verlag, 2008).

62. Jursa, "Der neubabylonische Hof," in *Der Achämenidenhof/The Achaemenid Court*, ed. B. Jacobs and R. Rollinger (Wiesbaden: Harrassowitz, 2010), 67–106.

63. Grayson, *Chronicles*, 99 obv. 2–5; Glassner, *Chronicles*, 226–27; Bill T. Arnold, "The Neo-Babylonian Chronicle Series," in Chavalas, *Ancient Near East*, 407–26, esp. 416.

64. Grayson, *Chronicles*, 100 obv. 17; Glassner, *Chronicles*, 228–29; Arnold, "Chronicle Series," 416.

65. Grayson, *Chronicles*, 100 obv. 13; 101 rev. 4; Glassner, *Chronicles*, 226–31; Arnold, "Chronicle Series," 416–17.

Chronicle also claims that Nebuchadnezzar "marched about victoriously in Hatti."[66] These years mark the Babylonian rise to uncontested regional power beyond Babylonia as far as the southeastern Mediterranean coastal zone. Biblical historiographers acknowledged the transition: "The king of Egypt did not leave his country anymore, for the king of Babylon captured all that had belonged to the king of Egypt, from the brook of Egypt to the Euphrates River" (2 Kings 24:7 [AT]).

Nebuchadnezzar's royal inscriptions, meanwhile, describe his call to rulership by the gods and tend to focus on two ancient ideas about the role of the king in Babylon. First, the gods called the king to rule over both local Babylonian and wider populations and territories. Second, the gods commissioned the king to renew temples or cities. These points appear succinctly in the following excerpt: "Marduk gave me the widespread peoples for shepherding, he sublimely commanded me to care for cult centers (and) to renew temples" (AT).[67] These and similar stock phrases about widespread authority communicate a sort of ideal view of world domination. Yet the implementation of imperial hegemony insofar as it is acknowledged in these texts appears to have a cultic orientation: Nebuchadnezzar's rule is oriented to his divine obligation "to care for cult centers (and) to renew temples." Of course, from the Babylonian perspective, this obligation was a demonstrable benefit for the people who came under the king's sway, and Nebuchadnezzar is depicted as a protector of humanity. One of his royal inscriptions, echoing the ancient language used by Hammurabi in the prologue to that king's laws, states:

> (As for) the widespread peoples whom Marduk, the lord, gave into my hand ... I continually strove for their welfare. (In) a just path and correct conduct I directed them ... I stretched a roof over them in the wind, (and) a canopy in the tempest. I brought all of them under the sway of Babylon. The yield of the lands, the abundance of the mountain regions, the produce of the countries, I received within it (Babylon). Into its eternal shadow I assembled all the peoples for good.[68]

It was during this period that the city of Babylon underwent its most remarkable reconstruction and expansion, a physical corollary of the idea that

---

66. Grayson, *Chronicles*, 100 obv. 12–13; 100 obv. 16; 101 rev. 5; 100 obv. 23; Glassner, *Chronicles*, 226–31; Arnold, "Chronicle Series," 416–17.

67. Albert T. Clay, *Miscellaneous Inscriptions in the Yale Babylonian Collection*, YOS 1 (New Haven: Yale University Press, 1915), 62–63, no. 44 i 11–13. See also P.-R. Berger, *Die neubabylonischen Königsschriften: Königsinschriften des ausgehenden babylonischen Reiches (625–539 a. Chr.)*, AOAT 4/1 (Kevelaer: Butzon & Bercker, 1973), Zyl II,10.

68. My translation. For the text, see Eckhard Unger, *Babylon: Die heilige Stadt nach der Beschreibung der Babylonier* (Berlin: de Gruyter, 1931), 283 ii 6–21.

it was the cosmic and political center of the world. This pairing was hardly a new element in the thought of ancient Mesopotamia, but it was emphasized with new vigor and with self-conscious concern for the beautification of the city, its temples, and, of course, its ziggurat, which was referred to in the book of Genesis as a *migdāl* (tower) "with its top in the heavens" (Gen. 11:4). About the city itself, Nebuchadnezzar boasts to Marduk, in one instance, "More than your cult center Babylon I did not glorify any cult center in the entire inhabited world."[69] The city was, then, a physical demonstration of the divine imprimatur for the king's imperial rule.[70] Furthermore, Nebuchadnezzar and his successors sought to accomplish the beautification of Babylon by appealing to ancient models, excavating inscriptions of ancient kings and seeking whenever possible to establish tangible links with Babylon's illustrious past rulers, most notably Hammurabi. This appeal to antiquity, as we have seen, made an impression on biblical writers too, who conceded the point that civilization had indeed spread from the east.

Figure 3.4. Mushhushu dragon on the Ishtar Gate

The effect was noteworthy. When German excavators of the early twentieth century uncovered the remarkable Ishtar Gate (fig. 3.4) at the north end of Babylon's Processional Way, they were inspired, as was typical for the era, to remove it and reerect the gate, almost in its entirety, in the Pergamon Museum in Berlin. The effect of Babylon's impressive dimensions and its architectural embellishments can scarcely have been any less impressive to the ancients.

Archaeological excavations and the reconstruction of the Ishtar Gate and other monuments of Babylon by the Deutsche Orientgesellschaft under the direction of Robert Koldewey from 1899 to 1917 helped illumine the cultural,

---

69. My translation. See Stephen H. Langdon, *Die neubabylonischen Königsinschriften*, VAB 4 (Leipzig: Hinrichs, 1912), 4 140 ix 54–56; Berger, *Die neubabylonischen Königsinschriften*, Nbk 15 = St. Tfl. X.

70. P.-A. Beaulieu, "Nebuchadnezzar's Babylon as World Capital," *JCSMS* 3 (2008): 5–12; Beaulieu argues, however, that the two identities of the city—as cultic/cosmic center and as imperial seat—were never fully reconciled in Babylonian thought.

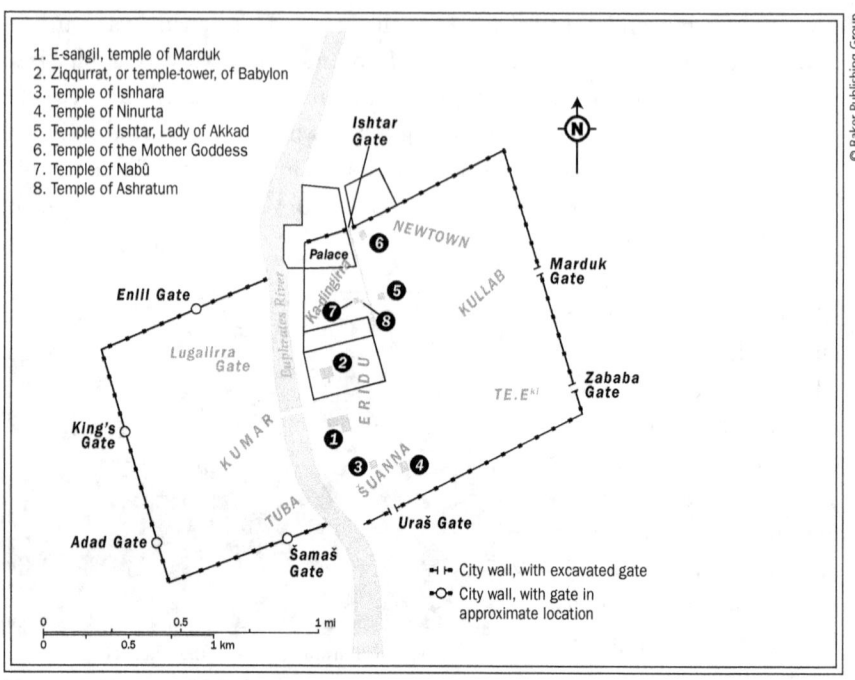

Figure 3.5. Site map of Babylon

cultic, and artistic achievements of the Neo-Babylonian imperial period, and especially the achievements of its chief architect: Nebuchadnezzar II.[71]

The city, which formed a rough rectangle, was bisected by the Euphrates River (the Arahtu branch), with a monumental bridge spanning the river. It was surrounded on all sides by a vast network of inner and outer fortified walls, which extended some 18 kilometers; there were also eight monumental gates and a moat. The walls adjacent to the river were covered with bitumen and sunk into the riverbed. On the east side of the river, the wide Processional Way (over 20 m. across), which ran from south to north and passed through the Ishtar Gate, dominated the layout of the city. This Processional Way, called the Ay-ibūr-šabû (May the Enemy Not Flourish), was decorated for some 180 meters along its length with glazed bricks embossed with fabulous images of lions together with floral and other designs. Flanking the great Processional Way, one would have passed, from south to north, the great temples of the chief deities and also Nebuchadnezzar's principal palace, which extended across the city wall to the north between the river and the Ishtar Gate. The Ishtar Gate itself was likewise gilded with glazed tiles forming images of

---

71. Koldewey, *Das wieder erstehende Babylon*.

composite dragons (called *mušḫuššu*s) and bulls, numbering at least 575, according to the German excavation team.[72] The technicolor effect of these artistic flourishes, the remarkable azure-blue and bright gold glazed bricks, and their immense scale and number were practically unprecedented and must have made a tremendous impression on residents and visitors alike.

Although Babylon was replete with shrines to a panoply of gods, the dramatic centrality of Marduk's chief temple, called the Esagila (House Whose Top Is High), and his ziggurat, called the Etemenanki (House, Foundation Platform of Heaven and Underworld), together announced the preeminence of the deity both locally and to the world. The Esagila temple, originally founded in the early second millennium, was the subject of enormous attention by Nebuchadnezzar. It measured some 86 by 79 meters, with gates 9 meters high and walls nearly 4 meters thick. An enormous administration oversaw the closely interwoven economic and cultic affairs of all Babylonian temples, but that of the Esagila was especially large.

If the Esagila symbolized the vast importance of the temple economy and cult for Babylonia, the ziggurat of Marduk, the Etemenanki (which itself had a shrine to Marduk on top) visibly projected his preeminence. While the outline of the ziggurat and some of its lowest courses were investigated by German scholars in the early twentieth century, it had already been dismantled by Alexander the Great in antiquity, and its remaining baked bricks were robbed for building purposes since then; the high water table also eroded the structure. It consisted in the Neo-Babylonian period of seven stages, each slightly smaller than the one below, giving a pyramidal shape with a total height of about 84 meters (276 ft.), which is the height of Westminster Cathedral in London, or 6 meters (20 ft.) less than Notre Dame Cathedral in Paris.[73] It was accessed from the ground level by an enormous outer stairway that ran along the southern façade. Its exterior was ornately decorated and was studded with gemstones; the upper level was probably sky blue, a manifestation of the linkage represented in architecture between the heavens and the earth. Babylonian scholars, moreover, carefully recorded its form and dimensions in cuneiform tablets and reflected on how its perfect dimensions (as wide as it was tall) embodied a sort of divine symmetry.

The remarkable sequence of architectural elements running from the Ishtar Gate along the Processional Way past the Etemenanki complex and the Esagila precinct all came alive especially during the spring *Akītu* or New Year festival.

72. Ibid., 51.
73. A. R. George, "A Stele of Nebuchadnezzar II," in *Cuneiform Royal Inscriptions and Related Texts in the Schøyen Collection* (Bethesda, MD: CDL Press, 2011), 153–69; for dimensions, 155; also George, *Babylonian Topographical Texts*, 109–19.

During the *Akītu*, the statue of the god Nabû, son of Marduk, traveled up the Euphrates to Babylon from nearby Borsippa on a barge. It then progressed to the Esagila and joined Marduk before they were drawn together in chariots by ceremonial beasts along the Processional Way to the extramural *Akītu* temple, north of the city. During the festival, priests performed elaborate rituals and the king was ritually humiliated before being reinstalled in office. As mentioned earlier, the Enuma Elish was recited on the fourth day, celebrating Marduk's grand victory over the forces of chaos embodied by the goddess Tiamat. Then the gods returned in triumph to Babylon, and the statue of Marduk was reinstalled with rejoicing in the Esagila. As a religious and political display, therefore, the festival celebrated the deity's cosmic supremacy, the mythic subjugation of chaos, and the legitimacy of the king who ruled from Babylon at Marduk's pleasure. So important was celebration of the *Akītu* in Babylon that the Babylonian Chronicle series effectively revolved around whether or not the king was present in Babylon to partake in the celebration.

The constellation of specific religious rituals surrounding the festival, the theological claims about Marduk's cosmic reign in the Enuma Elish, and celebration of the king's political prerogatives as viceroy of the chief deity may be said to constitute the basic framework of Babylonian religio-political thought in the imperial era. It was a pattern that elicited both admiration and derisive attempts to disparage it. In the biblical book of Isaiah, a laconic oracle about Bel (= Marduk) and Nebo (= Nabû) going into exile clearly targets the very complex of ideas that undergirded the Babylonian intellectual and political program as embodied in the *Akītu* festival: "Bel bows down, Nebo bends over; their images are upon animals and cattle. Your burdens are borne (like) a weight for the weary. They bend over, they bow down together; they are unable to deliver the burden; rather they themselves go into captivity" (Isa. 46:1–2).[74] Far from being in charge of a cosmic order reflected on earth by the just rule of a great king, the statues of the gods process not in grand ceremony but ignominiously into exile from Babylon.

Notwithstanding such critiques, the direct imposition of Babylonian control on Judah and other western polities is a well-documented chapter of the imperial period, one that closed for Judah in 586 with the complete devastation of the city of Jerusalem, its temple and royal acropolis, defenses and residences. Self-rule under a Judean monarch was terminated, and a Babylonian appointee, Gedaliah, served as a caretaker leader. Many Judeans were

---

74. For the translation, see Vanderhooft, *Neo-Babylonian Empire*, 175–80; for a brilliant analysis of the intersection of this passage with Babylonian omen literature, see H.-P. Schaudig, "'Bēl Bows, Nabû Stoops!': The Prophecy of Isaiah xlvi 1–2 as a Reflection of Babylonian 'Processional Omens,'" *VT* 58 (2008): 557–72.

deported in successive waves, although estimates vary about both the extent of Judah's population before the destruction and the number of people who remained behind.

The effects of this trauma on the literary deposit of the Hebrew Bible can scarcely be overstated. Kings (and Chronicles), Isaiah, Jeremiah, Ezekiel, Habakkuk, Lamentations, Psalms (famously Ps. 137), and Daniel are among the books that focus attention squarely on the repercussions of the Babylonian depredations and their aftermath.

5. Judean Deportees in Babylonia after 586

New evidence has recently begun to emerge from cuneiform tablets to illuminate the experiences of Judean deportees in Babylonia, and thereby to give us a clearer sense of the milieu in which they lived and worked. It does not seem that they were, in the narrow sense, put into slavery. Judeans dwelled and engaged in activities especially in proximity to Nippur, in the Nippur-Kesh-Kakara triangle, including, we have learned during the past two decades, in a town called āl-Yaḫūdu, or "the City of Judah," the name for a settlement of persons who traced their origins to the geographic region of Judah.[75] The range of those activities is broad and includes a variety of mercantile, juridical, and other spheres pertaining to daily life. Some of these Judeans worked in the expansive Babylonian bureaucracy, and we also know that some Judeans even gained access to scribal training and opportunities beginning in the Neo-Babylonian era.[76]

---

75. The basic bibliography includes the following: E. F. Weidner, "Jojachin, König von Juda, in babylonischen Keilschrifttexten," in *Mélanges Syriens offerts à Monsieur René Dussaud* (Paris: P. Geuthner, 1939), 2:923–35; F. Joannès and A. Lemaire, "Trois tablettes cunéiformes à onomastique ouest-sémitique," *Transeu* 17 (1999): 17–34; K. Abraham, "West Semitic and Judean Brides in Cuneiform Sources from the Sixth Century BCE: New Evidence from a Marriage Contract from Al-Yahudu," *AfO* 51 (2005/6): 198–219; L. E. Pearce, "New Evidence for Judeans in Babylonia," in *Judah and the Judeans in the Persian Period*, ed. Oded Lipschits and Manfred Oeming (Winona Lake, IN: Eisenbrauns, 2006), 399–412; K. Abraham, "An Inheritance Division among Judeans in Babylonia from the Early Persian Period," in *New Seals and Inscriptions, Hebrew, Idumean and Cuneiform*, ed. M. Lubetski (Sheffield, UK: Sheffield Phoenix, 2007), 206–21; for the geographical location of the settlement of āl-Yaḫūdu, see L. E. Pearce, "'Judean': A Special Status in Neo-Babylonian and Achaemenid Babylonia?," in *The Judeans in the Achaemenid Age: Negotiating Identity in an International Context*, ed. G. N. Knoppers, O. Lipschits, and M. Oeming (Winona Lake, IN: Eisenbrauns, 2011), 267–77. The fullest publication of texts to date may be found in Laurie E. Pearce and Cornelia Wunsch, *Documents of Judean Exiles and West Semites in Babylonia in the Collection of David Sofer*, CUSAS 28 (Bethesda, MD: CDL Press, 2014).

76. D. S. Vanderhooft, "*'el-mĕdînâ ûmĕdînâ kiktābāh*: Scribes and Scripts in Yehud and in Achaemenid Transeuphratene," in Knoppers, Lipschits, and Oeming, *Judeans in the Achaemenid Age*, 529–44.

As L. Pearce has written, "participation of Judeans in Babylonian economic, legal, and administrative processes and institutions facilitated and reflected their integration into Babylonian society."[77] K. Abraham similarly concludes that "the community of Judeans recorded their economic, administrative and private legal activities on clay tablets in Akkadian [that] conform to the well-attested cuneiform types.... They assimilated the contemporary Babylonian practices and absorbed the standard legal jargon."[78] This happened quite quickly after their arrival, within a generation of the collapse of the Judean kingdom. The integration that these scholars have demonstrated required the adoption of economic habits and administrative norms native to the Babylonian heartland, where Hebrew-speaking Judeans began to acculturate. Did such contact also afford opportunities for Judeans to engage Babylonian traditions, or even scholars, at a more detailed level? Did they, for example, appropriate key Babylonian mythological and cultural texts and ideas? One thinks in this connection of the later recollection of this era in the book of Daniel: "The king [Nebuchadnezzar] told Ashpenaz, his chief eunuch, to bring some Israelites of the royal line or of the nobility, youths . . . proficient in all wisdom, possessed of knowledge, discerning in thought, with the capacity to serve in the royal palace, and to teach them the writings and language of the Chaldeans" (Dan. 1:3–4 [AT]). This reconstruction in Daniel of the diaspora intellectual milieu is no doubt schematic, but it may well reflect the experience of some members of deported populations from the eastern Mediterannean region.

The unintended (or at least only corollary) consequence of the Babylonian practice of deporting populations into Babylonia from peripheral territories, therefore, was a rather rapid process of acculturation. The inevitable exposure to imperial religio-political claims and the exchange of information and ideas even at a mundane level led to the absorption and transmission of Babylonian ideas more widely.

6. The End of Babylonian Rule

Cuneiform texts prove that, in 539 BCE, Babylon passed rapidly from the control of Nabonidus to Cyrus II of Persia, bringing to an end native Babylonian rule of the region. The Babylonian Chronicle notes that Ugbaru, governor of Gutium, together with the army of Cyrus, entered Babylon without a battle on the sixteenth day of the month Tashrītu, in the seventeenth year of Nabonidus

---

77. Pearce, "'Judean': A Special Status," 268.
78. Abraham, "West Semitic and Judean Brides," 206.

(the Julian date is Oct. 12, 539).[79] The Chronicle reports that seventeen days later, on the third of Araḫsamnu (Oct. 29, 539), Cyrus himself entered Babylon, to great acclaim. Yet, as scholars have shown, the anti-Nabonidus tendencies of this and other relevant texts that describe this transfer hardly indicate that we have received a dispassionate description of these events.[80] Even so, Cyrus is presented in the Babylonian texts, including the famous Cyrus Cylinder, as Marduk's divinely elected deliverer sent to Babylon: "Without a battle or attack, he (Marduk) made him (Cyrus) enter Šuanna [i.e., Babylon], his city; he saved Babylon from hardship."[81] The famously generous characterizations of Cyrus in so-called Second Isaiah (Isa. 40–55) echo this formulation, although the divine agent responsible for Cyrus's rise is, of course, YHWH, the God of Israel, and the subjects of liberation are the Judeans (e.g., Isa. 44:28; 45:1).

7. Israel and the Babylonians

Babylon and its cultural orbit pervade the biblical imagination, even while Babylonia formed the very literal backdrop for so many Judeans deported from their homeland after Nebuchadnezzar's campaign in 587–586 BCE. From the primeval history of Genesis 1–11 to the concluding verses of 2 Chronicles (see 2 Chron. 36:20), Babylon and Babylonia exert a consistent force that shapes the Hebrew Scriptures. Thus, in a fundamental sense, Genesis 1–11 represents a kind of intercultural engagement with central claims of the Babylonians. If the Enuma Elish proclaims the preeminence of Babylon's patron deity, Marduk, and his cosmogonic accomplishment in eviscerating the chaotic goddess, Tiamat, then the Priestly narrative of creation in Genesis 1 lodges a counterclaim for the God of Israel, for whom *təhôm*, "the Deep" (cognate equivalent of Babylonian, *tiamat*), scarcely presents a real threat.[82] The Noahide flood narrative in Genesis 6–9 incorporates both structural and detailed parallels to the more ancient tale found in Gilgamesh Tablet XI and in Atraḫasis. Genesis 10, the so-called Table of Nations, discussed above, acknowledges Babylon as a site of cultural innovation, and that text paves the way for the brief but incisive narrative about the effort to build the city and its tower in Genesis 11.

79. Grayson, *Chronicles*, 109–10, iii 15–16; Glassner, *Chronicles*, 236–37; Arnold, "Chronicle Series," 420.
80. The most thorough presentation and treatment of the relevant texts describing Cyrus's rise is that of H. Schaudig, *Die Inschriften Nabonids von Babylon und Kyros' des Grossen samt den in ihrem Umfeld entstandenen Tendenzschriften*, AOAT 256 (Münster: Ugarit-Verlag, 2001).
81. My translation. See Schaudig, *Die Inschriften*, 552, line 17; Piotr Michalowski, "The Cyrus Cylinder," in Chavalas, *Ancient Near East*, 426–30, esp. 428.
82. See Mark S. Smith, *The Priestly Vision of Genesis 1* (Minneapolis: Fortress, 2009).

That effort, of course, is frustrated by God. Immediately thereafter, we learn that a certain denizen of Ur in the southern Babylonian alluvium, Abram, together with his wife, Sarai, will follow a divine mandate to journey west and install themselves in a land as yet unknown to them.

If Babylonian traditions shape these early narratives in Genesis in a global way, then we encounter a different form of engagement with Babylonia in the laws of Exodus, and particularly the Covenant Code. The primeval history in Genesis 1–11 acknowledges openly that Babylon and "the land of Shinar" were the loci for cultural experimentation, whereas the legal traditions do not concede such explicit connections. Yet, as discussed above, whether one adopts the sort of "shared tradition" approach championed by Raymond Westbrook, or rather the argument for more direct genetic dependence of David Wright, few scholars doubt that the Babylonian legal tradition furnished crucial raw materials for Israel's first foray into articulating its own laws. Certainly this is true of the Covenant Code, but also such texts as the covenant curses of Deuteronomy 28, as Eckart Otto among others has argued, which deliberately absorb and rework Mesopotamian treaty curse language, perhaps as an incipient form of intellectual rebellion.

Within Israel's prophetic traditions, Babylonia can serve as God's punitive agent to correct his wayward people. Yet the threat of Babylonian assault also generates a profound prophetic debate about the justice of God using such a horrifyingly blunt instrument (e.g., Hab. 1:12–17). In Jeremiah 50–51, and also, for example, in Isaiah 47, an extensive tradition also develops that wishes upon Babylon a fate similar to the one it meted out to Judah (see also Ps. 137). This pattern, of course, will find reapplication much later when the book of Revelation identifies a new imperial center, Rome, as the whore of Babylon (Rev. 17:5).

Babylonia bequeathed other quite concrete cultural innovations that would shape biblical traditions. Thus, for example, the old Canaanite month names used early in Israel's history give way to Babylonian month names in the Neo-Babylonian era. And not only Israel but also the Greeks absorbed some insights about the celestial order that emerged from Babylonian scholars, who were simply referred to in Greek sources as "Chaldeans."[83]

Jewish life persisted in Babylonia after the Neo-Babylonian and Persian periods, as is shown from references to Judeans in local texts. These Jewish communities persisted into the Common Era, according to talmudic references.

---

83. See, on "Chaldean" astronomical achievements and their influence in the West, F. Rochberg, "Elements of the Babylonian Contribution to Hellenistic Astronomy," in *In the Path of the Moon: Babylonian Celestial Divination and Its Legacy* (Leiden: Brill, 2010), 143–65.

And while this lore and also the portrait offered in the court tales of Daniel 1–6 insist that Jews lived according to their own norms and religious convictions, unaffected by local ideas and cultural habits, nevertheless Babylon contributed to the intellectual life of Jews and Judaism in myriad ways.

For Further Reading

Bahrani, Zainab. *Women of Babylon: Gender and Representation in Mesopotamia*. New York: Routledge, 2001.

Boiy, Thomas. *Late Achaemenid and Hellenistic Babylon*. OLA 136. Leuven: Peeters, 2004.

Brinkman, J. A. *A Political History of Post-Kassite Babylonia, 1158–722 B.C.* AnOr 43. Rome: Pontifical Biblical Institute, 1968.

Charpin, Dominique. *Writing, Law, and Kingship in Old Babylonian Mesopotamia*. Translated by Jane Marie Todd. Chicago: University of Chicago Press, 2010.

Finkel, Irving, et al. *Babylon*. London: British Museum Press, 2008.

Jursa, Michael. *Aspects of the Economic History of Babylonia in the First Millennium B.C.* AOAT 377. Münster: Ugarit-Verlag, 2010.

Koldewey, Robert. *Das wieder erstehende Babylon*. Edited by B. Hrouda. 5th ed. Munich: C. H. Beck, 1990.

Leick, Gwendolyn, ed. *The Babylonian World*. New York: Routledge, 2007.

Liverani, Mario. *Prestige and Interest: International Relations in the Near East, ca. 1600–1100 B.C.* Padova: Sargon, 1990.

Oppenheim, A. L. *Ancient Mesopotamia: Portrait of a Dead Civilization*. 2nd rev. ed. completed by E. Reiner. Chicago: University of Chicago Press, 1979.

Postgate, J. N. *Early Mesopotamia: Society and Economy at the Dawn of History*. New York: Routledge, 1992.

Soden, Wolfram von. *The Ancient Orient: Introduction to the Study of the Ancient Near East*. Grand Rapids: Eerdmans, 1994.

Van De Mieroop, Marc. *A History of the Ancient Near East, 3000–323 B.C.* Malden, MA: Blackwell, 2004.

———. *Philosophy before the Greeks: The Pursuit of Truth in Ancient Babylonia*. Princeton: Princeton University Press, 2016.

4

Ugarit and the Ugaritians

Mark S. Smith

1. Introduction

Ancient Ugarit, located on the coast of Syria about ten kilometers north of the modern port-city of Latakia, offers great riches for the study of the Bible and ancient Israel. The people of ancient Ugarit belonged to the same larger culture as the area of Canaan, in which the ancient Israelites emerged at the end of the Late Bronze Age and the beginning of the Iron Age. Based on features known at Ugarit that are attested also in Canaan and Israel, it has become evident that this region showed considerable cultural continuity. Indeed, the same proper names sometimes appear in both Ugaritic and biblical texts. For example, the name of Leviathan in the Bible (e.g., Ps. 74:14; Isa. 27:1) is matched by Ugaritic *ltn* (see below). Similarly, scholars generally agree that the name of Danil in Ugaritic refers to the same figure as Daniel in Ezekiel 14:14, 20 and 28:3 (see also *Jubilees* 4:20). Parallels such as these show the considerable overlap between Ugaritic and biblical traditions. At the same time, the earlier culture of Ugarit and the later society of Israel may reflect variations in these similarities; the Ugaritic versions are not necessarily direct

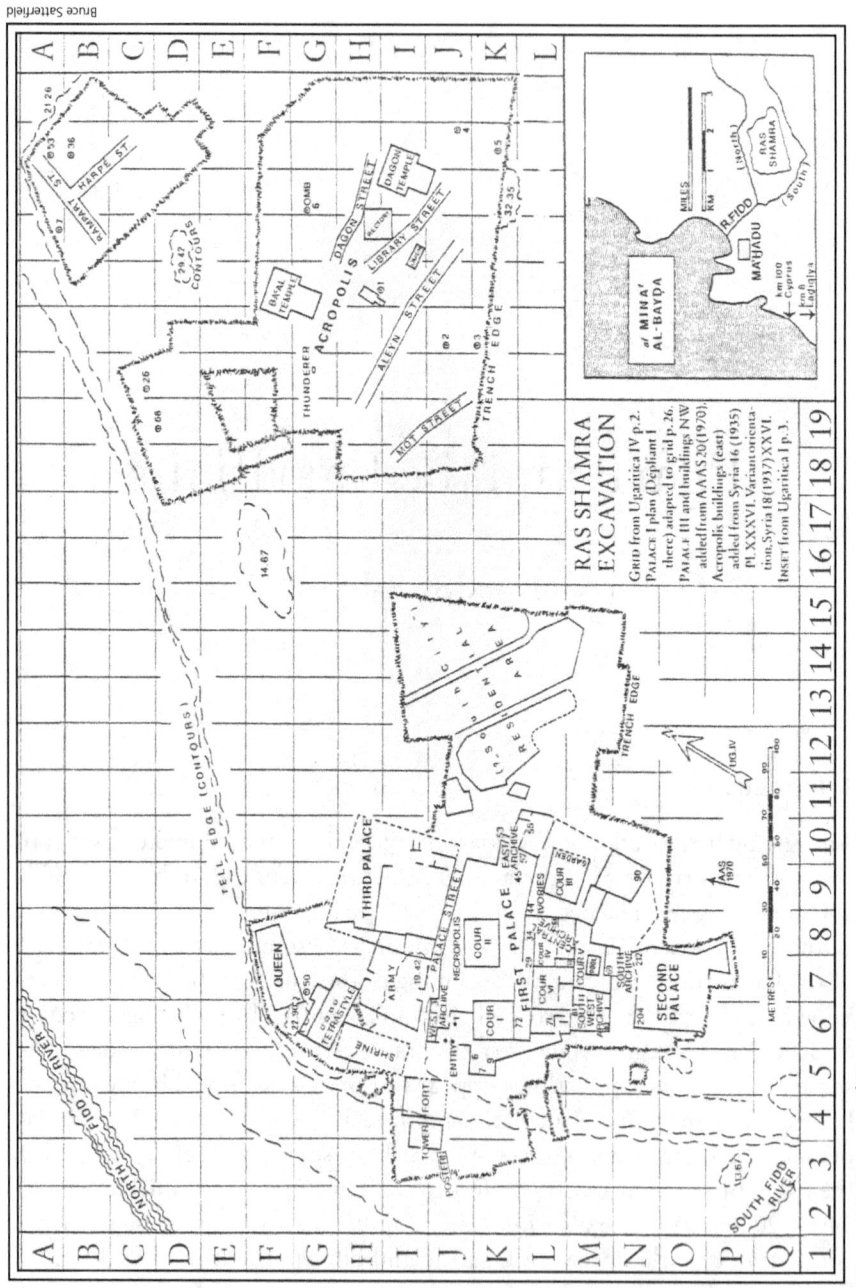

Figure 4.1. Site map of Ugarit

precursors to their biblical counterparts.¹ While this perspective is supported by further evidence, some nuancing is needed.

Scholars have used the term "Canaanite" to label the society and culture of Ugarit. However, the kingdom of Ugarit did not consider itself technically part of Canaan.² For example, a list of personal names followed by a word denoting their social or "ethnic" background (*KTU* 4.96.6–7) includes "Nʻmn the Egyptian," followed by "Yʻl the Canaanite" (evidently the same name as "Yael," known as "the wife of Heber the Kenite" in Judg. 4:17; 5:24).³ The Egyptian and Canaanite mentioned in this context were not indigenous to Ugarit. The distinction made between Ugarit and Canaan at Ugarit is evident also in a monetary dispute between "the sons of the land of Ugarit" and "the sons of the land of Canaan" (RS 20.182 + 20.181).⁴ At the same time, people from outside of Ugarit sometimes treated the city in the same context as Canaan. Ugarit was recognized among coastal sites down to Byblos ("all the lands from Gubla to Ugarit") in El Amarna letter 98.⁵ A report on Canaan by the king of Tyre in El Amarna letter 151 includes news not only about a fire at Ugarit but also about the king of Danuna, a kingdom in eastern Cilicia (in modern Turkey).⁶

Despite lying just north of ancient Canaan, Ugarit yielded many texts that furnish close parallels to passages in the Bible, pointing to a shared cultural heritage. Even the personal name Israel seems to be attested at Ugarit (*KTU* 4.623.3). There is an important temporal difference between Ugarit and Israel. Ugarit was destroyed at the end of the Late Bronze Age, shortly after the first clear extrabiblical mentions of Israel. The overlap between the end of Ugarit and the emergence of Israel can be seen in their association with the name of the Egyptian king Merenptah. Ugarit attests to a letter (RS 88.2158) from this king to the king of Ugarit (Niqmaddu III or Ammurapi,

---

1. Several parallels are well noted by Edward L. Greenstein, "Texts from Ugarit Solve Biblical Puzzles," *BAR* 36, no. 6 (2010): 48–53, 70. However, the parallels do not confirm the following view (p. 53): "The Biblical writers assume their audience's familiarity with this Ugaritic literature."

2. For surveys, see Dennis Pardee, "Canaan," in *The Blackwell Companion to the Hebrew Bible*, ed. Leo G. Perdue (Oxford: Blackwell, 2001), 151–68; and Wayne T. Pitard, "Canaanite Literature," in *From an Antique Land: An Introduction to Ancient Near Eastern Literature*, ed. Carl S. Ehrlich (Lanham, MD: Rowman & Littlefield, 2009), 255–311.

3. Anson Rainey, "A Canaanite at Ugarit," *IEJ* 13 (1963): 43–45; and Rainey, "Ugarit and Canaanites Again," *IEJ* 14 (1964): 101. Note also Rainey, "Who Is a Canaanite? A Review of the Textual Evidence," *BASOR* 304 (1996): 1–15.

4. Itamar Singer, "A Political History of Ugarit," in *HUS*, 674.

5. William L. Moran, *The Amarna Letters* (Baltimore: Johns Hopkins University Press, 1992), 171.

6. Ibid., 238.

the last king of Ugarit).⁷ Merenptah is also important for the historical record of early Israel. A famous stela of this king dating to ca. 1208 (fig. 4.2) ends by noting the destruction of Egypt's enemies in the Levant, including Canaan and Israel ("Israel is laid waste, his seed is not").⁸ Israel may have been known earlier in Egypt. An Egyptian inscription (Berlin Statue Pedestal Relief 21687) dating to the reign of Ramesses II (r. ca. 1279–1213) or earlier may attest to the name of Israel.⁹ Whether or not this particular claim holds up, Israel predates the time of its first recognition in Egyptian sources and overlapped with Ugarit probably from around 1250 to 1180.

The geographical distance between Ugarit and Israel is more pronounced: Ugarit lies at the northern end of the cultural context of ancient Canaan, while Israel is located in its southern extent. In addition, Ugarit was a cosmopolitan and prosperous city located close to the Mediterranean coast. By contrast, the heartland of ancient Israel was based in the hill country of southern Canaan and was isolated by comparison with Ugarit. At the same time, it is also to be noted that the geographical horizons in the texts of Ugarit and Israel overlap. Some Ugaritic texts refer to points south (Lebanon and Siryon in *KTU* 1.4 VI 18–21; Phoenician cities in 1.14 IV 34–36;

Figure 4.2. Merenptah Stela

---

7. Singer, "Political History of Ugarit," 708–11.
8. As translated by John A. Wilson in *ANET*, 378. See also the translation of James K. Hoffmeier, in *COS* 3.40–41.
9. So Peter van der Veen, Christoffer Theis, and Manfred Görg, "Israel in Canaan (Long) before Pharaoh Merenptah? A Fresh Look at Berlin Statue Pedestal Relief 21687," *JAEI* 2, no. 4 (2010): 15–25.

the Transjordanian sites of Ashtarot and Edrei in 1.108.2–3, and possibly Lake Huleh in 1.10 II 9 and 12), while a number of biblical texts name points north (e.g., Lebanon and Siryon in Ps. 29; arguably *ṣāpôn* [north] in Ps. 48:3 [Eng. 48:2] and elsewhere).[10] The discovery of the shorter cuneiform alphabet not only at Ugarit (e.g., *KTU* 4.710), but also at a number of sites south of Ugarit (including Taanek, *KTU* 4.767), is perhaps suggestive of cultural continuity in the scribal traditions of these places. In short, Ugarit, Canaan, and Israel share temporal and geographical horizons. This is not to suggest that, within the larger area running from Ugarit to southern Canaan, there was not considerable variation among polities. Indeed, Ugarit and Israel show a number of distinctive features, along with the many characteristics that they share. Before noting their shared features, an introduction to the site and its ancient history is provided.

2. General Overview of Geography and History

The ancient city of Ugarit (Tell Ras Shamra, "Fennel Hill") is located near the Mediterranean coast (fig. 4.3). Following the accidental discovery of a tomb at Minet el-Bheida (White Harbor) on the coast in 1928, a French archaeological team arrived there in April 1929.[11] The next month it moved about a mile inland to Ras Shamra, which in the very first season of excavation began to yield tablets. The identification of Ras Shamra as ancient Ugarit was later confirmed, thanks to the discovery of a tablet written in the local language with the name of the king Niqmaddu followed by his title, "king of Ugarit" (*KTU* 1.4 VIII, left edge). Other tablets bearing the name of Ugarit would confirm the identification. By the end of 1930, the essential decipherment of the letters of the local language (designated Ugaritic after the ancient name of the site) was achieved primarily by Hans Bauer and aided by Edouard Dhorme and to a lesser extent by Charles Virolleaud.[12] The decipherment of this script demonstrated that it is alphabetic (without vowels), consisting of thirty letters that were cuneiform (wedge shaped). The site yielded hundreds of texts in Ugaritic and in many other languages, most notably Akkadian, the lingua franca of the Middle and Late Bronze Age.

10. For Phoenician sites in administrative texts from Ugarit, see Singer, "Political History of Ugarit," 668–73.
11. For the excavator's account of the site's discovery, see C. F. A. Schaeffer, "The Discovery of Ugarit," in *Hands on the Past*, ed. C. W. Ceram (New York: Knopf, 1966), 301–6. See also Mark S. Smith, *Untold Stories: The Bible and Ugaritic Studies in the Twentieth Century* (Peabody, MA: Hendrickson, 2001), 13–14.
12. So Peggy L. Day, "*Dies diem docet*: The Decipherment of Ugaritic," *Studi epigrafici e linguistici* 19 (2002): 37–57. See also Kevin J. Cathcart, "The Ugaritic Language," in *HUS*, 76–80.

Figure 4.3. Ruins of ancient Ugarit

Excavations at the site point to settlement in the Neolithic period, in the eighth millennium.[13] The site continued through subsequent periods down into the Middle and Late Bronze Age. During the Middle Bronze Age, the site went through significant urban development. By the early Late Bronze Age (ca. 1600), the "North Palace" was built. It was abandoned later in the Late Bronze Age when a new royal complex was built on the city's western side. Several artifacts are known from the Middle Bronze period, including Egyptian objects with inscriptions. In addition, the king list first published in 1999 attests to twenty-six surviving names,[14] and the material evidence of the tablet suggests as many as fifty names.[15] From this evidence, it would appear that the royal line traced itself back at least to the Middle Bronze Age and perhaps even to the Early Bronze Age. The Late Bronze Age city is the most extensively excavated, revealing architecture spread over the site, including

---

13. Much of the following information derives from Marguerite Yon, *The City of Ugarit* (Winona Lake, IN: Eisenbrauns, 2006), 6–18. See also Wilfred van Soldt, "Ugarit: A Second Millennium Kingdom on the Mediterranean Coast," *CANE* 2:1255–66.

14. Daniel Arnaud, "Prolégomènes à la redaction d'une histoire d'Ougarit, II: Les borderaux de rois divinizes," *SMEA* 41, no. 2 (1999): 155–73; cf. Dennis Pardee, *Ritual and Cult at Ugarit*, WAW 10 (Atlanta: Society of Biblical Literature, 2002), 195–210.

15. Pardee, *Ritual and Cult*, 195–99.

two temples on the acropolis as well as a massive royal complex. The city had an ancient port at Minet el-Bheida. Five kilometers south, on a promontory overlooking the sea, was the site of Ras ibn Hani,[16] built up during the city's expansion in the Late Bronze Age; like Ugarit, it yielded tablets. The city ended in destruction around 1185 BCE. Subsequently there was sporadic occupation at the site.

3. The Site of Late Bronze Age Ugarit and Its Political History

The Late Bronze Age kingdom of Ugarit was bounded by the Mediterranean to the west and by mountains on its other three sides.[17] To the north lay the Bayer and Bassit range, which included Mount Sapanu (or Sapunu), standing at a height of about 1,780 meters and famous as the home of the god Baal Sapan. To the east lay the Alawai mountain range. To the south the same range turns toward the sea not far from where the kingdom of Ugarit met the kingdom of Siyannu (near the Nahr es-Sinn). Several rivers and streams, the Nahr al-Kabir being the most important, run from the mountain ranges down to the sea. As a result, the center of the kingdom largely consisted of a large fertile plain, enjoying an average annual rainfall of more than 800 millimeters during the rainy season. Covering about 2,000 square kilometers, the ancient kingdom of Ugarit was a city-state that stood at the crossroads of both sea trade around the eastern Mediterranean and land trade to the north, east, and south. To the west beyond Cyprus lay the Aegean; to the north was the Hittite Empire; to the south Levantine city-states and then the ancient kingdom of Egypt; and to the east were other major Syrian sites of Alalakh on the Orontes River, and then on to Emar and Mari on the Euphrates, the gateway for trade with the Mesopotamian heartland.

The city of Ugarit was bounded on its north and south by two wadis that join just to the west to form the Nahr-el Feid, which flows into the bay of Minet el-Bheida on the Mediterranean. Between the two wadis lay the city itself, which was surrounded by a monumental wall.[18] The city's west side was protected by a tower, approached by a ramp from the south. The tower stood near a postern

---

16. See A. Bounni, J. Lagarce, and E. Lagarce, *Ras ibn Hani, I: Le palais nord du Bronze recent, fouilles 1979–1995, synthèse préliminaire* (Beirut: Institut Français d'Archéologie du Proche Orient, 1998).

17. See Wilfred H. van Soldt, *The Topography of the City-State of Ugarit*, AOAT 324 (Münster: Ugarit-Verlag, 2005); and the fine summary of Pierre Bordreuil and Dennis Pardee, *A Manual of Ugaritic* (Winona Lake, IN: Eisenbrauns, 2009), 15–19.

18. For the city's organization, see M. Yon, "Topographie régionale et topographie urbaine," in *Ougarit au Bronze moyen et au Bronze récent*, ed. Yves Calvet and Marguerite Yon, TMOM 47 (Lyon: Maison de l'Orient et de la Méditerranée, 2008), 37–47.

gate (blocked in the thirteenth century) and a monumental gate dating to the thirteenth–twelfth centuries. Just inside the wall was a royal zone[19] of more than 10,000 square meters that included several palace buildings and a royal temple.[20] This area had a water drainage system with a massive sewer.[21] The palace complex, built in several stages over the fifteenth to the thirteenth centuries, covered nearly 7,000 square meters. One of the El Amarna letters (EA 89) attests to the wealth of the palace in the fourteenth century. In his report to his overlord, Amenophis III, Rib-Hadda of Byblos compared the palace in Tyre to the royal residence at Ugarit: "It is like the residence in Ugarit. Exceedingly [gr]eat is the wealth [i]n it."[22] In the same period, the palace at Ugarit is also known to have sustained great damage due to a fire (EA 151). The palace complex included several courtyards as well as areas for royal ceremonial use (such as the Throne Room), administrative activity, and private areas; it is also believed to have had a space reserved for a royal funerary cult.[23] The six palace archives yielded many tablets, written mostly in Ugaritic and Akkadian.[24]

While other parts of the tell show substantial architecture,[25] the main architectural focus in this period, in addition to the palace complex, was the acropolis to the northeast, with its two temples.[26] Two stelae of the storm god in one temple (RS 1.[089]+2.[033]+5.183; RS 4.427)[27] suggested Baal as its divine patron, while two stelae inscribed with the name of Dagan (*KTU* 6.13, 6.14)[28] found in the other temple pointed to this god as its patron (it has since been suggested that this was a temple of El). Between the temples stood several buildings, including "the House (or Library) of the High Priest." Many important texts were discovered in this building, including major literary texts, the Baal Cycle (*KTU* 1.1–1.6), Kirta (1.14–1.16), Aqhat (1.17–1.19), the Rituals and Myths of the Goodly Gods (1.23), and the Hymn of Nikkal (1.24), which are described below. The languages attested are not only the local language of Ugaritic and Akkadian, the lingua franca of the time, but also Cypro-Minoan, Egyptian, Hittite, Hurrian, Luwian, and Sumerian. Among

19. See Yon, *City of Ugarit*, 30–38, with schematic plans on pp. 30 and 37.
20. For this temple, see ibid., 49.
21. Ibid., 49–50.
22. Moran, *Amarna Letters*, 162.
23. Yon, *City of Ugarit*, 38, referring to locus 28 on the schematic map on p. 37.
24. Ibid., 43–45.
25. Ibid., 51–97.
26. Ibid., 106–15.
27. For pictures and descriptions, see ibid., 134, 135.
28. For a picture of one and descriptions of both, see ibid., 134, 135. See also Theodore J. Lewis, *Cults of the Dead in Ancient Israel and Ugarit*, HSM 39 (Atlanta: Scholars Press, 1989), 72–79; Pardee, *Ritual and Cult*, 124–25.

these is a series of polyglot texts with parallel columns of words written in Sumerian, Akkadian, Hurrian, and Ugaritic in syllabic transcription.[29] (The Ugaritic forms in syllabic transcription provide the main indigenous information for the vowels in Ugaritic words, along with Ugaritic loanwords into Akkadian texts and Ugaritic words written with any of the "three *aleph*s," which indicate a vowel in cases where the *aleph* does not close the syllable.) The polyglot texts, not to mention the wide variety of languages at the site, show its cosmopolitan character. The textual discoveries also show advanced scribal activity in service to the operation of the monarchy.[30]

The early history of Ugarit is unclear.[31] Apart from the possible mention of Ugarit in sources at Ebla, there are no independent sources for Ugarit prior to the middle of the second millennium. Thanks to the king lists, we have the names of twenty-six kings (as noted above), and originally the lists may have indicated forty-six or more monarchic names. However, the lengths of the reigns of even the attested kings are generally unknown. Historians have suggested seeing the beginning of the second millennium as the time for the foundations of the kingdom of Ugarit. This would locate the establishment of Ugarit within the context of the putative "Amorite" expansion in Mesopotamia and Syria. This "Amorite" influence is suggested by the reference to the figure of Ddn mentioned in an Ugaritic royal liturgy lamenting the recently deceased Niqmaddu (*KTU* 1.161) and the same figure as Dtn in the story of Kirta (*KTU* 1.15 III 4, 15), a name also known in the genealogy of the Hammurabi dynasty (preserved in Assyrian King List A).[32]

29. John Huehnergard, *Ugaritic Vocabulary in Syllabic Transcription*, 2nd ed., HSS 32 (Winona Lake, IN: Eisenbrauns, 2008). Note also Pardee, "Ugaritic Science," in *The World of the Aramaeans III: Studies in Language and Literature in Honour of Paul-Eugène Dion*, ed. P. M. Michèle Daviau, John W. Wevers, and Michael Weigl, JSOTSup 326 (Sheffield, UK: Sheffield Academic, 2001), 230–31, 248–51.

30. Wilfred van Soldt, "Babylonian Lexical, Religious and Literary Texts and Scribal Education at Ugarit and Its Implications for the Alphabetic Literary Texts," in *Ugarit: Ein ostmediterranes Kulturzentrum; Ergebnisse und Perspektiven der Forschung*, vol. 1, *Ugarit und seinem altorientalische Umwelt*, ed. M. Dietrich and O. Loretz, ALASP 7 (Münster: Ugarit-Verlag, 1995), 171–212; Robert Hawley, "On the Alphabetic Scribal Curriculum at Ugarit," in *Proceedings of the 51st Rencontre Assyriologique Internationale Held at the Oriental Institute of the University of Chicago, July 18–22, 2005*, ed. R. D. Biggs, J. Myers, and M. T. Roth, SAOC 62 (Chicago: Oriental Institute of the University of Chicago, 2008), 57–67; and Carole Roche, "Language and Script in the Akkadian Documents from Ras Shamra," in *Society and Administration in Ancient Ugarit*, ed. W. H. van Soldt (Leiden: Brill, 2010), 107–22.

31. This section largely follows Singer, "Political History of Ugarit," 603–733. See also Jacques Freu, *Histoire politique du royaume d'Ugarit*, Kubaba, Série Antiquité 11 (Paris: L'Harmattan, 2006).

32. Mark S. Smith, *The Ugaritic Baal Cycle*, vol. 1, *Introduction with Text, Translation, and Commentary of KTU 1.1–1.2*, VTSup 55 (Leiden: Brill, 1994), 112–13.

Ugarit appears in the documentation of a journey that King Zimri-Lim made to Ugarit ca. 1765.[33] The considerable corpus of Mari letters attesting to this trip, however, reveals little about Ugarit. The Mari expedition spent a month at Ugarit, but even the name of the Ugaritic king at the time goes unmentioned. Purchase of luxury goods is mentioned, however, indicating the high level of wealth on the part of both parties. Somewhat later a Mari letter reveals that the "man of Ugarit"—that is, the king—wished to visit the palace at Mari.

With the demise of the old Amorite centers in northern Syria ca. 1600, the void was filled by Hurrian Mittani. Little is known of this period, apart from a letter sent by Niqmepa of Alalakh to king Ibra<nu> (see the name *Ibrn* listed four times in *KTU* 1.113, and *i-bi-ra-na* four times in RS 94.2518.10).[34] Another letter written in Hurrian, perhaps sent from Mittani or the successor state of Hanigalbat, was found in the palace, but it is poorly preserved. Ongoing Hurrian cultural influence can be seen in Hurrian vocabulary in the polyglot texts at Ugarit as well as texts written in Hurrian (*KTU* 1.125, 1.128, 1.131), sometimes in combination with Ugaritic (see *KTU* 1.110, 1.111, 1.116, 1.132).[35]

In the fourteenth century, Ugarit entered the orbit of Egyptian power under Amenophis III. Along with letters from Ugarit known in the Amarna correspondence (El Amarna letters 45 and 49 and perhaps letters 46–48)[36] are five references to Ugarit (El Amarna letters 1, 89, 98, 126, and 151). Letter 45 evidently mentions king Ammishtamru (the name is partially reconstructed), while letter 49 constitutes the "message of Niqmaddu." This Ammishtamru, evidently the first of two Ugaritic kings with this name, reigned until around 1350. Ugarit also attests to a scarab commemorating the marriage of Amenophis III to Ty. The first Niqmaddu (the name of three Ugaritic kings) reigned ca. 1350–1315. Trade with Egypt was quite active in this period, as was Egyptian influence, marked by the cartouches of Akhenaten and Nefertiti as well as an Egyptian inscription, "Niqmaddu the Great One of the Land of Ugarit." At this time, Ugarit acknowledged the superior status of Egypt. El Amarna letters 45 and 49 show the proper diplomatic etiquette. The Ugaritic king calls the Egyptian king "the Sun, my lord" and refers to himself as "your

---

33. P. Villard, "Un roi de Mari à Ugarit," *UF* 18 (1986): 387–412.
34. Pardee, *Ritual and Cult*, 202, 203.
35. Manfried Dietrich and Walter Mayer, "Sprache und Kultur der Hurriter in Ugarit," in Dietrich and Loretz, *Ugarit*, 7–42; and Dennis Pardee, "L'ougaritique et le hourrite dans les textes rituels de Ras Shamra-Ougarit," in *Mosaïques de langues, mosaïque culturelle: Le bilingualisme dans le proche-orient ancien*, ed. Françoise Briquel-Chatonnet (Paris: Jean Maisonneuve, 1996), 63–80.
36. Moran, *Amarna Letters*, 118n1.

servant." Still, it is not clear that Ugarit was an Egyptian vassal as such. Ugarit also appears in geographical lists from the reigns of Amen-hotep III and Horemheb.[37]

With the first Hittite campaign into Syria ca. 1340, the situation changed rather dramatically. EA 98 complains that "all the lands from Byblos to Ugarit" banded together with the Hittite vassal Aziru, clearly against Egyptian interests from the perspective of Byblos (see also El Amarna letter 126). Aziru and Ugarit signed a treaty, suggesting that Ugarit came under the new power of the Hittites led by Suppiluliuma. Tensions between the old Egyptian order and the new Hittite hegemony in northern Syria may be reflected in a number of documents at Ugarit. The so-called General's Letter from Ugarit (RS 20.033) might date to this context, although the specific situation that it reflects remains unknown. This may also be the background for the fire at Ugarit mentioned in El Amarna letter 151. Perhaps an anti-Hittite coalition including Mukish attempting to win Ugarit back to the Egyptian sphere of influence was responsible. By the end of the reign of Niqmaddu, Ugarit was in the Hittite camp, as evidenced by a letter from Suppiluliuma (RS 17.132) as well as a treaty between them (RS 17.340). Subsequent treaties stipulated tribute to be paid but omitted the standard requirement for the dispatch of troops from Ugarit. This kingdom was chiefly of economic value to the Hittites. In exchange, Ugarit received a number of towns from Mukish to the north of Ugarit. From this point onward, Ugarit would remain a Hittite vassal.

Niqmaddu was succeeded briefly by his son Arhalba (ca. 1315–1313) and then by a second son, Niqmepa (ca. 1313–1260). Little is known of the first, apart from six judicial texts (RS 16.344, 15.91, 16.144, 167.160, 16.278, 16.142, in *PRU* 3, 75–77). It would appear from the treaty of Niqmepa with the Hittites that they may have forced Arhalba from his throne and replaced him with his brother (RS 17.349B+ = *PRU* 4, 85f.). Through a diplomatic marriage, Niqmepa established ties also with another local power, Amurru, located to the south of Ugarit and Siyannu. Amurru sent troops to meet the threat of local forces hostile to Ugarit (the tribal Umman Manda, RS 17.286 = *PRU* 4, 180). Ugarit also continued as a Hittite vassal and contributed troops to the Hittite conflict with the invading Egyptian force at the battle of Qadesh ca. 1290. Around 1258 these two great international forces concluded a peace treaty (an Egyptian version mentions Ugarit as one of the Hittite vassals), which contributed to Ugarit's return to its role as a center of trade in the eastern Mediterranean. A Hittite ritual mentions "the country of Ugarit"

---

37. See "Lists of Asiatic Countries under the Egyptian Empire" (*ANET*, 243).

in a series of places running from Mittani to Canaan and beyond,[38] while a Hittite prayer mentions Ugarit along with Alalakh and Sidon.[39]

By this time, Ammishtamru II (ca. 1260–1235) succeeded his father, Niqmepa. His mother served as "queen mother." With her agreement, the king exiled his two brothers to Alashiya under mysterious circumstances, perhaps involving a failed rebellion. Like his father, Ammishtamru married a princess from Amurru, but their failed relationship became an international affair requiring Hittite diplomatic intervention. With the marriage dissolved, the spouse returned home to Amurru, and her son and legitimate crown prince, Utri-Sharruma, chose to accompany his mother. Another son (whose mother remains unknown) instead succeeded Ammishtamru: Ibiranu (ca. 1235–1225/1220). His reign included the Hittite demand to provide military assistance.

His successor, Niqmaddu III (ca. 1225/1220–1215), has become one of the best-documented kings of Ugarit, thanks to the discovery of Urtenu's archive in the city's south-central area. (Urtenu was a high-level official who lived in the reigns of the last kings of Ugarit; he is named in a number of texts.) The transition from Niqmaddu III to Ammurapi (ca. 1215–1190/1185) was marked by a royal funerary text (*KTU* 1.161), which invokes the old tribal deceased ancestors known as the Rephaim and also Kings Ammishtamru and Niqmaddu III (the name of the intervening monarch, Ibiranu, is omitted). The reign of Ammurapi, the last king of Ugarit, was afflicted by the broad series of circumstances that beset the Hittite Empire as well. Records point to enemy invasions, perhaps by any number of the Sea Peoples (as suggested by RS 34.129), as well as food shortages, perhaps due to drought (see RS 34.152.9–14). The defeat of the Ugaritic army and the sack of the city are mentioned in a private letter (*KTU* 2.61; see also 2.10).[40] The archaeological record confirms massive conflagration and arrowheads. With few corpses attested, it is thought that most of the population managed to flee the city.

During its final century, the kingdom of Ugarit prospered. It was often favored by the Hittites in disputes with merchants and in other lawsuits, often mediated by the kingdom of Carchemish,[41] the center of Hittite rule in Syria. Ugarit's annual tribute continued to go to the Hittites, where it was distributed among the king, the queen, and royal officials. Despite Ugarit's

---

38. "Evocatio," trans. Albrecht Goetze (*ANET*, 352–53); see also Anson Rainey, "Political and Foreign Affairs," in *Ras Shamra Parallels: The Texts from Ugarit and the Hebrew Bible*, vol. 2, ed. Loren R. Fisher, AnOr 50 (Rome: Pontificium Institutum Biblicum, 1975), 125–29.
39. Bordreuil and Pardee, *Manual of Ugaritic*, 3.
40. On these points, see Singer, "Political History of Ugarit," 715–23.
41. See "Additional Mesopotamian Legal Documents," trans. J. J. Finkelstein (*ANET*, 547, no. 18: "Trial for Homicide").

vassalage to Hatti, there is little evidence of Hittite cultural impact on Ugarit. While a handful of Hittite texts have been discovered at Ugarit, there is no clear evidence that any of them were produced there. In this context, Ugarit blossomed as a center of international trade, with its material prosperity evident through the end of the Late Bronze Age.

4. Culture and Religion

Ugarit's prosperity is reflected not only in its textual records but also in its material remains.[42] Objects of gold and ivory represent art of the region at its height.[43] Palaces, temples, and tombs contain a rich array of artifacts, many imported. Metal and stone statues of various deities are known, most notably for El and Baal as well as a goddess (fig. 4.4).[44] A bed panel of carved ivory depicts a series of scenes, including the king as warrior and hunter; a couple in embrace, presumably a royal pair; and a goddess suckling two children, perhaps royals. A beautiful sculpted ivory head of a young male was inlaid with precious metal. The massive number of ivory pieces includes a duck-shaped cosmetic box with a lid and a miniature figurine of a musician. Pottery imports from the Aegean or Cyprus were also of very fine quality. Mycenaean rhytons as well as stands with carvings of various figures also point to the high culture of ancient Ugarit.

The ritual life of Ugarit centered largely on the temple of Baal and the royal palace. Their construction and furnishing are suggested by various terms, such as the temple's *pariktu* (cf. the biblical term for "veil" or "curtain" in 2 Chron. 3:14), mentioned in an Akkadian letter (RS 94.2221+).[45] The king was the central figure in the attested ritual texts, joined by various priests and singers. The sacrificial system, especially in terms of its offerings, shows considerable commonality with biblical descriptions.[46] The recipients of these sacrifices were

---

42. Yon, *City of Ugarit*, 123–72.

43. See Jacqueline Gachet-Bizollon, *Les ivoires d'Ougarit et l'art des ivoiriers du Levant au Bronze Récent*, RSO 16 (Paris: Éditions Recherche sur les Civilisations, 2007).

44. I use conventional spellings for the names of deities. El, for example, is more properly 'Il or 'Ilu (with the final nominative case ending). For the iconography of some major deities at Ugarit, see Izak Cornelius, *The Iconography of the Canaanite Gods Reshef and Baʻal: Late Bronze and Iron Age I Periods (c. 1500–1000 BCE)*, OBO 140 (Fribourg: University Press; Göttingen: Vandenhoeck & Ruprecht, 1994); and Cornelius, *The Many Faces of the Goddess: The Iconography of the Syro-Palestinian Goddesses Anat, Astarte, Qedeshet, and Asherah, c. 1500–1000*, OBO 24 (Fribourg: Academic Press; Göttingen: Vandenhoeck & Ruprecht, 2004).

45. Pierre Bordreuil, "Ugarit and the Bible: New Data from the House of Urtenu," in *Ugarit at Seventy-Five*, ed. K. Lawson Younger Jr. (Winona Lake, IN: Eisenbrauns, 2007), 94–96.

46. See Pardee, *Ritual and Cult*, 223–41.

Figure 4.4. Bronze figurine of Baal found at Ras Shamra (ancient Ugarit)

the many deities both at home at Ugarit and from further abroad.[47] The divine household, largely coterminous with the divine council, consists of the divine parents, the compassionate and benevolent El (cf. biblical El) and Athirat (cf. biblical Asherah).[48] The second level of the household consists of their "seventy children" (cf. the number of gods of the nations in Deut. 32:8–9 in the Septuagint and 4QDeut^j), also called the "sons of El" (cf. "divine sons" in Ps. 29:1). These include notably the warrior goddesses, Anat (also Baal's sister) and Astarte (both goddesses being named in the Bible; see below); the latter's male counterpart, Athtar; the warrior Rashpu (cf. *rešep* in Hab. 3:5); the sun goddess, Shapshu, and the moon god, Yarikh (cf. "the sun, the moon, and the stars" in 2 Kings 23:5; cf. 1 Kings 22:19; Zeph. 1:5); and Dawn (Shahar; cf. Isa. 14:12) and Dusk (Shalim; see the name of Jerusalem and perhaps the names of Absalom and Solomon). These children are commonly astral in contrast to the outsider Baal, the warrior storm god. As "the son of Dagan," he stands in an inimical relationship to the sons of El and Athirat, though El is regarded also as Baal's father, perhaps in a general way. Several of these deities are associated with animals considered to be emblematic of them in some manner. For example, El is called "Bull El" (cf. the horns associated with God—literally, El—in Num. 23:22; 24:8), and Baal is represented as a young bull or bull-calf (cf. the so-called golden calf in Exod. 32, a representation of Yahweh, not Baal).[49] The deities of the second level are regarded as providing benefit (sometimes

---

47. For a summary of deities, see the older study of Johannes C. de Moor, "The Semitic Pantheon of Ugarit," *UF* 2 (1970): 187–228. For comparisons of gods and goddesses in Ugaritic and biblical literatures, see Karel van der Toorn, Bob Becking, and Pieter W. van der Horst, eds., *Dictionary of Deities and Demons in the Bible*, 2nd ed. (Leiden: Brill; Grand Rapids: Eerdmans, 1999).

48. The best assessment remains Judith Hadley, *The Cult of Asherah in Ancient Israel and Judah* (Cambridge: Cambridge University Press, 2000).

49. Mark S. Smith, "Counting Calves at Bethel," in *"Up to the Gates of Ekron": Essays on the Archaeology and History of the Eastern Mediterranean in Honor of Seymour Gitin*, ed. Sidnie White Crawford (Jerusalem: The W. F. Albright Institute of Archaeological Research / The Israel Exploration Society, 2007), 382–94.

expressed in terms of violence against enemies), in contrast to the destructive gods, Yamm ("Sea"; see Ps. 74:13) and Mot ("Death"; see Isa. 25:8; Jer. 9:20 [Eng. 9:21]). These two are called "beloved of El," but it is unclear whether they were considered his children as such. This is also true of other destructive divinities, such as *ltn* (cf. Leviathan in Ps. 74:14; Isa. 27:1) and *tnn* (cf. biblical *tannînîm* in Ps. 74:13). A possible third level of the divine household may be recognized in its chief worker, the figure of the craftsman-god, Kothar, who unlike the other deities has homes in Egypt and Crete. He makes weaponry and palaces for deities as well as weapons for mortals. The fourth level of the divine household comprises various workers, including messengers (the word that in Hebrew becomes the term for "angels"). Other figures also understood to be divine are the skillful goddesses of conception and birth, the Kotharatu; the gods' "divine ancestor," literally "the god of the father" (*'il'ib*; cf. Exod. 15:2); and the ancient tribal leaders associated with the royal line called the *rp'um* (cf. biblical Rephaim in Isa. 14:9; 26:14, 19). The "olden" pair of deities, "Heaven" and "Earth" (cf. Deut. 32:1), also receives offerings.

5. A Survey of the Ugaritic Texts with Biblical Parallels

To gain insight into ancient Ugarit, it may be useful to provide an overview of the Ugaritic texts. The standard edition of the Ugaritic texts (*KTU*) uses the following categories: literary and religious texts (*KTU* 1); letters (*KTU* 2); legal texts (*KTU* 3); economic texts (*KTU* 4); scribal exercises (*KTU* 5); inscriptions on seals, labels, ivories, and so forth (*KTU* 6); unclassified texts (*KTU* 7); illegible tablets and uninscribed fragments (*KTU* 8); unpublished texts (*KTU* 9); and one Ugaritic (?) text in syllabic script (*KTU* 10). This listing includes a number of Hurrian texts (noted above), as well as two Akkadian religious texts in cuneiform alphabetic writing and another text with seven lines of Akkadian followed by ten lines in Ugaritic. The discussion below omits discussion of *KTU* 7–10, as they furnish relatively little information. In addition to the texts in *KTU*, about another sixty Ugaritic texts (along with about three hundred Akkadian texts) were discovered in the 1994 and 1996 excavations.[50] These Ugaritic texts are to be incorporated in the next *KTU* edition of the Ugaritic texts (presently in preparation). Bordreuil and Pardee's tally of the Ugaritic corpus comes to about fifty poetic texts and 1,500 prose texts.

The Ugaritic texts are not confined to the site of Ugarit proper. Several were also discovered at Ras ibn-Hani. Two texts from Ugarit are written in

50. Pierre Bordreuil and Dennis Pardee, "Catalogue raisonné des textes ougaritiques de la Maison d'Ourtenou," *AuOr* 17–18 (1999–2000): 23–38.

a shorter alphabet running from right to left (*KTU* 4.31 and 4.710), as are several others from Levantine and Cypriot sites outside of Ugarit. This shorter alphabet stands closer to the number of letters in the Hebrew and Aramaic alphabets. Whether of the longer or shorter variety, the writing of alphabetic signs in cuneiform suggests the influence of Mesopotamian cuneiform scribal traditions on the Levant in the Late Bronze Age. The following overview of the Ugaritic texts cites biblical verses with parallels suggesting a shared West Semitic tradition.[51] There are also many important parallels between the Akkadian texts at Ugarit and biblical texts, especially in the international language of treaty[52] and wisdom literature,[53] which largely partake of broader ancient Near Eastern tradition.[54]

KTU 1: Literary Texts (KTU 1.1-1.25, 1.61-1.63 [?], 1.83, 1.92, 1.93, 1.96, 1.101, 1.108, 1.114.1-28)[55]

The literary texts are characterized by poetic parallelism consisting of units comprising two or three lines, as found in biblical poetry.[56] The prose in these texts is confined to scribal additions, including superscriptions preserved at

---

51. For Ugaritic-biblical parallels, see Loren R. Fisher, ed., *Ras Shamra Parallels: The Texts from Ugarit and the Hebrew Bible*, vols. 1 and 2, AnOr 49–50 (Rome: Pontificium Institutum Biblicum, 1972, 1975); and Stan Rummel, ed., *Ras Shamra Parallels: The Texts from Ugarit and the Hebrew Bible*, vol. 3, AnOr 51 (Rome: Pontificium Institutum Biblicum, 1981).

52. F. Brent Knutson, "Political and Foreign Affairs," and "Literary Genres in *PRU IV*," in Fisher, *Ras Shamra Parallels*, 2:109–29 and 153–214, respectively. See also John Khanjian, "Wisdom," in ibid., 2:371–400.

53. Duane E. Smith, "Wisdom Genres in RS 22.439," in Fisher, *Ras Shamra Parallels*, 2:215–47. For wisdom literature at Ugarit, see Loren R. Mack-Fisher, "A Survey and Reading Guide to the Didactic Literature of Ugarit: Prolegomenon to a Study of the Sage," in *The Sage in Israel and the Ancient Near East*, ed. John G. Gammie and Leo G. Perdue (Winona Lake, IN: Eisenbrauns, 1990), 67–80.

54. Law codes and historical chronicles are also absent from the Ugaritic texts, compared with Mesopotamian and biblical corpora. Like treaty and wisdom texts, these may not represent genres of the older West Semitic tradition, but Iron Age imports into Israel. For this problem, see Mark S. Smith, "Biblical Narrative between Ugaritic and Akkadian Literature: Part I: Ugarit and the Hebrew Bible; Consideration of Recent Comparative Research," *RB* 114 (2007): 5–29; and Smith, "Biblical Narrative between Ugaritic and Akkadian Literature: Part II," *RB* 114 (2007): 189–207.

55. For convenient translations of these texts, see Simon B. Parker, ed., *Ugaritic Narrative Poetry*, WAW 9 (Atlanta: Scholars Press, 1997); André Caquot, Maurice Sznycer, and Andrée Herdner, *Textes ougaritiques*, vol. 1, *Mythes et légendes*, LAPO 7 (Paris: Cerf, 1974); and Pardee, in COS 1.241–83, 333–56. For most of these texts, note also Michael D. Coogan and Mark S. Smith, *Stories from Ancient Canaan*, 2nd rev. and expanded ed. (Louisville: Westminster John Knox, 2012). For the latter three texts, see also the important edition of Pardee, *Les textes para-mythologiques de la 24ᵉ Campagne (1961)*, RSO 4 (Paris: Éditions Recherche sur les Civilisations, 1988).

56. See Simon B. Parker, *The Pre-Biblical Narrative Tradition: Essays on the Ugaritic Poems Keret and Aqhat*, RBS 24 (Atlanta: Scholars Press, 1989), 7–98; and Wilfred G. E. Watson,

the heads of some tablets and colophons preserved at the end of some tablets. The literary texts include four sets of multitablet collections: (1) stories centered on the god Baal (the Baal Cycle, 1.1–1.3 + 1.8, 1.4–1.6); (2) episodes in the life of King Kirta (1.14–1.16); (3) the short life of the human hero, Aqhat (1.17–1.19); and (4) the travel and feasting of the ancient deceased heroes, the *rp'um* (1.20–1.22).

Shorter texts narrate Baal's fathering a bull (1.10); a birth involving several deities (1.11); Baal's conflict with monstrous foes called "Devourers" (1.12); an exaltation of the warrior goddess, Anat (1.13); the birth, banishment, and reincorporation of the dangerous "Goodly Gods" (1.23.30–76), following a series of ritual instructions concerning these deities (1.23.1–29);[57] the wedding song of Nikkal, the Mesopotamian moon goddess, and Yarikh, the Ugaritic moon god (1.24);[58] the binding of the monstrous *tnn* (1.83; cf. biblical "dragons" in Ps. 74:13 and "sea monsters" in Gen. 1:21);[59] the hunt of the goddess Astarte, followed by the roiling of the cosmic "deep" (1.92; cf. "deep" in Gen. 1:2);[60] the cry of the cow (1.93); the dangerous "eye" (or perhaps the goddess Anat)[61] consuming "her brother's flesh" without a knife and drinking "his blood without a cup" (1.96); a hymnic description of Baal (1.101); a hymnic description of a feast for the god *rp'u* (evidently the leader of the *rp'um*; see below) and his companions (perhaps themselves the *rp'um*), as well as Anat (1.108), followed by a wish for blessing for the dynasty; and El's drunken feast and the goddesses' hunt for ingredients for a cure (1.114.1–28), followed by a prescription for a hangover (1.114.29–31).[62] One of the newer texts (RIH

Traditional Techniques in Classical Hebrew Verse, 2nd ed., JSOTSup 170 (Sheffield, UK: Sheffield Academic, 1994).

57. See Mark S. Smith, *The Sacrificial Rituals and Myths of the Goodly Gods, KTU/CAT 1.23: Royal Constructions of Opposition, Intersection, Integration and Domination* (Atlanta: Society of Biblical Literature; Leiden: Brill, 2006).

58. See Dennis Pardee, "RS 5.194 (CTA 24): Un chant nuptial ougaritique. Nouvelle étude épigraphique suivie de remarques philologiques et littéraires," *Semitica et Classica* 3 (2010): 13–46.

59. See Wayne T. Pitard, "The Binding of Yamm: A New Edition of the Ugaritic Text *KTU* 1.83," *JNES* 57 (1998): 261–80.

60. See Dennis Pardee, "Deux tablettes ougaritiques de la main d'un meme scribe, trouvées sur deux sites distinct: RS 19.039 et RIH 98/02," *Semitica et Classica* 1 (2008): 9–38.

61. The interpretation depends on how to read '*nn*, taken by many as the "evil eye," but without sufficient explanation for the final *n*. An alternative is to read the *n* as *t* and to take the word as the name of Anat. See Pardee, *Ritual and Cult*, 161; and Pardee, "RS 22.225: Étude épigraphique suivie de quelques remarques philologiques," in *D'Ougarit à Jérusalem: Recueil d'études épigraphiques et archéologiques offert à Pierre Bordreuil*, ed. C. Roche, Orient & Méditerranée 2 (Paris: de Boccard, 2008), 3–20.

62. These texts can be found in Parker, *Ugaritic Narrative Poetry*. See also Manfried Dietrich and Oswald Loretz, *Studien zu den ugaritischen Texten: I. Mythos und Ritual in KTU 1.12, 1.24, 1.96, 1.100 und 1.114*, AOAT 269/1 (Münster: Ugarit-Verlag, 2000).

98/02) is a hymn to Astarte as a leonine warrior.[63] The subject of some texts is unclear (e.g., 1.9, 1.25, 1.61–1.63, 1.75, 1.79, 1.81). At this point, we review the four longer literary cycles.

THE BAAL CYCLE (*KTU* 1.1–1.6)[64]

The longest Ugaritic text, the Baal Cycle, relates Baal's attainment of divine kingship represented by the construction of his royal palace (1.3 III–1.4 VII), preceded by his conflict with the cosmic, personified Sea (1.1–1.3 II) and followed by his struggle with Death personified (1.4 VIII–1.6). The fragmentary first tablet of the Baal Cycle (1.1) begins with El's naming Sea as divine champion (1.1 V–IV). El then summons Kothar to build a palace, apparently for Yamm (1.1 III). El then summons Anat to desist from conflict (1.1 II). The second tablet is missing one column and most of a second. It has two clear columns, the order of which has been disputed recently by Dennis Pardee.[65] In one column (1.2 I), Sea's messengers come to the divine council headed by the patriarchal god, El, in order to demand the surrender of Baal, who stands at attention while the other deities of the divine assembly are enjoying a meal. The sight of Sea's messengers inspires fear in the divine council, and El decrees that Baal is to become Sea's servant. The scene breaks off with Baal's resisting this decision and with the warrior goddesses, Anat and Astarte, rebuking him.

An old type-scene of ancient Near Eastern literatures, the classic example of the divine council in biblical literature appears in the prophetic vision of Micaiah (1 Kings 22:19–23), who sees the host of heaven standing on either side of Yahweh. In Psalm 82, God stands in the divine council and accuses the other gods (see also Dan. 7). In divine council scenes, the head god of the divine assembly typically commissions a member to carry out or announce the divine decree. In biblical examples, the prophet may be commissioned (see Isa. 6 and Ezek. 1–3; cf. the lying spirit in 1 Kings 22:20–23). In the Baal Cycle, Baal would be expected to serve as the divine council's champion against an enemy such as Sea. This is the case with Marduk in the Babylonian Epic of Creation (Enuma Elish). However, the expectation of the type-scene is

---

63. Pardee, "Preliminary Presentation of a New Ugaritic Song to ʿAṯtartu (RIH 98/02)," in Younger, *Ugarit at Seventy-Five*, 27–39.

64. Smith, *Ugaritic Baal Cycle*, vol. 1; Mark S. Smith and Wayne T. Pitard, *The Ugaritic Baal Cycle*, vol. 2, *Introduction with Text, Translation and Commentary of KTU 1.3–1.4*, VTSup 114 (Leiden: Brill, 2009).

65. Pardee, "RS 3.367, Colonne 'IV': Étude épigraphique suivie de quelques remarques philologiques," in *He Unfurrowed His Brow and Laughed: Essays in Honour of Professor Nicolas Wyatt*, ed. W. G. E. Watson, AOAT 299 (Münster: Ugarit-Verlag, 2007), 227–47.

deliberately altered in the case of the Baal Cycle: Baal is surrendered to Sea, showing his weak position at this point in the story.

In another clear column of the same tablet (1.2 IV), Baal upends the divine assembly's decision by defeating Sea, aided by weapons made by Kothar. This god first predicts Baal's victory over Sea (in words notably similar to Pss. 92:10; 145:13). The theme of the divine battle against Sea is well known in Psalm 74:13, where Sea is one of Yahweh's cosmic enemies (see also Pss. 29; 89:9–11; Isa. 51:9–11). After his victory, Baal celebrates with a feast (1.3 I), attended initially by his servant who sings and serves him a superhuman-sized cup of alcohol that no woman, not even the goddess Athirat, is supposed to see. At the end of the feast, Baal eyes his girls.

Anat comes into the story with the description of her savage battle against enemies (1.3 II). She may be fighting on Baal's behalf on the terrestrial level, while Baal fights against cosmic Sea. By contrast, she attacks human warriors; she is knee-deep gleaning in blood and gore (cf. Lam. 1:15; Joel 4:13 [Eng. 3:13]; Rev. 14:14–20; 19:15; cf. secular examples in Judg. 8:1–2; 20:43–46; Jer. 49:9; Obad. 5). She attaches hands and heads to her waist as trophies; still she is unsatisfied. She takes human captives to her palace, where she sets up tables and chairs, evidently for a feast; then she is satisfied perhaps with her captives as the main course. The cannibalistic feast here is a divine counterpart to the biblical notion of the "ban" or "devoted things" (*ḥerem*) in warfare (e.g., Josh. 7:1); the corresponding Ugaritic term for the "ban" is applied to Anat's battling in 1.13.2–7 (see below). Vestiges of this bloody, divine warfare appear in Yahweh's battle against human enemies (see Isa. 34:5–7; 49:25–26; 63:1–6; see also Deut. 32:41–42; Pss. 58:10; 68:23; Ezek. 39:19).

In the second major part of the Baal Cycle (1.3 III–1.4 VII), Baal seeks to have a palace built in his honor as the pantheon's new king. The process is stalled by his need to gain El's permission for the construction project. *KTU* 1.3 III–V centers on Baal's effort to secure permission first through intercession attempted by his sister, Anat. It relates Baal's summons to Anat to his holy mountain (cf. Exod. 15:17), and her subsequent efforts to obtain El's permission for Baal's palace. Baal then commissions Kothar to make a number of valuable furnishings (1.3 VI + 1.8–1.4 I) in order to induce Athirat to go to El on Baal's behalf (1.4 II–III). This she does with great success (1.4 IV–V). With El's permission granted, the building of the palace proceeds, culminating in its inauguration by a great feast celebrated by a gathering of deities (1.4 VI). Baal then goes on a victory tour leading to the final addition to the palace, his window, from which he utters his theophanous, thunderous voice (1.4 VII; cf. the divine "voice" in Ps. 29). Baal is now recognized as divine king in heaven and on earth.

Figure 4.5. Baal with thunderbolt

The third major section of the Baal Cycle (1.4 VIII–1.6) begins when Baal wishes to extend his kingship to the underworld and its lord, the god Death. Baal's initial communication with Death results in Death's rebuke of Baal (1.4 VIII–1.5 I). In this speech, Death mentions Baal's earlier defeat of enemies, known from the Bible as Leviathan and the seven-headed dragon (cf. Job 3:8; 7:12; 41:1; Ps. 74:14; Isa. 27:1). Baal's decision to assert his kingship over the underworld proves foolhardy, as his efforts result in his descent to the underworld (1.5 II–VI). After learning the news of his death, Anat and El follow proper mourning and burial ritual (1.5 VI–1.6 I). Afterward two lesser gods try unsuccessfully to display their physical qualifications for kingship (1.6 I). These failures signal the reason why Baal is king: no other god can measure up, thus anticipating his return. Thanks to Anat's destruction of Death (1.6 II), Baal returns to life (1.6 III–IV), though he remains unable to defeat Death (1.6 V). With El's intervention, Baal is able to retain his rule (1.6 VI). This conflict recalls biblical passages celebrating divine victory over death (see Isa. 25:8, echoed in Rev. 21:4, the context of which in vv. 1–4 offers a parallel to all three of the major episodes of the Baal Cycle; note also Ps. 49:15 and Jer. 9:20 [Eng. 9:21]). The Baal Cycle presents a view of divine kingship that offers prosperity and well-being on the divine, human, and natural levels, despite destructive forces in the universe; this fragile kingship of Baal's stands under threat and needs help from a variety of deities. The cycle offered a vision of kingship for a small though prosperous city-state, often standing in the shadow of great powers, the Egyptians and the Hittites.

Kirta (*KTU* 1.14–1.16)[66]

At the outset, Kirta loses his wife and children (1.14 I), as suggested by his name (*krt, "to cut") and much like the figure of Job in Job 1–2. Kirta laments to his patron-god El that he needs an heir (cf. Absalom's lack of an heir in 2 Sam. 18:18). In a dream vision (1.14 I), El asks him what he wants (cf. Solomon's dream in 1 Kings 3:5–15), and the god instructs him to go on a military march to besiege the city of Udm (1.14 II–III). Kirta follows El's directions virtually to the letter (1.14 III), apart from a stop at the sanctuary of Athirat of Tyre and Sidon, when the king offers a vow to the goddess in exchange for her help. After completing his march and siege (1.14 IV–V), Kirta gains the object of his quest, the daughter of the king of Udm. Kirta is thus able to reestablish his royal family, celebrated at a wedding feast attended by several deities and blessed by El (1.15 I–III).

After the feast, Athirat remembers Kirta's unpaid vow, evidently the cause of his sickly condition (1.15 IV–VI; cf. the illness of Hezekiah in 2 Kings 20//Isa. 38). When his son and daughter learn of the serious illness, they come to him in lamentation (1.16 I–II). His dutiful daughter asks if the king is a son of El and can die. Here the paradox of kingship captures both the ideal that the dynasty and its king last forever and the reality that every king is ultimately mortal. The king's illness is not only a political problem; it also leads to agricultural infertility (1.16 III). The crisis induces the divine council to meet (1.16 IV), where El invites the gods to expel the illness (1.16 V). When none answers the call, El creates an "expeller" who flies to Kirta's palace and dispels the illness.

The third challenge to Kirta's kingship involves his son's rebellion (1.16 VI; cf. Absalom's rebellion against David in 2 Sam. 15–20). Kirta's son claims that during his illness the king has ignored his royal responsibility to adjudicate the cases of the widow, the poor, and the orphan. In the story's closing lines, Kirta utters curses against his son. In sum, the story of Kirta relates three paradigmatic challenges to kingship: the need for an heir, illness, and rebellion. Aided by El, Kirta is able to overcome these challenges.

Aqhat (*KTU* 1.17–1.19)[67]

The story opens with the patriarch Danil (cf. Daniel in Ezek. 14:14, 20; 28:3, from whom Daniel of the biblical book of Daniel apparently takes his name;

---

66. See Parker, *Pre-Biblical Narrative Tradition*, 145–216. Note also the older but important study of H. L. Ginsberg, *The Legend of King Keret: A Canaanite Epic of the Bronze Age*, BASORSup 2–3 (New Haven: American Schools of Oriental Research, 1946).
67. See Parker, *Pre-Biblical Narrative Tradition*, 99–144. Book-length works include Kenneth T. Aitken, *The Aqhat Narrative: A Study in the Narrative Structure and Composition of an Ugaritic Tale* (Manchester: University of Manchester, 1990); Chloe Sun, *The Ethics of*

cf. *Jubilees* 4:20). Danil laments that he has no son to perform traditional filial duties (1.17 I). Moved to compassion, Baal takes Danil's case to El, who blesses Danil (1.17 II). Divine help then arrives in the form of the Kotharatu, goddesses who aid in conception. The illegible columns (1.17 III–IV) perhaps relate the birth and youth of the new son, for when the story resumes (1.17 V), Danil is hearing the cases of the widow and the orphan, and he receives the craftsman-god, Kothar, who gives him a bow and arrows. Danil gives these weapons to his son, Aqhat, and commands him to offer the first of his hunt to the temple. While Anat feasts, evidently at her temple (1.17 VI), she sees Aqhat and his bow. She asks for the weapons, perhaps expecting the weapons as a votive gift to her or perhaps because of divine covetousness or a sense of divine entitlement. She offers silver and gold in exchange; he suggests that she have Kothar make her own weapons. She then offers Aqhat eternal life; he refuses, claiming the offer is a lie; death is the fate of all mortals. Here he evidently oversteps in suggesting that hunting is not for women, as it is certainly for Anat (see *KTU* 1.114). Anat laughs at him and threatens him. She travels to El, whom she threatens with violence; El tells her that she can do whatever is in her heart (1.18 I). After two lost columns (1.18 II–III), Anat informs her warrior, Ytpn, how the two of them will execute Aqhat (1.18 IV). Anat flies among a flock of raptors and releases Ytpn, who strikes Aqhat dead. She then weeps for the deceased Aqhat.

A drought ensues, and Danil notes the failing vegetation. Raptors circle above, and Pughat, Danil's daughter and Aqhat's sister, weeps, joining her father in lamentation. He expresses the lack of precipitation: "no dew, no rain, no upsurging of the deeps, no good voice of Baal" (commonly compared with 2 Sam. 1:21). Together father and daughter go to the fields to see their desiccated vegetation, when the news of Aqhat's death arrives (1.19 II). On hearing the report, Danil expresses the wish that the bird that feasted on his son's corpse would give it up (1.19 III). Upon recovering the body, he buries it and proceeds to curse the place where the lethal attack has occurred. Danil returns home in order to lament his son for seven years accompanied by weepers (1.19 IV). Afterward he dismisses them and offers a meal for the gods. At this point, Pughat obtains her father's blessing to avenge her brother's death.

Violence in the Story of Aqhat (Piscataway, NJ: Gorgias Press, 2008); David P. Wright, *Ritual in Narrative: The Dynamics of Feasting, Mourning, and Retaliation Rites in the Ugaritic Tale of Aqhat* (Winona Lake, IN: Eisenbrauns, 2001); and the controversial work of Baruch Margalit, *The Ugaritic Poem of Aqht*, BZAW 182 (Berlin: de Gruyter, 1989). See also Michael Patrick O'Connor, "The Human Characters' Names in the Ugaritic Poems: Onomastic Eccentricity in Bronze-Age Semitic and the Name Daniel in Particular," in *Biblical Hebrew in Its Northwest Semitic Setting: Typological and Historical Perspectives*, ed. Steven E. Fassberg and Avi Hurvitz (Jerusalem: Magnes, 2006), 269–83.

She cleans herself and puts on "a hero's outfit" under her "woman's outfit." She goes to Ytpn's military camp, where he greets her and invites her to drink. The story breaks off, leading to speculation that a fourth tablet would have described how Pughat succeeded and avenged her brother's death by killing Ytpn (cf. Jael's assassination of Sisera in Judg. 4–5 and Judith's killing of Holofernes in Jdt. 13).

Rituals often entailing interactions with deities predominate in the family story of Aqhat. The story's opening highlights the proper roles of the son, and the closing stresses the proper role of the daughter as well as the rituals undertaken by the father. Yet this is a family story of warriors, as the mother appears only briefly; its world focuses on the patriarch and his two children, all three presented as heroes. The older hero had become a model elder while the younger figure fails to complete his transition into adulthood. The two figures reflect the successful and unsuccessful sides of life for warriors; the daughter in her victory is the traditional exception in the warrior role.

The Rephaim Texts (*KTU* 1.20–1.22)[68]

These rather fragmentary texts might belong to some sort of sequel to the story of Aqhat since they mention Danil and they are taken up with the *rp'um*, deceased warrior heroes of old (named also in the royal funerary text, 1.161, discussed below; see also the Rephaim in Isa. 14:9; 1 Sam. 28). They relate an invitation to the *rp'um* to attend an elaborate feast. The *rp'um* travel on chariots to reach the threshing floor, where they are to be feted. They are also invited to a temple or palace, apparently by the god El. There in the heights of Lebanon they enjoy a magnificent banquet.

KTU 1: *Rituals and Related Texts* (KTU *1.27–1.176)*[69]

The sacrificial cult of Ugarit presents the king as the principal ritual actor, along with priests (*khnm*, the same term as in Hebrew) as well as "holy ones" (see also 4.752). The sacrificial cult is lunar in its overall calendrical reckoning.

---

68. See Wayne T. Pitard, "A New Edition of the 'Râpi'Ëma' Texts: *KTU* 1.20–22," *BASOR* 285 (1992): 33–77; and Dennis Pardee, "Nouvelle étude épigraphique et littéraire des textes fragmentaires en langue ougaritique dits « Les Rephaïm » (*CTA* 20–22)," *Or* 80 (2011): 1–65. Note also William J. Horwitz, "The Significance of the Rephaim: *rm.aby.btk.rpim*," *JNSL* 12 (1979): 37–43.

69. For the ritual texts, see Dennis Pardee, *Les textes rituels*, 2 vols., RSO 12 (Paris: Éditions Recherche sur les Civilisations, 2000). For a convenient presentation of many ritual texts, see Pardee, *Ritual and Cult*. See also Gregorio del Olmo Lete, *Canaanite Religion according to the Liturgical Texts of Ugarit* (Bethesda, MD: CDL Press, 1999); and David M. Clemens, *Sources for Ugaritic Ritual and Sacrifice*, vol. 1, *Ugaritic and Ugarit Akkadian Texts*, AOAT 284/1 (Münster: Ugarit-Verlag, 2001).

One ritual (1.41/1.87) includes offerings for the beginning of fall corresponding to the Israelite fall New Year and Festival of Booths or Tabernacles. In one section there are to be dwellings of branches where sacrifices are offered to a deity. A single-day royal offering (1.115) includes the instruction that "a woman/women may eat of it." This additional notation, otherwise unknown, would suggest that women did not generally partake in eating ritual offerings. Another ritual (1.162) includes an offering of a shield (cf. the dedication of Saul's weapons in Astarte's temple in 1 Sam. 31:10). Three texts focus on a royal ritual of seeing or contemplation (1.90, 1.164, 1.168), perhaps parallel to the biblical idea of "seeing" God in a sanctuary context (e.g., Pss. 11:7; 17:15; 42:3 [Eng. 42:2]; 63:2).

The rituals include one (1.40) concerned with uprightness, the adjudication of sin, and national unity, offered on behalf of the oppressed, the impoverished, and foreigners. A number of Ugaritic terms correspond to biblical names for offerings: "peace offering" (the same term as the biblical sacrifice of "well-being," as in Lev. 3:1); "burnt offering" (Lev. 1:3); and "elevation offering" (Num. 8:11–15, 21; 18:11, etc.); these texts also use the general term for "sacrifice" found in Hebrew. One ritual addresses the problem of sin (1.40), which is a regular concern in the biblical material; unlike the biblical ritual texts, the Ugaritic rituals do not refer to expiation or cleansing (see, however, atonement mentioned along with sin in the Ugaritic letter 2.72). Unlike biblical ritual, the Ugaritic texts lack references to the blood and fat of sacrifices, as well as incense (which, however, does appear in the story of King Kirta). As in the Bible, there is no sacrifice of wild animals, dogs, or pigs. There is no clear reference to child sacrifice at Ugarit. The requirements for bodily purity are similar in the biblical and Ugaritic rituals. There is no ritual of a "fertility cult" as understood by earlier generations of scholars. One text (1.132) may possibly allude to "sacred marriage," but no sexual relations are actually mentioned. The Ugaritic rituals mention garments to be worn by priests or deities or both; priestly garments are well known in the Bible, garments for deities less so (cf. "weaving for Asherah" in 2 Kings 23:7; and see also the listing of material for deities in *KTU* 4.182). As in ritual texts in the Bible, prayers are relatively rare in the ritual texts of Ugarit (see 1.119 and perhaps 1.127). The deity lists (1.65, 1.74, 1.102, 1.148) are apparently tied to the sacrificial cult, as they order names of deities as found in ritual texts. Typically the number of deities listed comes to about 33. These are evidently the main deities, as the total number of deities mentioned in rituals and related texts tallies to 234, with 178 specifically named as recipients of offerings.

A funerary ritual (1.161), set in poetic lines, summons two deceased kings of Ugarit as well as the ancient heroes of old, the *rp'um* (biblical Rephaim), known also from literary texts. Whereas the Ugaritic monarchy identifies with this ancient tradition, the Bible views them as the dead in general (Ps. 88:11 [Eng. 88:10]; Prov. 2:18; 9:18) or as ancient heroic figures in the land (e.g., Gen. 14:5; Deut. 2:10–11); in the latter case, the biblical texts show an association of Rephaim traditions with the prior inhabitants and a corresponding disassociation from Israelites.[70] One of the ancient heroes named in this text (*KTU* 1.161) is consulted in another text for healing (1.124). A third text (1.113) lists the dead kings of Ugarit labeled as "divine" (cf. Ps. 45:7 [Eng. 45:6]) on one side, and on the other side describes music played, apparently for the kings.

Descriptive rituals include ritual slaughter of animals in a rural context outside the city of Ugarit (*KTU* 1.79, 1.80; cf. Judg. 6:19–24; 13:19). Royal rituals in the "sown" are indicated by the ritual instructions in *KTU* 1.23 and by a listing of wine in 4.149.14–16.[71] Divination texts include practice texts, such as liver models (1.141–1.145, 1.155), a lung model report (1.127), a liver omen (1.155), dream omens (1.86), and an astrological report (1.78) and lunar omens (1.163), as well as manuals for omens derived from a reading of the physical features of malformed animal and human fetuses (1.103 + 1.145, 1.140).[72] Medical literature includes texts for the care of horses, also known as hippiatric texts (1.71, 1.72, 1.85, 1.97).[73] *KTU* 1.82, 1.100, and 1.107 are incantations against snakebites (cf. the healing from snakebites through the bronze serpent Nehushtan in Num. 21:8–9 and 2 Kings 18:4). *KTU* 9.435 (= RS 92.2014) is to protect against snakes and scorpions and also to ward off verbal attacks from enemies and sorcerers (cf. "sorcerer" in the list of proscribed specialists in Deut. 18:10–11). In this text, sorcerers are described as making sound with their mouths with the same term (**ghr*) used for the figure of Elisha producing mouth-to-mouth resuscitation (2 Kings 4:34–35; cf. 1 Kings 18:42).[74] On this score, the Ugaritic texts provide hints of the older background to magic in early Israel.

KTU 1.169 is to relieve impotence. *KTU* 1.114 provides a prescription for the effects of excessive intoxication, following a mythic narrative about the drunkenness of the god El. The mythic setting includes the *marzēaḥ*, known from other

---

70. Mark S. Smith, "Recent Study of Israelite Religion in Light of the Ugaritic Texts," in Younger, *Ugarit at Seventy-Five*, 18–19.
71. Smith, *Sacrificial Rituals and Myths*, esp. 5, 39, 121, and 164.
72. Pardee, "Ugaritic Science," 223–54.
73. Chaim Cohen, "The Ugaritic Hippiatric Texts: Revised Composite Text, Translation and Commentary," *UF* 28 (1996): 105–53 (with prior bibliography), and in *COS* 1.361–62; and Pardee, "Ugaritic Science," 229–30, 244–48.
74. Smith, "Recent Study of Israelite Religion," 12–13. Note also the important but difficult text RS 92.2016, published by André Caquot and Anne-Sophie Dalix, "Un texte mythic-magique," in *Études ougaritiques*, vol. 1, *Travaux 1985–1995*, ed. Marguerite Yon and Daniel Arnaud, RSO 14 (Paris: Éditions Recherche sur les Civilisations, 2001), 393–405.

Ugaritic texts (e.g., a contract for this institution in *KTU* 3.9) and two biblical texts (Jer. 16:5; Amos 6:7). Attested as early as Ebla and as late as the Greco-Roman period, it seems to have been an upper-class male social institution.[75]

KTU 2: Letters[76]

The eighty-three letters in *KTU* 2 record communication between a number of figures, most notably members of the royal family and other elite figures (such as "the chief of the priests" in 2.4, cf. biblical "high priest"), as well as their servants. The letters commonly name the sender and the recipient. They regularly request blessing of deities upon the recipient (see the list of deities from various places in 2.42). Where the sender is inferior in social status, he is said to bow down before the recipient. Many letters relate a further message from the sender before closing with a request to the recipient to send information as to her or his situation. Occasionally, the communication is international in nature (2.20, 2.39; see also 2.72). They mention threats from enemies (2.33), battle (2.82), foreigners (2.30), the "sin" of an Amorite princess married to the Ugaritic king (2.72), and apparently plague (2.10). Letters also report a variety of domestic matters involving communication and shipping (2.37). The letters contain expressions familiar from the Bible, such as the ideas of a force (plague?) being "very strong like death" (2.10; cf. Song 8:6) or the "face" of the king "shining" on the sender (2.13 and 2.16; cf. the priestly blessing of Num. 6:24–26).

KTU 3: Legal Texts[77]

The ten texts labeled as legal texts (*KTU* 3) are broad in scope. They include a record of disbursement of tribute from the Ugaritic king to his Hittite overlord (3.1); royal grants to individuals (3.2, 3.5; cf. RS 94.2965); records of guarantee made on behalf of one or more individuals (*KTU* 3.3, 3.7, 3.8);

---

75. See the surveys of John L. McLaughlin, *The* marzēaḥ *in the Prophetic Literature: References and Allusions in the Light of Extra-Biblical Evidence*, VTSup 86 (Leiden: Brill, 2001); and Lorena Miralles Maciá, *Marzeaḥ y thíasos: Una institución en el Oriente Próximo Antiguo y el Mediterráneo*, 'Ilu. Revista de Ciencas de las Religiones. Annejo XX (Madrid: Universidad de Complutense, Madrid, 2007). Note also Pierre Bordreuil and Dennis Pardee, "Le papyrus de marzeaḥ," *Sem* 38 (1990): 49–68, plates 7–9.

76. For an introduction, see John Huehnergard, "The Akkadian Letters," in *HUS*, 375–89. For translations, see Jesús-Luis Cunchillos, "Correspondance," in *Textes ougaritiques*, vol. 2, *Textes religieux, rituels, correspondance*, ed. A. Caquot, J.-M. de Tarragon, and J.-L. Cunchillos, LAPO 14 (Paris: Cerf, 1989), 239–421, 446–78; Pardee, in *COS* 3.87–116; and Robert Hawley, "Textes épistolaires ougaritiques: Préliminaires à une nouvelle étude," in Calvet and Yon, *Ougarit*, 195–225.

77. Dennis Pardee, with the collaboration of Robert Hawley, "Les textes juridiques en langue ougaritique," in *Trois millénaires de formulaires juridiques*, ed. Sophie Démare-Lafont and André Lemaire (Geneva: Droz, 2010), 125–40.

a record of "ransom" (*pdy*; *KTU* 3.4; cf. biblical redemption expressed by the verb **pdh*, used for the Israelites' redemption from Egypt in Deut. 7:8; 13:6 [Eng. 13:5]; cf. also the redemption of the firstborn in Exod. 13:13–15); a legal contract protecting the head of the *marzēaḥ* (noted above) from any potential legal claims made against him by any of its members (*KTU* 3.9); and a legal list of funds owed (3.10).

Legal matters are mentioned in other genres. One letter (2.19) may be mentioned, as it records the manumission of a royal slave (cf. Exod. 21:2–6). Two administrative texts (*KTU* 4.172 and 4.266) record purchases of licenses to handle payments of customs duty, while two others (4.336 and 4.338) record the purchase of a trading concession (see also the letter 2.36; cf. the problem of trade and transit recalled in Judg. 5:6).

KTU 4: Administrative (Economic) Texts[78]

The nearly eight hundred texts in this category mostly list places, property and equipment, personnel and occupations, foodstuffs, metals, and other goods. These records show a network of economic relations largely revolving around the royal administration.[79] Some of these include those on duty or eating at the "table" (4.13; cf. eating at the king's table in 1 Sam. 20:29, 34; 2 Sam. 9:11, 13; 19:29 [Eng. 19:28]; 1 Kings 2:7; etc.); singers, shipbuilders, and archers (*KTU* 4.35; see also 4.66); ship crews (4.40) and ships (4.81); ploughmen (4.65); weapons (4.169); wine sold to shrines and individuals (4.219); and silver given for "the cup of the gods" (4.280). Cultic matters play relatively little role in these texts (see 4.728, found in the House of the Hurrian Priest). Some lists (e.g., 4.102) show families consisting of fathers, their wives, and their children, as well as young men and women, probably retainers or servants. One text (4.360) lists various family lineages as three heads of households, with their patriarchal lord called "Bull" (cf. the title of the god El, "Bull El my Father," and the divine horns in Num. 23:22; 24:8, noted above), along with his four daughters. Many of the administrative texts show the operation of the monarchy, with its lists of officials (e.g., *KTU* 4.29, 4.36, 4.38, 4.47, 4.99; cf. 2 Sam. 8:15–18; 20:23–26) and numerous administrative lists (cf. Solomon's administration in 1 Kings 4).[80]

---

78. For these texts, see Kevin M. McGeough, *Ugaritic Economic Tablets: Text, Translation and Notes*, ed. Mark S. Smith (Leuven: Peeters, 2010).

79. See Kevin M. McGeough, *Exchange Relationships at Ugarit* (Leuven: Peeters, 2007); and J. David Schloen, *The House of the Father as Fact and Symbol: Patrimonialism in Ugarit and the Ancient Near East* (Winona Lake, IN: Eisenbrauns, 2001).

80. Dennis Pardee, "Background to the Bible: Ugarit," in *Ebla to Damascus: Art and Archaeology of Ancient Syria* (Washington, DC: Smithsonian Institute, 1985), 258.

KTU 5: *Scribal Exercises*[81]

These texts include partial or complete abecedaries: *KTU* 5.4, 5.5, 5.6, 5.8, 5.12, 5.13, 5.16, 5.17, 5.19–5.21, 5.24 = 8.1, 5.25, and RS 92.2440. One text (5.14) lists the Ugaritic letters, each one followed by an Akkadian syllabic sign (thought by some to stand for the name of the Ugaritic letter). Other scribal exercises show the writing out of consonants (5.2, 5.15), lists of words beginning with the same letter of the alphabet (5.1) or written with the same word (5.3), and personal names (5.7, 5.18, 5.22). Two texts show the scribal practice of correspondence (5.10, 5.11), while a third (5.9) combines a practice letter with an abecedary. In addition to the texts in this section of *KTU*, other texts are thought by *KTU*'s editors to be scribal exercises (e.g., 1.9, 1.13, 1.67, 1.69, 1.71, 1.73, 1.133).

KTU 6: *Inscriptions on Axes, Stelae, Seals, Ivories, Etc.*

The seventy-six texts in this category are mostly short inscriptions made on items, some indicating ownership. Some axes (6.6–6.10) are inscribed with the title "chief of the priests" (see above). Two standing stelae (6.13, 6.14) bearing inscriptions with the name of Dagan mark them as mortuary offerings on behalf of their donor (noted above; cf. Lev. 26:30; Ezek. 43:7). One inscription appears on the lion head on a rhyton dedicated to the god Resheph (*KTU* 6.62).

As this overview suggests, the texts show an astonishing array of information pertinent to the Bible. As Ugaritic and Akkadian texts discovered at Ras Shamra continue to be published, further insights into the Bible and ancient Israel will no doubt come to light, calling for additional syntheses of the larger literary and cultural contexts.

For Further Reading

Bordreuil, Pierre, and Dennis Pardee. *A Manual of Ugaritic*. Winona Lake, IN: Eisenbrauns, 2009.

Soldt, Wilfred van. "Ugarit: A Second Millennium Kingdom on the Mediterranean Coast." In *CANE* 2:1255–66.

---

81. See Robert Hawley, "Apprendre à écrire à Ougarit: Une typologie des abécédaires," in Roche, *D'Ougarit à Jérusalem*, 215–32. For a consideration of Ugaritic as a vernacular expressive of local political concerns, see Seth L. Sanders, "What Was the Alphabet For? The Rise of Written Vernaculars and the Making of Israelite National Literature," *Maarav* 11, no. 1 (2004): 25–56, esp. 45–47; and Sanders, *The Invention of Hebrew* (Urbana: University of Illinois Press, 2009), 50–61. See the response to Sanders's article by Alan Millard, "Alphabetic Writing, Cuneiform and Linear, Reconsidered," *Maarav* 14, no. 2 (2007): 83–94.

Watson, Wilfred G. E., and Nicholas Wyatt, eds. *Handbook of Ugaritic Studies*. HdO I/39. Leiden: Brill, 1999.

Yon, Marguerite. *The City of Ugarit at Tell Ras Shamra*. Winona Lake, IN: Eisenbrauns, 2006.

Yon, Marguerite, Dennis Pardee, and Pierre Bordreuil. "Ugarit." In *ABD* 6:695–721.

5

Egypt and the Egyptians

Joel M. LeMon

Up and down the Nile, ancient Egyptians venerated many different gods as the sole, unique creator god: Atum, Ptah, Khonsu, Neith, and Khnum, along with a number of others. Egypt was created by one god and it was created by many.[1] Such a claim sounds peculiar today, yet it reveals a fundamental aspect of ancient Egyptian religion and society: the constant, generative tension between unity and multiplicity. This tension between "the one and the many" in the divine realm had clear reflexes in the geography and political history of ancient Egypt.

One defining geographical feature, the river Nile, united ancient Egypt along seven hundred miles from Aswan to the Mediterranean and across five thousand years from the Naqada period to the Roman period. In this sense, the great river can be rightly called Egypt's sole, unique creator. Its unrelenting northward track to the Mediterranean, its yearly rhythms of inundation,

---

1. The question of the plurality and unity of Egyptian deities features prominently in most discussions of ancient Egyptian religion. For a classic exposition, see Erich Hornung, *Conceptions of God in Ancient Egypt: The One and the Many*, trans. John Baines (Ithaca, NY: Cornell University Press, 1982). See also Jan Assmann, *The Search for God in Ancient Egypt*, trans. David Lorton (Ithaca, NY: Cornell University Press, 2001).

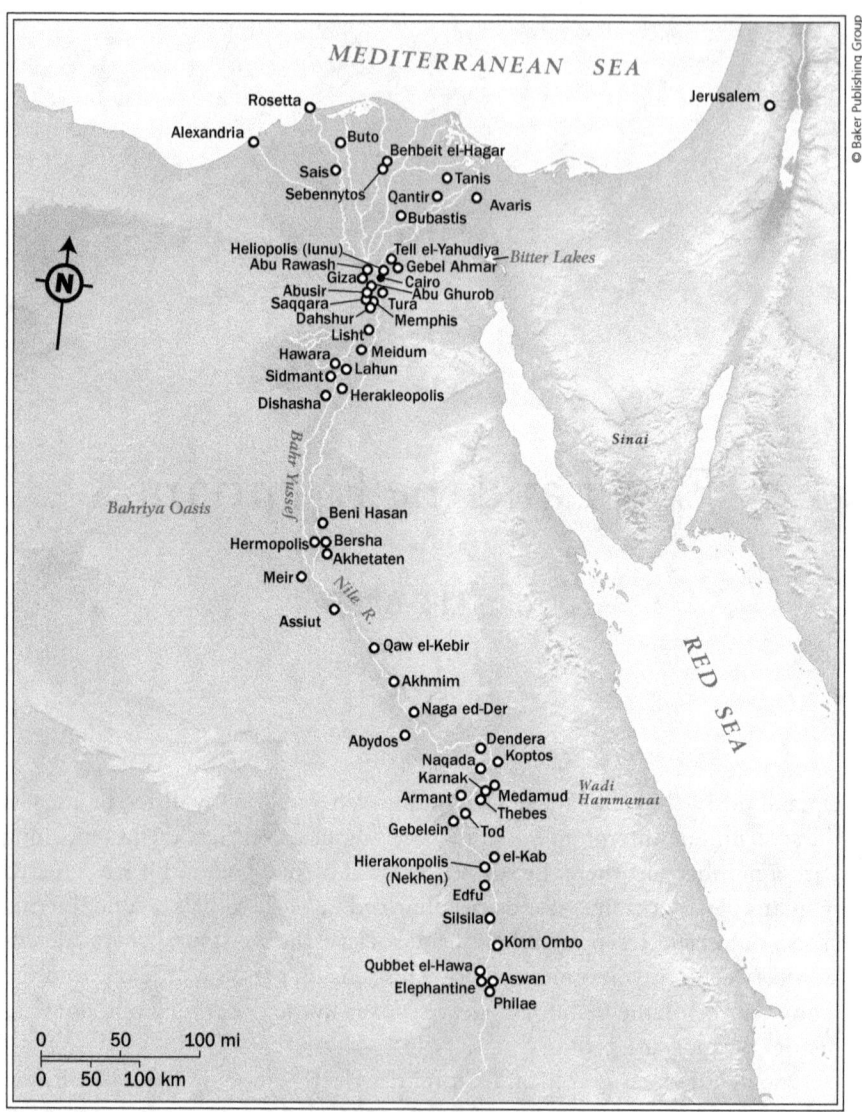

Figure 5.1. Egypt

its life-giving silt all gave birth to Egypt. Yet the flow of the Nile also divided Egypt into its constituent parts. The region known as Upper Egypt includes the upstream reaches of the Nile north of the first cataract near Aswan. Lower Egypt is the downstream region of the Delta in the north (as confusing as that may sound at first). A third section, Middle Egypt, describes the territory along the river between Assiut and Memphis. These divisions are not simply modern constructs but have been operative during many periods of Egyptian history.

The political history of ancient Egypt also reflects the same fundamental tension between unity and multiplicity that is so striking in Egyptian religion. In fact, Egyptian history can be characterized as the constant struggle to unite the three regions of the Nile and to manage the conflicts between the various cities along its banks. Scholars divide ancient Egyptian history into the following periods, which correspond to the centralization of political power or lack thereof.[2]

Old Kingdom	2686–2160
First Intermediate period	2160–2055
Middle Kingdom	2055–1650
Second Intermediate period	1650–1550
New Kingdom	1550–1069
Third Intermediate period	1069–664
Late period	664–332

The Old, Middle, and New Kingdoms saw consolidated governments arise and endure. During the First, Second, and Third Intermediate periods, local governance generally exerted a stronger influence than any one force. In the Late period, strong, centralized Egyptian authority occasionally emerged. However, during this time the foreign empires of Assyria, Babylonia, and Persia often overwhelmed the attempts of the Egyptian kings to maintain and extend their control.

Given that "ancient Egypt" encompasses so much territory across such a vast period of time, one would expect significant diversity of social and cultural structures. The Egyptians were certainly a diverse lot, as we shall see below. Yet, a sense of a cultural distinctiveness obtained throughout ancient Egypt, readily apparent in its art, architecture, and great religious and political institutions. In spite of its tensions and internal contradictions, the *idea* of Egypt as a land, culture, and people is a remarkably coherent one, forged in part from the common experiences of those living along the banks of the Nile.[3]

---

2. Throughout this chapter, all dates are BCE and are approximate prior to 664. In the main, they follow those presented in *The Oxford History of Ancient Egypt*, ed. Ian Shaw (Oxford: Oxford University Press, 2000). Egyptian chronology is fraught with problems and debates. In short, the so-called High and Low Chronologies stem from uncertainty as to whether certain astronomical observations were made in Memphis (High Chronology) or Thebes (Low Chronology) during the Eighteenth to Twentieth Dynasties.

3. On the general cultural homogeneity of ancient Egypt and its relationship to the static climate and geography of Egypt during the New Kingdom and Third Intermediate period, see

This chapter presents the critical events that shaped Egyptian political history from the New Kingdom through the Late period (1550–332), as these are the periods most pertinent to Israelite literature and history (Late Bronze Age to the Persian period correspondingly). Indeed, this summary makes frequent reference to Egypt's ongoing relationship to the Levant. The chapter concludes by sampling some of the ways that Egyptian culture influenced that of Israel and Judah.

1. Egyptian Political History with a View to the Levant (ca. 1550–332)

The Early New Kingdom (Eighteenth Dynasty, 1550–1295)

The New Kingdom began with the defeat and expulsion of the Hyksos, a group of West Semitic people who had settled in the northern Delta during the Middle Kingdom. These foreigners had gradually risen to power over the course of a century (1650–1550, the Fifteenth Dynasty) and controlled the Delta from their heavily fortified capital city of Avaris (Tell ed-Dab'a). In Thebes, the cultural and economic center of Upper Egypt, the kings of the latter Seventeenth Dynasty saw the presence of the Hyksos as an acute threat to their authority. Furthermore, the Theban kings perceived foreign rule as an affront to the intrinsic order of Egypt, since foreigners were understood to be the forces of chaos personified. This reign of chaos in the Delta was an abomination to Thebes.[4] As the Second Intermediate period drew to a close, Thebes made increasingly frequent attempts to unseat the Hyksos and restore Egypt to a united, orderly state. When Pharaoh Ahmose (1550–1525) finally conquered Avaris in 1530, he was not content until he had pushed the Hyksos back across the Sinai Peninsula and into Palestine.

Ahmose's singular victory over the hated Hyksos had significant political, cultural, and religious implications throughout Egypt and the larger Near East. Some have argued that a Canaanite version of the story of the rise and fall of the Hyksos dynasty ultimately appeared in the Hebrew Bible in the accounts of the migration of Hebrew-speaking people into and out of

---

David O'Connor, "New Kingdom and Third Intermediate Period, 1552–664 BC," in *Ancient Egypt: A Social History*, ed. B. G. Trigger, Barry J. Kemp, David O'Connor, and Alan B. Lloyd (Cambridge: Cambridge University Press, 1993), 183–278, esp. 188–190.

4. The term "Hyksos" comes from the Egyptian phrase meaning "rulers of foreign countries." Thus, it is more accurate to refer to the Hyksos as the rulers of Lower Egypt rather than its inhabitants. That larger group included both West Semitic peoples and ethnic Egyptians during this period. Note, too, that establishing the "ethnicity" of the inhabitants is only possible on the basis of the names preserved during this time. See Donald B. Redford, *Egypt, Canaan, and Israel in Ancient Times* (Princeton: Princeton University Press, 1992), 98–129.

Egypt.[5] Others maintain that the Hyksos period of Egyptian history suggests, at most, that a movement by Israelites into Egypt sometime during the second millennium "was neither impossible nor unlikely, and would have been compatible with the tenor of the times."[6] Though it is impossible to prove this correspondence with the biblical exodus traditions, the period of the Hyksos dynasty is nevertheless extraordinarily important for understanding the development of the relationship between Egypt and the Levant. The Hyksos, through their capital at Avaris, maintained extensive cultural and economic interactions with West Semitic peoples. Later Egyptian rulers exploited these well-established trading relationships with southern Palestine and tried to expand economic ties farther north and east throughout the Levant. Indeed, for the rest of the New Kingdom, Egyptian interaction with the Levant was frequent and complex, marked by both military conflict and economic interdependence.

With the expulsion of the Hyksos, Ahmose accomplished the religious and political reunification of Egypt after a century of division. In doing so, he inaugurated the New Kingdom and established his Eighteenth Dynasty (1550–1295) as the longest and most prosperous in Egyptian history. Ahmose's success against the Hyksos was matched by similar success in gold-laden Nubia. Through the military ventures of Ahmose and his son Amenhotep I (1525–1504), who succeeded him as king, the Nubians came firmly under Egyptian control and would remain so for generations. With unrivaled supremacy along the Nile, the early Eighteenth Dynasty kings had positioned Egypt to accrue great power and wealth over the ensuing centuries.

Most of the subsequent kings of the Eighteenth Dynasty continued the policies of imperial expansion through extensive use of military force.[7] Thutmose I (1504–1492) began his reign by consolidating Egyptian control beyond the third cataract of the Nile. To illustrate his unshakable foothold in Nubia, he sailed back to Thebes from a campaign with a defeated Nubian bowman hanging upside down from the bow of his ship. Such displays effectively conveyed his dominion. Encouraged by his successes and in search of still more, Thutmose sought to extend Egyptian influence into the Levant beyond that which existed during the Hyksos period. Though he probably met stiff

---

5. See Donald B. Redford, "An Egyptological Perspective on the Exodus Narrative," in *Egypt, Israel, Sinai: Archaeological and Historical Relationships in the Biblical Period*, ed. Anson Rainey (Tel Aviv: Tel Aviv University Press, 1987), 137–61.

6. Carol A. Redmount, "Bitter Lives: Israel in and out of Egypt," in *The Oxford History of the Biblical World*, ed. Michael D. Coogan (New York: Oxford University Press, 1998), 58–89, esp. 74.

7. The notable exception was the female pharaoh Hatshepsut (1473–1458), who increased the wealth of Egypt largely through establishing new trading connections with Punt.

resistance from Mittani, a powerful kingdom of northern Mesopotamia whose sphere of influence extended well into Syria, Thutmose ventured as far as Niy on the Orontes River, where he claimed to have hunted elephants. Had he achieved decisive victory over Mittani, he would certainly have celebrated it in his royal annals. The conquest of Syrian elephants was as much as he could claim. Though these campaigns brought less convincing results than those in Nubia, Thutmose's presence in Syria laid the foundation for the activities of later Eighteenth Dynasty kings in the region.

After a coregency with his aunt and stepmother, Hatshepsut (1473–1458), Thutmose III (1479–1425) assumed an even more adventuresome posture toward Syria-Palestine than that of his grandfather, Thutmose I.[8] His seventeen years of campaigning in the Levant achieved unprecedented victories. By conquering critically important fortified cities—especially Megiddo, through a chariot battle and an extended siege—he secured lucrative trade routes through Syria and brought extraordinary wealth into Egypt.

Amenhotep II (1427–1400), famous for his athleticism, continued his father's Levantine victories. Two campaigns in Syria-Palestine brought back huge amounts of plunder as well as gruesome evidence of Egyptian military supremacy. The royal barge returning up the Nile from the first campaign carried the corpses of seven defeated chiefs hanging upside down for display in Thebes. One of these unfortunate chiefs traveled as far as Napata. This dead Asiatic in Nubia vividly represented the power and reach of the Egyptian Empire.

The spoils of war and the steady flow of tribute from the peripheral regions of the empire further enriched the Eighteenth Dynasty kings. Thutmose IV (1400–1390) and especially Amenhotep III (1390–1352) sought to secure Egypt's position of power within the Near East more often through treaties and diplomatic marriages than through military campaigns. Though Egyptian princesses were not sent abroad in these diplomatic marriages, the Egyptian kings increasingly married foreign princesses.

Steadily, the perception of foreigners was changing. Ahmose had portrayed the Hyksos as the forces of chaos personified and thus to be destroyed at all costs. Yet in the latter Eighteenth Dynasty, foreigners were increasingly seen as exotic and benign, though certainly inferior and largely under the control of the king. As for the great rulers of Assyria, Babylonia, Hatti, and Mittani, written materials suggest that—at least for the purposes of diplomacy—they

---

8. Relatively little information is preserved from the reign of Thutmose II (1492–1479), son of Thutmose I and father of Thutmose III. There is, however, evidence to suggest that he continued to exploit Nubia militarily.

belonged to the same noble family of the Egyptian king. With their relationships reinforced by diplomatic marriages, the great kings were the brothers of the pharaoh.

Most of the rulers of Syria-Palestine did not enjoy this sort of relationship, however. They were instead firmly under Egyptian control by the time of the long reign of Amenhotep III, which marked the apogee of Egyptian prosperity and influence in the Near East. In fact, it is difficult to determine the exact nature of the Egyptian "influence" at this time. There is not enough evidence to know precisely how Egypt segmented the provinces of the Levant. It is also unclear whether Egypt maintained a permanent military presence there, and if so, precisely where and for how long. More certain, however, is that the children of Syro-Palestinian nobles were often forcibly deported to Egypt, acculturated, and then returned to their regions to reinforce the empire's control of the city-states from within. Despite the uncertainty about the precise means of influence, Egyptian artifacts appear virtually everywhere throughout Syria-Palestine during this period. Moreover, the prevalence of Egyptian-style (or Egyptianizing) artifacts produced by local craftsmen from Ugarit to southern Palestine reflects a widespread emulation of Egyptian religion, culture, and art.

The famous cache of 350 cuneiform letters found at el-Amarna, ancient Akhetaten, also attests the dynamics of the relationship between the smaller city-states and Egypt during the latter years of Amenhotep III and the early reign of his son and successor Amenhotep IV / Akhenaten (1352–1336). In addition to correspondence between Egypt and the great powers of Assyria, Babylonia, Hatti, and Mittani, the cache contains numerous letters from the vassal-kings of Syria-Palestine. The tenor of these letters is markedly different from the correspondence with the great powers. Seeking various forms of economic and military assistance, the vassal-kings were doing their best to exploit the pharaoh's power to their own advantage. Invariably, they did so by assuming a posture of utter humility before and dependence on Egypt.

These letters also witness the remarkable religious and political changes that were underway in Egypt. The minor kings employed a common series of epithets in their opening addresses: "To the king, my lord, my sun."[9] This latter title, particularly, reflects a steadily increasing solar aspect of the royal cult and ideology that began with Amenhotep II and reached a climax during the reign of Amenhotep IV / Akhenaten. Throughout the Eighteenth Dynasty,

---

9. See William Moran, *The Amarna Letters* (Baltimore: Johns Hopkins University Press, 2000), 283 (EA 213), 298 (EA 244), 308 (EA 255). The honorifics in the address might also include "my god" and/or "the Sun of the sky."

Figure 5.3. Akhenaten, Nefertiti, and three of their daughters beneath the rays of the Aten (Eighteenth Dynasty, 1352–1336; ÄM 14145)

the main Theban god, Amun, had been increasingly associated with the sun god Re and eventually became known in a combined form as the chief god Amun-Re. During the reign of Amenhotep III, the cults of more and more deities likewise became solarized.

Soon after the installation of Amenhotep IV, the young king replaced the traditional sun god Amun-Re with an iconographically distinct form. The Aten, an orb with hands/rays extending downward from it in all directions, became the official representation of the sun god (fig. 5.3). Corresponding to the shift in religious terminology and iconography, Amenhotep IV disassociated himself and his administration from Amun and Thebes. He took on the name Akhenaten, meaning "he who acts effectively on behalf of the Aten," and founded a new city in Middle Egypt, Akhetaten, meaning "Horizon of the Aten"—that is, the place where the Aten manifests itself (in the form of the king).

Not long after his move to Akhetaten, Akhenaten outlawed the veneration of Amun and all other gods. At the same time, he associated himself even more intimately with the sun god. With the sole god Aten as his father, Akhenaten was the direct manifestation of the sun and the world's only mediator of the divine presence. Thus the religious reorganization of the so-called Amarna period corresponds to profound political centralization. The king himself replaced the panoply of Egyptian gods, so all political and religious power stemmed from and accrued to Akhenaten. As a religious and political system, Atenism was obsessed with unity, light, and power. It completely denied the reality of disunity, darkness, and death. And so the religious reforms of Akhenaten were destined to fail.

They began to fail, appropriately enough, with the death of Akhenaten. Uncertainties abound in this period, especially with regard to the identity of the succeeding king Neferneferuaten (1338–1336), who may have been Akhenaten's wife Nefertiti ruling as king under a new name. In any case, it is clear that the boy-king Tutankhaten (1336–1327), Akhenaten's son, initiated a move back toward the old political and religious establishment. Since this program began so early in Tutankhaten's reign, we should assume that his military general and coregent Horemheb guided and motivated all the activities. The coregents systematically reversed the reform program of Akhenaten by reestablishing the cults, dismantling the temples to the Aten, and moving the power of the state back to the traditional cities of Memphis and Thebes in Lower and Upper Egypt, respectively. A complete repudiation of the Amarna episode was underway. Accordingly, Tutankhaten (The Living Image of the Aten) changed his name to Tutankhamun (The Living Image of Amun).

While Egypt was undergoing these radical internal changes, the geopolitical situation did not remain static. When the great empire of Mittani fell to the Hittites (ca. 1370), Egypt's relationship to the Near East began to change dramatically. The shift in power in northern Mesopotamia and Anatolia rendered worthless the long-standing treaties that Egypt had enjoyed with Mittani. Immediately, the Hittite king Suppiluliuma I (ca. 1400) began to exert pressure on northern Syria-Palestine, which had been within Egypt's sphere of influence for most of the Eighteenth Dynasty.

In this context, Tutankhamun's untimely and mysterious death had far-reaching implications. A move was underway in the royal court to secure a peace with the Hittites by offering Tutankhamun's widow as the wife of a Hittite prince, who would then become king of Egypt. This version of diplomatic marriage had no precedent; Egyptian princes had married foreign princesses, but never vice versa. The political implications of Egypt in the role of the submissive partner in a sexual relationship would likely have struck many within the court as completely unacceptable. On a more practical level, the prospect of such a marriage threatened members of the king's court who aspired to the throne themselves. While the betrothed Hittite prince was en route to Egypt to assume the role of king, someone murdered him. We do not know who the killer was, in part because so many had a strong motive. In any case, from that point forward the Hittites and the Egyptians assumed a posture of war, with the contested region of Syria-Palestine as their primary battleground.

General Horemheb clearly had the most to gain from the death of Tutankhamun and the Hittite prince, for he had officially secured rights to the throne if Tutankhamun died without an heir. He indeed became king after a short reign by Ay (1327–1323), an aged courtier of Tutankhamun and his father Akhenaten. Horemheb's twenty-seven-year reign (1323–1295) continued the program of reversing the religious and political innovations of the Amarna period. In addition to maintaining an ambitious building program, the general-turned-king succeeded in holding off the Hittites from expanding their sphere of influence beyond Qadesh in northern Syria-Palestine.

The Ramesside Period (Nineteenth and Twentieth Dynasties, 1295–1069)

Horemheb had not come to power through dynastic succession. And he, in turn, did not cede the throne to his offspring. Instead, he chose one of his trusted generals from Sile, a frontier town on the eastern side of the Delta. General Paramessu became known as Ramesses I at his enthronement. Though his rule lasted only one year (1295–1294), perhaps because of his advanced age, he reestablished the tradition of hereditary kingship. Since so many of his successors would assume his name, the remainder of the New Kingdom, the Nineteenth and Twentieth Dynasties, would be known as the Ramesside period.

Ramesses's son Seti I (1294–1279) began a massive restoration program with the goal of bringing the great religious, political, and cultural institutions back from their Amarna nadir. This work also had a clear military component. While fighting off Libyan tribes invading from the west, Seti I continued to seize the material resources of Nubia to the south. He looked to complement these successes by extending Egyptian hegemony farther north and east in Syria-Palestine. Seti I wrested control of Qadesh from the Hittites, though only temporarily. When it reverted to Hittite control during the reign of his son Ramesses II, the stage was set for one of the most famous battles in Egyptian history.

A coregency of uncertain duration affirmed the hereditary succession from Seti I to Ramesses II (1279–1213). Within a few years of assuming kingship, Ramesses II sought to address his father's unfinished business with the Hittites in northern Syria. In the famous battle of Qadesh (1274), the Hittite king Muwatalli repulsed Ramesses II's attempts to take the city, with the battle ending in stalemate. In fact, a failure of intelligence left Ramesses II perilously exposed to an overwhelming Hittite force. It was only the arrival of a division of reinforcements at a pivotal moment in the battle that saved him from certain defeat. After Ramesses II's retreat, as was common in ancient royal annals, the event was cast in the best possible light. In the official Egyptian account, Ramesses portrayed the battle as a victory in which the god Amun personally intervened to save him and rout the Hittites.

While the Egyptians never actually routed the Hittites, by the mid-thirteenth century the Assyrians under Shalmaneser I were threatening to do just that. In 1259, the Hittites and Egyptians perceived that joining forces was their best chance for confronting the emerging Assyrian Empire. Ramesses II confirmed the peace accord by taking a Hittite princess as a bride, a particularly fitting gesture since the Egyptian-Hittite animosity had begun with the murder of the betrothed Hittite prince three-quarters of a century earlier. This new peace accord brought security and renewed prosperity to Egypt thanks to extensive trade that moved through Syria-Palestine as well as through multiple seaports along the Mediterranean basin.

Ramesses II also revived the city of Avaris, the erstwhile Hyksos capital, renaming it Piramesse (the house of Ramesses). Situated as it was in the eastern Delta, this flourishing city had many West Semitic inhabitants, and a great degree of religious syncretism obtained there, with cultic sites for foreign deities like Baal, Resheph, and Astarte, among others. This is the region to be identified with the toponym Rameses/Raamses in the Hebrew Bible (Gen. 47:11; Exod. 1:11; 12:37; Num. 33:3, 5).

Ramesses's spectacularly long reign—his twelve eldest sons predeceased him—gave way to that of his son Merenptah (1213–1203). Though Merenptah was not a young man, like his father and grandfather before him he felt compelled to prove his royal mettle with campaigns in Syria-Palestine. His victory stela from his fifth year commemorates his subduing the Palestinian cities of Ashekelon, Gezer, and Yenoam (see fig. 4.2, p. 142). Israel, too, appears in his list of conquests, though not as a city but rather as a group of people.

Merenptah was also forced to deal with the outcomes of the most significant human migration in the ancient Mediterranean world. An economic and environmental catastrophe in the latter twelfth century BCE (the details of which are not fully known) forced the so-called Sea Peoples to leave their homes in the Aegean and Anatolia and settle around the Mediterranean basin, including Syria-Palestine and northern Africa. The Sea Peoples who had landed in northern Africa then joined forces with the Libyans to attack the western

Delta of the Nile with the aim of settling it for themselves. Merenptah met them in battle and defeated the army of invaders, who also brought along their families and possessions. After his triumph, Merenptah chose to resettle the survivors in the Delta. And so, in a manner of speaking, the Libyans and Sea Peoples actually achieved their ultimate goal. The migration came through defeat rather than victory.

There was no clear succession following Merenptah's death in 1203. While the historical record is murky, it seems that his sons Seti II (1200–1194) and Amenmessu (1203–1200?) may have contended with each other for control of the entire Nile, ruling in Lower and Upper Egypt, respectively. Seti outlasted Amenmessu, for Seti's only son Saptah finally ascended the throne (1194–1188). Born of a Syrian concubine and suffering from a crippling disease, the boy-king relied on his stepmother, Tausret, and her extraordinarily powerful courtier Bay, who was a Syrian. This outlander likely continued to play a pivotal role in the governance of Egypt during the brief rule of Tausret (1188–1186), who, like Hatshepsut (and possibly Nefertiti) before her, served as a female king.

Tausret's death resulted in a general diffusion of political power. Some evidence suggests that Bay usurped the throne and initiated a series of religious and political changes that reflected his West Semitic heritage. Sethnakht, who ultimately deposed him, interpreted Bay's actions as corrupt, alien, and contrary to the order on which Egyptian society had been built. Indeed, Sethnakht's actions against the foreigner Bay recall those of Ahmose against the Hyksos at the dawn of the Eighteenth Dynasty. Like Ahmose, Sethnakht founded a dynasty, the Twentieth and last of the New Kingdom. His short reign (1186–1184) gave way to the long and tumultuous rule of Ramesses III (1184–1153).

Ramesses III faced numerous internal and external threats. He led two campaigns against the Libyans, who had continued to insinuate themselves deeper into the western Delta since the time of Merenptah. An even more serious threat came from the Sea Peoples, who had changed the face of the Mediterranean world through a series of astounding military feats along the coast of Anatolia and Syria-Palestine. Now they directly threatened Egypt, a final prize. However, Ramesses III had prepared well for their attack. He repelled marine forces in the Delta and, through the use of strong fortifications, held off a land offensive in southern Palestine. In doing so he preserved the integrity of the Egyptian homeland and virtually all of the Egyptian provinces in Syria-Palestine. His memorials to the victory include some of the most visually stunning reliefs in all of ancient Egyptian art (fig. 5.4). During his relatively long reign, he also weathered numerous internal conflicts, surviving

Figure 5.4. Relief from the Mortuary Temple of Ramesses III at Medinet Habu (plate 39 from *Medinet Habu*, vol. 1, *Earlier Historical Records of Ramses III*)

an assassination attempt from within his own court and an extended work stoppage by his craftsmen at Deir el-Medina, who were responsible for most of the monumental construction in Upper Egypt.

For all the apparent success of Ramesses III, the manifold difficulties of his reign presaged the end of a united monarchy along the course of the Nile. In the remaining eighty-four years of the Twentieth Dynasty, eight kings, all named Ramesses, rose to the throne. Each Ramesses inherited a weaker kingship than his predecessor had enjoyed. This decline in royal power corresponded to a rise in priestly power, as the high priest of Amun at Thebes emerged as a political rival to the king. Rather than serving as the king's appointed representative in the cult, the high priesthood became a hereditary office and operated largely independently. A system of patronage emanating from Thebes extended the high priest's control ever wider as the Twentieth Dynasty wore on. By the time of Ramesses XI (1099–1069), the king's sphere of influence was limited almost exclusively to the Delta.

During this time, the Egyptian viceroy of Nubia named Panehsy descended the Nile. By means of a military coup, he attempted to seize Thebes from the control of the priesthood of Amun and especially the high priest Amenhotep. Panehsy's move on Thebes, though ultimately unsuccessful, resulted in a complicated period of civil war marked by shifting loyalties among the priests of Amun, the king, and military generals, who operated with increasing independence and often in outright defiance of the king.[10]

---

10. Jacobus van Dijk suggests that the decline in the power of the unified government at the end of the New Kingdom is ultimately the result of the Amarna episode. Akhenaten had so drastically overreached his religious and political authority that the office of kingship never fully recovered ("The Amarna Period and Later New Kingdom [c. 1352–1069 BC]," in Shaw, *Oxford History of Ancient Egypt*, 303–7).

The weakening of the office of the kingship in the latter Twentieth Dynasty corresponded to a decline in Egypt's sphere of influence, especially in Syria-Palestine but also in Nubia. After the fall of the Hittites to the Sea Peoples, Egypt no longer had the resources to secure its trade routes through Syria-Palestine. Egypt was left without a strong trading partner in Anatolia and northern Mesopotamia and without the resources to enforce the fealty of local Syro-Palestinian leaders through the threat of violence. Thus, Syria-Palestine ceased to have any active Egyptian control. Instead, the region reverted to the authority of local independent states. Thus, the decline of a strong, centralized government in Egypt directly promoted the rise of small kingdoms in the Levant, including Israel and Judah.

The Third Intermediate Period (Twenty-First to Twenty-Fifth Dynasties, 1069–664)

At the time of the death of Ramesses XI (ca. 1069), the forces of decentralization were so strong that Egypt essentially had two separately functioning administrations. Though Smendes (1069–1043), the founder of the Twenty-First Dynasty, was ostensibly the ruler of the entire country, his power actually extended only to the region surrounding the major Lower Egyptian cities of Memphis and Tanis. Herihor, the chief general of the army, had assumed the office of high priest of Amun, and with it the control of Upper and Middle Egypt. There a hereditary succession of southern rulers continued to style themselves as chief generals and high priests.[11] These leaders utilized strong fortresses in Middle Egypt to limit the practical extent of royal power in their realm.

The ascension of Psusennes I (1031–991), the son of a Theban commander, brought a period of relative cooperation between Tanis and Thebes. Psusennes I's brother ruled in the south as chief general and high priest, so the centralization of power was only partially accomplished. Without strong and unified control over the entire Nile Valley, Egypt was not in a position to exert its political influence eastward into the Levant. This region was left to its own affairs, free of significant Egyptian intervention. As for Nubia, Egypt—or, more accurately, Thebes—exerted a much more significant influence, but only because of the legacy of extensive military and economic activities that had occurred there throughout the New Kingdom.

Libyan presence in the North had been steadily increasing since the decline of the New Kingdom. An ethnically Libyan population consisted of

---

11. Though General Herihor initiated this form of government in the south, most of the subsequent rulers belonged to the family of his colleague, Piankh.

mercenaries in the Egyptian army, resettled Libyans that had been defeated in earlier confrontations, and bands of Libyan nomadic pastoralists. As this population became more established within the Delta, the Libyans went through a process of Egyptian acculturation. The process muted many aspects of their unique identity, such that little distinctively Libyan material culture has been discovered in the Delta during the Third Intermediate period. That said, their cultural assimilation was by no means complete. The clear differences in artistic styles between Upper and Lower Egypt during this time (e.g., coffin decoration) suggest that while Libyans adopted Egyptian practices and conventions, they also modified them in important ways. Moreover, the persistence of Libyan names in the Lower Egyptian onomasticon reveals that the old ethnic identifications were not completely erased or forgotten.

The growing political power of the Libyans in the north can be seen most clearly in the ascension of the first ethnically Libyan king, Osorkon the Elder (984–978). The son of a powerful chief of the Meshwesh tribe, Osorkon kept his Libyan name upon assuming the throne, a fact that betrays his heritage and suggests some level of resistance to full assimilation into Egyptian culture. Though his reign was relatively brief and he was not succeeded by his son, this kingship foreshadowed the extended Libyan rule that was soon to come. As the Twenty-First Dynasty came to a close with the reigns of Siamun (978–959) and Psusennes II (959–945),[12] Libyans were gaining ever more predominance in the Delta.[13]

Sheshonq I (945–924), the ruler of the Libyan tribe Meshwesh and a nephew of Osorkon the Elder, initiated an extended period of Libyan control from the Twenty-Second to the Twenty-Fourth Dynasties. These pharaohs kept their Libyan names, though their iconography and artistic programs follow closely the traditions of the ethnically Egyptian kings. The kings therefore maintained a delicate balance between ethnic particularity and assimilation for the purposes of promoting their own authority. The rise of Sheshonq I epitomizes this endeavor. Sheshonq I came to power peacefully through his family ties to the former king Osorkon the Elder and his marriage to the daughter of Psusennes II.

He sought to build on the relatively positive relationship between North and South that had been forged during the reign of Psusennes I (when

12. Psusennes II was in fact the brother of Psusennes I and former chief general and high priest of Thebes.
13. The presence of Libyan names, titles, and genealogies provides evidence of the composition of the population of the Delta, as do the distinctively northern scribal practices and linguistics that diverged markedly from the south. See John Taylor, "Third Intermediate Period (1069–664 BC)," in Shaw, *Oxford History of Ancient Egypt*, 339.

Psusennes I's brother Psusennes II was serving in Thebes). Installing a chief general and high priest in Thebes from his own family, Sheshonq I intended to reunite the Delta with Upper Egypt, a connection that had served the monarchy so well in the golden age of the New Kingdom. With the kingdom under a relatively stable and united government once again, Sheshonq I turned his attentions to the Levant, as had so many of his New Kingdom predecessors. The Hebrew Bible suggests that Sheshonq I gave asylum to Jeroboam, the future king of Israel, just prior to the secession of the northern tribes under his leadership (1 Kings 11:40). It is reasonable to suppose that Sheshonq I was indeed trying to use Jeroboam to destabilize and exploit the kingdom in Jerusalem. After the division of the united Israelite monarchy (the kingdom of Israel in the north and Judah in the south), the Bible describes Sheshonq I's successful campaign against Jerusalem, among other southern Palestinian cities (ca. 925), at which time he removed "the treasures of the house of the LORD and the treasures of the king's house; he took everything" (1 Kings 14:25–26; cf. 2 Chron. 12:2–9).[14] The era of expansion into Syria-Palestine under Libyan rule was thus politically significant for the region but brief, ending with the immediate death of Sheshonq I upon his return from the Levantine campaign.

The forces of decentralization along the Nile were again on the rise, splitting Egypt into mostly independent city-states under the control of local elites. During the New Kingdom, local rulers had served as royal appointees and continued to serve only at the discretion of the king. Though Sheshonq I tried to reestablish this practice, it was ultimately unsuccessful. Local offices reverted to hereditary succession once again after his death. In fact, these leaders often claimed the trappings of kingship for themselves. Thus, many of the "kings" of the late Twenty-Second to early Twenty-Fifth Dynasties (ca. 925–715) ruled at the same time in different parts of Egypt. John Taylor argues that this sort of rule was most natural for a government dominated by Libyans:

> The political picture that emerges as the Third Intermediate Period progresses is one of a federation of semi-autonomous rulers, nominally subject (and often related) to an overlord-king. This is perhaps an example of the impact of the Libyan presence on the administration, since such a system can be seen as consistent with the patterns of rule in a semi-nomadic society such as theirs.[15]

---

14. The king's name appears as Shishak in the biblical material. In this way, the Deuteronomistic Historian explains the impoverishment of Judah in the wake of the death of the great king Solomon, Rehoboam's father.

15. Taylor, "Third Intermediate Period," 338.

Whatever its ultimate cause, the dissolution of a strong central government created an opening for another longtime enemy of Egypt.

After two centuries of minimal Egyptian oversight, the Nubians finally seized an opportunity to exert their influence over their former overlords to the north. The Nubian (Kushite) ruler Piy (747–716) descended the Nile to take Upper Egypt city by city (ca. 730). Eventually, Piy reached Memphis, besieged it, and succeeded in bringing the Delta under his control. This action essentially inverted the relationship between Nubia and Egypt that had persisted throughout most of history. The rulers of the Egyptian provinces became vassals of Nubia, sending tribute to the Kushite capital at Napata near Gebel Barkal. When the Twenty-Fourth Dynasty kings (727–715) briefly resisted Nubian rule in the Delta, Piy's successor Shabaqo (716–702) brought his military down the Nile again. His crushing victory (ca. 716) quieted any further attempts to challenge Shabaqo's ultimate superiority. As a sign of his strength in the midst of the once-hostile Delta, Shabaqo established his Egyptian residence in Memphis.

The adoption of Memphis also played an important role in the Nubians' appropriation of Egyptian religion and aesthetics, especially those of the Middle Kingdom. The Nubians had a long history of emulating Egyptian forms, and the Twenty-Fifth Dynasty Nubian kings (747–656) did so to provide a sense of strength and continuity with the great pharaohs of Egypt's past. They were attempting to revive the idea of a powerful, united Egypt in a time when the traditional understandings of Egyptian identity and unity were in flux. Egypt was, after all, now ruled by a foreign power, a situation that was anathema in earlier epochs. The Nubians also faced the challenge of a general dissolution of political power. Thanks to the precedent of the Libyan pharaohs of the Twenty-Second to Twenty-Fourth Dynasties, local control of cities largely remained with various princes. The Nubians thus clung to a conservative ideology to mitigate the double threat of foreign rule and political fragmentation.

The Nubian kings also sought to expand their power from the Delta into the Levant, like so many strong kings in Egypt's past. This desire for a larger sphere of influence brought them directly into conflict with the Assyrians, who also had designs on the southern Levant. King Taharqo (690–664), in an attempt to support King Hezekiah of Judah (see 2 Kings 19:9; Isa. 37:9), met the forces of Sennacherib in the Levant in 701. Taharqo was totally outmatched. Yet, as a result of the encounter, the Assyrians saw Egypt as a threat that must be addressed. Thus, the Assyrians launched campaigns directly into Egyptian territory. The second of these, led by Esarhaddon, succeeded in capturing Memphis and forced a temporary retreat of Taharqo up the Nile

Figure 5.5. Bronze statuette of Taharqo (690–664)

(ca. 671). Taharqo continued to fight further up the Nile but ultimately lost Thebes to Assurbanipal in 663.

After the Assyrians conquered Egypt, they sought loyal vassals, new local leaders who would resist any further attempt by the Nubians to expand their reach through Egypt and into the Levant. In the Delta, the Assyrians threw their support behind a certain Nekau (672–664) as the ruler of Sais. They took his son, Psamtek I, to Nineveh in order to acculturate him and prepare him for a life of devoted service to Assyria. The Egyptians themselves had employed this same practice in Syria-Palestine during the New Kingdom. However, not long after Psamtek I's return to Egypt, the Assyrians saw their plans backfire. In fact, Psamtek I's return inaugurated Egypt's last great period of united rule. Psamtek I took the throne after his father Nekau was killed in 664 by Taharqo's son, Tanutamani (664–656). Through extensive use of Greek mercenaries, Psamtek I neutralized the Nubian threat to Upper Egypt by 656 and founded the Twenty-Sixth Dynasty (664–525), known as the Saite dynasty after its capital city, Sais (Sa el-Hagar), in the western Delta.

The Late Period (Twenty-Sixth to Thirty-First Dynasties, 664–332)

After dealing with the threat of Nubia and empowered by a united Egypt, Psamtek I (664–610) bucked all Assyrian attempts at oversight of Egypt. He could do so because of the critical overextension of the Assyrian Empire, which did not have the resources to maintain its grip over its vast domain from the Tigris to the Nile. Psamtek I's success was also the result of his extensive use of mercenaries, especially Greeks and Carians (from southwestern Anatolia).

Psamtek I's ability to unite Egypt stemmed in part from his installation of his daughter in Thebes as "god's wife of Amun." With his loyal daughter in a position comparable to a high-priestly office, Psamtek I secured and maintained constant authority over the length of Egypt. As we have seen, political unification invariably spurred military expansionism. Psamtek I's efforts in the Levant resulted in securing the Levantine coast, including the important city of Ashdod, thirty miles west of Jerusalem.

The Saite period saw a dizzying number of shifts in geopolitical alliances. Psamtek I began his reign as an Assyrian protégé. Yet he soon rejected his Assyrian suzerain once his own authority was established along the Nile. But as Assyria began to face increasing threats from their aggressive neighbors in Persia and southern Mesopotamia, the Assyrians sought assistance from the suddenly resurgent Egypt under Psamtek I. Assyria and Egypt thus entered into a treaty, with the result that Egyptians began fighting alongside the Assyrians against the Babylonians deep within Mesopotamia (ca. 616).

Psamtek I's son Nekau II (610–595) hoped to extend Egypt's military might throughout the Levant and beyond. On his way to assisting Assyria in Harran (northern Syria), Nekau II defeated the Judahite king Josiah at Megiddo in 609 (2 Kings 23:29; 2 Chron. 35:20–24) and enforced vassal status on Judah. Borrowing a page from Assyrian imperial practices, Nekau II chose a new loyal king for Judah, Eliakim/Jehoiakim, and imposed a heavy tribute payment (2 Kings 23:31–35; 2 Chron. 36:1–4).[16] Yet Nekau II's control of Judah and the Levant lasted only four years. After suffering a debilitating loss to the Babylonians in 605 at Carchemish in northern Syria, Nekau II had to retreat from Palestine altogether and ceded it to the Babylonian sphere of influence.

The next king of the Saite dynasty, Psamtek II (595–589), temporarily reestablished an Egyptian foothold in Palestine, with devastating results for Judah under King Zedekiah. Zedekiah clung to some hope of rebelling against the Babylonians with an agreement with Psamtek II and his son Apries (589–570). The Babylonians, however, responded decisively, destroying Jerusalem in 587 and then pushing into Egypt itself in the 580s. After a defeat by the Babylonian king Nebuchadnezzar II, Apries was deposed by a general, Ahmose II (570–526), who had served in Nubia under Psamtek II. Ahmose II's long reign benefited from the weakening and contraction of the Babylonians, thanks to the rise of the Persian king Cyrus the Great. In another remarkable shift of allegiances, the Egyptians joined the Babylonians in an attempt to arrest the advance of Cyrus against the Babylonian Empire. When Cyrus took Babylon in

---

16. For a recent, detailed discussion of this period, see Bernd U. Schipper, "Egypt and the Kingdom of Judah under Josiah and Jehoiakim," *TA* 37 (2010): 200–229.

539, Egypt had to cast about again for an ally. Thus they forged a partnership with the Greeks, who were also resisting the Persians' relentless push westward.

Though Cyrus the Great died before he could conquer Egypt, his successor, Cambyses (530–522), did so in 525 and inaugurated the first Persian period, the Twenty-Seventh Dynasty (525–404). We cannot be sure to what extent Cambyses saw himself as assuming the mantle of traditional Egyptian kingship. What is clear is that the Achaemenid kings—Cambyses, Darius I, Xerxes I, Artaxerxes I, Darius II, and Artaxerxes II—saw some of the traditions of Egyptian kingship useful for exercising their authority, including monumental building campaigns. Under Persian rule, the government of Egypt took on a similar shape to the Twenty-Second to Twenty-Fourth Libyan Dynasties (945–715). A Persian bureaucrat oversaw the administration, but in accordance with their practices elsewhere, the Persians sought to preserve much of the power of local authorities and the autochthonous legal and religious traditions.

Despite this relatively permissive system of administration, revolts during the first Persian period led to a period of a solely Egyptian, unified government in 404–343. We have comparatively few internal historical sources to describe the events of this period, known as the Twenty-Eighth to Thirtieth Dynasties. Greek accounts suggest a time of tremendous upheaval. The typically short reigns of Egyptian kings beginning with Amyrtaios (404–399) confirm this idea. The Twenty-Eighth to Thirtieth Dynasty kings tried to assume the titles and trappings of Egyptian kingship, though the resources were limited and the memory of strong unified government was relatively dim. Thus, there was virtually no opportunity for expanding the Egyptian sphere of influence. Only through extensive use of mercenary forces were the kings able to hold off the Persian incursions.

The pressure from Persia increased greatly in the latter fourth century BCE as kings Artaxerxes II and Artaxerxes III tried to secure the western rim of the empire and meet the persistent threat of the Greeks. Persian military might eventually overwhelmed Egypt in 343 when Nectanebo II, the last native pharaoh (360–343), fell to Artaxerxes III Ochus (343–338) after a series of pitched land and sea battles. The despised Thirty-First Persian Dynasty (343–332) would not last long, however. Persia lost its grip almost immediately when Alexander arrived in Egypt uncontested in late 332. Alexander appealed directly to the long-standing tradition of the king as the lord of order and the unifier of Egypt, quickly assuming the titles of pharaoh and son of god. After just a year, Alexander left Egypt to continue his pursuit of the Persians. Though he would never return, his legacy was undeniable, both in the city that bore his name, Alexandria, and in the program of Hellenism that had followed all of his conquests. To be sure, at Alexandria and throughout the country, Egyptian Hellenism was marked by a mutual adaptation of Greek and Egyptian values. The distinctive form of Hellenism that emerged along the Nile testified to the endurance of the idea of Egypt as a complex but unified political, religious, and cultural entity.

2. Egypt and Israel

This brief historical outline has shown that the fortunes of Israel were inextricably linked to the political dramas constantly unfolding along the course of the Nile. As Egypt moved back and forth along the political spectrum between unity and diversity of power, the entire Near East felt the effects. When Egyptian political power was centralized, its leaders were invariably drawn toward military adventurism in the Levant. When power was decentralized, the Levant was left to its own devices. During these times, petty kingdoms and mighty empires fought among themselves to establish their authority.

The decline of centralized power in Egypt during the Third Intermediate period essentially provided the opportunity for the kingdom of Israel to come into existence. Egypt also played a role in the division of the kingdom into North and South as Sheshonq I encouraged Jeroboam's rebellion and then sacked Jerusalem in its weakened state. As the Third Intermediate period wore on, Israel and Judah found themselves in and out of alliances and vassal relationships with Egypt: Hezekiah sought assistance from Taharqo; Josiah opposed Nekau II; Zedekiah looked to Psamtek II for support. In virtually every instance, Israel and Judah suffered for their decisions about how to position themselves in relation to Egypt. Such is life in the shadow of empires.

The Old Testament raises many questions about the relationship between Egypt and Israel. It is difficult to overstate the importance of the biblical tradition of the exodus from Egypt, particularly in the Pentateuch. However, it is also difficult to establish the historicity of these events. Most Egyptologists contend that there is a complete lack of historical evidence to corroborate the accounts of an Israelite exodus from Egypt. Similarly, no Egyptian evidence points straightforwardly to the monumental figures of Joseph and Moses, characters who play such an important role in these narratives.[17] To be sure, Egyptian history reveals that numerous persons of West Semitic origin rose to

---

17. See Redford, *Egypt, Canaan, and Israel in Ancient Times*. Others emphasize the plausibility of the exodus event itself while acknowledging the lack of definitive proof; so James Hoffmeier, *Israel in Egypt: The Evidence for the Authenticity of the Exodus Tradition* (Oxford: Oxford University Press, 1999).

great power in Egypt (e.g., the Hyksos or Bay, the Syrian courtier of Tausret). Yet any connection to the particular figures in the Pentateuch remains elusive.

Accordingly, historians of ancient Israel have approached the exodus story with a great level of caution—indeed, suspicion. James Hoffmeier is right to point out that the Bible's status as an authoritative text for modern people of faith actually encourages some historians to be more suspicious of its claims than they might be under other circumstances.[18] With that point granted, one must admit that there remain significant and seemingly intractable problems for locating the Egyptian sojourn historically. And unfortunately, discussions about the historicity of the exodus often do little more than reinforce one's preconceptions about the Bible's historical credibility or lack thereof.

A word of caution is in order at this point. It is unwise and unhelpful to import modern expectations about the genre of "history" back to the biblical text. Biblical authors and editors worked from a very different set of expectations about the world, God's relationship to natural and societal events, and even the function and role of writing. Those ancient expectations rarely match those of modern history writers. The more one recognizes these differences, the better one will be equipped to adjudicate the "historical" claims that an ancient text makes. Thus, the most critical tool for exploring the historicity of the exodus account or any other biblical text is the recognition of the ancient genre(s) to which a text belongs. The modern reader should ask: What fundamental questions is this text seeking to address? And how has the writer chosen to address these questions? Is the text attempting to explain a situation in the writer's current context (an etiological narrative)? Is the text providing some real or ideal accounting of a particular king's reign (a royal annal)? Is the text a poetic work meant to stir its readers/hearers by employing exalted rhetoric? Or is the text some mixture of these or other well-established genres?

The historical survey above indicated a number of texts from 2 Kings that provide strong correspondences to Egyptian history. The authors of the book of 2 Kings made explicit use of sources to create a narrative accounting of the past in the mode of other ancient Near Eastern royal annals. Thus one can profitably compare these biblical texts with Egyptian royal annals. Doing so yields corroboration for some (but not all) of the biblical accounts of Israel's and Judah's relationship to Egypt. The exodus narratives, however, belong to a different genre, one that is more concerned with establishing the origins and, thus, the identity of a people and their unique relationship with God.

---

18. James K. Hoffmeier, "The Exodus and Wilderness Narratives," in *Ancient Israel's History: An Introduction to Issues and Sources*, ed. Bill T. Arnold and Richard S. Hess (Grand Rapids: Baker Academic, 2014), 48.

One should read such etiological narratives with a different set of expectations about the historicity of the events the text purports to describe. Put simply, when exploring the relationship between Israel and Egypt, one cannot take the claims of a biblical text simply at face value. Neither can one discount the historical value of a text just because it appears in the Old Testament. Careful attention to genre helps one decide how much historical credibility one can give to the claims of a text.

While fierce debates regarding the exact locations of biblical Pithom and Rameses or the most likely "pharaoh of the exodus" are not without some merit, there are many more promising and generative ways of exploring the interactions between Egypt and Israel. Using comparative analysis, scholars have identified numerous links between Egyptian and Israelite literature. With regard to the Joseph story, for example, scholars have identified remarkable similarities in the scene of the seduction of Joseph by Potiphar's wife and the Egyptian Tale of the Two Brothers. In both stories a handsome young man suffers a false accusation of abuse after he rebuffs the sexual advances of the wife of his master. Another classic example of a profitable comparison between Egyptian and Israelite literature comes through juxtaposing the Song of Songs to Egyptian love poetry.[19] While there is little evidence that the Song of Songs relies directly on the Egyptian love poetry, reading the two in tandem has yielded a better understanding of the various features of the genre of ancient "love songs." The similarities between the Instruction of Amenemope and Proverbs 22:17–24:22 provide some of the most telling evidence of the interaction of Israelite and Egyptian wisdom traditions. The passages from Proverbs almost certainly drew from the Egyptian wisdom text. In some places, in fact, it seems that the book of Proverbs simply gives a Hebrew translation of the Egyptian proverb. One should also note that Psalm 104 shares many striking features with the much earlier Great Hymn to the Aten from the Amarna period. Both present a supreme god in his solar aspect, creating and sustaining entire ecosystems that consist of plants, animals, and humans. In this case, the biblical text seems to represent a once- or twice-mediated version of the hymn because of the great span of time between the two works.

The specific correspondences between Egyptian and Hebrew texts are only part of the evidence of interaction between Egypt and Israel. The interaction of imagery presents a still more promising means of comparison. Levantine iconography exhibits a strong Egyptianizing tendency in many periods from the Late Bronze Age to the Persian period. Thousands of scarab-shaped stamp

---

19. See Michael V. Fox, *The Song of Songs and the Ancient Egyptian Love Songs* (Madison: University of Wisconsin Press, 1985).

Figure 5.6. Ivory plaque, Megiddo, 1250–1150 BCE (after Gordon Loud, *The Megiddo Ivories*)

seals from Levantine sites amply testify to the profound influence of Egyptian images.[20] One of the most complex and beautiful examples of local artists adopting and adapting Egyptian styles comes from Late Bronze Age Megiddo. The so-called Megiddo Ivory (ca. 1250–1150 BCE) presents a scene that is meant to be read from right to left (fig. 5.6). At right, the king is returning from a chariot battle with bound, nude (and thus humiliated) prisoners walking in front of him. The public display of conquered foreign peoples and the victorious king in his chariot all reflect standard Egyptian displays of royal power. In this ivory plaque, one can recall, for example, the chariot battles of Thutmose III at Megiddo and the public display of enemy bodies by Thutmose I and Amenhotep II in Thebes and Nubia. On the left side of the plaque, the king enjoys the benefits of his victory over his foreign enemies. He celebrates a royal feast with ministers and music. While the object exhibits a degree of local adaptation of styles, the Egyptian elements pervade the entire composite scene: the positioning of bodies, the weaponry, the throne, the luxury items, and the vegetation. The winged sun disk suspended over the chariot is another Egyptian symbol indicating the sun god's blessing and empowerment of the king in his military activities.

During Egypt's Third Intermediate period, when its sphere of influence did not consistently include the Levant, the kingdoms of Israel and Judah had extensive interaction with Phoenicians on the coast of the Mediterranean (see 1 Kings 5). Because of the Phoenicians' long-standing maritime trade relationships with Egypt, Phoenician art shows extensive emulation of Egyptian styles. Thus, Egyptian imagery also found its way into Israel and Judah via Phoenician intermediaries. One representative example of such imagery comes from Samaria, capital of the northern kingdom of Israel. In this ivory carving, the two Egyptian goddesses Isis and Nephthys spread out their wings in a gesture of protection to the *djed* pillar, a symbol of the god Osiris (fig. 5.7). It is not clear whether the image was produced by a Phoenician or Israelite

---

20. See Othmar Keel, *Corpus der Stempelsiegel-Amulette aus Palästina/Israel: Von den Anfängen bis zur Perserzeit*, OBO.SA (Göttingen: Vandenhoeck & Ruprecht, 2010–).

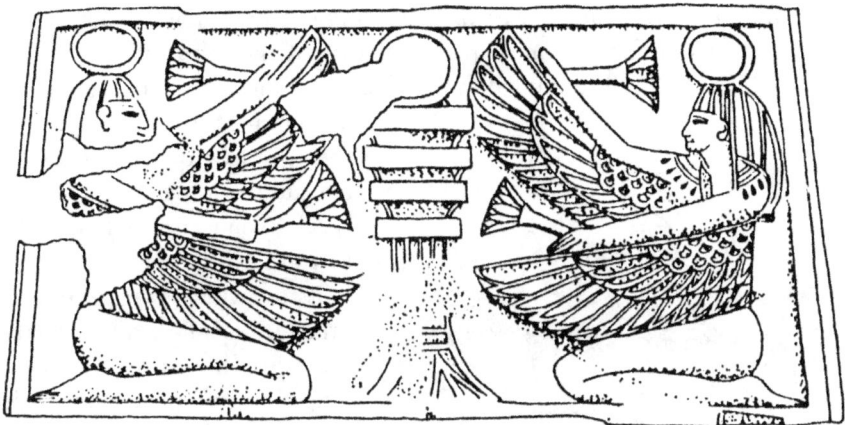

Figure 5.7. Ivory inlay of Isis and Nephthys flanking a djed pillar, Samaria, 9th–8th cent. BCE (after Othmar Keel and Christoph Uehlinger, *Gods, Goddesses, and Images of God in Ancient Israel*)

craftsman, but in either case the object shows the prevalence of Egyptian and Egyptianizing imagery well beyond the banks of the Nile.

Over the past thirty years, scholars have increasingly turned to exploring the complex interactions of imagery in the Levant as Egyptian hegemony variously extended and receded.[21] As we have seen, royal imagery was particularly important in ancient Egypt since so much of Egypt's history turned on the ability of strong centralized governments to unite the reaches of the Nile. As a result, there are numerous correspondences between the powerful imagery of kingship in Egypt and Israel. A sampling of just a few biblical texts points to the myriad ways that Egyptian imagery supplies the background for the development of Israelite notions of kingship.

In both art and text, Egyptian royal ideology consistently maintains that the king is the image and offspring of the deity. Psalm 2:7 presumes the same notions, portraying the king as a divine son at his coronation: "I will tell of the decree of the LORD: He said to me, 'You are my son; today I have begotten you.'" Psalm 110:1 also reflects an ideology of kingship that resonates with Egyptian imagery in its description of the king's dominance over his enemies: "The LORD says to my lord, 'Sit at my right hand until I make your enemies your footstool.'"

One can compare this literary imagery with a New Kingdom tomb painting in which King Amenhotep III displays numerous symbols of kingship

---

21. Othmar Keel has demonstrated an array of the correspondences between the literary imagery of the Old Testament and the pictorial imagery of ancient Egypt (among other Near Eastern cultures). See Othmar Keel, *The Symbolism of the Biblical World: Ancient Near Eastern Iconography and the Psalms*, trans. Timothy J. Hallet (Winona Lake, IN: Eisenbrauns, 1997).

(fig. 5.8). The crook and the *ankh*, the symbol of life, show his power and ability to sustain and promote the prosperity of the people under his dominion. The bull tail running down his leg also indicates his royal status by associating the king with one of the most fearsome beasts of the ancient world. And, finally, in a specific connection to Psalm 110, beneath Amenhotep III's feet is a footstool with the images of nine prostrate enemies, indicating the forces of chaos over which the king has triumphed. In fact, in Psalm 2 and Psalm 110 more broadly, one can discern the Egyptian idea of foreigners as the forces of chaos personified. Thus, in Egypt as in Israel, the king demonstrates his commitment to the divine ordering of the world by subduing these foes.

Figure 5.8. Tomb painting from Abd el-Qurna, during the reign of Thutmose IV, Theban Tomb 46, 1400–1390 (after Othmar Keel, *The Symbolism of the Biblical World: Ancient Near Eastern Iconography and the Book of Psalms*)

Othmar Keel and Christoph Uehlinger have suggested that the kings of Judah explicitly adopted the imagery of Egyptian kingship to affirm their own authority, especially during the time of Hezekiah. The systematic adoption of the symbols of Egyptian kingship also served to associate the Judean king more closely with the pharaoh Taharqo, to whom he was looking for support amidst the threats of Assyrian attack.[22] During this time, Egyptian imagery appears in a number of artifacts from the kingdom of Judah, including the famous *lmlk* seals that bear the image of various winged beings along with the Hebrew inscription *lmlk*, meaning "of the king" or "belonging to the king." The imagery on these seals clearly stands in the tradition of Egyptian royal iconography: the winged scarab beetle, the Horus falcon, or a winged solar disk (fig. 5.9). All of these images are linked with the Egyptian sun god, the divine sponsor of the king. In

---

22. Othmar Keel and Christoph Uehlinger, *Gods, Goddesses, and Images of God in Ancient Israel*, trans. Thomas H. Trapp (Minneapolis: Fortress, 1998), 265–81.

fact, these Egyptianizing images may be a representation of the king, or even, more provocatively, the divine sponsor of the king, Yahweh himself in a solar aspect.[23]

Whatever one makes of the Egyptianizing imagery on the *lmlk* seals, it is clear from all of this literary and iconographic evidence that the shadow of Egypt loomed large in the cultural consciousness and the symbolic systems of Israel and Judah. The pervasive spread of Egyptian imagery throughout the Levant attests not only the power of Egypt but also the compelling distinctiveness of its imagery. Even today, thousands of years after Egypt's golden age, many laypersons can identify an image as Egyptian at a simple glance. The distinctiveness of ancient Egypt has always endowed it with a certain mystique. Perhaps this compelling singularity of Egyptian culture contributed to the fact that the authors of the Hebrew Bible chose to portray Egypt as an archetypal foe. For Israel, no other foreign people had such a powerful and cohesive identity, one which they both emulated and vilified.

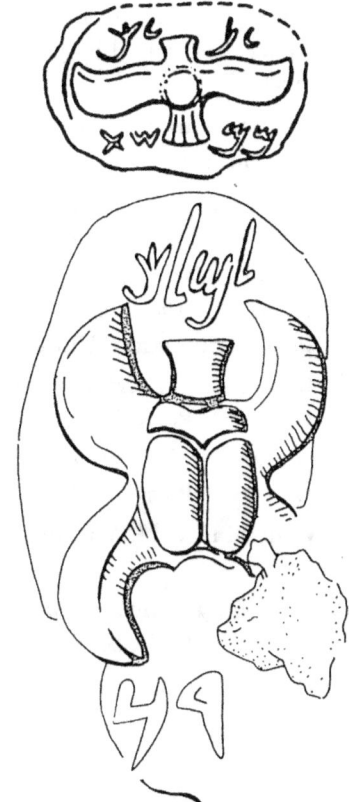

Figure 5.9. Judean *lmlk* seals, late 8th–early 7th century (after Othmar Keel and Christoph Uehlinger, *Gods, Goddesses, and Images of God in Ancient Israel*)

For Further Reading

Assmann, Jan. *The Search for God in Ancient Egypt*. Translated by David Lorton. Ithaca, NY: Cornell University Press, 2001.

Hoffmeier, James K. "The Exodus and Wilderness Narratives." In *Ancient Israel's History: An Introduction to Issues and Sources*, edited by Bill T. Arnold and Richard S. Hess, 46–90. Grand Rapids: Baker Academic, 2014.

23. See Tallay Ornan, "A Complex System of Religious Symbols: The Case of the Winged Disc in Near Eastern Imagery of the First Millennium BCE," in *Crafts and Images in Contact: Studies on Eastern Mediterranean Art of the First Millennium BCE*, ed. Claudia E. Suter and Christoph Uehlinger (Fribourg: Academic Press; Göttingen: Vandenhoeck & Ruprecht, 2005), 207–41.

Hornung, Erich. *Conceptions of God in Ancient Egypt: The One and the Many*. Translated by John Baines. Ithaca, NY: Cornell University Press, 1982.

Lichtheim, Miriam. *Ancient Egyptian Literature*. 3 vols. Berkeley: University of California Press, 1973–80.

Redford, Donald B. *Egypt, Canaan, and Israel in Ancient Times*. Princeton: Princeton University Press, 1992.

Redmount, Carol A. "Bitter Lives: Israel in and out of Egypt." In *The Oxford History of the Biblical World*, edited by Michael David Coogan, 58–89. New York: Oxford University Press, 1998.

Robins, Gay. *The Art of Ancient Egypt*. Rev. ed. Cambridge, MA: Harvard University Press, 2008.

Shaw, Ian, ed. *The Oxford History of Ancient Egypt*. New York: Oxford University Press, 2000.

Silverman, David P., ed. *Ancient Egypt*. New York: Oxford University Press, 1997.

Teeter, Emily. *Religion and Ritual in Ancient Egypt*. New York: Cambridge University Press, 2011.

Yamauchi, Edwin. *Africa and the Bible*. Grand Rapids: Baker Academic, 2006.

6

The Hittites and the Hurrians

Billie Jean Collins

The Hittites enter the world stage at the beginning of the seventeenth century BCE.[1] Details about their coalescence into a centralized political power remain unclear. They were but one among several ethnolinguistic groups inhabiting the central Anatolian plateau in the early second millennium, a period illuminated through the lens of archaeology and the documents left behind by the Assyrian businessmen whose merchant colonies (*kārum*) operated with the cooperation and under the protection of the local Anatolian rulers. These documents, which derive from the most important merchant colony at Kanes, present a picture of a mixed local population of Hattian, Hurrian, and Indo-European (Palaic, spoken in Pala in the Pontic Mountains; Luwian; and Hittite) speakers who were connected by a common material culture even while facing off against one another for strategic advantage in the quest for control of resources. The earliest historical document found in the later Hittite royal archives is the Anitta

---

1. The standard works on Hittite history are Trevor Bryce, *The Kingdom of the Hittites*, rev. ed. (Oxford: Oxford University Press, 2005); Bryce, *Letters of the Great Kings of the Ancient Near East: The Royal Correspondence of the Late Bronze Age* (London: Routledge, 2003); H. Craig Melchert, ed., *The Luwians* (Leiden: Brill, 2003); Horst Klengel, *Geschichte des hethitischen Reiches* (Leiden: Brill, 1999); Billie Jean Collins, *The Hittites and Their World* (Atlanta: Society of Biblical Literature, 2007); Jörg Klinger, *Die Hethiter* (Munich: Beck, 2007).

Figure 6.1. Anatolia

Chronicle. It records the conquest of the Halys (Hittite Marassantiya) River basin in this early period by King Anitta of Kanes, including the destruction of Hattusa, one of the centers of opposition to Kanesite hegemony. The Assyrians withdrew from Anatolia in about 1725 BCE, bringing an end to the Colony period and with it our documentation. Perhaps they were driven away by such local rivalries as that described in Anitta's text. Although Anitta cannot be linked directly with the Hittite dynasty that would within a few decades establish itself at Hattusa, his ambitions in Anatolia laid the groundwork for a powerful new kingdom to emerge.

1. The Hittite Old Kingdom

Hattusili is the first Hittite king for whom we have contemporary historical evidence. About his predecessors we know very little. His grandfather may have been a certain Huzziya, whose name appears in fragmentary form on a cruciform seal from Hattusa as the predecessor of Labarna.[2] Hattusili's father and immediate predecessor was Labarna, whose royal name would be adopted by future Hittite kings (including Hattusili himself) as a title. Whatever success his forebears may have had in strengthening their position in central Anatolia, Hattusili is the first king to whom we can attribute historical records, including his royal annals. It was he who likely moved the dynastic seat to

---

2. See A. M. Dinçol, B. Dinçol, J. David Hawkins, and Gernot Wilhelm, "The 'Cruciform' Seal from Boğazköy-Hattusa," *IstMitt* 43 (1993): 87–106, esp. 104–6.

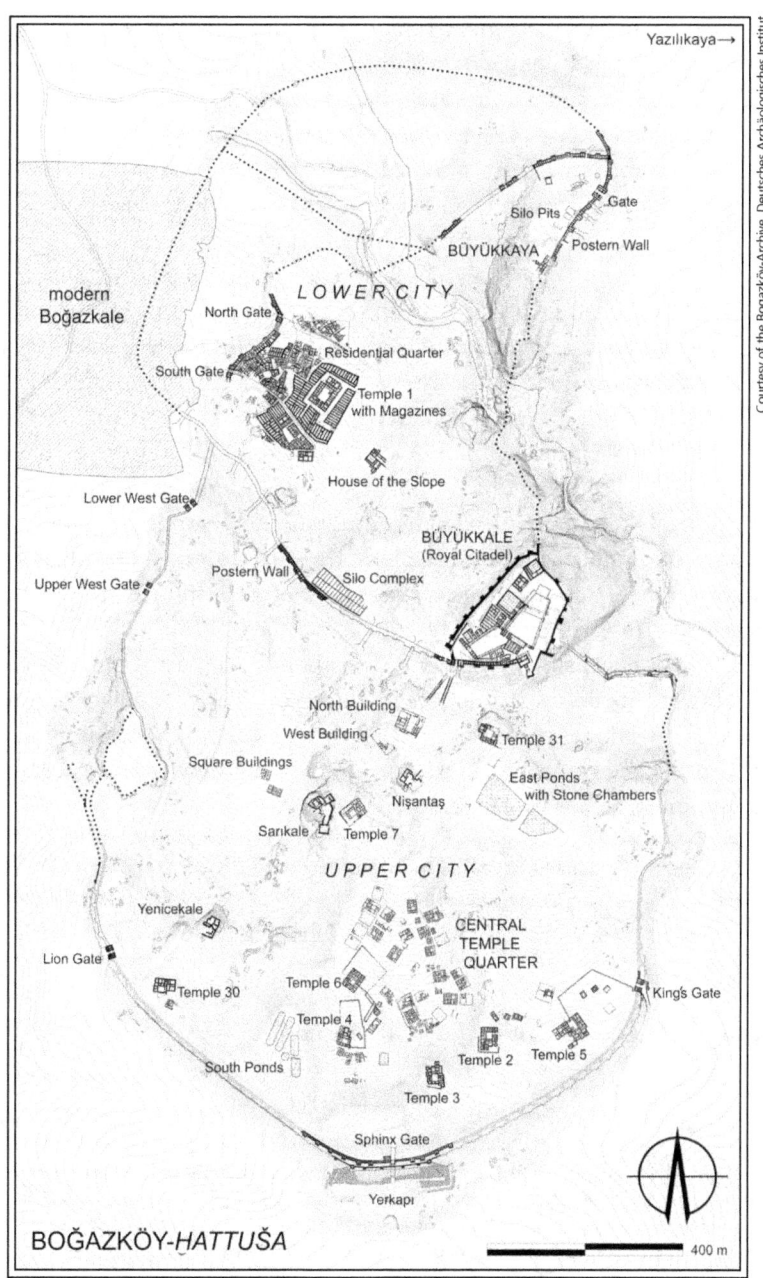

Figure 6.2. Plan of the Hittite capital at Hattusa. From Dirk Paul Mielke, "Key Sites of the Hittite Empire," in *The Oxford Handbook of Ancient Anatolia*, ed. Sharon Steadman and Gregory McMahon (Oxford University Press, 2011), 1033, doi: 10.1093/oxfordhb/9780195376142.013.0048.

Hattusa, who united the plateau under a centralized government and sought to expand his interests beyond the Euphrates, and, not least, who established the administrative and cultural foundations of the kingdom.

Hattusili understood the importance of Syria to Anatolia's increasing need for control of the Near Eastern trade routes providing access to outlets to the Mediterranean Sea. He conducted no fewer than three major campaigns in the region over the course of his approximately thirty-year reign (ca. 1650–1620 BCE). During the first campaign he succeeded in destroying Alalakh, Halpa/Aleppo's port city. But the second campaign represents his greatest military achievement. Leaving a wake of destruction during his march eastward toward the Euphrates River, Hattusili notes the river crossing with considerable pride in his annals, a milestone not achieved since Sargon the Great (from the opposite direction) centuries earlier. A letter—the only one of its kind to survive from the Hittite Old Kingdom—that he wrote in Akkadian to Tunip-Teshub (Tuniya) of Tikunani, a minor ruler in northern Mesopotamia, hints at his activities and influence beyond the borders of Hatti.[3] It is also likely that it was during these actions in Syria that Hattusili reintroduced the Akkadian cuneiform script to Anatolia.

In the end, Hattusili's campaigns, though militarily successful, resulted in no lasting Hittite political influence in the region. The groundwork for a Hittite empire had not yet been laid. With no worthy heirs among his immediate family, at the end of his life, Hattusili adopted his young grandson Mursili I and appointed him as his successor.

Figure 6.3. The Kings of the Hittites*

Approximate Date of Accession	Throne Name
Old Kingdom	
1690	Huzziya I
1670	Labarna
1650	Hattusili I
1620	Mursili I

3. Hittite involvement across the Euphrates in Hattusili's reign may have been greater than previously suspected. Texts from Terqa (a part of the kingdom of Mari in the middle Euphrates region) mention clashes with troops of Hatte/Hattu. Excavators also found an Old Hittite stamp seal at this site. See Itamar Singer, review of Horst Klengel, *Geschichte des hethitischen Reiches*, BO 57 (2000): 638–39; Klengel, *Geschichte des hethitischen Reiches*, 66. See also Jarod L. Miller ("Hattušili I's Expansion into Northern Syria in Light of the Tikunani Letter," in *Akten des IV. Internationalen Kongresses für Hethitologie, Würzburg, 4.–8. Oktober 1999*, ed. Gernot Wilhelm, StBoT 45 [Wiesbaden: Harrassowitz, 2001], 410–29), who cautions against concluding that Tikunani was a vassal of Hattusili I (424–26).

Approximate Date of Accession	Throne Name
1590	Hantili I
1560	Zidanta I
1550	Ammuna
1530	Huzziya II
1525	Telipinu
1500	Alluwamna
	Tahurwaili
	Hantili II
	Zidanta II
	Huzziya III
	Muwatalli I
Empire	
1400	Tudhaliya I/II
	Arnuwanda I
	Hattusili II?
	Tudhaliya III
1350	Suppiluliuma I
1322	Arnuwanda II
1321	Mursili II
1295	Muwattalli II
1272	Mursili III
1267	Hattusili III
1237	Tudhaliya IV
1209	Arnuwanda III
1207	Suppiluliuma II

*After Bryce, *Kingdom of the Hittites*, xv.

Mursili shared his grandfather's military ambitions. He succeeded in destroying the kingdom of Yamhad and its capital Halpa, a goal that his predecessor had failed to achieve. His ambitions did not stop here. He continued to Babylon, sacking the city (ca. 1595 BCE) and bringing an end to the Old Babylonian dynasty that Hammurabi had established two centuries prior. Whether his goal was wealth in spoils and captives, the prestige of conquest, or military strategy, history would remember the raid as one of Hatti's most glorious moments.

Sometime after his return to Hattusa, Mursili was assassinated by his brother-in-law Hantili, who assumed the throne. Hantili's reign began a period of instability within the royal family and the kingdom as a whole that lasted nearly a century. Each of the four kings who ruled in this period fought with limited success to keep the kingdom from disintegrating altogether in the face of incursions by Kaskeans from the north, Hurrians from the south and east, and the Arzawa lands in the west. It seems that Hattusili's fragile kingdom came perilously close to collapse within only a century of its foundation.

The reign of Telipinu (ca. 1525–1500 BCE) marks a turning point for the fragile kingdom. The new king issued a proclamation that sketched the unfortunate events of the previous reigns and established definitive rules for the royal succession that would eliminate infighting in the royal court. Though there would be another century of such infighting before his policies would take root, his impact on the development of the Hittite state infrastructure is unmistakable. He may be responsible for the first written formulation of the Hittite Law Code, and he concluded the kingdom's first international treaty agreement with the recently independent state of Kizzuwatna (the region of southern Anatolia corresponding to classical Cilicia), then under the rule of Isputahsu. By formalizing the border between the two kingdoms, this treaty ensured the security of Hatti's southern border. It is during the poorly documented century between Telipinu and Tudhaliya I/II that cuneiform was adapted to represent the Hittite language; by the reign of Tudhaliya I/II, Akkadian was no longer used for internal purposes.[4]

2. The Early Empire

Hatti's fortunes finally changed for the better with the accession to the throne of an individual named Tudhaliya (II) sometime at the beginning of the fourteenth century.[5] Whether Tudhaliya's accession marks the restoration of Hattusili I's dynasty on the throne of Hatti (from the usurper Muwatalli I) or he is a member of a new Hurrian dynasty originating from Kummanni in Kizzuwatna, remains a matter of debate.[6] What is not disputed is that it marks the beginning of a new era for the kingdom, both politically and culturally.

---

4. See (with literature) Theo van den Hout, "The Hittite Empire from Textual Evidence," in *The Oxford Handbook of Ancient Anatolia (10,000–323 B.C.E.)*, ed. Sharon R. Steadman and Gregory McMahon (Oxford: Oxford University Press, 2011), 900–916.

5. Whether Tudhaliya is labeled I or II depends on whether one accepts the existence of a grandfather of the same name who founded the dynasty. See the following note.

6. For a recent summary of the issues, with bibliography, see Piotr Taracha, "On the Dynasty of the Hittite Empire," in *Šarnikzel: Hethitologische Studien zum Gedenken an Emil Orgetorix Forrer*, ed. D. Groddek and S. Rößle, DBH 10 (Dresden: Verlag der TU Dresden, 2004). For a reconstruction of this period, see Jacques Freu, "La 'révolution dynastique' du Grand Roi de Hatti Tuthalia I," *Hethitica* 13 (1996): 17–38; Freu, "Le grand roi Tuthaliya, fils de Kantuzzili," in *Mélanges offerts au professeur René Lebrun*, ed. Michel Mazoyer and

According to his royal annals, Tudhaliya I/II's first military expeditions as king took him deep into western Anatolia to do battle with a newly formed anti-Hittite alliance, known as the Assuwan confederacy, which included the kingdom of Arzawa. Tudhaliya I/II's decisive defeat of this alliance had little long-term effect in the region, but it marks the beginning of a long and uniquely troubled relationship between east and west in Anatolia's Late Bronze Age. The situation in the west will remain unstable through the reigns of Tudhaliya's two successors, in large part as a result of the disruptive machinations of a man named Madduwatta, whom Arnuwanda censures for his ambitions in the west and the duplicities in which he engages against his Hittite overlord and protector in order to fulfill them.

The Kaska, an alliance of mountain-dwelling tribes from the Pontic region to the north who first enter the story during the reign of Hantili II roughly a century earlier, immediately took advantage of Tudhaliya's absence to invade Hatti's northern border. The official correspondence from the archive at the northern frontier town of Tapikka (modern Maşat) documents the serious problem the Kaska represented for Hatti in the reigns of Tudhaliya I/II and his son-in-law and successor Arnuwanda.[7] Tudhaliya I/II succeeded in pushing them out of Hittite territory, but only to be confronted by another threat in the east.

In the years between the reigns of Telipinu and Tudhaliya I/II, the power of the kingdom of Mittani, whose base lay east of the Euphrates, had spread over the whole of northern Syria, including Alalakh and Aleppo. The population of this kingdom was primarily Hurrian. Hurrian-speaking peoples had been present in Anatolia from the earliest written records, and the annals of Hattusili I record numerous confrontations as well as tensions with Hurrians living to the east and south of Hatti. These Hurrian territories in northern Mesopotamia and Syria coalesced, under the influence of unknown forces, into a united political entity by the end of the sixteenth century. Confrontation between the two powers over their common territorial interests was inevitable.

Mittani had been encouraging dissension in Isuwa, a Hittite subject state in the upper Euphrates, which took up arms against Tudhaliya I/II. Although Tudhaliya I/II was successful in this arena as well, once again it was only a temporary victory, as Isuwa remained sympathetic to Mittani and would later have cause once again to rise up in arms against Hatti. In preparation

---

Olivier Casabonne, 2 vols., Collection Kubaba, Série Antiquité 5–6 (Paris: L'Harmattan, 2004), 1:271–304.

7. For a dating of the correspondence from Maşat-Tapikka to the reigns of Tudhaliya I/II and Arnuwanda I, see Jörg Klinger, "Das Corpus der Maşat-Briefe und seine Beziehungen zu den Texten aus Hattusa," ZA 85 (1995): 74–108; cf. Bryce, *Kingdom of the Hittites*, 145, who follows a dating of this corpus to the reign of Tudhaliya III, Arnuwanda's successor.

for further confrontations with Mittani in Syria, Tudhaliya I/II concluded a new treaty with Sunashshura of Kizzuwatna, who had broken his alliance with Mittani. With his buffer thus secured, Tudhaliya I/II took his troops into Syria, destroying Halpa and making major inroads against other Mittanian territories.

During the reign of Tudhaliya I/II's successor, Arnuwanda, Mittani's new king, Artatama I, came to an agreement with Thutmose IV of Egypt, effectively halting Hittite ambition in Syria.[8] In the north, the Kaska were meanwhile once again threatening the borders. They ravaged many of the Hittite holy cities that lay along its northern frontier and carried off their personnel. The result was a complete cessation of the religious cult in these northern lands. Arnuwanda attempted to bind the tribal Kaska by treaty and took other measures to ensure the safety of the frontier, but with limited success.

Dating to this period are a number of documents recording grants of land that were given to officials in order to ensure loyalty and strengthen the position of the king. The period is most notable, though, for the sweeping impact of Hurrian culture and religion on Hittite society. Hurrian names now appear among members of the royal family; a new Hurrian pantheon is introduced beside the existing mixed pantheon of Hittite and foreign deities; there is an influx of Hurrian mythological material; and new Hurrian religious elements, including royal rituals, enter our documentation. The *itkalzi* and *itkahhi* ritual series, for example, were important royal purification rituals belonging to the very beginning of the Hurrian presence in Hattusa, during the reigns of Arnuwanda and his son Tudhaliya III.

During the reign of Tudhaliya III, the kingdom reached another low point. Hatti was attacked from every side in an episode that has come to be known as the "concentric invasion." Excavations have confirmed that Hattusa was burned at this time, as was the regional center at Tapikka (modern Maşat). When the Egyptian pharaoh Amenhotep III corresponded with the king of Arzawa, Tarhundaradu, at about this time, he wrote, "I have heard that everything is finished, and that the country Hattusa is paralyzed."[9] The pharaoh's interest in a marriage alliance with Arzawa suggests that Egypt thought Arzawa might even become the new power in Anatolia. However, despite the extent of the uprising, the Hittite king and his court somehow managed to survive the calamity, no doubt in no small part due to the help of his son Suppiluliuma,

---

8. Bryce, *Kingdom of the Hittites*, 144–45.

9. EA 31, translated by Volkert Haas in William Moran, *The Amarna Letters* (Baltimore: Johns Hopkins University Press, 1992), 101; however, on the translation "paralyzed" for *egai-* instead of Haas's "shattered," see Jaan Puhvel, *Hittite Etymological Dictionary* (Berlin: Mouton, 2004), 2:257, s.v. *eka-*.

who was his most trusted advisor and general. Suppiluliuma would also succeed his father, through a military coup that included the assassination of the chosen heir, Suppiluliuma's own brother.

The primary focus of Suppiluliuma's long reign (ca. 1350–1322 BCE) was the recovery and expansion of Hatti's territories in Syria. Suppiluliuma's first Syrian campaign took him to Wassukkanni, the Mittanian capital, only to find that the Mittanian king, Tushratta, had fled. Unable to confront its king, he turned his army westward into Syria and conquered all the kingdoms of northern Syria that had been under the overlordship of Mittani, including the important harbor city of Ugarit. Only Karkamis (Carchemish) on the Euphrates remained.

Tushratta had been weakened but was not yet defeated, and took advantage of Suppiluliuma's withdrawal from Syria to resume hostilities around Karkamis. Suppiluliuma responded with a renewed campaign in Syria, one that would last several years and result in the conquest of Karkamis and the final subjugation of Mittani.

Suppiluliuma's successes in Syria had brought Hatti into direct contact with Egyptian territories in Syria. Early on, Suppiluliuma had made a political overture to Egypt, evidently in an effort to forestall any hostile reaction to his military activities. It was while he was engaged in the siege of Karkamis in ca. 1327 BCE that an envoy from Egypt arrived with a letter from the Egyptian queen, widow of the deceased pharoah (Tutankhamun?), asking for a Hittite prince in marriage who would then also become king of Egypt. Suppiluliuma was caught off guard by the request and naturally suspicious. He sent an envoy to Egypt to verify the communication. Reassured by the queen's emissary that the offer was sincere, Suppiluliuma sent his son Zannanza to Egypt. The unfortunate prince, however, was murdered en route.

Dismissing the protestations of innocence from the new pharaoh, Ay,[10] a bereaved and angry Suppiluliuma took vengeance, sending Hittite troops into the Egyptian-held territories. Ironically, the Egyptian prisoners whom they transported back to Hatti from these campaigns were blamed for the plagues that wreaked havoc in the Hittite heartland for the next two decades.

Even as these events were unfolding, Suppiluliuma had succeeded in taking Karkamis and installing his son Sharri-Kushuh as its king. Following the

---

10. So Bryce, *Kingdom of the Hittites*, 183; cf. Horst Klengel, "History of the Hittites," in *Insights into Hittite History and Archaeology*, ed. Hermann Genz and Dirk Paul Mielke (Leuven: Peeters, 2011), 39. For the letter from Suppiluliuma to Ay (*KUB* 19.20 + *KBo* 12.23 + 154/s; *CTH* 154) in which the latter is quoted as having disclaimed any responsibility (obv. 24–25), see also Theo P. J. van den Hout, "Der Falke und das Kücken: Der neue Pharao und der hethitische Prinze?," *ZA* 84 (1994): 60–88.

fall of Karkamis, the Mittanian king Tushratta was assassinated. With his murder, his son Shattiwaza submitted to the Hittite king, and Mittani became a protectorate of the Hittites. Six years after his conquest of Karkamis, Suppiluliuma too died, probably from the very plague his troops had brought home. His son and successor, Arnuwanda II, also succumbed to it after little more than a year on the throne.

Suppiluliuma formed a series of alliances secured by treaty that brought the vassals and appanage kingdoms firmly under the control of the Hittite king. Whatever successes his predecessors may have had, through this system of alliances and the appointment of his sons Sharri-Kushuh in Karkamis and Telipinu in Aleppo to administer his Syrian holdings, which now included Ugarit, Nuhasse, Qadesh, and Amurru, Suppiluliuma went beyond mere conquest to establish for the first time a sustainable Hittite empire.

Suppiluliuma's youngest son, Mursili II, assumed the kingship in 1321 BCE. His reign is as notable for his personal troubles as it is for his military enterprises. Militarily he had to stabilize his rule, both in the north against the Kaska, who had organized themselves under a leader named Pihhuniya, and in the west against a new coordinated offensive initiated by the king of Arzawa, Uhhaziti, in collaboration with the king of Ahhiyawa and the city of Millawanda (Miletos). Mursili succeeded in eliminating Arzawa, and its constituent parts—the territories of Hapalla, Mira, and the Seha River Land—became Hittite vassals. The west was finally under Hittite control.

With the death of his brother Sharri-Kushuh, king of Karkamis, in Mursili's ninth year, the Hittite king was forced to turn his personal attention to events in Syria. There was an Egyptian-backed rebellion in Nuhasse and Qadesh to deal with. And Assyria, which had been waiting for an opportunity to fill the vacuum left by the destruction of the kingdom of Mittani, invaded territories under Hittite control east of the Euphrates. With the help of his generals, Mursili was able to withstand the threats on all fronts. Assyria was driven out of Karkamis, and Mursili was able to install the sons of Sharri-Kushuh and Telipinu as viceroys in Karkamis and Aleppo, respectively.

The records of Mursili's reign chronicle a troubled personal life. The death of his beloved wife Gassulawiya he blamed on the persecution of the reigning queen, the Babylonian princess called Tawananna, who was Suppiluliuma's last wife and a powerful thorn in Mursili's side. In addition, the plague that Suppiluliuma had brought home from his conquests in Syria continued to rage unabated throughout the kingdom well into the latter half of Mursili's reign. This engendered some of the most poignant literature in the Hittite corpus, the prayers directed at the gods to bring an end to the plague. Finally, at some point Mursili suffered a sudden, though apparently temporary, speech loss that required elaborate ritual treatment. Yet, despite these setbacks, Mursili persevered.

The campaigns conducted in the final years of his reign brought Mursili again to the west and north. Although he would have no more success than any other king in finally ending the Kaskean menace, Mursili did achieve a great symbolic victory when he wrested the sacred city of Nerik from Kaskean control and became the first Hittite king in two hundred years to worship in its temples.

3. The Thirteenth Century

Mursili II's son and successor, Muwatalli II, had first to deal with another renegade vassal in the west, one Piyamaradu, who may have taken control of Wilusa (ancient Troy) away from its pro-Hittite king Alaksandu.[11] Muwatalli managed to expel Piyamaradu—who probably found refuge with the Ahhiyawans—restored Alaksandu to the throne of Wilusa, banished the king of the Seha River Land, Manapa-Tarhunda, whose support in the conflict had been less than enthusiastic, and installed his son Masturi in his place. Piyamaradu's career, however, was not yet over, as we will see.

It was some time after his return from this campaign that Muwatalli decided to move his capital to Tarhuntassa, capital of the region by the same name in south-central Anatolia. Although the boundaries of the kingdom of Tarhuntassa are roughly known, the exact location of its capital city is still debated.[12] Hattusa had been the political and religious heart of the Hittite kingdom for the past 350 years, and Muwatalli's reasons for abandoning it must have been compelling ones. Whether those reasons were military, political, or religious, or a combination of these, is not entirely clear. Without the royal library and the historical and religious documents that no doubt still lie buried in the ruins of Tarhuntassa, Muwatalli's reign remains among the most enigmatic. But the fact that he brought to the new capital the statues of the gods of Hatti and the manes (venerated spirits) of the ancestors signifies that the move was intended to be permanent.[13] Still, Muwatalli did not simply

---

11. On the probability that Piyamaradu was an ambitious Arzawan prince, see J. David Hawkins, "Tarkasnawa King of Mira," *AnSt* 48 (1998): 17. On the difficulty of interpreting the relevant passage in the Manapa-Tarhunda letter, see Trevor Bryce, *The Trojans and Their Neighbors* (New York: Routledge, 2006), 184–85.

12. See Stefano de Martino, "Ura and the Boundaries of Tarhuntašša," *AoF* 26 (1999): 291–300; Ali M. Dinçol, Jak Yakar, Belkıs Dinçol, and Avia Taffer, "The Borders of the Appanage Kingdom of Tarhuntašša: A Geographical and Archaeological Assessment," *Anatolica* 26 (2000): 1–29.

13. Itamar Singer ("From Hattuša to Tarhuntašša: Some Thoughts on Muwatalli's Reign," in *Acts of the IIIrd International Congress of Hittitology, Çorum, September 16–22, 1996*,

abandon the north to its fate. He appointed his brother Hattusili, who had served as chief of the royal guard and governor of the Upper Land, king in Hakpis and gave him control over the northern half of the kingdom, with the exception of Hattusa itself, which was left in the hands of a trusted official.[14]

When Muwatalli II assumed the throne of his father, relations between Hatti and Egypt were still tense over their common interests in Syria. This cold war turned hot when the Nineteenth Dynasty pharoah Seti I (r. 1294–1279 BCE) struck out successfully to reclaim Egypt's lost territories of Qadesh and Amurru. The hostilities between the two superpowers culminated a few years later in an epic battle. Ramesses II (ca. 1279–1213 BCE) was now pharoah of Egypt and as intent as his father on establishing Egyptian hegemony over Syria-Palestine. A major clash was unavoidable. The scene of the battle was Qadesh, now in Hittite control. The other contested state, Amurru, under its king, Benteshina, was, at the time of the battle, a loyal vassal of Egypt. Despite his claims of victory, recorded in the Egyptian accounts of the battle, Ramesses had failed in his goals—Qadesh remained under Hittite control and the land of Amurru was returned to Hittite control—and Muwatalli was able to pursue the retreating Egyptian troops south into Egyptian-controlled territory.

Muwatalli died a few years after the battle of Qadesh, leaving the kingship to a second-rank son, Urhi-Teshub, who took the throne name Mursili III. We are forced to view Mursili III's reign through the hostile eyes of his uncle Hattusili III, who would usurp his throne in a bitter civil war a few years later. Initially, however, Hattusili claims to have supported the succession, even taking credit for installing his nephew in kingship. In the short period of his rule, Mursili III's most significant act was to return the seat of government back to Hattusa, a move no doubt supported by Hattusili. Indeed, there are some indications that many of Mursili's policy decisions were heavily influenced by his powerful uncle.[15]

Diplomatic relations with Assyria during Mursili III's reign were strained. Adad-nirari had succeeded in making Hanigalbat, the remnant of the former kingdom of Mittani, a vassal of Assyria, thus eliminating any buffer between the lands controlled by Hatti and Assyria. Mursili III's displeasure with the situation is evident in a letter to Adad-nirari in which he refuses to acknowledge

---

ed. S. Alp and A. Süel [Ankara: Uyum Ajans, 1998], 535–41) compares Akhenaten's choice of Akhetaten as his new capital.

14. See Itamar Singer, "The Fate of Hattusa during the Period of Tarhuntassa's Supremacy," in *Kulturgeschichten: Altorientalistische Studien für Volkert Haas zum 65. Geburtstag*, ed. Thomas Richter, Doris Prechel, and Jörg Klinger (Saarbrücken: Saarbrücker Druckerei, 2001), 403.

15. See Bryce, *Kingdom of the Hittites*, 253–56; Collins, *Hittites and Their World*, 57–58.

the Assyrian king as his "brother"—that is, as a king with whom he enjoys good diplomatic relations.[16]

The Apology of Hattusili, a document composed to justify his usurpation and to secure the line of succession for his son Tudhaliya IV, blames Hattusili's nephew, to whom he refers disrespectfully by his birth name, for initiating the hostilities that led to the civil war by systematically dismantling Hattusili's base of power and demoting him from office. In fact, Mursili III may well have been justified in wanting to limit the authority and power of his ambitious uncle. When Mursili III finally took the cities of Nerik and Hakpis from his authority, Hattusili declared war, writing to the king, "You opposed me. You (are) Great King, whereas I (am) king of the single fortress that you left me. So come! Ištar of Šamuḫa and the Stormgod of Nerik will judge us."[17] That divine judgment fell decisively in Hattusili's favor, as he informs us in his Apology, when Mursili III was captured at Samuha. Hattusili became Great King and Mursili III was sent into exile.

As a prince of the realm, Hattusili had been a successful military leader. As king, he became a consummate diplomat. Given his controversial route to the throne, it was essential that he establish good relations with vassals and foreign powers alike. Treaties with Amurru, Babylon, and Egypt were reinforced by diplomatic marriages. He no doubt pursued all of these alliances with a view to reinforcing the legitimacy of his rule in the eyes of the international community.

With Assyria, Hattusili tread softly. Adad-nirari had not recognized his legitimacy, initially failing to send a gift on the occasion of Hattusili's enthronement and remarking to him that he was "(but) a substitute for the Great King."[18] When the king of Hanigalbat, Shattuara II, rebelled against Adad-nirari's successor, Shalmaneser, the effort went unaided by Hattusili, who acknowledged the Assyrian as a Great King and officially recognized his sovereignty over Hanigalbat. Shalmaneser's response to the rebellion was to obliterate the kingdom of Hanigalbat once and for all. Hattusili's policy of forbearance may have helped temporarily to ease tensions between the two powers.

16. *KUB* 23.102 (*CTH* 171) i 1–19, for which see *HDT*, 146–47 (no. 24A). Against the generally accepted view that Mursili III (Urhi-Teshub), not Hattusili III, authored the letter, see Theo P. J. van den Hout, "Khattushili III, King of the Hittites," *CANE* 2:1114–15. For this nuance of the diplomatic use of the term "brother," see Bryce, *Letters of the Great Kings*, 74–78.

17. "Apology of Hattusili III," translated by Theo P. J. van den Hout (*COS* 1.77:203, §10).

18. As reported in a letter from Ramesses (*KBo* 8.14 [*CTH* 163] obv. 10'); see Elmar Edel, *Umschriften und Übersetzungen*, vol. 1 of *Die ägyptisch-hethitische Korrespondenz aus Boghazköy in babylonischer und hethitischer Sprache* (Opladen: Westdeutscher Verlag, 1994), 24–25 (no. 5), who records the Assyrian king's statement. The Assyrian king could also have been Shalmaneser (Bryce, *Kingdom of the Hittites*, 466n49).

Hattusili's paramount concern and the motivation behind all these actions was not only to garner international recognition of his kingship while building up his base of support at home but also to ensure that the right of succession to the throne of Hatti remain with his line. It was for these same reasons that he approached Ramesses II with a proposal for a treaty alliance. The treaty was concluded in 1259, Ramesses's twenty-first year.[19] The treaty followed the formula characteristic of Hittite treaties and included stipulations of nonaggression, mutual assistance against internal and external enemies, and the extradition of fugitives. The insertion of a clause whereby Ramesses guaranteed the succession of Hattusili's legitimate heir has no corresponding stipulation on the Egyptian side and underscores Hattusili's preoccupation with securing the succession for his heirs.

The treaty, which both Hattusili and his powerful and dynamic queen Puduhepa signed, initiated a period of cooperation known as the Egypto-Hittite peace, in which intense contact took place between the two courts. The correspondence from this period was preserved in the Hittite archives. Thirteen years after the treaty the royal couple sent one of their daughters to Egypt to wed Ramesses. A second wedding to another daughter of Hattusili and Puduhepa followed some years later. Puduhepa was instrumental in making the arrangements for both. She continued in her role as queen well into the reign of her son Tudhaliya (IV).

Hattusili's reign was not entirely free of military activity. Most notably, like his brother before him, Hattusili had to deal with the insurrectionist Piyamaradu, who had been harrassing Hatti's western allies since Muwatalli's reign. Their troops clashed at Iyalanda (classical Alinda in Caria). Hattusili pursued Piyamaradu as far as Millawanda, but the fugitive managed to escape by ship to the protection of the Ahhiyawan king. From the safety of an island refuge, he continued his raids on Hittite holdings on the mainland. With Ahhiyawa actively working against Hittite interests in the region, the situation in the west was doomed to deteriorate. When Hattusili finally died at a relatively advanced age, he left behind a large extended royal family and lingering questions about who had the right to sit on the throne of Hatti.

Tudhaliya IV, who succeeded his father in ca. 1237 BCE, had mixed success in international affairs. A veteran soldier like his father, Tudhaliya managed to bring some stability to the western territories, thus ensuring against any further aggression on the part of Ahhiyawa. On other fronts, however, he was less successful. Tukulti-Ninurta I of Assyria attacked the Hurrian lands to the northwest that were under Hittite hegemony, thus gaining control of the

---

19. *HDT*, 96–100.

Subari lands, and with them all of the major passes into Anatolia, and he now sought to secure his new northern border by taking the city of Nihriya. The Hittite troops were waiting for the Assyrians at Nihriya and met the Assyrian troops outside the city. Effectively deserted by his vassals, Tudhaliya's forces were defeated. The loss would seriously weaken the Hittites' ability to keep their Syrian vassals in check.

In addition, the southwest of Anatolia had once again become restive, requiring Tudhaliya's presence there. Although his Yalburt inscription commemorates his victories during this campaign, the region was almost certainly by this time in an irreversible descent into anarchy. Tudhaliya IV was also the first Hittite king to attempt a sea battle, against the island of Cyprus, and he succeeded in establishing a new, if temporary, pro-Hittite regime on the island.

Perhaps the greatest challenge to Tudhaliya's reign was his own cousin, Kurunta, the younger brother of Urhi-Teshub.[20] Immediately upon his accession to the throne, Hattusili III had installed Kurunta as king of Tarhuntassa (his father's capital) and ratified the appointment with a treaty that granted significant concessions to Kurunta.[21] When Tudhaliya IV came to the throne, he renewed Hattusili III's treaty with Kurunta, the original copy of which was engraved in bronze. The new treaty bestowed further favors on Kurunta putting him on a par politically with the viceroy of Karkamis, and hopefully ensuring his loyalty. This was especially important because his claim to the throne was as strong as, if not stronger than, Tudhaliya's. Indeed, Kurunta at some point seems to have assumed the title "Great King, Labarna, My Sun." The adoption of these titles by a vassal-king was unheard of and has prompted speculation that Kurunta proclaimed himself Great King as an assertion of his right to his father's throne, which had been based at Tarhuntassa.[22] Whatever the situation, the growing weakness of the Hittite power base at Hattusa apparently made it possible for a second "Great" King to emerge.

Tudhaliya also devoted considerable attention to cultic matters at home. In a prayer to the Sun Goddess of Arinna, he vowed to restore the cult of the goddess if she would support him against his enemy. This involved correcting persistent mistakes in the celebration of the spring and autumn festivals and

---

20. On the exact relationship between Urhi-Teshub and Kurunta, see Trevor Bryce, "The Secession of Tarhuntassa," in *Tabularia Hethaeorum: Hethitologische Beiträge Silvin Košak zum 65. Geburtstag*, ed. Detlev Groddek and Marina Zorman, DBH 25 (Wiesbaden: Harrassowitz, 2007), 119.

21. This assumes that the throne name Kurunta was adopted by Ulmi-Teshub and that the two are to be identified. There is no consensus that such an identification is justified. For a summary of the sequence of treaties with Kurunta/Ulmi-Teshub, see HDT, 107–8.

22. Bryce, "Secession of Tarhuntassa," 124–26.

Figure 6.4. Tudhaliya IV in relief at Yazılıkaya, depicted in an *Umarmungszene*—that is, in the embrace of his protective deity.

replacing divine images that had fallen into disrepair.[23] Tudhaliya's program of reorganizing the cult along these lines throughout the kingdom had the goal not only of restoring the favor of the Sun Goddess but also of reasserting royal authority by making his presence felt throughout the kingdom.[24]

Tudhaliya IV left his kingdom to his son Arnuwanda III, whose reign was too short to leave an heir or any archival or monumental records. Arnuwanda's brother Suppiluliuma II would follow him on the throne. Like his father, Suppiluliuma II was preoccupied with the loyalty of his circle of peers. In this respect, the civil war between Mursili III and Hattusili III had taken a serious toll on the political stability of the kingdom. The result was the undermining of royal authority, which, when combined with losses such as that suffered by Tudhaliya at Nihriya, caused the royal hold on the vassals to loosen as their confidence in their Anatolian overlord ebbed. The documents dating to Suppiluliuma's reign reflect these concerns, as they comprise mostly protocols and instructions regarding matters of internal security.[25]

Although the kingdom that Suppiluliuma II inherited was already in irreversible decline, all was not bleak. Tukulti-Ninurta had resumed diplomatic and economic relations with the Hittites. Middle Assyrian tablets from Tell Chuera and Tell Sheikh Ḥamad attest to Hittite diplomats and merchants operating in Assyrian-controlled areas east of the Euphrates,[26] an indication

23. KBo 12.58 + 13.162 (= CTH 385.9) obv. 2–11; see Joost Hazenbos, *The Organization of the Anatolian Local Cults during the Thirteenth Century B.C.*, CM 21 (Leiden: Brill, 2003), 12.

24. So Franca Pecchioli-Daddi, "The System of Government at the Time of Tutḫaliya IV," in *The Life and Times of Ḫattušili III and Tutḫaliya IV*, ed. Theo P. J. van den Hout, PIHANS 103 (Leiden: NINO, 2006), 117–30.

25. Itamar Singer, "The Battle of Niḫriya and the End of the Hittite Empire," *ZA* 75 (1985): 120.

26. Singer, review of Klengel, *Geschichte des hethitischen Reiches*, 642, with bibliography.

that relations with Assyria were on the mend following the fateful battle of Nihriya.

Sometime after Tudhaliya IV's conquest of Cyprus, the island was lost to Hittite control and Suppiluliuma II was forced to mount a new sea campaign involving three naval engagements, which he commemorated in an inscription on the Eternal Peak, the mortuary shrine that he dedicated to his father in Hattusa.[27] The need to protect the increasingly fragile supply routes must have been acute. Already in the reign of Hattusili III, the country's growing dependence on shipments of grain from abroad is evident. A letter from the period refers to grain that Ramesses II shipped from Egypt to help alleviate a famine in Hatti.[28] Another shipment was sent in the fifth year of Pharaoh Merenptah to "keep alive the land of Hatti."[29] By the time Niqmaddu III (or Ammurapi?) of Ugarit received a letter from the Hittite king (perhaps Suppiluliuma II) demanding that he furnish a ship and crew to transport 2,000 kor (ca. 450 metric tons) of grain from Mukish (Alalakh) to Ura on the southern coast of Hatti, the matter had literally become one of life and death.[30] The elaborate grain silos constructed in the northwest part of the capital may be a sign of this growing dependence on foreign grain.[31]

Suppiluliuma II appears to have directed much of his energy to the construction of religious monuments, an indication perhaps of his growing desperation, as he appealed to the gods and the manes of the ancestors for assistance. One of these monuments, a vaulted stone chamber about four meters deep, was decorated with reliefs of the Sun God and the king. The structure itself was an entrance to the underworld, by which the royal petitioner could appeal to the gods of that realm for mercy. The chamber also contained a rather problematic hieroglyphic inscription, known as the Südburg inscription, that seems to record Suppiluliuma II's victorious campaigns against rebellious vassals in southwestern Anatolia (fig. 6.5).[32] His campaign covered localities

---

27. *KBo* 12.38 (*CTH* 121) contains the narratives both of Suppiluliuma's conquest of Cyprus and that of his father.

28. *KUB* 3.34 (*CTH* 165) rev. 15–17; Edel, *Umschriften und Übersetzungen*, 182–85 (no. 78); Klengel, "'Hungerjahre' in Hatti," *AoF* 1 (1974): 167 with n. 13.

29. Karnak Inscription; James Henry Breasted, *Ancient Records of Egypt*, 5 vols. (repr. of 1906 Chicago edition; London: Histories and Mysteries of Man, 1988), 3:244, §580.

30. RS 20.212; see Jean Nougayrol, *Ugaritica V* (Paris: Geuthner, 1968), 105–7, no. 33. For further evidence of attempts to procure grain to alleviate food shortages, see Itamar Singer, "A Political History of Ugarit," in *HUS*, 715–19.

31. Klengel, *Geschichte des hethitischen Reiches*, 311; see also Walter Dörfler et al., "Environment and Economy in Hittite Anatolia," in Genz and Mielke, *Insights into Hittite History and Archaeology*, 108–13.

32. On the dating of the events recounted on the Südburg inscription after those of the Nişantaş inscription, see Itamar Singer, "Great Kings of Tarḫuntašša," *SMEA* 38 (1996): 67.

Figure 6.5. A section from the hieroglyphic inscription of Suppiluliuma II located in the "Südburg" adjacent to the sacred pool complex just south of the citadel. The inscription records Suppiluliuma II's campaigns in southwestern Anatolia.

in and around the Lukka lands, some of which Tudhaliya IV had previously engaged, according to the Yalburt inscription. Following this campaign, the inscription reports that he undertook the conquest of Tarhuntassa.[33] These events may have occurred not long before the empire's final collapse, as Suppiluliuma himself barely had time to return to Hattusa to complete his victory inscription on the so-called Südburg monument when he was forced to abandon the capital to its fate.[34]

What exactly caused the empire's collapse? Undoubtedly, internal dissension was a significant contributing factor, as would have been the secession of Tarhuntassa from the empire, as recorded on the Südburg inscription. At the same time, the population, especially in the west, was becoming increasingly restive as years of famine brought on by unfavorable climatic conditions in

---

33. Itamar Singer, "New Evidence on the End of the Hittite Empire," in *The Sea Peoples and Their World: A Reassessment*, ed. Eliezer D. Oren (Philadelphia: University Museum, 2000), 27. H. Craig Melchert questions the interpretation of the inscription as narrating the conquest of Tarhuntassa ("Tarḫuntašša in the SÜDBURG Hieroglyphic Inscription," in *Recent Developments in Hittite Archaeology and History*, ed. K. Aslihan Yener and Harry A. Hoffner Jr. (Winona Lake, IN: Eisenbrauns, 2002), 137–43.

34. For the suggestion that chamber 1 remained unfinished, see Singer, "Great Kings of Tarḫuntašša," 67.

the dry farming regions of Anatolia took their toll. With the disintegration of the bonds of vassalage and the breakdown of the system that enforced their terms, the starving peasants abandoned their villages in droves to seek more favorable conditions by land or sea. These forces, exacerbated by the interference of Tarhuntassa, may already have been at work when Suppiluliuma II came to reassert his authority over the region as recorded in his Südburg inscription.

Egyptian records from the reigns of Merenptah and Ramesses III describe battles with ship-borne enemies whose alliance modern scholarship has labeled the "Sea Peoples." Western Anatolia is the logical place of origin for the disturbance, since this is where the political structures first began to disintegrate in the struggle between Hatti and Ahhiyawa for control.[35] The growing ferment in the region was fed by food shortages resulting from a combination of crop failure and disrupted supply routes. Moreover, the south-coastal regions of Anatolia—Caria, Lycia, and Cilicia—were notorious for their piratical activities as early as the fifteenth century, with Cyprus and Egypt frequent targets. Ramesses II had also complained of Sherden (one of the Sea Peoples groups) making piratical attacks on his coastal towns. The famine that ravaged Anatolia probably turned these scattered raids into vast population movements of individuals and entire families that turned to a marauding lifestyle in the search for new places to settle.[36] For the most part a disorganized and heterogeneous collection of peoples, they were as much victims as they were contributors to the circumstances that brought the Bronze Age in the Near East to an end.[37]

Suppiluliuma II knew his empire was under serious threat. In a letter that he wrote to an Ugaritic official, he sought to interview someone who had been kidnapped by the Sikila (Shekelesh, also identified as among the Sea Peoples), "who live on boats," in an effort to gather intelligence.[38] His sea battles with the unnamed enemies off the coast of Cyprus probably had to do with the movements of these dislocated populations.

By the time it was put to the torch, Hattusa already lay derelict, its inhabitants having long since evacuated it, taking with them their valuables,

---

35. Bryce, *Kingdom of the Hittites*, 338–39; Itamar Singer, "The Origin of the Sea Peoples and Their Settlement on the Coast of Canaan," in *Society and Economy in the Eastern Mediterranean, ca. 1500–1200 BC*, ed. Michael Heltzer and Edward Lipiński, OLA 23 (Leuven: Peeters, 1988), 243–44.

36. Itamar Singer, "Western Anatolia in the Thirteenth Century B.C. according to the Hittite Sources," *AnSt* 33 (1983): 217.

37. Bryce, *Kingdom of the Hittites*, 335.

38. RS 34.129; F. Malbran-Labat, "Lettres (nos. 6–29)," in *Une bibliothèque au sud de la ville: Les textes de la 34ᵉ campagne (1973)*, RSO 7 (Paris: Éditions Recherche sur les Civilisations, 1991), 38–39, no. 12.

including the kingdom's most important official records.[39] Their age-old enemy, the Kaska, may have been responsible for the final torching of Hattusa as well as other cites in the Halys River basin.[40] The citadel, many of the temples, and areas of the fortifications, including the sacred Sphinx Gate, were consumed by fire. The Hittite Empire was no more.

4. Hittite Culture and Society

For more than three thousand years the Hittites were forgotten, a lost civilization. This changed when excavations began at Hattusa in 1906 and cuneiform tablets by the thousands were recovered immediately. When it abandoned the city, the Hittite central administration had left behind a significant written legacy comprising a diverse collection of historical, religious, administrative, diplomatic, and legal documents that span the full five hundred years of Hittite history (1650–1180 BCE). These were written on tablets of clay, metal, and wood, depending on the purpose, though those on clay are primarily the ones that have been recovered. The Hittite archives and libraries contain documents not only in Hittite but also in cuneiform Luwian, Palaic, Hattian, Hurrian, Sumerian, and Akkadian. While Hittite was the language and cuneiform the script for the administration of the kingdom, the hieroglyphic script used to write Luwian may have been more accessible to the largely Luwian-speaking population of Anatolia and so was used for inscriptions on stone monuments and seals, which would have circulated outside of the central administration.[41]

The Hittites contributed in important ways to the development of ancient Near Eastern literature, particularly in the genres of historiography, myth, and prayer.[42] Royal annals, edicts, historical narratives, and prologues to diplomatic treaties reveal a literary tradition interested in preserving a record of the past, in some cases to justify the present, in others as didactic tools. From the Anitta Chronicle to Suppiluliuma's Südburg inscription, historiographic texts bookend the Hittite scribal tradition.

---

39. Jürgen Seeher, "Die Zerstörung der Stadt Hattusa," in Wilhelm, *Akten des IV. Internationalen Kongresses für Hethitologie*, 623–34. See also Stefano de Martino, "Anatolia after the Collapse of the Hittite Empire," in 8. *Dall'Egeo all'Adriatico: Organizzazioni sociali, modi di scambio e interazione in età postpalaziale (XII–XI sec. a.C.)*, ed. E. Borgna and Guida P. Càssola (Rome: Quasar, 2009), 21–28.

40. Harry A. Hoffner Jr., "The Last Days of Khattusha," in *The Crisis Years: The 12th Century B.C.*, ed. W. A. Ward and M. S. Joukowsky (Dubuque, IA: Kendall/Hunt, 1992), 46–51.

41. Theo van den Hout, "The Written Legacy of the Hittites," in Genz and Mielke, *Insights into Hittite History and Archaeology*, 47–84, esp. 48.

42. Collins, *Hittites and Their World*, 143–55. For an exhaustive treatment of Hittite literature, see Volkert Haas, *Die hethitische Literatur: Texte, Stilistik, Motive* (Berlin: de Gruyter, 2006).

Traditionally, the numerous myths preserved by the Hittites have been assigned either to the old Anatolian milieu or to Hurrian circles. In either case, their interest extends well beyond the Anatolian peninsula. Among the former, the most important and clearly most popular in their day are the myths that have as their theme the disappearance of a deity from his place in the cosmos, the resulting disruption of the ordered world, and the enactment of a ritual whose goal is the restoration of the deity. Also popular were the stories (two versions exist) of the cosmic battle between the storm god and a mythological serpent called Illuyanka, which symbolizes desolation and death. The myth is the cult legend of the spring *purulli* festival. Only when the monster is defeated "may the land flourish and prosper" and the festival be celebrated.

Hurrian songs were imported into Anatolia with the influx of Hurrian elements in the empire period. The cycle of songs about Kumarbi, an underworld deity who competes with Teshub, the Hurrian storm god, for the kingship of heaven, provided the inspiration for Hesiod's *Theogony*. The individual songs that make up this cycle provided a primeval history of the Hurrian gods whose cults were becoming increasingly important to the Hittite state.[43] The Song of Release, which was composed in Hurrian and translated into Hittite in the Middle Hittite period, is a fascinating and complex poem that combines parable, myth, and allegory in a rare piece of wisdom literature that is concerned with lessons of correct behavior.

While the Hittites borrowed hymns from Mesopotamia into their scribal curriculum, these did not become a part of their religious observance. The genre of the personal prayer effectively evolved from invocations to the gods embedded in Old Anatolian rituals.[44] The earliest example was composed by Kantuzili, a son of Tudhaliya I/II and Nikkalmati, who served as high priest in Kizzuwatna. Personal prayers typically sought divine intervention in specific situations resulting from the anger of a particular deity and were independent compositions intended to be recited by an officiant on behalf of the king. Such prayers have survived from the reign of every king of the empire period except for the two Suppiluliumas, the first perhaps because he seems to have lacked religious devotion and the second possibly because of the shortage of documentation for his reign generally.

---

43. See the discussion of the cycle as a *Chaoskampf* connected to royal ideology in Piotr Taracha, *Religions of Second Millennium Anatolia*, DBH 27 (Wiesbaden: Harrassowitz, 2009), 82.

44. The best source of information for the Hittite prayers remains the anthology by Itamar Singer, *Hittite Prayers*, WAW 11 (Atlanta: Society of Biblical Literature, 2002).

Another document of singular importance is the Hittite Law Code.[45] It was probably Telepinu who implemented the legal reform that is recorded in this collection of legal cases. The Hittite Law Code was apparently a working document, not a piece of propaganda designed to aggrandize the king, as we see in Mesopotamia. The laws cover both civil and criminal matters, including homicide; assault; stolen and runaway slaves; marriage; land tenure; lost property; theft of or injury to animals; unlawful entry; arson; theft of or damage to plants; theft of or damage to implements; wages, hire, and fees; prices; and sexual offenses. It was not a complete law code, though, and would have supplemented existing forms of law, such as contracts and customary law. In any event, it is our best window into daily life in Anatolia during the Hittite period, about which our elite-centered documentation is otherwise largely silent.[46]

By far the largest percentage of texts in the Hittite corpus are concerned with religious matters. These include omens, hymns and prayers, festivals, rituals, myths, vows, and cult inventories. Even those texts not specifically religious in purpose inform us in some manner about Hittite religious beliefs, such was the centrality of religious observance to the functioning of the Hittite state. The vast pantheon of deities was attended to in temples located in Hittite towns throughout the realm by a staff that comprised a priesthood and an extensive retinue of temple personnel and dependents.[47] The most important priestly positions were reserved for members of the royal family and other elites. Unfortunately, it is not possible to know which deity or deities were worshiped in the thirty-six Hittite temples that are known. Nor was worship limited to the temples. Smaller shrines were no doubt also in use, as were stelae (*huwasi*s), which provided the locus for cultic activities. Open-air sanctuaries located in natural settings such as mountains, groves, and water sources, and rock sanctuaries such as that at Yazılıkaya located just outside the Hittite capital, also provided important sacred spaces for religious activities (fig. 6.6).[48]

Those activities centered on the daily sacrificial cult,[49] numerous festivals carried out according to a very busy religious calendar, and ad hoc rituals to

---

45. For the Hittite Law Code see Harry A. Hoffner Jr., *The Laws of the Hittites: A Critical Edition* (Leiden: Brill, 1997).

46. For a full discussion of Hittite society, see Trevor Bryce, *Life and Society in the Hittite World* (Oxford: Oxford University Press, 2002).

47. For a recent discussion of Hittite temples, see Caroline Zimmer-Vorhaus, "Hittite Temples: Palaces of the Gods," in Genz and Mielke, *Insights into Hittite History and Archaeology*, 195–218.

48. For a good overview of the known open-air sanctuaries, see A. Tuba Ökse, "Open-Air Sanctuaries of the Hittites," in Genz and Mielke, *Insights into Hittite History and Archaeology*, 219–40.

49. For which see Cord Kühne, "Hethitisch *auli*- und einige Aspekte altanatolischer Opferpraxis," *ZA* 76 (1986): 85–117; Billie Jean Collins, "Ritual Meals in the Hittite Cult," in *Ancient*

Figure 6.6. The rock outcropping of Yazılıkaya, located adjacent to Hattusa, was a sacred locus. Carved into the face of the rocks are various reliefs. Shown here is the procession of the gods in Chamber A, which culminates in the meeting in the center of the two supreme deities.

address specific problems that arose. The most important, though by no means the only, festivals were the annual festival of the AN.TAH.ŠUM-plant and the festival of "haste" (*nuntarriyashas*) celebrated in the spring and autumn respectively and lasting up to forty days in both cases. The king went on the road to celebrate these festivals, visiting the temples of important religious centers. The *purulli* has already been mentioned in connection with the myth of Illuyanka. It celebrated the renewal of life at the beginning of the agricultural

---

Magic and Ritual Power, ed. Marvin Meyer and Paul Mirecki, RGRW 129 (Leiden: Brill, 1995), 71–92.

year. The ancient KI.LAM festival took place in Hattusa, where delegations from towns within the core of the Hittite kingdom were received as a part of the festivities. The annual performance of the nine-day *hisuwa* festival, which was brought from Kizzuwatna by Puduhepa wife of Hattusili, and honored the deities of its capital Kummanni, ensured the prosperity of the ruling house.[50]

Ad hoc rituals performed for individuals to address a host of problems were carried out most commonly by professional "Wise Women" (^{MUNUS}ŠU .GI), but also by diviners (^{LÚ}HAL, ^{LÚ}AZU), augurs (^{LÚ}MUŠEN.DÙ), and certain categories of temple personnel. Ritual texts typically follow a pattern, beginning with an introduction of the author and a statement of the purpose of the ritual. This is followed by a list of ingredients to be used in the ritual and a description of the actions and incantations that form the ritual. The text ends with a colophon that repeats the name, profession, and place of origin of the ritualist, usually also with a statement as to whether the ritual is complete or not. A variety of techniques were employed in the course of the rituals depending on the problem being addressed and the particular ethnogeographical milieu on which the ritual drew. These included cleansing, transference, substitution, and attraction magic. Often incantations employing analogic magic accompanied the ritual actions. Hurrian festivals and rituals brought their own sets of techniques and ritual vocabulary. Much of the Hurrian ritual material may have been appropriated directly from a preexisting scribal tradition in Kizzuwatna.[51]

The pantheon that was the focus of these attentions was a mixed one including Anatolian, Hurrian, Syrian, and Mesopotamian deities. At its head were the Storm God of Hatti and the Sun Goddess of Arinna. Next in importance were the class of LAMMA, or tutelary, deities, originally from the Luwian milieu. Like the Sun Goddess, who was said to run before the kings in battle, the Sun God of Heaven (Istanu) was closely tied to royal ideology (see below). The Storm God of Hatti had numerous hypostases in the form of storm gods of various centers. There were also gods of war, plague, and retribution, ancient chthonic deities, and mother and fate goddesses. Mountains, rivers, and other natural phenomena were also considered divine.

However, it is not this pantheon, but the Hurrian one, that is displayed on the rock faces at Yazılıkaya, an important sanctuary adjacent to the Hittite capital. Here all the gods and goddesses process toward a central scene where

---

50. Taracha, *Religions of Second Millennium Anatolia*, 138; Gernot Wilhelm, *The Hurrians* (Warminster: Aris & Philips, 1989), 64.

51. Jared L. Miller, *Studies in the Origins, Development and Interpretation of the Kizzuwatna Rituals*, StBoT 46 (Wiesbaden: Harrassowitz, 2004), 254; Piotr Taracha, "Hittitology Up to Date: Issues and New Approaches," *RO* 65 (2012): 222–23.

Teshub and Hebat, the supreme divine couple, meet face-to-face. Their son, Sharruma, is depicted with them. Also important in this pantheon were the goddesses Shaushka, the equivalent of Babylonian Ishtar; Ishara, guardian of oaths; and Allani, queen of the underworld. Attempts were made to merge the Hurrian and Anatolian pantheons, with the Storm God of Hatti appearing in the guise of Teshub and the Sun Goddess identified with Hebat, but these were ideologically motivated and somewhat forced.

The kings responsible for the large corpus of cuneiform documents at our disposal enjoyed a special relationship with the gods, as we have seen, and the well-being of the land depended upon that relationship remaining a sound one.[52] This relationship is expressed in royal seal iconography in which the winged solar disk, representing the Sun God, appears above the hieroglyphs of the king's name. The identification of the king and the Sun God is evident also in the title "My Sun," used by kings beginning before Suppiluliuma I. With Muwatalli II at the beginning of the thirteenth century, the intimate relationship between king and deity is also expressed through the so-called *Umarmung* scene in which the king is embraced protectively by his personal deity.[53] Muwatalli II is also responsible for the tradition of royal representation on rock faces, a custom that continues with each king until the empire's end. In these representations, the king in military attire is identified with the Storm God and in priestly robes with the Sun God.

This imagery reflects the kings' primary royal duties. They were the commanders in chief of the army and served as the supreme judicial authority in the kingdom. The royal titulary begins with the title "Labarna" and the king's name followed by a series of epithets: "Great King," indicating his status in the greater political landscape; "King of the Land of Hatti," reflecting his administrative role; and "Hero," reflecting his military role. Texts of instructions and letters between the court and provincial administrators offer considerable insight into the internal operations of the kingdom. In all of these areas, the king was fully engaged, although some responsibilities could be, and were, delegated when necessary. The larger empire, as we have seen, was glued together through a system of vassalage, alliances that were often

---

52. On Hittite royal ideology, see in particular, Gary Beckman, "'My Sun-God': Reflections of Mesopotamian Conceptions of Kingship among the Hittites," in *Ideologies as Intercultural Phenomena: Proceedings of the Third Annual Symposium of the Assyrian and Babylonian Intellectual Heritage Project*, ed. A. Panaino and G. Pettinato (Milan: Università di Bologna, 2002); Collins, *Hittites and Their World*, 92–98; Taracha, *Religions of Second Millennium Anatolia*, 88–92.

53. Piotr Taracha, "Studying Hittite Religion: Selected Issues," in *Acts of the VIIth International Congress of Hittitology: Çorum, August 25–31, 2008*, ed. A. Süel (Ankara: T. C. Çorum Valiliği, 2010), 857–68.

sealed by diplomatic marriages. A sizable bureaucracy, beginning with the viceregal seats at Karkamis and Aleppo in northern Syria, administered this network of vassals, while a strong military made up of infantry and chariotry protected Hatti's borders. A workable structure for a time, it was ultimately unable to withstand the forces of entropy from within.

5. The Iron Age "Hittite" Kingdoms

The two centuries immediately after the collapse of Hittite power are poorly represented both archaeologically and textually, although modern excavations at important sites like Tell Taʿyinat, Aleppo, and Zincirli (ancient Samʾal) have begun to fill in our knowledge.[54] Tarhuntassa may have survived for a time following the collapse under the son of Urhi-Teshup, Hartapu, whose inscriptions, which proclaim him "Great King," have been found.[55] Hartapu may have succeeded his uncle Kurunta to the throne, and he may have played a role in the events that had brought Suppiluliuma II to the region to campaign as recorded in his Südburg inscription just prior to the empire's collapse. But there is little evidence to suggest that this dynasty continued much farther into the new era.

By the time we once again have a steady supply of written records to illuminate the history of the region, the ethnic makeup of eastern Anatolia and Syria had changed considerably. The political vacuum created by the collapse of Hittite power in Anatolia and Syria allowed for considerable mobility on the part of peripheral groups. In Anatolia, Phrygians (Muski) had settled in the highlands from the west, while the Kasku, to be identified with the Kaska tribes of the Late Bronze Age, had entered the interior of Anatolia as far as the southern bend of the Halys River; the Assyrians later encountered them as far east as the upper Euphrates. The south-coastal areas of Anatolia, on the other hand, enjoyed continuous settlement into the early Iron Age. The relatively isolated regions of Cilicia and Lycia may have retained a portion of their precatastrophe populations while also experiencing an influx of immigrants from inland areas, although there is as yet no archaeological support for this.[56] In Syria, in addition to Luwian

---

54. See the issue of *Near Eastern Archaeology* (72, no. 4 [2009]) devoted to recent important results from these excavations. For a history of the period, see Trevor Bryce, *The World of the Neo-Hittite Kingdoms: A Political and Military History* (Oxford: Oxford University Press, 2012).

55. For the inscriptions of Hartapu, see J. D. Hawkins, *Corpus of Hieroglyphic Luwian Inscriptions: Inscriptions of the Iron Age* (Berlin: de Gruyter, 2000), 1:433–42.

56. The retention of Luwian place-names and the appearance of Luwian onomastic elements in southern Anatolia into the classical period is one indication of this; see Bryce, "History," in Melchert, *Luwians*, 101–2.

speakers, we find Arameans and Phoenicians, both descendants of the Late Bronze Age populations of Syria.

With the merging of disparate and dynamic populations and in the absence of a strong central authority, the former Hittite provinces rapidly fragmented. The small kingdoms that arose at this time have been labeled collectively the Neo-Hittite states. In Anatolia these included Hilakku (Rough Cilicia); Kue/Hiyawa (the Cilician Plain, corresponding to Kizzuwatna in the Late Bronze Age but not as extensive); and the small kingdoms known to the Assyrians collectively as Tabal, in the area between the upper Halys and the Seyhan Rivers and including parts of the former kingdom of Tarhuntassa. In the east, from north to south were Melid (with its capital at Malatya), Kummuh, Gurgum, and Karkamis. Just north of the Orontes River lay W/Palastin (= Unqi/Pattina; Late Bronze Age Mukish) and Samal, and to their east toward the Euphrates was Bit-Agusi. Southward on the Orontes were Lu'as and Hamath. Damascus was the center of the country of Aram. East of the Euphrates opposite Karkamis was Bit-Adini, with its capital at Til Barsip. These states were for the most part strategically located along major trade routes, accounting for their reputation as centers of affluence and sophistication.

Despite Ramesses's pronouncement that Karkamis was among the casualties of the catastrophe that ended the Bronze Age, the city itself survived with its architecture and its royal house intact.[57] Members of the Hittite court may even have found refuge here after evacuating their capital. Karkamis, still in control of much of the eastern half of the empire, was for the moment the strongest power in the region. In such circumstances, its king, Kuzi-Teshub, must have seen himself as the logical successor to Hittite power, and he quickly adopted the title "Great King." While it probably did not take long for Karkamis's territories to diminish, nevertheless in the early part of the Iron Age its political influence reached at least as far as Emar and Malatya (whose sculptures and inscriptions date to the period immediately following the empire's collapse) along the Euphrates, and it would continue to be among the most important and influential of the so-called Neo-Hittite states until the end of the eighth century.

Excavations conducted since 1996 of the temple of the storm god in Aleppo have provided important artistic, religious, and historical data from the Late Bronze Age through the Iron Age that indicate continuity with the past. Among the finds is a dedicatory inscription of one Taita, "King and Hero of the Land

---

57. Ramesses II may have been referring, broadly, to the loss of Karkamis's territories; see, e.g., Bryce, "History," 88.

of Palistin,"[58] an eleventh-century ruler who is also responsible for two stelae found in the region of Hamath. The seat of Taita's power was probably at Tell Ta'yinat, ancient Kinulua. It appears that Aleppo, which had been the seat of a Hittite viceroy, had lost its dominant position to this new city at the beginning of the twelfth century BCE. Taita may have been an ancestor of the royal house of Unqi (Kinulua in the ninth century is identified as the seat of the land of Unqi/Pattin [= Palistin?]). In sum, the Land of Palistin seems to have been a powerful state in the eleventh century, encompassing not only Aleppo but also the Iron Age states of Unqi, Arpad, and Hamath.[59] The excavations at its capital Tell Ta'yinat also indicate strong Aegean cultural ties, suggesting that Philistines, who were among the Sea Peoples, settled here, giving the country its name.[60]

The recent discovery of a colossal inscribed statue of the storm god near the village of Çineköy in Cilicia (Kue) has shed some light on events in Cilicia during the Bronze–Iron transition. The inscription was made by Warika (Awariku), the king of Adana already known from an inscription from Karatepe, and thus belongs to the end of the hieroglyphic tradition (late eighth century). Warika identifies himself as king of Hiyawa (= Adana) and claims descent from Muksa (Phoenician MPŠ)—that is, Mopsos of Greek legend. The connection between Hiyawa and cuneiform Ahhiyawa, referring to the Mycenaean Greeks, combined with the appearance of Aegean-style pottery (as at Tell Ta'yinat), suggests that the legend of Mopsos, who traveled from western Anatolia following the Trojan War to Cilicia, founding cities, was based in historical reality, and a migration of people from western Anatolia to Cilicia did occur.[61]

The rulers of southeastern Anatolia and northern Syria wanted to be perceived as the successors of Hittite authority and employed a new royal ideology

---

58. Kay Kohlmeyer, "The Temple of the Storm God in Aleppo during the Late Bronze and Early Iron Ages," *NEA* 72, no. 4 (2009): 197–200.

59. J. David Hawkins, "Cilicia, the Amuq, and Aleppo: New Light in a Dark Age," *NEA* 72, no. 4 (2009): 164–73. See also Timothy Harrison, "Neo-Hittites in the 'Land of Palistin,'" *NEA* 72, no. 4 (2009): 187; Harrison, "Lifting the Veil on a 'Dark Age': Ta'yinat and the North Orontes Valley during the Early Iron Age," in *Exploring the Longue Durée: Essays in Honor of Lawrence E. Stager*, ed. J. David Schloen (Winona Lake, IN: Eisenbrauns, 2009), 171–84.

60. For the settlement of Anatolians along the Levantine coast, see Singer, "New Evidence on the End of the Hittite Empire," 21–33.

61. Recai Tekoğlu and André Lemaire, "La bilingue royale louvito-phénicienne de Çineköy," *CRAI* 144 (2000): 961–1007. For recent discussions, see Ilya Yakubovich, "Phoenician and Luwian in Early Iron Age Cilicia," *AnSt* 65 (2015): 35–53; Max Gander, "Aḫḫiyawa—Ḫiyawa—Que: Gibt es Evidenz für die Anwesenheit von Griechen in Kilikien am Übergang von der Bronze- zur Eisenzeit?," *SMEA* 54 (2012): 281–309; Carolina Lopez-Ruiz, "Mopsos and Cultural Exchange between Greeks and Locals in Cilicia," in *Antike Mythen: Medien, Transformationen, Konstruktionen*, ed. U. Dill and C. Walde (Berlin: de Gruyter, 2009), 382–96.

to accomplish this.⁶² This is most obvious in their use of royal names from the empire: note, in particular, Qatazili at Gurgum, Uspilulume and Mutallu at Kummuh,⁶³ Arnuwantis at Malatya, and Lubarna and Sapalulme at Unqi. In addition, because they had been so closely connected to royal ideology, Hittite artistic and architectural styles became the trademark of the Neo-Hittite kingdoms, which sought to incorporate a visual form of propaganda into their urban planning. The adoption of gate lions as well as sphinxes, some of them inscribed, and the use of carved orthostat blocks on temples, palaces, and gate entrances were part of the formation of a common urban ideology.

Equally important to royal ideology was the use of the Luwian hieroglyphs as the official language and script. The adoption of Luwian hieroglyphs over cuneiform Hittite may have had to do with the fact that Luwian had, by the end of the empire, become the vernacular in Anatolia.⁶⁴ With the notable exceptions of Sam'al/Zincirli and Kue/Cilicia, which chose to distance themselves from the other Neo-Hittite cities by adopting the Phoenician script, the Neo-Hittite kingdoms chose to use Luwian hieroglyphs in their monumental architectural decoration. The script was well suited to such a program of visual propaganda and easily integrated into the new urban ideology.⁶⁵ However, the adoption of Luwian hieroglyphs was not merely among the trappings of kingship, as the script and language would not have been used had no one been able to understand it.⁶⁶ The hieroglyphs were employed not only for monumental stelae but also for letters, contracts, and legal documents, which were written on perishable materials that have not survived, such as waxed writing boards and leather. It thus seems that the states that shared the greatest continuity with the Late Bronze Age empire opted to use the language and script most familiar to them.

62. For more on this as well as continuity with the Bronze Age, see Collins, *Hittites and Their World*, 85–88.
63. Trevor Bryce has speculated that the Iron Age Mutallu could even have been a direct descendent of Muwatalli II ("Secession of Tarhuntassa," 127–28).
64. On the presence of Luwian elements in northern Syria (at Emar, Ugarit, Tell Afis, and Hama), see Stefania Mazzoni, "Syria and the Periodization of the Iron Age: A Cross-Cultural Perspective," in *Essays on Syria in the Iron Age*, ed. Guy Bunnens, ANESSup 7 (Leuven: Peeters, 2000), 34n13; cf. Bryce, "History," 127.
65. Bryce ("History," 125) notes that in Lycia and Rough Cilicia, where we have continuity of population, no hieroglyphic inscriptions have been found, which could be taken as a sign that the adoption of the hieroglyphs was a deliberate effort at creating an identity for those who used them. See Yakubovich ("Phoenician and Luwian"), who suggests that Phoenician was adopted as the official language and script in Que by the new Greek ruling class as a means of distinguishing itself from the elites of neighboring Neo-Hittite states.
66. J. D. Hawkins, "Karkamish and Karatepe: Neo-Hittite City-States in North Syria," *CANE* 2:1297.

Competition between the Neo-Hittite states often erupted into military conflict, and they were never unified politically. Neo-Assyrian inscriptions nevertheless refer to them individually and together as "Hatti." But although they shared a degree of cultural identity, it was only in the face of Assyrian aggression that any kind of cooperation was achieved between them. And it would be the Assyrians who ultimately destroyed them. Karkamis fell in 717 BCE and Tabal, Melid, Gurgum, and Kumuh followed shortly thereafter. The Karatepe inscription of Azatiwada, a subordinate of Warika, king of Adana (= Kue; see above), dates to the beginning of the seventh century, just prior to the annexation of Kue by Assyria, and is the latest known example of Luwian hieroglyphic writing.

6. Hittitology and the Bible

Hittite civilization had a significant impact on the world of ancient Israel. Numerous parallels between Hittite traditions and the biblical text in the areas of religion, art, law, literature, and more have been identified.[67] Direct Hittite influence on the biblical text is most apparent in the story of David's rise to power, which was modeled on The Apology of Hattusili III, a document that likely circulated in Israel/Palestine in the thirteenth century.[68] Further, the structure of the Hittite treaties almost certainly served as a model for shaping the covenant between God and the Israelites.[69] Such direct exchanges of ideas most likely occurred during the period of the Hittite-Egyptian Peace following the signing of the treaty between Ramesses II and Hattusili III.[70] It was a time of intensified and cordial contacts conducive to the communication of artistic, literary, legal, and religious traditions. Such ideas would have taken hold in ancient Israel at almost the very moment that Israel as a nation entered the historical record.

Other parallels may be explained by less direct points of contact. The Neo-Hittite kingdoms may have served to preserve and forward ancient traditions to the Israelites. Sea Peoples from Anatolia who settled on the Levantine coast (the Sikila, Sherden, and Philistines) may provide another point of contact. The Hurrians too would have served as cultural mediators between the Hittites and the Levant at the end of the Bronze Age.

---

67. Itamar Singer, "The Hittites and the Bible Revisited," in *"I Will Speak the Riddle of Ancient Times": Archaeological and Historical Studies in Honor of Amihai Mazar on the Occasion of His Sixtieth Birthday*, ed. Aren M. Maeir and Pierre R. de Miroschedji (Winona Lake, IN: Eisenbrauns, 2006), 723–56; Harry A. Hoffner Jr., "Hittite-Israelite Cultural Parallels," COS 3:xxix–xxxiv.

68. Collins, *Hittites and Their World*, 146.

69. Ibid., 109–11; Joshua A. Berman, "God's Alliance with Man," *Azure* 25 (2006): 79–113, http://www.azure.org.il/article.php?id=131; both with previous literature.

70. Collins, *Hittites and Their World*, 213–18.

As to the question of who exactly were the Hittites in the Bible and how were they related, if at all, to the Late Bronze Age Hittite Empire, several solutions have been offered. Five biblical references to Hittites are consistent with an identification with the Neo-Hittite cities of the Iron Age (Josh. 1:4; Judg. 1:26; 1 Kings 10:29//2 Chron. 1:17; 1 Kings 11:1; 2 Kings 7:6). These Iron Age Hittites in the Bible are to be distinguished from the Hittites that the Bible identifies as among the pre-Israelite "nations" of Palestine together with the Amorites, Canaanites, Perizzites, Hivites, and Jebusites. This "list of nations" reflects a collective historical memory of the ethnic and political makeup of the northern Levant and Syria at the end of the Bronze Age.[71] This historical memory merged with Assyrian rhetoric, which referred to all of northern Syria as the land of the Hittites and to its kings as "wicked Hittites"—a rhetoric with which the scribes of the northern kingdom of Israel would have been well aware. With the conquest of the northern kingdom at the hands of the Assyrians, these traditions were carried south with the Israelite refugees, and, in the hands of the now burgeoning southern scribal institution, northern lore and Assyrian literary convention merged and were turned to a new ideological purpose—namely, the construction of a foundational story of Israelite origins in which the "nations" served as a negative counteridentity to the "conquering" Israelites. In sum, the biblical Hittites are connected to the second-millennium Hittites only by means of the merging of threads of literary tradition, and the suggestions that a group of Hittites lived in Palestine in the biblical period can firmly be rejected.

An alternative approach posits two possible scenarios:[72] in the first, the Hittites in the Bible migrated from Anatolia, adapting to the local culture so thoroughly that the biblical writers disregarded their Anatolian origins. In the second, the biblical writers inherited the use of the term "Hittite" from Neo-Assyrian and Neo-Babylonian usage, wherein it served as a synonym for "Canaanite" and "Amorite," and thus the biblical Hittites have nothing whatever to do with the Anatolian Hittites.

7. Conclusion

Anatolia under the Hittites was a pluralistic society, and the Hittite archives and libraries have accordingly preserved languages and traditions about which we would otherwise know little. The Hittites were also transmitters of traditions,

---

71. As argued in ibid., 200–204.
72. Singer, "Hittites and the Bible Revisited." For a summary discussion of both Singer and Collins, see Bryce, *World of the Neo-Hittite Kingdoms*, 64–75.

mediating between East and West in the marketplace of ideas. Their lasting impact on both the classical and biblical worlds is perhaps their most important legacy. Beyond this, the sheer quantity of the written record they left behind, rare in its richness and depth, offers an uncommon opportunity for cross-disciplinary research.

For Further Reading

Bryce, Trevor. *The Kingdom of the Hittites*. Rev. ed. Oxford: Oxford University Press, 2005.

———. *Life and Society in the Hittite World*. Oxford: Oxford University Press, 2002.

Collins, Billie Jean. *The Hittites and Their World*. Atlanta: Society of Biblical Literature, 2007.

Die Hethiter und ihr Reich: Das Volk der 1000 Götter. Stuttgart: Theiss, 2002.

Genz, H., and D. P. Mielke, eds. *Insights into Hittite History and Archaeology*. Colloquia Antiqua 2. Leuven: Peeters, 2011.

Haas, Volkert. *Die hethitische Literatur: Texte, Stilistik, Motive*. Berlin: de Gruyter, 2006.

———. *Geschichte der hethitischen Religion*. HdO 1.15. Leiden: Brill, 1994.

Neve, Peter. *Hattuša: Stadt der Götter und Tempel; Neue Ausgrabungen in der Hauptstadt der Hethiter*. Mainz: von Zabern, 1996.

Popko, Maciej. *Religions of Asia Minor*. Warsaw: Dialog, 1995.

Rieken, E. "Hethitisch." In *Sprachen des alten Orients*, edited by Michael P. Streck, 80–127. Darmstadt, Germany: Wissenschaftliche Buchgesellschaft, 2005.

Steadman, Sharon, and Gregory McMahon, eds. *The Oxford Handbook of Ancient Anatolia: (10,000–323 BCE)*. Oxford: Oxford University Press, 2011.

Taracha, Piotr. *Religions of Second Millennium Anatolia*. DBH 27. Wiesbaden, Germany: Harrassowitz, 2009.

7

Aram and the Arameans

K. Lawson Younger Jr.

The Arameans were a group of tribes who spoke various dialects of the West Semitic language called Aramaic and who formed various polities throughout the Fertile Crescent in the first millennium BCE. However, the primary geographic area where the history of the Arameans took place corresponds roughly to the modern state of Syria, although a part of southeastern Turkey should also be included. It was here that the Aramean civilization achieved its height, even if it was never a unified political power. Although Aramean tribal groups migrated into southern Mesopotamia, they did not develop into the type of polities encountered in Syria, and their contributions to our understanding of Aramean history and culture are quite limited (see discussion in "Southern Mesopotamian Arameans," pp. 256–57). In the end, the Arameans' greatest legacy is their language, which became a lingua franca of the ancient Near East.

The Arameans had numerous contacts with biblical Israel and appear quite often in the Hebrew Bible. This is especially the case with the southern Aramean polities, in particular Aram-Damascus. The biblical text sets out a kinship of the Hebrew patriarchs with the Arameans. Moreover, it recounts a dynamic, three-hundred-year relationship between the Israelite people and various Aramean polities of the first millennium that was both friendly and hostile. Thus, from the earliest origins of the Israelite people to their political end, the Arameans played an important role.

1. Origins

One of the cruxes of ancient Near Eastern history is the origins of the Arameans. The discussion is complicated because scholars have not always distinguished between issues of ultimate origins and the process of Aramean state formation. Moreover, the anthropological models of nomadism that have been utilized in the reconstruction have yielded very different results. Only an overview of these issues can be presented here.[1]

Nomadism

Scholars have proposed a number of different models to explain the origins of the Arameans. Two fundamentally different presuppositions about the nature of pastoral nomadism in its relationship to sedentary societies have shaped these models: (1) the relationship is basically hostile or (2) the relationship is symbiotic.

The earliest model that became scholarly consensus was an invasion model. This model portrayed the Arameans as "waves" of wild barbaric nomads flowing out from the fringe of the Syrian desert and overwhelming the agricultural zones, often wiping out the settled populations and bringing urban civilization to an abrupt end. As part of an evolutionary process, these hordes would sedentarize, their place on the steppe being taken by other nomads, who in turn would eventually follow the same process.[2]

A second, subtler view was a migration model that pictured the nomadic migrations as being more like a "river" rather than invasion waves.[3] The Arameans were seen as nomads who filled in the areas around the urban landscape and over time sedentarized.

---

1. For more detailed discussion, see K. L. Younger Jr., *A Political History of the Arameans: From Their Origins to the End of Their Polities* (Atlanta: Society of Biblical Literature, 2016), chap. 2; Younger, "The Late Bronze Age/Iron Age Transition and the Origins of the Arameans," in *Ugarit at Seventy-Five: Its Environs and the Bible*, ed. K. L. Younger Jr. (Winona Lake, IN: Eisenbrauns, 2007), 131–74; and Jeffrey J. Szuchman, "Prelude to Empire: Middle Assyrian Hanigalbat and the Rise of the Arameans" (PhD diss., University of California Los Angeles, 2007), 111–62.

2. W. F. Albright, "Syria, the Philistines, and Phoenicia," in *The Cambridge Ancient History*, vol. 2, pt. 2, *History of the Middle East and the Aegean Region, c. 1380–1000 B.C.*, ed. I. E. S. Edwards et al. (Cambridge: Cambridge University Press, 1975), 532.

3. Amélie Kuhrt, *The Ancient Near East, c. 3000–330 BC* (London: Routledge, 1995), 2:401.

Both of these models envisioned four great Semitic invasions/migrations: (1) the Akkadians at some unknown early date; (2) the Amorites at the beginning of the Old Babylonian period; (3) the Arameans from the twelfth century; and (4) the later Arabs after the advent of Islam.[4]

Both models were driven by an assumption that a permanent conflict existed between sedentary and nomadic societies, a clash that resulted in nomadic invasions/migrations from the desert into the otherwise bucolic and urban centers of Mesopotamia and the Levant.[5] Thus, in both models there was a heavy dependence on late nineteenth- and early twentieth-century notions of nomadism. Part of the problem lay in historic biases against pastoral nomads as seen in some of the ancient Near Eastern texts. Composed by urban elite scribes, these commonly presented pastoral nomads as a constant threat to sedentary agricultural peoples.

During the last three decades, a third model has attained consensus: the symbiotic relationship model. Based on the study of modern nomadic groups, it is posited that while there is often confrontation between pastoral nomadism and sedentary agriculture, the two are fundamentally complementary—a nomadic-sedentary symbiosis. M. B. Rowton used the terms "enclosed nomadism" and "dimorphic chiefdom" to describe a type of social organization "which represents a curious blend of city-state, tribe, and nomadism."[6] Tribes migrated within an area controlled by a central urban authority but were not subject to that authority. The tribes had sedentary and mobile members who interacted with the various levels of sedentary society. Rowton's work led to further research that produced a more integrated view of nomadic and sedentary adaptations in the ancient world.[7] The work of Rowton and his successors was applied to Aramean nomadism.[8] G. Schwartz emphasized that "the nomads, rather than keeping to the fringes of sedentary society, moved well within the borders of the settled zone, where nomad and sedentist existed in a mutually dependent symbiotic relationship."[9]

---

4. See S. Moscati, *The Semites in Ancient History: An Inquiry into the Settlement of the Beduin and Their Political Establishment* (Cardiff: University of Wales Press, 1959), 72.

5. Szuchman, "Prelude to Empire," 119.

6. M. B. Rowton, "Urban Autonomy in a Nomadic Environment," *JNES* 32 (1973): 201–15, esp. 201.

7. G. M. Schwartz, "Pastoral Nomadism in Ancient Western Asia," *CANE* 1:249–58.

8. For example, G. M. Schwartz, "The Origins of the Aramaeans in Syria and Northern Mesopotamia: Research Problems and Potential Strategies," in *To the Euphrates and Beyond: Archaeological Studies in Honour of M. N. van Loon*, ed. O. Haex et al. (Rotterdam: Balkema, 1989), 275–91; W. T. Pitard, "An Historical Overview of Pastoral Nomadism in the Central Euphrates Valley," in *"Go to the Land I Will Show You": Studies in Honor of Dwight W. Young*, ed. J. Coleson and V. Matthews (Winona Lake, IN: Eisenbrauns, 1996), 293–308.

9. Schwartz, "Origins of the Aramaeans," 281.

Recent study of the Mari texts indicates that the division between nomad and sedentary could be even more porous than Rowton had claimed. Although Rowton had succeeded in integrating the two elements of the tribe-state dichotomy, according to Daniel Fleming[10] the tribe and the state at Mari were one and the same. The term *ḫana* in the Mari texts is not the name of a separate tribe, but means "tent-dweller." Thus Mari was "a fully integrated tribal kingdom" rather than an urban kingdom ruling over integrated sedentary and tribal elements.[11]

This third model has become predominant as an explanation for Aramean origins, particularly as combined with the "collapse" model.[12] This theory envisions that during the Late Bronze Age, palaces in urban cities held the apparatus of exchange and organization of populations in the hinterlands. When those palaces were eliminated, new mechanisms of exchange and new social structures took their place. Urban settlements became smaller, more diffuse, and more numerous, and the nomads of the steppe responded to these changes by becoming sedentary. With the collapse of the Late Bronze kingdoms, these Aramean tribes filled the vacuum left by the collapse of these kingdoms, following a well-established pattern.

Therefore, internal factors of socioeconomic dynamics were preeminent, and the external or migratory factors were rather limited. H. Sader states:

> The primary, if not only, cause for the collapse is to be looked for in the social and economic crisis of the city-state. . . . The emergence of the Arameans is to be understood not as the cause but rather as the result of the collapse of the urban system.[13]

While the "collapse" explanation advances the understanding of the rise of the Arameans, it is clear that such a monocausal explanation is insufficient for all the data.[14] E. van der Steen points out that there is never simply

---

10. Fleming, *Democracy's Ancient Ancestors: Mari and Early Collective Governance* (Cambridge: Cambridge University Press, 2004), 48, 85.
11. Ibid.
12. M. Liverani, "The Collapse of the Near Eastern Regional System at the End of the Bronze Age: The Case of Syria," in *Centre and Periphery in the Ancient World*, ed. M. Rowlands, M. Larsen, and K. Kristiansen (Cambridge: Cambridge University Press, 1987), 66–73.
13. H. Sader, "The 12th Century B.C. in Syria," in *The Crisis Years: The 12th Century B.C. from beyond the Danube to the Tigris*, ed. W. A. Ward and M. S. Joukowsky (Dubuque, IA: Kendall/Hunt, 1992), 158, 162. See also W. T. Pitard, "Arameans," in *Peoples of the Old Testament World*, ed. A. Hoerth, G. Mattingly, and E. Yamauchi (Grand Rapids: Baker, 1994), 207–30, esp. 209–10. See also H. Sader, "The Aramaeans of Syria: Some Considerations on Their Origin and Material Culture," in *The Books of Kings: Sources, Composition, Historiography and Reception*, ed. A. Lemaire and B. Halpern, VTSup 129 (Leiden: Brill, 2010), 273–300.
14. T. L. McClellan, "Twelfth Century B.C. Syria: Comments on H. Sader's Paper," in Ward and Joukowsky, *Crisis Years*, 164–73.

one explanation for why nomads settle or why they take to nomadism and pastoralism again. She states:

> Factors like climate, disease, population pressure, economic decline or its opposite economic revival and international political circumstances have all been used as possible explanations, but not one of them can claim to provide the final answer and which of these, or which combination of these, is valid may differ with every event.[15]

Furthermore, there is a need to acknowledge the significant complexity in the symbiotic relationship. While there is a symbiotic "trade relationship" between nomads and sedentary communities, this is usually an *unequal* relationship: "Nomads are much more dependent on agricultural products from sedentary farmers than are farmers on pastoral nomadic products."[16] In addition, the "nomad-villager symbiosis" can be unstable because of the competition between the two groups for limited resources. Interactions between nomadic and sedentary societies often lead to the subjugation of the latter by the former. Raiding and demands for tribute are two ways in which nomads adapt to the sedentary world, adaptations that exist alongside the mutualism of the symbiotic trade relationship. Therefore, the relationship between nomads and villagers is highly complex and multifaceted: it can be symbiotic and competitive at the same time. The fact that mobile communities fluctuate only complicates the forms of these interactions.

Moreover, there is a variability to tribal nomadic adaptations that can be envisioned along a mode-of-subsistence axis (ranging from agriculture to pastoralism) and a mobility axis (ranging from sedentary to fully nomadic).[17] This means that among the Arameans there were tribes that were more or less sedentary, and others that were more or less nomadic, with great variation in between. This is, in fact, attested in the textual records.

In recent years there has been a tendency among scholars to downplay migration as an explanation. This has happened to the point that the Arameans are presented in the literature as simply the same nomadic pastoralists that are always "there" throughout the centuries.[18] But there is

---

15. E. van der Steen, "Survival and Adaptation: Life East of the Jordan in the Transition from the Late Bronze Age to the Early Iron Age," *PEQ* 131 (1999): 176–91, esp. 171.

16. Szuchman, "Prelude to Empire," 137.

17. See Younger, *Political History of the Arameans*, 74–77; R. L. D. Cribb, *Nomads in Archaeology* (Cambridge: Cambridge University Press, 1991), 15–22 and fig. 2.1; and Szuchman, "Prelude to Empire," 135–38.

18. Pitard ("Arameans," 209–10) states: "It seems quite unlikely that the Arameans were immigrants into Syria and Upper Mesopotamia at all, but rather that they were the West

clear textual evidence of tribal migrations among the Arameans (e.g., the Yaḫānu; see below). Some Aramean tribes never settle, and move not just between seasonal areas but to entirely new locations (e.g., the Ḫaṭallu—Wadi Tharthar to southern Mesopotamia).[19] Throughout the history of the ancient Near East, there have been many people movements.[20] Even if these cannot always be thoroughly documented archaeologically, they did take place.

Ultimate Origins

THE NAME

The ultimate origins of the Arameans are still a mystery. The very etymology of the name "Aram" (*'rm*) is uncertain and debated. Some scholars suggest an etymology from the root *rûm*, "to be high, exalted," and posit a meaning of "highland." Another suggestion is that the form is a broken plural from the noun *raym*, "wild bulls."[21] Both suggestions are very speculative.

The word "Aram" occurs in the Hebrew Bible as a personal name and a place-name. As a personal name, Aram (Heb. *'ărām*) is listed as the fifth son of Shem in the genealogy known as the Table of Nations (Gen. 10:22), in a part of the table usually attributed to the so-called Priestly writer.[22] He is also listed in the genealogy of Shem in 1 Chronicles 1:17 and is presented as the eponymous ancestor of the "Arameans." A second individual bears this name: Aram, the son of Kemuel, grandson of Abraham's brother, Nahor (Gen.

Semitic-speaking peoples who had lived in that area throughout the second millennium. . . . Following the collapse of the Hittite empire, this West Semitic element of the population slowly became politically dominant."

19. See also M. A. Lönnqvist, "Were Nomadic Amorites on the Move? Migration, Invasion and Gradual Infiltration as Mechanisms for Cultural Transitions," in *Proceedings of the 4th International Congress of the Archaeology of the Ancient Near East, 29 March–3 April 2004, Freie Universität Berlin*, vol. 1, *The Reconstruction of Environment: Natural Resources and Human Interrelations through Time; Art History: Visual Communication*, ed. H. Kühne, R. M. Czichon, and F. J. Kreppner (Wiesbaden: Harrassowitz, 2008), 195–214; Younger, *Political History of the Arameans*, fig. 2.6: "Select Known Aramean Tribal Migrations."

20. For example, in the early nineteenth century CE, the Shammar nomads drove tribes like the 'Ubaid, once the lords of the Jezireh, across the Tigris into Iraq. See S. W. Cole, *Nippur in Late Assyrian Times, c. 755–612 BC*, SAAS 4 (Helsinki: The Neo-Assyrian Text Corpus Project, 1996), 24n4.

21. For the former definition, see E. G. H. Kraeling, *Aram and Israel* (New York: Columbia University Press, 1918), 22; for the latter, see E. Lipiński, *The Aramaeans: Their Ancient History, Culture, Religion*, OLA 100 (Leuven: Peeters, 2000), 51–54.

22. See A. Berlejung, "Nachbarn, Verwandte, Feinde und Gefährten: Die 'Aramäer' im Alten Testament," in *Arameans, Chaldeans, and Arabs in Babylonia and Palestine in the First Millennium B.C.*, ed. A. Berlejung and M. P. Streck, LAOS 3 (Wiesbaden: Harrassowitz, 2013), 57–86; and Younger, *Political History of the Arameans*, 98.

22:21). A third individual also bears the name: Aram, the son of Shemer, in the genealogy of Asher (1 Chron. 7:34).

As a place-name, the word "Aram" is used three ways in the biblical texts. First, it is most frequently a designation of the city-state of Damascus. From roughly 950 to 732 BCE, Damascus was one of the most important Aramean states; and from the Israelite perspective, it was *the* Aram." This usage is mostly in the books of Kings, Chronicles, and Isaiah. It is erroneously translated in a number of English versions as "Syria." This has created much confusion among modern readers because of the tendency to associate this with the modern political entity, which did not exist in this period.

Second, "Aram" can be compounded with other toponyms where the Arameans were a major people group during the Iron Age: Aram-Beth-Rehob, Aram-Damascus, Aram-Maacah, Aram-Naharaim, Aram-Zobah, and Paddan-Aram. Some of these were political entities, others regions. This compounding of "Aram" with other toponyms is unique to the Bible. Aram is occasionally used alone to label Aram-Naharaim (Num. 23:7; Judg. 3:10) and Aram-Zobah (2 Sam. 10//1 Chron. 19). However, these can occur without the "Aram" component. Naharaim (Two Rivers) is the Hebrew rendering of Naharin, a toponym occurring only in second-millennium sources. It refers to the area known today as the Jezireh (Arabic "island," because of its location between the Tigris and Euphrates Rivers). A large section of the Jezireh was designated as *Aramu* in the late Middle Assyrian sources. This is the origin of the biblical name Aram-Naharaim, where the "Aram" compound works as a functional gloss on the older Naharaim/Naharin.

Third, "Aram" is used to refer to all the Aramean kingdoms or tribes as a whole (Judg. 10:6; 1 Kings 10:29//2 Chron. 1:17). In Jeremiah 35:11, the term is used to refer to the Aramean tribes of southern Mesopotamia that are in Nebuchadnezzar's army.

Outside of the Bible, the earliest attestation of "Aram" may be in an Egyptian toponym list from the reign of Amenhotep III (ca. 1390–1352 BCE), which places Aram in north-central Syria. This attestation, however, provides no useful data. The earliest attested use of the ethnicon "Arameans" occurs in the inscriptions of Tiglath-pileser I (1114–1076 BCE).

In Aramaic inscriptions "Aram" is used to designate the kingdoms of both Damascus[23] and Arpad.[24] It also occurs in the Melqart Stela,[25] but scholars

---

23. Zakkur Inscription: line 4 (*COS* 2:155).
24. "All Aram" (Sefire Stelae: I A 5; I B 4); "Upper and Lower Aram" (Sefire Stelae: I A 6). See *COS* 2:213–15.
25. *COS* 2:152–53.

are divided concerning its reference. Some understand this as an attribution to Damascus, others to Arpad.

In Assyrian texts "the land of Aram" most often designates an area west of the Euphrates River[26] but is also used in later Assyrian texts for a location in southern Mesopotamia. "Aram" is never used to designate Damascus. Instead, this kingdom is designated *Ša-imērīšu* (lit., "of his asses"), Bīt-Haza'ili (House of Hazael), or simply "Damascus." Why the Assyrians chose to call Aram-Damascus by the name *Ša-imērīšu* is still unknown.[27]

The Aramean Homeland of Kir

In Amos 9:7 (cf. 1:5), Yahweh is said to have brought the Arameans (of Damascus) to their present homeland from a place called Kir, and he is about to reverse their history by sending them back to this place.[28] Abraham Malamat remarked: "After almost half a millennium of Aramean settlement in Syria, there still circulated a national account of Aramean migration, much like the chronicle of the Israelite exodus from Egypt or that of the Philistines from Caphtor."[29] Two other passages mention Kir: 2 Kings 16:9 (describing Tiglath-pileser III's capture of Damascus and deportation of its inhabitants to Kir); and Isaiah 22:6 (mentioning Kir along with Elam as areas from which troops are mustered).

The exact location of Kir is still uncertain. Some scholars, based on Isaiah 22:6, have sought its location near Elam.[30] However, the verse's poetic parallelism does not demand an immediate geographical proximity with Elam. Other scholars have located Kir in the Mount Bishri area based on a tablet from Emar.[31] Because the text was initially thought to read: "Pilsu-Dagan, son of Baal-kabar, king of Emar, king of the people of the land of Kiri [*ki-ri*]," it appeared to locate Kir on the middle Euphrates, not too far from Mount Bishri. However, the correct reading of the cuneiform is "Ḫurri" (*ḫur-ri*, in-

---

26. It does occur in some early Neo-Assyrian royal inscriptions designating areas near Assyria that were Aramean polities (e.g., Assur-dan II).

27. W. T. Pitard, *Ancient Damascus: A Historical Study of the Syrian City-State from Earliest Times until Its Fall to the Assyrians in 732 B.C.E.* (Winona Lake, IN: Eisenbrauns, 1987), 14–17. See also Younger, *Political History of the Arameans*, 555–57.

28. Although many English translations spell the name as "Kir," the Hebrew is *qîr*. For some further discussion, see Y. Elitsur, "Qīr of the Aramaeans: A New Approach," *Shnaton* 21 (2012): 141–52 (in Hebrew); and Younger, *Political History of the Arameans*, 43–44.

29. A. Malamat, "Aramaeans," in *Peoples of Old Testament Times*, ed. D. J. Wiseman (Oxford: Oxford University Press, 1973), 134–55, esp. 139.

30. Ibid.

31. D. Arnaud, *Recherches au Pays d'Aštata: Emar VI: Textes sumériens et accadiens* (Paris: Recherche sur les Civilisations, 1985–87), text number 42. See also Lipiński, *Aramaeans*, 41n101.

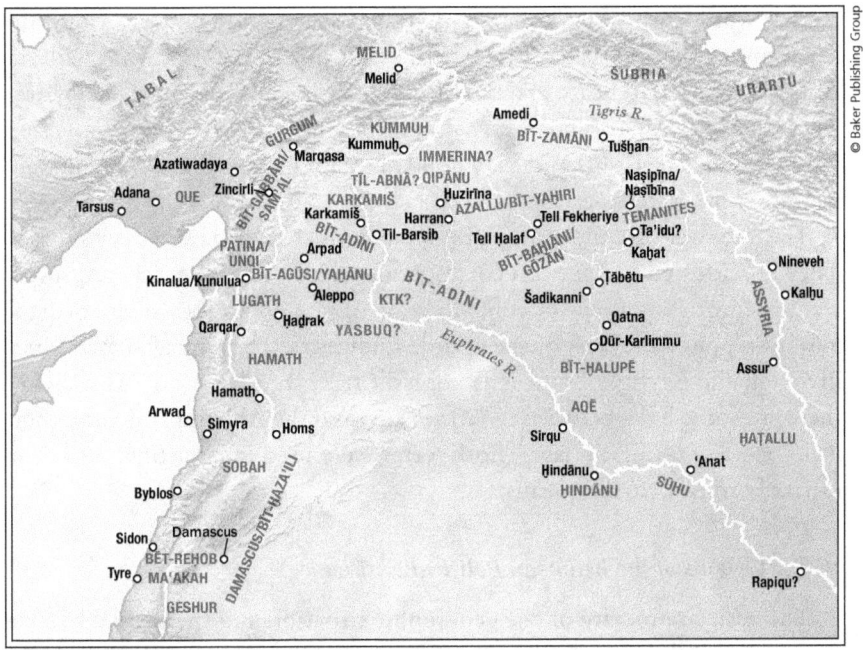

Figure 7.1. The Aramean kingdoms

stead of *ki-ri* or *qi-ri*). This is now confirmed by another tablet from Emar.[32] Thus, there is still no evidence for the location of Kir.

Links with Aḥlamû and Sutû

The early history of the Arameans is tied to that of the Aḥlamû and Sutû, who were groups of nomadic tribes already known in the Late Bronze Age sources. The Aḥlamû are first mentioned in the Old Babylonian period. The first indisputable use of the term "Arameans" occurs in the inscriptions of Tiglath-pileser I, who described fighting against the *aḥlamû*-Arameans.[33] Thus the two terms are linked. However, the precise relationship of the Aḥlamû to the Arameans is not entirely clear. The Assyrians saw it as very close. Thus a scribe of the ninth century might have termed "Aramean" the people whom his predecessor in the thirteenth century BCE would have termed "Aḥlamû." That the two groups were related can be seen in the fact that the tribe of

32. A. Tsukimoto, "Akkadian Texts in the Hirayama Collection," *Acta Sumerologica* 12 (1990): 177–227, esp. 191–92 (HCCT no. 7, lines 28–36).

33. See A. Kirk Grayson, *Assyrian Rulers of the Early First Millennium BC*, vol. 1, *1114–859 BC*, RIMA 2 (Toronto: University of Toronto Press, 1991), 23 (A.0.87.1, lines 46–47: *aḫ-la-mì-i* KUR *ar-ma-ia*.MEŠ) (hereafter in this chapter cited as RIMA 2).

Ḫirānu was identified as "Aḫlamû" in the Kassite period and as "Aramean" in the inscriptions of Tiglath-pileser III.[34] The link of the Arameans with the Aḫlamû seems to indicate that the Mount Bishri region was a particular area where the Arameans originate, *at least for the Arameans that Tiglath-pileser I encountered*. The Bishri range is a good place for pasture and has many wells near its southeastern section.

The Sutû were another group of nomadic tribes known from early sources. They are attested in the Mari correspondence of the eighteenth and seventeenth centuries as a type of confederation of nomadic tribes, active over the Syrian steppe to the west of the middle Euphrates. They are also mentioned in Syrian and Egyptian sources as nomadic tribes of the Levant. Thus, while there are some links between the Arameans and the Aḫlamû and Sutû, there is no one-to-one relationship. Both terms were used in later times anachronistically to refer to Arameans.

The Origins of the Aramean Political Entities

The very complexity of the geographic situation and the textual sources demands a multifaceted model that can cope comprehensively with all the data. Monocausal explanations must be avoided. The very designation "Arameans" masks the fact that they were not a unified group, except in general terms of language. The Aramean states arose over a wide and geographically diverse area, and there were many factors involved in their development. The very diversity of their tribes as reflected in the diversity of Aramaic dialects necessitates such an approach. Thus K. L. Younger has recently developed a "regional approach."[35] For upper Mesopotamia and the inland Levant, one can distinguish at least three major different geographic spheres:[36] (1) a Hittite region, (2) an Assyrian region (the Jezireh), and (3) a central and southern Levantine region. The southern Mesopotamian region is another area where Aramean tribes migrate (with some interconnections with sphere 2), though none of these develop into states.

HITTITE REGION (NORTH SYRIA)

After the collapse of the Hittite Empire (ca. 1180 BCE), political power in North Syria continued to be centered at Carchemish, with its rulers

---

34. Younger, "Late Bronze Age/Iron Age Transition," 136.
35. Ibid., 140–54; Younger, *Political History of the Arameans*, 111–15.
36. The Mediterranean coastal sphere where the Phoenician entities developed is not included in this discussion.

assuming the title "Great King."[37] In fact, the very connotation of the name "Hittite" shifted from central Anatolia to North Syria. Thus in areas that survived the collapse of the Hittite Empire, there was a cultural continuity that developed into the Neo-Hittite culture. In this region, there is clear evidence of a Luwian-Aramean cultural symbiosis. This can be discerned in material culture, from architecture and sculpture. It is also exhibited in the reception of deities and cults. The distinctions between the two groups are purely ethnolinguistic (see discussion in section 3, below, under "Culture and Society").

In time, the region was divided into numerous Neo-Hittite/Luwian states. While a number of these successor states maintained their independence (e.g., Carchemish retained the name "Hatti"), several Neo-Hittite territories eventually came under Aramean control. The kingdom of Hamath is a good example. It controlled the middle course of the Orontes River, having replaced the kingdom of Amurru, a vassal of the Hittites. Its rulers used non-Semitic names, and their monuments bore hieroglyphic Luwian inscriptions until the Aramean Zakkur seized power around 800, and his Aramaic inscription is followed by others in that language.[38]

Another example may be seen at Til-Barsib (modern Tell Aḥmar) on the upper Euphrates (just 20 km. south of Carchemish). This city was called Masuwari in Luwian and was the center of a Neo-Hittite kingdom. In the ninth century, when Assurnasirpal II and Shalmaneser III had to deal with the Aramean tribal state of Bīt-Adini, they describe Til-Barsib as the capital city of Ahuni, the ruler of Bīt-Adini. Interestingly, a number of Luwian inscriptions have been discovered at Masuwari/Til-Barsib, giving much information about the city's rulers.[39] Some scholars have proposed that some rulers' names are Aramean.[40] However, it seems best not to conflate the histories of Masuwari

37. J. D. Hawkins, "Kuzi-Tešub and the 'Great Kings' of Karkamiš," *AnSt* 38 (1988): 99–108.
38. P.-E. Dion, "Aramaean Tribes and Nations of First-Millennium Western Asia," *CANE* 2:1281–94, esp. 1283.
39. G. Bunnens, "Aramaeans, Hittites and Assyrians in the Upper Euphrates Valley," in *Archaeology of the Upper Syrian Euphrates: The Tishrin Dam Area; Proceedings of the International Symposium Held at Barcelona, January 28th–30th 1998*, ed. G. del Olmo Lete and J.-L. Montero Fenollós (Sabadell: AUSA, 1999), 613.
40. Ibid.; G. Bunnens, "Assyrian Empire Building and Aramization of Culture as Seen from Tell Ahmar/Til Barsib," *Syria* 86 (2009): 67–82; Bunnens, "Looking for Luwians, Aramaeans and Assyrians in the Tell Ahmar Stratigraphy," in *Syrian Archaeology in Perspective: Celebrating 20 Years of Excavations at Tell Afis; Proceedings of the International Meeting Percorsi di Archeologia Siriana, giornate di studio, Pisa, 27–28 Novembre 2006*, ed. S. Mazzoni and S. Soldi (Pisa: ETS, 2013), 177–98. For example, Bunnens understands the name Hamiyata to represent Aramaic ʿAmmī-yadaʿ, "My-(Divine)-Kinsman-Knows-(Me)." Dalley suggests ʿAmmī-Ad(d)a, "Ad(d)a/Hadad-is-my-(Divine)-Kinsman." See S. Dalley, "Shamshi-ilu, Language and Power

and Bīt-Adini, and to understand the Aramean group's takeover of the city of Til-Barsib to have occurred shortly before the Assyrian campaigns of Shalmaneser III.[41] Further complicating the picture, after the Assyrians captured the city, they renamed it Kār-Shalmaneser and made it their most important provincial capital city in the West.

There is a complexity in the textual and archaeological sources where two "layers" are extant: the layer represented by the culture of the ruling elites, and the layer represented by the indigenous or lower culture. For example, in the state of Sam'al, the Kulamuwa Inscription distinguishes between the *muškābîm* and the *ba'rīrîm*.[42] This stratification has been interpreted in terms of ethnicity. A consciousness of ethnic duality certainly existed in states where Arameans and Luwians are attested.

The continuity in the region can also be seen in the kingdom ruled by Taita (ca. 1100–1000 BCE). Recent excavations of the temple of the storm god of Aleppo[43] have uncovered an inscription of this king,[44] which when added to already known inscriptions of this ruler from Tell Taʻyinat (ancient Kunulua), as well as in the area of Hamath, demonstrates the considerable area of his political control,[45] an area that equals the size of the later Iron II states of Patina/ʻUmq, Arpad, and Hamath combined.

In this inscription, Taita identifies himself as "the King of [the land] of Palistin [var. Walistin]." J. D. Hawkins links this form—"Palistin"—with the biblical Philistines.[46] He thinks that the Aegean-style ceramic assemblages (the late Helladic IIIC pottery) discovered at Tell Taʻyinat are evidence of the arrival of a Sea People group (specifically the Philistines) in the Amuq Plain.[47]

in the Western Assyrian Empire," in *Essays on Syria in the Iron Age*, ed. G. Bunnens, ANES Sup 7 (Leuven: Peeters, 2000), 79–88. See Younger, *Political History of the Arameans*, 142–43.

41. F. M. Fales, "Die Ausbreitung Assyriens gegen Westen und seine fortschreitende Verwurzelung: Der Fall der nordwestlichen Jezira," in *Assur—Gott, Stadt und Land: 5. Internationales Colloquium der Deutschen Orient-Gesellschaft, 18.–21. Februar 2004 in Berlin*, ed. J. Renger, CDOG 5 (Wiesbaden: Harrassowitz, 2011), 211–37; Younger, *Political History of the Arameans*, 143–46.

42. The term *muškābîm* is clearly derived from *škb*, "to lie down," "settle." This group may refer to the sedentary Luwian population. The term *ba'rīrîm* may derive from *b'r*, "cattle," and refer to the pastoral, Aramean population.

43. See J. Gonnella, W. Khayyata, and K. Kohlmeyer, *Die Zitadelle von Aleppo und der Tempel des Wettergottes: Neue Forschungen und Entdeckungen* (Münster: Rhema, 2005), 90–115; and K. Kohlmeyer, "The Temple of the Storm God in Aleppo during the Late Bronze and Early Iron Ages," *NEA* 72 (2009): 190–202.

44. J. D. Hawkins, "Cilicia, the Amuq, and Aleppo: New Light in a Dark Age," *NEA* 72 (2009): 164–73.

45. Ibid., 171.

46. Ibid.

47. Ibid., 172. See also T. P. Harrison, "Neo-Hittite in the 'Land of Palistin': Renewed Investigations at Tell Taʻyinat on the Plain of Antioch," *NEA* 72 (2009): 174–89, esp. 187.

However, caution must be exercised, since there are problems with the spelling of the land's name in Taita's inscription.[48]

Assyrian Region (the Jezireh)

After the Middle Bronze Age, the Jezireh underwent a Hurrianization process.[49] Later, around 1500 BCE, the Hurrian kingdom of Mittani was founded with its core in the upper Habur region, where its capital, Washukanni, was located, possibly at Tell Fekheriye.

During the fourteenth and thirteenth centuries, the kingdom of Mittani (also known as Ḫurri, Naḫarin[a], and Hanigalbat) was reduced through repeated Hittite, Assyrian, and Egyptian attacks and intrigues. Because the Jezireh is the natural hinterland to Assyria, a series of Middle Assyrian kings subjugated it, making the Jezireh a vital part of the Assyrian Empire. Through mass deportations combined with colonization, an Assyrianization of the Jezireh took place. A tight administrative system was exercised by the Assyrians, as evidenced by tablets discovered at various provincial centers (e.g., Dūr-Katlimmu, modern Tell Sheikh Ḥamad), as well as smaller *dunnu* (fortified agricultural centers) (e.g., Tell Sabi Abyad or Giricano). Archaeologically, a material culture shift is seen especially in ceramic assemblages[50] and cylinder seal styles.[51]

At the end of the eleventh and during the first half of the tenth century, the Assyrian sources record significant conflicts with the Arameans in the Jezireh.[52] Two Assyrian kings in particular, Tiglath-pileser I and Assur-bēl-kala, faced numerous military incursions. Tiglath-pileser I claims to have defeated the "Aḫlamû-Arameans" over a wide area ranging from Carchemish and the foot of

---

48. Hawkins must explain the presence of the *n* as an Aramaic plural (-*īn*) to which the Luwian ethnicon ending -*iza*- has been added. In all other ancient writings, Egyptian (*Prst*), Hebrew (*Plšt*), and Assyrian (*Palastu/Pilistu*), the *n* is absent in the spelling for the "Philistines." See further discussion in Younger, *Political History of the Arameans*, 131–37.

49. For the Hurrians, see chap. 6 in this volume.

50. See P. Pfälzner, "Keramikproduktion und Provinzverwaltung im mittelassyrischen Reich," in *Assyrier im Wandel der Zeiten*, ed. H. Waetzoldt and H. Hauptmann (Heidelberg: Heidelberger Orientverlag, 1997), 337–45.

51. See P. Akkermans and G. Schwartz, *The Archaeology of Syria: From Complex Hunter-Gatherers to Early Urban Societies (c. 16,000–300 BC)* (Cambridge: Cambridge University Press, 2003), 355–57.

52. R. Zadok, "The Aramean Infiltration and Diffusion in the Upper Jazira, ca. 1150–930 BCE," in *The Ancient Near East in the 12th–10th Centuries BCE: Culture and History; Proceedings of the International Conference Held at the University of Haifa, 2–5 May, 2010*, ed. G. Galil, A. Gilboa, A. M. Maeir, and D. Kahn, AOAT 392 (Münster: Ugarit-Verlag, 2012), 569–79.

Mount Lebanon to Rapiqu (on the middle Euphrates), conquering "seventeen of their cities."[53] He asserts that he crossed the Euphrates at least twenty-eight times in pursuit of the Arameans and conquered six of their cities at the foot of Mount Bishri.[54] Excavations along the middle Euphrates have attested to the building of fortresses in this region by the Assyrians. At one of these, ancient Haradu (modern Khirbet ed-Diniyeh), two tablets were discovered that date to the period, confirming Assyrian sovereignty over this region.[55]

Nevertheless, the Assyrian Chronicle, which dates to the last years of Tiglath-pileser I, gives a different picture. While fragmentary, it clearly indicates that the Assyrians have lost territory and have been driven back.[56] In fact, the Chronicle's mention of an Aramean penetration to the city of Īdu (now equated with Sātu Qala[57]) demonstrates a significant incursion deep into the region east of the Tigris. Assur-bēl-kala's inscriptions also claim victories over the Arameans (the Aḫlamû designation is dropped).[58] But again, it is clear that the situation in Assyria was deteriorating. Certain pockets remained in Assyrian control (e.g., Dūr-Katlimmu), but much of the Jezireh was no longer under Assyrian control.

Central and Southern Levantine Region

During the Late Bronze Age, central and southern Syria was in the Egyptian sphere of influence. Contemporaneous inscriptions confirm this.[59] The current consensus (insofar as there is one) pictures a gradual but uneven retreat of Egyptian imperial control during the two centuries following the battle of Qadesh, accompanied by the invasions and migrations of the so-called Sea Peoples in the decades around 1200 BCE. Some of these settled in the Levant as the Philistines of the Bible or the Sherden and Tjekker of Egyptian texts.[60]

---

53. RIMA 2:59–60 (A.0.87.13, 4′–9′).
54. RIMA 2:23 (A.0.87.1, v.44–63).
55. A. Tenu, "Le moyen Euphrate à la'époque médio-assyrienne," in *Studia Euphratica: Le moyen Euphrate iraquien révélé par les fouilles préventives de Haditha*, ed. C. Kepinski, O. Lecomte, and A. Tenu, TMRG 3 (Paris: de Boccard, 2006), 217–45, esp. 223.
56. J-J. Glassner, *Mesopotamian Chronicles*, ed. Benjamin R. Foster, WAW 19 (Atlanta: Society of Biblical Literature, 2004), 189–90.
57. The discoveries of inscriptions have confirmed the identification. See W. H. van Soldt, "The Location of Idu," *NABU* (2008): 72–74 (no. 55); W. H. van Soldt, C. Pappi, A. Wossink, C. W. Hess, and K. M. Ahmed, "Satu Qala: A Preliminary Report on the Seasons 2010–2011," *Anatolica* 39 (2013): 197–239.
58. The Broken Obelisk; RIMA 2:101–3 (A.0.89.7, lines iii.1–32).
59. A. Taraqji, "Nouvelles découvertes sur les relations avec l'Égypte à Tell Sakka et à Keswé, dans la région de Damas," *Bulletin de la Societé Française d'Égyptologie* 144 (1999): 27–43.
60. J. Weinstein, "Egyptian Relations with the Eastern Mediterranean World at the End of the Second Millennium BCE," in *Mediterranean Peoples in Transition: Thirteenth to Early*

Circumstances facing the Arameans in this region were different than those in the Hittite or Assyrian regions. With the demise of the Egyptian Empire, Aramean peoples were competing not with large states like Assyria but with smaller political entities.[61] Here, the remaining small city-states were very vulnerable. Arameans were already in the region,[62] and they were able to seize political control, though the details of this are unknown. The result was the creation of new Aramean polities (e.g., Zobah, Geshur).

2. History

Foundations: Assyrian Weakness and Aramean State Formation (1055–935 BCE)

During this period in the Jezireh, the Aramean polity of Gozan/Bīt-Baḫiāni was founded in the upper Habur region. Along the Tigris, south of Assur, a number of Aramean entities (e.g., Yausu, Yaḫānu) were established. In the Hittite region, Luwian-Aramean principalities flourished. The ruler of Carchemish assumed the title of "Great King of Hatti," and numerous Neo-Hittite successor states were created, most notably the kingdom ruled by Taita (see above).

In the central and southern Levant, sometime around 1025, the Aramean kingdom of Zobah (located in the northern Beqaʿ Valley, north of modern Lebwe) gained supremacy. The only sources for this kingdom are in the Hebrew Bible (2 Sam. 8:3–12; 10:6–19//1 Chron. 18:3–11; 19:6–19). While there are numerous difficulties in these passages,[63] it seems that in the early tenth century, David, the king of Israel, fought a series of battles against Hadadezer (Aram. Hadad-ʿidr), king of Aram-Zobah. In the context of this war, Hamath also appears as a significant kingdom with its king Toʿi entering into an alliance with David (2 Sam. 8:9–10).

Toward the end of the reign of Solomon (ca. 970–930 BCE), a servant of Hadadezer of Zobah, Rezon, the son of Eliada, broke away from him and became the leader of a band of raiders who seized Damascus (1 Kings 11:23–25). His rule marked the beginning of the rise of Damascus to domination as *"the* Aram" in the region.

Tenth Centuries BCE, ed. S. Gitin, A. Mazar, and E. Stern (Jerusalem: Israel Exploration Society, 1998), 188–96.

61. Dion, "Aramaean Tribes," 1282.

62. Based on the inscriptions of Tiglath-pileser I (see above).

63. Even the types of sources utilized in the composition of the biblical texts pose difficulties. Nonetheless, some of the information given about (Aram)-Zobah and Damascus is accepted by historians.

Initial Conflicts with Assyria (Vassalage) and the Rise of Damascus (934–824 BCE)

The Assyrian and biblical texts are the primary sources for the history of this period. These are naturally concerned with their own national interests and only provide a partial record. On the one hand, the Assyrian texts are concerned with the Arameans in the Jezireh and the process of their vassalage; on the other hand, the biblical materials give very limited insight into the early rise of Damascus.

In the case of Aram-Damascus, at the beginning of the ninth century Asa of Judah (ca. 911–870) hired "Ben-Hadad, son of Tab-rimmon, the son of Hezion, king of Aram, who was ruling in Damascus," against Baasha of Israel (ca. 909–886), who had fortified Ramah on the border between Israel and Judah (1 Kings 15:16–22//2 Chron. 16:1–6). Thus, a few of the early kings of Damascus were Hezion I (Aram. Ḥadyān) (ca. 930–910), Tab-rimmon (ca. 910–890), and Ben-Hadad I (Aram. Bar-Hadad, "son of Hadad") (ca. 890–870). Ben-Hadad I attacked a number of Israelite cities north of the Sea of Galilee,[64] resulting in the withdrawal of Baasha from Ramah and favorable peace terms for Damascus. Over the ensuing years, Damascus became the most powerful Levantine state.

Meanwhile, in the Jezireh the Assyrian kings Assur-dan II, Adad-nirari II, and Tukulti-Ninurta II began the process of reconquering this region (934–884). Because the Jezireh is the natural hinterland to Assyria, the Middle Assyrian kings had conquered and colonized it. But with the Aramean penetrations, it was lost. For more than a hundred years, the Assyrian monarchs were unable to cope with this situation, ruling over only the Assyrian heartland.[65] However, there was great ideological pressure on these Assyrian kings to recreate the "Land of Assyria" as it had been in the second millennium, seizing from the new Aramean polities what was, as they saw it, rightfully theirs. Just as

---

64. Earlier opinions attributed a destruction in Stratum IX at the city of Hazor to Ben-Hadad I (Yadin) or to Hazael (Finkelstein). See Y. Yadin, *Hazor: "The Head of All Those Kingdoms" (Joshua 11:10); With a Chapter on Israelite Megiddo*, The Schweich Lectures of the British Academy (London: Oxford University Press, 1972), 143; and I. Finkelstein, *The Forgotten Kingdom: The Archaeology and History of Northern Israel*, ANEM 5 (Atlanta: Society of Biblical Literature, 2013), 75–76. However, there is no clear-cut evidence at the city of Hazor for any proposed breaks in the occupational sequence, with no evidence of a wholesale destruction in either Stratum IX or Stratum VII. See A. Ben-Tor, D. Ben-Ami, and D. Sandhaus, *Hazor VI: The 1990–2009 Excavations, the Iron Age* (Jerusalem: Israel Exploration Society; Hebrew University of Jerusalem, 2012), 3. If this is correct, there is no evidence at Hazor for a destruction by Hazael.

65. See F. Joannès, *The Age of Empires: Mesopotamia in the First Millennium B.C.*, trans. A. Nevill (Edinburgh: Edinburgh University Press, 2004), 29.

the Mittanian domination had stimulated the Middle Assyrian militaristic response in the early thirteenth century, so the Aramean penetrations served as a catalyst for the renewed militarism and expansion of Assyria in the first millennium.

Some of the Aramean groups that penetrated the Jezireh created tribal states (e.g., Bīt-Baḫiāni and Bīt-Zamani). Others formed confederations of various sedentary and/or mobile pastoral groups (e.g., the Laqēans or the Temanites). Still others organized into confederations of highly mobile tribal groups (e.g., the Ḫaṭallu confederation, originally located in the Great Bend of the Euphrates, then in the Wadi Tharthar area, and finally in southern Mesopotamia).

With Assur-dan II (934–912), the Assyrians began the process of reconquering the Jezireh. Of particular interest is the mention of the conquest of the tribe of Yaḫānu. At this time, this tribe was located in the area east of the Tigris, but later it or some of its clans migrated to northwestern Syria and formed a political entity that gave birth to the entity Bēt-Guš.[66]

Adad-nirari II (911–891) campaigned against three Aramean entities: the Temanites; Bīt-Baḫiāni; and the Bīt-Ḫalupē and Laqē. The Temanites (Aram. *tymn*, "southern") were a conglomerate of Aramean groups (ruled by sheikhs and monarchs) who occupied the area south of Mount Kašiyari (the modern ʿṬur-Abdīn range). They were likely the same group of Arameans that Assur-bēl-kala encountered back in the mid-eleventh century. Their major fortified city was Nasibina (Nisibis), a city located on the major route from Nineveh to Harran. In 896, in spite of its strong fortifications, Nasibina fell to Assyrian forces.[67]

Adad-nirari II also expanded his rule over the upper and lower Habur. In the upper Habur, the state of Bīt-Baḫiāni had been founded in the tenth century by an Aramean ruler named Baḫiānu (Aram. Baġyān/Baʿyān, "the desired one"). In 894 BCE its ruler, Abi-salāmu, became a tributary of Assyria. In the lower Habur, with a "show of strength" expedition down the river to the confluence with the Euphrates, Adad-nirari forced the various Aramean polities in the region to pay tribute, in particular, the rulers of the land of Laqē (a tribal confederation composed of a conventional twelve rulers).

Tukulti-Ninurta II (890–884) continued the process of recovery, gaining control in the upper Tigris region over the Aramean state of Bīt-Zamani. He also had a "show of strength" expedition on the Habur and set up in Sirqu

---

66. Lipiński, *Aramaeans*, 195.
67. For a detailed analysis, see K. L. Younger Jr., "Adad-nērārī II and the Aramean Temanites: The Beginnings of Neo-Assyrian Recovery," in *Festschrift for Mordechai Cogan*, ed. A. Baruchi-Unna, S. Aḥituv, I. Ephʿal, and J. H. Tigay (Winona Lake, IN: Eisenbrauns, forthcoming).

(Tell Ashara) a basalt stela that commemorated the victorious campaigns in the land of Laqē of his father and himself. The inscription is secondarily incised onto a stela that contains a relief of the storm god killing the mythical serpent.[68]

These three kings recovered Assyrian control of the eastern Jezireh and laid the solid foundation for the two long and successful reigns of Assurnasirpal II (883–859) and Shalmaneser III (859–824). These two kings brought about the full recovery of the Jezireh, as well as the initial subjugation of territories west of the Euphrates River, thus impacting many Aramean states—even as far south as Damascus.

Early in his reign Assurnasirpal II had to deal with rebellions in the upper Tigris and lower Habur regions. In Bīt-Zamani a certain Bur-Rammān (son of the thunderer) had usurped the throne. After defeating him, Assurnasirpal flayed him alive and placed his skin for display on the wall of the city of Sinabu. This city was one of the cities that "the Arameans had captured by force" and in which Assurnasirpal claimed to resettle Assyrians "whom the Arameans had trampled."[69] In the lower Habur region, Aramean revolts were apparently encouraged by Bīt-Adini and the land of Suḫu on the middle Euphrates. Through a series of campaigns in the region, Assurnasirpal II solidified absolute Assyrian control.

The early Neo-Assyrian kings subjected the rulers they conquered, but often allowed them, or chosen replacements, to continue to rule, requiring only loyalty and annual tribute. Hence, these locals ruled their people as "kings"; but to their Assyrian overlords they were "governors." A good example can be seen in the case of Gozan/Bīt-Baḫiāni (modern Tell Halaf). In the Tell Fekheriye bilingual inscription, the Aramaic version[70] designates both Hadad-Yithʻi (the author of the inscription) and his father Šamaš-nūri as "king of Gozan [*mlk . gwzn*]," while the Akkadian version calls both "governor of the land of Guzāna [*šakin māt Guzāni*]." Refusal to remain submissive brought Assyrian troops back in punitive campaigns that resulted in the loss of independence and the area's incorporation into the Assyrian provincial system.

Around 870 BCE Assurnasirpal II led a campaign across the Euphrates into northern Syria. Many rulers of the region paid tribute: Sangara of Carchemish, Lubarna of Patina, and Gusu of Yaḫānu. After plundering the land of

---

68. See M. G. Masetti-Rouault, *Cultures locales du moyen-Euphrate: Modèles et événements, IIe-Ier mill. av. J.-C.*, Subartu 8 (Turnhout: Brepols, 2001), 89–134.

69. Assurnasirpal's Kurkh Monolith; RIMA 2:261–62 (A.0.101.19, lines 91–97).

70. This is one of the earliest Old Aramaic documents (ca. 850–825). See A. Abou Assaf, P. Bordreuil, and A. R. Millard, *La statue de Tell Fekherye et son inscription bilingue assyro-araméenne* (Paris: Éditions Recherche sur les Civilisations, 1982). See also COS 2:153–54 (Aramaic only).

Figure 7.2. Relief of the Assyrian king Assurnasirpal II

Luḫutu (Lu'ash) for grain, Assurnasirpal established an Assyrian outpost at Aribua on the Orontes River. Marching through the Bdama Pass, he reached the Mediterranean near Latakia. There he received the tribute of numerous Phoenician coastal cities, including Tyre and Sidon. Some of the reliefs on the Balawat Bronze Bands of Assurnasirpal II picture this campaign.[71]

Shalmaneser III (859–824 BCE) faced three powerful states that threatened to stop his westward expansion: (1) Bīt-Adini (the major power on the western Euphrates), (2) Hamath (the major power in central Syria), and (3) Damascus (the major power in southern Syria). With the removal of one of these, Shalmaneser faced another, and then another. He was successful, after much effort, in removing the first two, even though they formed coalitions that put

---

71. J. E. Curtis and N. Tallis, eds., *The Balawat Gates of Ashurnasirpal II* (London: British Museum, 2008), 26–74, 106–43, 156–91.

large numbers of troops on the field of battle against him. However, he was ultimately unable to remove the third, Damascus.

Bīt-Adini was removed through a process of cutting off and isolating it while at the same time maintaining pressure on its capital city, Til-Barsib (modern Tell Aḥmar). From 858 to 855 BCE, through open-field battles against coalitions on the west side of the Euphrates that included a number of Aramean states (e.g., Sam'al and Bīt-Agusi), Ahuni, Bīt-Adini's leader, was cut off and eventually defeated. The city of Til-Barsib was turned into one of the most important Assyrian provincial cities.

The second threat, Hamath, was eliminated by means of a war of attrition, eventually bringing it to the point of capitulation. But this took a decade of campaigns (853, 849, 848, 845) to accomplish because the Luwian dynast in Hamath,[72] Irḫulēni (Urḫilina), enlisted the aid of a significant coalition that included Damascus and Israel.

Referring to Shalmaneser's initial attempt to subdue Hamath, his Kurkh Monolith describes this coalition, listing as the first of the conventional "twelve" participants, Adad-idri (Aram. Hadad-idri; Heb. Hadadezer) of Damascus.[73] Listed third is Ahab, "the Israelite." Although Shalmaneser III claimed victory against this coalition in the battle of Qarqar (853), most scholars believe that this battle was an Assyrian defeat, since he returned in 849, 848, and 845 to fight this same coalition without any real success.[74] In Shalmaneser's inscriptions, Adad-idri is always listed at the head of this coalition, indicating Damascus's leading role.

However, while the monolith lists Adad-idri (Heb. Hadadezer) and Ahab as contemporaries and allies, the Hebrew Bible only mentions a king by the name of Ben-Hadad (Bar-Hadad) as king of Damascus during Ahab's reign. Two different historical reconstructions have been proposed. One option is to equate Adad-idri (Hadadezer) with Ben-Hadad of 1 Kings 20 and 22 (since an earlier Ben-Hadad I is mentioned in 1 Kings 15:18–20, this Ben-Hadad of 1 Kings 20 and 22 is often designated Ben-Hadad II by those following this

---

72. Excavations of Hamath (modern Hama) have uncovered Iron Age levels (F and E) that evince a clear Luwian cultural context, manifested particularly in its reliefs and monumental lions. The native hieroglyphic Luwian inscriptions are also evidence. These are primarily the work of Urḫilina, the son of Parita, and Urḫilina's son, Uratami. Urḫilina (ca. 860–840) was a contemporary of Shalmaneser III; his father, Parita (ca. 880–860), was a contemporary of Assurnasirpal II; and his son, Uratami, reigned ca. 840–800.

73. *COS* 2:263–64.

74. K. L. Younger Jr., "Neo-Assyrian and Israelite History in the Ninth Century: The Role of Shalmaneser III," in *Understanding the History of Israel*, ed. H. G. M. Williamson, Proceedings of the British Academy 143 (Oxford: Oxford University Press, 2007), 237–71. The battle of Qarqar is not mentioned in the Bible.

option). One fundamental problem is that the name in the monolith, Adad-idri, does not equate with Ben-Hadad (other than the deity element). Although the name "Ben-Hadad" (Bar-Hadad) may have been a dynastic title, there is no unambiguous evidence to support this.

The second option understands 1 Kings 20 and 22 as misplaced, reflecting a later political situation in the days of Jehoahaz or Jehoash. Hence, Adad-idri (Hadadezer) of the monolith should not be equated with Ben-Hadad of 1 Kings 20 and 22. Rather, the Ben-Hadad of these passages should be identified with Ben-Hadad (Bar-Hadad), the son of Hazael, who ruled over Damascus in the early eighth century (see below). Thus in the stories of 1 Kings 20 and 22, the name of Ahab has been erroneously inserted by a biblical writer; these narratives really belong to Jehoahaz (2 Kings 13:10–25). Critics of this second option point out that it may ultimately create "more problems than it solves."[75] The arguments for the two options are complex, and the matter cannot be considered finally settled.

This Levantine anti-Assyrian coalition was still intact in 845 BCE (though Ahab of Israel had died). However, by 841 Shalmaneser III was able to march through Hamath's territory unopposed. Very likely, usurpations in Damascus (Hazael) and Israel (Jehu) had negatively impacted the coalition (see below).

In any case, Shalmaneser now faced the third and final encumbrance to his westward expansion. While he was able to gain significant victories in open-field battles against Damascus (led by Hazael, who was without an ally), Shalmaneser III ultimately did not succeed "in opening this bottle." In fact, after the campaigns of 841 and 838–837, Damascus "recovered" much of the territory that Shalmaneser "opened up" in the northern Levant to create its own, short-lived empire. Shalmaneser attempted to implement a strategy against Damascus similar to the one he had implemented against Bīt-Adini: isolating it while maintaining pressure on the capital city. However, unlike Til-Barsib, somehow Damascus was able to hold out.

Between 845 and 842, Hazael had usurped the throne of Damascus. An account is given in 2 Kings 8:7–15, though the name of the king murdered by Hazael is Ben-Hadad, not Hadadezer (Adad-idri). Again, scholars are divided in dealing with this problem. Some doubt the historicity of the passage, seeing it as prophetic propaganda. Others accept the general veracity of the account but speculate that the incorporation of the Ben-Hadad stories into the account of the period of Ahab has led to the use of his name in this story

---

75. D. A. Glatt, *Chronological Displacement in Biblical and Related Literatures*, SBLDS 139 (Atlanta: Scholars Press, 1993), 110n135. See also M. Cogan, *I Kings: A New Translation with Introduction and Commentary*, AB 10 (New York: Doubleday, 2001), 471–74.

Figure 7.3. Tell Dan Stela

as well, and that the correct name of the king assassinated by Hazael was actually Hadadezer (Adad-idri). Wayne Pitard has suggested that Hadadezer (Adad-idri) died sometime between 845 and 842 and was succeeded by a Ben-Hadad (Bar-Hadad), who was assassinated by Hazael.[76] Finally, scholars who equate Adad-idri (Hadadezer) of the Kurkh Monolith with the Ben-Hadad of 1 Kings 20 and 22 understand the passage as a description of the actual usurpation of Hazael.

The problem is complicated by the Tell Dan Stela (fig. 7.3). Unfortunately, this important Aramaic text is fragmentary, with the identity of the author missing. Nevertheless, a general consensus has emerged that the inscription belongs to Hazael (ca. 844–803 BCE). This is likely, since the restoration of "[Jo]ram, son of [Ahab] king of Israel" in lines 7–8 of the stela seems virtually

---

76. Pitard, *Ancient Damascus*, 132–38.

certain. However, the author of the stela uses the term "my father" three times (though without an identification). If Hazael is the author, to whom does the "my father" refer? André Lemaire has noted that it is not surprising that Hazael would call Hadadezer "my father," since this was a traditional way to present oneself as a legitimate successor.[77] Fortunately, an Assyrian inscription of Shalmaneser III declares: "Hadadezer (Adad-idri) passed away. Hazael, son of a nobody, took the throne."[78] The phrase "son of a nobody" (*mār lā mammāna*) is a technical term referring to a usurper.[79] Thus there can be little doubt that Hazael usurped the throne, though the details are far from certain.

In 842 war broke out between Aram and Israel at Ramoth-Gilead (2 Kings 8:28-29; 9:14-15a). Joram, king of Israel, was wounded and retired to Jezreel. It was in this context that Jehu assassinated Joram and Ahaziah, the king of Judah, on the same day (2 Kings 9). In the Tell Dan Stela (lines 8-9), Hazael declares, "And [I] killed [Ahaziah], the son of [Joram, and overthr]ew the House of David (Judah)."[80] Some scholars have taken this ill-preserved claim as a contradiction to 2 Kings 9 (Jehu's usurpation). However, others have demonstrated that Hazael is simply claiming a role in the removal of the Israelite king, which brought Jehu to power.[81]

Thus, with the usurpations in Damascus and Israel, the coalition that had blocked the Assyrian advances in 853, 849, 848, and 845 collapsed, and Shalmaneser III invaded Aram-Damascus. In 841 he defeated Hazael's army at Mount Senir (the Anti-Lebanon range) and confined Hazael within Damascus. He plundered the Hauran area (modern Jebel ed-Druz) and extracted tribute from Jehu.[82] Shalmaneser campaigned against Damascus again in 838 and 837, though his annals conflate the two years into one account. He captured some of Hazael's fortified cities (Danabu and Malaḫa). A piece of booty from

77. Lemaire, "The Tel Dan Stela as a Piece of Royal Historiography," *JSOT* 81 (1998): 3-14, esp. 6.
78. *COS* 2:270.
79. K. L. Younger Jr., "'Hazael, Son of a Nobody': Some Reflections in Light of Recent Study," in *Writing and Ancient Near Eastern Society: Papers in Honour of Alan R. Millard*, ed. P. Bienkowski, C. Mee, and E. Slater, LHBOTS 426 (New York: T&T Clark, 2005), 245-70.
80. *COS* 2:161-62.
81. Lemaire, "Tel Dan Stela," 10-11; Younger, "'Hazael, Son of a Nobody,'" 255-57; M. J. Suriano, "The Apology of Hazael: A Literary and Historical Analysis of the Tel Dan Inscription," *JNES* 66 (2007): 163-76; Suriano, review of *The Tel Dan Inscription: A Critical Investigation of Recent Research on Its Palaeography and Philology*, by Hallvard Hagelia, *JNES* 69 (2010): 251-52; and A. Knapp, "Royal Apologetic in the Ancient Near East" (PhD diss., Johns Hopkins University, 2012).
82. Famously pictured on the Black Obelisk of Shalmaneser III, but not mentioned in the biblical texts. See C. Uehlinger, "Neither Eyewitnesses, nor Windows to the Past, but Valuable Testimony in Its Own Right: Remarks on Iconography, Source Criticism and Ancient Data-Processing," in Williamson, *Understanding the History of Israel*, 173-228.

these campaigns (found in Assur) was a cylinder "from the temple of the moon-god Saḥr in the city of Malaḥa, a royal city of Hazael of Damascus."[83]

Period of Aramean Renaissance (824–745 BCE)

After the Damascus campaigns, Shalmaneser was occupied elsewhere in the Assyrian Empire; and then, at the end of his reign, there was a revolt (826–824 BCE). Until the accession of Tiglath-pileser III (745), Assyria was in a period of relative decline, the result of both internal and external factors. Internally, there was such an investment of power among the Assyrian high officials that this period has been coined the "period of local autonomy."[84] Externally, on Assyria's northern border there was a corresponding "period of ascendency of the kingdom of Urartu/Biainili" (ca. 830–708 BCE)[85]; and at this same time in the Levant there was a renewed independence among the Aramean states, with the ascendancy of Damascus, followed by Arpad, each as "*the* Aram." Thus this was the period of the flourishing of the Aramean states.

Hazael rebounded from Shalmaneser's devastating defeats with his own conquests, creating an empire. Expanding southward, he took advantage of a weakened Israel and annexed its Transjordanian territories (2 Kings 10:32–33). He forced Jehoahaz, Jehu's son, into vassalage (13:22). Around 814 Hazael captured the Philistine city of Gath (Tell eṣ-Ṣafi) (12:18 [Eng. 12:17]), to which archaeological evidence, especially a siege trench, seems to attest.[86] When he threatened Jerusalem, Joash of Judah paid him off with gold from the treasuries of the Temple of Yahweh (12:18–19 [Eng. 12:17–18]).

Hazael also expanded his empire northward. This is seen in his inscribed bronze horse frontlet and blinker, the so-called Hazael Booty Inscription (the inscription on each item is the same).[87] The label reads: "That which Hadad gave our lord Hazael from Umq in the year that our lord crossed the river." Thus the

---

83. COS 2:271.

84. J. A. Brinkman, *A Political History of Post-Kassite Babylonia, 1158–722 B.C.*, AnOr 43 (Rome: Pontifical Biblical Institute, 1968), 218–19.

85. See P. Zimansky, "Writing, Writers, and Reading in the Kingdom of Van," in *Margins of Writing, Origins of Cultures*, ed. Seth L. Sanders (Chicago: Oriental Institute of the University of Chicago, 2006), 257–76, esp. 257n1, which delimits the usage of "Biainili."

86. A. M. Maeir and C. S. Ehrlich, "Excavating Philistine Gath: Have We Found Goliath's Hometown?," *BAR* 27, no. 6 (2001): 22–31; David Ussishkin, "On the So-Called Aramaean 'Siege Trench' in Tell eṣ-Ṣafi, Ancient Gath," *IEJ* 59 (2009): 137–57; and A. M. Maeir and S. Gur-Arieh, "Comparative Aspects of the Aramean Siege System at Tell eṣ-Ṣāfi/Gath," in *The Fire Signals of Lachish: Studies in the Archaeology and History of Israel in the Late Bronze Age, Iron Age, and Persian Period in Honor of David Ussishkin*, ed. I. Finkelstein and N. Na'aman (Winona Lake, IN: Eisenbrauns, 2011), 227–44.

87. Younger, "'Hazael, Son of a Nobody,'" 257–61.

booty was marked as a gift from the god Hadad to Hazael after his incursion across the Orontes River[88] into the land of Umq/Patina. In addition, a fragmentary piece of a stela from Tell Afis seems to mention Hazael. If correct, this is a further attestation of his control over Hamath and Lu'ash.[89] While Hazael's reign began with a fight for survival, it became the period of Aram-Damascus's greatest power. Although it only lasted for a short time, Damascus controlled a Levantine empire of significance. Undoubtedly, this is why the Assyrians, after Hazael's reign, designated Aram-Damascus, Bīt-Ḫaza'ili, "the house of Hazael."

With the death of Hazael, Damascus's power began to decline. His son, Bar-Hadad/Ben-Hadad (ca. 803–775 BCE), is mentioned in 2 Kings 13:3, 24–25 and the Zakkur Inscription. Depending on how one understands the Adad-idri identification and the Bar-Hadad/Ben-Hadad references in connection with Ahab discussed above, he is either Bar-Hadad/Ben-Hadad II or III. The Assyrian king Adad-nirari III tells of his attack on Damascus and his confinement of "Mari" within the city, probably in 796 BCE.[90] Mari (lit., "my lord"), a hypocoristic of the king's own name,[91] is likely to be identified with this Bar-Hadad/Ben-Hadad. During this campaign, Jehoash of Israel paid tribute to Adad-nirari III.

Not too long after the rise of Damascus under Hazael, the Aramean kingdom of Arpad (Bīt-Agusi) began to ascend. This can be seen in the efforts of the Assyrian king Adad-nirari III (810–783) to bring Arpad under his control. Even though a major battle was fought in 805 at Paqarḫubuni where an Arpad-led coalition under Attār-shumkī[92] was defeated by Adad-nirari III and his mother, Sammu-ramat (Semiramis),[93] it took two more years of campaigning to "subdue" Arpad. And yet, Arpad increased in strength.

In Hamath, the Luwian dynasty—no doubt weakened by the Assyrian actions against it in the middle of the ninth century—disappeared around 800

---

88. The "river" (*nhr*) referred to here is not the Euphrates but the Orontes (based on context). See ibid., 259–60.

89. K. L. Younger Jr., "Some of What's New in Old Aramaic Epigraphy," *NEA* 70 (2007): 138–46, esp. 139; M. G. Amadasi Guzzo, "Area 1: Il frammento di stele in basalto con iscrizione," in *Tell Afis (Siria) 2002–2004*, ed. S. Mazzoni et al. (Pisa: Università di Pisa, 2005), 21–23.

90. *COS* 2:275–76. See A. R. Millard and H. Tadmor, "Adad-Nirari III in Syria: Another Stele Fragment and the Dates of His Campaigns," *Iraq* 35 (1973): 57–64, esp. 61–64; and Pitard, *Ancient Damascus*, 163.

91. See A. R. Millard, "Mari'," *RlA* 7:418–19. See also H. D. Baker, *PNA* 2, pt. 2 (2001), 737; Younger, *Political History of the Arameans*, 590–94, 636–44.

92. The name means "(the god) Attār is my support." See F. M. Fales and K. Radner, "Attār-šumkī," *PNA* 1, pt. 1 (1998), 236.

93. See the Pazarcık Stela (A. Kirk Grayson, *Assyrian Rulers of the Early First Millennium BC*, vol. 2, *858–745 BC*, RIMA 3 [Toronto: University of Toronto Press, 1991], 204–5, A.0.104.3 [hereafter cited in this chapter as RIMA 3]; *COS* 2:273). See also the Orthostat Slab (RIMA 3, A.0.104.4; *COS* 2:273–74); and the Tell Sheikh Ḥamad Stela (RIMA 3, A.0.104.5; *COS* 2:274).

BCE with an Aramean usurper, Zakkur, seizing power. In his Aramaic inscription, Zakkur describes how a massive "sixteen"-king[94] coalition was organized against him by Bar-Hadad II/III, the son of Hazael, with an ensuing siege of the city of Ḥazrak (Tell Afis).[95] He claims that the god Baʻalshamayn (lit., "Lord of heaven") delivered him from this attack. But the more likely cause was the 796 campaign of Adad-nirari III against Damascus. Sometime after this campaign, Adad-nirari and Shamshi-ilu moved the border, giving strategically important territory on the Orontes River to Attār-shumkī of Arpad.[96] This was, no doubt, part of an Assyrian policy that favored Arpad over Hamath, in spite of the fact that Zakkur had not joined any anti-Assyrian group, whether led by Arpad or Damascus. Zakkur was surely deeply humiliated by this merciless Assyrian policy.

In 773, according to an inscription of the Assyrian king Shalmaneser IV,[97] his commander in chief, Shamshi-ilu,[98] campaigned against Ḥadyān II (Ḥadiānu) of Damascus (ca. 775–750). This ruler is not mentioned in any biblical text, but his name is the same as the earlier monarch of Damascus, Hezion I (Ḥadyān I, the grandfather of Ben-Hadad I). Shalmaneser IV himself does not seem to have taken part in this military campaign. Around this time (perhaps connected with or the result of the action of Shamshi-ilu), Israel experienced its last major political, economic revival under Jeroboam II (ca. 793–753). Jeroboam was able to dominate Aram-Damascus during part of his reign (2 Kings 14:25, 28).

In the middle of the eighth century, Arpad's position of power as "*the* Aram" can be clearly seen. Matiʿʾel, son of Attār-shumkī, was the ruler of Arpad/Bīt-Agusi and appears in two treaties: one written on the Aramaic stelae of Sefire, concluded at an uncertain date with the mysterious Bar-ga'yah, king of KTK (unknown);[99] the other, preserved on a fragmentary cuneiform tablet, concluded with Assur-nirari V of Assyria and dated to 754. The storm god of Aleppo is invoked among many divine witnesses in both treaties, and the

---

94. A. Lemaire, "Joas de Samarie, Barhadad de Damas, Zakkur de Hamat: La Syrie-Palestine vers 800 av. J.-C.," in *Abraham Malamat Volume*, Eretz-Israel 24 (Jerusalem: Israel Exploration Society, 1993), 148*–157*, esp. 151*.
95. Aramaic *Ḥazrak* (Heb. *Ḥadrāk*; Zech. 9:1) reflects *Ḥadrak*.
96. Antakya Stela (RIMA 3:203, A.0.104.2; COS 2:272).
97. COS 2:283–84.
98. A. Fuchs, "Der Turtān Šamšī-ilu und die große Zeit der assyrischen Großen (830–746)," WO 38(2008): 61–145.
99. For the most recent discussion, see Younger, *Political History of the Arameans*, 541–51; A. M. Bagg, *Die Assyrer und das Westland: Studien zur historischen Geographie und Herrschaftspraxis in der Levante im 1. Jt. v.u. Z.*, OLA 216 (Leuven: Peeters, 2011), 47–52.

Aramaic treaty also mentions Aleppo in the context of extradition, making clear that the city was under the authority of Arpad.

Final Conflict with Assyria: End of Freedom (744–720 BCE)

With the coming of Tiglath-pileser III's reign (744–727), the power of the local governors was abruptly curbed, and the period of local autonomy ended. Tiglath-pileser III also initiated a policy of expanding the frontiers of the "Land of Aššur," conquering most of the Levant.

This began in 743 when Mati''el, king of Arpad, instigated a revolt against Assyria, in spite of his treaty commitments. Arpad/Bīt-Agusi was the leading power in northern Syria and was the moving force behind significant opposition to Assyria that included Urartu and others. This alliance was severely defeated by Tiglath-pileser.[100] Arpad was besieged for three years (742–740) and captured. After this, Arpad was reconstituted as an Assyrian province.

The last king of Damascus, Rezin (Aram. Raḏyān), came to power sometime before 738, since in that year his name is included among vassals who brought tribute to Tiglath-pileser. During the next few years, Rezin put together a new coalition of Levantine states to fight Assyria. This coalition included Tyre and Israel.

Attempting to force Judah into the coalition, Rezin and Pekah of Israel attacked Judah, besieging Jerusalem (2 Kings 15:37; 16:5–9). Modern scholars call this the Syro-Ephraimite War.[101] Rezin and Pekah planned to replace Ahaz of Judah with an anti-Assyrian puppet ruler, Tabeel (Isa. 7:6). Although Isaiah advised against it, Ahaz sent a large gift to Tiglath-pileser III, asking for help against this coalition. In 734 Tiglath-pileser campaigned along the Levantine coast, forcing the capitulation of Tyre along with numerous Philistine cities. In 733–732 Tiglath-pileser campaigned against Aram and Israel. Joining Tiglath-pileser were numerous vassal-kings. One of these was Panamuwa II, the king of Sam'al, who was, in fact, killed during the campaign. His son, Bar-Rakib, erected a stela written in the Sam'alian Aramaic dialect memorializing Panamuwa. Tiglath-pileser III destroyed much of the territory of Aram-Damascus. He also captured Israelite territory in the Galilee and Transjordan, deporting the inhabitants. In 732 Damascus was captured and Rezin put to

---

100. See H. Tadmor, *The Inscriptions of Tiglath-pileser III, King of Assyria: Critical Edition, with Introductions, Translations, and Commentary* (Jerusalem: The Israel Academy of Sciences and Humanities, 1994), 100–103, Iran Stela B 21'–43'. Eponym Chronicle: "Urartu was defeated in (the land of) Arpad."

101. S. A. Irvine, *Isaiah, Ahaz, and the Syro-Ephraimitic Crisis*, SBLDS 123 (Atlanta: Scholars Press, 1990).

death (recorded in 2 Kings 16:9; missing in Tiglath-pileser's inscriptions). The Assyrians annexed Aram-Damascus and divided it into provinces.

However, enough spirit of independence survived among the Arameans of the Levant that there was a revolt in 720 BCE led by Yau-bi'di (Ilu-bi'di) of Hamath that included some of the other Aramean states in the west (e.g., Arpad). Sargon II crushed this revolt at the battle of Qarqar (the same site as the earlier battle in the days of Shalmaneser III in 853 BCE). This defeat extinguished with a final blow any flickering hopes for Aramean independence, resulting in all the former Aramean territories becoming provinces of the Assyrian Empire.

Southern Mesopotamian Arameans

During the Iron Age in southern Mesopotamia, besides the urban indigenous Babylonians, there were two tribal groups: the Chaldeans and the Arameans.[102] There is some evidence to indicate that the Chaldeans were West Semites, possibly related to the Arameans; but they were sociologically and politically distinct—a distinction maintained in all the textual sources.[103] Some of these Chaldeans were "Babylonianized," taking Babylonian names and becoming involved in Babylonian political life.

However, the Aramean tribes were led by one or more, simultaneously ruling sheikhs/chiefs (*nasīku*) (see below). Most of what we know about these tribes comes from late Neo-Assyrian texts (from the time of Tiglath-pileser III through Assurbanipal), archival materials (e.g., from Nippur), and some native Babylonian texts.[104]

With so many tribal leaders, the Arameans were far less capable of united action than the Chaldeans. They generally resisted sedentarization and assimilation to Babylonian life, being clearly more dependent on pastoralism. Thus, they were far less Babylonianized than the Chaldeans, even though their presence in Babylonia seems to have preceded the Chaldeans. In contrast to the Chaldeans, the Arameans never provided a king over Babylonia.

---

102. For the origins of the Aramean entities in southern Mesopotamia, see B. T. Arnold, "Aramean Origins: The Evidence from Babylonia," *AfO* 52 (2011): 179–85.

103. Ibid., 182; Brinkman, *Political History of Post-Kassite Babylonia*, 265–67.

104. For more detailed study, see R. Zadok, "The Onomastics of the Chaldean, Aramean, and Arabian Tribes in Babylonia during the First Millennium," in *Arameans, Chaldeans, and Arabs in Babylonia and Palestine in the First Millennium B.C.*, ed. A. Berlejung and M. P. Streck, LAOS 3 (Wiesbaden: Harrassowitz, 2013), 263–336; M. P. Streck, "Outlook: Aramaeans outside of Syria," in *The Aramaeans in Ancient Syria*, ed. H. Niehr, HdO 106 (Leiden: Brill, 2014), pt. 2, "Babylonia," 297–318; and Younger, *Political History of the Arameans*, 659–744.

The four most important Aramean tribes in southern Mesopotamia were the Gambūlu (who lived along the Elamite border), the Puqūdu (also on the Elamite border and near Uruk; the "Pekod" of Jer. 50:21 and Ezek. 23:23), the Gurasimmu (near Ur), and the Ru'a (near Nippur).[105]

3. Civilization

Culture and Society

In north Syrian Iron Age I–II contexts, there is clear evidence of a Luwian-Aramean cultural symbiosis. This symbiosis can be seen in architecture, sculpture, religion, and material culture. The distinctions between the two groups are purely ethnolinguistic.[106] In the Jezireh, the influence of Assyria can be discerned from an early stage.

Important remains of palatial architecture and monumental art have been excavated at sites like Zincirli (Sam'al), Tell Halaf (Gozan), Hama (Hamath), and Tell Afis (Hadrak). These typically manifest a fortified acropolis where the palaces were located, in addition to a lower city that housed merchants and craftsmen. The monumental art, in particular, evinces Neo-Hittite traditions, with some later Assyrian influences. This can be seen in the orthostats that depict scenes of military, ceremonial, and everyday life, but also in the statuary and column bases that exhibit guardian lions and sphinxes.[107]

Aramean society was tribal. This is reflected in the Assyrian designation "house" (Akk. *Bītu*; Aram. *bēt*) of some eponymous ruler (not necessarily an ancestor): Sam'al, Bīt-Gabbāri; Guzāna, Bīt-Baḫiāni; Arpad, Bīt-(A)gusi/Bēt-Guš; Damascus, Bīt-Haza'ili; and so forth. Members of the tribal communities are often described as "son(s)" (*mār[ē]*) of the corresponding eponyms: a man from Bīt-Gabbāri is "a son of Gabbāri." Similar usage can be seen in Aramaic and Hebrew.

---

105. The Gambūlu also lived in Elam. See G. Frame, *Babylonia 689–627 B.C.: A Political History*, PIHANS 69 (Leiden: Nederlands Historisch-Archaeologische Instituut te Istanbul, 1992), 47.

106. D. Bonatz, "The Iconography of Religion in the Hittite, Luwian, and Aramaean Kingdoms," in *Iconography of Deities and Demons*, electronic prepublication, http://www.religionswissenschaft.unizh.ch/idd/prepublication.php 2007:9/29.

107. The dating of some of these is challenging. E.g., the statuary and orthostats appropriated by a king named Kapara at Tell Halaf continue to have widely varying dates assigned to them. See most recently, N. Cholidis and L. Martin, eds., *Tell Halaf: Im Krieg zerstörte Denkmaler und ihre Restaurierung*, Tell Halaf 5 (Berlin: de Gruyter, 2010), 360–61; A. Gilibert, "Death, Amusement and the City: Civic Spectacles and the Theatre Palace of Kapara, King of Gūzāna," *KASKAL* 10 (2013): 35–68.

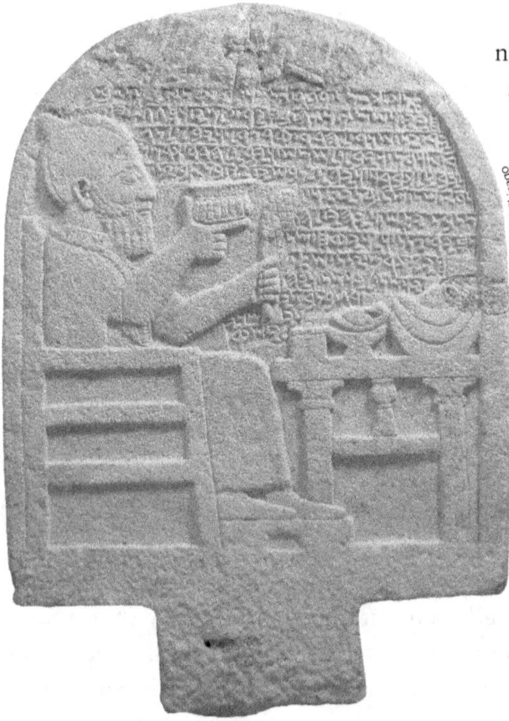

Courtesy of the Neubauer Expedition to Zincirli of the University of Chicago

Figure 7.4. Katumuwa Inscription

However, this terminology is not used by the Assyrians for Aramean tribal entities in southern Mesopotamia. This may reflect a lack of sedentarization and political development since the Arameans remained rather marginal to the urban society, and their leaders were called simply "chiefs/sheikhs" (*nasīku*).[108] In southern Mesopotamia, it was the Chaldeans who were referred to as the "House of PN" (e.g., Bīt-Yakīn).[109] In contrast, the Aramean rulers in the Jezireh and Levant were more frequently described as "kings" (*mlk*), even though often these polities were small, tribal entities. However, nonsedentary tribes in these regions seem to parallel the situation found among the southern Mesopotamian Arameans.[110] For example, in the Suḫu Annals,[111] the leaders of the nonsedentary Ḫaṭallu tribe are described as "heads/chiefs of camps" and their principal leader, a man named Shama'gamni, is identified as the "herald" (*nāgiru*) of the Sarugu clan, "their leader" (lit., "the one who goes before them").[112]

108. F. M. Fales, "Moving around Babylon: On the Aramean and Chaldean Presence in Southern Mesopotamia," in *Babylon: Wissenkultur in Orient und Okzident*, ed. E. Cancik-Kirschbaum, M. van Ess, and J. Marzahn, Topoi: Berlin Studies of the Ancient World (Berlin: de Gruyter, 2011), 91–111; P.-E. Dion, *Les Araméens à l'âge du fer: Histoire politique et structures sociales*, Études bibliques, n.s., 34 (Paris: J. Gabalda, 1997), 233; Brinkman, *Prelude to Empire: Babylonian Society and Politics, 747–626 B.C.* (Philadelphia: University Museum, 1984), 13–14.

109. Frame, *Babylonia 689–627 B.C.*, 37.

110. Arnold, "Aramean Origins," 184.

111. *COS* 2:279–82.

112. G. Frame, *Rulers of Babylonia: From the Second Dynasty of Isin to the End of Assyrian Domination (1157–612 BC)*, RIMB 2 (Toronto: University of Toronto Press, 1995), 293, 295, S.0.0.1002.1, lines 39–40; S.0.1002.2, lines 12–13.

The earlier royal traditions of upper Mesopotamia and the Levant are seen in these Aramean realms, where courts of servants and high officials have various administrative roles. While he designates himself in his inscription as the "servant [*'bd*] of Panamuwa [II]," Katumuwa was undoubtedly a man of status and power within the small kingdom of Sam'al (fig. 7.4).[113] This is evident from the archaeological context for the find-spot of his stela.[114]

Women are often depicted in the visual arts, especially in ancestor-cult contexts, though these are always elite women.[115] Women are rarely encountered in Aramaic inscriptions, except in contracts. From these, it is clear that most Aramean families were monogamous and that women could own property. But Aramean women lived in a man's world.

Religion[116]

The Arameans' proclivity to borrow and assimilate is demonstrated in religious matters.[117] Thus the various polities of the Jezireh and Levant have their own individual pantheons that are mixtures of indigenous Aramean, Luwian, and Assyrian deities. Temples, inscriptions, and iconography all attest to the richness of this religion in the Iron Age.

At the head of most principalities' pantheons was the storm god Hadad, known in Luwian as Tarhunza. Logically, wherever agriculture was reliant on rainfall, storm gods ranked among the most prominent deities.[118] This preeminence is attested in god lists (e.g., from Sam'al), where Hadad is always listed first. The famous Hadad Statue (with the inscription of

---

113. D. Pardee, "A New Aramaic Inscription from Zincirli," *BASOR* 356 (2009): 51–71; K. L. Younger Jr., "Two Epigraphic Notes on the New Katumuwa Inscription from Zincirli," *Maarav* 16 (2009): 159–79.

114. See J. D. Schloen and A. S. Fink, "New Excavations at Zincirli Höyük in Turkey (Ancient Sam'al) and the Discovery of an Inscribed Mortuary Stele," *BASOR* 356 (2009): 1–13.

115. E.g., see Zincirli and Tell Halaf. See H. Niehr, "Bestattung und Ahnenkult in den Königshäusern von Sam'al (Zincirli) und Guzāna (Tell Ḥalāf) in Nordsyrien," *ZDPV* 122 (2006): 111–39, and tafeln 17–23.

116. For excellent studies of the religion of the Arameans, see H. Niehr, "B. Die Aramäer in Syrien," in *Religionen in der Umwelt des Alten Testaments II: Phönizier, Punier, Aramäer*, ed. C. Bonnet and H. Niehr, Kohlhammer Studienbücher Theologie 4.2 (Stuttgart: Kohlhammer, 2010), 199–324; Niehr, "Religion," in *The Aramaeans in Ancient Syria*, ed. H. Niehr, HdO 106 (Leiden: Brill, 2014), 127–203.

117. M. Novák, "Arameans and Luwians—Processes of an Acculturation," in *Ethnicity in Ancient Mesopotamia: Papers Read at the 48th Rencontre Assyriologique Internationale, Leiden, 1–4 July 2002*, ed. W. H. van Soldt, R. Kalvelagen, and D. Katz (Leiden: Nederlands Instituut voor het Nabije Oosten, 2005), 252–66.

118. D. Schwemer, "The Storm-Gods of the Ancient Near East: Summary, Synthesis, Recent Studies, Part 1," *JANER* 7, no. 2 (2007): 121–68; Schwemer, "The Storm-Gods of the Ancient Near East: Summary, Synthesis, Recent Studies, Part 2," *JANER* 8, no. 1 (2008): 1–44.

Figure 7.5. Hadad Statue

Panamuwa I; fig. 7.5) demonstrates this deity's importance to the royal ancestor cult (see below).

The oldest attested Aramean epithet for Hadad is Ramman, "the Thunderer." The importance of the cult of the storm god in Bīt-Zamani can be seen in an oath imposed on Amme-Baʿal by Tukulti-Ninurta II: "If you give horses to my enemies (and) foes, may the god Adad (Hadad) [strike your] land with terrible lightning."[119] This deity is depicted standing on a bull and armed with thunderbolts, often in a pose in which he is seen preparing to strike with his weapon, the so-called smiting pose.

As Ramman, Hadad presided over the destinies of Damascus and was the object of a mourning ritual reminiscent of the mourning for Baal at Ugarit and of the later cult of Adonis. Numerous names of the kings of Damascus contained the theonym "Hadad." In the Tell Dan Stela, Hazael credits Hadad with "going before" him (protecting him in battle);[120] and in his Booty Inscription, he labels: "That which Hadad gave to our lord Hazael . . ."[121]

The storm god was recognized in some important local manifestations. The ancient universal fame of the storm god of Aleppo is one example. Recent excavations have uncovered the remains of a temple to this deity in various periods from the third to the first millennium.[122] In the eleventh-century phase of this temple, the image and inscription of King Taita (see discussion above) were discovered positioned opposite to the Neo-Hittite image

---

119. Tukulti-Ninurta II; RIMA 2:172 (A.0.0.100.5, line 25).
120. *COS* 2:161–62.
121. *COS* 2:162.
122. Kohlmeyer, "Temple of the Storm God," 190–202.

of the storm god in smiting pose. The heavenly manifestation of the storm god as "Baʻalšamayn" is evident in the Zakkur inscription. This is "Celestial Tarhunza" of a number of Luwian inscriptions. In ancient Guzāna, the Hadad of the city of Sikan is described as "the Lord of the Ḫabur River" (Tell Fekheriye Stela).

Another very important deity throughout the Aramean world was the moon god (Aram. Sahr; Akk. Sîn). This deity was, from early times, firmly associated with the city of Harran on the northern Balīḫ River. His popularity is seen in the iconography and glyptic.[123] Stelae and orthostats containing reliefs of crescents on poles with tassels are common throughout the region; simple crescents, or full lunar disks shown with crescents on the bottom, are found on stelae, orthostats, and numerous cylinder and stamp seals (often with Aramaic inscriptions). The deity is mentioned in the Zakkur inscription as well as in the inscriptions of two of this deity's priests (*kumr*) from Nerab. On an orthostat that contains a relief of a disk, crescent, pole, and tassels, Bar-Rakib, king of Sam'al, declared in a short inscription: "My lord is the Lord of Harran [i.e., Sahr] . . ." (*KAI* no. 218). This god's popularity is also demonstrated in the significant number of Aramaic personal names that contain his theonym.

Another significant deity was Shamash, the sun god. Mentioned in numerous texts and represented by a winged solar disk on reliefs and seals, Shamash not only was a god of justice but also played a crucial role in the royal ancestor cult. Being the only deity that crossed *daily* the threshold between the upper and lower worlds, between this life and the next, he was frequently represented on grave memorials as a winged solar disk at the top of the arc-shaped upper edge of the stela, appropriately marking the "paradox" place between the two worlds.[124] The winged solar disk was also used as a symbol of regeneration.[125]

Two female deities deserve mention, even though they are not mentioned as often as the Aramean male deities: Kubaba and Astarte. Kubaba, who was a Luwian mother goddess prominent at the city of Carchemish, is a deity attested in Aramaic inscriptions. Among the deities at ancient Sam'al, the goddess Kubaba is mentioned in the Katumuwa and Ördek Burnu stelae and is pictured on an orthostat relief from Zincirli. She is also attested in the Tell

---

123. See T. Staubli, "Sin von Harran und seine Verbreitung im Westen," in *Werbung für die Götter: Heilsbringer aus 4000 Jahren; Eine Ausstellung in den Museen für Kommunikation von Bern 28.2.03–25.1.04 und Frankfurt 26.2.04–13.6.04* (Freiburg: Universitätsverlag, 2003), 65–89.

124. For these, see D. Bonatz, *Das syro-hethitische Grabdenkmal: Untersuchungen zur Entstehung einer neuen Bildgattung in der Eisenzeit im nordsyrisch-südostanatolischen Raum* (Mainz: Philipp van Zabern, 2000).

125. J. Kutter, *Nūr ilī: Die Sonnengottheiten in den nordwestsemitischen Religionen von der Spätbronzezeit bis zur vorrömischen Zeit*, AOAT 346 (Münster: Ugarit-Verlag, 2008), 308.

Sifr inscription (probably located in the kingdom of Arpad) and in the treaty of Assur-nirari V with Mati"el, king of Arpad. Her name is the theonym in a number of personal names that have Aramaic predicates.[126] Astarte, the "Lady" of the Phoenician cities of Sidon and of Byblos, was the western counterpart of Mesopotamian Ishtar. She is attested primarily in artistic forms, as the woman at the window of numerous Aramean ivory plaques found at the Assyrian capital city of Kalhu (Nimrud), and as a nude goddess with the nude figures standing on lions' heads (e.g., the bronze Hazael horse frontlet and Zincirli horsehead statuary with horse frontlet).

Another later goddess, Atargatis (the *Dea Syria*, "Syrian goddess," of classical times) combines features of the two above goddesses. Atargatis bears an Aramaic name related to Astarte, and her holy city (Hierapolis) was at Bambyke, the ancient Nampigi (Mambidj) in Bīt-Adini. Atargatis was also related to Kubaba. She had a close relationship with fish, which were her sacred animal and which were kept in the ponds in and around her shrines and sanctuaries. According to the classical tradition, the goddess manifested herself as a fish.

A number of other Aramean deities deserve mention. Attār, a god of fertility and vegetation, is attested primarily in Aramean personal names (e.g., Attār-shumkī). The deity Rakib-El (lit., "charioteer of El"), who bore the title "Lord of the House [i.e., dynasty]," was the protector deity of the kings of Sam'al (Zincirli) and seems unique to this small kingdom. Rašap, the god of plague, is also attested at Sam'al and Arpad. Melqart, chief god of Tyre, a Phoenician deity, was worshiped in north Syria (Melqart stela). Finally, there is a growing number of attestations of an Aramean deity named Ashima, though the function of this god is still not understood.

There is much evidence of an ancestor cult among the Arameans.[127] Clear examples are seen especially at ancient Sam'al. The inscription of Panamuwa (I) on the statue of Hadad demonstrates this. The offerer is instructed to invoke: "May the dead spirit of Pana[muwa] eat with Hadad, and may the dead spirit of Panamuwa drink with Had[ad]"; thus the deceased king Panamuwa was memorialized before Hadad.[128]

Finally, it is important to note that there was a significant Aramean astrological tradition. This is most manifest in a bronze bowl that contains an astral scene with tiny labels in Aramaic (dating to the mid-eighth century).[129] It depicts a cen-

126. For references, see Younger, "Two Epigraphic Notes," 159–79.
127. See particularly Niehr, "Bestattung und Ahnenkult," 111–39, and tafeln 17–23.
128. *COS* 2:156–58. See now also the example of the Katumuwa inscription.
129. K. L. Younger Jr., "Another Look at an Aramaic Astral Bowl," *JNES* 71, no. 2 (2012): 209–30.

tral motif, comprised mainly of the constellation Orion (clearly representative of the well-known storm-god imagery, i.e., Hadad). Eight zones surround the central motif, each zone picturing an astral identity. The zones directly above and below the central motif show the sun and the moon (labeled Shamash and Sahr respectively). Such a bowl was utilized in divination on behalf of royalty.

Literature

The Arameans' greatest contribution to ancient Near Eastern civilization was the Aramaic language; and yet, almost no Aramaic literature older than the Persian Empire has been recovered.[130] The oldest Aramaic inscriptions are preserved on stone monuments (stelae and orthostats: e.g., Tell Fekheriye, Hadad, Zakkur, Panamuwa, Katumuwa, Bar-Rakib, Tell Dan, and Bukān). Many other writings were committed to perishable media (papyrus, wax tablets), or the writing material itself was perishable (i.e., ink painted onto clay or stone).[131] This helps explain the lack of literary works in Aramaic. The Proverbs of Ahiqar are a notable exception.

The oldest inscriptions are written in a variety of dialects and are mostly commemorative inscriptions, treaties, contracts, letters, and lists. The influences of Luwian and Assyrian are evident regionally, both in bilinguals and lexical details (loanwords and phrases). Nevertheless, the importance of Aramaic, even in areas where it was not the native language, is seen in a text like the Bukān Inscription.[132]

The utilization of Aramaic was increased exponentially by the Assyrian deportations of Arameans throughout the empire, but particularly to the Assyrian heartland. Thus by the seventh century it was becoming the lingua franca of the ancient Near East, playing a crucial role in both the late Neo-Assyrian and Neo-Babylonian Empires.

The survival of papyri in Egypt has provided a window into the Aramaic literary tradition that flourished during the Persian period, though the Aramean Proverbs of Ahiqar found at Elephantine in Upper Egypt are clearly much older than their archaeological context of 400 BCE, with their original core dating back to the seventh-century context of the Assyrian king Esarhaddon.

---

130. I. Kottsieper, "Aramaic Literature," in *From an Antique Land: An Introduction to Ancient Near Eastern Literature*, ed. C. S. Ehrlich (Lanham, MD: Rowman & Littlefield, 2009), 393–492.

131. F. M. Fales, "Between Archaeology and Linguistics: The Use of Aramaic Writing in Painted Characters on Clay Tablets of the 7th Century BC," in *XII Incontro italiano di linguistica camito-semitica (afroasiatica)*, ed. M. Moriggi, Medioevo romanzo e orientale, Colloqui 9 (Soveria Mannelli: Rubbettino, 2007), 139–60.

132. *COS* 3:219. Amazingly, the Aramaic language will later be written in Demotic script in Egypt (*COS* 1:309–27) and also in the cuneiform script.

The dominance of Aramaic presents a fascinating anomaly in the history of world languages.[133] At the very time that Aramaic became a dominant vehicle for administration and communication, it nevertheless failed to serve as a dominant cultural vehicle—such as happens typically with international languages (e.g., Akkadian, Greek, Latin, Sanskrit, Arabic)—even as it was being promoted as the official language of the Assyrian, Babylonian, and Achaemenid Persian Empires, and at the peak of its internationalization. This failure may be explained in part by the Assyrians' adoption of the language in the eighth century as a political strategy to integrate the western provinces into the empire. Since the Arameans were never unified and never created an empire, they never achieved a hegemonic base. Thus their language never had the cultural influence that most international languages wield.

For Further Reading

Akkermans, P. M. M. G., and G. M. Schwartz. *The Archaeology of Syria: From Complex Hunter-Gatherers to Early Urban Societies (c. 16,000–300 BC)*. Cambridge: Cambridge University Press, 2003.

Berlejung, A., and M. P. Streck, eds. *Arameans, Chaldeans, and Arabs in Babylonia and Palestine in the First Millennium B.C.* LAOS 3. Wiesbaden: Harrassowitz, 2013.

Daviau, P. M. M., J. W. Wevers, and M. Weigl, eds. *The World of the Aramaeans*. 3 vols. JSOTSup 324–26. Sheffield: Sheffield Academic Press, 2001.

Dion, P.-E. *Les Araméens à l'âge du fer: Histoire politique et structures sociales*. Études bibliques, n.s., 34. Paris: J. Gabalda, 1997.

Fales, F. M. "Old Aramaic." In *The Semitic Languages: An International Handbook*, edited by S. Weninger, G. Khan, M. P. Streck, and J. C. E. Watson, 555–73. Berlin and Boston: De Gruyter Mouton, 2011.

Gzella, H. *A Cultural History of Aramaic: From the Beginnings to the Advent of Islam*. HdO 111. Leiden: Brill, 2015.

Herrmann, V. R., and J. D. Schloen, eds. *In Remembrance of Me: Feasting with the Dead in the Ancient Near East*. OIP 37. Chicago: Oriental Institute, 2014.

Lipiński, E. *The Arameans: Their Ancient History, Culture, Religion*. OLA 100. Leuven: Peeters, 2000.

---

133. P.-A. Beaulieu, "Official and Vernacular Languages: The Shifting Sands of Imperial and Cultural Identities in First Millennium B.C. Mesopotamia," in Sanders, *Margins of Writing*, 187–216, esp. 208.

Niehr, H., ed. *The Aramaeans in Ancient Syria*. HdO 106. Leiden: Brill, 2014.

Younger, K. L., Jr. *A Political History of the Arameans: From Their Origins to the End of Their Polities*. ABS 13. Atlanta: Society of Biblical Literature, 2016.

Zadok, R. "The Aramean Infiltration and Diffusion in the Upper Jazira, ca. 1150–930 BCE." In *The Ancient Near East in the 12th–10th Centuries BCE: Culture and History; Proceedings of the International Conference Held at the University of Haifa, 2–5 May, 2010*, edited by G. Galil, A. Gilboa, A. M. Maier, and D. Kahn, 569–79. AOAT 392. Münster: Ugarit-Verlag, 2012.

8

Phoenicia and the Phoenicians

CHRISTOPHER A. ROLLSTON

"Phoenicia" is a broad (Greek) term used for certain cities of the eastern Mediterranean coastal region that shared a common language and culture, accompanied by political solidarity and a sense of shared ethnicity. The etymological meaning of the term "Phoenicia" has been much discussed, and it is normally argued that its original meaning was "purple" or "crimson" (and this geographicon was connected with the production of colored dye known to have occurred in this region).[1] In any case, among the prominent ancient cities of Phoenicia were Tyre, Sidon, Beirut, Byblos, and Arvad. Significantly, however, there was not an ancient nation per se that can be termed "Phoenicia," and there was not a king who was considered to be the king of the entire Phoenician realm. Rather, the major Phoenician cities were basically federated city-states ruled by separate kings (and these city-states often had spheres of influence that engulfed smaller cities in their region). For this reason, a number of Iron Age Phoenician inscriptions refer to (for example) "the king

---

I am grateful to my research assistant Jared Poznich for his assistance in assembling many of the bibliographic materials.

1. See Michael C. Astour, "The Origin of the Terms 'Canaan,' 'Phoenician,' and 'Purple,'" *JNES* 24 (1965): 346–50.

of Byblos" and "the king of Sidon" rather than to the "king of Phoenicia."[2] The Amarna letters (ca. fourteenth century BCE) arguably provide correlative data from the Late Bronze Age.[3] For example, a number these letters are from, or refer to, cities such as Byblos, Sidon, Tyre, Arvad, and Beirut, and the term "king" (Akk. *šarrum*) is sometimes used of these rulers (in spite of at least some sort of Egyptian hegemony in the region at this time).[4] Thus Rib-Hadda, the king of Byblos, mentions the "king of Beirut, the king of Sidon, and the king of Tyre" in some of his correspondence.[5] This pericope is also of particular import because within it Rib-Hadda conveys his gratitude to the pharaoh for sending a message to these kings (i.e., of Beirut, Sidon, and Tyre) in order to request that they support Rib-Hadda in his resistance to the forces of Abdi-Ashrati (of the kingdom of Amurru), with the added notation from Rib-Hadda that "the three of us are brothers."[6] Naturally, although diplomatic relations between these cities (e.g., Byblos, Tyre, Sidon, Beirut, and Arvad) were certainly amicable at times, tensions were also sometimes present between them during this chronological horizon (and arguably later as well). For example, Abi-Milku of Tyre writes to the pharaoh that "the ruler of {Sidon, Z}imredda is ho{stile to m}e."[7] Similarly, Rib-Hadda of Byblos is the putative sender of a letter in which he mentions that ships associated with the "Men of Arvad" have attacked him.[8] In sum, it is reasonable to posit that during certain chronological horizons of the Late Bronze Age there were periods of harmony between these cities of the Mediterranean littoral and there were periods of conflict and tension. Moreover, although there is a general dearth of data (but certainly not a complete absence of data), I would posit that the same thing can probably be said for the Iron Age history of these cities as well. In any case, the main point is that Iron Age Phoenicia was

---

2. See Herbert Donner and Wolfgang Röllig, *Kanaanäische und aramäische Inschriften: Volume 1*, 5th ed. (Wiesbaden: Harrassowitz, 2002), 1–4 (nos. 1–16).

3. For an English translation, see William L. Moran, *The Amarna Letters* (Baltimore: Johns Hopkins University Press, 2002).

4. For a nuanced discussion of Egyptian hegemony, see Donald Redford, *Egypt, Canaan, and Israel in Ancient Times* (Princeton: Princeton University Press, 1992), 125–213.

5. Moran, *Amarna Letters*, 166–67 (no. 92, lines 32–34). For further discussion of the terminology for political leaders, see ibid., xxvi–xxxii, esp. nn. 70 and 73.

6. Ibid., 166 (no. 92, line 44). For a fine discussion of the breadth of meaning for this term "brothers," see Amanda H. Podany, *Brotherhood of Kings: How International Relations Shaped the Ancient Near East* (Oxford: Oxford University Press, 2010), 191–216 and passim. Suffice it to say that "brother" and "brotherhood" are not simply kinship terms.

7. Moran, *Amarna Letters*, 232 (no. 146, lines 15–16).

8. Ibid., 174 (no. 101). Note that Donald Redford has suggested that "although we know little of Arvad at this time [the Late Bronze Age], Byblos, Beirut, Sidon, and Tyre fall into the category of privileged state" (vis-à-vis the Egyptian throne), as did also Ugarit (*Egypt, Canaan, and Israel*, 168).

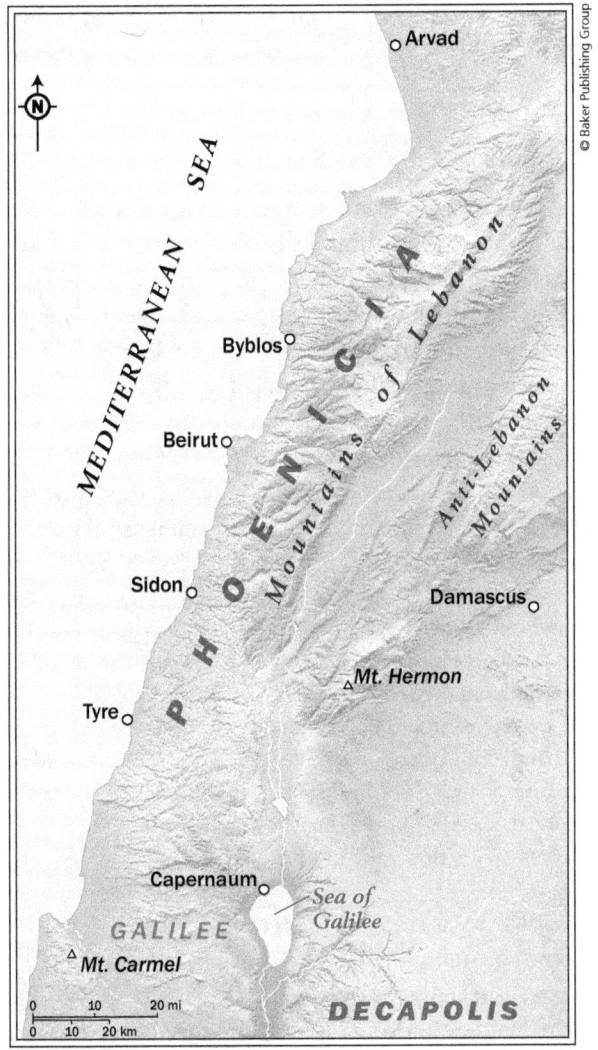

Figure 8.1. Phoenicia

basically a federation of city-states with a strong sense of cultural, linguistic, and political solidarity.

The intent of this chapter is to summarize the salient aspects of the history of the Phoenician city-states and the Phoenician script and language, with reference to Phoenician navigation, colonization, art, and religion. The predominant emphasis will be on primary textual sources. Of course, it must also be conceded from the outset that the actual Phoenician sources (i.e., in Phoenician) are not as abundant in caliber and content as the historian would wish. Nevertheless, the sources are sufficient to facilitate a reliable discussion of the broad contours of the Phoenicians, often with some rather precise details.

1. Evidence from Classical Authors

As a point of departure, it is useful to consider ways in which classical writers understood certain accomplishments of the Phoenicians, while also urging caution because of the dates of these authors, their interdependence, and the jaundiced manner in which some of them framed the Phoenicians. Naturally, Homer includes reference to the Phoenicians, replete with statements about Phoenician seafaring and certain Phoenician luxury goods; however, the Phoenicians are often presented in Homer in a negative fashion, and his work seems to be based on a dearth of source material. Thus, scholars such as Irene Winter have contended that "Homer's Phoenicians, then, do not represent the world of the Phoenicians, rather they present a masterful literary construct." Similarly, she states that, in Homer's descriptions of the Phoenicians,

> nowhere do we find evidence of direct informants serving as spokespersons for the culture.... Observations of behavior and activities that might be appropriate to ethnography are reduced to stereotyped character traits—greed, craft, duplicitousness, etc.—and made to stand for national or cultural practice. As a result, both individual references to Phoenicians in the *Iliad* and the *Odyssey*, as well as the overall picture of Phoenicians in the two texts, seem flattened and one-dimensional, thereby supporting the argument that the references serve a narrative rather than a documentary purpose.[9]

Discussions of the Phoenicians in Herodotus (ca. 484–425 BCE) are often considered to be considerably more useful. He mentions the Phoenicians in various contexts, especially (as one would expect) aspects of Phoenician history during the Persian period. Thus, while discussing the fighting men of the Persians, Medes, and Sacae, he refers to ships and then states that "the best sailing ships were furnished by the Phoenicians, and among them by the Sidonians" (*Histories* 7.96).[10] Discussing military conflicts in another place, he states that the political tensions between the Greeks and Phoenicians were said by "the Persian learned men" to have been caused by the Phoenicians.

---

9. Irene J. Winter, "Homer's Phoenicians: History, Ethnography, or Literary Trope [A Perspective on Early Orientalism]," in *The Ages of Homer*, ed. Jane B. Carter and Sarah P. Morris (Austin: University of Texas Press, 1995), 264, 255.

10. A. D. Godley, trans., *Herodotus*, vol. 3, LCL 119 (Cambridge, MA: Harvard University Press, 1971), 63.

Within this context (and as part of his description of a casus belli), Herodotus further mentions that it is believed that the Phoenicians

> came to our seas from the sea which is called Red, and having settled in the country which they still occupy, at once began to make long voyages. Among other places to which they carried Egyptian and Assyrian merchandise, they came to Argos, which was about that time preeminent in every way among the people of what is now called Hellas. . . . The Phoenicians then came, as I say, to Argos, and set out their cargo. (*Histories* 1.1)[11]

These statements of Herodotus are important for a number of reasons, especially since they provide data about the assumptions made about settlement patterns, navigational activities, and the transportation of foreign wares to various regions of the ancient Near Eastern world. Among the additional statements of Herodotus that are of particular import are those he makes about Cadmus. To be precise, he states that there were some Phoenicians who came with Cadmus to the country now called Boeotia and that "among many other kinds of learning, they brought into Hellas the alphabet, which had hitherto been unknown, as I think, to the Greeks." Significantly, he goes on to state:

> And presently as time went on the sound and the form of the letters were changed. At this time the Greeks that dwelt round them for the most part were Ionians; who having been taught the letters by the Phoenicians, used them with some few changes of form, and in so doing gave to these characters (as indeed was but just, seeing that the Phoenicians had brought them into Hellas) the name of Phoenician. (*Histories* 5.57–58)[12]

Striking is the fact that this passage of Herodotus is often cited as evidence that Herodotus believed the Phoenicians invented the alphabet. Mostly, however, this passage contains a statement about the fact that the Phoenicians brought the alphabet to Greece. Then, after Herodotus provides an interesting historical footnote regarding terminology for writing media (namely, "the Ionians have from ancient times called papyrus-sheets skins, because formerly for lack of papyrus they used the skins of sheep and goats; and even to this day there are many foreigners who write on such skins"), he states that he has himself "seen Cadmean characters in the temple of Ismenian Apollos at

---

11. A. D. Godley, trans., *Herodotus*, vol. 1, LCL 117 (Cambridge, MA: Harvard University Press, 1975), 3.
12. Godley, *Herodotus*, 3:63. Among the vast literature on this subject, see especially Rhys Carpenter, "Letters of Cadmus," *AJP* 56 (1935): 5–13; and P. Kyle McCarter Jr., *The Antiquity of the Greek Alphabet*, HSM 9 (Missoula, MT: Scholars Press, 1975).

Thebes of Boeotia, graven on certain tripods and for the most part like Ionian letters" (*Histories* 5.58–59).[13] There has been much discussion about the legends of Cadmus.[14] Sometimes the ancient sources associate him with the Mediterranean littoral and sometimes they associate him with Egypt. Frankly, however, I am not certain that there was an ancient figure with the given name Cadmus. After all, within the corpus of personal names in Phoenician and Punic, the name (which would be spelled with the consonants *qdm*) does not seem to occur.[15] Ultimately, from my perspective, it is reasonable to suggest that the name Kadmos (Qadmos) was (a) not the actual given name of the bearer of the alphabet, but rather a nickname (given by someone in the West for the legendary figure who brought the alphabet to Greece from Phoenicia) meaning basically "the Easterner"—that is, "the Qadmos." Conversely, it is also tenable to contend that (b) the Greek tradition personified something that was originally just a geographic reference about the origins of the alphabet; that is, originally it was simply noted that these letters came "from the East"—that is, "from Qdm"—and at some point this geographicon came to be considered some sort of personal name.[16]

Diodorus Siculus (fl. 60–30 BCE) is often cited in secondary-source discussions of the Phoenicians, especially with regard to the invention of the alphabet. Within book 3 of his *Library of History*, Diodorus quotes the account of a certain Dionysius as follows:

> Among the Greeks Linus was the first to discover the different rhythms and song, and when Cadmus brought from Phoenicia the letters, as they are called, Linus was again the first to transfer them into the Greek language, to give a name to each character, and to fix its shape. Now the letters, as a group, are called "Phoenician" because they were brought to the Greeks from the Phoenicians, but as single letters the Pelasgians were the first to make use of the transferred characters and so they were called "Pelasgic." (*Library of History* 3.67.1)[17]

Within book 5 Diodorus also discusses the origins of the Greek alphabet, but with certain important additional details. The broader context of

---

13. Godley, *Herodotus*, 3:65.

14. See especially Ruth B. Edwards, *Kadmos the Phoenician: A Study in Greek Legends and the Mycenaean Age* (Amsterdam: Adolf M. Hakkert, 1979).

15. See Frank L. Benz, *Personal Names in the Phoenician and Punic Inscriptions* (Rome: Biblical Institute Press, 1972), esp. 403.

16. It should be remembered in this connection that Greek often represents Semitic *qoph* with a Greek *kappa*. See also Gen. 15:19 in this connection, with its gentilic *qdmny*.

17. C. H. Oldfather, trans., *Diodorus of Sicily*, vol. 2, LCL 303 (Cambridge, MA: Harvard University Press, 1967), 305, 307.

his reference is important so as to understand more fully the import of his statements. Namely, within this section of book 5, Diodorus is discussing mythological material that mentions the contributions of the members of the pantheon. Obviously, Zeus is considered to be the font of great wisdom and knowledge. Aphrodite is said to have been entrusted with the youth of maidens and the years in which they are expected to marry. Athena is credited with conveying to humanity knowledge of the domestication and cultivation of olive trees, clothing, carpentry, and pipes (for music). Then, at that point in Diodorus, there is reference to the Muses and the statement that to them, "we are further told, it was given by their father Zeus to discover the letters and to combine words in the way which is designated poetry." Of substantial import is the fact that Diodorus then goes on to say:

> And in reply to those who say that the Syrians are the discoverers of the letters, the Phoenicians having learned them from the Syrians and then passed them on to the Greeks, and that these Phoenicians are those who sailed to Europe together with Cadmus and this is the reason why the Greeks call the letters "Phoenician," they tell us, on the other hand, that the Phoenicians were not the first to make this discovery, but that they did no more than to change the forms of the letters, whereupon the majority of humankind made use of the way of writing them as the Phoenicians devised it, and so the letters received the designation we have mentioned above. (*Library of History* 5.74.1)[18]

Strabo (ca. 64 BCE–24 CE), the Greek historian and geographer (born in Pontus of Asia Minor), has penned some of the most useful comments regarding the Phoenicians, and these merit citation in some detail. He begins by mentioning that he has traveled throughout Syria-Palestine and then makes some basic geographic comments and general comments about some of the most prominent Phoenician cities:

> Since, then, I have traversed Coele-Syria ... I shall pass on to Phoenicia. Of this country, I have already described the parts extending from Orthosia to Berytus [Beirut]; and after Berytus one comes to Sidon, at a distance of about four hundred stadia; but between the two places are the Tamyras River and the grove of Asclepius and a city of Leones. After Sidon one comes to Tyre, the largest and oldest city of the Phoenicians, which rivals Sidon, not only in size, but also in its fame and antiquity, as handed down to us in numerous myths. Now although the poets have referred more repeatedly to Sidon than to Tyre (Homer does not even mention Tyre), yet the colonies sent into Libya and Iberia,

---

18. C. H. Oldfather, trans., *Diodorus of Sicily*, vol. 3, LCL 340 (Cambridge, MA: Harvard University Press, 1970), 295, 297.

as far even as outside the Pillars, hymn rather the praises of Tyre. At any rate, both cities have been famous and illustrious, both in early times and at the present time; and no matter which of the two one might call the metropolis of the Phoenicians, there is a dispute in both cities.

Then Strabo continues his narrative with substantial focus on Tyre, including reference to Phoenician seafaring, a recent earthquake that destroyed much of the architecture of Tyre, and the famous campaign of Alexander the Great (ca. 332 BCE), as well as Tyre's industrial production of purple dye (from the murex snail of the Mediterranean Sea):

> Now Sidon is situated on the mainland near a harbour that is by nature a good one. But Tyre is wholly an island, being built up nearly in the same way as Arvad; and it is connected with the mainland by a [causeway], which was constructed by Alexander [the Great] when he was besieging it; and it has two harbours, one that can be closed and the other, called "Egyptian" harbour, open. The houses here, it is said, have many stories, even more than the houses at Rome, and on this account, when an earthquake took place, it lacked but little of utterly wiping out the city. The city was also unfortunate when it was taken by siege by Alexander; but it overcame such misfortunes and restored itself both by means of the seamanship of its people, in which the Phoenicians in general have been superior to all peoples of all times, and by means of their dye-houses for purple; for the Tyrian purple has proved itself by far the most beautiful of all; and the shell-fish are caught near the coast; and the other things requisite for dyeing are easily got; and although the great number of dye-works makes the city unpleasant to live in, yet it makes the city rich through the superior skill of its inhabitants. The Tyrians were adjudged autonomous, not only by the kings, but also, at small expense to them, by the Romans, when the Romans confirmed the decree of the kings. Heracles is paid extravagant honours by them. The number and size of their colonial cities is an evidence of their power in maritime affairs. Such, then, are the Tyrians.

Within the following pericope Strabo focuses on Sidon and its intellectual and cultural accomplishments through time. However, at times he broadens his focus and lauds the Phoenicians in general. Although some of the details Strabo provides might not be considered entirely accurate (e.g., the origins of astronomy and arithmetic), there can be no real doubt about the fact that Sidon was a center of culture and learning for many centuries and its influence throughout the region was quite pervasive.

> The Sidonians, according to tradition, are skilled in many beautiful arts, as the poet [Homer] also points out; and besides this they are philosophers in

the sciences of astronomy and arithmetic, having begun their studies with practical calculations and with night-sailings; for each of these branches of knowledge concerns the merchant and the shipowner; as, for example, geometry was invented, it is said, from the measurement of lands which is made necessary by the Nile when it confounds the boundaries at the time of its overflows. This science, then, is believed to have come to the Greeks from the Egyptians; astronomy and arithmetic from the Phoenicians; and at present by far the greatest store of knowledge in every other branch of philosophy is to be had from these cities. And if one must believe Poseidonius, the ancient dogma about atoms originated with Mochus, a Sidonian, born before the Trojan times. However, let us dismiss things ancient. In my time there have been famous philosophers from Sidon; Boethus, with whom I studied the Aristotelian philosophy, and his brother Diodotus; and from Tyre, Antipater, and, a little before my time, Apollonius, who published a tabulated account of the philosophers of the school of Zeno and of their books. (*Geography* 16.2.22–24)[19]

Similarly, Pliny the Elder (23–79 CE) mentions that the Phoenicians are to be credited with significant cultural accomplishments:

The whole of the sea lying off the coast is called the Phoenician Sea. The Phoenician race itself has the great distinction of having invented the alphabet and the sciences of astronomy, navigation and strategy. (*Natural History* 5.13.66–67)[20]

Regarding Tyre and Sidon, Pliny makes several interesting comments, including reference to Phoenician colonial activity:

Once [Tyre was] an island separated from the mainland by a very deep sea-channel 700 yards wide, but now joined to it by the works constructed by Alexander when besieging the place, and formerly famous as the mother-city from which sprang the cities of Leptis, Utica, and the great rival of Rome's empire in coveting world sovereignty, Carthage, and also Cadiz, which she founded outside the confines of the world; but the entire renown of Tyre now consists in a shell-fish and a purple dye! The circumference of the city, including Old Tyre on the coast, measures 19 miles, the actual town covering 2¾ miles. Next are Zarephath and Bird-town, and the mother-city of Thebes in Boeotia, Sidon, where glass is made. (*Natural History* 5.17.75–76)[21]

---

19. H. L. Jones, trans., *Strabo: Geography*, vol. 7, LCL 241 (Cambridge, MA: Harvard University Press, 1966), 267–71.
20. H. Rackham, trans., *Pliny: Natural History*, vol. 2, LCL 352 (Cambridge, MA: Harvard University Press, 1969), 271.
21. Rackham, *Natural History*, 2:279. Note that this city of Thebes was, according to tradition, founded by Cadmus, the son of Agenor king of Sidon.

During recent decades, scholars have become particularly cautious about embracing as historical some (or even many) of the statements in the classical authors about the Phoenicians.[22] This hermeneutic of suspicion is important and justified. I am also among those that believe a hermeneutic of suspicion is proper, while also believing that the classical authors often present some of the major contours of Phoenician culture with some accuracy, including those revolving around the Phoenician origins of the Greek alphabet, major Phoenician cities, Phoenician seafaring, and Phoenician commodities.

2. Evidence of the Phoenician Language and Inscriptions

We turn now to the nexus of data that revolves around the major facets of the Phoenician world, beginning with the Phoenician alphabet (and its precursors), as well as certain aspects of the Phoenician language, Phoenician art, the major cities, and certain aspects of Phoenician seafaring and colonial activities. Of necessity the presentation will be selective, but with the intent of representing the essential data using primarily Phoenician inscriptions from the homeland of the Phoenicians (i.e., modern Lebanon).

Phoenicians and the "Invention" of the Alphabet

"The Phoenicians invented the alphabet" is something that is often stated. Although I am sympathetic with the essence of that statement, technically speaking it is not terribly accurate. Research on the earliest history of the alphabet (sometimes called "Canaanite," sometimes called "Early Linear Alphabetic" or "Proto-Sinaitic") has progressed rapidly during the past century, precipitated by the discoveries of Sir Flinders Petrie in a site in the Egyptian Sinai known as Serabit el-Khadem. Many of the inscriptions he found at Serabit were Egyptian Hieroglyphics, but some were quite enigmatic and he initially referred to them as a "local barbarism."[23] However, Alan Gardiner soon began to analyze this corpus of inscriptions, and he became convinced that the script was alphabetic, not some "local barbarism." He rapidly made major strides forward in the decipherment of these inscriptions, based on his assumption that the signs were pictographic and that the "acrophonic principle" was operative. Moreover, he also argued that the intellectual soil that facilitated the invention was (certain aspects of) the ancient Egyptian

---

22. Among the finest discussions regarding this matter is that of McCarter, *Antiquity of the Greek Alphabet*, 1–27.

23. For discussion, see Alan H. Gardiner, "Serabit," in *Researches in Sinai*, ed. W. M. Flinders Petrie (London: J. Murray, 1906).

writing system.²⁴ Ultimately, based on the date of some of the Hieroglyphic inscriptions in (the region of) Serabit el-Khadem as well as the morphological similarities between these Early Linear Alphabetic signs and certain Egyptian Hieroglyphic signs, Gardiner stated that he believed that it was tenable to assign these alphabetic inscriptions to the latter portion of the Egyptian Twelfth Dynasty (basically the eighteenth century BCE). Several decades later, W. F. Albright made significant progress on the decipherment of these Early Linear Alphabetic inscriptions, building on Gardiner's seminal analyses.²⁵ Through the years, F. M. Cross made fundamental contributions to the discussion of the history and development of the Early Alphabet.²⁶ More recently, scholars such as Benjamin Sass and Gordon Hamilton have also contributed substantially to the discussion, as has the publication of the two Early Alphabetic inscriptions from Wadi el-Hol (Egypt), a corpus that hails from around the same time as the Serabit materials.²⁷ Regarding those that invented Early Alphabetic, there has been much debate, but I believe that the cumulative evidence suggests that the inventors were Semites (originally) from the Levant who were functioning in elite Egyptian circles (e.g., in the upper echelons of the mining industry) and were capable of using (at least to some degree) the Egyptian writing system.²⁸

Significantly, although Early Linear Alphabetic inscriptions have been found at a number of sites in Egypt and the Levant (roughly from the eighteenth through the eleventh centuries BCE), Early Linear Alphabetic was not a standardized system and did not become the official national script of a nation or

24. Alan H. Gardiner, "The Egyptian Origin of the Semitic Alphabet," *JEA* 3 (1916): 1–16. In essence, the acrophonic principle refers to the fact that the first sound of a picture came to be the letter that was symbolized by the picture. For example, the Semitic word for "head" is *ro'sh*. Therefore, the letter for the letter *r* was a picture of a head, since the first sound of the Semitic word for head starts with an *r*. Similarly, if someone wanted to write the letter for the "b" sound, they would draw a picture of the Semitic word for "house," which is *bet*.

25. W. F. Albright, *The Proto-Sinaitic Inscriptions and Their Decipherment*, HTS 22 (Cambridge, MA: Harvard University Press, 1966).

26. See especially the articles in F. M. Cross, *Leaves from an Epigrapher's Notebook: Collected Papers in Hebrew and West Semitic Palaeography and Epigraphy*, HSS 51 (Winona Lake, IN: Eisenbrauns, 2003), 195–356.

27. Benjamin Sass, *The Genesis of the Alphabet and Its Development in the Second Millennium B.C.*, ÄAT 13 (Wiesbaden: Harrassowitz, 1988); Gordon J. Hamilton, *Origins of the West Semitic Alphabet in Egyptian Scripts*, CBQMS 40 (Washington, DC: Catholic Biblical Association, 2006); John Darnell et al., *Two Early Alphabetic Inscriptions from Wadi el-Hol*, AASOR 59 (Boston: American Schools of Oriental Research, 2005). For a synthetic discussion, see also Christopher A. Rollston, *Writing and Literacy in the World of Ancient Israel: Epigraphic Evidence from the Iron Age*, ABS 11 (Atlanta: Society of Biblical Literature, 2011).

28. *Pace* Orly Goldwasser, "How the Alphabet Was Born from Hieroglyphs," *BAR* 36, no. 2 (March–April 2010): 36–50, 74. For more details, see Rollston, *Writing and Literacy*, 10–18.

a federation of city-states.[29] Moreover, the inscriptions written in the Early Linear Alphabetic script exhibit substantial variation, particularly in terms of stance (i.e., the position of the letter vis-à-vis the ceiling line—that is, the highest point of a given line at which most letters were usually written) and direction of writing (as sinistrograde [right to left], dextrograde [left to right], and columnar writing were all used). Moreover, during the early centuries of the usage of Early Linear Alphabetic, the number of consonantal graphemes was around twenty-eight or twenty-nine. However, during the terminal horizons of the second millennium BCE several developments occurred: (1) the stance of the graphemes (letters) became more stabilized and standardized; (2) the direction of writing was consistently sinistrograde; and (3) moreover, because of a number of consonant mergers, the number of consonantal graphemes was reduced to twenty-two. From this point on, because of these three developments, the convention within the field of Northwest Semitic epigraphy is to refer to this stage of the script as Phoenician rather than Early Linear Alphabetic. Joseph Naveh reflects the consensus of the field with his statement that the transition from Early Alphabetic to Phoenician "took place in the mid-eleventh century BC."[30] Note that these changes did not occur simultaneously, however. That is, the changes occurred during the course of time, but all were largely complete by around the mid-eleventh century.[31] Ultimately, it is most convincing to argue that this standardization of stance and direction of writing is to be attributed to the Phoenicians. In essence, then, the federation of Phoenician city-states was cohesive enough to standardize Early Linear Alphabetic writing, and in so doing this federation produced the first linear alphabetic national script: Phoenician. Someone might query about the precise aegis for these developments—namely, the establishment of the mature Phoenician national script. The most logical conclusion

29. The writing system that was developed for Ugaritic is alphabetic, but it is cuneiform (wedge-shaped) alphabetic. It is abundantly clear that those that developed the Ugaritic writing system were familiar with, and dependent on, the Early Linear Alphabetic writing system (note the similarity of many of the Ugaritic letters to their Early Linear Alphabetic counterparts). Significantly, the Ugaritic writing system was a standardized writing system (note the consistency of stance, direction of writing), and I believe it was a standardized writing system because its origins (i.e., of the graphemes themselves) and usage were part and parcel of a state aegis (i.e., Ugarit). Obviously, the usage of the Ugaritic writing system did spread to a few additional cities of the Levant, but its *Sitz im Leben* was Ugarit.
30. Joseph Naveh, *Early History of the Alphabet: An Introduction to West Semitic Epigraphy and Palaeography*, 2nd ed. (Jerusalem: Magnes, 1987), 42.
31. This is not to say that no one ever used the Early Linear Alphabetic script after the mid-eleventh century BCE. It seems reasonable to me to suggest that there may have been some outliers in the late eleventh or even the early tenth century, especially within the Levantine periphery.

is that there was a fairly sophisticated scribal apparatus (with some sort of formal, standardized scribal education) that functioned within this federation of Phoenician city-states.

Phoenician Language

Phoenician texts and the Phoenician language have been the subject of major studies for some time now. Among the most important of the late nineteenth-century works on Northwest Semitic is Mark Lidzbarski's *Handbuch*. This volume focuses on Iron Age, Persian period, Hellenistic period, and early Roman period Northwest Semitic languages, with Phoenician and Punic receiving substantial attention.[32] Coming very much on the heels of Lidzbarski's *Handbuch* was G. A. Cooke's handbook, which also had as its focus the Northwest Semitic languages from the Iron Age through the early Roman period, with substantial attention given to Phoenician.[33] Of course, during the late nineteenth century, Semitic inscriptions were beginning to be published in the *Corpus inscriptionum semiticarum* (Paris, 1881–), which was becoming the sine qua non—but because of its price most scholars were forced to settle for the status of *sine* (i.e., without it). For more than half a century, these two collections (Lidzbarski and Cooke) would be the vade mecum (i.e., ready reference) for scholars within the field. During the middle of the twentieth century, however, Herbert Donner and Wolfgang Röllig produced a compendium of Northwest Semitic inscriptions that would be the standard handbook for the remainder of the twentieth and the beginning of the twenty-first century—namely, *Kanaanäische und aramäische Inschriften* (*KAI*), with its first edition appearing in 1961. More than half of the inscriptions in *KAI* are Phoenician, Punic, and Neo-Punic.[34] John C. L. Gibson subsequently produced a similar handbook, consisting of three volumes, with the third devoted entirely to Phoenician. Although a very useful set of volumes, Gibson's work does not contain the sorts of philological and historical details that are the hallmark of Donner and Röllig's *KAI*.[35] Mention should also be made of two handbooks that focus just on Phoenician—namely, those of Maria Giulia Amadasi (focusing on Phoenician and Punic of the Phoenician colonies) and Pietro Magnanini

---

32. Lidzbarski, *Handbuch der nordsemitischen Epigraphik, nebst ausgewählten Inschriften* (Weimar: Verlag von Emil Felber, 1898).
33. Cooke, *A Text-Book of North-Semitic Inscriptions: Moabite, Hebrew, Phoenician, Aramaic, Nabataean, Palmyrene, Jewish* (Oxford: Clarendon, 1903).
34. Donner and Röllig, *Kanaanäische und aramäische Inschriften*, 4th ed. (Wiesbaden: Harrassowitz, 1979).
35. Gibson, *Textbook of Syrian Semitic Inscriptions*, 3 vols. (Oxford: Clarendon, 1971–82).

(focusing on Phoenician, but not Punic).³⁶ Of course, the production of scientific grammars began during the late nineteenth and early twentieth centuries and has persisted. Among the most important are those by Zellig Harris, Johannes Friedrich and Wolfgang Röllig, and Stanislav Segert.³⁷ Moreover, both Richard Tomback and Charles Krahmalkov have written dictionaries that focus on Phoenician and Punic.³⁸ For the Phoenician script, P. Kyle McCarter's volume discusses the Early Phoenician scripts in great detail, and J. Brian Peckham's volume is the most authoritative treatment of the Late Phoenician and Punic scripts.³⁹ More recently, Karel Jongeling and Robert Kerr have edited a useful (if brief) volume focusing on Late Punic epigraphy, replete with hand-copies of scores of inscriptions.⁴⁰ Thus, there are some very fine resources for the study of the Phoenician language, dialects, and script.

The Phoenician language is classified as Canaanite.⁴¹ Regarding the writing system, there are twenty-two consonantal graphemes in Phoenician. It is normally argued that this is because the Phoenician language consisted of twenty-two consonantal phonemes (with "phoneme" being defined as "the smallest meaningful unit of sound"). Regarding the phonology of Phoenician (and this is related to the issue of the number of consonants in the Phoenician alphabet), a number of consonantal mergers are reflected in the Phoenician alphabet (vis-à-vis Early Linear Alphabetic). For example, etymological *ð* has merged with the letter *z* (hence, the spelling of "sacrifice" is *zbḥ* in Phoenician, rather than the historical spelling *ðbḥ*). Similarly, etymological *ḍ* has merged in Phoenician with *ṣ* (hence, the spelling of "earth" is *'rṣ* in

---

36. Amadasi, *Le iscrizioni fenicie e puniche delle colonie in Occidente*, Studi Semitici 28 (Rome: Istituto di Studi del Vicino Oriente, Universita di Roma, 1967); Magnanini, *Le iscrizioni fenicie dell'Oriente: Testi, traduzioni, glossari* (Rome: Istituto di Studi del Vicino Oriente, Universita degli Studi di Roma, 1973).

37. Harris, *A Grammar of the Phoenician Language*, AOS 8 (New Haven: American Oriental Society, 1936); Friedrich and Röllig, *Phönizisch-Punische Grammatik*, 3rd ed., rev. Maria Giulia Amadasi Guzzo and Werner R. Mayer (Rome: Pontifical Biblical Institute, 1999); Segert, *A Grammar of Phoenician and Punic* (Munich: Beck, 1976).

38. Tomback, *A Comparative Semitic Lexicon of the Phoenician and Punic Languages*, SBLDS 32 (Missoula, MT: Society of Biblical Literature, 1978); Krahmalkov, *Phoenician-Punic Dictionary*, OLA 90 (Leuven: Peeters, 2000). For Northwest Semitic languages more broadly (including Phoenician and Punic), see esp. the two-volume set by J. Hoftijzer and K. Jongeling, *Dictionary of the North-West Semitic Inscriptions* (Leiden: Brill, 1995).

39. McCarter, *Antiquity of the Greek Alphabet*; Peckham, *The Development of the Late Phoenician Scripts* (Cambridge, MA: Harvard University Press, 1968).

40. Jongeling and Kerr, eds., *Late Punic Epigraphy* (Tübingen: Mohr Siebeck, 2005).

41. It should be remembered that the languages of the Iron Age Levant have normally been classified as either Canaanite or Aramaic. See Zellig S. Harris, *Development of the Canaanite Dialects: An Investigation in Linguistic History* (New Haven: American Oriental Society, 1939). For more recent discussion, see also W. Randall Garr, *Dialect Geography of Syria-Palestine, 1000–586 B.C.E.* (Philadelphia: University of Pennsylvania Press, 1985).

Figure 8.2. Correspondence of West Semitic Consonants

	*Proto-Semitic	Phoenician	Hebrew	Aramaic
1.	ʾ	ʾ	ʾ	ʾ
2.	b	b	b	b
3.	g	g	g	g
4.	d	d	d	d
5.	h	h	h	h
6.	w	w (y)	w (y)	w (y)
7.	ḏ	z	z	z/d
8.	z	z	z	z
9.	ḥ	ḥ	ḥ	ḥ
10.	ḫ	ḥ	ḥ	ḥ
11.	ṭ	ṭ	ṭ	ṭ
12.	y	y	y	y
13.	k	k	k	k
14.	l	l	l	l
15.	m	m	m	m
16.	n	n	n	n
17.	s	s	s	s
18.	ʿ	ʿ	ʿ	ʿ
19.	ġ	ʿ	ʿ	ʿ
20.	p	p	p	p
21.	ṣ	ṣ	ṣ	ṣ
22.	ẓ	ṣ	ṣ	ṣ/ṭ
23.	ḍ	ṣ	ṣ	q/ʿ
24.	q	q	q	q
25.	r	r	r	r
26.	ś	š	š	š
27.	š	š	š	š
28.	ṯ	š	š	t
29.	t	t	t	t

Christopher A. Rollston

Phoenician, rather than the historical spelling *ʾrḍ*). Furthermore, etymological *ṯ* has merged in Phoenician with *š* (hence, the spelling of "three" is *šlš* in Phoenician, rather than the original etymological spelling *ṯlṯ*). In short, the Phoenician writing system reflects a number of consonantal mergers. It should also be noted that the aspects of Phoenician phonology mentioned here are those that often distinguish the Canaanite dialects of Northwest Semitic from the Aramaic dialects of Northwest Semitic. Thus, within Imperial (and later)

Aramaic, etymological *ð* is preserved as *d* (hence, the spelling of "sacrifice" in Imperial Aramaic is *dbḥ*), etymological *ḍ* is preserved as *q* in Old Aramaic and as ʿ in Imperial Aramaic (hence the word "earth" is written as *ʾrq* in Old Aramaic and as *ʾrʿ* in Imperial Aramaic), and etymological *ṯ* is preserved as *t* (hence, the word for "three" is written *tlt* in Imperial Aramaic).

Regarding Phoenician orthography (especially the representation of vowels), throughout most of its history the Phoenician writing system was strictly consonantal. That is, short vowels were not represented in the writing system at all; and, although Iron Age Aramaic and Hebrew did develop a system for representing some final long vowels, Iron Age Phoenician did not. Thus, Phoenician did not use final *matres lectionis* (lit., "mothers of reading"; certain consonants representing certain long vowels—a system attested in the Iron Age Aramaic and Hebrew writing systems).[42] Thus, for example, $k\bar{\imath}$ is spelled *k* (e.g., Yehimilk Inscription, line 6)—that is, without a *mater lectionis* for the final $\bar{\imath}$. Similarly, neither is $\bar{u}$ represented in Iron Age Phoenician; thus, for example, Phoenician *paʿalū* (they made) is written *pʿl* (Kilamuwa Inscription, line 5), without the use of *waw* to represent the final $\bar{u}$. Similarly, although Iron Age Hebrew and Aramaic marked final $\bar{o}$, final $\bar{a}$, and final $\bar{e}$ with a *he mater*, Iron Age Phoenician did not. Moreover, Iron Age Phoenician did not mark medial vowels (long or short) either. Furthermore, in terms of "vocalic changes" in Phoenician (e.g., compared with other Iron Age Northwest Semitic orthographic systems, such as Hebrew and Aramaic), the following are some of the most important: the diphthong *ay* consistently contracts in Phoenician (thus the word "house" is spelled *bt* [*bêt*] in Phoenician, rather than *byt*); the diphthong *aw* consistently contracts to *ô* (thus the word "day" is consistently spelled *ym* [*yôm*], rather than *ywm*); and historical $\bar{a}$ becomes $\bar{o}$ (this feature is referred to as the "Canaanite Shift" and serves as an isogloss for the Northwest Semitic Canaanite languages such as Phoenician and Hebrew vis-à-vis the Aramaic language family). Also of import is the fact that, within later Phoenician, *ô* becomes $\bar{u}$.

The basic features of the Phoenician nominal system should also be emphasized so as to reveal some of the fundamental features of the language. Regarding the pluralizing of nouns (and adjectives), masculine plurals in Phoenician are marked with *m*, signifying $\bar{\imath}m$ (as demonstrated by comparative Semitic data and by Greek and Latin transliterations of masculine

---

[42]. For a discussion of Phoenician orthography during the early centuries of Phoenician, see (the still useful) Frank Moore Cross Jr. and David Noel Freedman, *Early Hebrew Orthography: A Study of the Epigraphic Evidence* (New Haven: American Oriental Society, 1952), 11–20. See also the comparative discussion of Christopher A. Rollston, "Scribal Education in Ancient Israel: The Old Hebrew Epigraphic Evidence," *BASOR* 344 (2006): 61–65.

plurals; note also the absence of the *mater lectionis*—that is, *m* is written rather than *ym*).⁴³ Contrast, of course, the fact that the Aramaic dialects form the masculine plural with *īn* (i.e., with final *nun*), as does the Moabite language. Masculine plurals in construct are not marked in the Iron Age Phoenician writing system because *ē* (the construct ending) was, of course, a vowel (but in Punic and Neo-Punic there were attempts to represent this vowel—namely, by using *aleph* or *ayin*). Feminine plurals are marked with *t*, signifying *ōt* (as demonstrated by comparative Semitic data and by transcriptions in Greek and Latin).⁴⁴ The feminine singular nominal was normally marked with *t* (hence in Phoenician the word for "widow" is *'lmt*; cf. Heb. *'lmnh*). Adjectives used the same system of marking plurals. Naturally, in addition to the singular and plural, the dual was arguably used as well.⁴⁵

The Phoenician verbal system shares many features with various Iron Age Northwest Semitic languages. In terms of "conjugations," the following are all attested: *qal, niphal, piel* (and arguably the *pual*), the *yiphil* (and arguably *yuphal*), the *yitpael, yitpolel*, and the *qal* with infixed *taw*. In terms of differences from Hebrew, it should be noted that rather than the *hiphil* of Hebrew, Phoenician has the *yiphil* (as the causative conjugation), and rather than the *hitpael* of Hebrew, Phoenician has the *yitpael*. Although the orthographic system in Phoenician makes it difficult to determine with certainty, it seems reasonable to conclude that the passive counterparts of the *piel* and *yiphal* (i.e., the *pual* and *yuphal*) were employed in the Phoenician verbal system. In terms of tenses, both the perfect (the suffix conjugation) and the imperfect (the prefix conjugation) were used, as were the imperative, the infinitives, and the participles.⁴⁶ So as to convey the essence of the verbal system, the forms of the *qal* perfect and imperfect will be provided here, using קטל as the paradigm word (the vocalizations in Latin script are provided so as to reveal the basic way that these forms would have been pronounced in ancient Phoenician, as well as to demonstrate the manner in which the consonantal nature of the Phoenician writing system concealed the vocalic elements of the Phoenician language). Naturally, perusal of these paradigms will also make it quite apparent that in the Phoenician writing system there is much ambiguity (e.g., the *qal* perfect 3fs, 2ms, and 1cs are all written the same), but fortunately the context of an occurrence will normally reveal the way a form is to be understood.

43. Note that some late inscriptions (e.g., Neo-Punic) do use the *yod mater*.
44. Note that some late inscriptions (e.g., Neo-Punic) do use the *waw mater*.
45. For further discussion and details, see esp. Friedrich and Röllig, *Phönizisch-Punische Grammatik*, 130–70.
46. For further discussion and details, see esp. ibid., 74–130.

Figure 8.3. *Qal* Perfect and Imperfect

Qal Perfect					
3ms	קטל	(qaṭala)	3cp	קטל	(qaṭalū)
3fs	קטלת	(qaṭalat)			
2ms	קטלת	(qaṭalta)	2mp	[unattested]	
2fs	קטלת	(qaṭalt)	2fp	[unattested]	
1cs	קטלת	(qaṭaltī)	1cp	קטלן	(qaṭalnū)
Qal Imperfect					
3ms	יקטל	(yiqṭul)	3mp	יקטל	(yiqṭulū)
3fs	תקטל	(tiqṭul)	3fp	[unattested]	
2ms	תקטל	(tiqṭul)	2mp	תקטל	(tiqṭulū)
2fs	תקטל	(tiqṭulī)	2fp	תקטלן	(tiqṭulna)
1cs	אקטל	(ʾiqṭul)	1cp	[unattested]	

Phoenician Inscriptions from the Homeland

There are a number of Phoenician inscriptions from the Phoenician homeland (modern Lebanon) that provide substantial data about the Phoenician script and language, as well as some data about Phoenician history (e.g., some of the rulers) and religion. Moreover, there are a number of important Phoenician inscriptions that were produced outside of the borders of Phoenicia during this early period, so brief reference also will be made to a few of these.

Among the most important of the early Phoenician inscriptions from the homeland is the Azarbaʿal Inscription, often referred to as the Bronze Spatula Inscription.[47] This prestige object was discovered during controlled excavations at Byblos (ancient Gebal, in Phoenicia). Six lines of Phoenician text (often considered enigmatic) are etched into the metal. I would suggest that although this inscription is difficult, it revolves around the subject of the payment of silver (I have collated this inscription in Lebanon and read *ksp* in line 2) and some sort of inheritance (note the root *nḥl* in line 4). The script reflects archaic features, such as the trident *kaph*, the *mem* with a strong vertical stance, *samek* with a short vertical shaft (i.e., not extending much below the bottom horizontal), and the box-shaped *ḥet*. Of import is the fact that the five strokes of *mem* are of the same approximate length, and the three strokes of *nun* are of the same approximate length (these are early features). Some have argued that this inscription reflects the terminal horizon of the

---

47. M. Dunand, *Biblia grammata: Documents et recherches sur le développent de l'écriture en Phénicie* (Beirut: Department of Antiquities, 1945), 155–57.

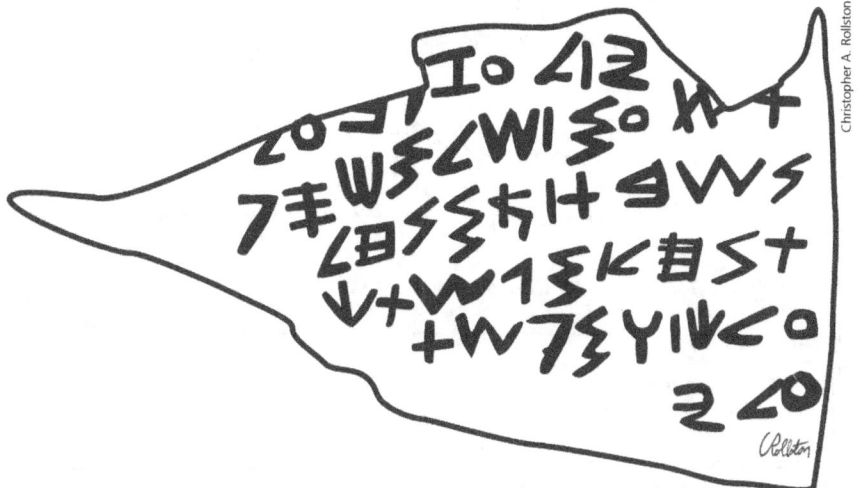

Figure 8.4. Drawing of Azarbaʻal Inscription

eleventh century, but I consider a date in the (early) tenth century also to be tenable. The script is really quite impressive and reflects the presence of a fairly sophisticated scribal apparatus.

There are several Early Royal Phoenician inscriptions from Byblos, coming from the chronological horizon following that of the Azarbaʻal Inscription (fig. 8.4).[48] Among the most impressive of these is that of the Ahiram Sarcophagus (fig. 8.5), an inscription commissioned by Ahiram's son named Ittobaʻal ('Ethbaʻal').[49] The majority of this inscription is written on the lid (the length of it) of a very impressive sarcophagus, but the initial component of the inscription is written on the end of the sarcophagus itself (i.e., not on the lid). Most of the letters were chiseled with care and substantial precision, although a diminution of letter-size is visible (and quantifiable) in the terminal portions of the inscription. It is likely that space constraints necessitated the diminution. That is, as the scribe began to realize that there was not sufficient space to complete the entire inscription using such large letters, he began to reduce the sizes of the letters. Here is my translation of the inscription:

48. For an attempt to lower the standard dates for these Early Royal Byblian Inscriptions, see Benjamin Sass, *The Alphabet at the Turn of the Millennium: The West Semitic Alphabet, ca. 1150–850 BCE* (Tel Aviv: Yass Publications in Archaeology, 2005). For a response to Sass, see Christopher Rollston, "The Dating of the Early Royal Byblian Phoenician Inscriptions: A Response to Benjamin Sass," *Maarav* 15 (2008): 57–93.

49. R. Dussaud, "Les inscriptions phéniciennes du tombeau d'Ahiram, roi de Byblos," *Syria* 5 (1924): 135–57.

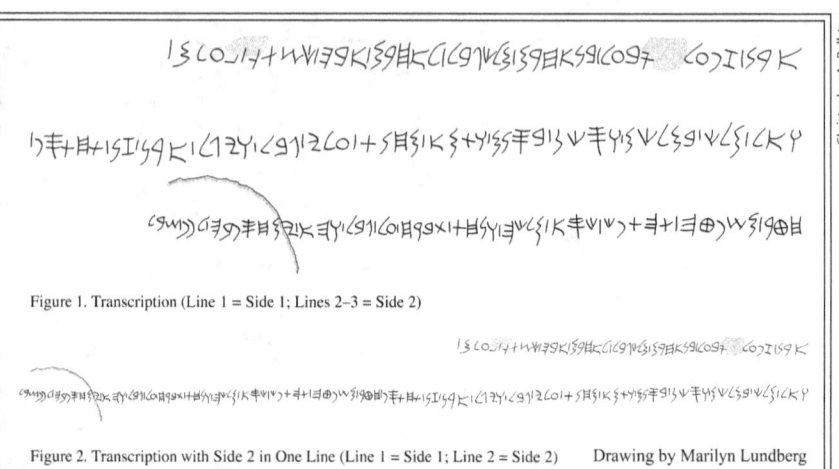

Figure 8.5. Drawing of Ahiram Sarcophagus Inscription

The sarcophagus that 'Ethba'al the son of Ahiram king of Byblos made for Ahiram, his father, when he placed him in his eternity. And if a king among kings, or a governor among governors or a commander of an army should come to Byblos, and uncover this sarcophagus, may the scepter of his rule be ripped away, may the throne of his kingdom be overturned, and may rest flee from Byblos. And as for him, may his royal records [lit., "book"] be effaced from before Byb[los].[50]

The Phoenician script of the Ahiram Sarcophagus can be distinguished from the script of the Azarba'al Inscription because of the presence of some discernible and diagnostic typological differences or developments. That is, the script of this inscription is later than that of the Azarba'al Inscription. The differences that are among the most important are the distinct lengthening of the vertical shaft of *samek*, the occasional lengthening of the fifth stroke of *mem*, the occasional lengthening of the third stroke of *nun*, and the lengthening of the verticals of *ḥet* (i.e., no longer box-shaped). Note, however, that *kaph* remains trident-shaped (the trident form of *kaph* is an early feature). Based on the script, I consider this inscription to be datable with substantial certitude to the tenth century BCE.[51] Also of substantial import is the high caliber of the art carved in relief on the Ahiram Sarcophagus. This is Phoenician art at its very best, and it has been discussed in substantial detail by the great art historian Edith Porada. Suffice it to say that this sarcophagus

---

50. For the text of this inscription, see *KAI* 1:1 (no. 1). Note that I have personally collated this inscription in Beirut using magnification, and I read *gbl* at the end of this inscription.

51. Rollston, "Dating of the Early Royal Byblian (Phoenician)."

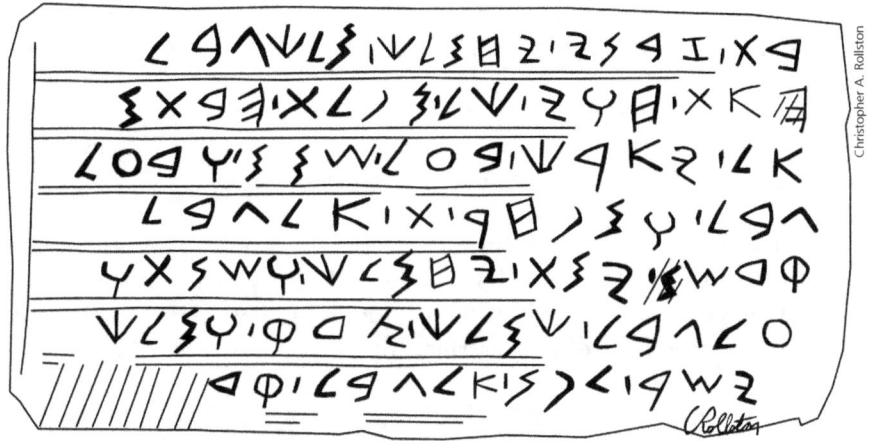

Figure 8.6. Drawing of Yehimilk Inscription

certainly reflects not just a sophisticated scribal apparatus but also the presence of some very skilled ancient artists.[52] In addition, it should be noted that curse formulas such as are found on the Ahiram Sarcophagus are quite common in the ancient Near Eastern world.

Hailing also from Byblos during this same basic horizon are the Yehimilk Inscription (fig. 8.6), the Abibaʻal Inscription, and the Elibaʻal Inscription. Yehimilk is a monumental Byblian (Phoenician) inscription, chiseled into a stone tablet.[53] It can be read as follows:

> The temple [lit., "house"] that Yehimilk king of Byblos built. He restored all the fallen temples. May Baʻal-Shamem and Baʻalat Byblos and the Assembly of the Holy Gods of Byblos lengthen the days of Yehimilk and his years over Byblos because the righteous and just king before the Holy Gods of Byblos is he.[54]

The Abibaʻal Inscription is inscribed on a statue of Pharaoh Sheshonq I (r. ca. 945–924 BCE; biblical Shishak, a pharaoh of the Twenty-Second Dynasty and a figure mentioned in 1 Kings 14:25–28), and so it is among the most interesting and important of the early Byblian (Phoenician) lapidary inscriptions, especially since it is a reflection of the historic relationship between Egypt

---

52. Edith Porada, "Notes on the Sarcophagus of Ahiram," *JANES* 5 (1973): 355–72. See also the superb article by Irene J. Winter, "On the Problems of Karatepe: The Reliefs and Their Context," *AnSt* 29 (1979): 115–51. Finally, see also Irit Ziffer, "From Acemhoyuk to Megiddo: The Banquet Scene in the Art of the Levant in the Second Millennium BCE," *TA* 35 (2005): 155–58.

53. M. Dunand, "Nouvelle inscription phénicienne archaïque," *RB* 39 (1930): 321–31.

54. For the text of this inscription, see *KAI* 1:1 (no. 4).

and Phoenicia.⁵⁵ Although fragmentary, this inscription is fairly formulaic, and so the restorations are reasonably secure:

> [The statue that] Abibaʻal king of [Byblos son of Yehimilk king] of Byblos brought from Egypt for Baʻalat [of Byblos, his lord. May Baʻalat of Byblos lengthen the days of Abibaʻal and his years] over Byblos.⁵⁶

Similarly, the Byblian (Phoenician) inscription of Elibaʻal was inscribed on a bust of Pharaoh Osorkon I (r. ca. 924–889).⁵⁷ Of consequence is the fact that within this inscription Elibaʻal provides his father's name: Yehi[milk]. Here is my translation of this inscription:

> {The statue} that Elibaʻal king of Byblos, son of Yehi[milk king of Byblos] made for Baʻalat of Byblos his lord. May Baʻalat [of Byblos] lengthen [the days of] Elibaʻal and his years over [Byblos].⁵⁸

The inscriptions of Yehimilk, Abibaʻal, and Elibaʻal reflect the same basic script typology as that of the Ahiram Sarcophagus Inscription, and they can be dated securely to the tenth century BCE. Significantly, however, the script of the Shipitbaʻal Inscription from Byblos (fig. 8.7) contains features that reflect further typological development (i.e., when compared with the script of Ahiram, Yehimilk, Abibaʻal, and Elibaʻal).⁵⁹ For example, the fifth stroke of *mem* has lengthened considerably, and it is readily apparent that some rotation of the head has begun (sometimes incipient, sometimes significant). Furthermore, the third stroke of *nun* has lengthened substantially, and there is some rotation of its head as well. The Shipitbaʻal Inscription can be classed as the latest of the great Early Royal Byblian inscriptions. From this chronological horizon also comes the ʻAbda Sherd. Note that the morphology of *bet* in these two inscriptions is the same; this feature was ephemeral. In sum, during the

---

55. C. Clermont-Ganneau, "Inscription égypto-phénicienne de Byblos," CRAI 47 (1903): 378–85.

56. For the text of this inscription, see *KAI* 1:1 (no. 5).

57. R. Dussaud, "Dédicace d'une statue d'Osorkon 1 per Elibaal, roi de Byblos," *Syria* 6 (1925): 101–17. Note also that the names in the cartouches of these statues of Sheshonq and Osorkon are those of Sheshonq I and Osorkon I. That is, it would be problematic for someone to suggest that these statues were those of Sheshonq II (r. ca. 890 BCE) and Osorkon II (r. ca. 874–850 BCE), as the readings of the latter two are quite different (J. von Beckerath, *Handbuch der aegyptischen Königsnamen* [Mainz: von Zabern, 1999], 185). I am grateful to James Hoffmeier for discussing this issue with me and providing this reference.

58. For the text of this inscription, see *KAI* 1:1 (no. 6). Note that { } in this case signify that this word is restored on the basis of the same terminology in several of the Royal Byblian Phoenician inscriptions.

59. Dunand, *Biblia grammata*, 146–51.

Figure 8.7. Drawing of Shipitba'al Inscription

tenth and very early ninth centuries the Phoenician script is well attested in the Phoenician homeland, and Shipitba'al is the latest of the Early Royal Byblian (Phoenician) inscriptions. In short, in terms of script typology, Shipitba'al (and the 'Abda Sherd) is the latest of the Early Byblian Phoenician texts. In terms of archaeological context, it is important to note that this inscription was found near the wall associated with the acropolis of Byblos (note the reference to this wall at the beginning of the inscription). Regarding regnal sequencing of the Byblian kings, it should be emphasized that Shipitba'al is of particular usefulness. Here is a translation of this inscription:

> The wall that Shipitba'al king of Byblos, son of Eliba'al king of Byblos, son of Yehimilk king of Byblos built for Ba'alat of Byblos, his lord. May Ba'alat of Byblos lengthen the days of Shipitba'al and his years over Byblos.[60]

Cumulatively, these Royal Byblian Phoenician inscriptions are interesting and important for a number of reasons, including the sorts of things that they reveal about Phoenician religion. For example, Ba'alat of Byblos is certainly the divinity that receives the most attention.[61] Within the Abiba'al Inscription, she is the only divinity that is mentioned, and the bringing of the statue of Sheshonq from Egypt is something stated to have been done for (or facilitated by) her. Moreover, she is the divinity petitioned for the lengthening of the lifetime of Abiba'al and his years upon the throne.[62] Of course, both Eliba'al

60. For the text of this inscription, see *KAI* 1:2 (no. 7).
61. Some have suggested that this term, literally meaning "Lordess of Byblos," may be a way of referring to Asherah, while others suggest that it may be referring to Astarte or even Anat. I do not believe there is sufficient evidence for a decision.
62. Although this material is in the restored component of the Abiba'al Inscription, it is a formulaic reference typical of these Byblian inscriptions, so I consider this restoration to be

and Shipitba'al mention Ba'alat in conjunction with these same basic motifs. Based on these inscriptions someone might wish to conclude that Ba'alat of Byblos was the primary, or even the sole, divinity at Byblos. She may very well have been perceived as the most active patron deity of Byblos, but the Yehimilk Inscription refers not only to Ba'alat of Byblos but also to Ba'al Shamem and the Assembly of the Holy Gods of Byblos. And I would suggest that it is not inconsequential that of these, Ba'al Shamem is mentioned first. It may be that Ba'al Shamem was considered decrepit or otiose, but it seems reasonable to posit that he was considered the head of the pantheon at Byblos, and his prominence in the treaty between Ba'al I of Tyre and Esarhaddon (dated to ca. 675 BCE) suggests that he also may have been considered the head of the pantheon at Tyre at that time.[63] In addition to the discussion of the ranking of Ba'alat of Byblos and Ba'al Shamem, it should also be emphasized that the reference to the "Assembly of the Holy Gods of Byblos" reveals quite nicely the Phoenician acceptance of the standard ancient Near Eastern notion of a divine council (something also accepted within early Israelite religion).[64]

There have also been some very important inscriptions from later centuries. For example, an inscription from "the son of Shipitba'al the king of Byblos" (often referred to as Shipitba'al III) hails from Byblos and dates to the late sixth or early fifth century BCE (written in the Late Phoenician script). Although this inscription is fragmentary, it does refer to a divinity named Ba'al 'Addir.[65] Also among the most substantive of the Late Phoenician inscriptions is that of Yehawmilk king of Byblos. The script of this inscription has been dated to the middle of the fifth century BCE.[66] Because of the length of this rather stunning inscription, a summary of its contents will need to suffice.[67] This inscription is essentially a dedicatory inscription, touting some of the building accomplishments of Yehawmilk. It begins with reference to the fact that Ba'alat of Byblos made him king. Yehawmilk states that he called upon Ba'alat of Byblos and she heard him, so in return he made for her a bronze

---

cogent. On epigraphic methodologies and restorations, see the principles outlined in Rollston, *Writing and Literacy*, 5.

63. For a similar reference, see Karatepe A III, 18 (*KAI* 1:6 [no. 26 AIII, 186]). For the treaty of Ba'al I of Tyre and Esarhaddon, see Simo Parpola and Kazuko Watanabe, *Neo-Assyrian Treaties and Loyalty Oaths*, SAA 2 (Helsinki: State Archives of Assyria, 1988), IV, 10.

64. On Phoenician deities and on Israelite religion in general, see esp. Mark S. Smith, *The Early History of God: Yahweh and the Other Deities in Ancient Israel*, 2nd ed. (Grand Rapids: Eerdmans, 2002), 61–64; and Joel S. Burnett, *A Reassessment of Biblical Elohim*, SBLDS 183 (Atlanta: Society of Biblical Literature, 2001).

65. For the text of this inscription, see *KAI* 1:7 (no. 9).

66. Peckham, *Development of the Late Phoenician Scripts*, 44–45, et passim.

67. For the text of this inscription, see *KAI* 1:2 (no. 10).

altar, a golden gateway, a winged disk of gold, and a portico with pillars and capitals. Yehawmilk petitions the goddess to lengthen his days and years over Byblos, with the additional statement that he is the lawful king (*mlk ṣdq*). Also of import in this connection is the fact that the king requests that Baʿalat of Byblos "give him favor (*ḥn*) in the eyes of the gods." Similarly, he utters a fairly standard curse upon those that might subsequently remove his name from these public works, imploring Baʿalat of Byblos "to destroy that person and his seed before all the gods of Byblos," another important reference to the plurality of divinities within the pantheon.

The inscription of Tabnit was incised in the base of a black basalt sarcophagus found in a necropolis in Sidon and is usually dated to the end of the sixth century BCE. The inscription begins in the following manner: "I am Tabnit, the priest of Astarte, king of the Sidonians, the son of Eshmunazar priest of Astarte, king of the Sidonians, lying here in this coffin."[68] He goes on to state that no silver or gold or riches were buried with him in the coffin, but rather just his corpse. The inscription states further that to disturb his corpse would be an abomination to Astarte. The inscription concludes with a curse upon any that might disturb his remains, and the hope that such a person may have "no seed among the living under the sun with the Rephaim."

Among the most interesting of Phoenician inscriptions is the Eshmunazar Sarcophagus inscription from Sidon, dating to the early fifth century BCE.[69] The sarcophagus itself is simply breathtaking in workmanship. The inscription on it begins with a date formula ("in the month of Bul, in the fourteenth year of King Eshmunazar, king of the Sidonians"), a patronymic ("son of King Tabnit"), and a statement that the king had died a premature death. Within this first-person inscription, King Eshmunazar also states that he was "an orphan, the son of a widow." After formulaic language cursing anyone who might attempt to open or remove the sarcophagus (and within this a reference to "the Holy Gods"), King Eshmunazar mentions that he is the grandson of King Eshmunazar, king of the Sidonians (note the practice of papponymy, naming a grandson after a grandfather), and he mentions his mother—namely, "Amotashtart the priestess [*khnt*] of Astarte, our great lady the queen, the daughter of King Eshmunazar king of Sidon." Of some import (even if this is more of a title than a role) is the fact that his mother was said to be a priestess. (From the fourth century comes a funerary inscription of a woman named "Batnoam, mother of king ʿAzbaʿal of Byblos, son of Palitbaʿal, the

68. For the text of this inscription, see *KAI* 1:3 (no. 13).
69. For the text of this inscription, see *KAI* 1:3–4 (no. 14).

priest [*khn*] of Baʻalat.")⁷⁰ As the text of this inscription continues, there are references to building projects, including a temple for the god ʾEshmun, as well as multiple temples for "the Gods of the Sidonians in Sidon, land of the Sea," a temple for "Baʻal of Sidon," and a temple for "Astarte the Name of Baʻal" (note the terminology that reflects the notion of a local manifestation of a deity). Also of particular import is the fact that this inscription goes on to state that "the Lord of kings" (*ʾdn mlkm*)—a means of referring to Persian hegemony and the king himself—gave the Sidonians both "Dor and Joppa," territories said to be located in the "rich lands of Dagon." These territories are said to have been "added to the borders of the land" of the Sidonians.

Although the number of epigraphic remains in Phoenician from Beirut is minuscule, it should be emphasized that some fragmentary inscriptions have been preserved. Among the most interesting ones is a broken marble plate with an inscription on its rim that can be read " {to} my lady, to Astarte. May she bless [ ]."⁷¹ In sum, although one might wish for larger quantities and a greater diversity of Phoenician epigraphic materials, what we do have provides substantial data about the Phoenician language and script and gives us some sense for the political structure (including the names of some royal figures), most significant cities, and significant deities, as well as references to temples, temple personnel, and sacrifices.

Phoenician Inscriptions from outside Phoenicia

Because of Phoenician colonial activity, a number of Phoenician inscriptions have been discovered at sites that were originally Phoenician colonies or had some sort of a Phoenician presence. Among the most important is the Honeyman inscription of Cyprus, dating to the ninth century BCE. This inscription is quite fragmentary, but enough of it can be read to understand that its contents revolve around death and burial.⁷² The Nora Inscription from Sardinia is also arguably a reflection of Phoenician colonial activity (fig. 8.8). Although not complete, its contents are tantalizing. It refers to Tarshish, to Sardinia, and to some sort of peace, along with reference to a figure referred to as "Milkaton son of Shubna," who is said to be the "general of (king) Pummay."⁷³

---

70. For the text of this inscription, see *KAI* 1:3 (no. 11).

71. For the *editio princeps* of this inscription, see Hélène Sader, "Phoenician Inscriptions from Beirut," in *Ancient Egyptian and Mediterranean Studies in Memory of William A. Ward*, ed. Leonard H. Lesko (Providence: Brown University Department of Egyptology, 1998), 203–13, esp. 204–6.

72. A. M. Honeyman, "Phoenician Inscriptions of the Cyprus Museum," *Iraq* 6 (1939): 106–8.

73. See Frank M. Cross, "An Interpretation of the Nora Stone," *BASOR* 208 (1972): 13–19.

Similarly, the Kition Bowl (Cyprus; fig. 8.9) is also a reflection of the Phoenician presence on Cyprus. Its inscription is written in a fine cursive Phoenician script of the eighth century BCE. The bowl is quite fragmentary, and so the readings and interpretation are not at all certain, but this bowl is also the reflection of the presence of a sophisticated Phoenician scribal apparatus on Cyprus during the eighth century. Inscriptions from Carthage are also quite common (though narrow in scope), with a fair number hailing from the "Tophet" or "Precinct of Tanit," which contains stelae with vows accompanying the sacrifices of small children.[74]

Of course, the Phoenician script and language were for some time the prestige script and language of the region, and so it comes as no surprise that they were used in regions that were neither within the geographic confines of Phoenicia nor part of strong colonial activity. For example, the Kilamuwa Inscription (ninth century) is written in the Phoenician language rather than the local dialect and arguably also in the Phoenician script. Moreover, the Karatepe Inscription from the eighth century is written in the Phoenician language (and there is an accompanying Hieroglyphic Hittite text with the same basic material). The Tell Fekheriye

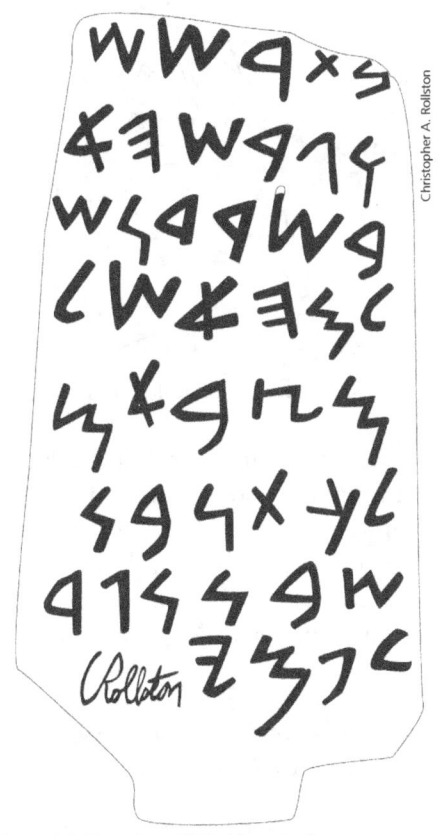

Figure 8.8. Drawing of Nora Inscription

---

74. I do not doubt that human sacrifice occurred in Phoenicia, much as it did at the Phoenician colony of Carthage. For discussion, see Philip J. King and Lawrence E. Stager, *Life in Biblical Israel* (Louisville: Westminster John Knox, 2001), 359–62. Of course, I would also hasten to add that early Israelite religion also embraced human sacrifice (Judg. 11:29–32, 39; Mic. 6:6–8), although the Deuteronomist repudiated it (2 Kings 16:3; 21:6). See also Lucian, *The Syrian Goddess* (= *De Dea Syria*), trans. Harold W. Attridge and Robert A. Oden (Missoula, MT: Scholars Press, 1976).

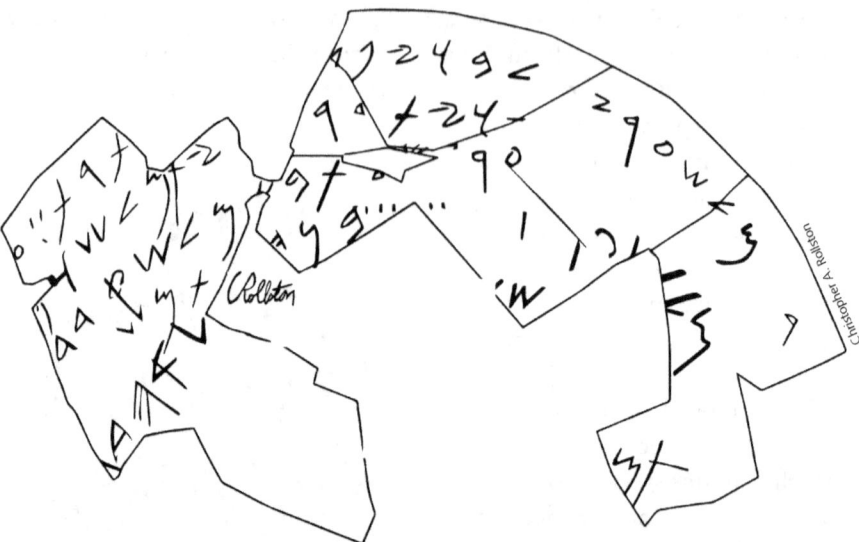

Figure 8.9. Drawing of the Kition Bowl

Stela inscription is written in the Phoenician script, but the Aramaic language. In short, the Phoenician script was quite pervasive in the Levant during the ninth and eighth centuries as the prestige script, and sometimes the Phoenician language was used as an international language during this time frame. This was also the case in Israel, as the Phoenician script was used there during the tenth century and also the early ninth century.[75]

3. Evidence of Egyptian, Assyrian, Babylonian, Hebrew, and Greek References

The Phoenician inscriptions from the Phoenician homeland and Phoenician colonies provide some data about Phoenician history, but no annals in the Phoenician language have been discovered, nor have major literary works in the Phoenician language survived. To be sure, there are materials from later periods that demonstrate that such texts were produced in antiquity by the Phoenicians. For example, Philo of Byblos (writing in the late first or early second century CE, but whose work is known through subsequent citations of it, especially those of Eusebius of Caesarea) purports to have translated the work of Sanchuniathon. Porphyry of Tyre (ca. 234–305 CE), the famous Neoplatonic philosopher, considered this to be so and mentions that Sanchuniathon wrote

75. Rollston, *Writing and Literacy*, 27–46.

in the Phoenician language and Philo of Byblos translated this work into Greek in eight volumes. Although some have argued that Sanchuniathon was not a historical figure, most consider him to have lived and to have been the author of a Phoenician history. Indeed, Albright has argued that "Sanchuniathon was a refugee from Tyre who settled in Beirut about the second quarter of the sixth century BC" and that his work contains much valuable data about Phoenician history and "is not a forgery of early Roman times."[76] It is often argued (quite reasonably) that the preserved portions of this history (mostly from Eusebius) are quite useful for discussions of Phoenician religion. Moreover, in terms of other sources, Josephus (ca. 37–ca. 100 CE) refers to Phoenician annals and claims to have used them in his own work, with some fairly detailed references to kings of Tyre. Within his material, Josephus also putatively cites material from Dius, a historian of Phoenicia, and the historian Menander of Ephesus.[77] In any case, at this juncture the intent is to focus on primary sources from Mesopotamia and Egypt regarding Phoenicia, especially those from the late second millennium to the middle of the first millennium, while also referring at times to material from Josephus and (on occasion) the Hebrew Bible.

Among the most important references is one in the corpus of the Royal Inscriptions of Tiglath-pileser I (1114–1076 BCE). Predictably, the focus of Tiglath-pileser's campaign was the acquisition of Phoenician timber (i.e., cedars of Lebanon, referred to in this text as "tribute"). In addition, there is a striking statement about his killing a sea horse during a boating trip originating at Arvad (within some other texts there are statements about his receiving monkeys from the Phoenicians as well). Here is one of his lengthiest statements:

> I marched to Mount Lebanon. I cut down (and) carried off cedar beams for the temple of the gods Anu and Adad, the great gods, my lords. I continued to the land of Amurru (and) conquered the entire land of Amurru. I received tribute from the lands of Byblos, Sidon, (and) Arvad. I rode in boats of the people of Arvad (and) traveled successfully a distance of three double hours from the city Arvad, and island, to the city Samuru which is in the land of Amurru. I killed at sea a nahiru, which is called a sea-horse.[78]

---

76. W. F. Albright, "Neglected Factors in the Greek Intellectual Revolution," *Proceedings of the American Philosophical Society* 116 (1972): 239. For a critical edition of Philo of Byblos, see Harold W. Attridge and Robert A. Oden Jr., *Philo of Byblos, The Phoenician History: Introduction, Critical Text, Translation, Notes*, CBQMS 9 (Washington, DC: Catholic Biblical Association, 1981).

77. See esp. Josephus, *Against Apion* 1.17–18; H. St. J. Thackeray, trans., *Josephus: The Life; Against Apion*, LCL 186 (Cambridge, MA: Harvard University Press, 1976), 205–13.

78. A. Kirk Grayson, *Assyrian Rulers of the Early First Millennium BC*, vol. 1, *1114–859 BC*, RIMA 2 (Toronto: University of Toronto Press, 1991), 37 (see also 42, 44, 53, 60, 63).

Of a similar nature (at least with regard to the desire for the acquisition of Phoenician timber) is the Egyptian "Story of Wenamun."[79] This narrative is set during the transitional period between the Twentieth and Twenty-First Dynasties—that is, during the reigns of Ramesses XI (r. ca. 1099–1069) and Smendes I (r. ca. 1069–1043), with reference also being made to Herihor (ca. 1081–1074), who was a high priest of Amun. Within this delightful piece of literature, Wenamun arrives first at Dor (where he was robbed) and then sails to Byblos (passing Tyre). However, the king of Byblos, a certain Zakarbaʻal (Tjekerbaal), does not wish to welcome Wenamun (arguably showing the perceived weakness of Egypt at this time, at least as understood by this Phoenician king) or to provide him with the desired timber. In fact, Zakarbaʻal is reported to have gone out to the harbor each morning and to have said to Wenamun "Leave my harbor!" However, a prophet figure of this region convinces Zakarbaʻal that Wenamun's journey is of God (i.e., Amun), and so (after much negotiation and dispute) Wenamun is given the requested timber, and he sails from the Byblian harbor.

Early Byblian inscriptions provide (as discussed above) the names of (most of) the Byblian kings of the tenth century, but without much additional historical data. Moreover, the Deuteronomistic Historian mentions some connections between the Israelites and the Phoenicians during the tenth century, especially Tyre. For example, it is mentioned in 1 Kings 5 that King Hiram of Tyre sent emissaries to King Solomon at the time of Solomon's coronation, and Solomon requested from Hiram's servants "that cedars from the Lebanon be cut for me" (5:6). Striking is the fact that Chronicles suggests that Solomon made the initial contact with Hiram and not the reverse (2 Chron. 2:1–16), and there are further differences between these two accounts. In any case, Hiram is stated to have agreed and is reported to have said that he would send the timber via the sea to a port that Solomon may choose. Solomon, in turn, is reported to have provided for the sustenance of Hiram's workers and also to have supplied Hiram with massive amounts of wheat and oil to return the favor. In addition, Solomon is said to have sent tens of thousands of workers to assist Hiram's workmen. Significantly, the book of Kings also mentions that the Israelites and the Tyrians were assisted by Gebalites—that is, Byblians (1 Kings 5:18).

Naturally, because the Phoenicians were famous for their artistic traditions, it comes as no surprise that the artistic motifs and décor of the Jerusalem Temple are in keeping with that tradition (1 Kings 6), something that the text nods to with its reference to an artisan of bronze named Hiram (7:13–47). Moreover, it should also come as no surprise that the Deuteronomistic History

---

79. Miriam Lichtheim, *Ancient Egyptian Literature*, vol. 2, *The New Kingdom* (Berkeley: University of California Press, 1976), 224–30.

(1 Kings 9:26–28; 10:11, 22) and also Chronicles (2 Chron. 8:17–18; 9:10, 21) suggest that the Phoenicians assisted Solomon with things maritime as well. It is also worth noting that, according to the Deuteronomistic Historian, Solomon ceded some twenty cities to Hiram (1 Kings 9:10–14), basically as payment for services and commodities rendered (note the pejorative pun on the place-name Cabul in 9:13). This is not to suggest that all of the material in the Deuteronomistic History and Chronicles is historical, but it is reasonable to contend that Solomon (following in the tradition of kings near and far) used Phoenician cedars for his monumental building campaigns, and it is also reasonable that Phoenician artisanship was employed and embraced by the Israelites during this period as well. In addition, it is arguably important that Josephus cites Menander of Ephesus (who Josephus says was using Tyrian royal records) as recording some of the very same things (e.g., the symbiotic relationship between Hiram of Tyre and Solomon).[80] Of course, the Deuteronomistic Historian also severely critiqued Solomon for his marital alliances, suggesting that these caused him to turn from Yahweh at times. Wives from Sidon are among those that are mentioned, and they are reported to have caused him to follow "Astarte the goddess of the Sidonians" (1 Kings 11:1, 5).

Josephus (stating that he is following the account of Menander of Ephesus, who was using royal records from Tyre) states that after the reigns of (1) Abibalus (Abibaal) of Tyre and his son (2) Hiram (who is said to have reigned thirty-four years), the throne of Tyre passed to (3) Balbazer son of Hiram (who reigned for seventeen years), then to (4) Abdastratus ('Abdastarte) the son of Balbazer (who reigned nine years), and to (5) Methusastartus son of Deleastartus (who came to power because of a coup and then reigned for twelve years), (6) and then his brother Astharymus (who reigned for nine years). He was slain by his brother (7) Phelles (who had a brief reign of eight months), who was in turn slain by (8) Ithobal priest of Astarte (who reigned thirty-two years). He was succeeded by his son (9) Balezor (who reigned six years), who was succeeded by his son (10) Metten (who reigned twenty-nine years), and then came (11) Pygmalion (who reigned forty-seven years), whose reign arguably ended in the early eighth century BCE. At that juncture there is an interesting notation in Menander of Ephesus (as cited by Josephus) that "it was in the seventh year of his [Pygmalion's] reign that his sister took flight, and built the city of Carthage in Libya." Then, there is the following synchronism:

> The whole period from the accession of Hirom to the foundation of Carthage thus amounts to 155 years and eight months; and, since the temple at Jerusalem

80. See esp. Josephus, *Against Apion* 1.17–18.

was built in the twelfth year of King Hirom's reign, 143 years and eight months elapsed between the erection of the temple and the foundation of Carthage. (*Against Apion* 1.18)[81]

It does not seem prudent to push the numbers very hard, but the building of the Jerusalem temple is said to have begun in the fourth year of Solomon's reign and completed in his eleventh (1 Kings 6:1, 38); thus, using round numbers, it could be contended that the Jerusalem temple was completed in the mid-tenth century BCE. Therefore, the establishment of a Phoenician colony at Carthage (a name that derives from the original Phoenician term *qrt ḥdšt*, which means "new city") would be dated in the late ninth century. Significantly, Sabatino Moscati has stated that he considers the archaeological evidence to support a date in the eighth century (if not the ninth century).[82] In terms of additional data, it should be noted that, according to the Deuteronomistic Historian, a certain King Ethbaal of Sidon established an alliance with King Omri of Israel (r. ca. 876–869 BCE), sealing that agreement with the marriage of Ethbaal's daughter Jezebel to Omri's son Ahab (r. ca. 869–850 BCE; see 1 Kings 16:29–31), something that the Deuteronomistic Historian is particularly critical of, especially since Ahab and Jezebel's daughter Athaliah was subsequently married to King Jehoram of Judah (r. ca. 849–843 BCE; see 2 Kings 8:16–18).[83]

Although there are not abundant details about Phoenicia during the ninth century, some things are certainly known, especially through Neo-Assyrian royal records. For example, Assurnasirpal II (883–859 BCE) mentions several military campaigns to the Mediterranean coastal regions. Among the most detailed of these is this one:

> At that time, I made my way to the slopes of Mount Lebanon (and) went up to the Great Sea of the land Amurru. I cleansed my weapons in the Great Sea (and) made sacrifices to the gods. I received tribute from the kings of the sea coast, from the lands of the people of Tyre, Sidon, Byblos, Mahallatu, Maizu, Kaizu, Amurru, and the city Arvad which is (on an island) in the sea—silver, gold, tin, bronze, a bronze casserole, linen garments with multicoloured trim, a large female monkey, a small female monkey, ebony, boxwood, ivory of nahirus (which are) sea creatures. They submitted to me. I climbed up to Mount Amanus (and) cut down logs of cedar, cypress, dapranu-juniper, (and) burashu-juniper.

---

81. Thackeray, *Josephus*, 213. This translation spells Hiram as "Hirom."
82. Moscati, *The Phoenicians* (New York: Rizzoli, 1997), 48.
83. It should be noted in this connection that it is very doubtful that the so-called Jezebel Seal was that of Queen Jezebel. See Christopher A. Rollston, "Prosopography and the Yzbl Seal," *IEJ* 59 (2009): 86–91.

I made sacrifices to my gods. I made a memorial to my valour (and) erected (it) therein. I transported cedar logs from Mount Amanus and brought (them) to Esharra to my temple the shrine, a joyful temple, to the temple of the gods Sin and Shamash, the holy gods.[84]

During the reign of Shalmaneser III (r. 858–824 BCE), Neo-Assyrian campaigns to the west were quite frequent and were normally punitive in nature. After all, a coalition of Levantine states had allied itself against the Neo-Assyrian kingdom. The Kurkh Monolith of Shalmaneser III details some of these campaigns, including the great Battle of Qarqar (853 BCE). Because of the importance of this account, a substantial segment of it will be cited here:

Moving on from the city of Argana I approached the city Qarqar. I razed, destroyed, and burned the city Qarqar, his royal city. An alliance had been formed of these twelve kings: 1,200 chariots, 1,200 cavalry and 20,000 troops of Hadadezer (Adad-idri), the Damascene; 700 chariots, 700 cavalry and 10,000 troops of Irhulenu, the Hamatite; 2,000 chariots and 10,000 troops of Ahab (Ahabbu) the Israelite (Sir'alaia); 500 troops of Byblos; 1,000 troops of Egypt; 10 chariots and 10,000 of the land Irqanatu; 200 troops of Matinu-baal of the city Arvad; 200 troops of the land Usanatu; 30 chariots and [ ]000 troops of Adunu-baal of the land Shianu; 1,000 camels of Gindibu of the Arabs; { } hundred troops of Ba'asa, the man of Bit-ruhubi, the Ammonite. They attacked to [wage] war and battle against me . . . but I defeated them from the city Qarqar as far as the city Gilzau.[85]

From the annals of Shalmaneser III, it is readily apparent that multiple punitive campaigns were made against Levantine alliances that often included Phoenician cities, but his initial campaigns do not seem to have been entirely punitive in nature (but even so, they would have had hegemony or exploitation as a goal). Thus, these words are from a stone table found in a wall in Assur: "In my first regnal year I crossed the Euphrates and marched to the western sea (i.e., the Mediterranean). I washed my weapons in the sea and made sacrifices to my gods. I climbed up the Amanus range and cut beams of cedar and juniper. I climbed up Mount Lallar and erected therein my royal statue."[86]

Again, however, it must be emphasized that most of his subsequent campaigns were punitive military campaigns that were intended to subjugate as

---

84. Grayson, *Assyrian Rulers*, 1:218–19.
85. A. Kirk Grayson, *Assyrian Rulers of the Early First Millennium BC*, vol. 2, *858–745 BC*, RIMA 3 (Toronto: University of Toronto Press, 1996), 23–24.
86. Ibid., 51.

well as to garner tribute. Note, in this regard, the following text, replete with its reference to Phoenicia:

> In my eighteenth regnal year, I crossed the Euphrates for the sixteenth time. Hazael of Damascus [notice the transition—no longer is Hadad-ezer the Damascene king], trusting in the might of his soldiers, carried out an extensive mustering of his troops. He fortified Mount Saniru, the mountain peak, which is before Mount Lebanon. I put to the sword 16,020 of his fighting men and took away from him 1,121 of his chariots and 470 of his cavalry with his military camp. To save his life he ran away but I pursued him. I imprisoned him in Damascus, his royal city, cut down his gardens, and burned his shocks. I marched to Mount Haurana and razed, destroyed, burned, and plundered cities without number. I marched to Mount Baalira'asi, which is a cape (jutting out into) the sea before the land of Tyre, and erected my royal statue there. I received tribute from Baali-Manzeri of Tyre, and from Jehu (Iau) of the house of Omri (Humri). On my return, I ascended Mount Lebanon and erected my royal statue with the statue of Tiglath-pileser, a strong king who preceded me.[87]

During his twenty-first regnal year, Shalmaneser III states that he crossed the "Euphrates for the twenty-first time and marched to the cities of Hazael of Damascus. [He] captured four cities and received tribute from the people of the lands Tyre, Sidon, and Byblos."[88] Similarly, there are inscriptions on two bronze bands from Imgur-Enlil that contain tribute statements from Shalmaneser III: "I received tribute from the boats of the people of Tyre and Sidon" and "I received tribute from the cities of the people of Tyre and Sidon: silver, gold, tin, bronze, wool, lapis lazuli, and carnelian."[89] Of course, the same basic policies continued during the reigns of various Neo-Assyrian kings. Thus, for example, Adad-nirari III (r. 810–783 BCE) mentions that he received "the tribute of Mari, the Damascene" and the "tribute of Joash (Iu'asu), the Samaritan, and of the people of Tyre and Sidon." In addition, he states: "I marched to the great sea in the west. I erected my lordly statue in the city Arvad, which is on an island in the sea. I ascended Mount Lebanon and cut down 100 strong beams of cedar for the requirements of my palace and temples. I received tribute from all the kings of the land Nairi."[90]

During the eighth century, the royal records of Tiglath-pileser III sometimes provide significant data about Phoenician cities. For example, Tiglath-pileser III states in a text dating to ca. 738 BCE that he received tribute from

87. Ibid., 54.
88. Ibid., 67.
89. Ibid., 141 and 147.
90. Ibid., 211.

various places and regions in the west, including "Rahianu (Rezin) of the land Damascus, Menahem of the city Samaria, [Hiram of the city] Tyre, Sibitti-bi'il of the city Byblos." This tribute was reported as follows:

> Gold, silver, tin, iron, elephant hides, ivo[ry], multi-colored garments, linen garments, blue-purple and [red]-purple wool, ebony, boxwood, all kinds of precious things from the royal treasure, li[ve] sheep [whose wool] is dyed red-purple, flying birds of the sky whose wings are dyed blue-purple, horses, mules, oxen and she[ep and goats, camels], she-camels, together with their young, I received (from them).[91]

Within a text that has been dated to ca. 737 BCE, Tiglath-pileser III states that he "marched about from the Great Sea of the Rising Sun to the cities Reshi-suri and Byblos on the shore of the Great Sea of the Setting Sun, and thus [he] exercised authority over the four quarters of the world." Later, he continues and states that he received from various kings, including Menahem of the land of Samaria, Tuba'il of the city of Tyre, and Sibitti-ba'il (Sibitti-bi'il) of the city of Byblos, "tribute and payment of silver, gold, tin, iron, elephant hide(s), ivory, blue-purple and red-purple garments, multi-colored linen garments, camels, and she-camels."[92]

Hailing from the seventeenth *palu* (= year of the reign) of Tiglath-pileser III (ca. 729 BCE) comes a large fragment of a clay tablet from Kalhu. He states that he received tribute from various kings and city-states, including "Sibitti-bi'il of the city [Byblos, Hiram of the land Tyre] . . . [Ma]ttan-bi'il (Mattan-Ba'al) of the city Arvad . . . Jehoahaz of the land Judah, Qaus-malaka of the land Edom." Later Tiglath-pileser III states that he "sent a eunuch . . ., the chief eunuch, to the city Tyre. [Tiglath-pileser received] from Metenna of the city Tyre 150 talents of gold and [2,000 talents of silver as his audience gift]."[93]

Hailing from the Nabu temple at Kalhu is a large fragment that comes from the same basic chronological horizon. Within it Tiglath-pileser III states: "I annexed to Assyria the extensive [land of Bit]Haza'ili (Damascus) in its entirety, from Mount [Lebanon as far as the cities Gilead and Abil-shitti, which are on the border] of the land Bit-Humria (Israel) and placed a eunuch of mine as provincial governor over them." He goes on to note that "[As for Hi]ram of the land Tyre, who conspired with Rahianu (Rezin) against me, I

---

91. Hayim Tadmor and Shigeo Yamada, *The Royal Inscriptions of Tiglath-pileser III (744–727 BC) and Shalmaneser V (726–722 BC), Kings of Assyria*, RINAP 1 (Winona Lake, IN: Eisenbrauns, 2011), 46–48.
92. Ibid., 87.
93. Ibid., 122–23.

captured and plun[dered the city] Mahalab, his fortified city, together with other large cities of his. He came before me and kissed my feet."⁹⁴

Sargon II (722–705 BCE) continued the same basic policy, making campaigns into the Levant. With Sennacherib (704–681 BCE) there are some particularly interesting details about his interactions with Phoenicia. Thus, the Oriental Institute Prism of Sennacherib has the following:

> In my third campaign, I marched against Hatti. Luli, king of Sidon, whom the terror-inspiring glamor of my lordship had overwhelmed, fled far overseas and perished. The awe-inspiring splendor of the "Weapon" of Ashur, my lord, overwhelmed his strong cities (such as) Great Sidon, Little Sidon, Bit-Zitti, Zaribtu, Mahalliba, Ushu (i.e., the mainland settlement of Tyre), Akzib (and) Akko, all his fortress cities walled (and well) provided with food and water for his garrisons, and they bowed in submission to my feet. I installed Ethba'al (*Tuba'lu*) upon the throne to be their king and imposed upon him tribute (due) to me (as his) overlord (to be paid) annually without interruption.
>
> As to all the kings of Amurru—Menahem (*Mi-in-ḫi-im-mu*) from Samsimuruna, Tuba'lu from Sidon, Abdili'ti from Arvad, Urumilki from Byblos, Mitinti from Ashdod, Buduili from Beth-Ammon, Kammusunadbi from Moab (and) Aiarammu from Edom, they brought sumptuous gifts (*igisû*) and—fourfold—their heavy *tâmartu*-presents to me and kissed my feet.⁹⁵

It should be mentioned in this connection that the Bull Inscription contains slightly more information about Luli, king of Sidon; namely, it states that he was afraid to fight Sennacherib "and [he] fled to the country Cyprus (*Iadnana*) which is (an island) in the midst of the sea, and sought refuge (there). But even in this land, he met infamous death before the awe-inspiring splendor of the 'Weapon' of my lord Ashur."⁹⁶ To be sure, these texts are interesting on a number of levels. Of course, they supply the names of several Phoenician kings (in addition to the kings of Moab, Ammon, Edom, Ashdod, and Samaria), and there are references to some of the tribute paid. However, this text also makes it clear that Sennacherib removed Luli, king of Sidon, from power and placed a puppet king named Ethba'al on the throne. That is, Sennacherib's hegemony was such that he was able to orchestrate even this.

Political alliances and hegemony can shift rapidly. Therefore, it comes as no surprise that, in a text composed in ca. 673–672 BCE, Esarhaddon (680–669) states:

---

94. Ibid., 130–31.
95. "Texts from Hammurabi to the Downfall of the Assyrian Empire," trans. A. Leo Oppenheim (*ANET*, 287).
96. Ibid., 288.

Abdi-Milkuti, king of Sidon, did not fear my lordship and did not listen to the words of my lips, who trusted in the rolling sea and threw off the yoke of the god Assur—I leveled Sidon, his stronghold, which is situated in the midst of the sea, like a flood, tore out its walls and its dwellings, and threw them into the sea; and I even made the site where it stood disappear. Abdi-Milkuti, its king, in the face of my weapons, fled into the midst of the sea. By the command of the god Assur, my lord, I caught him like a fish from the midst of the sea and cut off his head. I carried off his wife, his sons, his daughters, his palace retainers, gold, silver, goods, property, precious stones, garments with trimming and linens, elephant hides, ivory, ebony, boxwood, everything of value from his palace in huge quantities, and took away his far-flung people who were beyond counting, oxen, sheep and goats, and donkeys in huge numbers to Assyria.

A few lines later Esarhaddon states that he handed over "the cities Ma'rubbu and Sarepta to Ba'alu, king of Tyre." Then he notes that he "increased his lordly tribute beyond his earlier, annual giving and imposed it on him."[97]

One of the most interesting documents from this period is the treaty of Esarhaddon with Ba'al of Tyre. Within this treaty, Ba'al of Tyre is said to be the "servant" of Esarhaddon. The treaty contains certain stipulations, responsibilities, stated benefits (e.g., a number of ports of trade are given to Ba'al of Tyre, including those of "Akko, Dor, in the entire district of the Philistines, and in all the cities within Assyrian territory, on the seacoast, and *in* Byblos, [across] the Lebanon"), and curses upon Ba'al of Tyre for breach of the treaty. Of particular import is the fact that (as per standard custom) a number of deities are invoked within the treaty, and among these are Baal-sameme, Baal-malage, Baal-saphon, Melqart, Eshmun, Astarte, Bethel, and Anat-Bethel, along with, of course, Ishtar and Gula.[98]

Esarhaddon's hegemony is assumed also in a text that was arguably composed ca. 671 or 670 BCE. He states:

> [I summoned] the kings of Hatti [and Across the River (Syria-Palestine): Ba'alu, king of Tyre, Ma]nasseh, king of Judah, [Qa'us-gabri, king of Edom, Musur] I, king of Moab, [Sil-Bel, king of Gaza, Mitinti], king of Ashkelon, [Ikausu, king of Ekron, Milki]-ashapa, king of Byblos, [Mattan-Ba'al, king of] Arvad, [Abi-Ba'al, king of Samsimurruna,]Budi-il, king of Bit-Ammon, Ahi-milki, king of

---

97. Erle Leichty, *The Royal Inscriptions of Esarhaddon, King of Assyria (680–669)*, RINAP 4 (Winona Lake, IN: Eisenbrauns, 2011), 16–17. Note that many of the goods from Abdi-Milkuti, the king of Sidon, are later reported to have been in Esarhaddon's palace (see ibid., 147, 148).

98. "Treaty of Esarhaddon with Baal of Tyre," trans. Erica Reiner (*ANET*, 533–34).

Ashdod—[twelve kings from the shore of the sea; Ekishtura, king of] Idalion, [Pilagura, king of Kitrusi, Kisu, king of] Salamis [. . . .].[99]

But Esarhaddon's relationship with Ba'alu king of Tyre soon soured as well. Thus, Esarhaddon affirms:

> In the course of my campaign, I set up fortifications against Ba'alu, the king of Tyre, who trusted in his friend Taharqa, the king of Kush, threw off the yoke of the god Assur, my lord, and kept answering me with insolence. I cut off the supply of food and water that sustained their lives.[100]

Another text hailing from the same basic chronological horizon contains the following reference:

> I conquered Tyre, which is in the midst of the sea, and took away all of the cities and possessions of Ba'alu, its king, who had trusted in Taharqa, king of Kush; and I conquered (Lower) Egypt, Upper Egypt, and Kush, struck Taharqa, its king, five times with arrows, and ruled his entire land. I wrote to all of the kings who are in the midst of the sea, from Iadnana (Cyprus) and Ionia to Tarsus and they bowed down at my feet. I received their heavy tribute. . . . I carried off gold, silver, goods, possessions, people—young and old—horses, oxen, and sheep and goats, their heavy booty that was beyond counting, to Assyria. I placed kings, governors, officials, and harbormasters over their lands.[101]

During the reign of Assurbanipal (668–627 BCE), he mentions that in his first campaign he marched against Egypt and its king Tirhakah. During his march toward Egypt, he states that "22 kings from the seashore, the islands and the mainland, servants who belong to me, brought heavy gifts (*tâmartu*) to me and kissed my feet. I made these kings accompany my army over the land—as well as (over) the sea-route with their armed forces and their ships." Among these twenty-two kings listed are the Phoenician kings "Ba'al, king of Tyre, . . . Milkiashapa, king of Byblos, Iakinlu, king of Arvad."[102] Note that it seems Ba'al of Tyre must have survived the punitive raid of Esarhaddon and so continued as a thorn in the flesh of the Neo-Assyrian monarch Assurbanipal. Indeed, Assurbanipal has a lengthy discussion regarding this, stating that:

99. Leichty, *Royal Inscriptions of Esarhaddon*, 46.
100. Ibid., 87.
101. Ibid., 135.
102. "Texts from Hammurabi to the Downfall of the Assyrian Empire," trans. A. Leo Oppenheim (*ANET*, 294).

In my third campaign I marched against Ba'il, king of Tyre, who lives (on an island) amidst the sea, because he did not heed my royal order, did not listen to my personal [lit., "of my lips"] commands. I surrounded him with redoubts, seized his communications [lit., "roads"] on sea and land. I (thus) intercepted [lit., "strangled"] and made scarce their food supply and forced them to submit to my yoke. He brought his own daughter and the daughters of his brothers before me to do menial services. At the same time, he brought his son Iahimilki who had not (yet) crossed the sea to greet me as (my) slave. I received from him his daughter and the daughters of his brothers with their great dowries. I had mercy upon him and returned to him the son, the offspring of his loins. Iakinlu, king of Arvad, living also on an island who had not submitted to (any of) the kings of my family, did (now) submit to my yoke and brought his daughter with a great dowry to Nineveh to do menial services, and he kissed my feet.

The next part of the narrative is especially interesting, as it relates to the issue of successors:

After Iakinlu, king of Arvad, had perished, Aziba'l, Abiba'l, Aduniba'l, Sapatiba'l, Budiba'l, Ba'liashupu, Ba'lhanunu, Ba'lmaluku, Abimilki, Ahimilki, the sons of Iakinlu who live (on an island) amidst the sea, came from the sea to me with their heavy presents [*tâmartu*] and kissed my feet. I liked Aziba'l [lit., "I looked with pleasure upon Aziba'l"] and made him king of Arvad. I clad Abiba'l, Aduniba'l, Sapatiba'l, Budiba'l, Ba'liashupu, Ba'lhanûnu, Ba'lmaluku, Abimilki (and) Ahimilki in multicolored garments, put golden rings on their hands and made them do service at my court.[103]

After the fall of the Neo-Assyrian Empire in the late seventh century BCE, the Phoenicians seemed to have similar difficulties with the Neo-Babylonian Empire. Thus, Nebuchadnezzar of Babylon began an attack on Tyre in ca. 585 BCE. The siege, however, was a difficult one and lasted for some thirteen years, something that is reflected in a satirical biblical text, which mentions the aging of the Babylonian soldiers during this siege (Ezek. 29:18). The period of Persian hegemony, though, seems to have been more tranquil for Phoenicia, at least at times. A particularly interesting narrative comes from Herodotus. He states that the Persian king Cambyses (r. 530–522 BCE) had decided to make military expeditions against the "Carcedonians" (i.e., Carthaginians), the Ammonites, and the Ethiopians (living along the Libyan coast). However, at the time that he commanded his fleet to sail against Carthage, "the Phoenicians would not consent"—that is, the Tyrians would not consent. The

---

103. Ibid., 295–96.

rationale of the Tyrians and the response of Cambyses are interesting and revealing. The Phoenicians said

> they were bound . . . by a strict treaty, and could not righteously attack their own sons; and the Phoenicians being unwilling, the rest were of no account as fighters. Thus the Carcedonians escaped being enslaved by the Persians; for Cambyses would not use force with the Phoenicians, seeing that they had willingly surrendered to the Persians, and the whole fleet drew its strength from them. (*Histories* 3.19)[104]

Obviously, the fidelity of the Phoenicians to the colony at Carthage is commendable (in light of the fact that they were under Persian hegemony at that point), and the fact that it is stated that there was a binding treaty is particularly interesting. Furthermore, the fact that Cambyses decided not to press the Phoenicians into battling against Carthage is striking (no doubt there were a number of reasons for his decision, not all of which had to do with his benevolence to the Phoenicians). It should be emphasized in this connection that the Phoenicians certainly were willing to assist the Persians militarily, though. For example, during the time of Xerxes I (486–465 BCE) and his campaign against the Greeks, the Phoenicians were among those that assisted in building a canal across the Mount Athos peninsula.[105]

Nevertheless, periods of severe tension and warfare occurred between the Persians and Phoenicians as well. For example, Diodorus Siculus notes that at one point during his reign, the Persian king Artaxerxes III (r. 358–338 BCE) learned of an alliance between the Phoenicians and the Cypriots, which had formed in order to revolt against him; therefore, Artaxerxes decided to make a punitive campaign against them (ca. 352 BCE). The cities of Tyre, Sidon, and Arvad are said to have deliberated on matters, and they also sent emissaries to the Egyptian king Nectanebos II (r. 360–343 BCE) requesting his help. Diodorus mentions that because Sidon was distinguished for its wealth and its citizens had amassed great riches from its shipping, they were able rapidly to begin preparations for war with the Persians. Artaxerxes learned of these preparations and sent them strong warnings. In the meantime Tennes, the king of Sidon (who had received some four thousand Greek mercenary soldiers), who had enjoyed some initial military successes, learned of the burgeoning Persian forces and sent a secret message to Artaxerxes stating that he would betray his city to the Persians and also assist him in vanquishing the Egyptians.

---

104. A. D. Godley, trans., *Herodotus*, vol. 2, LCL 118 (Cambridge, MA: Harvard University Press, 1971), 25–26.

105. Herodotus, *Histories* 7.23; Godley, *Herodotus*, 2:337–38.

Artaxerxes was very pleased and putatively agreed. Although Tennes went through with his secret attempt (i.e., without the knowledge of most of the Sidonian citizenry) to surrender the city, Artaxerxes slew both Tennes and his messenger, along with several hundred Sidonians. The Sidonians that remained in the city ultimately decided that they did not wish to surrender and so they

> burned all their ships so that none of the townspeople should be able by sailing out secretly to gain safety for himself. But when they saw the city and the walls captured and swarming with many myriads of soldiers, they shut themselves, their children, and their women up in their houses and consumed them all in flames. They say that those who were then destroyed in the fire, including the domestics, amounted to more than forty thousand. (Diodorus, *Library of History* 16.41–45, esp. 45)[106]

As a result of this carnage, the rest of the Phoenicians submitted again to the Persians. Of course, Alexander the Great (356–323 BCE) also made a campaign into Phoenicia. Arrian (96–180 CE) states that

> Alexander marched from Marathus and received the surrender of Byblos, Sidon also, invited by the Sidonians themselves, who loathed Persia and Darius. Thence he proceeded towards Tyre, and on the way Tyrian envoys met him, sent by the community to say that Tyre had decided to accept Alexander's orders. (*Anabasis of Alexander* 2.15)[107]

However, Alexander stated that he also wished to offer a sacrifice to Heracles in the famed Tyre temple. The Tyrians did not wish for any Persian or Macedonian to be within their city, and so they refused Alexander's request. Alexander was outraged at this and decided that he would vanquish Tyre (ultimately building the famed causeway to the island). Of course, Alexander eventually did succeed in conquering Tyre, and in addition to those that were killed, some 30,000 Tyrians and Carthaginians were sold into slavery. Then, Arrian notes, "Alexander sacrificed to Heracles and held a procession in his honor . . . and Alexander held games in the temple enclosure" (*Anabasis of Alexander* 2.24).[108]

References to Phoenicians and Phoenician history continue after this time, but such references gradually become quite sparse. Among the most interesting

---

106. Charles L. Sherman, trans., *Diodorus of Sicily*, vol. 7, LCL 389 (Cambridge, MA: Harvard University Press, 1963), 351–65, esp. 363.

107. E. Iliff Robson, trans., *Arrian, History of Alexander and Indica*, vol. 1, LCL 236 (Cambridge, MA: Harvard University Press, 1967), 183.

108. Ibid., 213.

references in literature is the account of the Syro-Phoenician woman that Jesus of Nazareth encountered in the region of Tyre. According to the narrative, she wished for Jesus to heal her daughter. Jesus replied by indicating that this would be tantamount to throwing children's food to dogs. However, the Syro-Phoenician woman's brilliant reply ("Even the dogs under the table eat the children's crumbs") persuaded the Galilean Jesus to grant her request (Mark 7:24–30). At the end of the day, it can be stated that the Phoenicians have had a profound impact upon Western culture, as even the script of this essay (derived from the Latin script, which derived from the Greek script, which derived from the Phoenician script) demonstrates.

For Further Reading

Avishur, Yitzhak. *Phoenician Inscriptions and the Bible*. Tel Aviv: Archaeological Center Publication, 2000.

Ballard, Robert D., and Toni Eugene. *Mystery of the Ancient Seafarers*. Washington, DC: National Geographic, 2004.

Doumet-Serhal, Claude, et al. *Stones and Creed: One Hundred Artefacts from Lebanon's Antiquity*. Translated by Jennifer Curtiss Gage. Beirut: Anis Commercial Press, 1998.

Markoe, Glenn E. *Peoples of the Past: Phoenicians*. London: British Museum Press, 2000.

Moscati, Sabatino. *The Phoenicians*. New York: Rizzoli, 1997.

Redford, Donald B. *Egypt, Canaan, and Israel in Ancient Times*. Princeton: Princeton University Press, 1992.

9

Transjordan: The Ammonites, Moabites, and Edomites

Joel S. Burnett

1. Introduction

Most prominent among ancient Israel's neighbors east of the Jordan were the Ammonites, Moabites, and Edomites. Like the Israelites, they shared in a common cultural heritage rooted in Syria-Palestine's Bronze Age past while asserting distinct identities recognized in biblical, epigraphic, and archaeological sources. During the exceptional circumstances of the Iron Age, independent regional kingdoms associated with these peoples thrived briefly, eventually giving way to the returning dominance of greater powers in successive eras of advancing imperialism that shaped the Near East for the rest of the first millennium BCE.

2. Transjordan and Its Early History

The land of Transjordan begins in the Jordan–Dead Sea–Arabah Rift, rises dramatically to the Transjordanian Plateau, and levels out to the Syro-Arabian Desert. From north to south, the Plateau is divided into subregions by major

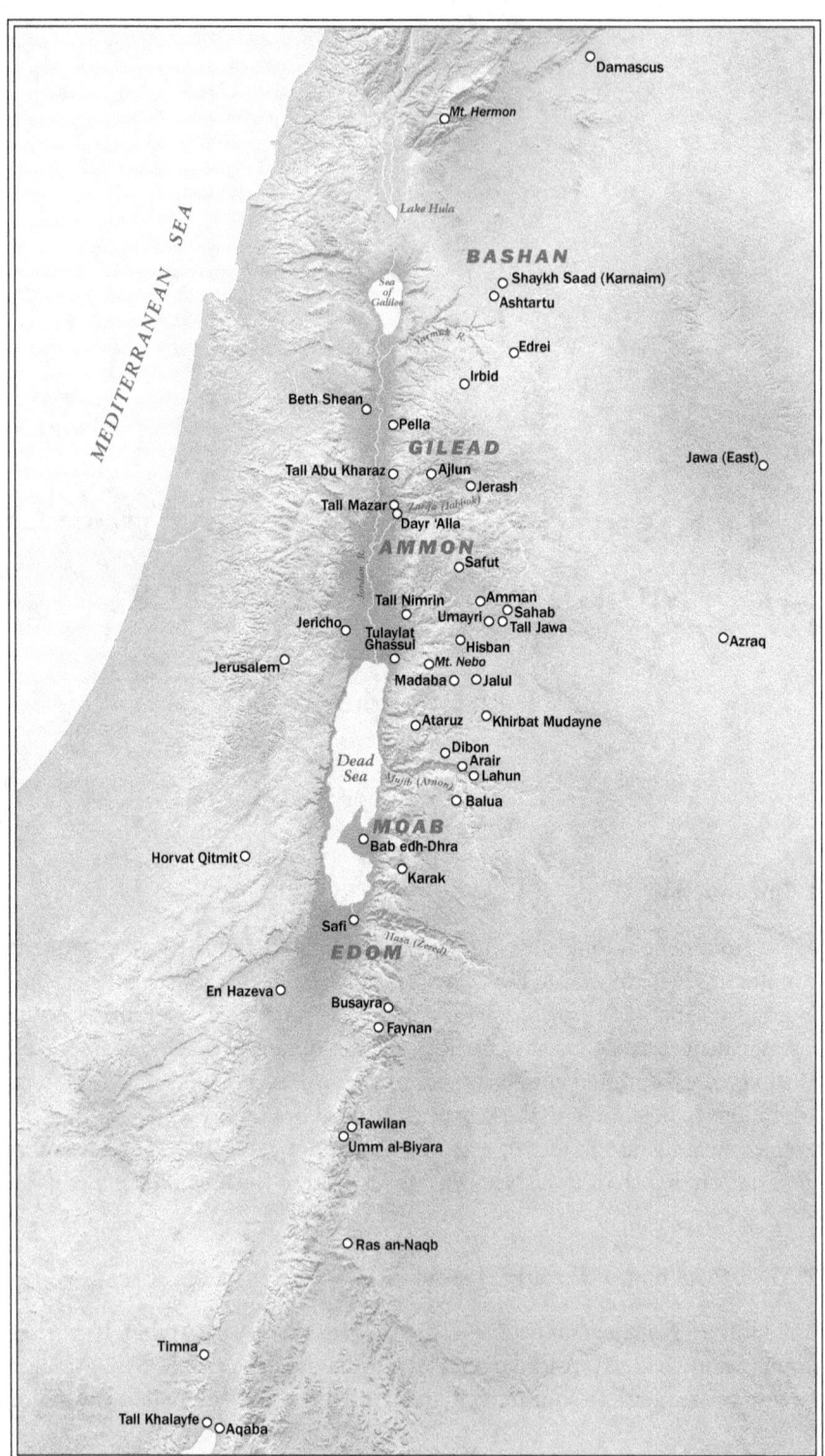

Figure 9.1. Transjordan

east-west river valleys draining into the Rift: the Yarmuk between Bashan and the forested hills of northern Gilead; the Zarqa (biblical Jabbok), south of which the ridges of southern Gilead settle into the Madaba Plains; the Mujib (biblical Arnon), a majestic canyon dividing central Transjordan, including the Karak Plateau to its south; and Wadi Hasa (biblical Zered), another dramatic canyon, south of which the southern (Edomite) Plateau extends for another 105 miles to Aqaba.

In line with Transjordan's northwest to southeast falloff in rainfall levels, human settlement from earliest times clustered along the northern Jordan Valley and western Plateau, extending south and east to marginal conditions along the desert steppe. That geographic continuum also involved an increasing shift in balance from plow agriculture to sheep-goat herding, with implications for ways of life, social organization, and economy.[1] Transjordan's place along an intercontinental land bridge meant a perennial flow of long-distance exchange providing incentive to produce surplus grain, wine, olives, and wool as its principal exports, supplemented occasionally by metals from the southern Levant's chief sources of copper and iron in Transjordan.[2] These long-lasting patterns of geography, population, and economy would prove foundational for the rise of Transjordan's territorial kingdoms during the Iron Age.

Archaeological evidence from the Middle Bronze (MB) Age (2000–1550 BCE) shows only sparse settlement south of the Wadi Mujib, almost none south of Wadi Hasa, but considerable settlement in the northern half of the country in proximity to the main artery of trade connecting Egypt with the great kingdoms of Syria-Mesopotamia and other parts of the Near East. As an extension of the peak in urban buildup that characterized MB II Cisjordan, northern Transjordan included walled settlements on the scale of small cities (e.g., Pella, Tall Irbid, and Amman Citadel), towns (e.g., Tall Dayr Alla in the central Jordan Valley, Tall Umayri south of Amman, and Sahab at the desert fringe), and villages (e.g., Tall Hayyat in the northern Jordan Valley and to the south at Tall Nimrin).

This north-south divide is reflected in Transjordan's first appearances in textual sources during this period. The Egyptian Execration Texts (ca. 1800

---

1. Øystein LaBianca and Randall W. Younker, "The Kingdoms of Ammon, Moab and Edom: The Archaeology of Society in Late Bronze/Iron Age Transjordan (ca. 1400–500 BCE)," in *The Archaeology of Society in the Holy Land*, ed. Thomas E. Levy (London: Leicester University Press, 1998), 399–415.

2. See the biblical description of the promised land as "a land whose stones are iron and from whose hills you may mine copper" (Deut. 8:9). The Faynan area of the northeast Arabah joins Timna to the southwest as chief copper sources in the Levant, and the southern Levant's largest deposit of iron ore is at Mugharat Wardeh in the Ajlun hills, north of the upper Zarqa. Iron was also produced through copper smelting and extraction of hematite from stone in various parts of the Transjordanian Plateau.

BCE) mention cities governed by single "rulers" in northern Transjordan (e.g., Ashtartu, Ṣur-Bashan, and Pella) and a more rural southern Transjordan ruled instead by "chiefs" of "clans."[3]

Those same patterns of society and settlement persisted into the Late Bronze (LB) Age (ca. 1550–1200 BCE), an era of unprecedented internationalism spurred by New Kingdom Egypt's resumption of political and economic hegemony over the eastern Mediterranean. Egyptian interests in Transjordan centered on control of overland trade routes and thus were concentrated mainly in the north, where Egyptian scarabs, Mycenaean pottery, jewelry, and other luxury items characterize settlements of this period. International prestige items found along with pottery wares of the region (e.g., chocolate-on-white ware) at towns like Tall Fukhar on the Yarmuk, Jerash in northern Gilead, Dayr Alla and Tell Saidiyya in the Jordan Valley, and in multigenerational tombs at Pella, Tall Abu Kharaz, Irbid, Amman, Sahab, as well as a well-preserved palace or temple at Tall Umayri, indicate cultural continuity and local political stability within the framework of long-distance trade. The archaeological picture is one of political domination by urban elites over an increasingly disaffected and mobile rural population, a picture also borne out in LB texts.

Topographical lists of Thutmose III (1479–1425 BCE) reflect possible Egyptian familiarity with a route south of Damascus through interior Transjordan.[4] The Amarna letters (fourteenth century BCE) document Egyptian interests in travel through northern Transjordan, where city-state alliances sometimes spanned the Jordan and Yarmuk Valleys. For example, Mut-Baʻlu, ruler of Pella and son of Lab'ayu of Shechem, pledges in the tradition of his father to provide safe passage to the pharaoh's caravans (EA 255). Another letter concerns Mut-Baʻlu's putative alliance with Ayyabu, ruler of Ashtartu (biblical Ashtaroth) in Bashan, who had robbed a Babylonian caravan and suffered the rebellion of his own cities (EA 256), some of which he had already lost to the ruler of Haṣura (biblical Hazor; EA 364). Egypt's continued need to assert its interests along these northern valley routes is substantiated by stelae of Seti I (1294–1279 BCE) found at Beth Shean, Tall Shihab on the Yarmuk, and Shaykh Saade (ancient Karnaim) in Bashan. The Beth Shean stela inscription describes Egyptian reprisals against a regional alliance including Pella (COS 2.4B). Texts of Ramesses II (1279–1213 BCE) maintain this focus on northern Transjordan, along with increasing attention to Transjordan's southern half, including explicit references to Moab and Edom.

---

3. Specifically, the Brussels series of Execration Texts. See K. A. Kitchen, "The Egyptian Evidence on Ancient Jordan," in *Early Edom and Moab: The Beginning of the Iron Age in Southern Jordan*, ed. Piotr Bienkowski (Sheffield, UK: J. R. Collis, 1992), 21–23.

4. Ibid., 23–25.

Figuring prominently in that context is a population element that Egyptian texts refer to as Shasu, a social designation perhaps related to an Egyptian verb meaning "to wander." Shasu are characteristically nomadic people occasionally appearing in texts and pictorial art in association with cities and towns. Toponym lists from the time of Amenophis III (1390–1352 BCE), recopied in the time of Ramesses II, name six "Shasu lands"—including Y*hw*, which draws comparisons with the Israelite divine name Yahweh, and S‛*rr*, which is comparable to the place-name Seir so closely associated with Edom (see below). Royal inscriptions boast of victories in these areas; for example, Ramesses II twice refers to himself as one "who plunders the mountain of Seir with his valiant arm," with Shasu appearing in parallel phrases. Ramesses III (1184–1153 BCE) claims, "I destroyed the Seirites, the clans of the Shasu, the clans of the Shasu, I pillaged their tents, with their people, their property, and their livestock."[5] A letter from an eastern Delta official during the reign of Merenptah (1213–1203 BCE) reports the passage of Shasu herders from "Edom" (Papyrus Anastasi VI). Although wandering Shasu are occasionally present in other areas of Palestine, their territorial base seems to have been the southern half of Transjordan, where they were a noteworthy component of the nomadic population of LB southern and central Transjordan that would begin to settle in sedentary communities during Iron I.

3. Iron Age Kingdoms of Transjordan

With the disintegration of Egyptian hegemony following 1200 BCE, the southern Levant became the eventual setting for independent regional kingdoms, including Ammon, Moab, and Edom. During Iron Age II (ca. 1000–550 BCE), those Transjordanian kingdoms emerged on the basis of territorial divisions and people groups. Those people identities gradually diminished following the loss of political independence under the Babylonian Empire and through increasing enculturation under successive international empires beginning with the Persian period (539–332 BCE). Even so, each of the three Transjordanian kingdoms represented a distinct legacy that echoed into later times and that can be traced back to cultural and economic roots in the Bronze Age.

Ammon

LB–Iron I

No second-millennium sources mention Ammon or Ammonites. Yet a northwest-to-southeast line of fortified settlements centering on the larger

---

5. Ibid., 27.

Figure 9.2. Excavation of Iron I building compound at Tall Abu Kharaz (directed by Peter M. Fischer), overlooking the central Jordan Valley from the east

site of Amman (including Khirbat Umm Dananir, Tall Safut, Sahab, and Tall Umayri) formed a secondary trade artery connecting the desert rim and north-central Plateau with Jordan Valley routes during LB times. Well fortified and easily defended by a system of surrounding wadi approaches, Amman would have been an important regional political center governing this network of trade and travel across the north-central Plateau already in Bronze Age times.[6]

A sociopolitical elite that exploited this regional system during LB times is evident in the elaborate caches of luxury goods and human remains found in the Amman Airport building ca. 3 miles northeast of central Amman and perhaps in similar square-plan structures 2.5 miles further southeast at Mabrak, and ca. 14 miles northwest of Amman at Rujm Henu East and Khirbat Umm Dananir, in the Baqah Valley.[7] The violent destruction and/or dismantling of these buildings at the end of LB contrasts with impressive cultural and

---

6. Patrick E. McGovern, "Settlement Patterns of the Late Bronze and Iron Ages in the Greater Amman Area," *SHAJ* 4 (1992): 179–83; Kent V. Bramlett, "Eastern Front: The Transjordanian Highlands in Late Bronze Age Hegemonic Contest" (PhD diss., University of Toronto, 2008). Cf. Eveline J. van der Steen, *Tribes and Territories in Transition: The Central East Jordan Valley in the Late Bronze and Early Iron Ages; A Study of the Sources*, OLA 130 (Leuven: Peeters, 2004), 279–80.

7. Patrick E. McGovern, "The Baqʻah Valley Project 1987: Khirbet Umm ad-Dananir and al-Qeṣir," *ADAJ* 32 (1989): 123–36, 272–78; Bruce Routledge, *Moab in the Iron Age: Hegemony, Polity, Archaeology* (Philadelphia: University of Pennsylvania Press, 2004), 67–70, 228nn30–31.

technological continuity into Iron IA in the Baqah and at Safut, Amman (Jebel Nuzha tomb), Sahab, and Umayri.[8]

Critical to the north-central Plateau's economic and social stability across the LB–Iron I transition was a regional metal industry based in the most abundant iron ore source east or west of the Jordan Rift at Mugharat Wardeh, ca. 21 miles northwest of Amman and 2.5 miles north of Wadi Zarqa.[9] Evidence for that industry includes early Iron Age pottery from mining areas and carburized steel jewelry from Baqah Valley burials.[10] Local control of this metal industry would account for the cultural continuity evident in LB–Iron I tombs, even as those assemblages exhibit a decrease in Aegean pottery and other foreign goods and an increasingly localized pottery repertoire reflecting a regionally self-contained economic framework.[11]

Shifting economic patterns during the LB–Iron I transition resulted in turmoil in central Transjordan, evident in violent destructions on the southern periphery of the Amman Plateau system, first at Tall Umayri, then later in Iron I at Sahab and Tall Jawa.[12] By contrast, the north-central Plateau's geographic contours, long-standing settlement history, and proximity to major trade routes predisposed it toward a stable settlement hierarchy and regional economic system centering on Amman during LB and Iron I times. These factors would have favored a long-standing sense of affiliation among agricultural and trade networks unifying towns and populations of the Amman Plateau, with a shared regional identity serving as a basis for stability through this transitional period.

Also, a steady reliance on plow agriculture in north-central Transjordan went hand in hand with more long-lasting and stable kinship bonds across society, promoting land ownership, investment in cultivation, and collective protection of agricultural lands.[13] By comparison, as one proceeded further south and rainfall levels diminished, so did investment in plow agriculture, with a greater investment in range-tied herding favoring

---

8. McGovern, "Baq'ah Valley Project," 134; Routledge, *Moab in the Iron Age*, 88, 232n3; van der Steen, *Tribes and Territories*, 52–60, 305–6.

9. Yosha Abdel Salam Al-Amri, "The Role of the Iron Ore Deposit of Mugharet el-Wardeh / Jordan in the Development of the Use of Iron in Southern Bilad el-Sham" (PhD diss., Ruhr-Universität Bochum, 2007), 54–82.

10. Patrick E. McGovern, *The Late Bronze and Early Iron Ages of Central Transjordan: The Baq'ah Valley Project, 1977–1981* (Philadelphia: University Museum, University of Pennsylvania, 1986), 245–67.

11. McGovern, "Settlement Patterns," 180–81.

12. P. M. Michèle Daviau, *Excavations at Tall Jawa, Jordan*, vols. 1–2, CHANE 11/1–2 (Leiden: Brill 2003), 1:41–43; Douglas R. Clark and Larry G. Herr, "From the Stone Age to the Middle Ages in Jordan: Digging Up Tall al-'Umayri," *NEA* 72, no. 2 (2009): 82–89.

13. LaBianca and Younker, "Kingdoms of Ammon, Moab and Edom," 402–3.

more flexible kinship bonds and less regional integration (see the section "Moab" below, pp. 322–29).

These enduring patterns of interdependence along the Amman corridor would favor the memory and invocation of long-standing societal bonds recognized during Iron II times. Persisting through the political shifts from LB to Iron I to Iron II times was the recognition of long-standing affiliation along the wadi systems of the north-central Plateau that had formed the basis for the regional economy during the Bronze Age and that stood as the sociopolitical background for the Iron Age notion of a broad regional population united through common descent as the "children of Ammon."

Iron II

During Iron Age II the Ammonites were distinguished from the other Transjordanian kingdoms by a special emphasis on the kin-based structure of their society in relationship to its ruling house, as expressed in the usual reference to the Ammonites in biblical and epigraphic texts as the "children" or "house of Ammon," name forms that never appear for the Moabites or Edomites. For example, the Ammonite Tall Siran inscription (ca. 600 BCE; COS 2.25) refers repeatedly to "the king of the children of Ammon" (*mlk bn 'mn*), and Jeremiah 27:3 refers to "the king of Edom, the king of Moab, the king of *the children of* Ammon" (AT; emphasis added).

Assyrian texts beginning with Tiglath-pileser III (744–727 BCE) refer to the "house of Ammon" (*bīt Am-ma-na-a-a*), in keeping with the conventional pattern in Assyrian and Aramaic sources of designating polities of Syria-Palestine by a recognized ruling dynasty or lineage over a declared kin-based (rather than city- or territory-based) population.[14] The ruling "house" is identified by the name of a reputed dynasty founder or eponymous ancestor (for example, "house of Agusi," "house of Hazael," "house of David," and "house of Omri").[15] The apparent etymology of *'Ammōn* from the common West Semitic noun **'amm-* meaning "people" or "kinsman" suggests that both "house" and "children of Ammon" identify the Ammonites as the people and kingdom of a common, primordial "kindred" or ancestor (a point played on with obvious pejorative intent in Gen. 19:38).

The Ammonite heartland was the territory in the north-central Plateau south of the Wadi Zarqa (biblical Jabbok) and centering on Amman.[16] The

---

14. Paul-Eugène Dion, "The Ammonites: A Historical Sketch," in Daviau, *Excavations*, 1:482–83.
15. Dion, "Ammonites," 495.
16. Burton MacDonald, *"East of the Jordan": Territories and Sites of the Hebrew Scriptures*, ASOR Books 6 (Boston: American Schools of Oriental Research, 2000), 157–70.

name of the Ammonite capital is known from biblical sources as Rabbah ("the Great" City; see, e.g., 2 Sam. 12:29) or *rabbat bənê 'ammôn* ("the Great [City] of the children of Ammon"; see, e.g., 2 Sam. 12:26). Its identification with present-day Amman, specifically the Citadel Hill (Jabal Qal'a) and the nearby spring at the source of the Wadi Zarqa, is certain, thanks to a continuous literary tradition to present times and to Iron Age monumental remains excavated on the Amman Citadel, including fortification walls, a water system, the Amman Citadel Inscription, an administrative building, and a megalithic building, perhaps a temple, running beneath the Roman-period temple of Hercules.[17] A series of circular and rectangular towers around Amman and similar buildings in outlying agricultural areas have been dated variously from Iron I to later Iron IIC/Persian period times, perhaps indicating ongoing use over that span.[18] An Ammonite realm of cultural and sociopolitical influence is evident in distinct forms of language, script, pottery, and art radiating outward from the capital to sites within a fifteen-mile radius during Iron II (see below).

Biblical traditions suggest that an encroaching Israelite kingdom intent on monopolizing Transjordanian trade routes connecting to the Amman Plateau trade network was a catalyst for its sociopolitical development from a network of interconnected towns to a monarchy on the model of a territorial kingdom. Saul defeats "Nahash the Ammonite" (1 Sam. 10:27b–11:15), who subsequently rules as David's ally (2 Sam. 10:1–2). Upon the accession of Nahash's son Hanun, David attacks the Ammonites, reportedly in retaliation for the disdainful treatment of his emissaries (2 Sam. 10:1–5), eventually conquering Rabbat-Ammon, crowning himself as the Ammonites' king (2 Sam. 12:30//1 Chron. 20:2),[19] and asserting dominion over the Ammonite people (2 Sam. 10:1–11:1; 12:26–31; 1 Chron. 19:1–20:3). David apparently replaces Hanun on the Ammonite throne with another son of Nahash, Shobi, who later will provide support to David in the account of Absalom's rebellion (2 Sam.

---

17. Dion, "Ammonites," 484–86; Rudolph H. Dornemann, "The Beginning of the Iron Age in Transjordan," *SHAJ* 1 (1982): 135–40; F. Zayadine, J.-B. Humbert, and M. Najjar, "The 1988 Excavations on the Citadel of Amman—Lower Terrace, Area A," *ADAJ* 33 (1989): 357–63 and plates 50–52; Ahmed Momani and Anthi Koutsoukou, "The 1993 Excavations," in *The Great Temple of Amman: The Excavations*, ed. A. Koutsoukou et al. (Amman: American Center of Oriental Research, 1997), 157–71; Sahar Mansour, "Preliminary Report of the Excavations at Jabal al-Qal'a (Lower Terrace): The Iron Age Walls," *ADAJ* 46 (2002): 141–50.

18. McGovern, "Settlement Patterns," 180–81.

19. Debate over the correct reading of the text, whether David assumes the crown of "their king" or of Milcom the Ammonite god, leads to the same political result. See Siegfried H. Horn, "The Crown of the King of the Ammonites," *AUSS* 11, no. 2 (1973): 170–80 and plates 17–20; P. Kyle McCarter Jr., *II Samuel: A New Translation with Introduction, Notes, and Commentary*, AB 9 (New York: Doubleday, 1984), 310–13.

17:27–29). Political ties between the "house of David" and the Ammonites are also indicated by the noteworthy mention of Rehoboam's Ammonite mother (1 Kings 14:21, 31). The very articulation of Ammonite identity as the "children of Ammon" may have crystallized only in opposition to the encroaching threat posed by the "children of Israel" and its political establishment ("house").

Israelite suzerainty over Ammon would have been short-lived and difficult to sustain, even during any monopoly over Palestine by the "house of David," due to Ammonite Rabbah's securely ensconced position. The Egyptian pharaoh Shishak's (Sheshonq I, ca. 945–924 BCE) invasion of Palestine included an incursion into Israelite Transjordan, with Succoth, Penuel, Mahanaim, and Adam being cities mentioned on his itinerary. This incursion would have disrupted any Israelite trade monopoly in the region, with a resulting boon to Ammonite fortunes and political independence, conditions perpetuated during the following century by Hazael of Damascus's severe weakening of Israel and Judah (2 Kings 10:32–33; 12:17–18; 13:3, 22). The ongoing vitality of Rabbat-Ammon over this span is corroborated by an archaeological sounding on Amman Citadel showing continuous occupation with enhanced fortifications from the tenth to ninth centuries BCE and by the Amman Citadel Inscription (ca. 825 BCE; COS 2.24).[20]

The Ammonites and their kings appear regularly in Assyrian sources beginning with Tiglath-pileser III.[21] Throughout the Assyrian period, the Transjordanian states retained their own kings and remained loyal vassals, requiring little direct involvement for Assyria to meet its objectives in this secondarily strategic area.[22] In return, Assyria received from its vassals the payment of annual tribute and assistance in Assyrian military and construction activities. For example, Amminadab of Ammon (along with Qausgabri of Edom, Musuri of Moab, and Manasseh of Judah) appears among the "kings of the west" who gave assistance to Assurbanipal in his 667 BCE Egyptian campaign (ANET, 294). Among Transjordan's kingdoms, Ammon gained the greatest territorial and economic benefits from Assyria's conquests of Damascus (732 BCE) and Samaria (722–721 BCE), as reflected in an Assyrian letter from

---

20. Dornemann, "Beginning of the Iron Age," 135–40.

21. In a possible earlier reference, Shalmaneser III's Kurkh Monolith Inscription mentions a certain Ba-'a-sa son of Ruhubi of A-ma-na-a-a, named as a member of the coalition of twelve kings at the battle of Qarqar in 853 BCE. It is debated whether this reference is to Ammon or to a kingdom in the Anti-Lebanon region. See K. Lawson Younger Jr., "Kurkh Monolith," COS 2.113A:264n33.

22. See Piotr Bienkowski, "Transjordan and Assyria," in *The Archaeology of Jordan and Beyond: Essays in Honor of James A. Sauer*, ed. J. A. Greene, M. D. Coogan, and L. E. Stager (Winona Lake, IN: Eisenbrauns, 2000), 44–58.

ca. 700 BCE showing Ammon's payment of tribute to be much greater than that of either Moab or Judah (*ANET*, 301).

Loyal Assyrian vassalage proved to be a wise, even if necessary, stance for an Ammonite kingdom that reached new prosperity under Assyrian protection and market influence during the late eighth through seventh centuries BCE. Grave goods from tombs around Amman show a new level of affluence correlating with long-distance market connections. These and other finds show indirect Assyrian cultural influence, with ceramic technology, vessel types, jewelry, seal glyptic, and architecture imitating Assyrian forms.[23] A class of local administrators and officials is indicated by the reference in Amos 1:15 to the "princes" (*śārîm*) of the Ammonites and by Ammonite name seals that include titles for their owners, including "servant" (*'bd*, *CAI* 13, 17, 40, 102, 129; *n'r*, "attendant," *CAI* 53, 54), "standard bearer" (*hnss*, *CAI* 68), "scribe" (*spr*, *CAI* 139), and perhaps even "female servant" (*'mt*, or "wife," *CAI* 36, 44).[24]

The weakening of Assyria during the last quarter of the seventh century allowed for a new era of Ammonite independence and nationalism. The Ammonite ostraca from Tall Mazar in the Jordan Valley and from Tall Hisban reflect Ammonite expansion beyond the heartland of the Amman Plateau by this time, and ceramic evidence from Tell Jalul shows a shift from Moabite to Ammonite pottery between the eighth and seventh centuries BCE. Ammon contended against Israel over disputed territory in Transjordan, as it had since the Assyrian conquests (2 Kings 15:29; Jer. 49:1–6; Amos 1:13–15; Zeph. 2:8–9). With the fall of Nineveh in 612 BCE, the Egyptian Twenty-Sixth Dynasty's hegemony over the region would have been only nominal for Transjordan, and Ammon retained control of these territories along the western edge of the Transjordanian Plateau and in the Jordan Valley.

Nebuchadnezzar's victory at Carchemish in 605 BCE would have made Ammon's submission to Babylon a necessity. Ammonites joined the Babylonian forces sent against Judah following Jehoiakim's rebellion leading up to 597 BCE (2 Kings 24:1–2). In 594 BCE Zedekiah may have gathered royal envoys from Ammon, Moab, Edom, Tyre, and Sidon in Jerusalem to consider a unified policy against Babylon (Jer. 27:1–11). Subsequent Ammonite resistance to Babylon is suggested by Nebuchadnezzar's dilemma portrayed in Ezekiel

---

23. Bienkowski, "Transjordan and Assyria"; P. M. Michèle Daviau, "Assyrian Influence and Changing Technologies at Tall Jawa, Jordan," in *The Land That I Will Show You: Essays on the History and Archaeology of the Ancient Near East in Honour of J. Maxwell Miller*, ed. J. Andrew Dearman and M. Patrick Graham (Sheffield, UK: Sheffield Academic, 2001), 214–38.

24. For the definitive, comprehensive edition of Ammonite inscriptions, see Walter E. Aufrecht, *A Corpus of Ammonite Inscriptions*, 2nd ed. (Lewiston, NY: Edwin Mellen, forthcoming), cited here as *CAI*.

21:23–27 (Eng. vv. 18–22). But the reported flight of Judean refugees to the territories of Ammon, Moab, and Edom when Nebuchadnezzar captured Jerusalem in 586 BCE (Jer. 40:11–12) suggests that these kingdoms were spared in the Babylonian assault and may have cooperated in some way.

Babylonian, Persian, and Hellenistic Periods

In the wake of Jerusalem's destruction, the Ammonite king Baalis sought to destabilize Babylonian control in the region by supporting the Judean Ishmael, who assassinated the Babylonian-appointed governor, Gedaliah, in 582 BCE (Jer. 40:7–41:18). While the Babylonian response is not well represented in historical sources, Josephus later relates that Nebuchadnezzar brought Ammon (and Moab) under subjection five years after the fall of Jerusalem (*Jewish Antiquities* 10.181–82). The hint that Babylon subjugated Ammon, rather than conquering it, along with the prediction of restored fortunes for the Ammonites in Jeremiah 49:6, is consistent with the archaeological record at Tall Umayri, which shows no evidence of destruction but rather a thriving economy in the Ammonite heartland continuing under the Babylonian Empire.[25]

Ammonite culture persists in the region even after Ammon's incorporation into the Babylonian and Persian Empires.[26] At Tall Umayri, a seal impression naming Baalis (*bʻlyšʻ*, *CAI* 129; cf. *baʻălîs*, Jer. 40:14) was found in association with an administrative building complex serving the site's function as a regional center for wine production through the sixth and fifth centuries BCE. Stamped jar seal impressions from Umayri with Aramaic script dating ca. 500 BCE read "Shuba of Ammon" (*šbʼ ʻmn*) and "Aya of Ammon" (*ʼyʼ ʻmn*), apparently naming the governor or treasurer of the Persian province of Ammon.[27] The Hisban and Mazar ostraca show that the Ammonite language, even while written in Aramaic script, persists in usage into the fifth century BCE. In contrast to Persian period Cisjordan, Ammon saw no disruption in its ceramic traditions, with production and use of characteristic Iron II Ammonite wheel-burnished pottery continuing into at least the early Persian period at Hisban and Umayri.

"Ammonite" identity continued to be recognized well beyond the time of the Iron Age kingdom with which it began. In Nehemiah 2:10, 19, "Tobiah the

---

25. See Larry G. Herr, "The Ammonites," in *Ancient Ammon*, ed. Burton MacDonald and Randall W. Younker, SHCANE 17 (Leiden: Brill, 1999), 227–32.

26. Herr, "Ammonites," 234–35; cf. Dion, "Ammonites," 508–9.

27. Clark and Herr, "From the Stone Age to the Middle Ages," 92–93; Piotr Bienkowski, "The Persian Period," in *Jordan: An Archaeological Reader*, ed. Russell B. Adams (London: Equinox, 2008), 334–52, here 335.

Figure 9.3. Kings of Iron Age Transjordan Appearing in Epigraphic Texts

Ammon	Moab	Edom
	Kemoshyat • Mesha Inscription (ca. 840) • Karak Fragment (ca. 840) **Mesha** • Mesha Inscription (ca. 840)	
Shanib • Tiglath-pileser III (ca. 733, *ANET*, 282) • Amman Statue Inscription (ca. 700, *CAI* 43)	**Salamanu** • Tiglath-pileser III (ca. 733, *ANET*, 282)	**Qausmalak** • Tiglath-pileser III (ca. 733, *ANET*, 282)
Zakur son of Shanib • Amman Statue Inscription (ca. 700, *CAI* 43)		
Yarḥ'azar (?) • Amman Statue Inscription (ca. 700, *CAI* 43)		
Pado'el • Sennacherib (701, *ANET*, 287)	**Kammusunadbi** • Sennacherib (701, *ANET*, 287)	**Ayarammu** • Sennacherib (701, *ANET*, 287)
	Musuri	**Qausgabri**
• Esarhaddon (ca. 677, *ANET*, 291) • seal of royal official (*CAI* 13:a, b; cf. *CAI* 33)	• Esarhaddon, ca. 677, *ANET*, 291 • Assurbanipal (668–?, *ANET*, 294)	• Esarhaddon, ca. 677, *ANET*, 291 • Assurbanipal (668–?, *ANET*, 294) • *qwsgb[r]*, Umm al-Biyara bulla/seal
'Amminadab I • Assurbanipal (668–?, *ANET*, 294) • named on two seals of royal officials (*CAI* 17, 40) • Siran Bottle (ca. 600, *CAI* 78)	**Kamashaltu** • Assurbanipal (668–?, *ANET*, 298)	
Ḥiṣṣal'el • Siran Bottle (ca. 600, *CAI* 78)		
'Amminadab II • Siran Bottle (ca. 600, *CAI* 78)		
Baalis/Baalyasha • Tall Umayri seal of royal official (*b'lyš'*, *CAI* 129, ca. 585; cf. *b'lys*, Jer. 40:14)		

The highlighting in the table indicates kings appearing in the same text.

Ammonite" figures significantly as a local official serving the Persians under Artaxerxes I (464–424 BCE). Nehemiah 13:1–2 invokes the exclusion of Ammonites and Moabites from the Judean worship community in Deuteronomy 23:3–4, in connection with Jewish intermarriage with women from Moab, Ammon, and Ashdod, including the indication that these groups continued to speak distinct language dialects (Neh. 13:23–24). This heightened concern to clarify group identities reflects ongoing continuity and change in those identities amidst competing social and political interests during the Persian period.

Similar connections across the Jordan Valley pertain to likely descendants of "Tobiah the Ammonite," known as the Tobiads of Maccabean times (2 Macc. 3:11; Josephus, *Jewish Antiquities* 12.160), who built the palace known as Qasr Abd (Castle of the Slave) at Iraq Amir just west of Amman ca. 187–175 BCE.[28] The book of 2 Maccabees, written between 124 and 63 BCE, can sensibly, even if artfully, speak of "the land of Ammon" (2 Macc. 4:26; see also 5:7). These associations echo in the modern Arabic name for the city—Amman— even though in Hellenistic times Ptolemy II (282–246 BCE) renamed the city Philadelphia, as it would still be known among the Roman Decapolis.

Moab

LB–Iron I

Moab (Egyptian *Mw-i-bw*) first appears in Egyptian texts of Ramesses II as a territorial designation in the context of central Transjordan.[29] Inscribed wall reliefs at Luxor show that the pharaoh's military assault on fortified "towns" in "Moab" possibly identified with Dibon (*Tbn*, modern Dhiban) and Butartu (*Btrt*, modern Rabbah, ca. 6 mi. north of Karak and named in a Byzantine era text as Raba Batora).[30] This Egyptian evidence, combined with the archaeological survey data described above, indicates that LB Moab was a region of sparse town and village settlements amidst a predominantly pastoral nomadic population likely related to the Shasu of such visible concern in Egyptian texts of this time.

Archaeological and artistic evidence from the Karak Plateau reflects the waning of Egyptian imperial power during later LB–early Iron I times. The Balua Stela, discovered at the archaeological site of Balua in the northeastern

---

28. See Piotr Bienkowski, "Jordan: Crossroads of the Near East," in *Treasures from an Ancient Land: The Art of Jordan*, ed. P. Bienkowski (Wolfeboro Falls, NH: Alan Sutton, 1991), 1–30, here 16–17 and fig. 11.
29. Kitchen, "Egyptian Evidence," 27–28.
30. Ibid. To date, archaeological evidence of LB settlement has yet to be unearthed at Dhiban. See Bruce Routledge, Danielle S. Fatkin, Benjamin W. Porter, Katherine Adelsberger, and Andrew Wilson, "Long-Term Settlement Change at Dhībān," *SHAJ* 11 (2013): 131–57.

Karak Plateau, includes a section of undeciphered writing and a relief scene typologically datable over an LB–Iron II span, which portrays an Egyptian god and goddess conferring emblems of authority on a Shasu leader.[31] Facing Balua on the Mujib's northern rim, the sites of Lahun (fig. 9.4) and Arair were constructed as fortified sites during Iron I, with Lahun, like Balua, being rebuilt on a more elaborate scale during Iron II and the early Iron Age fortified site of Khirbat Mummariyya guarding the southern side of the riverbed crossing.[32] Within this context, the Balua Stela scene may be understood to invoke Egyptian symbolism of imperial power in support of a Shasu leader's claim to rule from this location, controlling access to the Mujib crossing.[33] The Rujm Abd basalt relief (also known as the Shihan Warrior Stela), discovered about 6 miles west of Balua and south of the Wadi Mujib near Jebel Shihan, depicts a (possibly divine) warrior figure wielding a spear.[34] Both relief sculptures incorporate motifs known from Egypt and Syria, and both embody an ideological symbolism and devotion of resources representing significant political organization. The Balua and Rujm Abd monuments represent a royal sculpture tradition that continues in Moab during Iron II.[35]

Archaeological surveys and excavations reveal a dramatic increase in settlement north and south of the Mujib during Iron I, resulting chiefly from sedentarization of nomadic population elements. While occupation would have continued at core LB sites in central Transjordan, many new settlements emerged, including numerous agricultural villages in ecologically marginal areas.[36] New agricultural settlements clustered along the Mujib and Wadi Wala systems, often in well-defended positions atop the canyon cliffs of the Mujib and its tributaries—for example, Arair, Lahun, Khirbat Mudayna Muarraja,

31. Bruce Routledge and Carolyn Routledge, "The Balu'a Stela Revisited," in *Studies on Iron Age Moab and Neighbouring Areas in Honour of Michèle Daviau*, ed. Piotr Bienkowski (Leuven: Peeters, 2009), 71–96.

32. Ingrid M. Swinnen, "The Iron I Settlement and Its Residential Houses at al-Lahun in Moab, Jordan," *BASOR* 354 (2009): 29–53; Denyse Homès-Fredericq, "The Iron Age II Fortress of al-Lahun (Moab)," in Bienkowski, *Studies on Iron Age Moab*, 165–82; Friedbert Ninow, "The 2007 Season of the Wādī ash-Shuqayfāt Survey in the Greater Wādī al-Mūjib Area," *ADAJ* 52 (2008): 81–89.

33. J. A. Dearman, "Settlement Patterns and the Beginning of the Iron Age in Moab," in Bienkowski, *Early Edom and Moab*, 65–75, here 70–71.

34. Routledge, *Moab in the Iron Age*, 179–80. See also Fawzi Zayadine, "Sculpture in Ancient Jordan: Treasures from an Ancient Land," in Bienkowski, *Treasures from an Ancient Land*, 35–36.

35. For further discussion of Moabite and Ammonite stone-sculpture traditions, see the subsection "Art" (under "Cultural Expressions") below.

36. Paul E. Dion and P. M. Michèle Daviau, "The Moabites," in *The Books of Kings: Sources, Composition, Historiography and Reception*, ed. André Lemaire and Baruch Halpern VTSup 129 (Leiden: Brill, 2010), 216–19; Routledge, *Moab in the Iron Age*, 87–113.

Figure 9.4. Architectural remains of the Iron II fortress at Lahun overlooking Wadi Mujib (biblical Arnon) from its northern rim

and Khirbat Mudayna Aliyah.[37] These sites and others in areas extending further east and south along the desert steppe (e.g., Lejjun) featured town walls and large buildings for public storage, reflecting significant human labor and social cooperation in the founding of new settlements. Yet the layouts of these quickly emerging and gradually abandoned towns and the typical (pillared, sometimes four-room) house plan indicate autonomous, mobile family households as the basic unit of social identity and solidarity, with inequalities of wealth and status.[38] The preoccupation with defense, signaled by substantial town walls at these sites, shows Iron I in central Transjordan to have been a period of instability and violence, spilling over to the north as seen in Iron I destruction layers at Jalul, Umayri, Tall Jawa, and Sahab. Most of the new Iron I sites in Moab founded in this way were abandoned without reoccupation, in contrast to continuing or renewed settlement at the Mujib rim sites of Arair, Lahun, and Balua.[39]

To summarize, during Iron I some form of local political authority over the Mujib crossing allowed for control of north-south traffic through

37. Ibid.
38. Bruce Routledge, "Thinking 'Globally' and Analysing 'Locally': South-Central Jordan in Transition," in *Israel in Transition: From Late Bronze II to Iron IIa (c. 1250–850)*, vol. 1, *The Archaeology*, ed. Lester L. Grabbe (New York: T&T Clark, 2008), 144–76.
39. Dion and Daviau, "Moabites," 216.

Transjordan, utilization of water resources, and protection of agricultural investment in the area. Even this measure of local political hegemony at the heart of the territory known both beforehand and afterward as Moab was in keeping with the character of central Transjordan—a region fragmented among towns and areas where kinship bonds operated mostly on a local level, without regional political integration or development of urban centers like those appearing in Iron II Moab. Even still, this highly segmented pattern would go on to provide the social and political foundations for monarchy during Iron II.[40]

Iron II

Documentary sources and excavations to date provide little insight into Iron IIA Moab. The transformation from circumstances prevailing in Iron I to broader cohesion and enduring urbanized settlement reflecting statehood during Iron IIB means that Iron IIA was a time of formative dynamics for state formation. This span of a century or more would have been the period in which David allegedly killed two out of every three Moabites (2 Sam. 8:2) and in which Moab later was dominated by Omri and "his son" (Mesha Stela Inscription, henceforth MI, lines 4–5, 6; COS 2.23).[41] As was the case for the Ammonites (see above), this threatening familiarity with the Israelite kingdom would have been a catalyst for state formation in Moab.

By ca. 840 BCE, fortifications and urban constructions were reportedly in place at Dibon, Madaba, and other towns that come under Mesha's claims (MI, lines 3, 7–8, 9–10, 18–19, 21–28). Archaeological remains from Iron IIb Dhiban (ancient Dibon) include part of a city fortification wall, a large public building, and cultic artifacts[42] perhaps slightly postdating Mesha or relating to structures he claims to have built there, including defense walls, gates, towers, cisterns, and even an arbor (MI, lines 21–24) and a worship installation he calls "this *bamah* for Chemosh" (line 3).[43] The town of Atarot, which Mesha claims to have conquered from Israel (MI, line 11), is identified with Khirbat Ataruz, where an Iron II temple complex with abundant cultic artifacts and an inscription have been excavated (see more below). Architectural evidence corroborating this picture of Iron II royal hegemony includes proto-Aeolic, or volute, capitals excavated at Ayn Sara near Karak and to the southeast at

---

40. Routledge, "Thinking 'Globally,'" 172.
41. Ibid., 171–73.
42. William H. Morton, "The 1954, 55, and 65 Excavations at Dhiban in Jordan," in *Studies in the Mesha Inscription and Moab*, ed. A. Dearman, ABS 2 (Atlanta: Scholars Press, 1989), 239–46, 310–24; Routledge, *Moab in the Iron Age*, 161–72.
43. Routledge et al., "Long-Term Settlement Change at Dhībān," 136–40.

Mudaybi.⁴⁴ The latter site and Khirbat Mudayna (Wadi Thamad, ca. 10 mi. northeast of Dhiban) include Iron II fortification walls, towers, and multichamber ceremonial gateways dating to the late ninth or early eighth century. Mudayna and other sites near the Wadi Thamad, most notably Rumayl with its collapsed stone tower and distinct sawtooth-shaped enclosure wall, served as agricultural storage and processing stations, all built according to different plans and functions.⁴⁵

The nature of Moab as a region of distinct territorial and political segments as reflected in the Iron I evidence (see above) remained foundational under its monarchy during Iron IIB, as described in the most comprehensive surviving source for the Moabite polity, the Mesha Inscription (ca. 840 BCE). In fact, Mesha introduces himself in MI as "the king of Moab, the Dibonite" (lines 1–2), thus highlighting both national and local identity. (The term "Moabite" never appears in the text.) Throughout, Mesha discusses the population, territory, and expansion of his kingdom in terms of distinct territorial divisions ("lands," Moabite sg. *’rṣ*) and centers—the land of Madaba (lines 7–8), the land of Aṭarot (line 10; cf. line 11), and other town centers comparable to his own Dibon (lines 21, 28)—namely, Nebo (line 14), Yaḥaṣ (line 20), Aroer (line 26), Bet Bamot (line 27), Bet Diblaten (line 30), Bet Baʻlmaon (line 30), and Ḥawronen (lines 31, 32). Where kin- or ethnic-group identities are mentioned, it is always based on attachment to a local place—for example, "Dibonite" (*dybny*, line 1), "men of Sharon" (*’š šrn*, line 13), "men of Maharat" (*’š mḥrt*, lines 13–14), "[m]en of Dibon" (*[’]š dybn*, line 28), and "men of Gad" (*’š gd*, line 10). The implication that these distinct "lands" together constitute the "land," or "country" (line 5), of Chemosh indicates an understanding of Moab as a territorial unity, even if a socially segmented one.

Dibon's centrality in MI (lines 20–31) doubtlessly owes in part to its status as Mesha's hometown and the monument's location there. Even so, Dibon deserved much of the credit for Mesha's political success. Its strategic location in the heart of Moab and its proximity to the Mujib (line 26) provided it direct access to and potential control over the flow of trade through the region, and its surrounding fields provided abundant surplus goods through extensive herding and farming. Thus, MI describes Moab not as a mere patchwork of territories but as "a hierarchically segmented system of territories" ruled by Mesha, with Dibon as a strategic subdivision and Mesha's expanding power base.⁴⁶

---

44. Routledge, *Moab in the Iron Age*, 175–78.
45. P. M. Michèle Daviau, "*Hirbet el-Mudēyine* in Its Landscape: Iron Age Towns, Forts, and Shrines," *ZDPV* 122 (2006): 14–30 and plates 4–9.
46. Routledge, *Moab in the Iron Age*, 147.

The realization that Mesha inherited and built on an existing political structure based at Dibon is explicitly acknowledged in the king's self-introduction in MI as "Mesha, son of Chemosh[yat]" (lines 1–2) and is corroborated by a fragment of a second monumental inscription from Dibon (modern Dhiban) with letter forms indicating a date prior to that of MI.[47] The name of Mesha's father in MI (*kmš[yt]*) is partially restored from the roughly contemporary Karak Inscription fragment (fig. 9.7, p. 341), which begins following a break with formulary similar to that at the opening of MI: "[Che]moshyat, king of Moab, the D[ibonite]" (*[k]mšyt mlk m'b hd[ybny]*).[48] These ninth-century BCE monumental inscriptions represent a well-established claim of royal hegemony over Moab spanning both sides of the Mujib, from Dibon to Karak. Along with later inscriptions from sites in Moab, they show a basic consistency in language and orthography, even with some variations in script, indicating overarching unity but also heterogeneity of identity and local political organization among those lands encompassed by the hegemonic claims of Moab's monarchy.

Mesha and his successors were able to extend Moabite territory further northwest into formerly Israelite holdings in Transjordan, thanks to Hazael's conquests in Bashan and Gilead (2 Kings 10:32–33). Cities and towns north of those Mesha had added to his kingdom are regarded as Moabite in Isaiah 15–16 and Jeremiah 48, indicating Moab's northern boundary had shifted into the Wadi Hisban region.[49] By the late eighth century BCE, Moabite pottery, inscriptions, and sculpture at Madaba, Mudayna, and other smaller sites south of Wadi Thamad show a clear cultural boundary over against their Ammonite counterparts just a few miles to the north and east at Jalul and among agricultural processing sites north of Wadi Thamad.[50]

Like Ammon, Moab was under Assyrian vassalage by the late eighth century and remained so into the mid-seventh century BCE, appearing in fourteen Assyrian inscriptions over that span, beginning with Tiglath-pileser III's mention of King Salamanu of Moab (¹*sa-la-ma-nu* ᴷᵁᴿ*ma-'a-ba-a-a*) along with the rulers of Ammon, Edom, Ashkelon, and Judah as tributaries ca. 734–732

---

47. Roland E. Murphy, "A Fragment of an Early Moabite Inscription from Dibon," *BASOR* 125 (1952): 20–23.

48. William L. Reed and Fred V. Winnett, "A Fragment of an Early Moabite Inscription from Kerak," *BASOR* 172 (1963): 1–9; Heather Dana Davis Parker and Ashley Fiutko Arico, "A Moabite-Inscribed Statue Fragment from Kerak: Egyptian Parallels," *BASOR* 373 (2015): 105–20.

49. Nadav Na'aman, "Royal Inscription versus Prophetic Story: Mesha's Rebellion according to Biblical and Moabite Historiography," in *Ahab Agonistes: The Rise and Fall of the Omri Dynasty*, ed. Lester L. Grabbe (London, 2007), 175–76.

50. P. M. Michèle Daviau, "Moab's Northern Border: Khirbat al-Mudayna on the Wadi ath-Thamad," *BA* 60 (1997): 222–28.

BCE.[51] Moab, along with Edom, joined an unsuccessful alliance of southern Levantine states led by Judah against Sargon II (722–705 BCE), which ended with the Assyrian conquest and annexation of Ashdod in 712 BCE (*ANET*, 286–87). With this brief exception, Moab, like the other Transjordanian states, remained a compliant vassal of Assyria until its withdrawal from the west around 640 BCE.

Assyrian vassalage for Moab meant retaining political control of the Transjordanian Plateau south of Wadi Hisban and increased economic prosperity and military security for all the Transjordanian kingdoms, with episodic Assyrian military action supporting those tribute-paying vassals' oversight of trade along the routes flowing through them. For example, Assurbanipal (668–ca. 627 BCE) reports a series of victories against the forces of Yaite, "king of Arabia," among western vassal territories including Ammon, Moab, and Edom (Rassam Cylinder; *ANET*, 297–98).

Nonetheless, Assyrian support came at a steep price. Even after declining to join Hezekiah's anti-Assyrian coalition, Kammusunadbi of Moab and the rulers of Ammon, Edom, and other Levantine states paid heavy tribute during Sennacherib's third campaign (701 BCE; *ANET*, 287). Musuri of Moab, along with the kings of Ammon and Edom, aided in transport of building materials to Nineveh for the construction of a palace for Esarhaddon (680–669 BCE; *ANET*, 291) and provided troops for Assurbanipal's first campaign against Egypt in 669/667 BCE (*ANET*, 294). Another inscription, from later in Assurbanipal's reign, credits "Kamashaltu, king of Moab, a servant belonging to me" with defeating the Arab king Ammuladin of Qedar, who "had revolted and had continuously made razzias against the kings of the Westland" (*ANET*, 298).

Babylonian, Persian, and Hellenistic Periods

Following the mid-seventh century BCE, Moab remains largely hidden from view in surviving historical sources. The badly damaged Lachish Ostracon 8, written in Hebrew and dating to the late seventh or early sixth century BCE, preserves a reference to Moab, suggesting its recognition at that time (leading to Nebuchadnezzar's conquest of Judah) as a political unit, most likely a vassal to Babylon as it had been to Assyria.[52]

Moab apparently remained loyal to Babylon when Jehoiakim rebelled in 605 BCE, and Moabites were among those joining the Babylonian forces sent

---

51. For the Assyrian references to Moab collected by Mordechai Cogan along with two appearing later, see Routledge, *Moab in the Iron Age*, 202.
52. F. W. Dobbs-Allsopp, J. J. M. Roberts, C. L. Seow, and Richard E. Whitaker, eds., *Hebrew Inscriptions: Texts from the Biblical Period of the Monarchy* (New Haven: Yale University Press, 2005), 325–26.

against Judah (2 Kings 24:1–2). Resentment over this action may perhaps be reflected in the oracles against Moab in Jeremiah 48, which describe the devastation of various towns and fortresses of Moab. It is uncertain whether the Babylonians deported Moabites, as intimated by Jeremiah 48:7: "Chemosh shall go out into exile, with his priests and his attendants." A continuing threat facing Moab and Ammon alike during the sixth century BCE was that posed by desert tribes designated the "children of the east" in Ezekiel 25:10.

Josephus tells of Babylon's subordination of Moab (and Ammon) five years after the fall of Jerusalem (i.e., 582 BCE; *Jewish Antiquities* 10.181–82), and Jeremiah 48:47 mentions Moab's eventual restoration. Like Ammon, Moab was probably incorporated into the Babylonian and Persian Empires, with little immediate change resulting from the intervening fall of Babylon in 539 BCE. As yet, no written evidence survives for Moab's status as a distinct Persian province, such as that found for Ammon. Nehemiah 13:23–24 reflects the recognition of a "Moabite" people identity and language persisting well into the Persian period. By the early first century BCE, all of Transjordan was considered part of the Nabatean realm of "Arabia," as reflected in Josephus's account of Alexander Jannaeus's (103–76 BCE) conflict against the Nabatean Obodas I. Alexander reportedly defeated and extracted tribute from "the Arabians, such as the Moabites and Gileadites" (*Jewish Antiquities* 13.374), though later he would be forced to return "the land of Moab and Gilead" (*Jewish Antiquities* 14.382). As these Jewish textual sources suggest, a distinct Moabite identity and population continued to be recognized through Persian, Hellenistic, and perhaps Roman times, though with changes in that identity through surrounding political circumstances, even with the enduring sense of Moab as a territorial designation, likewise reflected in the persisting city names Rabbath Moab and Karak Moab.[53]

Edom

LB–Iron I

Edom is a place-name—from the Semitic word meaning "red (land)"—in reference to the soils and mountains of Nubian sandstone south of the Wadi Hasa, Edom's location in biblical texts.[54] The closely associated place-name Seir means "hairy," perhaps originally in reference to the brushy wooded slopes descending from the Edomite plateau to the Arabah or to a portion of the plateau itself (e.g., Gen. 32:4 [Eng. 32:3]; 36:8–9, 21; Num. 24:18;

---

53. J. Maxwell Miller, "Moab," *ABD* 4:882–93, here 890–91.
54. MacDonald, *"East of the Jordan,"* 185–94.

Judg. 5:4).⁵⁵ The recognition of territory west of the Arabah as belonging to Edom (Num. 34:3–4; Josh. 15:1–3) and Seir (e.g., Deut. 1:44; cf. Num. 14:45) possibly followed Edomite expansion into the eastern Negev beginning in the seventh century BCE, as indicated by archaeological and epigraphic evidence.⁵⁶

Both Edom and Seir appear in Egyptian texts during LB, including the reference from the eighth regnal year of Merenptah (ca. 1206 BCE) to "Shasu clansfolk of Edom," the claim by Ramesses II to have plundered "the mountain of Seir," and the boast by Ramesses III: "I destroyed the Seirites, the clans of the Shasu, I pillaged their tents, with their people, their property, and their livestock likewise, without limit."⁵⁷ These and additional Egyptian texts indicate that, during the later LB and early Iron I, Edom was inhabited by a pastoral nomadic, tent-dwelling population with a kin-based social structure that posed a sufficient threat to Egypt to warrant regular military action.

This textual evidence is consistent with the archaeological picture of virtually no settlement along the Wadi Hasa and south during LB and Iron I.⁵⁸ Survey data indicates that Edom, like Moab, underwent considerable settlement increase during the Iron Age, resulting mainly from the settling of a nomadic population that the Egyptian texts show was already present (even if archaeologically invisible) during LB times. Far from being a deserted wilderness, Edom and the Arabah during the LB–Iron I transition had a significant population with a mostly mobile lifestyle as pastoral tent dwellers.

Edom's location at the crossroads of trade from the Red Sea to Damascus and from Arabia to the Mediterranean across the southern Negev meant that a perennial part of Edom's economic makeup was some form of involvement in that flow of trade, which ebbed and rose depending on surrounding market realities. The collapse of the LB economic system, including the end of Cyprus's role as the chief producer of copper in the eastern Mediterranean,

---

55. Ernst Axel Knauf, "Seir," *ABD* 5:1072–73. Cf. the view of John R. Bartlett that Seir always denoted territory west of the Arabah (*Edom and the Edomites*, JSOTSup 77 [Sheffield, UK: Sheffield Academic, 1989], 33–44).

56. MacDonald, *"East of the Jordan,"* 185–87; Itzhaq Beit-Arieh, "The Edomites in Cisjordan," in *You Shall Not Abhor an Edomite for He Is Your Brother: Edom and Seir in History and Tradition*, ed. Diana V. Edelman, ABS 3 (Atlanta: Scholars Press, 1995), 33–40.

57. Kitchen, "Egyptian Evidence," 26–27.

58. Piotr Bienkowski, "Iron Age Settlement in Edom: A Revised Framework," in *The World of the Aramaeans II: Studies in History and Archaeology in Honour of Paul-Eugène Dion*, ed. P. M. M. Daviau, J. W. Wevers, and M. Weigl, JSOTSup 325 (Sheffield, UK: Sheffield Academic, 2001), 257–69.

meant a new importance for Arabah sources, first at Timna[59] under Egyptian control and soon afterward under local control in the Faynan district.[60]

Archaeological surveys, excavations, and high-precision radiocarbon dating in the Faynan district show a twelfth- to ninth-century BCE metal industry comprising several large-scale production sites (esp. Khirbet en-Nahas, KEN, ca. 10 ha. [fig. 9.5]; and Khirbet al-Jariyeh, KAJ, ca. 3 ha.); a number of smaller sites on the Wadi Fidan and main Wadi Faynan systems; numerous mines, campsites, and other smaller sites with various functions; some twenty cemeteries; and perhaps the site of Tall Faynan, often identified with biblical Punon (Num. 33:42–43).[61]

An enormous cemetery excavated near the western entrance of the Faynan district (labeled Wadi Fidan 40) reveals a nonsedentary, kin-based component of the local population, with connections to the Faynan metal industry.[62] Egyptian scarabs from these burials and from nearby metal industry sites might indicate this population's long-standing contact with an Egyptian presence, from the fifteenth century to the tenth century BCE, as reflected in New Kingdom textual references to Edom, Seir, and their Shasu inhabitants (see above).[63]

Supplementing this population's long-standing pursuits of herding and small-scale agriculture, economic specializations developed during Iron Age I in relationship to trade out of northwestern Arabia and the revived metal industry. Edom's economy may have involved a seasonal pattern whereby some portion of the largely nomadic population engaged in metal production in the lowlands during the cooler fall and winter and moved their flocks and herds into the highlands during the summer months.[64] In keeping with this highland-lowland seasonal pattern, these activities of herding, metal industry,

59. Benno Rothenberg, "Timna," *EAEHL* 4:1184–1203; Erez Ben-Yosef, Ron Shaar, Lisa Tauxe, and Hagai Ron, "A New Chronological Framework for Iron Age Copper Production at Timna Israel," *BASOR* 367 (2012): 31–71.

60. Erez Ben-Yosef, Thomas E. Levy, Thomas Higham, Mohammad Najjar, and Lisa Tauxe, "The Beginning of Iron Age Copper Production in the Southern Levant: New Evidence from Khirbat al-Jariya, Faynan, Jordan," *Antiquity* 84 (2010): 724–46.

61. Thomas E. Levy, "Pastoral Nomads and Iron Age Metal Production in Ancient Edom," in *Nomads, Tribes, and the State in the Ancient Near East: Cross-Disciplinary Perspectives*, ed. J. Szuchman (Chicago: Oriental Institute of the University of Chicago, 2009), 152. Punon has been connected with a Shasu region *pwnw* mentioned by Ramesses II, perhaps in reference to the Faynan area; see Ernst Axel Knauf, "Punon," *ABD* 5:556–57.

62. Thomas E. Levy, "Ethnic Identity in Biblical Edom, Israel, and Midian: Some Insights from Mortuary Contexts in the Lowlands of Edom," in *Exploring the Longue Durée: Essays in Honor of Lawrence E. Stager*, ed. J. David Schloen (Winona Lake, IN: Eisenbrauns, 2009), 251–62.

63. Levy, "Pastoral Nomads," 157–58, 160.

64. Faunal analysis shows seasonal rather than year-round occupation of lowland sites. See Levy, "Ethnic Identity."

Figure 9.5. Fortification wall of the copper-processing center at Khirbat en-Nahas in the Wadi Faynan area of the northeast Arabah (10th–9th century BCE). The background includes surrounding natural hills, architectural rubble, and extensive slag deposits from the metal processing operations.

and trade were components of a regional economy, interwoven along social and geographic lines according to tribal political authority. The Edomite "king" list in Genesis 36:31–39, though completed centuries later, preserves a picture of regional power and political authority across Edom as having been negotiated among local and tribal rulers prior to the time of centralized monarchies in Israel or Edom. That cultural memory preserved in this text corresponds with the archaeological evidence from KEN and the Wadi Fidan 40 cemetery, indicating that socioeconomic and political organization in Iron I Edom followed kin-based segmentary patterns negotiated among tribal chieftains, a regional "chiefly confederacy" that eventually provided the basis for an emerging Edomite kingdom.[65]

Iron II

At KEN, radiocarbon dates from charcoal samples show that, following a period of some smelting activity during the late twelfth and eleventh centuries BCE, the tenth and ninth centuries BCE marked the high point of the Faynan copper industry, with a late tenth-century disruption and reorganization due perhaps to Sheshonq I's invasion.[66] The KEN fortress, originally built in the

---

65. Levy, "Pastoral Nomads," 159–60.
66. As indicated by Egyptian ornaments from the time of Sheshonq I and a major disruption of copper production at the end of the tenth century indicated in slag evidence at KEN. See Levy, "Pastoral Nomads," 161, and 153–55 for details on what follows.

tenth century BCE, was substantially reorganized and expanded during the ninth century BCE. Ongoing but more limited mining and smelting activity in the Faynan lowlands during the eighth and seventh centuries is evident at a number of sites.

Ceramics at tenth- and ninth-century KEN are defined by locally produced wheel-made pottery anticipating the characteristic wares—especially Busayra painted ware (also called "Edomite pottery")—at highland Edomite sites dated to the eighth through sixth centuries BCE, namely, the fortresses and palaces at Busayra, Tawilan, and Umm al-Biyara (fig. 9.6), as well as at Tall Khalayfi near the Red Sea (frequently spelled Tell el-Kheleifeh).[67] The KEN pottery also includes significant amounts of Qurayyah painted ware (also known as "Midianite pottery") and locally produced handmade pottery (sometimes called "Negeb ware"), the latter being characteristic of early Iron II Negev sites, as well as a few examples of Cypriot black-on-red juglets, which begin to appear as imports in Cisjordan during late Iron IIa. This KEN repertoire reflects a mobile and mixed population based in Edom and involved in trade between northwest Arabia and the Mediterranean coast. The ongoing regional pottery tradition indicates cultural continuity between the highly fortified metal industry of the tenth- and ninth-century BCE Edomite lowlands and the subsequent period of monumental architecture and expanded, intensified settlement over the Edomite plateau.[68]

Although the lack of extensive inscriptions surviving from Edom leaves many of the circumstances of the kingdom and its origin in obscurity, biblical and Assyrian sources align in ways that allow some insights. According to biblical tradition, King David subdued Edom, "killed eighteen thousand Edomites in the Valley of Salt," placed garrisons "throughout all Edom," and made the Edomites his "servants" (2 Sam. 8:13–14). Eventually, David's general Joab reportedly "killed every male in Edom" (1 Kings 11:15–16). Domination over Edom from Jerusalem allegedly continued into the ninth century BCE, as suggested by the statement that under Jehoshaphat of Judah (870–846 BCE) "there was no king in Edom; a deputy was king" (1 Kings 22:48 [Eng. 22:47]).[69] The report of Jehoshaphat's trade with Ophir and the wrecking of his ships at Ezion-geber implies Judahite control of the Red Sea port and

---

67. Neil G. Smith and Thomas E. Levy, "The Iron Age Pottery from Khirbat en-Nahas, Jordan: A Preliminary Study," *BASOR* 352 (2008): 41–91. See also Levy, "Pastoral Nomads," 160.

68. But cf. Piotr Bienkowski, "Edom during the Iron Age II Period," in *The Oxford Handbook of the Archaeology of the Levant, c. 8000–332 BCE*, ed. Margreet L. Steiner and Ann E. Killebrew (Oxford: Oxford University Press, 2014), 782–94, here 787.

69. Bartlett, *Edom and the Edomites*, 115–16, and 118–22 on the reference simply to "the king of Edom" in the problematic passage 2 Kings 3.

Figure 9.6. Iron II architectural remains atop Umm al-Biyara in Petra

the connecting overland routes through the Arabah (1 Kings 22:48–49 [Eng. 22:47–48]; cf. 2 Chron. 20:36–37).

Edom is the first of the Transjordanian kingdoms to appear in an undisputed reference in Assyrian records, as a tributary to Adad-nirari III (810–783 BCE) in connection with his western campaign and siege of Damascus (*ANET*, 281–82). This text documents Edom's existence as an independent kingdom by ca. 800 BCE and suggests its origins as such during the preceding decades or earlier.

The critical turning point may have occurred during the reign of Jehoshaphat's son Jehoram (846–841 BCE), when "Edom revolted against the rule of Judah, and set up a king of their own" (2 Kings 8:20–22). Within the next few years, Hazael's expansionist campaigns and eventual subjugation of Israel and Judah ensured Edom's lasting independence (2 Kings 10:32–33; the Tel Dan Stela Inscription, *COS* 2.39). Damascus's dominance over the southern Levant (ca. 840–800 BCE), even if causing the decline of the Faynan copper industry, solidified Edom's break from Judah and strengthened the hand of all Transjordan's kingdoms against Israel and Judah in a realignment of trade through the region.

Edom's realization of independence would have involved, if not new levels of political organization, a new ideal of political cohesion developing from its long-standing regime of negotiated tribal authority. Ironically, Edom's former subjugation to "the house of David" and its proximity to Mesha's Moab would have provided both the impetus and the models for Edomite political and military organization as a unified kingdom. Eventually, Edomite governance became centralized on the highland plateau, somewhat in the image of the surrounding kingdoms but also in resistance to them. While this mid-ninth- to mid-eighth-century BCE time of transition remains vague in archaeological sources (even if represented in biblical texts), the following period of prosperity from secured markets and trade under Assyrian vassalage comes into view in Assyrian texts and in archaeological evidence (see below).

The renewed Assyrian check on Damascus by Adad-nirari III facilitated a resurgence of the Cisjordanian kingdoms, including a resumption of Judah's domination of Edom. This would be the backdrop for the biblical reports that Judahite forces under Amaziah of Judah (800–783 BCE) "killed ten thousand Edomites in the Valley of Salt," captured Sela (2 Kings 14:7; 2 Chron. 25:11), and threw another ten thousand Edomite prisoners to their deaths from the precipice there (2 Chron. 25:12).[70] Azariah (Uzziah, 783–742 BCE) managed a temporary resumption of Judahite control of the Red Sea port of Elath (2 Kings 14:22).[71] Later Ahaz (735–715 BCE), preoccupied with the Syro-Ephraimite threat to his north and Tiglath-pileser III's ensuing 734 BCE campaign, would see Edom regain Elath for good (2 Kings 16:5–7; cf. 2 Chron. 28:16–18).

During Assyria's expansion into the southern Levant, most of the region's kingdoms, including those of Transjordan, retained their independence but paid heavy tribute. Edom, Moab, and Ammon appear together regularly as tribute-paying vassals in Assyrian inscriptions beginning with Tiglath-pileser III.[72] King Qausgabri of Edom is thus named among those supplying labor and materials for Esarhaddon's building projects in Nineveh (ca. 673 BCE) and providing assistance in Assurbanipal's wars against Egypt (beginning in 667 BCE; *ANET*, 291, 294).

Vassalage to Assyria brought new protection from desert tribes, and the Assyrian annexations of Damascus in 732 BCE and of Samaria in 722, along with the weakening of Judah, strengthened the economic position of the Transjordanian kingdoms, integrating them more fully into an international market system dominated by Assyria. Edom's ability, under Assyrian suzerainty, to

---

70. Biblical Sela has been identified with Umm al-Biyara in Petra and, more likely, with Khirbat Silʿ north of Busayra. See Bartlett, *Edom and the Edomites*, 123; Diana V. Edelman, "Edom: A Historical Geography," in Edelman, *You Shall Not Abhor an Edomite*, 3–4.

71. Bartlett, *Edom and the Edomites*, 124–25.

72. Tiglath-pileser III (*ANET*, 282), Sennacherib (ibid., 287), Esarhaddon (ibid., 291), Assurbanipal (ibid., 294).

maintain and maximize control over southern trade routes passing through its territory and along the full extent of the Arabah, as represented by Tall Khalayfi, eventuated in an Edomite foothold on the western edge of the Arabah by the seventh century BCE at En Hazeva and in the Negev at Horvat Qitmit, southeast of Arad.

An increasing Edomite presence in the Negev is evident in the epigraphic and ceramic remains from late seventh- and early sixth-century BCE Arad and Beersheba (see below). The site of Horvat Uza in the Negev, originally a Judean military fort, apparently fell into Edomite hands during the late seventh or early sixth century, as indicated by the Edomite ostracon found there. These sites represent advancing Edomite encroachment on the territory of Judah during that kingdom's final decades.

Along with Edom's continued control of the Arabah, the late eighth- to seventh-century BCE period of Assyrian hegemony also coincides with the development of intensified settlement on the Edomite Plateau, as represented in archaeological evidence by towns, farmsteads, and palaces excavated at the sites of Busayra, Ghrareh, Tawilan, and Umm al-Biyara and also by pottery collected at sites southeast of the Dead Sea and along the Wadi Dana leading up from Faynan to the Plateau.[73]

The most extensive Edomite archaeological evidence comes from Busayra (biblical Bozrah; e.g., Amos 1:12), on the western edge of the Plateau above Faynan, ca. 19 miles south of Wadi Hasa and ca. 2.5 miles west of the King's Highway.[74] The site rests on a land spur with impressive remnants of an administrative center with monumental buildings, an encircling fortification wall, and a commanding view of the lower town that ran along the slopes surrounding it on three sides. Two or more interrelated palatial or temple buildings comparable to Assyrian open court structures show evidence of a fiery destruction.

Busayra offers the most complete repertoire of pottery from Edom, including the fine painted ware often designated "Edomite" pottery or "Busayra ware."[75] Given the limited ceramic sequence for Iron II Edom that currently exists, pottery from the main occupational phase of Busayra can be dated to the seventh and sixth centuries BCE, based on a small number of inscribed ostraca, seals, weights, and seal impressions on pottery. Related pottery, though

---

73. Burton MacDonald, "Evidence from the Wadi el-Hasa and Southern Ghors and North-East Arabah Archaeological Surveys," in Bienkowski, *Early Edom and Moab*, 113–42.

74. Piotr Bienkowski, Crystal-M. Bennett, and Márta Balla, *Busayra Excavations by Crystal-M. Bennett, 1971–1980* (Oxford: Oxford University Press, 2002).

75. Piotr Bienkowski, "The Edomites: The Archaeological Evidence from Transjordan," in Edelman, *You Shall Not Abhor an Edomite*, 41–92, esp. 49–53.

restricted to undecorated wares, appears at the agricultural settlement at Tawilan (near Petra) and at mountaintop sites in the Petra region: as-Sadeh, Ba'ja III, Jabal al-Qseir, Qurayyat al-Mansur, and Umm al-Biyara,[76] where a royal palace is dated to ca. 670 BCE by a clay seal impression of Qausgabri. Known from Assyrian inscriptions, it is the first seal or impression of an Iron Age Levantine king to be recovered through archaeological excavation and is an important anchor for absolute dating of an Edomite site and associated pottery.[77]

These sites have yielded locally made pottery imitating a type known as Assyrian palace ware, in keeping with the late eighth- and seventh-century dating of those sites' main phases. The Qurayya ("Midianite") ware present at Timna and KEN also appears in small quantities at Busayra and Tawilan. The dominant pottery forms and styles at the Edomite highland sites have their closest parallels in locally made pottery at Faynan sites dating to the tenth and ninth centuries BCE (see above), suggesting a core ceramic tradition for the area of Edom that persists among outside contacts and cultural influences. Although a site in southern Jordan with a stratified, datable pottery sequence from LB to Iron II is still lacking, the combined datable evidence from the Wadi Faynan and the Edomite plateau holds promise as a basis for establishing a dated pottery sequence for Edom over most of that span.

Babylonian, Persian, and Hellenistic Periods

Babylonian and Persian sources provide little information regarding Edom and Transjordan during the sixth century BCE. In the biblical description of Jehoiakim's rebellion against Nebuchadnezzar, Edomites are not mentioned among the Aramean, Ammonite, and Moabite divisions accompanying the Babylonian forces sent "against Judah to destroy it" (2 Kings 24:1–2). Perhaps Babylon excluded them from vassal duties for logistic and geographic reasons, or its nonparticipation may relate to Edom's "brotherhood" with Judah-Israel (see Deut. 23:8–9 [Eng. 23:7–8]).

Although Edomite emissaries are among those Zedekiah gathered in Jerusalem to consider a regional response to Babylon in the portrayal of Jeremiah 27:1–3, Edom (like Ammon and Moab) does not seem to have joined Zedekiah in rebellion against Nebuchadnezzar (see Jer. 40:11–12). Against the backdrop of a purported "ancient enmity," Ezekiel 35 accuses Edom (under the

---

76. Bienkowski, "Edom during the Iron Age II Period," 789.
77. Bartlett, *Edom and the Edomites*, 213; Bienkowski, "Edomites," 41–92. See also Crystal-M. Bennett and Piotr Bienkowski, *Excavations at Tawilan in Southern Jordan* (Oxford: Oxford University Press, 1995); Piotr Bienkowski, ed., *Umm al-Biyara: Excavations by Crystal-M. Bennett in Petra, 1960–1965*, Levant Supplementary Series 10 (Oxford: Oxbow, 2011).

name "Mount Seir") not only of rejoicing but also of giving "over the people of Israel to the power of the sword" in the Babylonian conquest of Judah, and threatens the desolation of "Mount Seir, and all Edom, all of it" (Ezek. 35:5, 14–15). Similarly, Ezekiel 25:12 speaks of Edom's "taking vengeance" on Judah, and Psalm 137 and Obadiah 11–14 indicate Edom's exultation, even its complicity, in Jerusalem's fall. Although 2 Kings 25:9 and 2 Chronicles 36:19 place ultimate responsibility on Babylon for the destruction of Jerusalem, 1 Esdras 4:45 speaks of "the temple, which the Edomites burned when Judea was laid waste by the Chaldeans."[78] Edom's active participation in the Babylonian destruction of Judah, as indicated by a preponderance of the biblical texts, would have been consistent with Edom's necessary vassal status and its opportunity for gain at the expense of its hapless neighbor and longtime rival to the west and north.[79]

A badly damaged cuneiform chronicle reports that, during the third year of his reign, the last Babylonian king, Nabonidus (555–539 BCE), besieged and probably captured the "[town of A]dummu" (i.e., town of Edom), most likely Busayra, on his way to Tayma in northwest Arabia, where he would sojourn for a decade.[80] Destruction layers at Tawilan, at Umm al-Biyara, and in localized areas of Busayra may relate to Nabonidus's possible annexation of Edom on his campaign to Tayma, a measure perhaps directed toward Egypt and aimed at controlling northwest Arabian trade to Gaza.[81] Consistent with this general scenario is a limestone cliff face at Sela, slightly north of Busayra and just west of the King's Highway, which preserves badly eroded remnants of Babylonian cuneiform writing and a large sculpted relief of a Babylonian king with motifs similar to those in depictions of Nabonidus.[82] The book of Malachi's portrayal of Edom as "a desolation and . . . a desert for jackals" (1:3) may refer to Nabonidus's conquest of Edom.

Nonetheless, at Busayra and Tawilan, Iron II Edomite pottery persists into the Persian period, and the continued use of Busayra's public buildings at least to the fourth century BCE is indicated by the presence of Greek Attic pottery.[83] Upon its conquest by Nabonidus, Busayra likely became the resi-

---

78. Cf. Bartlett, *Edom and the Edomites*, 151–61.
79. See Edelman, "Edom: A Historical Geography," 6–7.
80. "Text from the Accession Year of Nabonidus to the Fall of Babylon," trans. A. Leo Oppenheim (*ANET*, 305–6).
81. See Routledge, *Moab in the Iron Age*, 211.
82. Stephanie Dalley and Anne Goguel, "The Selaʿ Sculpture: A Neo-Babylonian Rock Relief in Southern Jordan," *ADAJ* 41 (1997): 169–76.
83. Bennett and Bienkowski, *Excavations at Tawilan*; Bienkowski, Bennett, and Balla, *Busayra Excavations*; Bienkowski, "Persian Period," 339–40, 342, 344–45.

dence of a Babylonian-appointed governor.[84] The shift from Neo-Babylonian to Achaemenid rule with the fall of Babylon in 539 BCE would have brought little immediate change in Edom, as in Ammon (see above). Like Moab, Edom was likely incorporated into the larger territory, then (after 486 BCE) satrapy, "Beyond the River," with no evidence that Edom (or Moab) ranked as a separate province within that satrapy (as exists for Ammon; see above).[85] A cuneiform tablet found at Tawilan is dated to the first regnal year of Darius I (521–486 BCE), Darius II (425–405 BCE), or Darius III (335–331 BCE) and was drawn up in the city of Harran in north Syria.[86] It presents the testimony of a man with an Edomite name and patronymic, Qausshama (Qaus has heard) son of Qausyada (Qaus knows), regarding a disputed sale of two rams. Although the tablet's relationship to occupation at the site remains uncertain, it indicates free travel between Edom and other parts of the Persian Empire, along with the continuation of Edomite name-giving and language, thus adding to the picture of general cultural continuity in Transjordan from late Iron II well into the Persian period, as observed at Ammonite Umayri (see above). Even so, Nabonidus's conquest of Edom and incursions by desert tribes may have been early contributing factors to Edomite migration into the Negev and southern Judea, which would come to be known as Idumea by Hellenistic times.[87]

Cultural Expressions

As part of a broader cultural continuum across Syria-Palestine, Iron Age Ammonites, Moabites, and Edomites are represented by linguistic, artistic, and religious expressions that align with territories, people-group identities, and political kingdoms.

Texts, Language, and Scripts

The surviving epigraphic evidence reveals distinct but closely related "Canaanite" languages of Northwest Semitic, representing each of the

84. Bienkowski, "Edom during the Iron Age II Period," 792.
85. Ibid., 792.
86. Stephanie Dalley, "The Cuneiform Tablet," in Bennett and Bienkowski, *Excavations at Tawilan*, 67–68.
87. Even with the persistence of occupation at certain sites in Edom, like Busayra and Tawilan, archaeological surveys show a pronounced decrease in the population of southern Transjordan during the Persian and Hellenistic periods, reversing the increase in population during Iron II. See Burton MacDonald, Larry G. Herr, D. Scott Quaintance, Geoffrey A. Clark, and Michael C. A. Macdonald, *The Ayl to Ras an-Naqab Archaeological Survey, Southern Jordan (2005–2007)*, ASOR Archaeological Reports 16 (Boston: American Schools of Oriental Research, 2012), 474–75.

Transjordanian kingdoms.[88] Similarly, each kingdom can be associated with distinct script forms that developed from earlier existing script traditions, with Moabite and Edomite scripts deriving from the Hebrew script and the Ammonite script developing from the Aramaic script (all deriving ultimately from a tenth-century Phoenician script tradition).[89] The epigraphic evidence thus indicates interrelated but mutually distinguished script forms and languages cultivated as markers of distinct Ammonite, Moabite, and Edomite kingdom identities.

Royal monumental inscriptions in Ammonite include the Amman Citadel Inscription (ninth century BCE; COS 2.24), the Amman Theatre Inscription (sixth century BCE; COS 2.26), and the bronze bottle inscription from Tall Siran, a few miles northwest of the Amman Citadel (ca. 600 BCE; COS 2.25). The majority of Ammonite inscriptions comprise hundreds of personal seals and impressions (some from excavations, most from the antiquities market) bearing the names, and sometimes titles, of prominent Ammonites who lived from the late eighth to the sixth century BCE—for example, two seventh-century seals of officials with the title "servant of Amminadab," arguably the Ammonite king contemporary with Assurbanipal of Assyria (ca. 667 BCE) (CAI 17; 40). A clay seal impression from excavations at Tall Umayri, dating to ca. 600 BCE, names its owner as "Milkom'ur servant of Baalyasha" (CAI 129), the latter being identified with the Ammonite king Baalis mentioned in Jeremiah 40:14. Ammonite and Aramaic ink inscriptions on ostraca (reused pottery sherds) from Tall Hisban, Tall Mazar, and Tall Jalul show that, despite the advancing presence of Aramaic writing during the sixth century BCE, the Ammonite language continued in use through this time.[90] Those ostracon inscriptions also show the sixth-century reabsorption of the Ammonite script back into the Aramaic script tradition from which it had emerged by the end of the eighth century BCE.[91]

---

88. Simon B. Parker, "Ammonite, Edomite, and Moabite," in *Beyond Babel: A Handbook for Biblical Hebrew and Related Languages*, ed. John Kaltner and Steven L. McKenzie (Atlanta: Society of Biblical Literature, 2002), 43–60.

89. Larry G. Herr, "The Formal Scripts of Iron Age Transjordan," BASOR 238 (1981): 21–34; Christopher A. Rollston, *Writing and Literacy in the World of Ancient Israel: Epigraphic Evidence from the Iron Age* (Atlanta: Society of Biblical Literature, 2010), 19–46.

90. See Walter E. Aufrecht, "Ammonite Texts and Language," in MacDonald and Younker, *Ancient Ammon*, 163–89; Roy E. Gane, "Jalul Ostracon 1," BASOR 351 (2008): 73–84; Christine J. Goulart and Roy E. Gane, "Three Epigraphic Finds from Tall Jalul, Jordan," BASOR 365 (2012): 27–32.

91. Frank Moore Cross, "Ammonite Ostraca from Tell Ḥisbān," in *Leaves from an Epigrapher's Notebook: Collected Papers in Hebrew and West Semitic Palaeography and Epigraphy* (Winona Lake, IN: Eisenbrauns, 2003), 70–94. Cf. Joseph Naveh, *Early History of the Alphabet: An Introduction to West Semitic Epigraphy and Paleography*, 2nd rev. ed. (Jerusalem: Magnes Press, 1987), 109–11.

Like Ammonite, Moabite is a Northwest Semitic language dialect resembling Hebrew, though distinguished further by certain features such as the masculine plural absolute nominal ending *-n* (cf. Heb. *-îm*, Ammonite *-m*). The Mesha Inscription (ca. 840 BCE) is written in the Moabite language, using the Hebrew script. Ironically it is one of the earliest surviving examples of the formal Hebrew script and thus reflects Moab's prior subordination to Israel, as is well documented in the inscription. In addition to MI, the Karak Fragment, and the Dibon Fragment (see above), another ninth-century BCE Moabite inscription, discovered in recent excavations in the Iron II sanctuary at Khirbat Ataruz, consists of seven lines incised onto a stone cylindrical pedestal (ostensibly of an altar or other cultic object).[92] The site is commonly identified with the town of Atarot, which MI describes as having belonged to Gad before it was conquered by the Moabite king (MI, lines 10–14).

Figure 9.7. The Karak Inscription fragment in basalt illustrates the Moabites' adoption of the Hebrew script for writing the Moabite language in royal inscriptions. The preserved portion of the inscription begins, after a break, by making reference to "[Che]moshyat, king of Moab" ([k]mšyt . mlk. m'b). The sculpted form of a navel above the writing and, beneath it, the waistband and downward lines of an Egyptian-style kilt show that the fragment once belonged to a relief or statue of a male anthropomorphic figure (Parker and Arico, "A Moabite-Inscribed Statue Fragment from Kerak").

In addition, the Moabite corpus includes two eighth-century BCE inscriptions from Balua, both tantalizingly brief or fragmented label inscriptions.[93] Several inscribed objects from Khirbat Mudayna (Wadi Thamad) include a limestone incense altar inscribed "Incense altar, which Elishama made for

92. Chang-Ho Ji, "Architectural and Stratigraphic Context of the 'Ataruz Inscription Column"; and Christopher A. Rollston, "The New 'Ataruz Inscription: Late Ninth Century Epigraphic Evidence for the Moabite Scribal Apparatus" (presentations, ASOR Annual Meeting, Chicago, IL, November 16, 2012).
93. Fawzi Zayadine, "The Moabite Inscription," *ADAJ* 30 (1986): 302–4; Fawzi Zayadine and Udo Worschech, "Khirbet el-Balu' (1986–1987)," *Syria* 65 (1988): 415–19; Udo Worschech, "An Inscription from al-Bālū' (Arḍ al-Karak)," *ADAJ* 50 (2006): 99–105.

YSP, daughter of 'WT" (*mqt[r] 'š 'š 'lšm' lysp bt 'wt*), an ostracon, stone weights, and a small triangular limestone "tablet" excavated from a filled silo of the town gate area and bearing incised letters of Moabite script but not admitting to a sensible reading.[94] In contrast to the abundance of Ammonite name seals, less than fifty Moabite seals have been identified, including one excavated in a Babylonian temple in Ur, bearing a personal name invoking Chemosh.[95]

Two inscriptions of unknown origins yet suggesting a connection to Moab are the Marzeaḥ Papyrus[96] and a fragment of a basalt monument bearing what appears, from its content and script, to be a Moabite royal inscription.[97] Unfortunately, in an era when convincing forgeries are both feasible and lucrative, the authenticity of sensational finds of this nature remains highly uncertain, limiting their usefulness for scholarly research.[98]

The inscriptions excavated from Moabite sites are, on the whole, consistent with the language and orthography known from MI and shorter ninth-century epigraphs. But they also contain noteworthy variations in script forms and possibly in language, indicating considerable heterogeneity of identity and political organization at the local level among those lands encompassed by the hegemonic claims of Moab's monarchy.[99]

The surviving Edomite textual corpus to date is confined to a small number of seals, ostraca, and a few stone and ceramic objects incised with brief label or dedicatory inscriptions.[100] Like the Moabites, the Edomites adopted

---

94. Paul E. Dion and P. M. Michèle Daviau, "An Inscribed Incense Altar of Iron Age II at Ḥirbet el-Mudēyine (Jordan)," *ZDPV* 116 (2000): 1–13; P. M. Michèle Daviau and Paul E. Dion, "Economy-Related Finds from Khirbat al-Mudayna (Wadi ath-Thamad, Jordan)," *BASOR* 328 (2002): 39–40; Michael Weigl, "Eine Inschrift aus Silo 4 in *Ḥirbet el-Mudēyine* (*Wādī eṯ-Ṯemed*, Jordanien)," *ZDPV* 122 (2006): 31–45.

95. Nahman Avigad and Benjamin Sass, *Corpus of West Semitic Stamp Seals* (Jerusalem: Israel Academy of Sciences and Humanities, 1997), 381 (no. 1034).

96. Pierre Bordreuil and Dennis Pardee, "Épigraphie moabitique: Nouvel examen du 'papyrus du marzeaḥ,'" *Sem* 50 (2001): 224–26.

97. Shmuel Ahituv, "A New Moabite Inscription," *Israel Museum Studies in Archaeology* 2 (2003): 3–10; J. Andrew Dearman, "Moab and Ammon: Some Observations on Their Relationship in Light of a New Moabite Inscription," in Bienkowski, *Studies on Iron Age Moab*, 97–116.

98. Less troubling but still problematic are unprovenanced finds discovered in earlier decades, e.g., many of the Ammonite name seals mentioned above. On this general problem and suggestions for handling such material, see Rollston, *Writing and Literacy*, 137–44.

99. Dion and Daviau, "Moabites," 210–11; cf. Erasmus Gass, *Die Moabiter—Geschichte und Kultur eines ostjordanischen Volkes im 1. Jahrtausend v. Chr.*, ADPV 38 (Wiesbaden: Harrassowitz, 2009), 5–101, which offers treatment of all these inscriptions except the most recent one, from Ataruz.

100. See Bartlett, *Edom and the Edomites*, 209–28; David S. Vanderhooft, "The Edomite Dialect and Script: A Review of the Evidence," in Edelman, *You Shall Not Abhor an Edomite*, 137–57.

the Hebrew script, in keeping with the biblical depiction of Edom's subordination to Israel and Judah beginning with David. Less than a dozen seals or impressions identified as Edomite, most with scripts dating to the seventh century BCE, include examples recovered from excavated sites in Edom (Busayra, Umm al-Biyara, Tall Khalayfi) and in the Negev at Aroer—most notably the bulla found at Busayra naming "Qausga[bri], king of E[dom]" (*qws g[br] / mlk '[dm]*).[101]

Ten, mostly brief, ink ostraca inscriptions dating from the seventh to fifth/fourth centuries BCE have been excavated at Umm al-Biyara, Busayra, Tall Khalayfi, and at Aroer and Horvat Uza in the Negev.[102] Even briefer in nature are a nearly equal number of incised label inscriptions from Petra, Umm al-Biyara, Busayra, and Tall Khalayfi, including metal and stone weights, a limestone incense altar, and terra-cotta vessel fragments, all dating from perhaps the eighth to sixth centuries BCE. Two of these incised inscriptions from Tall Khalayfi feature South Arabic scripts reflecting Edom's trade connections with Arabia and the Red Sea during that time.

ART

Ammonite artistic forms include a distinct tradition of stone statuary well attested in and around Amman by numerous crowned statue heads; a collection of two-sided, double-faced female heads from an Iron Age administrative building on the Amman Citadel; and several statuettes of royal or divine figures.[103] Artistic motifs deriving from Egypt and appearing among many of these Amman sculptures include the *atef* crown (often associated with the god Osiris), suggesting the portrayal of El or Milcom as the chief Ammonite deity.[104] In 2010 a larger than life-size basalt statue of an Ammonite king was excavated near the Amman Roman Theatre, the largest Iron Age statue ever

---

101. See Vanderhooft, "Edomite Dialect," 151–53. The name is restored from the Edomite king mentioned in Assyrian texts (*ANET*, 29, 294).

102. For these and the following alphabetic inscriptions mentioned in this paragraph, see Vanderhooft, "Edomite Dialect," 140–45, 154.

103. Abdel-Jalil 'Amr, "An Ammonite Votive Dolomite Statue," *PEQ* 119 (1987): 35–38; 'Amr, "Four Ammonite Sculptures from Jordan," *ZDPV* 106 (1990): 114–18; Rudoph Henry Dornemann, *The Archaeology of the Transjordan in the Bronze and Iron Ages* (Milwaukee: Milwaukee Public Museum, 1983), 153–63, 284–87; Routledge, *Moab in the Iron Age*, 180–82.

104. P. M. Michèle Daviau and Paul E. Dion, "El, the God of the Ammonites? The Atef-Crowned Head from Tell Jawa, Jordan," *ZDPV* 110 (1994): 158–67; Joel S. Burnett, "Iron Age Deities in Word, Image, and Name: Correlating Epigraphic, Iconographic, and Onomastic Evidence for the Ammonite God," *SHAJ* 10 (2009): 153–64; Burnett, "Egyptianizing Elements in Ammonite Stone Statuary: The *Atef* Crown and Lotus," in *9 ICAANE: Proceedings of the 9th International Congress on the Archaeology of the Ancient Near East (2014)*, ed. Oskar Kaelen (Wiesbaden: Harrassowitz, 2016), 59–71.

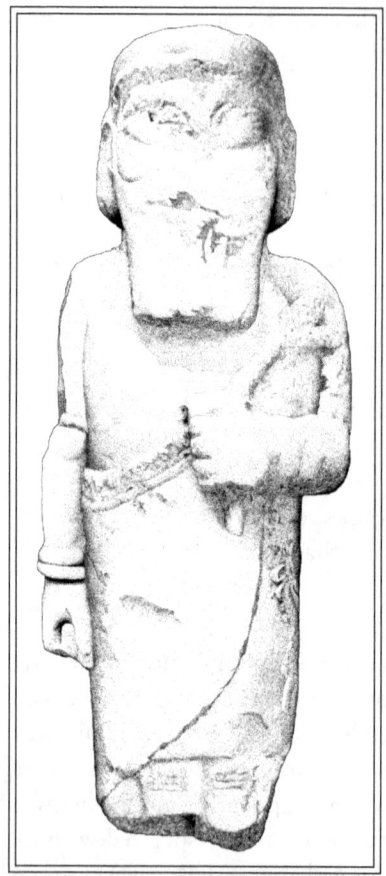

Figure 9.8. Larger-than-life-size basalt statue (over 6 feet in height) of an Ammonite king, excavated in front of the Roman Theatre in Amman in April 2010

recovered from the southern Levant and the only one of its kind from east or west of the Jordan.[105]

Monumental basalt sculpture from the land of Moab includes most prominently the Balua stela and Rujm Abd reliefs (see above, pp. 322–23) and from Karak a stone orthostat in the form of a lion in a style comparable to Neo-Hittite and Aramean palace and temple traditions in Syria.[106] Other examples include an unprovenanced statue fragment at the Karak Museum depicting a figure wearing an Egyptian-style kilt like that of the Rujm Abd warrior, another unprovenanced statue fragment reportedly from Karak with the torso and head of a male figure with an Egyptian hairstyle, and an arm fragment of a statue from Dhiban.[107] These examples of monumental sculpture from Ammonite and Moabite areas represent artistic traditions in support of royal institutions and ruling centers.

Surviving Edomite sculpture, on the other hand, is of smaller scale, typically in terra-cotta, and has been excavated mainly at sites west of the Arabah. An assemblage of nearly eight hundred objects from the shrine site Horvat Qitmit in the Negev features a variety of small sculptures, including a terra-cotta statue head of a three-horned goddess, ceramic cylindrical anthropomorphic statues and stands, and a statuette of a winged sphinx.[108] The cylindrical

105. See Joel S. Burnett and Romel Ghareeb, "An Iron Age Basalt Statue from the Amman Theatre Area," *ADAJ* (forthcoming).
106. Parker and Arico, "Moabite-Inscribed Statue Fragment from Kerak"; Routledge, *Moab in the Iron Age*, 182.
107. Routledge, *Moab in the Iron Age*, 178–80.
108. Pirhiya Beck, "Catalogue of Cult Objects and Study of the Iconography," in *Horvat Qitmit: An Edomite Shrine in the Biblical Negev*, ed. Itzhaq Beit-Arieh, Monograph Series 11 (Tel Aviv: The Institute of Archaeology of Tel Aviv University, 1995), 27–197.

statuettes and stands, a recurring type at Edomite sites, have been found at Qitmit, Tel Malḥata (also in the Negev), En Hazeva on the western edge of the Arabah, and Busayra on the Edomite Plateau; but they have also been found at various non-Edomite sites west and east of the Jordan, including the shrine site (Wadi Thamad site 13) near Khirbat Mudayna (Wadi Thamad) in Moabite territory.[109]

Among the most abundantly preserved artistic objects throughout the southern Levant are terra-cotta figurines. Anthropomorphic and animal figurines have been recovered from territories of all three Transjordanian kingdoms, the main types being freestanding and attached mold-made figurines and pillar figurines.[110] Though female figurines dominate in frequency, male figurines appear more often in Transjordan than in Cisjordan. Though usually freestanding, figurines were sometimes attached to the exterior of ceramic cult stands and miniature shrines, with examples from Tall Umayri, Khirbat Ataruz, Horvat Qitmit, and Pella. The representation and function of figurines remain debated.

Another artistic form common to all three kingdoms, and to the Iron II southern Levant more broadly, consists of the iconography of stamp seals, which were usually made from semiprecious stone and served primarily to represent an individual's identity and sometimes authority, especially in the case of government officials or other people of social influence or wealth.[111] The seals were carried by the owners or worn attached to the body or clothing, and may have been regarded as amulets protecting their owners. Iron Age seals displayed miniature artistic symbols and scenes incised onto the flat surface and, in Transjordan beginning in the mid-eighth century, also the name and sometimes title of the seal owner. In contrast to nationally distinct forms of language, script, and sculpture, seal iconography among the three Transjordanian kingdoms (and their Iron II counterparts throughout the southern Levant) represents a common stock of symbols and motifs aimed at a shared language of international prestige rather than distinct national identities.[112]

---

109. P. M. Michèle Daviau, "Diversity in the Cultic Setting: Temples and Shrines in Central Jordan and the Negev," in *Temple Building and Temple Cult: Architecture and Cultic Paraphernalia of Temples in the Levant (2.-1. Mill. B.C.E.)*, ed. J. Kamlah (Wiesbaden: Harrassowitz, 2012), 450.

110. P. M. Michèle Daviau, "New Light on Iron Age Religious Iconography: The Evidence from Moab," *SHAJ* 7 (2001): 317–26.

111. The definitive catalogue of various seals from second- and first-millennium BCE Transjordan is Jürg Eggler and Othmar Keel, *Corpus der Siegel-Amulette aus Jordanien: Vom Neolithicum bis zur Perserzeit*, OBO.SA 25 (Fribourg: Academic Press; Göttingen: Vandenhoeck & Ruprecht, 2006).

112. See the conclusions of the various essays on different national groups in Benjamin Sass and Christoph Uehlinger, eds., *Studies in the Iconography of Northwest Semitic Inscribed Seals*, OBO 125 (Fribourg: University Press of Fribourg, 1993).

Religion

Another way the kingdoms of Transjordan and the broader southern Levant distinguished themselves was by identifying with a leading warrior deity. Ammonite artistic tradition portrays this divine role in the stern-faced statue heads wearing the Egyptian *atef* crown.[113] The ninth-century BCE Amman Citadel Inscription (COS 2.24) presents Milcom as the leading Ammonite god, in keeping with the usual depiction in the Hebrew Bible (e.g., see 1 Kings 11:5; cf. Judg. 11:24). The inscription's contents relate to building and protection from surrounding enemies, primary endeavors of kings and gods. On the other hand, Milcom appears rarely in personal names as compared with *'l* (the/my "god" or the deity "El"), by far the most common divine element among Ammonite names. This onomastic evidence, along with El's leading role in the Dayr Alla plaster inscriptions (see below), suggests that this deity, who was so prominent at LB Ugarit and in Israel's background, continued to be important during Iron II across the central Jordan Valley, Gilead hills, and Ammonite plateau. In comparison with El's known persona as a kindly senior god, Milcom, whose name contains the West Semitic root *mlk* (to rule), fit the paradigm of the Iron Age national god—a bellicose deity of political dominion as projected in the Amman Citadel Inscription and Ammonite statuary. Ammonite Milcom may have been equated with El, as Yahweh was in Israelite circles.

Moabite Chemosh clearly embodies the role of national god, as attested in biblical texts (e.g., Num. 21:29; 1 Kings 11:7, 33; Jer. 48:46) and in MI, which honors Chemosh for the Moabite king's achievements. Paramount among those claims are military victories and expansion of national territory explicitly directed by the deity and mainly at the expense of Israel, whose prior control of Moabite territories had occurred "because Chemosh was angry with his land" (line 5). Mesha relates how, upon conquering the Israelite town of Nebo, he ritually slaughtered its people under the sacred "ban" (*ḥrm*) and removed cultic objects of Yahweh, placing them "before Chemosh" (lines 14–18). The inscription communicates a national theology uniting territory, people, and a chief deity in a mutually exclusive relationship over against contiguous, neighboring kingdoms.[114] This viewpoint, also well known from the Hebrew Bible, was foundational for national religion throughout the Iron Age southern Levant. Though preserved in much smaller numbers than Ammonite or Hebrew personal names, Moabite anthroponyms feature Chemosh

---

113. Daviau and Dion, "El, the God of the Ammonites?," 158–67; Burnett, "Iron Age Deities," 153–64.

114. Routledge, *Moab in the Iron Age*, 133–53.

as the most frequent divine element and in proportional numbers to those of the leading deities in those other name groups.[115]

The role of Qaus/Qos as the Edomites' leading deity is indicated by the appearance of the god's name as the dominant divine element in Edomite names, including those of two Edomite kings mentioned in Assyrian inscriptions—Qausmalak (ca. 734 BCE) and Qausgabri (ca. 672 BCE), the latter also named in an Edomite seal impression from Umm al-Biyara (see above). Blessings in the name of Qos appear in the Horvat Uza ostracon and incised on a body sherd from Busayra.[116] The Hebrew Bible is strangely mute regarding Qaus/Qos—or any Edomite deity, for that matter—the only exception being the personal name Barqos, meaning "Qos gleamed forth" (Ezra 2:53// Neh. 7:55).[117] Along with this ironic silence, Yahweh's associations with the territory of Edom and its vicinity in biblical poetry (Judg. 5:4; Hab. 3:3, 7) and biblical traditions of Edom's "brotherhood" with Israel-Judah are peculiarities unique to Edom among Israel's neighbors that point to possible close connections, if not an original equation, between Israelite Yahweh and Edomite Qaus.

A compelling etymology of Qaus/Qos connects it with Arabic *qaus* (bow), though with some philological difficulty. And Qos's appearance as a divine element in personal names in Old South Arabian rock inscriptions may or may not indicate Arabian origins for this deity, given Edom's proximity to northwest Arabia and a perennial flow of trade connecting the two.[118] Qos names continue to be attested well into the Persian period and even appear in Hellenistic sources.

In addition to the national god, other deities or divine elements appear among the Transjordanian name groups, for example, Baal, Bel, Mot, Adad.[119] The extent of divine pluralism thus signaled is debated, but the general pattern indicates a limited polytheism dominated by devotion to the national god for each group. For Transjordan and the rest of the southern Levant, this pattern

---

115. See Burnett, "Iron Age Deities," 157; cf. Rainer Albertz and Rüdiger Schmitt, *Family and Household Religion in Ancient Israel and the Levant* (Winona Lake, IN: Eisenbrauns, 2012), 508–10.

116. Itzhaq Beit-Arieh and Bruce Cresson, "An Edomite Ostracon from Ḥorvat 'Uza," *TA* 12 (1985): 96–101; Vanderhooft, "Edomite Dialect," 142–43; Bartlett, *Edom and the Edomites*, 223 (no. 3).

117. The name Kushaiah (1 Chron. 15:17) has the variant form Kishi in 1 Chron. 6:29 (Eng. 6:44), and in any case involves a spelling with *shin* that is never used for Qos in other texts. See Ernst Axel Knauf, "Qôs," *DDD*, 674.

118. See Bartlett, *Edom and the Edomites*, 205–7; Knauf, "Qôs," 674–77.

119. See Albertz and Schmitt, *Household and Family Religion*, 508–10; Ziony Zevit, *The Religions of Ancient Israel: A Synthesis of Parallactic Approaches* (London: Continuum, 2001), 586–609.

shows a strong connection between national religious identity and family religion, the socioreligious context primarily associated with personal names.

Archaeological evidence for family religion throughout Transjordan, like its larger milieu, involves common religious expressions and practices as reflected in household religious assemblages consisting of figurines, ornamental vessels, censer cups, chalices, jewelry, seashells, and occasionally small cultic stands or ceramic shrines along with everyday pottery relating to food preparation and consumption.[120] This common profile of artifact assemblages appears in houses, neighborhood shrines, and tombs or caves, pointing to family-based ritual and commemoration focusing on family deities and ancestors.

Architectural remains of temples and shrines substantiate more public settings of religious identity and activity in and around Ammonite, Moabite, and Edomite territories of Transjordan. In northern and central Jordan Valley areas ascribed to Israel in biblical tradition, a long-standing temple from MB to LB times is rebuilt on a more modest scale at Iron II Pella, and smaller sanctuaries from the early Iron Age have been identified at Tall as-Saidiyya and at Tall Mazar.[121] Further south at Tall Damiya (biblical Adam), near the Zarqa's convergence with the Jordan and a natural crossing point for the latter, an Iron IIC mud-brick sanctuary with platforms and ceramic statuary and figurines has been excavated.[122]

Up the Zarqa about 9 miles northeast of Damiya at Dayr Alla, a significant LB sanctuary site, an Iron II building complex featured a plaster-wall inscription with warnings from the prophetic figure "Balaam son of Beor" also known from Numbers 22–24 (the Dayr 'Alla Plaster Inscription, *COS* 2.27).[123] The inscription conspicuously lacks reference to national deities of any surrounding kingdoms (e.g., Yahweh, Milcom, Chemosh, or Qos) but rather presents the broadly recognized pantheon of El and "the gods," generically stated.[124] A dearth of excavated cultic items militates against the structure's identification as a worship sanctuary, but the displayed inscription suggests the site's religious significance, perhaps in service to merchants and travelers passing from surrounding regions.

---

120. Albertz and Schmitt, *Household and Family Religion*, 57–219, esp. 176–219.

121. Stephen Bourke, "The Six Canaanite Temples of *Ṭabaqāt Faḥil*: Excavating Pella's 'Fortress' Temple (1994–2009)," in Kamlah, *Temple Building and Temple Cult*, 159–201 and plates 31–43; van der Steen, *Tribes and Territories in Transition*, 63–68.

122. Lucas Petit and Zeidan Kafafi, "Beyond the River Jordan: A Late Iron Age Sanctuary at Tell Damiyah," *NEA* 79, no. 1 (2016): 18–26.

123. H. J. Franken, "Deir 'Alla, Tell: Archaeology," *ABD* 2:126–29; Jo Ann Hackett, "Deir 'Alla, Tell: Texts," *ABD* 2:129–30; C.-L. Seow, "Deir 'Alla Plaster Texts," in M. Nissinen, *Prophets and Prophecy in the Ancient Near East*, WAW 12 (Atlanta: Society of Biblical Literature, 2003), 207–12.

124. Joel S. Burnett, "Prophecy in Transjordan: Balaam son of Beor," in *Enemies and Friends of the State: Prophecy in Context*, ed. C. A. Rollston (Winona Lake, IN: Eisenbrauns, forthcoming).

A temple to Milcom likely once stood on the Amman Citadel, on the spot where remains of an Iron Age megalithic building running underneath the later Roman temple to Hercules have been excavated.[125] At Rujm al-Kursi, about 6 miles west of Amman Citadel, an Iron IIC building with identical limestone blocks bearing a lunar crescent relief might have been a temple.[126] South of Amman at Tall Umayri, late Iron I remains include an open courtyard sanctuary paved in cobblestones with a small central stone altar and fragments of ceramic miniature shrines with attached figurines.[127] Further excavations stand to shed more light on worship places in Ammonite territory.

At Khirbat Ataruz ca. 7 miles east of the Dead Sea on the Moabite Plateau, an elaborate worship complex centered on a temple roughly 36 x 24 feet surrounded by adjoining rooms, courtyards, offering platforms, and secondary structures.[128] Impressive worship artifacts discovered inside the temple include a standing stone, a terra-cotta four-horned altar, a terra-cotta bull statue (fig. 9.9), a large storage krater with bull and gazelle iconography, ornamental cultic vessels, a ceramic miniature shrine with attached male figurines, and the inscribed pedestal mentioned above. Scholars identify Ataruz with the Atarot mentioned in MI as a town of Israelite Gad that the king of Moab conquered and from which he pillaged an important cultic item—"the altar hearth of its DWD" (*'r'l dwdh*; lines 10–13).

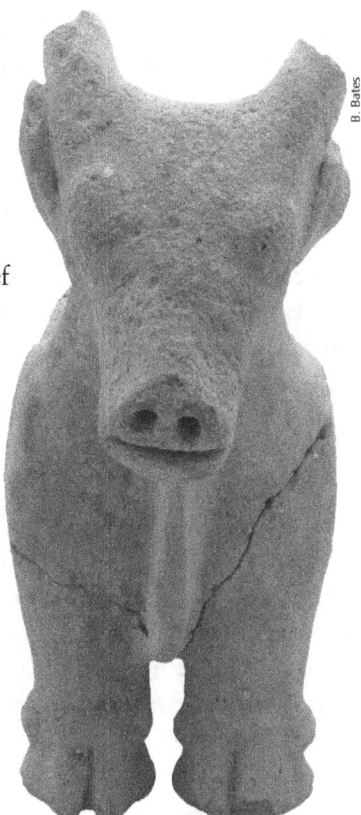

Figure 9.9. Terra-cotta bull statue (ca. 14 inches long, 6.5 inches wide, 15 inches high) from the main sanctuary of the Iron II temple complex at Khirbat Ataruz

At Dibon (modern Dhiban), a cylindrical cult stand was excavated among the remnants of a ninth-century BCE palace, but any temple or worship "high

---

125. Momani and Koutsoukou, "The 1993 Excavations," 157–71.
126. Craig William Tyson, *The Ammonites: Elites, Empires, and Sociopolitical Change (1000–500 BCE)* LHBOTS 585 (New York: Bloomsbury T&T Clark, 2014), 37–39.
127. Clark and Herr, "From the Stone Age to the Middle Ages," 89–90.
128. Chang-Ho Ji, "The Early Iron Age II Temple at Ḥirbet ʿAṭārūs and Its Architecture and Selected Cultic Objects," in Kamlah, *Temple Building and Temple Cult*, 204–21 and plates 44–49.

place" as described by MI (*hbmt z't*, line 3) has eluded discovery in subsequent excavations.[129] In northeastern Moabite territory, a small sanctuary just inside the fortified gate of Iron II Khirbat Mudayna (Wadi Thamad) included limestone altars and an inscribed incense burner (see above). Just a few miles away at Wadi Thamad site 13, an enclosed structure identified as a "wayside shrine" yielded diverse ceramics and votive objects (including numerous figurines, clay statuettes, amulets, scarabs, and several ceramic shrines), indicating not a local assemblage but various objects brought to the site from other regions.[130]

At En Hazeva in the northwestern Arabah, a collection of ceramic statuettes, cylindrical stands, cultic vessels, and miniature stone altars found smashed and buried in a pit outside the Iron II fortress there suggests an Edomite shrine belonging to its final (late seventh-/early sixth-century BCE) phase.[131] Twenty-seven miles to the northwest at Horvat Qitmit, similar cylindrical statuettes and stands, figurines, and Edomite pottery, along with a vessel fragment inscribed "to Qos" (*lqws*), were among a vast assemblage of objects associated with a shrine complex comprising two substantial buildings, a courtyard area with abundant bone evidence of feasting, and circular stone enclosures with worship installations.[132]

These patterns in cultural expressions tend to illustrate a general correspondence of territories, group identities, and political kingdoms in Iron Age Transjordan.

For Further Reading

Adams, Russell B., ed. *Jordan: An Archaeological Reader*. London: Equinox, 2008.

Aufrecht, Walter E. *A Corpus of Ammonite Inscriptions*. 2nd ed. Lewiston, NY: Edwin Mellen, forthcoming.

Bartlett, John R. *Edom and the Edomites*. JSOTSup 77. Sheffield, UK: Sheffield Academic, 1989.

Bienkowski, Piotr, ed. *Early Edom and Moab: The Beginning of the Iron Age in Southern Jordan*. Sheffield, UK: J. R. Collis, 1992.

---

129. Routledge, *Moab in the Iron Age*, 161–73, 242–43.

130. Daviau, "*Hirbet el-Mudēyine* in Its Landscape," 24–28; Annlee Dolan, "Defining Sacred Space in Ancient Moab," in Bienkowski, *Studies on Iron Age Moab*, 130–31.

131. Rudolph Cohen and Yigal Yisrael, "The Iron Age Fortresses at 'En Ḥaṣēva," *BA* 58 (1995): 223–35; cf. Daviau, "Diversity in the Cultic Setting," 450.

132. Beit-Arieh, *Horvat Qitmit*, including within the same volume Beck, "Catalogue of Cult Objects."

———, ed. *Studies on Iron Age Moab and Neighbouring Areas in Honour of Michèle Daviau*. Leuven: Peeters, 2009.

———, ed. *Treasures from an Ancient Land: The Art of Jordan*. Wolfeboro Falls, NH: Alan Sutton, 1991.

Daviau, P. M. Michèle. *Excavations at Tall Jawa, Jordan*. Vols. 1–2. CHANE 11/1–2. Leiden: Brill, 2003.

Dion, Paul E., and P. M. Michèle Daviau. "The Moabites." In *The Books of Kings: Sources, Composition, Historiography and Reception*, edited by André Lemaire and Baruch Halpern, 205–24. VTSup 129. Leiden: Brill, 2010.

Edelman, Diana V., ed. *You Shall Not Abhor an Edomite for He Is Your Brother: Edom and Seir in History and Tradition*. ABS 3. Atlanta: Scholars Press, 1995.

Herr, Larry G. "The Iron Age II Period: Emerging Nations." *NEA* 60 (1997): 114–83.

LaBianca, Øystein, and Randall W. Younker. "The Kingdoms of Ammon, Moab and Edom: The Archaeology of Society in Late Bronze/Iron Age Transjordan (ca. 1400–500 BCE)." In *The Archaeology of Society in the Holy Land*, edited by Thomas E. Levy, 399–415. London: Leicester University Press, 1998.

Levy, Thomas E., Mohammad Najjar, and Erez Ben-Yosef. *New Insights into the Iron Age Archaeology of Edom, Southern Jordan*. 2 vols. Los Angeles: The Cotsen Institute of Archaeology Press, University of California Los Angeles, 2014.

Lipiński, Edward. *On the Skirts of Canaan in the Iron Age: Historical and Topographical Researches*. OLA 153. Leuven: Peeters, 2006.

MacDonald, Burton. *Ammon, Moab, and Edom: Early States/Nations of Jordan in the Biblical Period (End of the 2nd and during the 1st Millennium B.C.)*. Amman: Al-Kutba, 1994.

———. *"East of the Jordan": Territories and Sites of the Hebrew Scriptures*. ASOR Books 6. Boston: American Schools of Oriental Research, 2000.

MacDonald, Burton, and Randall W. Younker, eds. *Ancient Ammon*. SHCANE 17. Leiden: Brill, 1999.

Porter, Benjamin W. *Complex Communities: The Archaeology of Early Iron Age West-Central Jordan*. Tucson: University of Arizona Press, 2013.

Routledge, Bruce. *Moab in the Iron Age: Hegemony, Polity, Archaeology*. Philadelphia: University of Pennsylvania Press, 2004.

Tyson, Craig William. *The Ammonites: Elites, Empires, and Sociopolitical Change (1000–500 BCE)*. LHBOTS 585. New York: Bloomsbury T&T Clark, 2014.

Van der Steen, Eveline J. *Tribes and Territories in Transition: The Central East Jordan Valley in the Late Bronze and Early Iron Ages; A Study of the Sources*. OLA 130. Leuven: Peeters, 2004.

10

Philistia and the Philistines

Carl S. Ehrlich

The Philistines were a people of a northeastern (Anatolian or Aegean) Mediterranean origin who settled on the southern coastal strip of Canaan around the time of the transition from the Late Bronze Age to the Iron Age I—that is, sometime around the first half of the twelfth century BCE. Their territory of habitation, which we call Philistia, was bounded on the west by the Mediterranean Sea and on the east by the Shephelah, the Judean foothills. In the north the maximum extent of their territory during the Iron Age I (ca. 1200/1150–1000) reached Tell Qasile on the Yarkon River in modern-day Tel Aviv; and on the south their border extended to the Wadi el-Arish[1] or the Naḥal Besor,[2] the Brook of Egypt, on the other side of which lies the Sinai Peninsula. From ancient sources, including the Hebrew Bible, it appears that the Philistines organized their society into a city-state system, which originally included five major cities: Ashdod, Ashkelon, and Gaza, which were situated

---

1. Trude Dothan, *The Philistines and Their Material Culture* (Jerusalem: Israel Exploration Society, 1982), 16–17.
2. Nadav Na'aman, "The Brook of Egypt and Assyrian Foreign Policy on the Border of Egypt," *TA* 6 (1979): 68–90; repr. in *Ancient Israel and Its Neighbors: Interaction and Counteraction*, Collected Essays Vol. 1 (Winona Lake, IN: Eisenbrauns, 2005), 238–64.

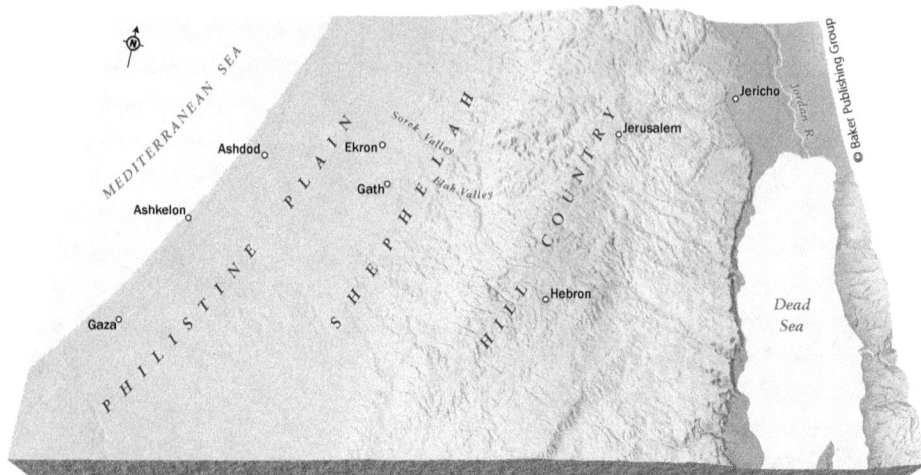

Figure 10.1. The Philistine plain

along the coast from north to south, and Ekron and Gath, which were located on or near the border between the coastal plain and the Shephelah.

Until recently the bulk of our information about the Philistines had come from the Hebrew Bible, in which they play an oftentimes central role as the enemy par excellence of the Israelites, particularly during the stage of state formation or, in biblical terms, of the transition from the period of the judges to that of the united monarchy of Israel.[3] However, in order to gain a complete picture of the state of Philistine studies and of our knowledge of the Philistines, three major corpora of evidence must be weighed and synthesized: the biblical text, ancient Near Eastern texts, and the results of archaeological investigation. This chapter will survey all three corpora before concluding with a summary synthesis.

1. Evidence from the Hebrew Bible

Although the Hebrew Bible would appear to be a—if not the—primary witness to Philistine history, its complex literary history means that questions regarding issues such as the dating of individual texts and their ideology and theology must be taken into account before one is able to employ those texts in historical reconstruction. And the results of such questions are bound to be controversial without external or extrabiblical corroboration. Looking at

---

3. See Avraham Faust, *Israel's Ethnogenesis: Settlement, Interaction, Expansion and Resistance*, Approaches to Anthropological Archaeology (London: Equinox, 2006), 111–56.

the biblical evidence as a whole, the following picture emerges of Philistine civilization.

The Philistines belong to the ancient inhabitants of the land of Canaan, as is evidenced by their appearance in the ancestral narratives of Genesis. In order to avoid confronting them, the Israelites took the long way around to the promised land after leaving Egypt at the time of the exodus, with the disastrous results that are familiar to all readers of the Pentateuch. Since Joshua and the Israelites were unable to conquer the Philistine cities at the time of their incursion into Canaan, the Philistines, who were organized into a coalition of five city-states (the so-called Pentapolis), proved to be a thorn in the side of the Israelite tribes. Indeed, it was pressure from the Philistines that led to the coalescence of the tribes into a monarchy under the leadership of Saul, who ultimately fell in battle against them. It was left to his successor, David, who had briefly been a Philistine vassal, to defeat them and break their stranglehold on Israel. Subsequent to his time the Philistine threat was minimized, although not eliminated. The Philistines appear in accounts of minor border conflicts and in prophetic condemnations (in texts that are subsumed under the rubric of oracles against the nations). Ultimately, they disappear from the biblical narrative, although tradition associates forms of divination with the Philistines, whose chief deity was named Dagon. Owing to their lack of male circumcision, the Philistines are viewed by the biblical texts as the archetypal other.[4] In fact, it was this otherness of the Philistines that eventually was to give rise to the use of their name to designate uncouth and uncultured people, centuries after they had disappeared from the historical stage.[5]

According to the Table of Nations in Genesis 10, a summary statement of ancient Israel's geographic and ethnographic knowledge,[6] the Philistines were descended from the Caphtorim (v. 14), which is generally taken to be a reference to the island of Crete,[7] unless one should follow the Septuagint, which translates the name as Cappadocia in Anatolia. This is echoed by Amos 9:7, in which God has brought the Philistines up from Caphtor. In this manner the Hebrew Bible associates the Philistines with a foreign origin in the eastern

---

4. Trude Dothan and Robert L. Cohn, "The Philistine as Other: Biblical Rhetoric and Archaeological Reality," in *The Other in Jewish Thought and History: Constructions of Jewish Culture and Identity*, ed. L. J. Silberstein and R. L. Cohn (New York: New York University Press, 1994), 61–73.

5. Trude Dothan and Moshe Dothan, *People of the Sea: The Search for the Philistines* (New York: Macmillan, 1992), 3–6.

6. See Bill T. Arnold, *Genesis*, NCBC (Cambridge: Cambridge University Press, 2009), 113–17.

7. On the problems with this identification, see Ann E. Killebrew, *Biblical Peoples and Ethnicity: An Archaeological Study of Egyptians, Canaanites, Philistines, and Early Israel, 1300–1100 B.C.E.*, ABS 9 (Atlanta: Society of Biblical Literature, 2005), 238n33.

Mediterranean and, by extension, with seafaring. Both of these associations were to play an important role in the search for Philistine origins.

Genesis 21:32–34 identifies the land of the Philistines as the region in which Abimelech the king of Gerar dwelt and in which Abraham and Sarah settled following Isaac's birth. Indeed, the hapless Abimelech of Gerar is indentified as "king of the Philistines" in Genesis 26:1 and 8, in which Isaac emulates his father and attempts to suppress the fact of his marriage from the apparently randy king. This clearly anachronistic reference to the Philistines and their territory is echoed in the statement that the Israelites skirted the territory of the Philistines on their way out of Egypt as per divine directive (Exod. 13:17).[8]

The fact that Philistia remained a separate entity and was not incorporated into either Israel or Judah is acknowledged by the book of Joshua, where the territory of the Philistine Pentapolis—consisting of Ashdod, Ashkelon, Ekron, Gath, and Gaza—is reckoned with the land that yet remained to be conquered (Josh. 13:2–3). In Judges the Philistine Pentapolis is counted among the nations that God left in the land to test the Israelites (Judg. 3:1–6), once again identifying Philistia as a region outside that of ancient Israel. Somewhat later in the narrative the Philistines are presented among the oppressors of Israel (10:6–7).

However, it is only in the Samson cycle (Judg. 13–16) that the Philistines assume a more important role in the biblical narrative. In this cycle of stories comprising Samson's birth narrative (chap. 13), the story of his marriage to a Philistine woman (chaps. 14–15), an amusing anecdote about his dalliance with a prostitute in Gaza (16:1–3), and the tragic tale of his relationship with the temptress Delilah (16:4–31), the Philistines play a central role as the hero's antagonists. Although the cycle is introduced at the beginning of Samson's birth narrative by the motif of the Israelites' oppression by the Philistines (13:1), it is not until Samson is full-grown that the focus turns to his relations with the Philistines.

In the first such episode (Judg. 14–15), Samson, the Danite strongman, marries a Philistine woman against his parents' wishes. The text, however, informs us that this was according to God's design, since he wished to have a pretext to take action against the uncircumcised ones (14:3–4). The upshot of the relationship is that he kills 1,030 Philistines (14:19; 15:15) in revenge for his mistreatment at the hands of the Philistines and their subsequent murder of his wife.

---

8. These references may be narrative prolepsis, referring to the general region that would one day become the land of the Philistines (Arnold, *Genesis*, 198).

In the second episode (Judg. 16:1–3), Samson sleeps with a prostitute in Gaza. When the Philistines attempt to kill him, he anticipates their actions and escapes from the city before their plan can be put into action. In a nice folkloric—and hyperbolic—touch, Samson makes off with the gates of Gaza.

The third episode (Judg. 16:4–31) is the most famous among the Samson tales. He falls in love with a woman named Delilah who lives in the Sorek Valley between Israel and Philistia. The Philistine lords bribe her to betray Samson to them by seducing him and learning the secret of his great strength. After three failed attempts, Delilah learns that his power lies in his hair. After Samson's hair is shorn, the Philistines capture him, blind him, and enslave him. At a festival for their god Dagon, the Philistines bring Samson into the temple to perform for them. Samson is led between two pillars, and—after praying for the return of his strength—he collapses the temple on the Philistines and on himself, thus killing more Philistines in his death than during his life.

While these folktales may contain a memory of a period of tension between the Israelites and the Philistines, they cannot be placed in any definite historical context. Nonetheless, they do provide some details regarding the geography of Philistia: Ashkelon and Gaza lie deep in Philistine territory on the Mediterranean coast, while Timnah and the Sorek Valley lie in the oftentimes contested borderland between Israel and Philistia. In addition, they propagate the view that the Philistines were a unified ethnic group, concentrated in five cities, and had a chief deity named Dagon.

The next major biblical appearance of the Philistines is in the Ark Narrative of 1 Samuel 4:1–7:1. According to this amusing folktale, the Israelites were arrayed against the Philistines in battle at Ebenezer. Since the conflict was going poorly for them, they decided to bring into battle their equivalent of a weapon of mass destruction—namely, the ark of the covenant. When the Philistines saw this, they were seized with fright. Nonetheless, they were able to prevail and capture the ark, which they subsequently brought in triumph to their homeland, placing it as a spoil of victory next to the statue of Dagon in his temple in Ashdod. The following morning, the Ashdodites found the statue of their god facedown on the ground. After they righted the statue, this process was repeated, with the addition of the breaking off of Dagon's extremities. In addition, a plague of boils or hemorrhoids[9] broke out among the Ashdodites, although it has recently been quite convincingly argued that what plagued the Philistines according to this story should be interpreted as some sort of malady affecting their male sexual organs, an interpretation made

---

9. Thus, respectively, the *ketiv* (עפלים) and the *qere* (טחרים) of the MT of 1 Sam. 5:6, 9, 12; 6:4–5.

all the more compelling in light of archaeological evidence of Philistine votive phalluses (particularly from Ashkelon and Tell eṣ-Ṣafi/Gath) and the Hebrew Bible's fixation on the uncircumcised nature of the Philistines.[10]

In light of the ark's disastrous effect upon Ashdod, it was subsequently sent to Gath and from there to Ekron with the same deleterious consequences. Thereupon the Philistines placed the ark on a cart pulled by two cows along with five golden ʿŏpālîm (boils, hemorrhoids, or votive penises) and five golden mice, equivalent to the number of Philistine cities and symbolic of the plagues affecting them, and sent it on its way back to Israel. While this narrative pokes fun at the Philistines and their cult, it also relays an Israelite understanding of the power of the ark, which symbolized the divine presence—a power that was brilliantly illustrated by Steven Spielberg at the end of *Raiders of the Lost Ark*, in which he may have drawn on the account of what happened to Aaron's sons Nadab and Abihu in Leviticus 10:1–2. Once again, Dagon plays a central role in this presentation of the Philistine cult. And the biblical authors' knowledge of local geography is revealed in the placement of the narrative's range within the three northern or easternmost Philistine cities (Ashdod, Ekron, and Gath), which would have been the closest to the borders of Israel.

The major role assigned to the Philistines in the biblical narrative, however, is as the enemy par excellence at the time of the rise of the Israelite monarchy. Indeed, from the perspective of the biblical text it could be argued that it was pressure from Philistine expansionism that gave the disparate Israelite tribes the impetus to organize themselves around a central leadership in order to counter the Philistine threat. Of course, this presupposes a unified Philistine polity, something that is not evidenced in any of our extrabiblical sources. Be that as it may, the biblical narrative implies that much of Samuel's authority as a leader in Israel arose not only from his religious leadership but also from his success in countering the Philistine threat (1 Sam. 7:2–14).

Saul, the first king of Israel anointed by Samuel, supposedly spent a goodly portion of his reign countering the Philistine threat (1 Sam. 13–14; 17; 28–29; 31). According to 1 Samuel 13, it was Saul's inappropriate cultic actions following a victory over the Philistines that led Samuel to reject him, although 1 Samuel 15 attributes the falling out to Saul's actions following a victory over the Amalekites. First Samuel 17 relates one of the most famous stories involving the Philistines, one that symbolizes the transference of divine favor from Saul to David. In this extended narrative, Goliath, a Philistine warrior of gigantic proportions, challenges the Israelites to send a suitable

---

10. See Aren M. Maeir, "A New Interpretation of the Term ʿopalim (עפלים) in the Light of Recent Archaeological Finds from Philistia," *JSOT* 32, no. 1 (2007): 23–40.

champion to meet him in single combat. The expectation of the reader is that this would be Saul, who was a renowned warrior and a giant among the Israelites, standing a head taller than anyone else (1 Sam. 9:2). However, Saul was as scared of Goliath as any of his subjects; hence it was left to the shepherd-boy David to defeat the Philistine warrior, in spite of his alleged inexperience. Although this is arguably the most famous story concerning David, it should be noted that this victory is ascribed to one of David's own warriors later in the narrative (2 Sam. 21:19), a piece of information that is "corrected" in 1 Chronicles 20:5.

The account of David and Goliath's mano-a-mano encounter has played an important role in determining the origins of the Philistines. The source of Goliath's name has been sought in the Aegean world in formations such as Alyattes or in the Anatolian one in names such as *w/uliat*, an argument that has received a boost thanks to the finding of an ostracon at Tell eṣ-Ṣafi/Gath, which seems to preserve two names with similar endings.[11] It thus appears probable that Goliath's name may be used as a piece of evidence in searching for a non-Canaanite origin for the Philistines.[12] The same is somewhat harder to do in the case of the description of his armor and weaponry. On the one hand, it has been argued that the description of Goliath's armor and weaponry is reflective of that of a Mycenaean soldier of the end of the Late Bronze Age;[13] on the other hand, it has been claimed that the description is a hodgepodge of different styles that were in use at various times and, therefore, must be taken as evidence of the late date of the text's development.[14] More recently, the attempt has been made to understand the mixture of armament styles as indicative of a mixture of Levantine and Aegean charioteer styles from the Iron Age I.[15] Likewise, it has not proven possible to date the text on the basis of its depiction of the single combat between two champions, despite attempts to do so.[16]

---

11. See Aren M. Maeir, Stefan J. Wimmer, Alexander Zuckerman, and Aaron Demsky, "A Late Iron Age I/Early Iron Age II Canaanite Inscription from Tell eṣ-Ṣâfi/Gath, Israel: Paleography, Dating, and Historical-Cultural Significance," *BASOR* 351 (2008): 39–71.

12. In addition, the standard word employed in the biblical text to refer to the Philistine rulers (other than Abimelech and Achish, who are termed "kings") is *sərānîm*, which has been related to the word "tyrant" and is thus another piece of evidence pointing to the Aegean world for the origin of the Philistines.

13. Yigael Yadin, "Goliath's Javelin and the מנור ארגים," *PEQ* 87 (1955): 58–69.

14. Israel Finkelstein, "The Philistines in the Bible: A Late-Monarchic Perspective," *JSOT* 27 (2002): 131–67. See also the discussion in Steven L. McKenzie, *King David: A Biography* (Oxford: Oxford University Press, 2000), 74–75.

15. Jeffrey R. Zorn, "Reconsidering Goliath: An Iron Age I Philistine Chariot Warrior," *BASOR* 360 (2010): 1–22.

16. Roland de Vaux, *The Bible and the Ancient Near East*, trans. Damian McHugh (Garden City, NY: Doubleday, 1971), 122–35.

Tucked away among the various colorful stories of David's flight from Saul and his life as a fugitive and brigand are a handful of passages that tell of his service as a vassal to Achish, king of Gath (1 Sam. 21:11–16 [Eng. 21:10–15]; 27:1–28:2; 29).[17] The biblical text tries to walk a tightrope in its depiction of David's service to Achish. On the one hand, he is presented as a loyal vassal. On the other, through a convoluted story in 1 Samuel 29–31 David is exonerated of participation in the Philistine coalition that defeated the Israelites and killed Saul, his crown prince Jonathan, and others of his sons. Indeed, David's supposed innocence is underlined in 2 Samuel 1, which has David compose a heartfelt lament upon learning of the deaths of Saul and Jonathan. One chapter earlier, we are informed that the Philistines deposited Saul's armor in the temple of the goddess Astarte (Ashtaroth; 1 Sam. 31:10). Owing to the fact that this information is immediately followed by the notice that his body was hung on the walls of Beth-shan, many have sought to locate the temple of Astarte in the Jordan Valley.

The portrait of David conveyed by the biblical text is that of an opportunist, shifting his allegiance from Saul to Achish. Yet, once Achish and his allies had cleared the way for David's assumption of rule over the southern kingdom of Judah by removing David's main rival Saul, David still had to engage in a war to eliminate the rule of the house of Saul over the northern kingdom of Israel. Once that had been completed and David had established his capital at Jerusalem, thus uniting Israel and Judah in one state by establishing his administrative center on the border between the two, David was able to turn his attention to his erstwhile suzerains, the Philistines. Second Samuel 8:1[18] informs us that David subjugated the Philistines and took *meteg hā'ammâ* from their hands. Unfortunately, in spite of many attempts to understand what that was, it remains a conundrum. First Chronicles 18:1 attempts to solve this mystery by rewriting the text as "Gath and its dependencies [*ûbənōtêhā*]." While the biblical text is attempting to distinguish David's subjugation of the Philistines from his conquests of other peoples, it appears that the text reflects a remembrance of a distinct relationship between David/Israel and the city of Gath. In spite of the lack of a conquest motif, 1 Kings 5:1–4 (Eng. 4:21–24) makes the grandiloquent—and impossible—claim that Philistia was part of the Solomonic kingdom.

---

17. See Baruch Halpern, *David's Secret Demons: Messiah, Murderer, Traitor, King* (Grand Rapids: Eerdmans, 2001), 287–94; Walter Dietrich, *David: Der Herrscher mit der Harfe*, Biblische Gestalten 14 (Leipzig: Evangelische Verlagsanstalt, 2006), 140–44.

18. On 2 Sam. 8:1 and 1 Chron. 18:1, see Carl S. Ehrlich, *The Philistines in Transition: A History from c. 1000–730 BCE*, SHCANE 10 (Leiden: Brill, 1996), 31–34, 119–121; Halpern, *David's Secret Demons*, 144–59.

It is presumably to David's period as the vassal of Achish that his acquisition of loyal followers such as the Gittites Obed-edom (2 Sam. 6:9–12; 1 Chron. 13:12–14; 15:24–25) and Ittai (2 Sam. 15:17–22; 18:2a) is to be dated. Ironically, according to the biblical text these Gittite mercenaries prove to be more loyal to David than his fellow Judahites. In addition, his personal troop is augmented by the addition of the Cherethites and Pelethites, whose origin is murky but presumably somehow related to the Aegean world.[19]

Subsequent to the time of David, the Philistines lose their central position in the narrative of the Deuteronomistic History (Joshua, Judges, 1 and 2 Samuel, and 1 and 2 Kings). They now become peripheral actors in the biblical worldview. They do, however, appear with some frequency in their bit part. A couple of narratives appear to indicate that there were porous borders between Israel/Judah and Philistia. One of these is the account of the flight of Shimei's slaves from Jerusalem to Gath, presumably because it was the closest non-Israelite city, whence they were subsequently extradited back to Jerusalem (1 Kings 2:39–41). And the Shunammite woman sojourned in Philistia during a time of drought (2 Kings 8:2–3). But more often than not the Philistines provide the backdrop to tales of conflict. Twice Israelite coups take place during sieges of Philistine Gibbethon (1 Kings 15:27; 16:15–17). And in two passages that play a pivotal role in the current archaeological discussion, King Hazael of Aram-Damascus captures Gath and the northern Philistine coast (2 Kings 12:18 [Eng. 12:17]; 13:22 [+ G^{Lg}]).[20]

The book of Chronicles also preserves accounts of conflict involving the Philistines that are not mentioned in the Deuteronomistic History. While it could be argued that these help fill in gaps in our historical knowledge, their evident theological-ideological use in this late retelling of Israel's story calls into question their employment as historical sources. In these passages the Philistines act as foils in the text's theological evaluations of the kings of Judah. The Philistines pay tribute to "good" King Jehoshaphat (2 Chron. 17:11) and are the victims of the expansionism of "good" King Uzziah (26:6–7). However, they fare better against "bad" King Jehoram, into whose territory they advance (21:16–17), and against "bad" King Ahaz, from whom they take cities in the Negev and the Shephelah (28:18).

There are some passages that hint at Philistine religion or, at any rate, at a Judahite understanding of same. Chief among these is the account of

19. Ehrlich, *Philistines in Transition*, 37–41.
20. This latter text is found only in the LXX and not in the MT.

Ahaziah's sending messengers to Ekron to enquire of the god Baal-zebub[21] whether he would live or die, for which he is condemned by the prophet Elijah (2 Kings 1:2–3, 6). This association of the Philistines with the oracular arts may also be reflected in Isaiah 2:5–6.

In addition, the Philistines appear in prophetic oracles against the foreign nations, in which the prediction of woe for Judah's enemies presages Judah's weal. Jeremiah 47 focuses its attention on the two southern coastal Philistine cities that were closest to the Egyptian border—namely, Gaza and Ashkelon. Amos 1:6–8 calls destruction down on Gaza, Ashdod, Ashkelon, and Ekron. Significantly, Gath is missing from these passages.

What then are the main points that the biblical text makes about the Philistines? First, they were longtime inhabitants of the land in spite of the fact that they came originally from Caphtor (see Amos 9:7). Second, they were organized in a Pentapolis, a confederation of five city-states, which in later texts became a Tetrapolis, a confederation of four city-states. Third, their heyday as Israel's enemy extended from the period of the judges until the early monarchic age. Fourth, although their power was broken by David, they still remained a thorn in Israel's side. And fifth, their cult was dominated by their devotion to the gods Dagon and Baal,[22] with a small nod in the direction of the goddess Ashtoreth/Astarte.

2. Evidence from the Ancient Near East

The Philistines also appear in a number of extrabiblical texts. From around 1200 BCE date a handful of Egyptian texts that mention the Philistines among other Sea Peoples, as they are termed following nineteenth-century Egyptologist Gaston Maspero.[23] From a number of centuries later, they appear again in Neo-Assyrian and Neo-Babylonian inscriptions.

Dating to the transitional period between the Late Bronze Age and Iron Age I, when the international aquatic trade routes were interrupted and old and established civilizations throughout the eastern Mediterranean world entered into a period of rapid decline and collapse, a number of texts refer to seafaring groups that posed a threat to the established order.[24] It is, however,

---

21. This ("Baal the Fly" or "Lord Fly") is presumably an intentional corruption of Baal-zebul, "Prince Baal." See, e.g., Mordechai Cogan and Hayim Tadmor, *II Kings: A New Translation with Introduction and Commentary*, AB 11 (New York: Doubleday, 1988), 25.

22. From the Late Bronze Age Ugaritic texts we know that Baal was Dagon's son.

23. See Robert Drews, *The End of the Bronze Age: Changes in Warfare and the Catastrophe, ca. 1200 B.C.* (Princeton: Princeton University Press, 1993), 53–61.

24. About the Sea Peoples, see N. K. Sandars, *The Sea Peoples: Warriors of the Ancient Mediterranean, 1250–1150 BC*, rev. ed. (London: Thames & Hudson, 1985); Eliezer D. Oren,

a debated topic whether these seafaring groups were the cause, a cause, or a consequence of the general civilizational collapse.[25] The first mention of one of the Sea Peoples is on a stela dating to near the beginning of the reign of Ramesses II (1279–1213) from Tanis (*HTAT* 089), which mentions the Sherden or Shardana. Ramesses claims to have defeated them and brought them to Egypt. In his report about the battle of Qadesh (Kadesh) in 1275, Ramesses mentions the Sherden again but as mercenaries in his army (*COS* 2.5; *HTAT* 090). Five of the Sea Peoples, including the Sherden, are mentioned as allies of the Libyans, whom the pharaoh supposedly defeated, in an inscription of Ramesses's successor Merenptah (1213–1203) from Karnak (*HTAT* 091).

Dating to the final days of the city of Ugarit on the modern Syrian coast at Ras Shamra are examples of diplomatic correspondence that indicate concerns about seafaring marauders, which possibly include mention of at least one of the Sea Peoples known from Egyptian texts (*HTAT* 095–098).

Roughly contemporaneous with these letters from the early twelfth century BCE are some pivotal texts dating to the reign of Ramesses III (ca. 1184–1153). The first two are found on the northern walls of his mortuary temple at Medinet Habu. They deal with battles waged by the pharaoh in his fifth (1180 BCE; *HTAT* 092) and eighth (1177 BCE; *ANET*, 262–63; *HTAT* 093) regnal years. According to these texts, in his fifth year Ramesses defeated a coalition of Peleset (= Philistines) and Tjekker. Most interest is focused, however, on the account of Ramesses's eighth year, in which he defeated a large coalition consisting of a number of Sea Peoples, including the Philistines, the Tjekker, the Sheklesh, the Denyen, and the Weshesh. This propagandistic account makes the claim that they attacked Egypt after leaving their islands, overrunning the Hittite Empire in Anatolia, and then moving down the coast, leaving a swath of destruction in their wake. Only the might of the pharaoh, who met them in battle both on land and on sea, was able to stop their advance. This account has oftentimes been taken as a crucial piece of evidence in postulating a Sea Peoples invasion, which came from the Aegean world and swept through the Levant from north (the Hittite Empire) to south (Egypt), bringing destruction and the end of the Late Bronze Age. This information is often combined with that of Papyrus Harris I (*ANET*, 260–62; *HTAT* 094), which dates to the reign of Ramesses IV (1155–1148) but summarizes the

---

ed., *The Sea Peoples and Their World: A Reassessment* (Philadelphia: University Museum, 2000). The texts referring to the Philistines and other Sea Peoples are conveniently collected, translated, and annotated in Manfred Weippert, *Historisches Textbuch zum Alten Testament*, GAT 10 (Göttingen: Vandenhoeck & Ruprecht, 2010), 199–213, texts 089–099 (henceforth, *HTAT*).

25. See Amélie Kuhrt, *The Ancient Near East, c. 3000–330 BC* (London: Routledge, 1995), 2:386–93.

reign of Ramesses III. According to this latter text, Ramesses III defeated the Sea Peoples, among whom were the Philistines, and brought them to Egypt, subsequent to which he settled them in fortresses. In the attempt to find a *terminus post quem* by which the Philistines were settled on the southern coastal strip of Canaan, these texts play a central role.[26] Although Papyrus Harris I does not indicate where Ramesses settled the defeated Sea Peoples, a common assumption is that this is a reference to the original settlement of the Philistines in Canaan. According to this reconstruction, Ramesses withstood an attempted invasion of Egypt by the Sea Peoples, defeated them, and then settled them as Egyptian mercenaries or subjects in Canaan—thus in one stroke explaining the origin of the Philistines and dating their arrival to the eighth year of Ramesses III.

Others have called this reconstruction into question.[27] First, as indicated above, one of the Sea Peoples already appears in a text of Ramesses II as being defeated and brought to Egypt. Second, Papyrus Harris does not indicate where the garrisons were, in which Ramesses settled the defeated Sea Peoples. It could have been in Canaan, but the context makes it more likely that it was in Egypt.[28] Third, the layout of the temple at Medinet Habu indicates that the inscriptions are not necessarily to be read as factual historical accounts but as theological boilerplate, whose purpose is to depict the pharaoh as the defender of Egypt from threats from the four corners of the earth. In this case, the battle (or battles) against the Sea Peoples—whatever its possible historical context, if there was, in fact, such historical context—served the purpose of presenting Ramesses as the protector of Egypt from northern threats. The references to the destructive path of the Sea Peoples would then be hyperbole meant to enhance the glory and might of the pharaoh in the face of a threat of cosmic proportions. And fourth, the archaeological evidence for a massive and coordinated invasion of the eastern Mediterranean by groups from the Aegean world is inconclusive at best.[29]

Both enhancing and complicating the attempt to understand the inscriptions from Medinet Habu are reliefs from the same temple complex depicting Ramesses's two battles (or two-pronged battle) on land and sea

26. See the discussion of the "maximalist" and "minimalist" positions regarding the interpretation of the Ramesses III materials in Ehrlich, *Philistines in Transition*, 9–13.

27. Cf. Barbara Cifola, "Ramses III and the Sea Peoples: A Structural Analysis of the Medinet Habu Inscriptions," *Or* 57 (1988): 275–306.

28. See, e.g., Israel Finkelstein, "The Settlement of the Philistines in Canaan," *TA* 22 (1995): 213–39, esp. 226–27.

29. See Killebrew, *Biblical Peoples*, 197–245, for a discussion of the subject, wherein she does, however, identify evidence for a large influx of colonizers originating most recently on Cyprus.

against the Sea Peoples.[30] The exact relationship between the reliefs and the inscriptions is unclear, and the same strictures on interpreting the visual evidence obtains as in the case of the written. Nonetheless, the reliefs are an invaluable source for visualizing the Sea Peoples. From the distinctive uniforms of the warriors of the different Sea People groups to the fashions of their women and children,[31] from their ox-drawn carts to their seemingly two-prowed ships with birds' heads at both bow and stern,[32] the world of the Sea Peoples, including the Philistines with their distinctive "feathered" headdresses, comes alive.

Subsequent to the time of Ramesses III, the Sea Peoples in general and the Philistines in particular more or less disappear from the Egyptian sources, except for a couple of brief mentions.[33] It was not until the heyday of the Neo-Assyrian Empire a few centuries later that Philistia and Philistines would once again play a significant role in texts from the ancient Near East.[34]

In 796 BCE Adad-nirari III (810–783) reached the Mediterranean Sea in the area of modern-day Lebanon and claimed to have received one-time tribute payments from various southern Levantine states, including Philistia (*māt Palastu*).[35] Since *Palastu* is generally a designation for the region of Philistine habitation and not that of a clearly defined geopolitical entity, the reference in this case is presumably to the area of Philistine habitation—namely, that of the Philistine city-states—rather than to a unified political entity.

However, it was only during the reign of Tiglath-pileser III[36] (744–727) that Philistia was made subject to the direct military power of the Assyrian Empire. He marched down the Mediterranean coast and conquered Gaza, thus bringing the valuable spice trade from the Arabian Peninsula under his

---

30. On the Medinet Habu reliefs, see Dothan, *Philistines and Their Material Culture*, 5–13; Ed Noort, *Die Seevölker in Palästina*, Palaestina antiqua 8 (Kampen: Kok Pharos, 1994), 56–83.

31. Deborah Sweeney and Asaf Yasur-Landau, "Following the Path of the Sea Persons: The Women in the Medinet Habu Reliefs," *TA* 26 (1999): 116–45.

32. Shelley Wachsmann, *Seagoing Ships and Seamanship in the Bronze Age Levant* (College Station: Texas A&M University Press, 1998), 163–97.

33. See the Onomasticon of Amenope, dating to ca. 1100 BCE (Dothan, *Philistines and Their Material Culture*, 3–4), and the funerary inscription of Pedeeset, who may have been an Egyptian serving in Philistia or a Philistine serving in Egypt during the Twenty-Second or Twenty-Sixth Dynasty (Ehrlich, *Philistines in Transition*, 65).

34. For transcriptions and translations of and commentaries on the Assyrian texts from Adad-nirari III until Tiglath-pileser III as they relate to the Philistines, see Ehrlich, *Philistines in Transition*, 167–94. And on the history of the Neo-Assyrian Empire, see Kuhrt, *Ancient Near East*, 2:473–546.

35. See *ANET*, 281–82; *COS* 2.114G; *HTAT* 121.

36. About whom see Hayim Tadmor, *The Inscriptions of Tiglath-pileser III, King of Assyria: Critical Edition, with Introductions, Translations, and Commentary* (Jerusalem: The Israel Academy of Sciences and Humanities, 1994).

control and establishing a beachhead on the border with Egypt.[37] Hanunu, the king of Gaza, fled before the Assyrian assault but was reinstated on his throne, presumably because the Assyrians did not view him as an active enemy and wanted to maintain an orderly administrative transition to their controlling economic interest in Gaza, which became an Assyrian economic center (*bīt kāri*).[38] It was probably in reaction to this unprovoked Assyrian assault on the southern Levant that a coalition of Levantine states formed against Assyrian rule, in which case this event forms the background of the biblical Syro-Ephraimite War (cf. 2 Kings 16). Among the petty kinglets revolting against Assyrian rule at this time was Mitinti, the king of Ashkelon. Tiglath-pileser acted decisively against the coalition, deposed Mitinti, and replaced him with a certain Rukibtu. Thus did Philistia come under Assyrian sovereignty.

In the ancient world the death of a mighty ruler was oftentimes accompanied by the revolt of those he had subjugated. So it happened after the death of Tiglath-pileser's successor Shalmaneser V (726–722), who died around the time of the Assyrian siege and destruction of Israelite Samaria. Shortly thereafter, a number of states rose up in revolt against the new ruler, Sargon II (722–705). Among them was Hanunu of Gaza, who probably felt the pull of neighboring Egypt more than he did that of distant Assyria. Sargon recounts that he crushed the revolt and took Hanunu captive to Assyria, where his fate—although unmentioned—was probably most unpleasant (COS 2.118).

In the following years, the anti-Assyrian forces in Philistia concentrated themselves in Ashdod (COS 2.118; HTAT 160–63), whose king, Azuri, withheld tribute from Assyria, whereupon Sargon set his brother Ahimiti on the throne. He in turn was deposed by the people of Ashdod, who set a commoner named Iamani (Yamani) over themselves. When Sargon advanced upon Ashdod in 713, Iamani fled through Egypt to Ethiopia but was captured there and extradited to the Assyrians. Sargon captured Ashdod, its port Asdudimmu (= Ashdod-Yam), and Gath, which by now had been reduced to a satellite of Ashdod. As for Ashdod itself, it now lost even its semi-independence and became an Assyrian province.

Less than a decade later Sargon died unexpectedly in battle, which precipitated a struggle for power in Assyria and, consequently, appeared to give the opportunity to the Levantine states to emerge from under the harsh hand of Assyria. This time the ringleader of the revolt was Hezekiah of Judah, with the support of Egypt. Both Ashkelon and Ekron joined the anti-Assyrian

---

37. Gaza was the outlet of the spice trade to the international markets.
38. A prior economic interest in controlling Philistine trade may be indicated by Nimrud Letter 12 (= ND 2715). See Ehrlich, *Philistines in Transition*, 89, 190–92.

coalition, the latter after deposing its pro-Assyrian king Padi and handing him over to Hezekiah, the former possibly also after doing the same to its pro-Assyrian ruler Sharru-lu-dari son of Rukibtu, who had been set upon the throne by Tiglath-pileser III and, therefore, owed the Assyrians his loyalty. After the inevitable defeat of the anti-Assyrian coalition by the new king of Assyria, Sennacherib (704–681), Padi and Sharru-lu-dari were (re-)instated in their respective cities, while Ṣidqa the king of Ashkelon, who had joined in the revolt, was deposed and deported along with his family. Hezekiah's holdings were truncated and divided between the pro-Assyrian kings Padi of Ekron, Mitinti of Ashdod, and Ṣilli-bel of Gaza (COS 2.119B–D).

In all it took about a third of a century, stretching from Tiglath-pileser's attack on Gaza in 734 until Sennacherib's siege of Jerusalem in 701, for the Assyrians to establish their will upon the states of the Levant. Henceforth, peace would reign among the states of the southern Levant, including the city-states of Philistia, until the time of the decline of the Assyrian Empire, which would bring an end to the *pax Assyriaca*. Indeed, the Philistines, who had in the late eighth century BCE been a thorn in the side of the Assyrians, were both to benefit from Assyrian rule and to participate as loyal vassals in Assyrian activities—including in building projects in the Assyrian heartland (*HTAT* 188) and in the invasion of Egypt in 664 (*HTAT* 191). Ironically, it is this latter military campaign that provides us with our only extrabiblical evidence for the Philistine city-states acting in unison, albeit only four (Ashdod, Ashkelon, Ekron, and Gaza) were of sufficient significance to be mentioned at this late date. Nonetheless, in contrast to the majority of the biblical depictions of the Philistine city-states as an undifferentiated geopolitical entity, Gaza, Ashkelon, and Ekron are mentioned in sequence, with Ashdod mentioned later in the lists, presumably because the latter city had entered into a more severe form of vassalage as an Assyrian province, in spite of its being ruled by a client king.[39]

Following the death of the last significant Neo-Assyrian king, Assurbanipal (668–627), the Assyrian Empire entered into rapid decline and was replaced by the Neo-Babylonian Empire.[40] In the first full year of his rule (604/3), Nebuchadnezzar II (605–562) marched against Philistia, whose city-states presumably were by now allied with Egypt, and destroyed Ashkelon, bringing an end to the semi-independent city-state system that had endured in the region for the previous centuries (*HTAT* 258). An Aramaic letter, written on

---

39. In addition, these lists provide us with the names of the cities' rulers (namely, Ahimilki of Ashdod, Mitinti of Ashkelon, Ṣilli-bel of Gaza, and Ikausu [= Achish] of Ekron), thus adding to our knowledge of the Philistine onomasticon.

40. About which, see Kuhrt, *Ancient Near East*, 2:573–622.

papyrus and found in Egyptian Sakkara, provides some moving insight into the desperate state of the Philistines in anticipation of the Babylonian onslaught. In it, Adon, most probably the ruler of Ekron, asks the pharaoh in vain for help against the forces of the king of Babylon (*COS* 3.54; *HTAT* 260). The last glimmer of the Philistines appears in a Babylonian ration list, where rations for the exiled kings of Ashdod and Gaza are mentioned; unfortunately, their names are lost (*ANET*, 307–8).[41]

3. Evidence from Archaeological Investigation

From these three or so disparate types of written and iconographic sources (biblical, Egyptian, and Mesopotamian), we are able to piece together a rough outline of some major stations along the path of Philistine history. However, it is only thanks to the archaeological excavations that have been undertaken within Philistine territory that a fuller picture emerges not only of the Philistines' history but also of their culture. Owing to their continuous habitation over the course of the millennia, the sites of Ashdod, Ashkelon, and Gaza have never disappeared from human consciousness. The same cannot be said of Ekron and Gath, whose locations were forgotten until recent decades. Our picture of Philistine material culture is rounded out by excavations at a number of smaller sites that lie in Philistia and/or exhibit signs of Philistine remains.[42]

The first excavations in Philistia were carried out at the very end of the nineteenth century.[43] Archaeologists quickly recognized that there is a unique style of pottery that distinguishes Philistine material culture from that of the surrounding cultures, at least during the Iron Age IB. While the presence of such pottery does not necessarily indicate the ethnicity of the users, the amount of same may be used to identify a site as predominantly Philistine as distinct, for example, from Israelite. Over the course of time, excavations have revealed not only great amounts of the distinctive pottery first identified by the earliest archaeologists but also other styles of Philistine pottery, thus allowing us to refine our understanding of the development of the Philistine pottery tradition beyond the stage first identified, which is only the second of the styles associated with Philistine habitation. Indeed, when Trude Dothan wrote her magisterial survey *The Philistines and Their Material Culture*, she

---

41. See also Nadav Na'aman, "Ekron under the Assyrian and Egyptian Empires," *BASOR* 332 (2003): 81–91, esp. 85n8.

42. Among others, these include peripheral border sites such as Timnah (Tel Batash), which changed hands over the course of time. See George L. Kelm and Amihai Mazar, *Timnah: A Biblical City in the Sorek Valley* (Winona Lake, IN: Eisenbrauns, 1995).

43. See the brief summary in Dothan, *Philistines and Their Material Culture*, 23–24.

did not yet have the advantage of the recent explosion of knowledge about the subject that allows us to identify the following major stages in the development of Philistine pottery.

The first style is known variously as Philistine monochrome ware, Mycenaean IIIC:1b, or Mycenaean IIIC Middle.[44] It is a locally produced style of pottery in which many of the shapes and designs reflect Aegean models of the late Mycenaean period. Found in greatest profusion at the sites of Ashdod and Tel Miqne-Ekron, it represents the first phase of Philistine settlement, which—according to the traditional chronology[45]—took place between ca. 1175 and 1150 BCE. It is characterized by its monochrome decoration, in which dark designs are painted on a lighter background. This style lasts for about a generation and is more or less coterminous with the Iron Age IA.

The second style is known as Philistine bichrome ware and is the classic style associated with the Philistines. It is evidenced for Iron Age IB from the mid-twelfth to the tenth centuries BCE.[46] Philistine bichrome pottery not only incorporates the Aegean designs known from the previous phase but also adds a number of elements indigenous to or already in evidence in Canaan, including both eclectic pottery shapes and two-colored designs on a light background, a color scheme that hearkens back to Canaanite models. The decoration of this bichrome ware includes circular bands lower on the vessels and higher up, both geometric and animal shapes, often enclosed in metopes (a square frame), of which the bird looking backward is the most distinctive and famous example, although others are attested.[47] This style, which is distinctive to the culture of the southern coastal plain (although examples are found in other areas of the land), is that which is most often associated with the Philistines and represents the heyday of their culture. And yet it also is used in positing the melding of the Philistines' foreign origins with their local cultural matrix, a process that has variously been called assimilation,[48] acculturation,[49] and

---

44. On the terminology, see Killebrew, *Biblical Peoples*, 206.

45. But see Finkelstein, "Settlement of the Philistines," who dates their arrival to the late twelfth century BCE and, hence, sees no connection between their settlement and the texts of Ramesses III.

46. See Faust, *Israel's Ethnogenesis*, 140 (fig. 14.1), for a schematic map of Philistine expansion during the monochrome and bichrome phases.

47. See the discussions of the various types of Philistine iconography in David Ben-Shlomo, *Philistine Iconography: A Wealth of Style and Symbolism*, OBO 241 (Fribourg: Academic Press; Göttingen: Vandenhoeck & Ruprecht, 2010). Specifically on the bird, see Dothan, *Philistines and Their Material Culture*, 198–203; Ben-Shlomo, *Philistine Iconography*, 132–42.

48. Dothan, *Philistines and Their Material Culture*, 217–18.

49. Bryan Jack Stone, "The Philistines and Acculturation: Culture Change and Ethnic Continuity in the Iron Age," *BASOR* 298 (1995): 7–35.

creolization.[50] Indeed, the mixture of influences from various spheres would appear to indicate that the Philistines did not consist of a unitary ethnic stock.[51]

The study of the third period is still in its infancy.[52] As the Philistines progressively melded with their environment, their pottery assumed a regional character. Nonetheless, in Iron II (ca. 1000–600 BCE) one finds a dark-red slipped ware characterized by simpler decorative patterns of lines and circles. Among the designations for this type of ceramic ware are Ashdod Ware and Late Philistine Decorated Ware.

After the early soundings at Philistine sites in the late nineteenth and early twentieth centuries, not much attention was devoted to Philistine archaeology until the excavation at Ashdod in the 1960s ushered in a renewed interest in the archaeology of Philistia. This was followed in the early 1980s by the excavation at Tel Miqne-Ekron, in the mid-1980s by that of Ashkelon, and in the late 1990s by that of Tell eṣ-Ṣafi/Gath, which was the last of the five cities of the Philistine Pentapolis to be identified with some measure of security. While the excavations at Ashdod and Tel Miqne-Ekron have been concluded, those at Ashkelon and Tell eṣ-Ṣafi/Gath are still ongoing. Other than some small soundings, the site of Gaza has not been examined, owing to the fact that the modern city is built on top of the ancient remains. In addition to the cities of the Pentapolis, a number of smaller and in some cases peripheral sites have also been excavated in Philistia and have yielded much valuable information about the Philistines, their society, and material culture. These include Tell Qasile, Yavneh, and possibly Tel Zayit,[53] among others.

Tell Qasile,[54] whose ancient name is unknown, was an inland port city that lay on the northern side of the Yarkon River in modern-day Tel Aviv

---

50. Killebrew, *Biblical Peoples*, 206. See also Joe Uziel, "The Development Process of Philistine Material Culture: Assimilation, Acculturation and Everything in Between," *Levant* 39 (2007): 165–73, who advocates for the term "cultural fusion."

51. See Killebrew, *Biblical Peoples*, 219–30, for a "Typology of Philistine Pottery."

52. David Ben-Shlomo, Itzhaq Shai, and Aren M. Maeir, "Late Philistine Decorated Ware ('Ashdod Ware'): Typology, Chronology, and Production Centers," *BASOR* 335 (2004): 1–35; Itzhaq Shai and Aren M. Maeir, "The Iron Age IIA Pottery Assemblage at Tell es-Sâfi/Gath," in *Proceedings of the 4th International Congress of the Archaeology of the Ancient Near East, 29 March–3 April 2004, Freie Universität Berlin*, vol. 2, *Social and Cultural Transformation: The Archaeology of Transitional Periods and Dark Ages Excavation Reports*, ed. Hartmut Kühne, Rainer M. Czichon, and Florian Janoscha Kreppner (Wiesbaden: Harrassowitz, 2008), 419–28.

53. On the question whether Tel Zayit was a Philistine city, see Israel Finkelstein, Benjamin Sass, and Lily Singer-Avitz, "Writing in Iron IIA Philistia in Light of the *Tēl Zayit/Zētā* Abecedary," *ZDPV* 124 (2008): 1–14.

54. Amihai Mazar, *Excavations at Tell Qasile*, pt. 1, *The Philistine Sanctuary: Architecture and Cult Objects*, Qedem 12 (Jerusalem: Israel Exploration Society, 1980).

and was the northernmost Philistine site.[55] It was settled during the second or bichrome phase of Philistine culture (Iron IB). Since the site had not been previously settled, the city planning and architecture are presumably reflective of as pristine an example of Philistine culture as we are likely to find. Nonetheless, the presence, for example, of the four-room house there does indicate the influence of the indigenous culture on the Philistines at this early date.[56] Of particular interest are the cultic remains found at Tell Qasile, among which the pride of place goes to an irregularly shaped temple that went through three distinct building phases and has been related to both Aegean and Canaanite prototypes. Arguably the most interesting of the cultic objects found is a clay vessel in the shape of a woman, whose breasts serve as spouts. This may be taken as evidence of the importance of the divine feminine in the cult as practiced at Tell Qasile. It appears that by Iron IIA the site had become Israelite, which it was to remain for the duration of its existence.

Ashdod was also—and still is—a port city located on the Mediterranean Sea.[57] Although it was destroyed at the end of Iron Age I, it continued to grow during Iron Age II, eventually becoming the center of an Assyrian province. Like Tell Qasile, it evidenced architectural features that many had presumed were more indicative of Israelite settlement, such as a six-chambered gate, which has oftentimes been referred to as "Solomonic." At this site too, an Iron I cultic complex was uncovered that provides insight into Philistine religious practice. A unique cultic stand, dubbed the Musicians' Stand, with a fenestrated base in which a group of musicians is depicted, was uncovered here. It is also here that the first and thus far only complete example of a relatively common Philistine type of sitting female figurine, nicknamed Ashdoda, was discovered. Significantly, it evidences both Aegean and local artistic influences and has been interpreted as another example of the Philistine worship of a goddess.[58]

---

55. It is not, however, the northernmost site where Philistine remains have been found. Tel Dor, which lies on the coast halfway between Tel Aviv and Haifa, is also a Sea Peoples site. However, as we know from the Story of Wenamun (*COS* 1.41; *HTAT* 100), it was settled by the Tjekker. And as is known from the excavations of the site, it evidences a different material culture. See Ephraim Stern, *Dor, Ruler of the Seas: Twelve Years of Excavations at the Israelite-Phoenician Harbor Town on the Carmel Coast*, rev. ed. (Jerusalem: Israel Exploration Society, 2000).

56. This also puts to rest the facile identification of the four-room house as an Israelite ethnic marker.

57. See Moshe Dothan, "Ashdod," *NEAEHL* 1:93–102.

58. See most recently Ben-Shlomo, *Philistine Iconography*, 45–51; David Ben-Shlomo and Michael D. Press, "A Reexamination of Aegean-Style Figurines in Light of New Evidence from Ashdod, Ashkelon, and Ekron," *BASOR* 353 (2009): 39–74.

Figure 10.2. Ekron Inscription

The city of Ashkelon is still being excavated; and the publication project is just getting off the ground.[59] Nonetheless, it is possible to observe that most of the remains thus far recovered from the site and of significance for the subject matter of this chapter date to the Iron I and Iron IIB–C (or Iron III) periods.[60] This would appear to mirror the changing fortunes of the city during the Iron Age. Among the preliminary conclusions that have been drawn from the excavations are that the arrival of the Philistines is indicated not only by a change in material culture but also in eating habits, with pork and beef consumption playing a more significant role than during the previous Bronze Age or in contemporaneous Israel and Judah, and that—contrary to previous assumptions—the Philistines' choice of beverage was wine rather than beer, which has once again been taken as a sign of their Aegean origin.

59. Lawrence E. Stager, *Ashkelon Discovered: From Canaanites and Philistines to Romans and Moslems* (Washington, DC: Biblical Archaeology Society, 1991); Lawrence E. Stager, J. David Schloen, and Daniel M. Master, eds., *Ashkelon 1: Introduction and Overview (1985–2006)* (Winona Lake, IN: Eisenbrauns, 2008); Lawrence E. Stager, Daniel M. Master, and J. David Schloen, *Ashkelon 3: The Seventh Century B.C.* (Winona Lake, IN: Eisenbrauns, 2011).

60. Extensive remains from the Hellenistic and Roman periods as well as the Middle and Late Bronze Ages have also been uncovered.

It was only in the late 1950s that it was first suggested that the low-lying mound of Tel Miqne could be the site of ancient Ekron,[61] an identification that was strengthened during the course of the excavations at the site beginning in 1981 and that was confirmed during the last season of excavation (1996) with the discovery of an inscription mentioning the name of the site and some of its rulers (fig. 10.2). Ekron was a large city during Iron Age I but shrank during Iron Age IIA, perhaps because of pressure from Judah (near whose border it lay) and probably also owing to its proximity to Tell eṣ-Ṣafi/Gath. It remained a small town until it grew exponentially during Iron Age IIB, when the city profited most handsomely from the benefits associated with the *pax Assyriaca* (late eighth to late seventh century BCE). It was during this time that Ekron became—as far as we know—the ancient Near East's largest producer of olive oil. Since the area surrounding Ekron itself could not have produced enough olives for the amount of production that took place at the site, it is assumed that olives were imported from as far away as the Judean hills. Owing to the large number of horned incense altars found at the site, it is possible that there were Israelites who took part in the olive oil production. During the months when the olive presses were quiet, the city became a center of textile production, as is indicated by the many loom weights recovered from the site.[62] Also found at Tel Miqne-Ekron were buildings that presumably served a cultic purpose. Dating to Iron Age I is a hearth sanctuary, one of a number of buildings found at Philistine sites that included this architectural feature, which plays such an important role in the Aegean world.[63] In addition, a shrine was found that included many cultic objects similar to finds on Cyprus and in the Aegean world, such as incised bovine shoulder blades (scapulae), the wheels of a bronze cultic stand, and an iron knife with an ivory handle. In the Iron Age IIB levels were found another sanctuary and—more importantly—the dedicatory inscription to *Ptgyh*[64] the "lady" of Ekron (*COS* 2.42; *HTAT* 192) and on an ostracon a dedication to the goddess Asherat,[65] in addition to one

---

61. Joseph Naveh, "Khirbat al-Muqannaʿ–Ekron: An Archaeological Survey," *IEJ* 8 (1958): 87–100.

62. Seymour Gitin, "Tel Miqne-Ekron: A Type-Site for the Inner Coastal Plain in the Iron Age II Period," in *Recent Excavations in Israel: Studies in Iron Age Archaeology*, ed. S. Gitin and W. G. Dever, AASOR 49 (Winona Lake, IN: Eisenbrauns, 1989), 23–58.

63. On Philistine hearths and the problems of their interpretation within the context of hearths on Cyprus and in the Aegean world, see Aren M. Maeir and Louise A. Hitchcock, "Absence Makes the *Hearth* Grow Fonder: Searching for the Origins of the Philistine Hearth," *ErIsr* 30 (2011): 46*–64*.

64. Christa Schäfer-Lichtenberger, "The Goddess of Ekron and the Religious-Cultural Background of the Philistines," *IEJ* 50 (2000): 82–91.

65. Seymour Gitin, "Philistia in Transition: The Tenth Century BCE and Beyond," in *Mediterranean Peoples in Transition: Thirteenth to Early Tenth Centuries BCE*, Festschrift for Trude

Figure 10.3. Tell eṣ-Ṣafi

that appears to mention the god Baal,[66] thus indicating even at this late date the importance of the worship of a goddess at Ekron.

The last city of the Philistine Pentapolis to be indentified is Gath at the site of Tell eṣ-Ṣafi (fig. 10.3).[67] During the course of this still-ongoing excavation, it has been discovered that the ancient city at this site is much larger than was originally supposed. Thus far minimal amounts of Iron IA monochrome pottery have been found, indicating that Gath became a Philistine city during the second or bichrome stage of Philistine settlement. It remained a large and ever-expanding city until around 800 BCE, to which a massive destruction level must be dated; its fate thus was a mirror image of that of Ekron except during Iron IB, when both cities were large. Associated with this destruction is a unique siege trench surrounding the city on three

---

Dothan, ed. Seymour Gitin, Amihai Mazar, and Ephraim Stern (Jerusalem: Israel Exploration Society, 1998), 162–83, esp. 175, fig. 16.

66. But see Edward Lipiński, "Review of Markus Witte and Johannes F. Diehl, eds., *Israeliten und Phönizier: Ihre Beziehungen im Spiegel der Archäologie und der Literatur des Alten Testaments und seiner Umwelt* (OBO 235; Fribourg: Academic Press, 2008)," *BO* 66 (2009): 326–30, who views the "for Baal and for Padi" inscription as mistranslated, owing to a "pleonastic *wāw*" he has identified in the original (*lb'l wlpdy*). Hence, he advocates translating the inscription as: "for the Lord, i.e. for Padiy" (330).

67. Aren M. Maeir and Carl S. Ehrlich, "Excavating Philistine Gath: Have We Found Goliath's Hometown?," *BAR* 27, no. 6 (2001): 22–31.

sides—that is, wherever the site was not bounded by the Elah Valley. Analysis of the pottery remains from the siege trench, combined with the biblical notices of the conquest of the city by Hazael (2 Kings 12:18 [Eng. 12:17]; 13:22 [according to the Lucianic recension of the Septuagint]), has led excavators to posit that this enormous siege trench was dug under the command of Hazael, whose campaign against Gath brought an end to the city's prominence.[68] Henceforth, it disappears from the biblical and extrabiblical record, except as a satellite of Ashdod. Among the other major finds from the first decade or so of excavation at Tell eṣ-Ṣafi is a temple dating to Iron IIA, which—as the excavator likes to point out—was supported by two centrally located pillars, similar to the description of the Philistine temple at the end of the Samson narrative.

A smaller Philistine site that has recently assumed some prominence in the discussion is the site of Yavneh, at which an enormous collection of clay votive shrines or cult stands has been found.[69] Once again, the human figures attached to these shrines are predominantly female. The accumulation of such evidence among Philistine finds leads one to posit that—contrary to the picture presented in the Hebrew Bible, in which the Philistines primarily worshiped the gods Dagon and Baal—goddesses were preeminent in the Philistine cult.[70]

What can be said then in summary about Philistia and the Philistines? Sometime in the Iron Age IA, groups of an Aegean or Anatolian origin to whom later tradition—perhaps *pars pro toto*—assigned the name "Philistines" settled in colonies on the southern coastal strip of Canaan, where they established a city-state system that initially included five major cities.[71] Over the course of time they developed a distinctive hybrid culture that both retained elements of their land(s) of origin and assimilated elements from the indigenous culture. Whatever their original language, which presumably was an Indo-European one, they adopted the Canaanite dialect of Northwest

---

68. Aren M. Maeir, "Hazael, Birhadad, and the ḥrṣ," in *Exploring the Longue Durée: Essays in Honor of Lawrence E. Stager*, ed. J. David Schloen (Winona Lake, IN: Eisenbrauns, 2009), 273–77.

69. Raz Kletter, Irit Ziffer, and Wolfgang Zwickel, "Cult Stands of the Philistines: A Genizah from Yavneh," *NEA* 69 (2006): 146–59; Kletter, Zwickel, and Ziffer, *Yavneh I: The Excavation of the 'Temple Hill' Repository Pit and the Cult Stands*, OBO.SA 30 (Fribourg: Academic Press; Göttingen: Vandenhoeck & Ruprecht, 2010).

70. On Philistine religion, see Itamar Singer, "Towards the Image of Dagon, God of the Philistines," *Syria* 69 (1992): 431–50; Carl S. Ehrlich, "Philistine Religion: Text and Archaeology," *Scripta Mediterranea* 27–28 (2006–7): 33–52.

71. Still imperfectly understood is the relationship between the southern Canaanite Philistines and the Iron Age I northern kingdom of Palistin in the region of Hamath and Tell Taʿyinat. See, e.g., Benjamin Sass, "Four Notes on Taita King of Palistin with an Excursus on King Solomon's Empire," *TA* 37 (2010): 169–74.

Semitic as well as its writing system, while retaining some nouns and names that hearkened back to their original culture. A particular aspect of their cult that seems to have been retained over the course of their existence was the worship of a goddess. After a period of expansionism lasting until the end of Iron Age I, they were bounded within their coastal strip, a process that was probably influenced by the rise of various national states in the Levant, in particular by the Israelites and Judahites. Thereafter the Philistine city-states attempted to negotiate their separate fates, sometimes as allies of the one or the other but oftentimes pursuing differing political programs, particularly in regard to coalition politics. Ultimately, they, like the Israelites and Judahites, fell prey to larger geopolitical forces and disappeared from the historical record around 600 BCE. Among their most prominent cultural legacies are the use of their gentilic in the Western languages to indicate boorish people (i.e., "philistines") and the use of their originally restricted regional name to designate the whole of the southern Levant—namely, "Palestine."[72]

For Further Reading

Ben-Shlomo, David. *Philistine Iconography: A Wealth of Style and Symbolism*. OBO 241. Fribourg: Academic Press; Göttingen: Vandenhoeck & Ruprecht, 2010.

Bierling, Neal. *Giving Goliath His Due: New Archaeological Light on the Philistines*. Rev. ed. Marco Polo Monographs 7. Warren Center, PA: Shangri-La Publications, 2002.

Brug, John F. *A Literary and Archaeological Study of the Philistines*. BARIS 265. Oxford: B.A.R., 1985.

Dothan, Trude. *The Philistines and Their Material Culture*. Jerusalem: Israel Exploration Society, 1982.

Dothan, Trude, and Moshe Dothan. *People of the Sea: The Search for the Philistines*. New York: Macmillan, 1992.

---

72. The flood of publications on Philistine topics continues unabated. Among the more significant publications that have appeared since the completion of this chapter are the following: Dominik Elkowicz, *Tempel und Kultplätze der Philister und der Völker des Ostjordanlandes: Eine Untersuchung zur Bau- und zur Kultgeschichte während der Eisenzeit I–II*, AOAT 378 (Münster: Ugarit-Verlag, 2012); Ann E. Killebrew and Gunnar Lehmann, eds., *The Philistines and Other "Sea Peoples" in Text and Archaeology*, ABS 15 (Atlanta: Society of Biblical Literature, 2013); Aren M. Maeir, ed., *Tell es-Safi/Gath I: The 1996–2005 Seasons*, 2 vols., ÄAT 69 (Wiesbaden: Harrassowitz, 2012); Michael D. Press, *Ashkelon 4: The Iron Age Figurines of Ashkelon and Philistia* (Winona Lake, IN: Eisenbrauns, 2012).

Drews, Robert. *The End of the Bronze Age: Changes in Warfare and the Catastrophe, ca. 1200 B.C.* Princeton: Princeton University Press, 1993.

Ehrlich, Carl S. *The Philistines in Transition: A History from c. 1000–730 BCE.* SHCANE 10. Leiden: Brill, 1996.

Gitin, Seymour, Amihai Mazar, and Ephraim Stern, eds. *Mediterranean Peoples in Transition: Thirteenth to Early Tenth Centuries BCE.* Festschrift for Trude Dothan. Jerusalem: Israel Exploration Society, 1998.

Harrison, Timothy P., ed. *Cyprus, the Sea Peoples and the Eastern Mediterranean: Regional Perspectives of Continuity and Change* (= *Scripta Mediterranea* 27–28 [2006–7]). Toronto: Canadian Institute for Mediterranean Studies, 2008.

Killebrew, Ann E. *Biblical Peoples and Ethnicity: An Archaeological Study of Egyptians, Canaanites, Philistines, and Early Israel 1300–1100 B.C.E.* ABS 9. Atlanta: Society of Biblical Literature, 2005.

Margalith, Othniel. *The Sea Peoples in the Bible.* Wiesbaden: Harrassowitz, 1994.

Oren, Eliezer D., ed. *The Sea Peoples and Their World: A Reassessment.* Philadelphia: University Museum, 2000.

Sandars, N. K. *The Sea Peoples: Warriors of the Ancient Mediterranean 1250–1150 BC.* Rev. ed. London: Thames & Hudson, 1985.

Wachsmann, Shelley. *Seagoing Ships and Seamanship in the Bronze Age Levant.* College Station: Texas A&M University Press, 1998.

Yasur-Landau, Assaf. *The Philistines and Aegean Migration at the End of the Late Bronze Age.* Cambridge: Cambridge University Press, 2010.

11

Persia and the Persians

Pierre Briant

Around 550 BCE the history of the ancient Middle East witnessed a revolution that would prove to represent a profound change in the region. For the first and last time in history, all the peoples and lands between the Indus and the Mediterranean and between the Syr Darya River in central Asia and Aswan in Upper Egypt were united under one state: the Achaemenid Persian Empire, named after the Achaemenid dynasty. The first world empire in history, it was constructed over a period of around thirty years (ca. 540–510 BCE) following the successive military conquests led by the first three representatives of a small dynasty originating in Anshan, in present-day Fārs:[1] Cyrus the Great (ca. 550–530 BCE), Cambyses (530–522 BCE), and Darius I (522–486 BCE).

The empire reached its largest territorial expanse around 480 BCE, on the eve of a new expedition to Europe (the second Median War). Apart from the territorial losses in Europe due to the two successive Median Wars under Darius and then under his son Xerxes,[2] as well as to temporary secessions,

---

This essay was translated by Stephen Germany.

1. See Pierre Briant, *From Cyrus to Alexander: A History of the Persian Empire*, trans. Peter T. Daniels (Winona Lake, IN: Eisenbrauns, 2002), 13–161.

2. Ibid., 515–86.

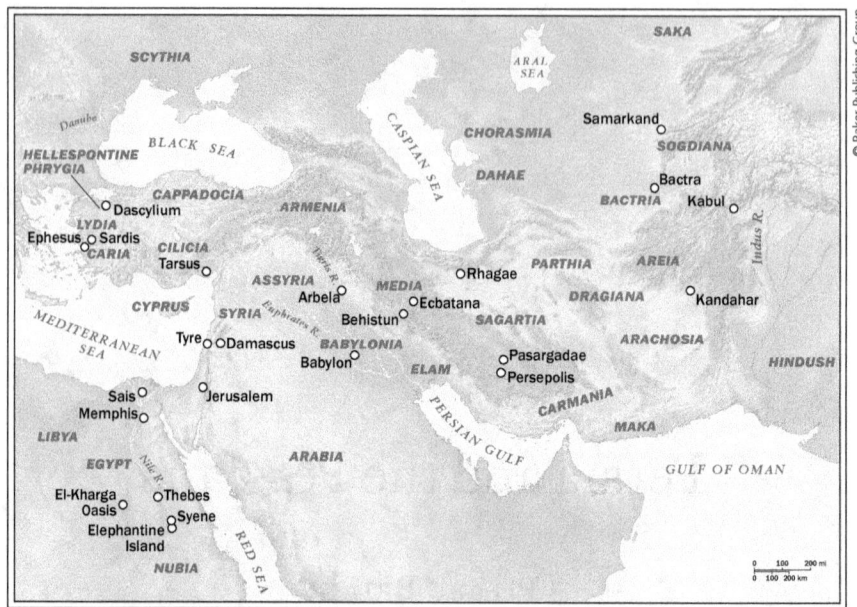

Figure 11.1. The Achaemenid Empire

the extent of the empire remained unchanged until the arrival of Alexander the Great.[3] Only Egypt succeeded in reclaiming its independence over a long period of time, between the end of the fifth century BCE and the reign of Artaxerxes III (ca. 400–343 BCE). This period of Egyptian independence occurred between two periods of Persian rule: the first (525–400 BCE) was begun by Cambyses's conquest of Egypt, and the second, much more violent period (343–332 BCE) was inaugurated by Artaxerxes's reconquest of Egypt and was concluded by Alexander the Great's conquest.[4]

In a struggle against Darius III, the last representative of the Achaemenid dynasty, Alexander of Macedonia overtook the Achaemenid Empire during a period of about ten years (334–323 BCE).[5] Subsequently, over a period of about twenty more years (ca. 323–300 BCE), Alexander's successors divided the territories of the empire among themselves and transformed them into competing, hostile kingdoms: the Hellenistic kingdoms centered in Mesopotamia and Iran (the Seleucid kingdom), Egypt (the Lagid kingdom, or Ptolemaic dynasty), Asia Minor (the Attalid kingdom), and Macedonia (the Antigonid

3. Ibid., 693–768.
4. Ibid., 615–90, 717–18, 858–61.
5. Ibid., 769–871.

kingdom). Eventually, the Roman Empire reunited some of these areas, although Iran, the Iranian Plateau, and central Asia escaped its domination.

The most striking feature of Achaemenid space and time is that political unity was constructed and maintained without sacrificing the extraordinary linguistic and cultural diversity of the lands that composed the empire. The historical dynamics of the period resulted in the dialectical fusion of two fundamentally antagonistic principles: unity and diversity. From the Indus to the Mediterranean, languages, scripts, and cultures maintained their vitality throughout the empire's existence. Such diversity presents both a challenge and an opportunity for understanding the functioning and dynamics of the Empire of the Great Kings from within.

1. The Burgeoning Field of Study

In 1948 Albert Ten Eyck Olmstead's posthumous work *History of the Persian Empire* was published in Chicago. In comparison with the historiography of the preceding decades, this work represented notable progress in the author's evaluation of the available documentary material. In the preface to his *History*, Olmstead lucidly traced the epistemological revolution that was underway in scholarship on the Persian Empire. From his point of view, the great archaeological and photographic expeditions conducted by the Oriental Institute of Chicago under the direction of James Henry Breasted—particularly those at Persepolis—marked "a new epoch in the recovery of the ancient Near East." As professor of history at the University of Chicago, Olmstead was able to utilize almost immediately the results of archaeological and philological research conducted by his colleagues at the Oriental Institute. This allowed him to highlight a fact that he believed to be decisive at the beginning of the 1940s: "Through these years also the oriental sources for the Achaemenid period have only slowly been pieced together. Their contribution is especially valued because they redress the balance so heavily weighted until now in favor of the Greek writers."[6] Among these new sources, Olmstead cited not only Persian sources proper (that is, sources from Fārs) but also Egyptian, Judean, Phoenician, and Babylonian sources, as well as the documents from Asia Minor written in local languages and scripts (Lycian and Lydian), not to mention the documents written in Aramaic, the language of the Achaemenid administration. In the closing pages of the work, Olmstead returned insistently to this idea, and he ended

---

6. Albert T. E. Olmstead, *History of the Persian Empire* (Chicago: University of Chicago Press, 1948), xii.

with this memorable phrase: "Close to twenty-three centuries have elapsed since Alexander burned Persepolis; now at last, through the united effort of archaeologist, philologist and historian, Achaemenid Persia has risen from the dead."[7]

In a certain way, the constant progress made over the course of the past seventy years confirms and amplifies the remark that Olmstead made regarding method seventy years ago: the Achaemenid sources proper "redress the balance so heavily weighted until now in favor of the Greek writers." In certain cases, the recourse to classical texts loses its pertinence once new documents are included in the dossier (such as the Babylonian revolts against Xerxes).[8] Due to persisting lacunae, the use of classical sources remains a viable method (with the aim of extracting from them the "Achaemenid" kernel of information), particularly for the periods in which the Achaemenid documentation remains insufficient (such as the reign of Darius III)[9] or for festive events that set the rhythm of court life. Even in these areas, however, the value of the Greco-Roman sources is somewhat lessened insofar as the new documentary discoveries allow for a new understanding of the end of the Achaemenid Empire or of certain rules of the court (such as the King's Table).[10]

The Greco-Roman sources are useful for reconstructing a continuous event-based narrative, yet they are much less useful for understanding the day-to-day functioning of the imperial machine. Studies on imperial taxation are now conducted based on Elamite, Babylonian, and Aramaic documents recording everyday activity and are supplemented by Greek or bilingual

---

7. Ibid., 524.

8. See Caroline Waerzeggers, "The Babylonian Revolts against Xerxes and the 'End of Archives,'" *AfO* (2003–4): 150–73; Wouter Henkelman, Amélie Kuhrt, Robert Rollinger, and Josef Wiesehöfer, "Herodotus and Babylon Reconsidered," in *Herodotus and the Persian Empire*, ed. Robert Rollinger, Brigitte Truschnegg, and Reinhold Bichler (Wiesbaden: Harrassowitz, 2011), 449–70.

9. See Pierre Briant, *Darius in the Shadow of Alexander*, trans. Jane Marie Todd (Cambridge, MA: Harvard University Press, 2014); Briant, "The Empire of Darius III in Perspective," in *Alexander the Great: A New History*, ed. Waldemar Heckel and Lawrence A. Trittle (Malden, MA: Wiley-Blackwell, 2009), 141–70; Briant, *Alexander the Great and His Empire: A Short Introduction* (Princeton: Princeton University Press, 2010), 171–80.

10. The importance of the text of Polyaenus, which has always been highlighted in the scholarship (Briant, *From Cyrus to Alexander,* 286–97; *BHAch* 2:100–107), was analyzed again with unparalleled precision by Suzanne Amigues, "Pour la table du Grand Roi," *Journal des Savants* (2003): 3–59. See also Wouter Henkelman, "'Consumed before the King': The Table of Darius, That of Irdabama and Irtaštuna, and That of His Satrap, Karkiš," in *Der Achämenidenhof / The Achaemenid Court: Akten des 2. Internationalen Kolloquiums zum Thema "Vorderasien im Spannungsfeld klassischer und altorientalischer Überlieferungen,"* ed. Bruno Jacobs and Robert Rollinger (Wiesbaden: Harrassowitz, 2010), 667–776.

inscriptions from Asia Minor. In the same way, it is through the analysis of royal inscriptions, the decoration of Achaemenid residences, and the iconography borne on seals that one must reconstruct royal and imperial Achaemenid ideology.

More generally, due to the exponential growth of Achaemenid sources, historians are less obsessed with the constant concern to evaluate Greek sources in light of Achaemenid sources. The main task of historians today is to combine the Achaemenid corpora of every type (written, archaeological, iconographic, numismatic, etc.) and in every language and script utilized throughout the empire, from Asia Minor to India and from central Asia to the western desert of Egypt. From now on, it is possible to write the history of the Achaemenid Empire for its own sake and no longer under the now outmoded form of an appendix to Greek history. The study of Greco-Persian relations (especially in the area of cultural history) certainly remains important,[11] but it is only one element of a much broader evaluation of intercultural relations at work within the empire.

In conclusion, today it is possible to affirm with certainty that the Achaemenid period of the history of the Middle East and central Asia is one of the best documented, both at the center of the empire and in the different provinces and satrapies. Far from being a handicap, the linguistic diversity during this period further augments the informative possibilities of the written sources, particularly the multilingual texts found at the center of the empire and in the provinces. At the same time, the spectacular growth of archaeological and iconographic source material allows for a precise analysis of the diffusion and adaptation of Persian images in the provinces and of the fertile encounters between Persian traditions and local ones.

2. At the Center of the Empire

The King

The entire Persian political and imperial system was organized around the person of the king, who was constantly surrounded by coded ceremony, whether while walking in the palace or in audience with a dignitary or ambassador (fig. 11.2).[12] Generally, the oldest son succeeded his father, but there was no rule of succession strictly speaking, and challengers to the throne were numerous,

---

11. See Seyed Mohammad Reza Darbandi and Antigoni Zournatzi, eds., *Ancient Greece and Ancient Iran: Cross-Cultural Encounters* (Athens: National Hellenic Research Foundation, 2008).

12. Briant, *From Cyrus to Alexander*, 216–25; Amélie Kuhrt, *The Persian Empire: A Corpus of Sources from the Achaemenid Period* (London: Routledge, 2010), 531–44.

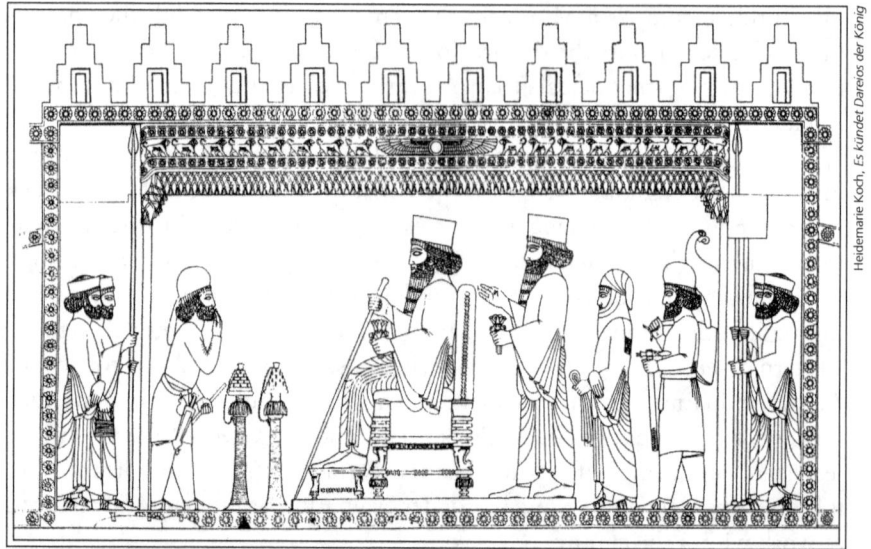

Figure 11.2. Audience relief at Persepolis

both while the king was alive and after his death (often following murders planned by members of the court).[13] For example, it was only at the end of a bloody conflict that the succession of Cambyses (d. 522 BCE) was resolved: the final victor, Darius, had to eliminate several competitors and at the same time suppress the "liar-kings," the leaders of rebellions against Darius's rule in Persia, Elam, Babylonia, Media, and central Asia.[14] These "liar-kings" are represented at Behistun as a line of individuals attached to each other by a rope and labeled with a short inscription stating their name and ethnicity (fig. 11.3). Facing them, Darius the conqueror, clothed in the royal robe and holding a bow in his left hand, crushes underfoot the one presented as the usurper, Gaumata. Darius is followed by two nobles who assisted him in his conquest and who received prestigious courtly titles, in conformity with Darius's declaration that "the man who was loyal, him I rewarded well; [he] who was evil, [him] I punished well." It was probably also at the time of Darius's rise to power that a fictitious genealogy was invented, making the hero Achaemenes the founder of the dynasty. Upon accession, each new king situated himself within the dynastic genealogy and employed formulas emphasizing his legitimacy.

Royal virtues are enumerated and exalted in several inscriptions. In a genre similar to the later "Mirror for Princes" genre (reused by Xerxes) is an

13. Briant, *From Cyrus to Alexander*, 563–67, 615–34, 769–80.
14. Ibid., 114–28.

Figure 11.3. Behistun relief

inscription carved on the façade of the tomb of Darius I at Naqsh-i Rustam. Below are some excerpts from the inscription:

> §7. A great god is Ahuramazda, who created this excellent work which is seen, who created happiness for man, who bestowed wisdom and efficiency on Darius the King.
>
> §8a. Saith Darius the King: By the favor of Ahuramazda I am of such a sort that I am a friend to right, I am not a friend to wrong. It is not my desire that the weak man should have wrong done to him by the mighty; nor is that my desire, that the mighty man should have wrong done to him by the weak.
>
> §8b. What is right, that is my desire. I am not a friend to the man who is a Lie-follower, I am not hot-tempered. What things develop in my anger, I hold firmly under control by my thinking power. I am firmly ruling over my own (impulses).
>   [. . .]
>
> §8g. This indeed is my activity: inasmuch as my body has the strength, as battle-fighter I am a good battle-fighter. Once let there be seen with understanding in the place (of battle) what I see (to be) rebellious, what I see (to be) not (rebellious); both with understanding and with command then am I first to think with action, when I see a rebel as well as when I see a not-(rebel).

Figure 11.4. Cyrus's tomb

§8h. Trained am I both with hands and with feet. As a horseman I am a good horseman. As a bowman I am a good bowman both afoot and on horseback. As a spearman I am a good spearman both afoot and on horseback.

§8i. And the (physical) skillfulnesses which Ahuramazda has bestowed upon me and I have had the strength to use them—by the favor of Ahuramazda what has been done by me, I have done with these skillfulnesses which Ahuramazda has bestowed upon me.[15]

The king had the mental and intellectual capacity to differentiate between good and evil and between truth (*arta*) and falsehood (*drauga*); he also had the physical and military capacity to punish rebels and enemies. He received these uncommon qualities from the divinity, particularly Ahura Mazda, the great god of the dynasty, who is sometimes thought to appear in the form of a winged sun disk at Behistun and elsewhere. Later, during the fourth century BCE, the kings invoked Ahura Mazda alongside two other divinities, one masculine (Mithra) and the other feminine (Anahita). It was thus through their patrilineal descent and through this close connection between the representatives of the dynasty and Ahura Mazda that the kings derived their

15. Darius inscription b at Naqsh-i Rustam, in Roland G. Kent, *Old Persian: Grammar, Texts, Lexicon*, 2nd ed., AOS 33 (New Haven: American Oriental Society, 1953), 138–40.

legitimacy. Without being divinized themselves, they were the intermediaries between the Persian people and their deities.[16]

Palaces and Residences

The Achaemenid king was also a builder-king who erected or improved the royal residences of Pasargadae, Persepolis, and Susa, where the king's majesty was put on full display.[17] This was certainly also the case in Babylon and Ecbatana, since the king and his court moved from one residence to another throughout the year, but only the first three sites are well documented through archaeology.

Built by Cyrus the Great, Pasargadae comprises an immense space containing a fortification (Tall i-Thakht), a district containing residential palaces, and Cyrus's tomb (fig. 11.4).

Classical sources situate the tomb in a vast, verdant garden (a *paradise*), which is a well-known feature of royal and satrapal residences. The most recent archaeological surveys have shown that these gardens, traversed by canals, were very extensive, and the residential palaces opened onto their greenery and flowing water (fig. 11.5).[18]

---

16. On the religion of the Achaemenid court, see *BHAch* 1:71–76; 2:112–18. Thereafter, see Albert de Jong, "Religion at the Achaemenid Court," in Jacobs and Rollinger, *Der Achämenidenhof / The Achaemenid Court*, 533–58. On the contribution of the Persepolis Tablets, see Wouter Henkelman, *The Other Gods Who Are: Studies in Elamite-Iranian Acculturation Based on the Persepolis Fortification Texts*, AchHist 14 (Leiden: Nederlands Instituut voor het Nabije Oosten, 2008); Henkelman, "Parnakka's Feast: Šip in Persia and Elam," in *Elam and Persia*, ed. Javier Álvarez-Mon and Mark B. Garrison (Winona Lake, IN: Eisenbrauns, 2011), 89–166; and Mark B. Garrison, "By the Favour of Auramazdā: Kingship and the Divine in the Early Achaemenid Period," in *More Than Men, Less Than Gods: Studies on Royal Cult and Imperial Worship*, ed. P. I. Iossif, A. Chankowski, and C. Lorber (Leuven: Peeters, 2011), 15–104, which includes an exhaustive bibliography.

17. Briant, *From Cyrus to Alexander*, 165–85; Kuhrt, *Persian Empire*, 488–501; see also John Curtis and S. Ramzjou, "The Palace," in *Forgotten Empire: The World of Ancient Persia*, ed. John Curtis and Nigel Tallis (London: British Museum Press, 2005), 50–103; Dietrich Huff, "Überlegungen zu Funktion, Genese und Nachfolge des Apadana," in Jacobs and Rollinger, *Der Achämenidenhof/The Achaemenid Court*, 311–51; Rémy Boucharlat, "Le destin des résidences et sites perses d'Iran dans la seconde moitié du IVe siècle avant J.-C.," in *La transition entre l'empire achéménide et les royaumes hellénistiques*, ed. Pierre Briant and Francis Joannès, Persika 9 (Paris: de Boccard, 2006), 443–70; Amélie Kuhrt, "The Palace(s) of Babylon," in *The Royal Palace Institution in the First Millennium B.C.: Regional Development and Cultural Interchange between East and West*, ed. Inge Nielsen (Aarhus: Aarhus University Press, 2001), 77–93; D. Stronach, "From Cyrus to Darius: Notes on Art and Architecture in Early Achaemenid Palaces," in Nielsen, *Royal Palace Institution*, 95–112; and Rémy Boucharlat, "The Palace and the Royal Achaemenid City: Two Case Studies—Pasargadae and Susa," in Nielsen, *Royal Palace Institution*, 113–23.

18. On this point, see the studies of Rémy Boucharlat, most recently "Gardens and Parks at Pasargadae: Two 'Paradises?,'" in Rollinger, Truschnegg, and Bichler, *Herodotus and the Persian Empire*, 557–74 (with bibliography).

After his accession, Darius decided to establish a new residence in Persia, at a place called Parsa (Persepolis in Greek), and another residence at Susa in Elam (fig. 11.6). These construction projects were undertaken concurrently, beginning around 515 BCE. At Susa, the construction of an Achaemenid royal residence resulted in a profound transformation of the former Elamite city. Foundation deposits from the site provide precise information regarding the construction techniques of an artificial platform:

Figure 11.5. Irrigation canal in the gardens of Pasargadae

> This palace which I built in Susa, its materials were brought from far away; downwards, the earth was dug, until I reached the rock in the earth. When it had been dug, and the rubble packed—on one side its depth was 40 cubits, on the other, its depth was 20 cubits; on this rubble, the palace was set.[19]

The king delighted in the fact that the building materials used in the palace's construction were brought from every corner of the empire (cedars from Lebanon; wood from Gandhara and Carmania; ebony and other wood from Egypt, ivory from Nubia, India, and Arachosia; and lapis lazuli from Sogdiana). The same was the case regarding the palace's artisans, who consisted of Ionian and Lydian masons, Median and Egyptian goldsmiths, and Elamite brickmakers, among others. These lists were intended to exalt the greatness of the empire, the variety of its products, the excellence of its artisans, and the supreme power of the Great King. The use of workers from every land of the empire is confirmed by the Persepolis tablets: the Treasury tablets provide precise information on the ethnicities and skills of the artisans and other construction workers. Such ethnic diversity is also in evidence in the Fortification tablets, which include a much wider array of workers (called by the generic term *kurtaš*) and their different occupations (agriculture, cattle

---

19. Darius inscription f at Susa §7, in Kuhrt, *Persian Empire*, 492.

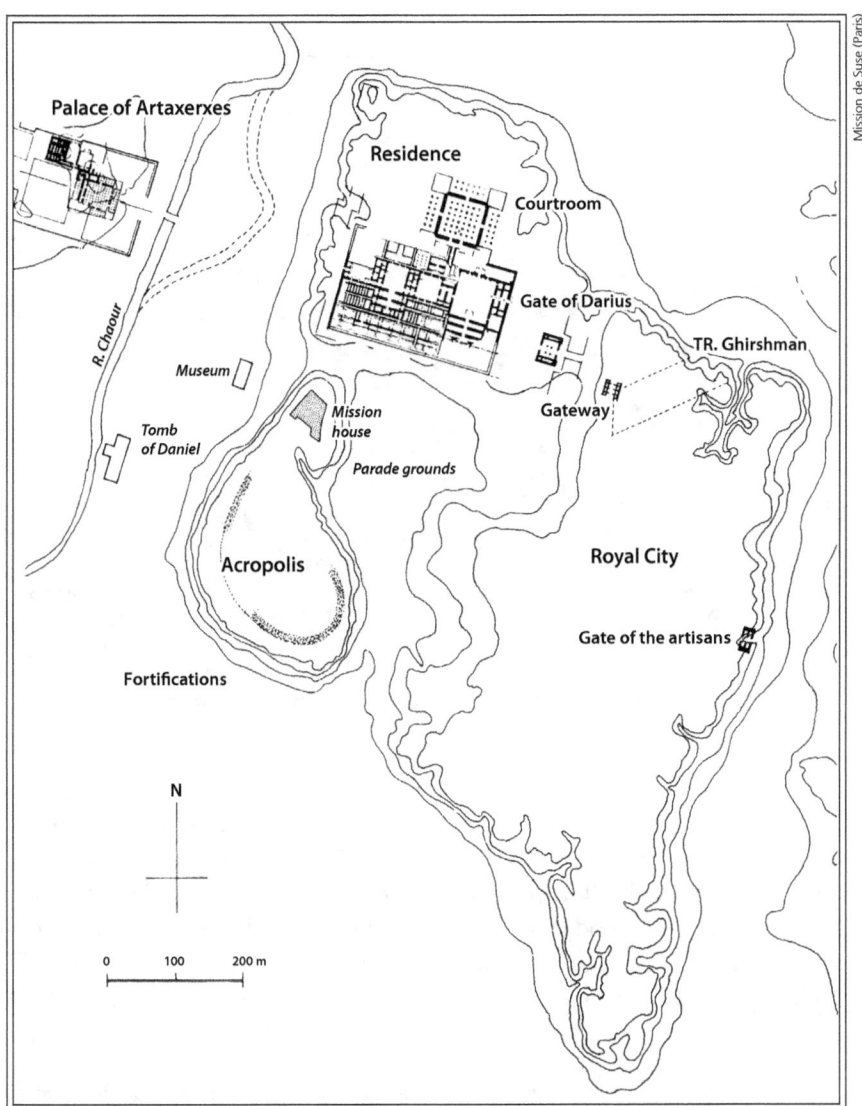

Figure 11.6. Plan of Susa

breeding, textile production, etc.). Groups of workers were sometimes sent from Susa to Persepolis and vice versa. Thanks to the Babylonian tablets, it is also known that the construction projects at Susa were completed through the conscription of workers from Babylonia.[20]

20. On these topics, see Briant, *From Cyrus to Alexander*, 165; Kuhrt, *Persian Empire*, 488–97 (Susa inscriptions in English translation); and Jean Perrot, ed., *The Palace of Darius*

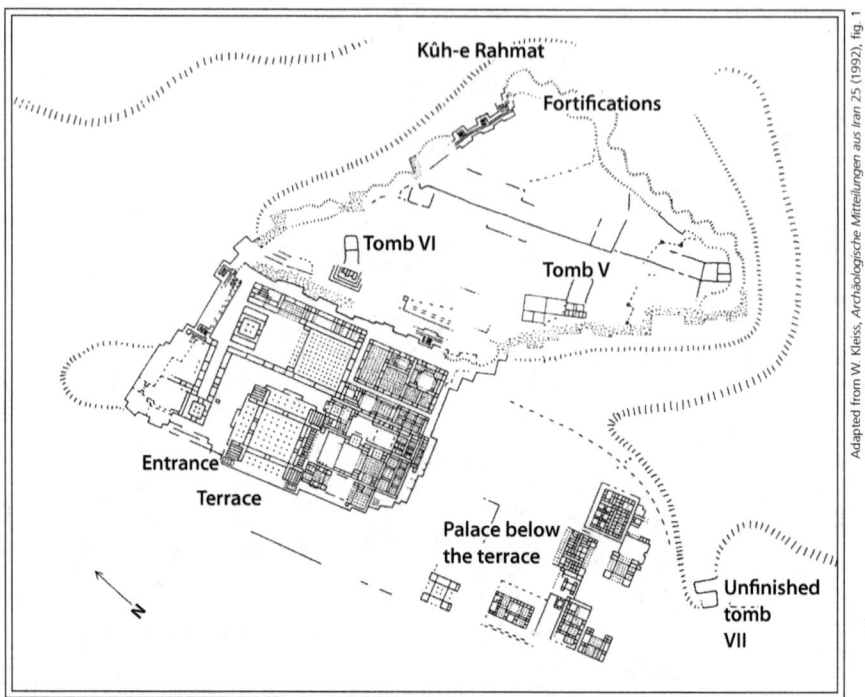

Figure 11.7. Plan of Persepolis

At Persepolis, the monumental terrace completely overtook the mountain, which was partially leveled, while mud-brick fortifications formed the terrace's upper walls. The terrace overlooks the vast, fertile plain of Marv Dasht, where more modest princes' residences were discovered. These construction projects were never completed; between Darius and Artaxerxes III, each king added a palace or restored or modified the palace of one of his predecessors.

---

at Susa: The Great Royal Residence of Achaemenid Persia, trans. Gérard Collon (London: I. B. Tauris, 2013). On the movement of construction workers between Susa, Persepolis, and the provinces, see Pierre Briant, "Susa and Elam in the Achaemenid Empire," in Perrot, *Palace of Darius at Susa*, 3–25. On the ethnic diversity of the *kurtaš* of Persepolis, see the case of the Skudrians, treated exhaustively in Wouter Henkelman and Matthew W. Stolper, "Ethnic Identity and Ethnic Labelling at Persepolis: The Case of the Skudrians," in *Organisation des pouvoirs et contacts culturels dans les pays de l'empire achéménide*, ed. Pierre Briant and Michel Chauveau, Persika 14 (Paris: de Boccard, 2009), 271–330; see also Robert Rollinger and Wouter Henkelman, "New Observations on 'Greeks' in the Achaemenid Empire according to the Cuneiform Texts from Babylonia and Persepolis," in Briant and Chauveau, *Organisation des pouvoirs*, 331–52; and M. Wasmuth, "Egyptians in Persia," in Briant and Chauveau, *Organisation des pouvoirs*, 133–44.

Figure 11.8. Elamite delegation on the "tribute" reliefs at Persepolis

The same was the case at Susa, where the so-called Palace of the Chaour, dating to the reign of Artaxerxes II, was constructed and in which fragments of murals depicting representatives of conquered peoples were discovered.[21] These representations correspond to the famous Persepolis reliefs, traditionally called "tribute reliefs," in which each ethnic group in the empire is represented in the form of a delegation coming to bring gifts to the Great King (fig. 11.8).

3. Administration of the Empire

Satrapies, Tributes, and Taxes

According to Herodotus, Darius completely reorganized the empire after his accession: "He proceeded to establish twenty governments of the kind which the Persians call satrapies, assigning to each its governor, and fixing the tribute which was to be paid him by the several nations" (*Histories* 3.89).[22] In reality, only the term "satrap" is known in Old Persian; the term "satrapy" is not attested in royal inscriptions, which only refer to "people-lands" (*dayava*), defined by the tribute (*baji*) that they were required to pay to the Great King as a sign of their obedience. Known in different languages throughout the empire (e.g., Old Persian, Elamite, Babylonian, Egyptian, Greek, Lycian, and Lydian), the term "satrap" (protector of power) had a wide variety of uses. In its Persian context, it referred to the "faithful ones" (*bandaka*) connected to the Great King by close ties of subordination. Most

---

21. On the Palace of the Chaour at Susa, see Rémy Boucharlat, "Other Works of Darius and His Successors," in Perrot, *Palace of Darius at Susa*, 359–403. On the history of the excavations at Persepolis, see Ali Mousavi, *Persepolis: Discovery and Afterlife of a World Wonder* (Boston: de Gruyter, 2012).

22. Herodotus, *The Histories*, trans. George Rawlinson (New York: Knopf, 1997), 269.

often drawn from the Persian high nobility, those who bore the title "satrap" were not necessarily heads of provincial governments, and in certain textual corpora, the heads of provincial governments do not consistently bear the title "satrap."[23]

The satrap had a large administration under his command, as well as a chancellery whose existence is attested by the large number of secretary-scribes and by the remains of local archives at sites such as Memphis, Daskyleion, and Susa. For example, in the case of Egypt,[24] we possess correspondence in Demotic from the time of Darius I between the satrap Pherendates and the administrators of the temple of Khnum at Elephantine,[25] as well as the Aramaic correspondence of Arshama (the satrap of Egypt between 428 and 412 BCE) and his subordinates. The ensemble of the Achaemenid sources from Egypt attests to the level of detail involved in the tasks carried out by the satrap and his administration; similar tasks are also attested in the Elamite tablets from Persepolis.[26] Several garrisons are also known in the Nile Delta at Memphis and at Syene-Elephantine in the "province of the South," well known thanks to the numerous documents in Aramaic that have come to light, particularly from the Judean community there.

In the same way, the term *baji* (part), used in the royal inscriptions, carries a political meaning in addition to a technical meaning, and the term "tribute," used by Herodotus and in other classical sources (Gk. *phoros*), oversimplifies the Achaemenid system of fiscal levies, which stands out for its diversity and complexity. The numerical evaluations of Herodotus for the tribute of each provincial government reflect Herodotus's own conceptions and are of no value once one takes into account actual Achaemenid documents, such as Elamite texts from Persepolis, Babylonian archives, or Aramaic documents from Egypt

---

23. See Briant, *From Cyrus to Alexander*, 466–69; Briant, "Empire of Darius III," 160–62; Kuhrt, *Persian Empire*, 881–82. For Egypt, see Günther Vittmann, "Rupture and Continuity: On Priests and Officials in Egypt during the Persian Period," in Briant and Chauveau, *Organisation des pouvoirs*, 102–4.

24. A synthetic study of Egypt during the Achaemenid period is still lacking, but see Günther Vittmann, *Ägypten und die Fremden im ersten vorchristliche Jahrtausend* (Mainz: von Zabern, 2003), 84–179; Vittmann, "Ägypten zur Zeit der Perserherrschaft," in Rollinger, Truschnegg, and Bichler, *Herodotus and the Persian Empire*, 373–430. See also the articles collected in Briant and Chauveau, *Organisation des pouvoirs*, 23–214, esp. H. S. Smith and C. J. Martin, "Demotic Papyri from the Sacred Animal Necropolis of North Saqqarah: Certainly or Possibly of Achaemenid Date," 23–78 (the *editio princeps* of papyri from Saqqara, which consist primarily of official reports). The recent monograph by Stephen Ruzicka, *Trouble in the West: Egypt and the Persian Empire, 525–332 BCE* (Oxford: Oxford University Press, 2012), focuses on Greek activity in the Nile Delta, without taking the Aramaic and Egyptian documentation into due account.

25. Briant, *From Cyrus to Alexander*, 474; Kuhrt, *Persian Empire*, 852–54.

26. Briant, *From Cyrus to Alexander*, 385–87, 417–18, 448–51; Briant, "Empire of Darius III," 148–51.

and elsewhere.[27] A Greek text from the last quarter of the fourth century BCE, the *Economics* of Pseudo-Aristotle, reflects the diversity of the levies in western Asia Minor.[28] Among the taxes levied by the satraps, the author identifies six types, associated with agriculture, mineral resources, commercial exchanges, troops, or other transactions;[29] the existence of some of these taxes is confirmed by Greek epigraphic evidence. Due to the particularities of each region, only regional studies allow for an understanding of how the imperial machinery functioned in one region or another at any given time period. In certain cases, specialized vocabulary indicates that a particular fiscal system was imposed by the Persians; such is the case for a tax on the sale of slaves in Babylonia, the collection and management of which were centralized within a specialized administration that bore a title of Iranian origin.[30]

The Case of Persia

According to Herodotus, the Persians were not subject to tribute (*dasmos*); they benefited from immunity (*ateleia*; *Histories* 3.97). In reality, the situation was not so simple: the Persepolis Fortification Tablets demonstrate that taxes existed within Persia.[31] One such tax was called *baziš* and was levied on cattle by specialized officers (*bazikara*). Other tablets refer to a tithe; yet others to a levy in kind (*ukpiyataš*) that is also known to have existed in Elam and Babylonia. The sole Babylonian tablet from the Treasury archives (PT 85) refers to a tax called *mandattu*, which designates in Akkadian and Aramaic a concept that is often translated as "tribute" yet in fact refers to diverse realities depending on the context.[32] The Persepolis tablets and the Babylonian documents reveal another type of levy in the form of corvées. In Babylonia this provision (*urašu*) was supplied primarily by

27. See Christopher Tuplin, "Managing the World: Herodotus on Achaemenid Imperial Organisation," in Rollinger, Truschnegg, and Bichler, *Herodotus and the Persian Empire*, 39–63.
28. On this text, see Raymond Descat, "Aspects d'une transition: L'économie du monde égéen (350–300)," in Briant and Joannès, *La transition*, 368–71.
29. Briant, *From Cyrus to Alexander*, 397–98; Kuhrt, *Persian Empire*, 672–73.
30. Kuhrt, *Persian Empire*, 704–5. On taxes and duties in Babylonia, see Michael Jursa, *Aspects of the Economic History of Babylonia in the First Millennium B.C.: Economic Geography, Economic Mentalities, Agriculture, the Use of Money, and the Problem of Economic Growth* (Münster: Ugarit-Verlag, 2010); Michael Jursa, "On Aspects of Taxation in Achaemenid Babylonia: New Evidence from Borsippa," in Briant and Chauveau, *Organisation des pouvoirs*, 237–70.
31. Briant, *From Cyrus to Alexander*, 439–42. See also Christopher Tuplin, "Taxation and Death: Certainties in the Persepolis Fortification Archive?," in *L'archive des fortifications de Persépolis: État des questions et perspectives de recherches*, ed. Pierre Briant, Wouter Henkelman, and Matthew W. Stolper, Persika 12 (Paris: de Boccard, 2008), 317–86.
32. Briant, *From Cyrus to Alexander*, 439–41; Kuhrt, *Persian Empire*, 772–73. For Aramaic occurrences, see Ezra 4:13, 20; 6:8; 7:24.

the great sanctuaries for the transportation of materials, for royal construction projects, and for work on irrigation canals. In Persia proper, thousands of workers (*kurtaš*) were conscripted from every region of the empire; they worked not only on the construction projects at Persepolis but also in agriculture and in craft workshops (spinning, weaving, tanning, etc.) and were transferred from place to place by order of the central administration in Fārs.[33] In Babylonia, the levying of manual labor could accompany the levying of products "for the table of the king"—that is, in order to provide for the royal court as it moved from one residence to another throughout the year. This form of taxation was also used by high-ranking provincial administrators.[34]

Commerce and Customs

Among the satrapal taxes mentioned by Pseudo-Aristotle are those that are drawn "from places of commerce" (*apo tōn emporiōn*) as well as "taxes on the markets" (*Economics* 2.1.4). To these taxes can be added customs duties, attested by Pseudo-Aristotle in Babylonia (2.34a) and by a Greek-Lycian bilingual inscription in Lycia (a tithe levied by the satrap in a port),[35] as well as the duties levied in the ports of the Euphrates attested in cuneiform sources.[36] The most remarkable document is a very long Aramaic papyrus from Egypt, dated to the eleventh year of a Great King of the fifth century, either Xerxes (475 BCE) or Artaxerxes I (454 BCE).[37] This document contains excerpts of a register recording the entry of ships into Egypt via a port in the Delta, very probably Tanis, and their subsequent exit into the Mediterranean. At the time of their entry and exit, the ships were inspected and their cargoes were carefully recorded. Some of these ships were specified as Ionian—that is, as

---

33. Briant, *From Cyrus to Alexander*, 429–39; Kuhrt, *Persian Empire*, 793–802.

34. Briant, *From Cyrus to Alexander*, 286–97; Kuhrt, *Persian Empire*, 711–13. See also Henkelman, "'Consumed before the King,'" 667–776.

35. Kuhrt, *Persian Empire*, 704.

36. Jursa, *Aspects of the Economic History of Babylonia*, 251–52; Kathleen Abraham, *Business and Politics under the Persian Empire: The Financial Dealings of Marduk-nāsir-apli of the House of Egibi (521–487 B.C.E.)* (Bethesda, MD: CDL Press, 2004), 41–44; Francis Joannès, "Les droits sur l'eau en Babylonie récente," *Annales: Histoire, Sciences sociales* 57 (2002): 592–607.

37. Published in 1986 by Bezalel Porten and Ada Yardeni, *Textbook of Aramaic Documents from Ancient Egypt*, vol. 3 (Winona Lake, IN: Eisenbrauns, 1986), this document (C3.7) is reproduced in English translation in Kuhrt, *Persian Empire*, 681–703, and is commented upon at length in Pierre Briant and Raymond Descat, "A Customs Register from the Satrapy of Egypt in the Achaemenid Period (TAD C3, 7)," in Briant, *Kings, Countries and Peoples*, trans. Amélie Kuhrt, OeO (Stuttgart: Steiner Verlag, forthcoming), chap. 18, with my foreword §6 and nn. 70–72 for more recent studies.

coming from ports in Asia Minor; the others, which transported merchandise from the Levant, were probably Phoenician. The dates on which the ships entered and exited were recorded, as well as the names of their captains. The Ionian ships paid a tax called *mandattu*, calculated in gold and silver according to the value of the goods imported into Egypt. The Phoenician vessels paid a tithe on every product (amphorae of wine, timber, bronze, iron, tin, pottery, etc.). Upon leaving Egypt, they paid a tax called "silver of the men" (perhaps a poll tax); the Ionian ships also paid a tax on the natron that they brought back from Egypt.

The existence of numerous diaspora communities in Egypt, especially in the Delta (Greeks, Carians, Arameans, and Judeans), was already well known, but the Aramaic papyrus described above has the additional merit of providing firsthand details regarding commercial exchanges in the eastern Mediterranean between Asia Minor, the Levant, and Egypt. This commerce also extended from the Mediterranean coast to Babylonia; Babylonian tablets from shortly before the Persian conquest indicate the importation of products from Asia Minor, Lebanon, and Egypt, especially raw materials, metals (iron and tin), products for the textile industry (alum and dyes), and food products (wine and honey).

Agricultural Development

Agricultural activity and cattle breeding are especially well documented in Babylonia by temple archives and the archives of the large commercial centers;[38] important information on such activities in Persia is also available thanks to the Persepolis tablets.[39] For Egypt, there is the fairly well-known case of the Kharga Oasis, the southernmost oasis in the western desert. In 1992, south of the oasis at Ayn Manâwir, a village was discovered with around twenty houses, fields, and a temple to Osiris, which contained Demotic archives on 465 ostraca dating between the reign of Xerxes and 370/360 BCE, at which time the site was abandoned.[40] The development of

---

38. See Bojana Janković, *Vogelzucht und Vogelfang in Sippar im 1. Jahrtausend v. Chr.* (Münster: Ugarit-Verlag, 2004).

39. Briant, *From Cyrus to Alexander*, 425–28, 439–46, 456–63.

40. *BHAch* 1:32–33, 88–89. These documents, edited by Damien Agut-Labordère and Michel Chauveau, are available at http://www.achemenet.com. A print publication will be published later by the *Institut français d'archéologie orientale*. See already several preliminary publications by Michel Chauveau: "Les qanāts dans les ostraca de Manâwir," in *Irrigation et drainage dans l'Antiquité: Qanāts et canalisations souterraines en Iran, en Égypte et en Grèce*, ed. Pierre Briant, Persika 2 (Paris: Thotm éditions, 2001), 137–42; Chauveau, "Les archives démotiques d'époque perse: À propos des archives démotiques d'Ayn-Manawîr," in Briant, Henkelman, and Stolper, *L'archive des fortifications de Persépolis*, 517–23; Chauveau, "Les archives

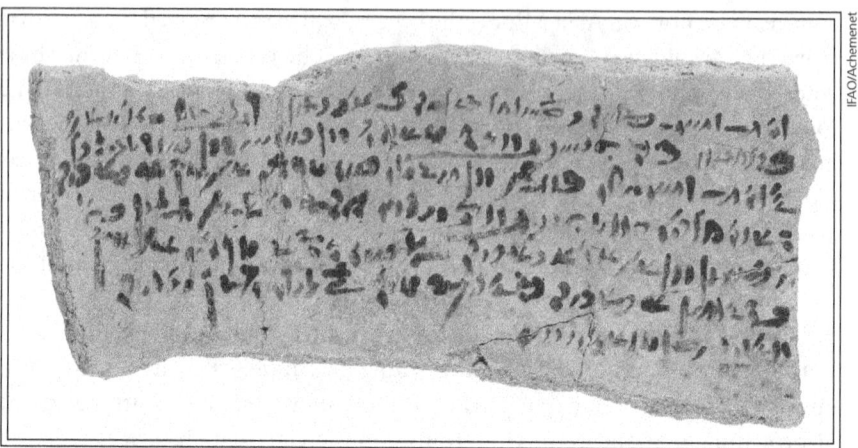

Figure 11.9. Ostracon of the hunt

this arid microregion was made possible through the use of underground water sources by constructing a series of drainage shafts and tunnels that functioned similarly to the structures called *qanāts* in the Arabo-Persian world.[41]

The prosopography of the contracts from Ayn Manâwir is uniquely Egyptian, without any mention of a Persian or Iranian name. The most important members of the community belonged to the local clergy of Osiris-Iou. The village must have been administered by one of these community members under the supervision of a local governor, who bore an Egyptian title. The extant taxes seem to have been levied exclusively by the temple. Does such an observation indicate that this village, which was established during the Persian period, developed in a completely local manner, without any contact—even distant—with the Persian administration? One factor that demands consideration is the choice of a water extraction technique that is known to have developed in the Iranian world during the Achaemenid period, as a famous passage from Polybius (*Histories* 10.28) dealing with the piedmont region in northern Iran demonstrates:

> Because in this region no water is visible on the surface, but there are, even in the desert, a number of underground channels connected to wells not known to those unfamiliar with the topography. A true story is told by the locals about them, namely, that at that time when the Persians ruled Asia they granted to

---

démotiques du temple de Ayn Manâwir," *ARTA* 2011.002. http://www.achemenet.com/pdf/arta/2011.002-Chauveau.pdf.

41. *BHAch* 1:33.

those who supplied water to previously unirrigated land the right to use the land for five generations.⁴²

Despite certain obscurities, this text reveals that the Achaemenid royal government promoted the development of irrigated agriculture in regions that had previously been unproductive and uninhabited. In order to do this, the government gave incentives to communities that were willing to invest the time and money necessary for the construction of irrigation tunnels, which in Iran were often quite long (up to 20 or 30 km.). Although the evidence is lacking, it is possible that this technique was imported into Egypt during the Persian period, when different villages were created south of the Khargah oasis. Following this hypothesis, it seems reasonable to propose that the development of the oasis could only have been carried out at the initiative of the imperial authorities, or at least with their consent.⁴³

Treasures and Treasuries

Part of the imperial taxes, as well as imperial gifts, was accumulated in immense royal treasuries, which are known thanks especially to classical texts recounting their seizure by Alexander in Babylon, Susa, Persepolis, Pasargadae, and Ecbatana. There was also at least one treasury in each provincial government, directed by an officer who held the title of chief treasurer (*ganzabara*). These regional treasuries were supplied by local levies; for example, customs duties in Egypt were sent to "the King's House"—that is, to the treasury of the royal administration of Egypt. At the command of the central government, such a treasury could be transferred, in whole or in part, from one place to another.⁴⁴ A number of Elamite documents record the activity of the royal treasurer of Persepolis, who disbursed salaries, paid in silver, to construction workers (PT 1, 27, 52, and 78). Many other treasuries and treasurers are known in Fārs. These treasuries had a different function, serving as storage depots for products from the Iranian plateau created by the "treasury artisans" (*kurtaš kapnuškip*) such as weavers, tanners, and stoneworkers.⁴⁵ Such workshops also existed at Persepolis, as the mortars and pestles inscribed in

---

42. Kuhrt, *Persian Empire*, 724.
43. See Pierre Briant, "Polybius X 28 and the *qanāts*: The Evidence and Its Limitations," in Briant, *Kings, Countries and Peoples*, chap. 13, with my foreword §5 and n. 58; see also several other papers in Briant, *Irrigation et drainage dans l'Antiquité*. On the use of irrigation water in the various regions of the Achaemenid Empire, see Briant, "The State, the Earth and Water between the Nile and Syr Darya," in Briant, *Kings, Countries and Peoples*, chap. 15, with bibliography.
44. For example, PF 1357 mentions that a Babylonian treasury was transferred to Persepolis.
45. Briant, *From Cyrus to Alexander*, 428–33, 440–41; Kuhrt, *Persian Empire*, 786–93.

Aramaic from that site indicate.⁴⁶ The term "treasury" (Elamite *kapnuški*) can also be understood in the sense of "storehouse" (like the term *thesauros* in Greek). It was apparently from such stores maintained in the numerous treasuries that the workers (*kurtaš*) in Persia were able to redeem their food rations at prices set by the administration according to one's age, sex, and role in the production process. In several satrapies in the empire (Babylonia, Egypt, and Bactria), this system of rations is well attested in cuneiform and Aramaic sources.⁴⁷

Storage Depots and Roads

Distributed throughout the empire, these treasuries and storehouses were used within the Achaemenid system of roads and communications.⁴⁸ Royal roads connected all of the satrapies to each other, from Sardis to Bactria and the Indus River and from Babylon to Memphis. Over the entire length of these routes were stores of food products (wine, beer, flour, grain, meat, etc.) for the army and for traveling officials as well as stores of feed for animals. One of the responsibilities of the governors and satraps was to maintain the level of these supplies (Pseudo-Aristotle, *Economics* 2.2.38). A good example of this is found in an Aramaic document from Bactria dated to November or December 330 BCE:⁴⁹ animals for slaughter (horses, cows, donkeys, sheep, geese, chickens), different qualities of oil and wine, flour, spices, and animal feed were distributed in the form of rations to travelers going from Bactria to Varnu. The Babylonian tablets are also very informative about shipping and transportation by land and by river.⁵⁰

---

46. Briant, *From Cyrus to Alexander*, 433.
47. See Michael Jursa, "The Remuneration of Institutional Labourers in an Urban Context in Babylonia in the First Millennium BC," in Briant, Henkelman, and Stolper, *L'archive des fortifications de Persépolis*, 387–427.
48. Briant, *From Cyrus to Alexander*, 357–87; *BHAch* 2:125–27, 147; Kuhrt, *Persian Empire*, 730–62. On the system of roads, see Briant, "From the Indus to the Mediterranean: The Administrative Organization and Logistics of the Great Roads of the Achaemenid Empire," in *Highways, Byways, and Road Systems in the Pre-Modern World*, ed. Susan Alcock, John Bodel, and Richard Talbert (New York: Wiley-Blackwell, 2012), 185–201; Briant, "Susa and Elam in the Achaemenid Empire," in Perrot, *Palace of Darius at Susa*, 3–25 (esp. 14–22). On the river-roads between southern Mesopotamia and the Persian Gulf, see Briant, *Alexander the Great and His Empire*, 89–96; and Briant, "The *Katarraktai* of the Tigris: Irrigation-Works, Commerce and Shipping in Elam and Babylonia from Darius to Alexander," in Briant, *Kings, Countries and Peoples*, chap. 28, with my foreword §7 and nn. 90–91.
49. Joseph Naveh and Shaul Shaked, *The Khalili Collection: Ancient Aramaic Documents from Bactria* (London: Khalili Collections, 2012), C1 (pp. 177–85).
50. See Bojana Janković, "Travel Provisions in Babylonia in the First Millennium BC," in Briant, Henkelman, and Stolper, *L'archive des fortifications de Persépolis*, 429–64. The subject

The most precise information comes from a series of tablets from Persepolis, the Q series (Travel Rations). These tablets indicate that traveling officials received an authorization (*halmi*) delivered by the king or by a satrap. When arriving at an official waypoint, the head of the caravan had to produce this sealed document, which gave him access to the stores; he received rations for himself and the members of his group according to the numbers given in the document. A concrete example of this procedure is found in an Aramaic document that the satrap of Egypt, Arshama (then in Babylonia), gave to his steward whom he sent back to Egypt.[51] The different stages along the route between Babylon and Damascus are precisely indicated, as well as the amount of daily rations (wheat and beer) for each category of travelers, including feed for horses. The text of the authorization enters into minute detail: "Give them this ration, each official in turn, according to the route which is from province to province (*medinah*) until he reaches Egypt. And if he be in one place more than one day, for those days do not give them extra rations!"[52]

4. Religion, Politics, and Culture

The Great King in His Lands

In the royal inscriptions from Persia, Darius is called "Great King, king of kings, king of the countries, son of Hystaspes, an Achaemenid." The king insisted on his privileged connection with the great Persian divinity Ahura Mazda and with Persia proper, "which is good, containing good horses, good men."[53] As the master of a number of "people-lands" (*dayava*) who brought him tribute and who are represented as subjects in the royal residences, the Persian king also appropriated the titles of the kings who preceded him in the conquered lands. This use of multiple titles is illustrated forcefully in the quadrilingual inscriptions on the statue of Darius discovered at Susa and on the stelae from the Suez Canal, which was reopened by Darius. The Persian, Elamite, and Babylonian versions insist on Darius's status as conqueror and head of the empire: "This is the statue of stone, which Darius the king ordered to be made in Egypt, so that whoever sees it in time to come will know that the Persian man holds Egypt."[54]

---

of shipping in Babylonia is treated in Jursa, *Aspects of the Economic History of Babylonia*, 62–140.

51. Briant, *From Cyrus to Alexander*, 364–68.
52. B. Porten and A. Yardeni, *Textbook of Aramaic Documents from Ancient Egypt*, vol. 1 (Winona Lake, IN: Eisenbrauns, 1986), A6.
53. Briant, *From Cyrus to Alexander*, 172–83; Kuhrt, *Persian Empire*, 476–87.
54. Inscription of Darius at Susa (statue), in Kuhrt, *Persian Empire*, 478.

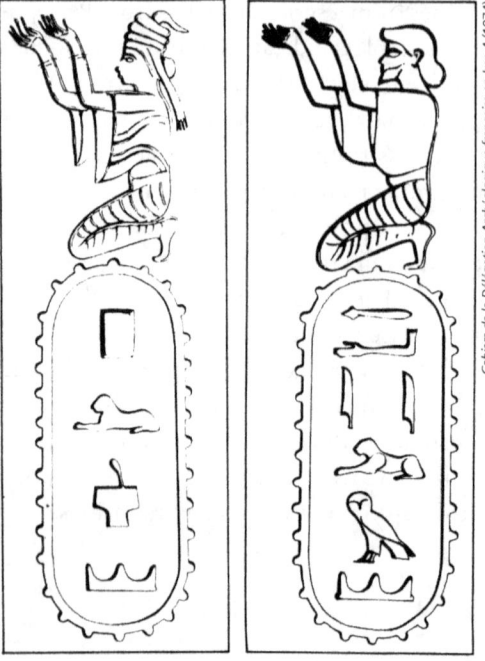

Figure 11.10. Two subject peoples on the statue of Darius: Persia (left), Elam (right)

At the same time, hieroglyphic inscriptions recognize Darius as "king of Upper and Lower Egypt, Lord of the Two Lands on the seat where Horus reigns over the living at the head of the gods, eternally."[55] Here, subject peoples are represented in Egyptian style and thus in quite a different form from the depictions found on the palace walls of Persepolis and Susa (fig. 11.10).

For this reason, in each region of the empire, the Great King was led to continue the tasks of the preceding rulers whom he had conquered. In Babylon he was expected to ensure the proper celebration of the New Year festival (even if it is uncertain that this festival was carried out throughout the Achaemenid period). In Egypt epigraphic sources attest that the burial of the sacred Apis bulls continued uninterrupted under Darius. The Demotic correspondence with the priests of Khnum at Elephantine demonstrates that the satrap of Egypt, Pherendates, in the name of Pharaoh Darius, made a recommendation for the recruitment of a new administrator (*lesonis*) of the sanctuary of Khnum at Elephantine. In the same way, the imposition of Persian power does not imply the disappearance of Egyptian systems of jurisprudence; on the contrary, these systems were unified and thus in a certain way revived under the command of Darius. At the time of Cambyses and Darius, this participation of the conquering kings in the rites and traditions of the pharaohs was facilitated by gaining the support of Egyptian aristocrats, of whom the most well-known is Udjahorresnet, who boasted of having composed the pharaonic titulary of Darius.[56]

---

55. On the statue of Darius and its inscriptions, see J. Yoyotte, "The Egyptian Statue of Darius," in Perrot, *Palace of Darius at Susa*, 241–71; quotation on p. 262.

56. Briant, *From Cyrus to Alexander*, 472–84, 510–11, 956–57; *BHAch* 2:59–60; Kuhrt, *Persian Empire*, 117–27, 852–54.

Between Jerusalem, Elephantine, and Xanthos

As the protector of his faithful subjects, the Great King did not question the existence of local sanctuaries and cultures, except in the case of revolt against the imperial power.[57] At the end of his entry into Babylon in 539 BCE, Cyrus took different measures in favor of Babylonian temples, a fact that is echoed in the famous Cyrus Cylinder and in other cuneiform texts.[58] Moreover, as indicated in Ezra 1:2–4 and 6:2–5, Cyrus authorized the Judeans in Babylon to end their exilic existence created by Nebuchadnezzar and to return to Jerusalem and Judea.[59] Nevertheless, some Judeans remained in Babylon, as is attested in a cuneiform archive originating in the town called al-Yahudu near Borsippa, part of which has recently been published, albeit in incomplete form. At the same time, the former kingdom of Judah became a province (*medinah*), directed by a governor (*peḥah*), within the administration of Eber-Nari, whose satrap resided in Damascus. The government of the *medinah* benefited from a certain amount of autonomy regarding internal affairs, yet it remained under the authority of imperial regulations (such as payment of tribute and taxes).[60]

Apart from the relevant passages in Ezra and Nehemiah, which are still the source of many debates,[61] only a handful of other documents are available that shed light on the day-to-day functioning of the Judean community during the Persian period. Important information comes from the late fifth-century

---

57. See the detailed discussions in *BHAch* 1:94–97; 2:176–87; and now in Briant, *Kings, Countries and Peoples*, chaps. 2–4 with my foreword §3.

58. Briant, *From Cyrus to Alexander*, 43–44.

59. Ibid., 44–49, 487–93; Kuhrt, *Persian Empire*, 70–85.

60. The secondary literature on this topic is extensive. For recent studies, see Laurie Pearce, "New Evidence for Judeans in Babylonia," in *Judah and the Judeans in the Persian Period*, ed. Oded Lipschits and Manfred Oeming (Winona Lake, IN: Eisenbrauns, 2006), 399–411; Gary N. Knoppers and Lester L. Grabbe, eds., *Exile and Restoration Revisited: Essays on the Babylonian and Persian Periods in Memory of Peter R. Ackroyd* (London: T&T Clark, 2009). On the governors of Yehud and Samaria, see André Lemaire, "Administration in Fourth-Century B.C.E. Judah in Light of Epigraphy and Numismatics," in *Judah and the Judeans in the Fourth Century B.C.E.*, ed. Oded Lipschits, Gary Knoppers, and Rainer Albertz (Winona Lake, IN: Eisenbrauns, 2007), 53–74; Hanan Eshel, "The Governors of Samaria in the Fifth and Fourth Centuries B.C.E.," in Lipschits, Knoppers, and Albertz, *Judah and the Judeans in the Fourth Century B.C.E.*, 223–36.

61. Briant, *From Cyrus to Alexander*, 583–87; see thereafter Peter R. Bedford, *Temple Restoration in Early Achaemenid Judah* (Leiden: Brill, 2001); Lester L. Grabbe, *A History of the Jews and Judaism in the Second Temple Period*, vol. 1, *Yehud: A History of the Persian Province of Judah* (London: T&T Clark, 2004); Lipschits and Oeming, *Judah and the Judeans in the Persian Period*, 491–628; Lipschits, Knoppers, and Albertz, *Judah and the Judeans in the Fourth Century B.C.E.*, 237–348; Isaac Kalimi, ed., *New Perspectives on Ezra-Nehemiah: History and Historiography, Text, Literature, and Interpretation* (Winona Lake, IN: Eisenbrauns, 2012).

archives of the Judean community at Elephantine, whose members formed part of the imperial military system, stationed at the garrison of Syene-Elephantine. These documents shed light on the leaders of the community, who, in their letters, claim to be antagonized by Egyptians associated with the temple of Khnum. According to the Judeans, the Egyptians had the support of the governor of the province, Vidranga, and his son Nafaina (who succeeded him as head of the garrison of Syene-Elephantine). The events are only known through the accusations made by the Judeans; the historian must therefore interpret these sources with caution. Rather than a violent ethnic and religious conflict (Egyptians versus Judeans), the conflict was probably juridical, in which the governor made a decision using Egyptian jurisprudence, which Darius had ordered to be "codified" a century earlier.[62]

Whatever the case, three years after the incident, in 407 BCE, the Judeans of Elephantine sent a petition to the governor of Judea, Bagohi, mentioning that they had already written to the high priest and his colleagues in Jerusalem and also to "Delaiah and Shelemiah, the sons of Sanballat, governor of Samaria." As a papyrus from Wadi Daliyeh demonstrates,[63] Samaria was the name of both the fortified city (*bîrah*) and the province (*medinah*). The governor of Judea and the governor of Samaria took joint action in seeking a response from Arshama, the satrap of Egypt. This episode testifies both to the relative autonomy of the governors of Judea and Samaria and to their dependence upon the satrapal powers: although they were considered to be the natural advocates of the Judean diaspora, they could not make a decision on their own initiative; they could only intervene with the satrap in order to represent the interests of the Judeans of Elephantine.

Another document sheds a different light on the intervention of satrapic authorities in the internal affairs of a subject community. It is a trilingual inscription from Xanthos, published in 1979 with extensive commentaries on

---

62. Briant, *From Cyrus to Alexander*, 474, 510–11; *BHAch* 1:95; 2:185. This event has been interpreted in a number of studies, such as Ingo Kottsieper, "Die Religionspolitik der Achämeniden und die Juden von Elephantine," in *Religion und Religionskontakte im Zeitalter der Achämeniden*, ed. Reinhard G. Kratz (Gütersloh: Kaiser, Gütersloher Verlagshaus, 2002), 150–78; Ernst Axel Knauf, "Elephantine und das vor-biblische Judentum," in Kratz, *Religion und Religionskontakte*, 179–88; Reinhard G. Kratz, "The Second Temple of Jeb and of Jerusalem," in Lipschits and Oeming, *Judah and the Judeans in the Persian Period*, 247–64; and Lisbeth S. Fried, *The Priest and the Great King: Temple-Palace Relations in the Persian Empire* (Winona Lake, IN: Eisenbrauns, 2004), 92–106. The documentary evidence is clearly presented in Kuhrt, *Persian Empire*, 829–31, 855–58, and now Briant, *Kings, Countries and Peoples*, chap. 6, with my foreword §4 with nn. 45–46.

63. Briant, *From Cyrus to Alexander*, 714; Douglas M. Gropp, *Wadi Daliyeh II: The Samaria Papyri from Wadi Daliyeh*, DJD 28 (Oxford: Oxford University Press, 2001), 1–116 (Wadi Daliyeh 1).

its Greek, Lycian, and Aramaic versions. During the reign of Artaxerxes (very probably Arses, the successor of Artaxerxes III), the assembly of the city of Xanthos met to decide on the institution of a new cult and the construction of a new sanctuary, as well as the stipulations for the compensation of the priest and the organization of regular sacrifices. These details are explained very clearly in the Lycian and Greek versions, which correspond closely to one another. The Aramaic version (sometimes called the "satrapal version") does not allow for the conclusion that the decision was made at the initiative of (or under the control of) the satrap Pixodaros, who only intervened as a guarantor: if an article of the document were violated, then the transgressor would undergo the punishment of the deities mentioned therein but also that of the satrap.[64]

Persians and Non-Persians

The Achaemenid principle of government was simple: the authority of the Great King was without limits. In reality, however, a significant degree of autonomy was granted to local entities, and collaboration within the power structure was organized between the Persians and Iranians on the one hand and the local aristocrats on the other.[65] Although the highest posts in the empire were reserved for the top elites, the representatives of the local nobility preserved their social and cultural status, as well as their linguistic, religious, and cultural traditions.[66] Even at the center of the empire, in Persia, the Persepolis tablets attest to the existence of multilingualism and of non-Persian cults supported by the royal administration.[67] There were, of course, also other multicultural influences, which resulted from a long period of encounter between cultures as well as from mixed marriages. In the conquered lands, the Persians did not hesitate to show their respects to local divinities. At Sardis, for example, a high official of the satrapy, the Persian Droaphernes, had a statue erected (perhaps of himself) and consecrated it to a Greek—or more probably Lydian—Zeus.[68] In Egypt, Atiyawahy, a Persian who was governor of Coptos between 524 and 473 BCE, had

64. See Briant, *From Cyrus to Alexander*, 706–9; *BHAch* 2:179–82. The texts, with commentary, are found in Kuhrt, *Persian Empire*, 859–63; and now Briant, *Kings, Countries and Peoples*, chap. 3, with my foreword §3 with n. 32.
65. Briant, *From Cyrus to Alexander*, 79–84, 852–71.
66. Ibid., 507–10.
67. Henkelman, *Other Gods Who Are*, 305–84; Jan Tavernier, "Multilingualism in the Fortification and Treasury Archives," in Briant, Henkelman, and Stolper, *L'archive des fortifications de Persépolis*, 59–86.
68. *BHAch* 1:95–96; 2:177–79; Kuhrt, *Persian Empire*, 865–69; and my recent assessment in *Kings, Countries and Peoples*, chap. 2, with my foreword §3 (and nn. 27, 29–31).

a series of hieroglyphic inscriptions carved in the Wadi Hammamat, all of which display his reverence for Egyptian deities; moreover, he proclaims himself to be "son of Artames and of the lady Qandju"; he was thus perhaps the child of an Iranian-Egyptian mixed marriage.[69]

Another remarkable Egyptian document, published in 1995,[70] is a funerary stela discovered at Saqqara, composed in three registers (fig. 11.11). Below an Egyptian winged sun disk, there is a scene displaying the deceased in the Egyptian style, with Isis and Nephthys at the head and foot of the bed and Anubis bringing a cup toward the mouth of the deceased. In the lower register, an individual who is identified as Persian by his clothes and by the furniture (an ornate chair and footstool) holds a lotus blossom in his left hand and lifts up a shallow cup in his right hand (a gesture found on numerous figural representations from the Achaemenid period). A demotic inscription between the second and third registers and a hieroglyphic inscription on the two lateral surfaces of the stela refer to the *ka* of the deceased, who is referred to as "Djedherbes, son of Artam, born of Lady Tanofrether." This is thus a clear attestation of a Persian-Egyptian marriage, in which the individual depicted has an Egyptian name and has adopted a number of Egyptian traditions yet is represented iconographically as Persian.

Figure 11.11. Saqqara stela

Persian Images in the Provinces

The rich Achaemenid iconographic repertoire known from the royal residences at the center of the empire—expressed in sculpture, bas-reliefs, seal impressions, and coins—is also attested in the provinces. The images from the

---

69. Briant, *From Cyrus to Alexander*, 481–84.
70. *BHAch* 1:34–35, 98–99; Kuhrt, *Persian Empire*, 870–71.

center of the empire could be reproduced identically or nearly identically, but they could also be modified and transformed as a result of interaction with local iconographic repertoires. Numerous examples of this phenomenon are found in the seal impressions on the Babylonian tablets and also on Phoenician coins. The lands of western Asia Minor have supplied the richest evidence of this mixed art form, which has too long been considered to be Greco-Persian but is in fact the result of encounters between Persian, Greek, Lycian, Lydian, Carian, and Phrygian traditions.[71]

In northwestern Asia Minor, the satrapy of Phrygia-Hellespont has provided very important corpora of sources.[72] Molded with a seal impression and sometimes bearing an inscription in cuneiform or in Aramaic dating to Xerxes or an Artaxerxes, these small clay objects are the residual testimony to the written archives of the satraps of Daskyleion. Seal impressions from the Phrygian sites of Daskyleion and Seyitömer Höyük bear images originating in Achaemenid traditions, particularly an audience scene (fig. 11.12), but also images in which Persian, Phrygian, and Greek traditions are fused, found especially in depictions of hunting and warfare.[73]

Moreover, a sarcophagus discovered near the village of Çan is remarkable for its raised, sculpted decorations in fairly well-preserved colors.[74] On the longest side, two hunting scenes are represented, separated by a tree. In one

71. On images of power, see Briant, *From Cyrus to Alexander*, 699–700, 704, 710, 712, 714–16, 722–23, 1029–32; *BHAch* 1:98–104; 2:191–206. For Sardis and Lydia, see Elspeth Dusinberre, *Aspects of Empire in Achaemenid Sardis* (Cambridge: Cambridge University Press, 2003), 128–71; Dusinberre, *Empire, Authority and Autonomy in Achaemenid Anatolia* (Cambridge: Cambridge University Press, 2013); Inci Delemen and Olivier Casabonne, eds., *The Achaemenid Impact on Local Populations and Cultures in Anatolia (Sixth–Fourth Centuries B.C.)* (Istanbul: Turkish Institute of Archaeology, 2007); Jens Nieling and Ellen Rehm, eds., *Achaemenid Impact in the Black Sea: Communication of Powers* (Aarhus: Aarhus University Press, 2010); Briant and Chauveau, *Organisation des pouvoirs*; John Boardman, *Persia and the West: An Archaeological Investigation of the Genesis of Achaemenid Art* (New York: Thames & Hudson, 2000), 152–74.
72. T. Bakır, "Dascylium (547–334 B.C.)," *Anadolu* (2012): 1–13. See also Kaan Iren, "A New Discovery in Dascylium: The Persian Destruction Layer," in *Proceedings of the 6th International Congress on the Archaeology of the Ancient Near East*, ed. Paolo Matthiae and Licia Romano, 3 vols. (Wiesbaden: Harrassowitz, 2010), 2:249–63; Deniz Kaptan, *The Daskyleion Bullae: Seal Images from the Western Achaemenid Empire*, 2 vols., AchHist 12 (Leiden: Nederlands Instituut voor het Nabije Oosten, 2002). On the clay objects discussed next, see Deniz Kaptan, "Clay Tags from Seyitömer Höyük in Phrygia," in *The World of Achaemenid Persia: History, Art and Society in Iran and the Ancient Near East*, ed. John Curtis and St John Simpson (London: I. B. Tauris, 2010), 361–68.
73. Briant, *From Cyrus to Alexander*, 699–700; *BHAch* 1:15–17; 2:33–35.
74. See N. Sevinç, M. Körpe, M. Tombul, B. Rose, et al., "A New Painted Graeco-Persian Sarcophagus from Can," *Studia Troica* 11 (2001): 383–420; B. Rose, "The Tombs of the Granicus River," in Delemen and Casabonne, *Achaemenid Impact*, 247–64; see also the drawings and commentary in Kuhrt, *Persian Empire*, 866–67.

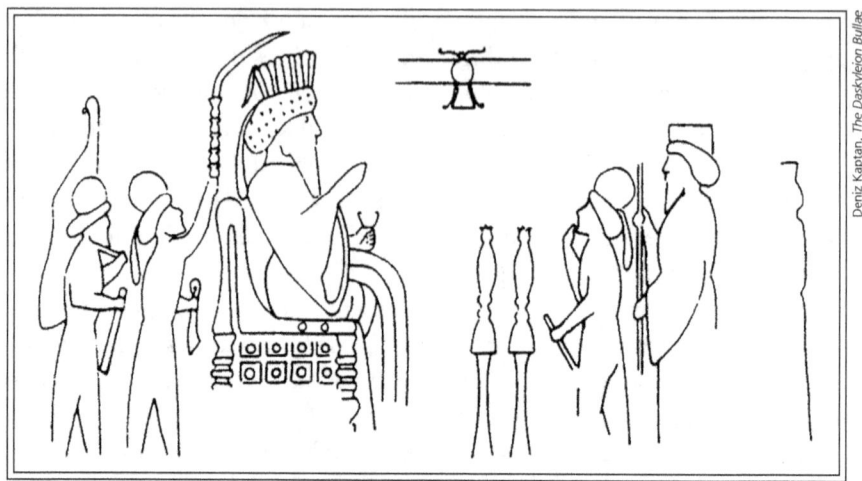

Figure 11.12. Audience scene from Daskyleion

of them, two riders armed with lances chase two stags; in the other, a rider brandishes his lance against a wild boar being attacked by dogs. On the short side is a rider wearing heavy armor, followed by a foot soldier carrying a shield and a sword; the rider points his long lance at a soldier who has been thrown to the ground and who is unarmed except for his shield. These two scenes—hunting and warfare—are very frequently represented on funerary stelae in Asia Minor as well as on seals from Daskyleion, Babylonia, and Persepolis. The ethnicity of the individuals is clearly indicated by their clothes and weapons: the hunters and the warrior are riders who wear distinctive Persian clothes and bear Persian weapons. The author of one of the studies of this sarcophagus draws the following conclusion:

> The boar hunter and the cuirassed rider appear to represent the same man, and the sarcophagus can be read as a biographical narrative highlighting the deceased man's success in the hunt and on the battlefield with the speared-eye motif establishing a link between the two foes, human and animal.[75]

Dated to the last quarter of the fourth century, the sarcophagus attests to the existence of a social class of local (Phrygian) origin that borrowed a number of features from the dominant Persian ethnoclass. The sarcophagus also attests to the existence of a tradition of painting, already known in Lycia at an earlier period through the tombs of Elmalı and Kızılbel, which contain wall paintings of funerary banquet scenes, audience scenes, battle scenes, and

75. Rose, "Tombs of the Granicus River," 255.

scenes of hunting deer, bears, and lions. Not far from these sites, the tomb of Karaburun is no less impressive: probably constructed and decorated at the initiative of a local dynast, the tomb's paintings attest to Persian influence through scenes whose themes are comparable to those of Kızılbel and other Lycian monuments, particularly at Xanthos.[76]

An exceptional discovery was made in another tomb: two painted beams sawed into four pieces that were preserved in a museum in Munich and had been taken from Turkey following illegal excavations and transactions.[77] Archaeologist Lâtife Summerer repatriated and recontextualized the beams in a tomb chamber near Tatarlı (Afyon Province, Turkey) and recovered its painted friezes. This tumulus tomb was pillaged in 1970, and some of its beams were deposited at that time in the nearby museum in Afyon (in the ancient satrapy of Greater Phrygia).[78]

One of the beams bears a combat scene marked by a strong Persian influence. In Summerer's interpretation, the victorious troops march from left to right against the army being conquered. Among the conquerors are seven riders arming their bows against the enemies and a chariot in which an archer, standing near the chariot driver, prepares to release his arrow. Approaching from the right, the enemies also consist of several riders, archers wearing Scythian caps, and foot soldiers. Still more exceptional, at the center of the composition one can see a fight between a Scythian, whose stomach is pierced by a sword, and his opponent, who is bearded and clothed in the Achaemenid royal robe (fig. 11.13). The latter carries a *gorytos* (quiver) and a bow on his back and is shown plunging his short sword into the back of his opponent, whose beard he grasps with his left hand.

His status is confirmed by the royal crown, which he wears on his hair done in a bun. This scene is truly unique in Achaemenid art: on the reliefs of the royal residences and on sealings, the "royal hero" only battles mythical animals, never human enemies. The narrative character of this composition (a memory of a victory by Darius I over the Scythians?) is also without parallel.

The tomb at Tatarlı could have belonged to a Persian of the imperial diaspora or to a member of the Phrygian elite who sought to indicate his privileged relations with the Persian imperial power. In any event, this new

76. Briant, *From Cyrus to Alexander*, 504–5, 955.
77. Ibid., 1008–9.
78. See Lâtife Summerer, "From Tatarlı to Munich: The Recovery of a Painted Wooden Tomb Chamber in Phrygia," in Delemen and Casabonne, *Achaemenid Impact*, 131–58; Summerer, "Wall Paintings," in *Tatarlı: The Return of Colours*, ed. Lâtife Summerer and Alexander von Kienlin (Istanbul: Yapı Kredi Yayınları, 2010), 120–85. For photographs and preliminary drawings, see Briant, *Darius in the Shadow of Alexander*, 200–201.

find is an important element in the long-running debates over the imprint of Persia in the imperial provinces.⁷⁹

Among the iconographic sources from Anatolia, the reliefs discovered at the site of Meydancıkkale are also remarkable (fig. 11.14).⁸⁰ Known by the name of Kiršu during the Neo-Babylonian period, the site was reoccupied during the Achaemenid period and again during the Hellenistic period. Poorly preserved Aramaic inscriptions attest to the Achaemenid phase of the site. Four reused blocks contain iconographic representations that clearly evoke Persepolis. Five individuals in a line walking from right to left (block 2) and from left to right (block 1) wear pleated robes; they are bearded and wear their hair in a bun as well as a tiara. Each of the figures has his right hand raised, holding an object. The third and fourth blocks are very incomplete. This image strongly evokes the files of Persian and Median nobles on the stairs of the *apadana* (audience hall) at Persepolis. It thus seems that the blocks from Meydancıkkale were also part of a procession depicted on the stairs or façade of an official building. This could have been a summer residence of the satrap of Tarsus or the capital of a Cilician dynasty that desired to indicate its loyalty to Achaemenid authority. In any case, this is the only example ever discovered of a Persepolis-type relief in any of the provinces of the empire.

Figure 11.13. Persian king killing an enemy on a painted beam from Tatarlı

The imprint of Persia was expressed not only through coins, inscriptions, painting, and sculpture (stelae); it was sometimes also visible in monumental architecture. This was the case in the Caucasus, where

---

79. Briant, *From Cyrus to Alexander*, 949–55, 995–97, 1007–32.

80. See *BHAch* 1:26–27; 2:47–51, 176–77, 199–200. A drawing of the reliefs is reproduced in ibid., 2:199, and Kuhrt, *Persian Empire*, 837. For a description of the site, see Olivier Casabonne, *La Cilicie à l'époque achéménide* (Paris: de Boccard, 2004), 151–65.

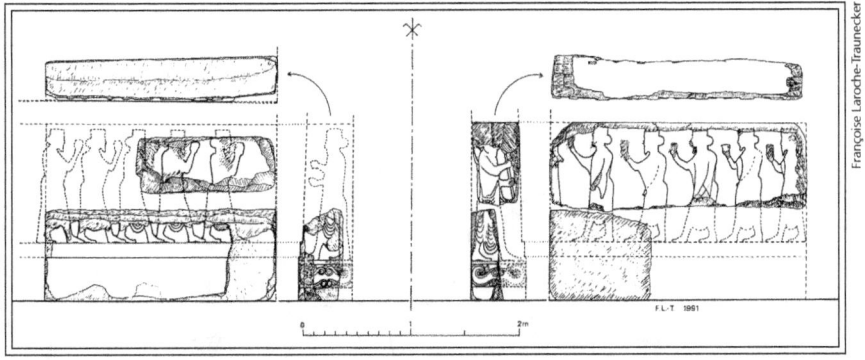

Figure 11.14. Meydancıkkale reliefs

archaeological excavations and surveys have been conducted over the course of the past fifteen years.[81] In 2006–7, a "Persian Propylaion" (columned entrance-gate) built of mud-bricks and extending 22 x 23 meters was discovered at Karacamirli; the measurements of the Achaemenid-type column bases suggest a building at least 5 meters high. All indications suggest that "this monumental structure at Karacamirli had been planned and built by architects and craftsmen who were familiar with Achaemenid architecture." This must have been the residence of a Persian high official of the satrapy. "Karacamirli shows us that, even at the periphery of the empire, Persian rule left its grandiose mark."[82]

The number and quality of iconographic and architectural discoveries of Achaemenid inspiration recently discovered in the provinces of the empire testify both to the presence of a Perso-Iranian diaspora throughout the empire and to the intensity of intercultural relations, as indicated by the existence of mixed marriages. At the same time, written documents, especially the numerous bilingual and trilingual inscriptions from Asia Minor, testify to the persistence of local languages and scripts.[83] The Demotic and hieroglyphic inscriptions carved on the funerary stela of Djeherbes in Memphis also demonstrate that borrowing elements from the Achaemenid iconographic

81. *BHAch* 2:44–46.
82. F. Knauß, I. Gagoshidze, and I. Babaev, "A Persian Propylaion in Azerbaijan: Excavations at Karacamirli," in Nieling and Rehm, *Achaemenid Impact in the Black Sea*, 111–22; Adele Bill, "Achaemenids in the Caucasus?," in Nieling and Rehm, *Achaemenid Impact in the Black Sea*, 15–27; Florian S. Knauß, "Residenzen achämenidischer Beamter und Vasallen," in *Kelainai-Apameia Kibotos: Développement urbain dans le contexte anatolien*, ed. Lâtife Summerer, A. I. Ivantchik, and Alexander von Kienlin (Bordeaux: Ausonius, 2011), 391–410; F. Knauß, I. Gagošidse, and I. Babaev, "Karačamirli, ein persisches Paradies," *ARTA* 2013.004, http://www.achemenet.com/document/ARTA_2013.004-Knauss-Gagosidse-Babaev.pdf.
83. Pierre Briant, "L'Asie mineure en transition," in Briant and Joannès, *La transition*, 322–27.

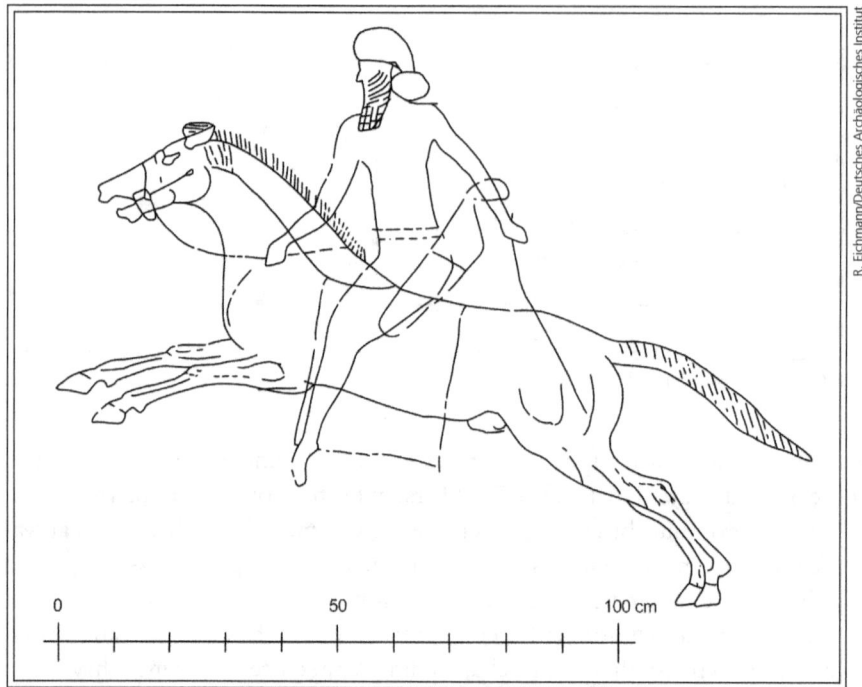

Figure 11.15. Taymā' rider

repertoire could occur while simultaneously affirming one's local identity. In the absence of written evidence, the great diversity of modes of contact often makes the task of determining the ethnic and cultural characteristics of the individual who commissioned a sculpture or a painting very difficult.[84] It is also difficult to determine the political intentions of the local dynasts who borrowed Persian motifs for the coins they struck; they doubtless did so both in order to display their loyalty to Persian authority and in order to

---

84. *BHAch* 1:102–4; 2:200–204. On the question of the extent of the Achaemenid impact, see Dusinberre, *Aspects of Empire*, 196–217; Lâtife Summerer and Alexander von Kienlin, "Achaemenid Impact in Paphlagonia: Rupestral Tombs in the Amnias Valley," in Nieling and Rehm, *Achaemenid Impact in the Black Sea*, 215–16; and Roger Matthews and Claudia Gratz, *At Empire's Edge: Project Paphlagonia; Regional Survey in North-Central Turkey* (London: British Institute at Ankara, 2009). See also the studies collected in Christopher Tuplin, ed., *Persian Responses: Political and Cultural Interaction with(in) the Achaemenid Empire* (Swansea, Wales: Classical Press of Wales, 2007), as well as Tuplin, "Historical Significance of the Tatarlı Tomb Chamber," in Summerer and von Kienlin, *Tatarlı*, 187–95; see now my recent new assessment: "À propos de l'"empreinte achéménide' (*Achaemenid impact*) en Anatolie (Notes de lecture)," in *Zwischen Satrapen und Dynasten: Kleinasien im 4. Jahrhundert v. Chr.*, ed. Engelbert Winter and Klaus Zimmerman, Asia Minor Studien 76 (Bonn: Habelt, 2015), 175–93.

justify their leadership in their own societies.[85] In certain cases, the existence of congruent images in several regions or corpora does not necessarily imply the borrowing of Achaemenid traditions.[86] Moreover, the presence of Perso-Iranian images at some sites is not necessarily an indication of Achaemenid hegemony, as the beautiful image of a Perso-Iranian rider in a cave engraving near Taymā' in Arabia demonstrates (fig. 11.15).[87]

5. The End of the Empire

The Persian defeats in three pitched battles (334–331 BCE), the death of Darius (330 BCE), and the conquest of the entire empire by the army of Alexander the Great have often led observers to suppose that the Persian Empire had entered into irreversible decadence and thus was unable to fight back in an organized manner. Moreover, the "enthusiastic" welcome that the various populations of the empire gave to the "liberator," Alexander, proved that Achaemenid power had become odious to its Egyptian or Babylonian subjects. This thesis, born and diffused primarily in eighteenth-century European historiography, was modeled on images and representations created and transmitted by the Greek and Latin authors who treated the "deeds of Alexander." In modern Europe, these images were articulated by way of analogy between the "declining" Persian Empire and the "decadent" Ottoman Empire. This thesis colored the dominant view of the Achaemenid period, which saw this period as part of the motionless history of a despotic and backward East. This thesis was logically connected to the "Orientalist" postulate (in the sense of Edward Said) that desired to see Alexander the Great—the first European conqueror of Asia—as a harbinger of progress. For example, it is claimed that Alexander was the first to impose complete domination over

---

85. Briant, *From Cyrus to Alexander*, 714–16; *BHAch* 2:76. See also Josette Elayi, *Le monnayage de la cité phénicienne de Sidon à l'époque perse (V^e–IVe s. av. J.-C.)* (Paris: Gabalda, 2004), 493–525; Haim Gitler, "Identities of the Indigenous Coinages of Palestine under Achaemenid Rule: The Dissemination of the Image of the Great King," in Iossif, Chankowski, and Lorber, *More Than Men, Less Than Gods*, 105–20; Koray Konuk, "Influences et éléments achéménides dans le monnayage de la Carie," in *Mécanismes et innovations monétaires dans l'Anatolie achéménide*, ed. Olivier Casabonne (Paris: de Boccard, 2000), 171–83; and Deniz Kaptan, "Common Traits on Seals and Coins of the Achaemenid Period in an Anatolian Context," in Casabonne, *Mécanismes et innovations monétaires*, 213–23.

86. For the iconography of the gardener-king, see Pierre Briant, "On the King as Gardener: Observations on the History of a Set of Documents," in Briant, *Kings, Countries and Peoples*, chap. 11, with my foreword §5 and nn. 64–65.

87. Bruno Jacobs and M. C. A. Macdonald, "Felszeichnung eines Reiters aus der Umgebung von Taymā'," *Zeitschrift für Orient-Archäologie* 2 (2009): 364–76; these authors date the engraving between 550 and 520 BCE.

populations that, although near the center of power of the Great King (in the Zagros Mountains and the Persian Gulf), had always refused to recognize Achaemenid rule, to the point of posing a permanent threat to Susa and Persepolis. The "backward" nature of Achaemenid power was also indicated by the phenomenon of royal hoarding, which was seen as contrary to the free circulation of money and merchandise. By placing Achaemenid hoards in circulation, Alexander restored life to regions and populations that had not previously known monetary circulation or large-scale trade. Alexander was also the first to open the route to India and to stipulate that products from India be redistributed throughout the entire Mediterranean region from the port of Alexandria in Egypt.[88]

In reality, none of the arguments that have been advanced are tenable in light of the considerable progress made in Achaemenid history and archaeology during the last thirty years.[89] Moreover, while there were certainly revolts throughout Achaemenid history, none of the conquered lands (with the exception of Egypt) escaped imperial hegemony on a lasting basis. At the time of Alexander's arrival, Darius's power extended from the Indus valley to the Mediterranean and from the Syr Darya River in central Asia to Syene-Elephantine in Upper Egypt, and Alexander's itinerary followed the outline of the imperial borders very precisely. The difficulties of coexistence between different populations (such as at Elephantine) should neither be denied nor exaggerated. At the time of Alexander, the various peoples within the empire were not united in a shared and irrepressible hatred against the Persians. At the centers of power, dynastic conflicts and court intrigues did not endanger the continuity of the Achaemenid dynastic stock: from Darius I to Darius III, the same family (broadly speaking) succeeded to the throne of the Great Kings. The Persian nobility that constituted the backbone of the empire also remained generally faithful to Darius, at least until the capture of Persepolis.

---

88. On the subject of Persian decline, see Pierre Briant, "History and Ideology: The Greeks and 'Persian Decadence,'" in *Greeks and Barbarians*, ed. Thomas Harrison (New York: Routledge, 2002), 193–210; Briant, *Darius in the Shadow of Alexander*; Briant, "Empire of Darius III," 141–70; Briant, "Alexander and the Persian Empire between 'Decline' and 'Renovation': History and Historiography," in Heckel and Trittle, *Alexander the Great*, 171–88; Briant, "The Theme of 'Persian Decadence' in Eighteenth-Century European Historiography: Remarks on the Genesis of a Myth," in Curtis and Simpson, *World of Achaemenid Persia*, 3–15; see also Josef Wiesehöfer, "The Achaemenid Empire in the Fourth Century B.C.E.: A Period of Decline?," in Lipschits, Knoppers, and Albertz, *Judah and the Judeans in the Fourth Century B.C.E.*, 11–32. On the analogy between the Persian Empire and the Ottoman Empire, see Pierre Briant, *Alexandre des lumières: Fragments d'histoire européenne* (Paris: Gallimard, 2012), 513–66.

89. Briant, *From Cyrus to Alexander*, 693–876; Kuhrt, *Persian Empire*, 418–63.

These observations do not signify that the empire was immune to political crises; they simply reveal that the accession of Darius III did not mark the beginning or the continuation of a period of anarchy and disorder that Alexander would have used to his advantage. Nor is there any indication that the empire was in an "economic crisis" (assuming that such a term is even relevant in describing an empire in antiquity that was so varied and diverse).[90] Without denying the importance of the minting of coins under Alexander and his successors, it should be kept in mind that the circulation of coinage was widespread in the western regions of the empire, from the Black Sea to Phoenicia and Palestine. Moreover, in the regions where coins did not circulate or did so only to a limited extent (Egypt, Babylon, and Iran), other modes of exchange (such as bullion) allowed for a rapid development in trade. The surpluses in kind were used as food rations distributed to workers, soldiers, and traveling officials. A portion of these surpluses was sold in the large trade centers in Babylonia; another portion was sold by the satraps of Asia Minor on the Aegean market. This practice in turn led to the development of large-scale trade of food products in the Aegean world, beginning especially in the middle of the fourth century BCE. The Achaemenid Empire was not reduced to a barter economy, nor was it irreparably impoverished by the levies (which were not insignificant) imposed from the center of the empire.[91] In short, in 334 BCE Darius's empire was not a feeble entity ready to give up without a fight, nor was it a "giant with feet of clay" on the point of collapsing under its own weight.

For Further Reading

Álvarez-Mon, Javier, and Mark B. Garrison, eds. *Elam and Persia*. Winona Lake, IN: Eisenbrauns, 2011.

Briant, Pierre. "Bulletin d'histoire achéménide (*BHAch*) I." In *Recherches récentes sur l'empire achéménide*, Topoi Supplément 1, edited by J. Andreau, M.-F. Boussac et al., 5–125. Lyon: Topoi; Paris: de Boccard, 1997.

———. *Bulletin d'histoire achéménide II*. Persika 1. Paris: Thotm éditions, 2001.

———. *From Cyrus to Alexander: A History of the Persian Empire*. Translated by Peter T. Daniels. Winona Lake, IN: Eisenbrauns, 2002.

90. Briant, *From Cyrus to Alexander*, 800–813.
91. Ibid. An innovative analysis is found in Raymond Descat, "L'économie du monde égéen," in Briant and Joannès, *La transition*, 353–73.

———. *Kings, Countries and Peoples*. Translated by Amélie Kuhrt. OeO. Stuttgart: Steiner Verlag, forthcoming.

Briant, Pierre, and Rémy Boucharlat, eds. *L'archéologie de l'empire achéménide: Nouvelles recherches*. Persika 6. Paris: de Boccard, 2005.

Briant, Pierre, and Michel Chauveau, eds. *Organisation des pouvoirs et contacts culturels dans les pays de l'empire achéménide*. Persika 14. Paris: de Boccard, 2009.

Briant, Pierre, Wouter Henkelman, and Matthew W. Stolper, eds. *L'archive des fortifications de Persépolis: État des questions et perspectives de recherches*. Persika 12. Paris: de Boccard, 2008.

Briant, Pierre, and Francis Joannès, eds. *La transition entre l'empire achéménide et les royaumes hellénistiques*. Persika 9. Paris: de Boccard, 2006.

Curtis, John, and St John Simpson, eds. *The World of Achaemenid Persia: History, Art and Society in Iran and the Ancient Near East*. London: I. B. Tauris, 2010.

Curtis, John, and Nigel Tallis, eds. *Forgotten Empire: The World of Ancient Persia*. London: British Museum Press, 2005.

Jacobs, Bruno, and Robert Rollinger, eds. *Der Achämenidenhof / The Achaemenid Court: Akten des 2. Internationalen Kolloquiums zum Thema "Vorderasien im Spannungsfeld klassischer und altorientalischer Überlieferungen," Landgut Castelen bei Basel, 23–25. Mai 2007*. Classica et Orientalia 2. Wiesbaden: Harrassowitz, 2010.

Kellens, Jean, ed. *La religion iranienne à l'époque achéménide*. Iranica antiqua Suppléments 5. Ghent: Iranica antiqua, 1991.

Kuhrt, Amélie. "The Achaemenid Persian Empire (c. 550–c. 330 B.C.E.): Continuities, Adaptations, Transformations." In *Empires: Perspectives from Archaeology and History*, edited by S. E. Alcock, T. N. d'Altroy, K. D. Morrison, and C. M. Sinopoli, 93–123. Cambridge: Cambridge University Press, 2001.

———. *The Persian Empire: A Corpus of Sources from the Achaemenid Period*. London: Routledge, 2010.

Lincoln, Bruce. *"Happiness for Mankind": Achaemenian Religion and the Imperial Project*. Acta Iranica 53. Leuven: Peeters, 2012.

Perrot, Jean, ed. *The Palace of Darius at Susa: The Great Royal Residence of Achaemenid Persia*. Translated by Gérard Collon. Translation edited by Dominique Collon. London: I. B. Tauris, 2013.

Porten, Bezalel, and Ada Yardeni. *Textbook of Aramaic Documents from Ancient Egypt*. 4 vols. Winona Lake, IN: Eisenbrauns, 1986–99.

Rollinger, Robert, Brigitte Truschnegg, and Reinhold Bichler, eds. *Herodot und das persische Weltreich/Herodotus and the Persian Empire*. Classica et Orientalia 2. Wiesbaden: Harrassowitz, 2011.

Tuplin, Christopher, ed. *Persian Responses: Political and Cultural Interaction with(in) the Achaemenid Empire*. Swansea, Wales: Classical Press of Wales, 2007.

12

Arabia and the Arabians

David F. Graf

The ethnic designation "Arab" and the geographical term "Arabia" have a confusing ancestry and legacy in the pre-Islamic era. After the Islamic conquests, "Arabia" simply designated the vast Arabian Peninsula (the *Jazīrat al-'arab* or "Island of Arabs") and "Arabs" were speakers of Arabic (the *lisān al-'arab* or "language of the Arabs"). The pre-Islamic world presents a much more complex picture.

The first reference to the ethnic term "Arab" is in 853 BCE, when "Gindibu (from the) land of Arabia" (^M^*Gi-in-di-bu-*' ^KUR^*Ar-ba-a-a*), with his one hundred camels, is mentioned as a participant in an anti-Assyrian coalition against Shalmaneser III in the battle of Qarqar on the upper Euphrates in Syria.[1] His locale and further details are lacking, but his territory generally is regarded to be in the Syro-Arabian desert. In subsequent periods, the term "Arab" was used for peoples who resided outside the Peninsula, including

---

1. A. Kirk Grayson, *Assyrian Rulers of the Early First Millennium BC*, vol. 2, 858–745 BC, RIMA 3 (Toronto: University of Toronto Press, 1996), no. 2, ii 94. For discussion see Israel Eph'al, *The Ancient Arabs: Nomads on the Borders of the Fertile Crescent, 9th–5th Centuries B.C.* (Jerusalem: The Hebrew University Press; Leiden: Brill, 1982), 75–76.

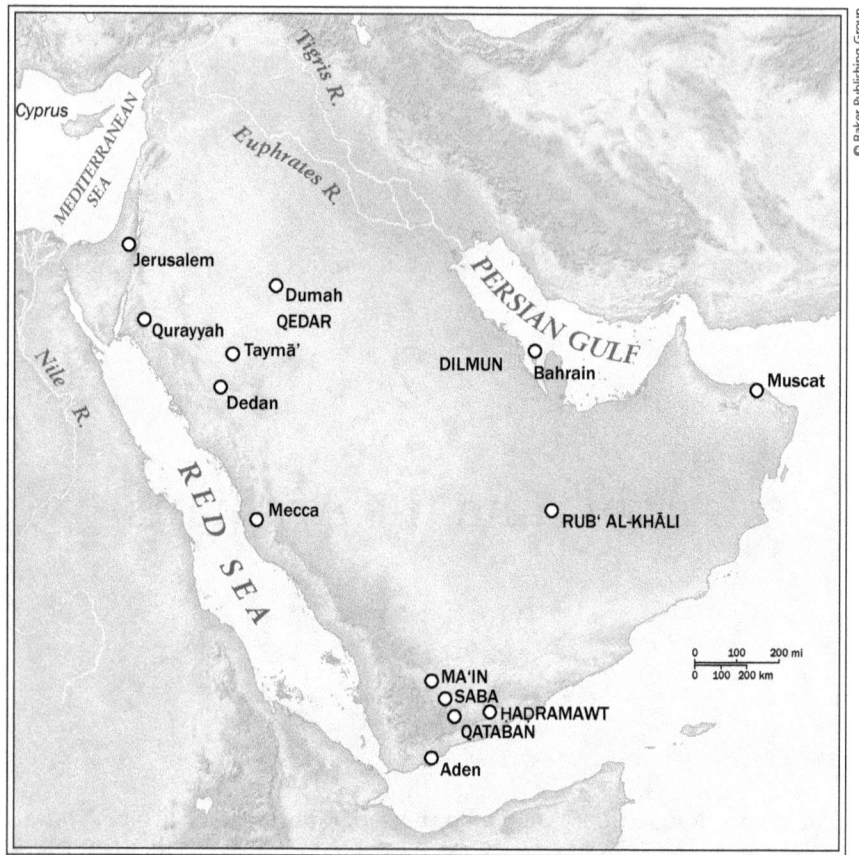

Figure 12.1. Arabia

Egypt, Palestine, Transjordan, Syria, Mesopotamia, and even Western Iran.[2] These "Arabs" appear to represent emigrants from the Arabian Peninsula, virtually an Arab diaspora, who in all likelihood spoke a variety of Semitic languages, not just Arabic. The term "Arab" also is generally interpreted to designate "nomads," whenever and wherever it appears in ancient sources of the Near East, referring both to peoples living in and outside the Arabian Peninsula, who are perceived as the counterparts of modern bedouin in spite of the fact that many Arabs dwelled in urban centers located in fertile

---

2. For Egypt, see Willy Clarysse and Dorothy Thompson, *Counting the People in Hellenistic Egypt*, vol. 2, *Historical Studies* (Cambridge: Cambridge University Press, 2006), 159–61. For Syria-Palestine, see below. For Iran, see Wouter F. M. Henkelman and Matthew W. Stolper, "Ethnic Identity and Ethnic Labeling at Persepolis: The Case of the Skudrians," in *Organisation des pouvoirs et contacts culturels dans les pays de l'empire achéménide*, ed. Pierre Briant and Michel Chauveau, Persika 14 (Paris: de Boccard, 2009), 300.

oases.³ In fact, the term "Arab" in antiquity frequently designates people of various sedentary lifestyles, not just "nomads." In the region of the Fertile Crescent, sedentarized Arabs are already established along the desert fringe in the eighth century BCE. For example, Neo-Assyrian administrative correspondence during the reign of the Neo-Assyrian king Sargon II (722–705 BCE) depicts Arabs as a troublesome community in the middle Euphrates and Tigris regions, but at least by Sennecherib's reign (705–681 BCE), they are living in towns on the western border of Babylonia.⁴ The attempt to narrow the definition of "Arab" to a particular social group or lifestyle without any ethnic connotations has been unsuccessful, as there remains a gnawing suspicion that the term "Arab" was at least initially a self-designation based on a "complex of language and culture."⁵ It is in this sense that the term "Arab" is employed in what follows.

In regard to the geographical term "Arabia," it seems clear from cuneiform texts of the Neo-Assyrian and Neo-Babylonian eras that the "land of the Arabs" refers both to the Syro-Arabian desert and the Arabian Peninsula. Tiglath-pileser's Arabian campaign in 732 BCE is against the Qedarite Arab center of Dumah in North Arabia, but Sargon II's Arabian campaign was definitely into the northwest Arabian Peninsula (^KUR^*Ar-ba-a-a*).⁶ In Nebuchadnezzar's campaign against the Arabs in 599/8 BCE, the "land of the Arabs" (^KUR^*A-ra-bi*) probably refers again to the Syro-Arabian desert.⁷ But in the Harran inscriptions describing Nabonidus's Arabian campaign in ca. 552 BCE, "land of Arabia" (*māt a-ra-bi*) refers clearly to the northwest region of the Arabian Peninsula.⁸ In the case of the Arabs mentioned at Persepolis in Iran, they probably were mainly from the Achaemenid satrapy of Makā

---

3. See T. Nöldeke, "Arabia, Arabians," *Encyclopaedia Biblica*, vol. 1 (London: Adam and Charles Black, 1899), 272–73, followed by Ephʻal, *Ancient Arabs*, 5–11, who designate the Arabs as "nomads" and "desert-dwellers," citing Isa. 13:20 and Jer. 3:2. The view is now outdated.

4. Ephʻal, *Ancient Arabs*, 59 = ABL 88 and 547 = Simo Parpola, ed., *The Correspondence of Sargon II*, vol. 1, *Letters from Assyria and the West*, SAA 1 (Helsinki: University of Helsinki Press, 1987), nos. 82 and 84.

5. M. C. A. Macdonald, "Arabs, Arabias, and Arabic before Late Antiquity," *Topoi* 16 (2009): 319. For a rather learned but idiosyncratic thesis, see Jan Retsö, *The Arabs in Antiquity: Their History from the Assyrians to the Umayyads* (London: Routledge, 2003), who argues that "Arab" designates a militant community under the banner of a divine hero, based on the domestication of the camel.

6. The occurrences in cuneiform are listed in Ephʻal, *Ancient Arabs*, 6; and for Tiglath-pileser III and Sargon II's Arab campaigns, see ibid., 36, where the toponyms and ethnic groups mentioned in the account clearly designate the northwest part of the Arabian Peninsula.

7. Ephʻal, *Ancient Arabs*, 171–75, citing Jer. 49:28–33.

8. C. J. Gadd, "The Harran Inscriptions of Nabonidus," *AnSt* 8 (1958): 58 (H 2, A 43 and 45). The entry on *mātu* in CAD 10, pt. 2:414–21, is organized according to "country (as a political unit), open country, home country, population of a country." Cf. *AHw*, 633–34.

(Oman) and East Arabia—that is, from the Arabian Peninsula.[9] Finally, in a fragment of a cuneiform chronicle related to Alexander the Great's anticipated Arabian expedition, Babylonian scribes indicate Macedonian troops had been dispersed to the "land of Arabia" (^{KUR}*A-ra-bi*[. . .]), ostensibly as an exploratory mission preparing for the campaign.[10] By the time of the Hellenistic kingdoms and Roman Empire, "Arabia" as the homeland of the Arabs is well established. Nevertheless, it is not clear how the inhabitants of the Arabian Peninsula designated themselves, as "Arab" is a designation used by the populations of the Fertile Crescent, not by the indigenous population.

The exception is in the Incense Kingdoms of South Arabia (modern Yemen), where the term "Arab" first appears at the beginning of the seventh century BCE in a temple dedication at Wadi ash-Shaqab near Baraqish in Jawf in Yemen, in which the community is divided into "farmers" (*gbr*) and "nomads" (*'rb*).[11] Afterward, there is a long hiatus before the term "Arab" appears again in the second and/or first centuries BCE. The designation then usually refers to the "bedouin" tribes north of Yemen, namely, the tribes of Qaḥtān, Madhḥij, and the Kinda kingdom at Qaryat al-Faw, some 280 kilometers northeast of Najran on the western edge of the Rubʿ al-Khāli or Empty Quarter. These tribes not only were designated "Arabs" but were also speakers of Arabic. In the several dozen references to "Arabs" in South Arabian inscriptions, the expression "country of *'rb*" seems always to designate the "country of the nomads."

As these texts indicate, outside of the scattered oases, there was a large population of nomads. Arabia is dominated by deserts: only approximately one-fifth of the Peninsula was actually habitable in antiquity, primarily in the Ḥijāz Mountains of the west and the Yemeni highlands in the southwest, and a few other oases scattered mostly on the edges of the Peninsula. The rest of the Peninsula is mainly desert: in addition to the Syro-Arabian Desert (*Hamad*) in the north, there is the Great Nafud Desert in the northeast, the vast sand desert called the Rubʿ al-Khāli or Empty Quarter in the southwest, and the Ḥisma Desert in the northwest. Even the central highlands, which are

---

9. François de Blois, "Maka and Mazūn," *Studia Iranica* 18 (1989): 157–67, citing PFa 17 and 29.

10. Robartus J. van der Spek, "Darius III, Alexander the Great and Babylonian Scholarship," in *A Persian Perspective: Essays in Memory of Heleen Sancisi-Weerdenburg*, AchHist 13, ed. Wouter Henkelman and Amélie Kuhrt (Leiden: Nederlaands Instituut voor het Nabije Oosten, 2003), 310–11 = BM 41080 (unpublished).

11. Christian Robin, "Le pénétration des Arabes nomades au Yémen," *Revue du monde musulman et de la Méditerranée* 61 (1991): 71–88, esp. 72–77. See also Alessandro de Maigret, "The Arab Nomadic People and the Cultural Interface between the 'Fertile Crescent' and 'Arabia Felix,'" *AAE* 10 (1998): 220–24.

called the Najd (Upland), are a vast flat open steppe slanting downward from the Ḥijāz Mountains in the west toward the Persian Gulf in the east. This is the realm of the bedouin or nomadic pastoralists, a population difficult to trace in the absence of any material cultural remains—that is, no permanent architecture—and virtual absence in the historical record. As a consequence, our focus on Arabia must be on a number of important urban settlements on the fringes of the vast steppe that emerged primarily in the first millennium BCE, although both in the northwest of Saudi Arabia and in southwest Yemen there were important earlier cultural predecessors. It is these urban centers or oases that drew the attention of the Mesopotamian and Levantine societies. In northwest Arabia these were the oases of Qurayyah (the capital of "Midian"), Dumah, Taymā', and Dedan. In Yemen, these were the large urban communities of agriculturalists in the third and second millennia BCE, who settled in the valleys east of the Yemeni highlands, in areas nourished by the monsoon rains. In the first millennium, the famous Incense Kingdoms of South Arabia emerged. As a result, in the Hellenistic and Roman eras, Southern Arabia was known as "Arabia Felix." In Strabo, the name *Arabia Eudaimōn* is explicitly connected with that part of the country that produces incense (*arōmatios*) (*Geography* 1.2.32). These urban settlements in North and South Arabia interacted with the larger Near Eastern world and therefore will be the focus for what follows.

1. Overview of Arabian History and Culture

The Arabian urban societies were highly complex and literate, as attested by thousands of inscriptions. The various scripts and languages of Arabia are normally categorized into North and South Arabian, but neither category is homogeneous. The Ancient North Arabian inscriptions are organized according to the three major oases in northwest Arabia: Taymanitic after Taymā', Dadanitic after Dedan (or Al-'Ulā), and Dumaitic after Dumah in Jawf.[12] In addition, there is what has been called the "Dispersed Oasis North Arabian" inscriptions, previously inappropriately designated as "Thamudic," which appear from Syria throughout Transjordan and the Ḥijāz. They represent

12. M. C. A. Macdonald, "Reflections on the Linguistic Map of Pre-Islamic Arabia," *AAE* 11 (2000): 28–79, and n. 1. The name "Dadan" appears in cuneiform sources and the LXX instead of biblical "Dedan"; see Alexander Sima, "Zum antiken Namen Dedan," *BN* 104 (2000): 42–47. As a result, the term "Dadanitic" has replaced "Dedanite" and "Dadan" (biblical "Dedan"). See M. C. A. Macdonald, "Ancient North Arabian," in *The Cambridge Encyclopedia of the World's Ancient Languages*, ed. Roger D. Woodward (Cambridge: Cambridge University Press, 2004), 488–533.

the dissemination of the urban scripts into the adjoining desert population. The so-called Chaldean inscriptions found in Mesopotamia, which are perhaps a product of Arabian settlers in the region, are related to the scripts in North and South Arabia. Another category is Ḥasitic, referring to inscriptions found in the coastal areas of northeast Arabia, which appear similar in script to monumental South Arabian (dedications of buildings and so forth) but are generally dated to the Hellenistic era. In regard to date, Taymanitic is assigned as early as the sixth century BCE but may be earlier. The corpus is now about four hundred texts, but most are brief graffiti. In contrast, many Dedanic inscriptions comprise monumental lengthier texts and are generally dated from the sixth century to the first century BCE. They are also more numerous than Taymanitic texts. Dumaitic is attested by only three texts and may be of a similar earlier date, but the corpus is too small to determine either their character or chronology.

The ancient South Arabian texts are lengthier and more monumental in nature than North Arabian. With the discovery of sticks inscribed in South Arabia, the corpus now well exceeds over seventeen thousand texts.[13] They represent the southern branch of the Semitic languages and are comprised of four dialects: Sabaic, Minaic, Qatabanic, and Ḥaḍramatic, which are named after the four Incense Kingdoms of southwest Arabia of the first millennium BCE.[14] These inscriptions perhaps date as early as 1100–1000 BCE. The Sabaic inscriptions increase dramatically beginning in the eighth century BCE and are mainly written in boustrophedon style until the fourth century BCE. There are archaic inscriptions found in the Wadi Madhāb northwest of Mārib that are as early as Sabaic, but represent a local phenomenon and are called "Madhabic," as linguistically they are not Sabaic. They disappear as Minaean culture becomes dominant in the region.[15] Southeast of Mārib is the Qatabanian capital of Timnaʿ where the Qatabanic dialect was dominant. Further to the east is the kingdom of Ḥaḍramawt and its capital at Shabwa, the home of

---

13. For the older texts, see C. Robin, *Inventaire des inscriptions sudarabiques*, 7 vols. (Paris: de Boccard; Rome: Herder, 1992–2007). For the sticks, see Peter Stein, *Die altsüdarabischen Minuskelinschriften auf Holzstäbchen aus der Bayerischen Staatsbibliothek in München*, vol. 1, *Die Inschriften der mittel- und spätsabäischen Periode*, EFAH 5 (Tübingen: Wasmuth, 2010). A future volume will publish the Old Sabaic texts from the first millennium BCE. The corpus exceeds 7,000 texts.

14. For a concise but informative overview with bibliography, see Norbert Nebes and Peter Stein, "Ancient South Arabian," in Woodward, *Cambridge Encyclopedia of the World's Ancient Languages*, 454–87. More recent discussion of Sabaic is provide by Peter Stein, "Materialien zur sabäischen Dialektologie: Das Problem des amiritischen ("haramitischen") Dialektes," *ZDMG* 157 (2007): 13–47.

15. Alessandra Avanzini, "Saba' and the Beginning of Epigraphic Documentation of the Jawf," *AAE* 7 (1996): 63–68.

the Ḥaḍramatic dialect, and where the incense route began. The Qatabanic, Minaic, and Ḥaḍramatic inscriptions increase dramatically after the middle of the first millennium BCE, until the Sabaeans lost their dominance over South Arabia. Since the Incense Kingdoms are all located in the valleys on the eastern edges of the Yemeni highlands that lead to the Ramlat as-Sabʿatayn on the edge of the Rubʿ al-Khālī, or the Ṣayhed Desert of medieval Yemeni geographers, some prefer to call the South Arabian languages "Ṣayhadic," but most prefer to designate the languages as simply "South Arabian." The dialects disappear with the collapse of the old South Arabian kingdoms, Minaic by the second century BCE, Qatabanic in the second century CE, and Ḥaḍramatic in the third century CE. In contrast, Sabaic texts last until the mid-sixth century CE, surviving for more than 1,400 years.

All the South Arabian inscriptions are written in an alphabet with twenty-nine letters, as opposed to the West Semitic Phoenician and Hebrew alphabet of twenty-two letters. North Arabian has twenty-eight phonemes, but appears related to South Arabian. It is now believed that the Semitic consonantal alphabet was invented in the first half of the second millennium BCE, probably first in northern Egypt and spreading from there to the Levant, where at least in Egypt and Ugarit it consisted of thirty phonemes.[16] By the middle of the millennium, several different traditions developed from the protoalphabet, one maintaining the longer system of twenty-seven to thirty phonemes and a reduced version of twenty-two letters. The two systems also differed in letter order. The shorter version followed the ʾbgd system and the longer version this order and the hlḥmq alphabetical order. The latter is now known from Beth-Shemesh in Palestine before 1200 BCE, and at Ugarit (Ras Shamra) before 1300 BCE, where it existed with other systems of alphabetic orders.[17] In South Arabia, the hlḥmq order is known from abecedaries at Saba and Qataban, as well as in North Arabia at Dedan.[18] Just when and how Arabia

---

16. See André Lemaire, "The Spread of Alphabetic Scripts (c. 1700–500 BCE)," *Diogenes* 218 (2008): 45–58; Dennis Pardee, "The Ugaritic Cuneiform Writing System in the Context of Other Alphabetic Systems," in *Studies in Semitic and Afroasiatic Linguistics Presented to Gene B. Gragg*, ed. Cynthia L. Miller, OIP 60 (Chicago: Oriental Institute of the University of Chicago, 2007), 181–200; and John Ray, "The Alphabet That Never Was: A Possible Egyptian Influence on the Near East," in *Judah between East and West: The Transition from Persian to Greek Rule (ca. 400–200 BCE)*, ed. Lester L. Grabbe and Oded Lipschits (London: T&T Clark, 2011), 199–209.

17. A. G. Lundlin, "L'abécédaire de Beth Shemesh," *Le Muséon* 100 (1987): 243–50; and P. Bordreuil and Dennis Pardee, "Textes alphabétiques en ougaritique," in *Études ougaritiques*, vol. 1, *Travaux 1985–1995*, ed. Marguerite Yon and Daniel Arnaud, RSO 14 (Paris: Éditions Recherche sur les Civilisations, 2001), 341–48.

18. Saba: F. Bron and C. Robin, "Nouvelles données sur l'ordre de letteres de l'alphabet," *Sem* 24 (1974): 77–82, and Stein, *Die altsüdarabischen Minuskelinschriften*, 1:591 (X.BSB 181);

developed the *hlḥmq* alphabetical order remains controversial, with theories of a migration from the north or contact between Arabians and the Levant offered as explanations.[19] As will be discussed later, there is now good evidence for South Arabian inscriptions as early as 1000 BCE.

During the first millennium, South Arabia emerged as a commercial power as a result of the production of frankincense and myrrh in the region, which were transported by camel caravans to the Levant and Mesopotamia.[20] Frankincense was produced primarily in Dhofar and Ḥaḍramawt, and myrrh in the southern and western parts of Yemen.[21] The impact of the trade is indicated by the small cuboid incense burners that begin to appear in the Fertile Crescent during the seventh century BCE, and with great increase in the Neo-Babylonian, Persian, and Hellenistic periods, especially in central and southern Mesopotamia and southern Palestine, although there are antecedents in the middle of the second millennium at sites in the middle Euphrates.[22] In addition, the precursor of the small cuboid incense burner may be the tall conical altar found in an eighth-century BCE context in the Moabite sanctuary at Khirbet al-Mudayna in Transjordan, inscribed as an "incense altar (*mqṭr*)" made for a female recipient.[23] The same term *mqṭr* is used for incense altars in South Arabia.[24] Frankincense was sacred to the gods and used in temples,

---

A. K. Irvine and A. F. L. Beeston, "New Evidence on the Qatabanian Letter Order," *PSAS* 18 (1988): 35–38; Dedan: W. W. Müller, "Some Remarks on the Safaitic Inscriptions," *PSAS* 10 (1980): 70; M. C. A. Macdonald, "ABCs and Letter Order in Ancient North Arabian," *PSAS* 16 (1986): 112–13.

19. For various proposals see Ernst Axel Knauf, "The Migration of the Script and the Formation of the State in South Arabia," *PSAS* 19 (1989): 79–90; Hani Hayajneh and Josef Tropper, "Die Genese des altsüdarabischen Alphabets," *UF* 29 (1997): 183–98; Benjamin Sass, *The Alphabet at the Turn of the Millennium* (Tel Aviv: Tel Aviv University, 2005), 116–32; Alessandra Avazini, "Origin and Classification of the Ancient South Arabian Languages," *JSS* 54 (2009): 205–20.

20. Caroline Singer, "The Incense Kingdoms of Yemen: An Outline History of the South Arabian Incense Trade," in *Food for the Gods: New Light on the Ancient Incense Trade*, ed. David Peacock and David Williams (Oxford: Oxbow, 2007), 4–27.

21. Nigel Groom, *Frankincense and Myrrh: A Study of the Arabian Incense Trade* (London: Longman, 1981), 96–120.

22. Michael O'Dwyer Shea, "The Small Cuboid Incense-Burner of the Ancient Near East," *Levant* 15 (1983): 76–109; and A. R. Millard, "The Small Cuboid Incense-Burners: A Note on Their Age," *Levant* 16 (1984): 172–73. For Mesopotamia, see Antonio Invernizzi, "Near-Eastern Incense-Burners and Pyraeums (I Millennium B.C.–I Millennium A.D.)," *Al-Rāfidān* 18 (1997): 241–61.

23. Michelle Daviau and Margaret Steiner, "A Moabite Sanctuary at Khirbet al-Mudayna," *BASOR* 320 (2000): 10–14; and P. E. Dion and M. Daviau, "An Inscribed Incense Altar of Iron Age II at Ḥirbet el-Mudēyine (Jordan)," *ZDPV* 116 (2000): 1–13.

24. *CIS* IV 338/9, *RES* 4230 A, 1; and Ja 696 and 697 from Mārib. For abbreviations, see G. L. Harding, *An Index and Concordance of Pre-Islamic Arabian Names and Inscriptions* (Toronto: University of Toronto Press, 1971).

but in addition to cultic functions, frankincense was burned in palaces and in domestic contexts, where it was used for fumigation and religious and medicinal purposes.[25] It was through this trade that South Arabians were connected to the North Arabians, in transporting the aromatics to the Mediterranean. Such long-distance trade required an elaborate infrastructure, but the details remain obscure.

2. Focus on the Late Bronze Age–Persian Period (ca. 1500–332)

During the ninth and sixth centuries BCE, the Arabs and Arabia become one of the focal points of the Assyrian royal annals. As noted above, the first reference of the ethnic term "Arab" is in the annals of Shalmaneser III in 853 BCE to designate "Gindibu (from the) land of Arabia" (^{M}Gi-in-di-bu-' ^{KUR}Ar-ba-a-a). After a hiatus of a century, the term "Arabs" appears again in the Assyrian annals, and they are the subject of sustained attacks for the next century. At the beginning of his reign in 745 BCE, Tiglath-pileser III conducted a campaign against the Arameans who were settled along the Euphrates and Tigris in southern Babylonia. His inscriptions mention thirty-five tribes and six cities that were conquered, including the tribes of the Nabātu and Ḥagarānu.[26] The *Nabātu/Nabājatu* are generally located south of Palmyra and west of the Euphrates.[27] The name Ḥagarānu becomes a generic ethnic term synonymous with "Arabs" (Ḥagar) in the Achaemenid period. They were probably located in the Gulf region of northeast Arabia.[28] These Aramean "chiefdoms" (*naskiāni*) were ruled by "sheikhs" (*nasīku*), a title used earlier for the "princes" of the Midianites in northwest Arabia (*nsykmw*; Ps. 83:12 [Eng.

25. Walter W. Müller, "Notes on the Use of Frankincense in South Arabia," *PSAS* 6 (1976): 124–36. See also M. D. Fowler, "Excavated Incense Burners: A Case for Identifying a Site as Sacred?," *PEQ* 117 (1985): 25–29; and Jonathan Hassell, "A Re-examination of the Cuboid Incense-Burning Altars from Flinders Petrie's Palestinian Excavations at Tell Jemmeh," *Levant* 37 (2005): 133–62.

26. J. A. Brinkman, *A Political History of Post-Kassite Babylonia, 1158–722 B.C.*, AnOr 43 (Rome: Pontifical Biblical Institute, 1968), 270, nos. 12 and 35; Hayim Tadmor, *The Inscriptions of Tiglath-pileser III, King of Assyria: Critical Edition, with Introductions, Translations, and Commentary* (Jerusalem: Israel Academy of Sciences and Humanities, 1994), Summary Inscription 7, lines 6 and 8 = Hayim Tadmor and Shigeo Yamada, *The Royal Inscriptions of Tiglath-pileser III (744–727 BC) and Shalmaneser V (726–722 BC), Kings of Assyria*, RINAP 1 (Winona Lake, IN: Eisenbrauns, 2011), no. 47, obv. 6 and 8.

27. Simo Parpola, *Neo-Assyrian Toponyms*, AOAT 6 (Kevelaer: Butzon & Bercker, 1970), 253–54, 405, and map on 409; cf. Eph'al, *Ancient Arabs*, 162.

28. D. F. Graf, "Arabia during Achaemenid Times," in *Centre and Periphery: Proceedings of the Groningen 1986 Achaemenid History Workshop*, ed. H. Sancisi-Weerdenburg and A. Kuhrt, AchHist 4 (Leiden: Nederlands Instituut vor het Nabije Oosten, 1990), 131–48, esp. 143–45.

83:11]), who bear Arabic names, suggesting North Arabian origins for at least some of the tribes listed by Tiglath-pileser III. It has been argued that many of the immigrants into southern Babylonia were of Arab composition on the basis of the proper names of the tribes, their chieftains, and their settlements.[29] This hypothesis has been disputed, but it seems likely that at least some were Arabs.[30] In the reign of Sargon II (722–705 BCE), Arabs were dwelling in villages on the desert fringe of western Syria near Damascus, Hamath, and Zobah, where they were subjects of the local governors. These Arabs were led by a rather sophisticated and influential Arab chieftain named Ammili'ti son of Amiri, whose people were employed as farmers and gardeners in Hamath and Zobah and formed an army of three hundred camels.[31] It is clear that the Arab penetration of Syria, southern Babylon, and Mesopotamia began at least in the eighth century BCE, with steady and even increased migration to the region in later periods.[32] Many of these Arabs were migrants from the major oases of Arabia, most of which were located on the periphery of the Peninsula: the Arabian Gulf region of the northeast, the northwestern Ḥijāz region, and the southwest area of what is today modern Yemen.

Dilmun and Northeast Arabia

The earliest sign of civilization in Arabia is in the Eastern Province along the coasts of the Persian Gulf, where the distinctive fifth-millennium BCE pottery from Ubaid near Ur in southern Mesopotamia is found between Dhahran and Qatar and the coasts of the United Arab Emirates. After an apparent hiatus in the fourth millennium BCE, there is a revival of the same trading

---

29. S. Moritz, "Die Nationalität der Arumu-Stämme in Südost-Babylonien," in *Oriental Studies Published in Commemoration of the Fortieth Anniversary (1883–1923) of Paul Haupt as Director of the Oriental Seminary of the Johns Hopkins University Baltimore*, ed. Cyrus Adler and Aaron Embe (Baltimore: Johns Hopkins Press, 1926), 184–211.

30. Israel Eph'al, "'Arabs' in Babylonia in the 8th Century B.C.," *JAOS* 94 (1974): 108–9, disputes the argument; but see F. Vattioni, "Ai primordi della storia degli Arabi Apptunti sui Nabatei," in *Studi arabo-islamici in onore di Roberto Rubinacci nel suo settantesimo compleanno*, ed. C. Sarnelli Cerqua (Naples: Istituto Universitario Orientale, 1985), 721.

31. Parpola, *Letters from Assyria and the West*, nos. 172–74, 177–80. For a rather imaginative discussion of the texts, see Ryan Byrne, "Early Assyrian Contacts with Arabs and the Impact on Levantine Vassal Tribute," *BASOR* 331 (2003): 16–18.

32. R. Zadok, "Arabians in Mesopotamia during the Late-Assyrian, Chaldean, Achaemenian and Hellenistic Periods Chiefly according to the Cuneiform Sources," *ZDMG* 131 (1981): 42–84; and Zadok, "On Early Arabians in the Fertile Crescent," *TA* 17 (1990): 223–31. For the ethnic diversity, including Arabs in Babylonia, see also I. Eph'al, "The Western Minorities in Babylonia in the 6th–5th Centuries B.C.: Maintenance and Cohesion," *Or* 47 (1978): 74–90. For the ethnic character of the term "Arab," see M. A. Dandamayev, "Arabs in Mesopotamia during the Neo-Babylonian and Achaemenid Periods," *VDI* 233 (2000): 135–39 (in Russian, with an English summary).

network, although now of a much wider international scope. In the middle of the third millennium BCE, pottery from southern Mesopotamia and the Diyala region northeast of Baghdad appears again in the Early Dynastic period (ca. 2900–2500 BCE), this time accompanied by lapis lazuli from Afghanistan and carnelian beads from India. The focal point of this major culture seems to be Tarut Island, just northeast of Qatif, and the eastern coasts of Arabia.[33] Tarut Island and the adjacent Arabian mainland are probably to be identified with the land of "Dilmun" that appears in cuneiform sources from the late fourth millennium BCE, but by about 2200 BCE the focal point of Dilmun shifted further south to the island of Bahrain. Archaeological finds suggest an early period between 2200 and 2050 BCE and a later period from 2050 to 1750 BCE, followed by a break before a revival in the Kassite period (1500–1300 BCE).

This chronology is supported by cuneiform texts that indicate Dilmun played a major role in international trade between Mesopotamia, Iran, Oman, and India at the time. Texts from around 2500 BCE indicate ships of Dilmun transported timber from foreign lands to the king of Lagash, and an Early Dynastic Letter (ca. 2400 BCE) indicates the queen of Dilmun sent gifts of dates, textiles, and copper to the queen of Lagash.[34] In the third millennium, Dilmun appears as an emporium for the redistribution of goods to Sumer and Akkad in Mesopotamia from more distant regions, including Magan/Makkan (identified with Oman) and Meluḫḫa (the Harappan culture of the Indus Valley).[35] This trading network extended to Syria, where the standard unit of weight at Ebla was that of the Dilmun shekel, and Dilmun copper and tin are mentioned in texts. Later, in the reigns of Hammurabi of Babylon (1792–1750 BCE) and Shamshi-Adad I of Assyria (1813–1781 BCE), caravans from Dilmun were plying their trade to Babylonia, Sippar, and Mari on the middle Euphrates, and even up the Tigris to Assyria. Later, King Zimri-Lim of Mari was sending oil to the king of Dilmun, providing the earliest reference to the royal dynasty on the island.[36] In the Kassite period, an inscribed stone at Bahrain refers to a palace servant of Inzak of Agarum, the name of one of the deities associated with Dilmun and the latter a toponym associated

---

33. Daniel T. Potts, *The Arabian Gulf in Antiquity*, 2 vols. (Oxford: Clarendon, 1990), 1:62–92.

34. Potts, *Arabian Gulf in Antiquity*, 1:88; Potts, *Roads of Arabia: The Archaeological Treasures of Saudi Arabia*, ed. Ute Franke and Joachim Gierlichs (Tübingen: Wasmuth, 2011), 86–101.

35. Potts, *Arabian Gulf in Antiquity*, 1:133–50.

36. Daniel T. Potts, "Dilmun's Further Relations: The Syro-Anatolian Evidence from the Third and Second Millennia B.C.," in *Bahrain through the Ages: The Archaeology*, ed. Haya Ali Khalifa and Michael Rice (London: Routledge & Kegan Paul, 1986), 389–96; and Potts, *Arabian Gulf in Antiquity*, 1:87–88 (Ebla) and 228–31 (Mari).

with East Arabia.³⁷ Other texts indicate the presence of Amorite diviners and fishermen on the island, a pastoralist population normally associated with Syria.³⁸ Under the Kassite dynasty in Babylon, a Kassite governor had replaced the king on Dilmun by ca. 1420–1410 BCE, as attested by recently found cuneiform tablets from Bahrain, late fourteenth-century BCE letters from the governor of Dilmun to Nippur, and a British Museum cylinder seal of unknown provenance.³⁹ After the Middle Assyrian king Tukulti-Ninurta I (ca. 1243–1207 BCE) captured Babylon in ca. 1225 BCE, he adopted new titles, proclaiming himself "King of Sumer and Akkad" and also "King of Dilmun and Meluḫḫa," and boasting that his kingdom reached all the way to the borders of Magan.⁴⁰ This may represent merely his assertion of Assyrian rights to the previously ruled Babylonian region. After this date, Dilmun is not mentioned again in the second millennium BCE.

Of prominence among the ruins at Bahrain is an extensive necropolis of an estimated 200,000 tumuli (burial mounds) scattered across the island, seemingly far larger than any reasonable projection of the indigenous population on the island in antiquity. The tumuli have been arranged into five types representing both single and multiple burial mounds, some assigned a date as early as ca. 2200–1750 BCE, with the possibility that some date as late as the Parthian period. Dozens of the larger mounds have outer ring walls and have been identified as royal or elite mounds, but it is the staggering number of smaller burial mounds that begs for an explanation.⁴¹ There are also thousands of similar burial mounds in the area of the Dhahran Airport on

---

37. H. E. Hirsch, "Die Inschriften der Könige von Agade," *AfO* 20 (1970): 8–13; and I. J. Gelb and B. Kienast, *Die altakkadischen Königsinschriften des dritten Jahrtausends v. Chr.* (Stuttgart: Steiner, 1990), 164.

38. Juris Zarins, "MAR-TU and the land of Dilmun," in Ali Khalifa and Rice, *Bahrain through the Ages*, 233–50; and Fleming Højlund, "The Formation of the Dilmun State and the Amorite Tribes," *PSAS* 19 (1989): 45–59.

39. Cuneiform texts: B. André-Salivni and P. Lombard, "La découverte épigraphique de 1995 à Qal'at al-Bahrein: Un jalon pour la chronologie de la phase Dilmoun Moyen dans le Golfe arabe," *PSAS* 27 (1997): 167; letters: Eric Olijdam, "Nippur and Dilmun in the Second Half of the Fourteenth Century BC: A Re-evaluation of the Ili-ippašra Letters," *PSAS* 27 (1997): 199–203; cylinder seal: Julian Reade, "Commerce or Conquest: Variations in the Mesopotamian-Dilmun Relationship," in Ali Khalifa and Rice, *Bahrain through the Ages*, 332–33 and fig. 137; with J. A. Brinkman, "A Kassite Seal Mentioning a Babylonian Governor of Dilmun," *NABU* (1993): 89–91 (no. 106). For discussion, see D. T. Potts, "Elamites and Kassites in the Persian Gulf," *JNES* 65 (2006): 115–16.

40. Khaled Nasshef, *Die Orts- und Gewässernamen der mittelbabylonischen und mittelassyrischen Zeit*, RGTC 5 (Wiesbaden: Dr. Ludwig Reichert Verlag, 1982), 182 and 261.

41. Fleming Højlund, ed., *The Burial Mounds of Bahrain: Social Complexity in Early Dilmun*, JASP 58 (Aarhus: Aarhus University Press, 2007); Fleming Højlund et al., "Late Third-Millennium Elite Burials in Bahrain," *AAE* 19 (2008): 144–55; Steffen Terp Laursen, "Early Dilmun and Its Rulers: New Evidence of the Burial Mounds of the Elite and the Development

the Arabian mainland apparently of similar date. C. C. Lamberg-Karlovsky's intriguing proposal is to connect the extensive burials with a funerary cult associated with Sumerian mythology about Dilmun, which is the setting of the Enki and Ninḫursag myth and depicted as Paradise or the "Abode of the Blessed," where Ziusudra resided, the hero of the Sumerian flood story and the counterpart of the Babylonian Utnapishtim, familiar from the Gilgamesh Epic, and the biblical Noah.[42] It is proposed that significant numbers of the Mesopotamian population as well as some local Arabians were buried on the Paradise Island in order to gain immortality. The fact that only a fraction of the extensively numerous burials have been excavated renders any interpretation purely conjectural. Of those excavated, many mounds contained no human burials or artifacts, and the burial goods of others are hardly reflective of Mesopotamian wealth or that of a major trading power. If the chronology of the mounds is expanded from four hundred years to several thousand, the number of mounds becomes more understandable.[43] It can only be hoped that future excavation of the largest necropolis in antiquity will illuminate the problem.

Another aspect of ancient Bahrain that deserves attention is the Greek tradition that Tyre in Phoenicia was founded around 2750 BCE by former residents of the Red Sea.[44] The tradition was amplified later in the time of Alexander the Great, when his admiral Androsthenes of Thasos conducted an exploration of the Arabian Gulf in preparation for a campaign against the Arabs. The report is preserved only in fragments, but the enterprise is corroborated by a Babylonian cuneiform chronicle.[45] Theophrastus indicates that he passed "Tylos, the island in the Red Sea" or "Arabian Gulf."[46] Later, Strabo mentions more specifically that Bahrain was called "Tyros" at the time and the adjacent island of Musharraq was called "Arados," with "temples like Phoenician ones," and that the residents said that the Phoenician island cities of the same name in the Mediterranean were colonies that they founded

---

of Social Complexity, c. 2300–1750 BC," *AAE* 19 (2008): 156–67; and Laursen, "Mesopotamian Ceramics from the Burial Mounds of Bahrain, c. 2250–1750 BC," *AAE* 22 (2011): 32–47.

42. C. C. Lamberg-Karlovsky, "Dilmun: Gateway to Immortality," *JNES* 41 (1982): 45–50; and Lamberg-Karlovsky, "Death in Dilmun," in Ali Khalifa and Rice, *Bahrain through the Ages*, 156–65.

43. Henry Innes Macadam, "Dilmun Revisited," *AAE* 1 (1990): 56–59.

44. Herodotus, *Histories* 2.44 and 7.89.

45. Van der Spek, "Darius III," 289–346, for the translation of BM 41080 that mentions Alexander's troops were sent to the "land of Arabia." The expedition's preparations began before Alexander's arrival back from India. See Arrian, *Anabasis of Alexander* 6.19.3–20.10; cf. Strabo, *Geography* 16.1.11 [741].

46. Theophrastus, *Enquiry into Plants* 2.5.5; 4.7.7.

earlier.⁴⁷ This Greek tradition that the Arabian Gulf was the original homeland of the Phoenicians is systematically rejected by Phoenician specialists, who maintain that the Phoenician cities of Tyre and Arados were founded by the indigenous population of the region. In contrast, classicists have supported the tradition, although suggesting the date of the Arab migration may have been sometime in the early or mid-second millennium BCE.⁴⁸ The commercial interaction of Dilmun with Ebla and Mari in the third and second millennia BCE makes it difficult to reject the tradition as purely groundless propaganda recycled by the Greeks.⁴⁹ At least for the present, the question deserves to be left open.

After the thirteenth century BCE, Dilmun is not mentioned again in Assyrian sources until the reign of Sargon II (722–705 BCE). After Sargon's defeat of the rebel Babylonian king Merodach-baladan, Upēri the king of Dilmun brought gifts to the victorious Assyrian king.⁵⁰ Afterward, during the reign of the Assyrian king Esarhaddon (680–669 BCE), a military expedition was conducted along the eastern edge of the Arabian Peninsula ca. 676 BCE.⁵¹ The region is designated Bāzu and described as adjacent to a salt desert, where "no king before [Esarhaddon] had gone since earlier days." In this area he defeated eight kings, with many warriors, looted the cities, and carried off the gods of the cities. A ninth king, Laialê, king of the city of Iadi', fled before the onslaught, but eventually was forced to come to Nineveh to offer his submission.⁵² As a result, Esarhaddon placed the province of Bāzu under Laialê's control. The location of the region of Bāzu in East Arabia

47. Strabo, *Geography* 16.3.2–4 [766]; cf. 16.4.27 [784]. Tilmun was the Akkadian name for Bahrain.

48. For sympathetic views of the tradition, see G. W. Bowersock, "Tylos and Tyre: Bahrain in the Graeco-Roman World," in Ali Khalifa and Rice, *Bahrain through the Ages*, 399–406; and Potts, *Arabian Gulf in Antiquity*, 2:139–41. For the history of the controversy, see Jean-François Salles, "Les Phéniciens de la Mer Érythrée," *AAE* 4 (1993): 170–209. See also Henry Innes Macadam, "Phoenician Origins: Ancient Tradition and Modern Evidence," *PJBR* 9, nos. 1–2 (2010): 95–144, for recent reflections and a proposal of a date of ca. 1600 BCE for the migration from the Arabian Gulf to Lebanon.

49. As observed by Robert R. Stieglitz, "Ebla and Dilmun," in *Eblaitica: Essays on the Ebla Archives and Eblaite Language*, vol. 1, ed. C. H. Gordon et al. (Winona Lake, IN: Eisenbrauns, 1987), 43–46.

50. Andreas Fuchs, *Die Inschriften Sargons II aus Khorsabad* (Göttingen: Cuvillier, 1994), 170, Ann. no. 383, and Anhang C (390–94) for maps and geographical lists, and 430 for other references to Dilmun; cf. Potts, *Arabian Gulf in Antiquity*, 1:333–38. The name Upēri appears to be Elamite; see Potts, "Elamites and Kassites," 119.

51. Erle Leichty, *The Royal Inscriptions of Esarhaddon, King of Assyria (680–669 BC)*, RINAP 4 (Winona Lake, IN: Eisenbrauns, 2011), 8; cf. Eph'al, *Ancient Arabs*, 130, who prefers a date before 676 BCE.

52. Leichty, *Royal Inscriptions of Esarhaddon*, no. 1, col. iv, 53–77; cf. no. 4, col. ii', 25'–36'.

has been disputed, and assigned rather to the northern part of the Wadi Sirḥān in Arabia, where the Assyrian kings were active against the Arabs, but this fails to meet the description of the region in Esarhaddon's annals.[53] A location on the northeastern Arabian coast opposite Dilmun (Bahrain) remains more attractive, based on the Sargon Geography (SG), where the distances in the text correlate well with that between Nineveh and Bahrain.[54] The "land of Bāzu" near Mount Ḫazu in the Assyrian text has been identified with the al-Hasa oasis along the northeastern coasts of Arabia, and several of the kings (SG 4–5) are identified with the cities of Dharan and Qatif in the Gulf region.[55] A fragmentary text of Esarhaddon appears to allude to the conquest of Dilmun, "whose place is far off," a phrase similar to that describing the Bāzu campaign, which would place it in the remote Gulf region.[56] Other texts of Esarhaddon connect Bāzu and Dilmun, and celebrate him as "king of the kings of Dilmun, Makkan, and Meluḫḫa," providing further support for the identification.[57] Another notable feature of Esarhaddon's Bāzu conquest is the mention of queens who ruled several of the cities (nos. 4 and 7). The regions of Bāzu and Mount Ḫazu in the Assyrian text have been identified with the biblical Buz and Hazo, the sons of Nahor (Gen. 22:21–22). The king of Buz also is listed with the kings of Tema and Dedan in Arabia (Jer. 25:23–24).[58]

Dilmun's subjection to Assyria continued into later periods. In the reign of Assurbanipal (668–627 BCE), after the defeat of his brother Shamash-shum-ukin, king of Babylon, Dilmun continues to be listed as one of the tribute-paying provinces.[59] In the Neo-Babylonian era, Nebuchadnezzar (ca. 605–562 BCE) appears to have been active at Faliaka at the head of the Gulf, and established a city named Teredon in southern Babylon, which later became

---

53. Alois Musil, *Arabia Deserta: A Topographical Itinerary* (New York: American Geographical Society, 1927), 482–84; cf. D. Potts, "The Road to Meluhha," *JNES* 41 (1982): 279–88. For criticism, see Ephʻal, *Ancient Arabs*, 131–37.

54. For the text, see A. Kirk Grayson, "The Empire of Sargon of Akkad," *AfO* 25 (1974–77): 56–64, and Wayne Horowitz, *Mesopotamian Cosmic Geography* (Winona Lake, IN: Eisenbrauns, 1998), 67–95.

55. Mario Liverani, "The Sargon Geography and the Late Assyrian Mensuration of the Earth," *SAAB* 13 (1999–2000): 57–87, esp. 71–76 with figs. 10–12; the confusing references to Meluḫḫa in the west on the borders of Egypt (SG 1) and in the Lower Sea or Persian Gulf (SG 30) are interpreted as a conflation of contemporary Neo-Assyrian meanings and the archaic Sargon of Akkad meaning.

56. *ARAB* ii § 572; cf. Potts, *Arabian Gulf in Antiquity*, 1:340–41 for discussion.

57. Leichty, *Royal Inscriptions of Esarhaddon*, nos. 57 and 60.

58. Ernst Axel Knauf, "Buz (place)," *ABD* 1:794, against the philological objections of Ephʻal, *Ancient Arabs*, 133.

59. Potts, *Arabian Gulf in Antiquity*, 1:342–48.

an Arab emporium for the distribution of frankincense.[60] But Dilmun is not specifically mentioned again until the reign of Nabonidus when, in ca. 544 BCE, a "governor of Dilmun" (*bēl piḫāti*) is mentioned.[61] After the Achaemenid Persian conquest of Babylon in ca. 539 BCE, the status of Dilmun becomes unclear. Under Darius I (521–486 BCE), Elamite texts record shipments of figs, grain, and wine made to Persepolis from a place called Ti-il-ma-in. The toponym has been associated with Akkadian Tilmun—that is, the Dilmun of earlier periods.[62] In addition, the toponym Makkaš (OP Makā; Akk. Mačiyā) appears in six Persepolis texts, four of which record travel rations.[63] The remaining two texts make it clear that Makā is a province governed by a satrap. Two of the travel texts indicate 162 men designated "Arabs" who were sent from Susa to Makā, suggesting the province is to be located in Arabia, and probably refers to Oman, which was called Mazūn in late antiquity.[64] The ethnic term "Arab" appears elsewhere in the Persian Persepolis texts, but the Persian province of Arabia (OP *Arabāya*) probably designates the Arabs of the northwest part of the Peninsula.[65]

Northwest Arabia

The land just east of the Gulf of Aqaba in northwest Arabia was called by the classical and medieval geographers the area "Madian" or "Madiama." This area forms part of the northern Ḥijāz, which is bordered by the Gulf of Aqaba on the west and the Hisma desert on the east. The rugged Ḥijāz Mountains are interlaced with many wadis, and drainage is to the east toward the Tabuk basin. Fourteen sites, dating to the Late Bronze and early Iron Ages (1300–1000 BCE), have been identified in the region, most of which are in the coastal wadis.

The main sedentary urban center in the region is Qurayya, located about 70 kilometers northwest of Tabuk. The ruins were visited first by Bernard Moritz in 1906, followed by H. St. J. Philby in 1951.[66] The archaeological investigation

---

60. Arrian, *Anabasis of Alexander* 8.41.8. See Potts, *Arabian Gulf in Antiquity*, 1:348–49.
61. A. Ungnad, *Aus den neubabylonische Privaturkunden* (Berlin/Leipzig, 1908), no. 81; and Potts, *Arabian Gulf in Antiquity*, 1:349–50.
62. R. T. Hallock, *Persian Persepolis Tablets*, OIP 92 (Chicago: University of Chicago Press, 1969) = PF 19, 202, 389, 1882, 1985. For discussion see Potts, *Arabian Gulf in Antiquity*, 1:351–52.
63. Satrap of Makā: PF 679 and 680; travel rations: PF 1545, 2050, and PFa 17, 29. PFa = R. T. Hallock, "Select Fortification Texts," *CDAFI* 8 (1978): 109–36.
64. PFa 17 (Arabs) and 29 (without the ethnic term). For discussion, see De Blois, "Maka and Mazūn," 157–67.
65. Arabs at Persepolis: PF 2011, 1477, 1507, 1534, and PFa 17. For discussion, see Henkelman and Stolper, "Ethnic Identity and Ethnic Labeling at Persepolis," 300; cf. Potts, *Arabian Gulf in Antiquity*, 1:350–400.
66. H. St. John Philby, *The Land of Midian* (London: Ernest Benn Limited, 1957), 169–82.

began in 1968 by a British survey team, followed by the Saudi Comprehensive Survey in 1980, and the site is currently being excavated by the Saudi Department of Antiquities.[67] The settlement is located on an isolated large hill (1,000 x 350 m.) that rises some 50 meters above the surrounding terrain, protected by walls. The summit is divided into three parts by two walls 3 meters high built of thin slabs. Towers are attached to the walls and a possible gateway is visible. The buildings on top are either watchtowers or tombs. At the foot of the citadel is a settlement mound (400 x 300 m.) enclosed by a stone wall, now mostly buried by windblown sands. East of the settlement, agricultural fields can be traced, marked by single lines of stones that enclose them and crossed by irrigation channels. A spring at the foot of the citadel appears to be the source of the water for irrigating the fields, rather than flash floods. The system is similar to that employed in Yemen and later in the Negev. The pottery at the settlement is distinctive and was initially called "Midianite" ware, but is now more appropriately designated as "Qurayya [polychrome] painted ware."[68] Its fabric is cream to red, with wheel-made jars, bowls, and platters as forms. The painting is red/black/yellow/brown on a cream slip. The motifs used appear to be of Aegean inspiration—birds, running spirals, chevrons, and lozenges—and Egyptian lotus patterns. The influence of Mycenaean ware in the eastern Mediterranean has been suggested. The production and distribution center for the pottery seems to be Qurayya, where a number of kilns have been discovered inside and outside the walls of the settlement, and where large amounts of the pottery have been found. Scattered finds of the pottery extend as far south as Al-'Ula in the northern Ḥijāz, to Taymā', some 260 kilometers to the southeast, and north in Transjordan in Edom at Khirbet al-Shudayyid, Tawilan near Petra, and north at the Amman Airport temple. In the west, it appears at Tell Kheleifah on the Gulf of Aqabah, at the Egyptian Nineteenth Dynasty sanctuary of Hathhor at Timna' in the Wadi Arabah, and at the southern end of the Dead Sea. Finds have also been made in the central Negev

67. P. J. Parr, G. L. Harding, and J. E. Dayton, "Preliminary Survey in N.W. Arabia, 1968," *BIAUL* 8–9 (1970): 219–41; Michael Lloyd Ingraham et al., "Saudi Arabia Comprehensive Survey Program: Preliminary Report on a Reconnaissance Survey of the Northwestern Province (with a note on a brief survey of the Northern Province)," *Atlal: The Journal of Saudi Arabian Archaeology* 5 (1981): 71–75; and Abdulaziz Saud Al-Ghazzi, "The Kingdom of Midian," in *Roads of Arabia: Archaeology and History of the Kingdom of Saudi Arabia*, ed. Ali Ibrahim Ali-Ghabban et al. (Paris: Somagy Art Publishers for the Musée du Louvre, 2010), 211–17.

68. As proposed by Peter J. Parr, "Pottery of the Late Second Millennium B.C. from North West Arabia and Its Historical Implications," in *Araby the Blest: Studies in Arabian Archaeology*, ed. D. T. Potts (Copenhagen: Museum Tusculanum Press, 1988), 74. See Beno Rothenberg and Jonathan Glass, "The Midianite Pottery," in *Midian, Moab and Edom: The History and Archaeology of Late Bronze and Iron Age Jordan and North-West Arabia*, ed. John F. A. Sawyer and David J. A. Clines, JSOTSup 24 (Sheffield, UK: JSOT Press, 1983), 65–124.

at Jedur, near Hebron, Tell Masos, Gezer, and Lachish, and in the northern Sinai at the Nineteenth–Twentieth Dynasty Egyptian fort at Bir el-'Abd. The date of the Qurayya ware here is then disputed, ranging from the thirteenth to twelfth centuries to 750 BCE or later. The Egyptian connections are striking.

In the biblical tradition, Midian is a descendant of Abraham and Keturah (Gen. 25:1–6; 1 Chron. 1:32–33), and a people that plays an important part in the narratives of Joseph (Gen. 37:25–36), the exodus (Exod. 2–4, 18; Num. 25), and the conquest (Judg. 6–8), and as a result has been connected with the "Qurayyan phenomenon."[69] But the attempt to associate Mount Horeb/Mount Sinai with Jebel al-Lawz in northwest Arabia has little merit.[70] Another controversy has centered on the duration of the settlement at Qurayya, as it is argued that its distinctive pottery seems to have declined and disappeared by ca. 1050 BCE in the Third Intermediate period of Egypt. As a consequence, the emergence of "oasis urbanism" in northwest Arabia in the Late Bronze and early Iron Ages has been considered a short-lived result of Egyptian imperialism, the so-called Midianites being identified with the Shoshu "pastoralists" (or Shasu) mentioned in Egyptian records of the Nineteenth Dynasty, who were settled in towns created by the Egyptians in the Sinai, northwest Arabia, and Transjordan.[71] This interpretation assumes a gap in urbanism in northwest Arabia until the middle of the first millennium BCE, but it has been sharply contested based on the more recent investigations at Taymā' and Al-'Ulā described below, which have considerably reduced if not eliminated this apparent gap.[72] The "Qurayya phenomenon" seems best understood as an indigenous development with antecedents that reach back into earlier millennia.

Dumah

The name Al-Jawf means the "cavity" or "basin" and denotes the *whole* region of the Wadi al-Sirḥan, a valley extending northwest into northeast Jordan. Dumah is an oasis located at the southern end of the basin, but Jawf

---

69. Ernst Axel Knauf, *Midian: Untersuchungen zur Geschichte Palästinas und Nordarabiens am Ende des 2. Jahrtausends v. Chr.*, ADPV (Wiesbaden: Harrassowitz, 1988), 1–6, 16; and George E. Mendenhall, "Midian," *ABD* 4:817. Keturah seems to be a personification of the incense trade; see Ernst Axel Knauf, "Keturah," *ABD* 4:31.

70. For a critique of this view, see James K. Hoffmeier, *Ancient Israel in Sinai: The Evidence for the Authenticity of the Wilderness Tradition* (Oxford: Oxford University Press, 2005), 121–22, 130–40.

71. Parr, "Pottery of the Late Second Millennium B.C.," 84–85, and Parr, "Aspects of the Archaeology of North-West Arabia in the First Millennium B.C.," in *L'Arabie préislamique et son environnement historique et culturel*, ed. T. Fahd, TCRPOGA 10 (Leiden: Brill, 1989), 39–66.

72. Garth Bawden, "Continuity and Disruption in the Ancient Hejaz: An Assessment of Current Archaeological Strategies," *AAE* 3 (1992): 1–22; and Peter J. Parr, "The Early History of the Hejaz: A Response to Garth Bawden," *AAE* 4 (1993): 48–58.

Figure 12.2. Al-Jawf, the fortress of Qasr Mārid at Dumah

is a composite oasis, connecting Dumah and nearby Sakkaka.[73] Its location was an important nexus for trade from South Arabia leading to Syria and Mesopotamia, and from Mesopotamia westward to Egypt. The Great Nafud Desert is on the south and east of Dumah, with sand dunes 25 to 35 meters high, and stretching 200 miles to the south, almost one-third of the way across the Peninsula.

Between the ninth and seventh centuries BCE, Dumah was the object of a series of Neo-Assyrian campaigns and appears to be the primary Arab settlement in North Arabia as the center of the Qedarite Arab kingdom.[74] The Assyrians knew the oasis as *Adummatu* and the West Semitic peoples as *Dumah*. After the mention of Gindibu the Arab in 853 BCE, the Arabs appear next in the records of Tiglath-pileser III (744–727 BCE), when he conducted a campaign in 738 BCE against an anti-Assyrian coalition that included Zabibe, queen of the (Qedarite) Arabs.[75] This campaign was followed by another Arabian campaign in 732 BCE against Samsi, another Qedarite "Queen of the Arabs," who was forced to flee from Mount Saqurri "like a wild

---

73. For an introduction to the region, see F. V. Winnett and W. L. Reed, *Ancient Records of North Arabia* (Toronto: University of Toronto Press, 1970), 7–20, 71–73.

74. Described in detail by Eph'al, *Ancient Arabs*, 74–169. For the effects on Palestine, see D. F. Graf, "Arabs in Palestine from the Neo-Assyrian to the Persian Period," *ARAM* 27/1–2 (2015): 289–93.

75. Tadmor, *Inscriptions of Tiglath-pileser III*, 107–8, Stele III A, 2 and 19.

she-ass" into the desert.[76] The toponym Mount Saqurri has been identified with Jebel Haurān in southern Syria, and her desert retreat with the Wadi Sirḥān.[77] As a result of these campaigns, tribute was received from a number of Arabian tribes, including Massa, Tema, Saba, Hayappa, Badanu, Hatte, and Idia'iilu, which are located "on the borders of the countries of the setting sun" (= western lands), many of which are identified with the ethnics in the biblical genealogies (Gen. 25:13–15; 1 Chron. 1:29–30).[78] After the defeat, the Assyrians appointed an official (^{LÚ}qépu) to oversee Samsi and monitor Dumah's political and economic activities. The conflict with Samsi is depicted in the reliefs from the Central Palace in Nimrud, which depict the Assyrian cavalry pursuing Arab camel riders, seizing captives, booty, and tribute, and perhaps Queen Samsi as a dejected woman with her hand to her forehead, leading four camels.[79] The listing of Taymā' and Saba among the Arab tributaries suggests the commercial connections of Dumah with trans-Arabian commerce. In 716 BCE the Assyrian king Sargon II had subjected Pir'u king of Egypt, Samsi queen of the Arabs, and It'amara the Sabaean, "the kings of the seashore and desert," from whom he received tribute, including, among other items, "aromatic substances."[80] The list of Arabs subjected by Sargon also includes the Thamud, Ibadidi, Marsimani, and 'Ephah—who previously "knew neither overseers nor officials"—without listing any booty or tribute, but indicating captives were transported to Samaria.[81] Only 'Ephah is known in the biblical tradition, identified as one of the sons of Keturah (Gen. 25:4; 1 Chron. 1:33) and associated with the land of Midian (Isa. 60:6). Other Arab tribes were entrusted with monitoring and guarding the border with Egypt.

The later Neo-Assyrian kings continued their assault against the Arabs. In 703 BCE the Assyrian king Sennacherib (705–681 BCE) campaigned against the Babylonian rebel Merodach-baladan, who was supported by a number

---

76. Tadmor, *Inscriptions of Tiglath-pileser III*, 141–43, Summary Inscription 4, lines 19–29; Eph'al, *Ancient Arabs*, 21–36, 82–92; Tadmor and Yamada, *Royal Inscriptions of Tiglath-pileser III*, no. 42, lines 19–29; cf. F. M. Fales and J. N. Postgate, *Imperial Administrative Records*, pt. 2, *Provincial and Military Administration*, SAA 11 (Helsinki: Helsinki University Press, 1995), no. 162.

77. Eph'al, *Ancient Arabs*, 85.

78. Tadmor, *Inscriptions of Tiglath-pileser III*, 312–13; Eph'al, *Ancient Arabs*, 215–30. Some of the identifications must be regarded with caution.

79. R. D. Barnett and M. Faulkner, *The Sculptures of Aššur-Naṣir-Apli II (883–859 B.C.), Tiglath-Pileser III (745–727 B.C.), Esarhaddon (681–669 B.C.), from the Central and South-west Palaces at Nimrud* (London: British Museum, 1962), 8–12, with plates 8–20, 23–30.

80. Fuchs, *Die Inschriften Sargons II*, 116, Ann. no. 123. For translation, summary, and discussion, see Eph'al, *Ancient Arabs*, 36–39 (texts), 87–89 (possible identifications), 101–11.

81. Fuchs, *Die Inschriften Sargons II*, 110, Ann. nos. 120–22; cf. 424 for other references to the Arabs.

of Arab allies: among those captured was Basqanu, the brother of Iati'e, queen of the Arabs. The list of the towns and settlements conquered by the Assyrians in southern Babylon includes the names of 81 walled towns and 820 minor settlements.[82] These included communities of Arameans and Arabs. Some of the toponyms reflect the names of Qedarite Arab chieftains and even the name Qidrina, probably to be associated with a Qedarite settlement. Between 691 and 689 BCE, Sennacherib followed his Babylonian expedition by pursuing the Arab rebels Ḥazael and Te'elḫunu, the Qedarite king and queen respectively, who had fled from the borders of Babylon to take refuge in their fortress at Adummatu, located in the Jawf oasis at the southeastern end of the Wadi Sirḥān in North Arabia.[83] Sennacherib's army besieged the fortress at Adummatu, capturing the queen, seizing booty and the divine images of the sanctuary (which were taken back to Assyria), and forcing Ḥazael to become a tributary to Assyria.[84] The queen Te'elḫunu was now a hostage in Assyria, along with their daughter Tabūa. Afterward, in the reign of the Assyrian king Esarhaddon (680–669 BCE), the Qedarite king Ḥazael went to Nineveh and petitioned the new king to return the queen and the divine images.[85] Esarhaddon granted the request, returning to Adummatu "the gods of the Arabs," which are specifically named: Atar-Samayin, Dūya, Nuḫāya, Ruldāwu, Abīrillu, and Atar-qurumā, but the lady Tabūa replaced her mother on the throne. The tribute was increased, but the divine images were returned to Adummatu and Tabūa was appointed "queen of the Arabs." After the death of King Ḥazael in 677 BCE, his son Uaite' became king and in 669 BCE rebelled against Esarhaddon, who sent his army to suppress the Qedarite revolt at Adummatu.[86]

Finally, Assurbanipal conducted several campaigns against the Arabs. The intial conflict (ca. 650–647 BCE) was related to his internecine war with his brother Shamash-shum-ukin, the king of Babylon, who was supported by Arab allies, including Uaite' (I) son of Ḥazael, the Qedarite king. After the defeat of Shamash-shum-ukin, Uaite' sought refuge with Natnu, king of the

---

82. Eph'al, *Ancient Arab*, 40–41; and Eph'al, "'Arabs' in Babylonia in the 8th Century B.C.," *JAOS* 94 (1974): 108–15, esp. 111–12.

83. Eckart Frahm, *Einleitung in die Sanherib-Inschriften*, AfOB 26 (Vienna: Institut für Orientalisk der Universität Wien, 1997), 129–36 = T 62, for the text, translation, and commentary.

84. Eph'al, *Ancient Arabs*, 118–23.

85. Leichty, *Royal Inscriptions of Esarhaddon*, no. 1, col. iv, 1–31, for the full account; cf. no. 4, col. ii', 1–24'; no. 66, col. iii, 1'–24'; no. 31, rev. 1'–24'; no. 31, rev. 2b–11; no. 97, 7–19a.

86. Eph'al, *Ancient Arabs*, 43–46, 125–142; cf. Frances Reynolds, ed., *The Babylonian Correspondence of Esarhaddon, and Letters to Assurbanipal and Sin-Šarru-Iškun from Northern and Central Babylonia*, SAA 18 (Helsinki: Helsinki University Press, 2003), nos. 143–45 = *ABL* 350, *CT* 54 498, and *ABL* 811. See now Leichty, *Royal Inscriptions of Esarhaddon*.

Nabayat, but was forced finally to submit to the Assyrian king in Nineveh. Assurbanipal then installed Abiyateʻ son of Teʼri as the Qedarite king. A second war (ca. 641–638 BCE) began when Abiyateʻ and Uaiteʻ (II) led the Qedarites to attack the western borders of Assyria, supported by Natnu, king of the Nabayat. The conflicts are well documented but involve twenty-six episodes in the annals that are difficult to reconstruct.[87] The fate of Abiyateʻ is unknown, but Natnu was replaced by his son Nuḫru as king of the Nabayat. The Nabayat territory is depicted at some remote distance from Assyria, but this may only mean southwestern Babylonia.

The size and extent of the Qedarite confederation is difficult to estimate in the Neo-Assyrian period. The sources suggest it interacted with Damascus and Moab in the west, Babylon to the east, and Taymāʼ to the south, which helps demarcate its extent. The Qedarite capital at Adummatu/Dumah (medieval Arabic Dumat al-Jandal) has been the focus of recent archaeological work, but without producing any evidence of the Neo-Assyrian period. In contrast, some important Iron Age sites were located near Dumat al-Jandal in the Kaf region of the Wadi Sirḥān.[88] Future investigation of the site may reveal the actual location of the Qedarite fortress and the pre-Hellenistic settlement.

There are several interesting aspects of the Qedarite confederation. What is of striking interest about the dynasty is the string of Qedarite queens named in Assyrian texts—Zabibe, Samsi, Iatiʼe, and Adiya, with the queens Teʼelḫunu and Tabūa/Tarbūa represented as high priestesses of Dilbat (i.e., Ishtar), who was worshiped locally under the name of ʻAṯtrsmn or Atar-Samayin—"Ishtar of the heavens." With the queens from the land of Bāzu and elsewhere, the political-social-religious structure of North Arabian society seems to have included queens in its administrative hierarchy, in contrast to the dominance of kings elsewhere. Secondly, the Assyrian annals identify the gods of the Arabian pantheon as Atar-Samayin, Dai, Huhai, Ruldāwu, Abīrillu, and Atar-qurumā. Some of these gods appear in North Arabian inscriptions in the region of Dumah, and elsewhere in later periods.[89] Finally, in contrast to the

---

87. For possible reconstructions, see Manfred Weippert, "Die Kämpfe des assyrischen Königs Assurbanipal gegen die Araber," *WO* 7 (1973): 39–85; Ephʻal, *Ancient Arabs*, 46–52, 142–69; and Pamela Gerardi, "The Arab Campaigns of Aššurbanipal: Scribal Reconstruction of the Past," *SAAB* 6, no. 2 (1992): 67–103. The conflict is also depicted in reliefs; see R. D. Barnett, *Sculptures from the North Palace of Assurbanipal at Nineveh (668–627 B.C.)* (London: British Museum, 1976), 15–16, 45, and plates 32–33, with a description by Ephʻal, *Ancient Arabs*, 151n518.

88. Robert McC. Adams et al., "Preliminary Report on the First Phase of the Comprehensive Archaeological Survey Program," *Atlal: The Journal of Saudi Arabian Archaeology* 1 (1977): 36–40.

89. Winnett and Reed, *Ancient Records of North Arabia*, Thamudic inscriptions, nos. 3, 21–23.

"Midianite phenomenon," the evidence for the Qedarite kingdom continues in the Babylonian, Persian, and Hellenistic eras, although the evidence is now in the western part of Arabia and the Levant. At an ancient shrine at Tell el-Maskhuta, just west of the Suez on the borders of Egypt, dating to about 400 BCE, some silver vessels were discovered with Aramaic dedicatory inscriptions to Han-'Ilāt ("the [Arab] goddess"), one of which bears the name "Qainū son of Gešem, king of Qedar."[90] The likelihood is that this is the son of Geshem the Arab, one of the adversaries of Nehemiah in Judah during the mid-fifth century BCE (Neh. 2:19; 6:1, 2, 6). The dynastic lineage may include "Iyas, son of Mahaly, the king," whose name is inscribed on an incense altar at Lachish in Palestine, the possible grandfather and great grandfather of "Qainū son of Gešem, king of Qedar."[91] In recent decades, thousands of Idumaean ostraca have been discovered from Maresha and Khirbet el-Qom. From the former, an ostracon may mention "Qedarites" and "Arabs."[92] Several from the latter refer to a "House of 'Uzza'" (*byt 'z'*), apparently a "shrine of 'Uzza'," the North Arabian deity.[93] Since the onomasticon of the ostraca contains a large number of Arabic names, it appears that Geshem the Arab represented a substantial population on the borders of Judah in the fourth century BCE, evidently to be associated with the Qedarites, who appear from the Egyptian frontier to Babylon.

Taymā'

The oasis of Taymā' is located about 220 kilometers southeast of Qurayya, 300 kilometers southwest of Dumat al-Jandal and 150 kilometers northeast of Al-'Ulā, connecting it with the major trade routes leading to the Levant, Mesopotamia, and Yemen. Modern Taymā' still retains its ancient name and serves as the administrative center of the district. The large al-Haddāj

---

90. I. Rabinowitz, "Aramaic Inscriptions of the Fifth Century B.C.E. from a North-Arab Shrine," *JNES* 15 (1956): 1–9 and 154–55.

91. A. Lemaire, "Un nouveaux roi arabe de Qedar dans l'inscription de l'autel a encens de Lakish," *RB* 81 (1974): 63–72.

92. Esther Eshel, "Inscriptions in Hebrew, Aramaic and Phoenician Script," in *Maresha Excavations Final Report III: Epigraphic Finds from the 1989–2000 Seasons*, ed. Amos Kloner et al. (Jerusalem: Israel Antiquities Authority, 2010), 43–44 (no. 11). See Graf, "Arabs in Palestine from the Neo-Assyrian to the Persian Period," 293–98; and B. Porten and A. Yardeni, *Textbook of Aramaic Ostraca from Idumea*, vol. 1 (Winona Lake, IN: Eisenbrauns, 2014), esp. ix–xiv for bibliography.

93. A. Lemaire, "Les religions du Sud de la Palestine au IVe siècle av. J.-C. d'après les ostraca Araméens d'Idumée," *CRAI* 145 (2001): 1157–58; cf. Lemaire, "Administration in Fourth Century B.C.E. Judah in Light of Epigraphy and Numismatics," in *Judah and the Judeans in the Fourth Century B.C.E.*, ed. Oded Lipschits, Gary Knoppers, and Rainer Albertz (Winona Lake, IN: Eisenbrauns, 2007), 65–67.

Figure 12.3. The palace of Qasr al-Hamra at Taymā', northwest of the settlement, the possible residence of Nabonidus, where several Aramaic stelae have been found

Well in the town was the center of the ancient and medieval settlement. The importance of the oasis on the Arabian trade route is indicated by its connection with Saba in Assyrian texts and the Hebrew Bible (Job 6:18–19). Although important discoveries were made at the site in the nineteenth century, excavations of the ruins began only in the 1970s, and after an interval, are continued now by the joint Saudi-German expedition at the site.[94]

It is one of the largest archaeological sites in Arabia. The reason for its size and importance is evident by its location and physical situation. Taymā' is located in a depression, which once formed a large lake in the prehistoric period, and it remains a fertile oasis. As early as the third millennium BCE, it became a cosmopolitan center, and by the early second millennium BCE attracted a population from Anatolia, the Levant, and Mesopotamia. It was approximately in the late third millennium BCE that the depression was encircled

94. Summarized by Arnulf Hausleiter, "The Oasis of Tayma," in Ali-Ghabban et al., *Roads of Arabia*, 219–61. For a listing of the various projects since 1979 with bibliography, see R. Eichmann et al., "Tayma–Spring 2004, Report on the Joint Saudi-Arabian-German Archaeological Project," *Atlal: The Journal of Saudi Arabian Archaeology* 19 (2006): 94–95.

by a 14-kilometer-long city wall to protect the oasis.[95] Although the society at Taymā' is unknown at this time, it must have been a politically well-organized community. Recent excavations have provided evidence for the continuity of occupation at the settlement from the Late Bronze Age through the first millennium BCE. At Qraya in the central area of the site, dating to the period between 1200 and 1000 BCE, there are public buildings, a variant of the Qurayya painted pottery, and finds that indicate contact with Mesopotamia and Egypt. Excavations from several ninth- and sixth-century cemeteries (Sana'iye and Tal'a) have produced the distinctive painted pottery with geometric motifs associated with Taymā'.[96] These discoveries make any presumed gap between Late Bronze Age Midian and Taymā' in the sixth century BCE difficult to maintain.

Even before Taymā' emerged from darkness in the early Iron Age with the recent excavations, new cuneiform sources were revealing that the oasis was prominently involved in the larger Near Eastern world in the same era. The first piece of evidence was a hieroglyphic Luwian tablet from the royal archives of Yariris of Carchemish on the middle Euphrates, who boasts of his cosmopolitan fame by indicating his ability to read twelve different languages, including that of Tyre (Sura), Assyria (Assur), and *Taiman*. The last has convincingly been understood as Taymā', indicating the interaction of the oasis in North Syria, and referring to the peculiar script utilized at the oasis.[97] The second contribution is the cuneiform correspondence of Ninurta-kuduri-uṣur, governor of Suhu and Mari on the middle Euphrates in the mid-eighth century BCE. The governor recounts how a caravan of Taymanites (*Tema'a*) and Sabaeans (*Šaba'a*) stopped at wells in the area and entered the town of Ḫindanu in his district, clearly without paying the local tribute. As a consequence, the governor raided the caravan and confiscated as booty two hundred camels, Tyrian blue wool, and other unspecified exotic items.[98] In addition, during the reign of Nebuchadnezzar, in 598 BCE, a Taymanite was

---

95. Nicole Klauser et al., "Optimally Stimulated Luminescence Dating of the City Wall System of Ancient Tayma (NW Saudi Arabia)," *JAS* 38 (2011): 1818–26.

96. Hausleiter, "Oasis of Tayma," 230–32, 242, and 246–47 with illustrations. For a comparison between the pottery traditions of northwest Arabia and the southern Levant in the early first millennium, see Juan Manuel Tebes, *Aram* 27/1–2 (2015): 255–82.

97. Alasdair Livingstone, "New Light on the Ancient Town of Taimā'," in *Studia Aramaica: New Sources and New Approaches*, ed. M. J. Geller et al., JSSSup 4 (Oxford: Oxford University Press, 1995), 137–40.

98. Mario Liverani, "Early Caravan Trade between South-Arabia and Mesopotamia," *Yemen* 1 (1992): 111–15; and Livingstone, "New Light," 137–140. For the context, see Nadav Na'aman, "The Suhu Governors' Inscriptions in the Context of Mesopotamian Royal Inscriptions," in *Treasures on Camels' Humps: History and Literary Studies from the Ancient Near East Presented to Israel Ephʻal*, ed. Mordechai Cogan and Dan'el Kahn (Jerusalem: Hebrew University Magnes Press, 2008), 221–35, esp. 233–34.

receiving rations while engaged as a workman in the local bitumen industry. As indicated earlier, after Tiglath-pileser III's campaign in 732 BCE against Samsi, queen of the Arabs, the Neo-Assyrian king received gifts from a string of Arab tributaries, including Taymā', which is listed between Massā' and Saba'.[99] In addition, Taymā' appears in the so-called Sargon Geography describing the extent of Sargon of Akkad's world empire, an archaizing source from the Neo-Assyrian Empire dating to the reign of Sargon II, with "Tema" appearing between Moab and Edom, in a section beginning with Baza (also located in Arabia).[100] Finally, a relief—discovered at Taymā' by Charles Huber and Julius Euting in 1884 and now in the Louvre—displays Assyrian iconography suggesting possible Assyrian presence at the oasis.[101] The antiquity of Taymā' in the early Iron Age is then well attested in Neo-Assyrian texts and the archaeological record.

Nevertheless, the fame of Taymā' is primarily the result of one of the strangest events in Near Eastern history, the ten-year stay of the Neo-Babylonian king Nabonidus at Taymā' (ca. 552–542 BCE). Such royal presence for an extended period must have had an impact on this large city of northwest Arabia. The details of Nabonidus's itinerary, the chronology of his stay at Taymā', and the results of his Arabian campaign can be constructed from a number of contemporary Babylonian cuneiform sources: the Nabonidus Chronicle, the Royal Chronicle, the Verse Account, and the Harran Inscriptions.[102] Of these, the inscriptions of Nabonidus's reign discovered at the great temple of the moon god Sîn at Harran on the upper Euphrates are of primary importance.[103] These sources are now supported by stunning new discoveries at Taymā', most importantly by a stela found in the 2004 excavations inscribed with a fragmentary Neo-Babylonian votive text, with iconography closely paralleling that of other reliefs of Nabonidus.[104] From these sources, at least the general outline of Nabonidus's adventurous Arabian expedition can be pieced together.

99. Eph'al, *Ancient Arabs*, 36.
100. W. Horowitz, "Moab and Edom in the Sargon Geography," *IEJ* 43 (1993): 153.
101. D. T. Potts, "Tayma and the Assyrian Empire," *AAE* 2 (1991): 10–23.
102. W. G. Lambert, "Nabonidus at Tayma," *PSAS* (1972): 53–64. For a discussion of the sources, see Eph'al, *Ancient Arabs*, 170–91; and Paul-Alain Beaulieu, *The Reign of Nabonidus, King of Babylon, 556–539 B.C.* (New Haven: Yale University Press, 1989), 144–85. There are also Babylonian cuneiform tablets from Uruk mentioning Taymanite residents in 598 BCE and later, as well as provisions for caravans sent to Taymā' in the fifth and tenth years of Nabonidus's reign. See Alasdair Livingstone, "Arabians in Babylonia/Babylonians in Arabia," in Fahd, *L'Arabie préislamique*, 97–105.
103. Gadd, "Harran Inscriptions," 35–92.
104. R. Eichmann, H. Schaudig, and A. Hausleiter, "Archaeology and Epigraphy at Tayma (Saudi Arabia)," *AAE* 17 (2006): 169–74.

Figure 12.4. Taymanite text from the Mahaijah region, southwest of Taymā', which mentions Nabonidus. It reads "I, MARDN, the servant of Nabonid, king of Babylon."

After his three-year stay in Syria, it appears Nabonidus headed south through Transjordan to North Arabia in ca. 552 BCE. The only clue to his route is provided by the Nabonidus Chronicle, listing the toponym [ú]-du-um-mum, which is restored and interpreted as a reference to Edom.[105] The recent discovery of the cuneiform inscription and sculpture at Sela' in southern Jordan offers support for the restoration.[106] In the Harran Inscriptions it is indicated that he took the road to Taymā', Dadanu (Al-'Ulā), Padakku (Fadak), Ḫibra (Khaybar), Yadiḫu (al-Ḥayit), and Yatribu (Yathrib, Medina), "where for ten years I moved among them and did not enter my city Babylon." The Royal Chronicle adds that the "king of Dadana" was defeated during a difficult campaign, and the Verse Account adds that Nabonidus killed the

---

105. Lambert, "Nabonidus at Tayma," 55; cf. Eph'al, *Ancient Arabs*, 185–88; and Beaulieu, *Reign of Nabonidus*, 166.

106. S. Dalley and A. Goguel, "The Sela' Sculpture: A Neo-Babylonian Rock Relief in Southern Jordan," *ADAJ* (1997): 169–76; see also F. Zayadine, "Le relief néo-babylonien à Sela' près de Tafileh: Interprétation historique," *Syria* 76 (1999): 83–90. For the wider implications, see also A. Lemaire, "Nabonidus in Arabia and Judah in the Neo-Babylonian Period," in *Judah and the Judeans in the Neo-Babylonian Period*, ed. O. Lipschits and J. Blenkinsopp (Winona Lake, IN: Eisenbrauns, 2003), 285–98, esp. 287–88.

king of Taymā' with the sword and slaughtered the herds of the inhabitants of the city. Afterward, he built a palace at Taymā', fortified the city, and garrisoned it, making it virtually a second capital of his kingdom. Taymā' was strategically positioned along the caravan route leading from South Arabia, but the motives for his campaign are debated, with political, economic, and religious reasons being advanced. The impact of Nabonidus on Taymā' has been exaggerated, as the city had risen to prominence in the centuries before his arrival. But his presence and influence must have had a dramatic effect on the oasis. There is evidence of the walls being reinforced, and Qasr al-Hamra in the northwest of the settlement has been suggested as his residence (fig. 12.3). Excavations have revealed a complex of ruins on this small natural hill and a possible shrine with an Aramaic stela similar to the one found by Huber and Euting at Taymā' a century earlier. But it is dated to ca. 400 BCE, representing a dedication to the gods of Taymā' by the governor of the oasis, who was a son of the king of Liḥyan and bears a dynastic name associated with the Qedarite confederation.[107] The possible connections between Qedar, Dedan, and Taymā' remain interesting and receive support from other discoveries at Taymā'. The Liḥyanite king TLMY left dedications for every decade of his reign in the Qraya temple in the heart of ancient Taymā', where a large royal Liḥyanite statue 4 meters high was also found.[108] For the sojourn of Nabonidus, there are some forty-five Taymanite texts found at Jabal Ghunaym, 14 kilometers southeast of Taymā', dating to the sixth and fifth centuries BCE. These texts refer repeatedly to the god Ṣalm and refer to wars conducted against Dedan, Massā', and Nabayat, ostensibly part of Nabonidus's campaign.[109] More dramatically, in the region south of Taymā', three hundred more Taymanite texts were recorded, several of which are engraved by officials that mention the Neo-Babylonian king Nabonidus in Taymanite script.[110] A string of small

---

107. Frank Moore Cross, "A New Aramaic Stele from Taymā'," *CBQ* 45 (1986): 387–94.
108. Hausleiter, "Oasis of Tayma," 233–34 and 258.
109. Winnett and Reed, *Ancient Records of North Arabia*, 88–107, nos. 1–44.
110. First published by Khalid M. Eskoubi, *An Analytical and Comparative Study of Inscriptions from the "Rum" Region, Southwest of Tayma* (Riyadh, 1999) [in Arabic]. See also H. Hayajneh, "First Evidence of Nabonidus in the Ancient North Arabian Inscriptions from the Region of Tayma'," *PSAS* 31 (2001): 81–95; Y. Gruntfest and M. Heltzer, "Nabonid, King of Babylon (556–539 B.C.E.) in Arabia in Light of New Evidence," *BN* 110 (2001): 25–30; W. W. Müller and Said al-Said, "Der babylonische König in taymanischen Inscriften," in *Neue Beiträge zur Semitistik*, ed. N. Nebes (Wiesbaden: Harrassowitz, 2002), 105–22; and Lemaire, "Nabonidus in Arabia and Judah," 288–89. For references to Dedan and Qedar in the Eskoubi ancient North Arabian texts, see H. Hayajneh, "Remarks on Ancient North Arabian Inscriptions from the Region of Tayma' in Northwest Arabia," in *From Ugarit to Nabataea: Studies in Honor of John F. Healey*, ed. G. A. Kiraz and Z. Al-Salameen (Piscataway, NJ: Gorgias, 2012), 123–39; and Hayajneh, "First Evidence of the Locative QDR (Qedar) in Ancient North Arabian Inscriptions,"

Figure 12.5. Mantar Bani 'Atiya, a small isolated watchtower ca. 8 km north of Taymā' on the road to Tabuk. The tower is 3.75 m square. The walls are covered with Taymanite and Thamudic texts dating from the sixth century and later.

forts external to the walls and encircling the city also may reflect Nabonidus's fortification of the oasis.

Other innovations under Nabonidus at the oasis are of a cultural nature. It appears that an Aramaic pantheon was also introduced to Taymā' during Nabonidus's stay at the oasis. The Aramaic stelae discovered in 1880 and 1979 at Taymā' mention the deities Ṣalm (a sun deity), Śangilā (meaning "Sîn [the moon god] is great"), and Ashīma (perhaps Venus), who appear in the Taymanite inscriptions as well.[111] This astrological interpretation of the Aramaic stela in 1979 is supported by the cuboid altar found along with it at al-Hamra that has astrological symbols covering its surfaces.[112] These

---

in *Studies in Honour of Christian Robin: Arabie-Arabiens*, ed. Iwona Gajda (forthcoming). In addition, two Thamudic texts, JS 695 + 696, found in Wādī Qanā, southwest of Tabūk in northwest Saudi Arabia, have been combined to be read as *l ḥdś ḏ 'l gśmw* or "by ḤDŚ of the tribe of GŚMW," a royal Qedarite name. See G. M. D. King, "Early North Arabian Thamudic E" (PhD diss., University of London School of Oriental and African Studies, 1990), 691.

111. Mohammed Maraqteen, "The Aramaic Pantheon of Taymā'," *AAE* 7 (1996): 17–31. See also Winnett and Reed, *Ancient Records of North Arabia*, 74–80, Thamudic inscriptions, nos. 3, 20–23.

112. Hausleiter, "Oasis of Tayma," 254–55.

Figure 12.6. Some texts on the outside walls of Mantar Bani 'Atiya. The Taymanite text at the top mentions the god Ṣalm (see *BIAUL* 8–9 [1972]: 44, no. 32).

Aramaic stelae are not isolated finds, as another nineteen Aramaic texts have been found at Taymā' on funerary stelae, in dedications and graffiti dating mostly after 400 BCE and as late as the early centuries of the Common Era.[113] The introduction of Aramaic into Taymā' by Nabonidus obviously was a long-lasting contribution. It also was argued that Nabonidus brought with him from Babylon Jewish exiles, whom he established in military mercenary colonies in the various oases of the Ḥijāz.[114] This is assumed on the basis of a Jewish presence at Taymā' and al-'Ulā in the Nabataean-Roman era, but if this was the case it has left no trace in the archaeological or epigraphic evidence of the Persian and Hellenistic eras.[115] The most interesting evidence

---

113. R. Degen, "Die aramäischen Inschriften aus Taimā' und Umgebung," in *Neue Ephemeris für Semitische Epigraphik*, vol. 2, ed. R. Degen, W. W. Müller, and W. Röllig (Wiesbaden: Harrassowitz, 1974), 79–98; and A. Lemaire, "Les inscriptions araméennes anciennes de Teima: Sur les pistes de Teima," in *Présence arabe dans le croissant fertile avant l'Hégire*, ed. H. Lozachmeur (Paris: Éditions Recherche sur les Civilisations, 1995), 63–68.

114. Gadd, "Harran Inscriptions," 86–88; cf. H. Hirschberg, "Arabia," *Encyclopaedia Judaica* 3 (1971) 234; I. Ben-Zvi, "The Origins of the Jewish Tribes in Arabia," *ErIsr* 6 (1990): 130–48 (in Hebrew, with an English summary on 35*); Beaulieu, *Reign of Nabonidus*, 174.

115. David F. Graf, "Ebrei in Arabia," in *Gli Ebrei nell'impero romano*, ed. Ariel Lewin (Firenze: Giuntina, 2001), 260.

for Jewish presence at Taymā' is three fragments of the Prayer of Nabonidus discovered at Qumran that mention a Jewish exorcist present at the oasis, but their interpretation remains controversial.[116] Taymā', as one of the largest archaeological sites in North Arabia, maintains its interest as one of the most fascinating ancient settlements in Arabia.

Dedan

Al-'Ulā is one of the principal towns in northwestern Arabia, located in the Ḥijāz Mountains in a fertile valley between towering sandstone mountains as high as 200 meters. It is in the middle of a sloping depression that begins ca. 50 kilometers north and runs 160 kilometers to the south. The drainage into this depression provides the basis for a flourishing oasis known by early Islamic geographers as the Wadi al-Qurā (Valley of Villages). The ancient ruins of Dedan lie to the northeast of the valley under the steep cliff of the Harrat al-'Awayridh and are known as al-Khurayba, identified as ancient Dedan by Edward Glaser in 1890 (fig. 12.7). During the seventh and fifth centuries BCE, the kingdom of Dedan was flourishing, but in the fourth century it was transformed or acquired by the tribe of Liḥyan, which continued to rule at the oasis until the first century BCE. The Liḥyanite kingdom's territory must have been extensive, since its impact is known to have reached to Medina in the south and the Gulf of Aqaba in the north, which Pliny called "Laeanitic" or "Aelanitic" after the Liḥyanites (*Natural History* 6.156). The ruins of al-Khurayba stretch for 300 meters and are 200 meters wide, but there are also the ancient remains of agricultural estates or plantations to the north and south of the town, where fields of fig trees are nourished by *qanats*, a complex underwater irrigation system. Large boulders nearby are covered with Liḥyanite inscriptions. Dedan was one of the major stops for ancient caravans coming from South Arabia and proceeding to the Levant. Inscriptions indicate that a Minaean South Arabian colony was established and flourished at the oasis in the fourth century BCE.

Excavations of the site began only in 2004 but are already yielding important results.[117] The many inscriptions of the valley are our main source of

---

116. J. Collins, "4Q242 Prayer of Nabonidus," in *Qumran Cave 4.XVII: Parabiblical Texts, Part 3*, ed. G. Brooke et al., DJD 22 (Oxford: Oxford University Press, 1996), 83–93; and Émile Puech, "La prière de Nabonide (4Q242)," in *Targumic and Cognate Studies: Essays in Honour of Martin McNamara*, ed. K. J. Cathcart and M. Maher, JSOTSup 230 (Sheffield, UK: Sheffield Academic, 1996), 208–27; cf. A. Steinmann, "The Chicken and the Egg: A New Proposal for the Relationship between the 'Prayer of Nabonidus' and the 'Book of Daniel,'" *RevQ* 20, no. 4 (2002): 557–70.

117. Summarized in Said F. al-Said, "Dedan (Al-Ula)," and Hussein bin Ali Abu Al-Hasan, "The Kingdom of Lihyan," in Ali-Ghabban et al., *Roads of Arabia*, 262–85. For an earlier brief summary, see A. T. al-Ansary, "The State of Lihyan: A New Perspective," *Topoi* 9 (1999): 191–95.

Figure 12.7. Dedan (Al-'Ulā), view of the oasis and the ruins of Khurayba, visible betweeen the palm tree oasis and large massif

information about the internal organization of Liḥyanite society at Dedan.[118] Among the earliest is the funerary inscription of Kabir'il king of Dedan (JS 138 lih.) and that of Gashm b. Shahr and 'Abd the governor (fḥt) of Dedan (JS 349 lih.).[119] Kabir'il was once the only known Dedanite king, but the recent excavations have produced more than one hundred new inscriptions, including one of another Dedanite king, 'Aṣī, who made a dedication to Ṭaḥlān, a previously unknown Arabian deity.[120] The hundreds of Liḥyanite inscriptions provide for us the names of six kings (mlk) of Liḥyan, three others of royal lineage without a title, and six governors (r'y), whose reigns are arranged from the mid-fourth to mid-second century BCE. Both Dedan and Liḥyan are now mentioned in a recent South Arabian Sabaean text dating to ca. 600 BCE, so adjustments may have to be made in the chronology. The

118. Saba Farès-Drappeau, *Dédan et Liḥyān: Histoire des Arabes aux confins des pouvoirs perse et hellénistique (IVᵉ-IIᵉ s. avant l'ère chrétienne)*, TMOM (Lyon: Maison de l'Orient et de la Méditerranée, 2005), provides a new corpus and full discussion of all aspects of the epigraphic evidence.
119. Winnett and Reed, *Ancient Records of North Arabia*, 113–20.
120. Said F. al-Said, "Recent Epigraphic Evidence from the Excavations at Al-'Ula Reveals a New King of Dadān," *AAE* 22 (2011): 196–200.

Figure 12.8. Dedan (Al-'Ulā), view of the Lion Tombs in the necropolis at Khurayba

king of Liḥyan was not an absolute monarch, as the inscriptions mention not only a governor but also an "assembly of partisans" (š't) headed by a "chief" (kbr) and composed of the "leaders" ('b'l) of the various clans. The pantheon of Liḥyan included al-Lāh ("the god") and Dhu-Ghābat (the [hidden] god of the forests or groves) as the principal deities, but also Ḥrg (the god of water), hn-'ktb (the god of writing, scribes), and many other deities of foreign extraction. Of note are a handful of texts that indicate women served as priestesses in offering sacrifices to Dhu-Ghābat.[121] Although the Liḥyanite kingdom appears to have existed for a rather short period, normally assigned to the late Persian and early Hellenistic eras, there are three Aramaic texts of a Mas'ūdū "king of Liḥyan" dated to around 120–100 BCE (JS 334, 335, 337), and a few Safaitic North Arabian inscriptions of the early Roman era in southern Syria that mention a number of attacks by the "tribe of Liḥyan" in the region.[122] Clearly, the origins and demise of the Liḥyanites remains obscure.

---

121. Saba Farès, "Les femmes prêtresses dans les religions arabes préislamiques: Les cas de Liḥyanites," *Topoi: Orient-Occident Supplément* 10 (2009): 183–95.
122. Michael Macdonald, Muna Al-Mu'azzin, and Laïla Nehmé, "Les inscriptions safaïtiques de Syrie, 140 ans après leur découverte," *CRAI* 140 (1996): 458–62.

South Arabia

During the first millennium BCE, a series of kingdoms emerged in South Arabia: Saba with a capital at Mārib, Qataban with a capital at Timnaʻ, Ḥaḍramawt with a capital at Shabwa, and the Minaeans with a capital at Maʻin. These were sophisticated states, with impressive architecture and art, and highly literate, producing a corpus of more than ten thousand inscriptions, almost six thousand of which are Sabaic, dating from the eighth century BCE to the end of the third century CE. The Sabaeans were clearly the most important of the four kingdoms, around which a cultural unity developed in South Arabia.[123] Their history is divided into two periods, reflecting the royal titles used by their rulers. In the archaic period their leaders are called *mukarribs*. The title "*mukarrib* of Saba" seems to mean "head, chief of a federation" (from *krb*, "to carry out orders, obligations"), one who exercised hegemony over other tribes and kingdoms. The title is employed only by the *mukarrib* himself, with the subjects referring to him by his name only. At some point during the history of Saba, the kings stopped using the title of *mukarrib* and instead began using the title of *mlk sbʼ*, "King of Saba." The transition appears to be around the sixth century BCE. This change is reflected in the paleography of the texts and also how they were engraved. Inscriptions in the later period are always right to left, whereas in the earlier period they could run in either direction. The date when this happened remains a matter of debate, but appears to be ca. 365 BCE. About thirty-one rulers used the title of *mukarrib*, and several dozen the title of "King of Saba."[124] The *mukarribs* appear to be political and religious leaders around whom the Sabaeans are united in the worship of the god Almaqah and a pantheon of lesser deities. The sequence and number of the *mukarribs* are not exact, but the later kings are mostly direct descendants, and the chronology more precise. These kings were assisted by an assembly composed of landowners and tribal representatives. In addition, the surrounding states were no longer simple allies or subjects but took on independent status, and Saba was no longer preeminent.

The chronology of the *mukarribs* has been a vexed question for scholars of South Arabia. The few early texts are difficult to date with any absolute certainty. The rulers that appear in the texts are difficult to arrange in any

---

123. See Christian Robin, "Sheba II. Dans les inscriptions d'Arabie du Sud," *DBSup* 12:1047–1254, for a detailed treatment with an exhaustive bibliography. In general, see Jean-François Breton, *Arabia Felix: From the Time of the Queen of Sheba; Eighth Century B.C. to First Century A.D.* (Notre Dame, IN: University of Notre Dame Press, 1999).

124. For a general guide, see K. A. Kitchen, *Documentation for Ancient Arabia*, pt. 1, *Chronological Framework and Historical Sources* (Liverpool: Liverpool University Press, 1994), 8–111 for the Sabaean mukkaribate, and 242–43 for a list of 31 *mukarribs* from ca. 820 to 365 BCE.

sequential order. In the nineteenth century pioneering scholars like Edmund Glaser and F. Hommel suggested the *mukarribs* were a tenth-century phenomenon. As evidence accumulated, the references to the *mukarribs* and Saba in the Assyrian annals suggested a date beginning with the eighth century BCE. The first text mentioned that Sargon II (722–705) received tribute in 716 BCE from "Ita'amra the Sabaean," who was identified with the *mukarrib* Yathī'amar Bayān.[125] The second important text mentioned in ca. 688 BCE that tribute of precious stones was received by King Sennacherib from "Karabilu king of Saba," who was identified with the *mukarrib* Karib'īl Watar.[126] Initially, these equivalencies with the Assyrian annals and the Sabaean *mukarribs* were considered decisive.[127] But criticisms emerged just as quickly. Since these royal names are frequently repeated in the Sabaean dynasty, it was argued that the rulers mentioned in South Arabian texts were only the namesakes of the earlier kings in Assyrian texts. As a result, a counterproposal was made by Jacqueline Pirenne based on a paleographical comparison with the Classical Greek script that suggested the development of monumental South Arabian script was influenced by the Greek world and that the South Arabian inscriptions date only from the fifth century BCE and afterward.[128] The former is called the "long chronology" and the latter the "short chronology."[129] The long chronology is favored by most scholars today, but the short chronology still has a few staunch and persistent advocates.

What helped change the picture in favor of the long chronology is the recent archaeological discoveries in Yemen of civilizations earlier than the first millennium BCE associated with epigraphic finds. The period between the Neolithic and Iron Ages in South Arabia was once an archaeological void, but

125. Fuchs, *Die Inschriften Sargons II*, 110 (Ann. no. 123) and 198. For discussion, see Hannes D. Galter, "'. . . an der Grenze der Länder im Westen': Saba' in den assyrischen Königsinschriften," in *Studies in Oriental Culture and History: Festschrift for Walter Dostal* (Frankfurt am Main: Peter Lang, 1993), 32–33. For a new text, see Norbert Nebes, "Ita'amar der Sabäer: Zur Datierung der Monumentalinschrift des Yiṯa"amar Watar aus Ṣirwāḥ," *AAE* 18 (2007): 25–33.

126. Frahm, *Einleitung in die Sanherib-Inschriften*, T 90–95 with 145–46; Eph'al, *Ancient Arabs*, 42–43 (VA 8248), 228–29; and see Manfried Dietrich, ed., *The Babylonian Correspondence of Sargon and Sennacherib*, SAA 17 (Helsinki: Helsinki University Press, 2003), xxiii and no. 4.5 for a letter of Sennacherib's reign mentioning the tribute of Saba. For discussion, see Galter, "'. . . an der Grenze,'" 34–35.

127. See Albert Jamme, *Sabaean Inscriptions from Maḥram Bilqîs (Mârib)* (Baltimore: Johns Hopkins Press, 1962), 389–94.

128. Jacqueline Pirenne, *Paléographie des inscriptions sud-arabes: Contribution à la chronologie et à l'histoire de l'Arabie du Sud antique*, vol. 1 (Brussels: Paleis der Academiën, 1956).

129. For recent discussion of the chronological problem, see Alessandra Avanzini, "La chronologie 'courte': Une réexamen," in *Arabia Antiqua: Early Origins of South Arabian States*, ed. Christian Robin (Rome: ISMEO, 1996), 7–13; and Giovanni Garbini, "La chronologie 'longue'": Une mise au point," in Robin, *Arabia Antiqua*, 15–22.

since the middle of the twentieth century the picture has changed dramatically. This began with the American expedition to Hajar ibn Ḥumayd in the Wadi Bayḥān in 1950. The site was located 12 kilometers south of Timnaʿ, the ancient capital of Qataban. The classic tell, over 50 feet high with twenty occupational levels, provided a basic stratigraphy for the pre-Islamic period. A radiocarbon date from the lower levels (Stratum Q) provided a date of 852 +/- 160 or the ninth century. Beneath it (in Stratum S) some South Arabian inscriptions were discovered incised into clay sherds, and a few raised in relief, suggesting a date between 1100 and 900 BCE—evidence in support of the long chronology.[130] The results received a scathing review by Jacqueline Pirenne, who advocated a date of the classical period and the fifth century BCE for the beginnings of the South Arabian script.[131] This view remained dominant in Europe until the last several decades, when multiple international excavation projects in Yemen discovered evidence of the early South Arabian script from the beginning of the first millennium (if not earlier) and a civilization reaching back into the Early Bronze Age. Those projects began with an Italian mission led by Alessandro de Maigret between 1981 and 1985 in the traditional Sabaean region between Ṣanʿāʾ and Mārib in northwest Yemen, where more than forty sites were found with a protohistoric pottery and stone industry, with Bronze Age parallels in the Early Bronze I/Middle Bronze I period at Syro-Palestinian sites, and radiocarbon dates between 2700 and 1800 BCE for the Early Bronze Age culture.[132] Later in the 1980s, the Russian mission discovered a large agricultural settlement at Raybūn in the western part of the Wadi Ḥaḍramawt, where a unique red-burnished slip pottery was prominent, decorated with zoomorphic and geometric designs similar to Late Bronze pottery in the Levant and assigned a date between 1200 and 1000 BCE. Some of the sherds also had inscriptions in monumental South Arabian scripts from the same lower strata (II–III) and are dated to the last quarter of the second millennium BCE.[133] In addition, three more early settlements were discovered in Wadi al-ʾAyn, a large tributary in the

---

130. Gus Van Beek, *Hajar Bin-Ḥumayd: Investigations at a Pre-Islamic Site in South Arabia* (Baltimore: Johns Hopkins University Press, 1969), 131; cf. Van Beek, "A Radiocarbon Date for Early South Arabia," *BASOR* 143 (1956): 6–9.

131. Pirenne, "Notes d'archéologie sud-arabe IX: Hajar bin Ḥumeid," *Syria* 51 (1974): 137–70.

132. A. de Maigret, "A Bronze Age for Southern Arabia," *East & West* 34 (1984): 340–434; de Maigret, *The Bronze Age Culture of Ḥawlān aṭ-Ṭiyāl and al-Ḥadā* (Rome: ISMEO, 1990); de Maigret, *Arabia Felix: An Exploration of the Archaeological History of Yemen* (London: Stacey, 2002), 134–62.

133. A. V. Sedov, "On the Origin of the Agricultural Settlements in Ḥaḍramawt," in Robin, *Arabia Antiqua*, 76–77; Sedov, "Notes on Stratigraphy and Pottery Sequence at Raybūn I Settlement (Western Wādī Ḥaḍramawt)," *Arabia* 1 (2003): 174–77.

western part of the Wadi Ḥaḍramawt, with pottery similar to that from the early Raybūn settlement.[134]

In North Yemen, just southwest of Mārib, the Italian mission in the Wadi Yalā between 1985 and 1989 excavated a large house ("A") in the settlement of al-Durayb.[135] The settlement was abandoned in the seventh or sixth century BCE and never reoccupied.[136] There were at least four strata in House A. The upper level A was dated by calibrated radiocarbon tests to between 825 and 585, and contained twenty-two sherds with writing. Level B yielded radiocarbon tests of 1100–830 BCE and contained three sherds with writing. A date before the mid-eighth century, and as early as the beginning of the first millennium, was proposed for the writing.[137] In essence, the finds of writing at Hajar bin Ḥumayd, Raybūn, and Yalā have shifted the introduction of writing in South Arabia to the long chronology. It is now clear that the Bronze Age in Yemen extended across the third and second millennia BCE.

In the heartland of Saba, on the plateau at Mārib, 1,500 meters above sea level, during possibly the third millennium but certainly in the second millennium BCE, irrigation dams were being constructed and progressively updated until the construction of the famous dam in 500 BCE that lasted until 500 CE.[138] Initially, a lock was constructed in the late third millennium BCE, located just several kilometers from the mouth of the Wadi Dhana, and another was constructed upstream in the second millennium. The later dam constructed in around 500 BCE was a masterpiece of engineering that carried floodwater through the Wadi Dhana to almost 47,990 acres or 194.2 square kilometers of cultivated land. A network of six lateral canals directed the waters to irrigate fields as far as 15 kilometers away. The dam consisted of an earthen wall fortified with stone, some 20 meters high and 650 meters long. These irrigation systems designed to catch and distribute the monsoon

---

134. A. V. Sedov, "Monuments of the Wādī al-'Ayn: Notes on an Archaeological Map of the Ḥaḍramawt, 3," *AAE* 7 (1996): 253–78.

135. Alessandro de Maigret and Christian Robin, "Les fouilles italiennes de Yalâ (Yémen du Nord): Nouvelles données sur la chronologie de l'Arabie du Sud préislamiques," *CRAI* 133 (1989): 255–91.

136. Romolo Loreto, "House and Household: A Contextual Approach to the Study of South Arabian Domestic Architecture; A Case Study from Seventh- to Sixth-Century BC Yalā/ad-Durayb," *PSAS* 39 (2009): 131–46.

137. Giovanni Garbini, "Le iscrizioni su ceramic da as-Durayb-Yalā," *Yemen* 1 (1992): 79–91. Two of the sherds from Level A contained names that Garbini considered North Arabian (nos. 6 and 10), and he argued for an eighth-century date. Alessandro de Maigret suggested a date as early as the tenth–ninth centuries (*Arabia Felix*, 173–84). Benjamin Sass (*Alphabet at the Turn of the Millennium*, 96–132) prefers a date of the mid-eighth century.

138. Summarized in Breton, *Arabia Felix*, 9–27. For the Sabaean capital at Mārib, see W. W. Müller, "Marib," *EI* 6:559–67.

rains are among the most important remains of antiquity in Yemen. Similar systems existed for other wadis that directed the periodic floods from the highlands to the fields below.

In addition to the antiquity of Saba and South Arabia, the discovery of new epigraphic evidence has provided support for the long chronology. Saba was already attested in Assyrian texts from the time of Tiglath-pileser in the eighth century BCE.[139] A newly discovered cuneiform text now records a South Arabian caravan operating on the middle Euphrates in Mesopotamia in the middle of the eighth century BCE. The caravan was led by both Taymanites and Sabaeans and was composed of two hundred camels loaded with purple-dyed woolen garments, iron, and alabaster.[140] It has been noted that the references to the Sabaeans in Assyrian texts suggest there was a Sabaean merchant colony located in North Arabia, perhaps at Dumah, Taymā', or Dedan, as Mārib in South Arabia was more than 1,000 kilometers from Assyria.[141] This may be the case, in order to facilitate long-distance trade, but the once-popular hypothesis that the Sabaeans were a North Arabian tribe who migrated south only in the fifth century BCE, introducing the alphabet and high culture to South Arabia, is now refuted by the new archaeological discoveries as well as new epigraphic evidence.[142] A new Sabaean inscription indicates that merchants also traveled from Saba to the Levant in the early first millennium BCE. It attests a Sabaean from Nashq (modern al-Bayḍa) in Jawf during the reign of Yitha'amar, king of Saba, ca. 600 BCE, who traveled with his caravan to Dedan, Gaza, and the "villages of Judah."[143] The interaction of Sabaeans with the major cultures and peoples of the Fertile Crescent is now an established fact.

The penetration of Sabaeans into the Levant and Mesopotamia may be considered an outgrowth of Sabaean expansion in the seventh century BCE. During

---

139. Tadmor, *Inscriptions of Tiglath-pileser III*, Summary Inscriptions 4:27′, 7:3′, 13:9′ (listed with tributaries: "Masa, Tema, Saba, Hayippa"). The evidence from the Assyrian texts is summarized by Galter, "'. . . an der Grenze,'" 29–40.

140. Liverani, "Early Caravan Trade," 111–15.

141. Eph'al, *Ancient Arabs*, 229 and n. 48.

142. For the north Sabaean hypothesis, see Giovanni Garbini, "I Sabei del Nord come problema storico," in *Studi in onore di Francesco Gabrieli nel suo ottantesimo compleanno* (Rome: Università di Roma "La Sapienza," Dipartimento di studi orientali, 1984), 373–80; and J. Pirenne, "Des Grecs à l'aurore de la culture monumentale sabéenne," in Fahd, *L'Arabie préislamique*, 262–63. Robin ("Sheba II," cols. 1109–11) considers this the last-ditch effort to preserve the short chronology. The battle now has been lost.

143. F. Bron and A. Lemaire, "Nouvelle inscription sabéenne et le commerce en Transeuphratène," *Transeu* 38 (2009): 11–29. For archaeological evidence of the incense trade in Palestine in the seventh century BCE, see Seymour Gitin, "Incense Altars from Ekron, Israel and Judah: Context and Typology," *ErIsr* 20 (1989): 52*–67*.

the reign of Karib'īl Watar, son of Dharmaral (ca. 700–680 BCE), the Sabaean kingdom expanded throughout southwest Arabia from its center in the Mārib and Sana'a region. Two long inscriptions erected inside the temple of Almaqah at Sirwah (*RES* 2945–46) describe eight successful military campaigns conducted with the ostensible purpose of gaining control of the caravan routes in the neighboring kingdoms. The kingdom of Aswan southeast of Mārib was subjected, and the southwest area penetrated to the Gulf of Aden, and then the kingdom of Nashshan in Jawf, 100 kilometers north of Mārib, where the capital was destroyed and replaced with a garrison of Sabaean colonists. The next campaign was conducted west against the Tihama, the coastal plain along the Red Sea, and perhaps even to the Eritrean/Ethiopian coastal plain on the African side of the Red Sea. The final campaign extended north against the tribes of Najran in southwest Saudi Arabia, the first prominent oasis on the caravan route leading out of Yemen to the Mediterranean. Afterward, Karib'īl consolidated his conquests and fortified the conquered cities. Colonists were sent throughout the conquered territories, even to Ethiopia. The result was that Sabaean language and culture extended into these regions. Although the local dialects continued, Sabaic became the international language of prestige in the region, and the principal language of law, religion, and historical texts. Throughout his reign, Ḥaḍramawt, the producer and distributor of the lucrative frankincense trade, was the ally of Saba, as was the kingdom of Qataban, but even here Sabaean influence and presence were great. For these reasons, Karib'īl Watar is appropriately designated "Karib'īl the Great."

Afterward, the Sabaean kingdom was reduced significantly and withdrew to its center around Mārib, as the other Incense Kingdoms emerged and established some kind of independence vis-à-vis Saba. The Sabaic inscriptions diminish from the archaic period significantly, so the sequence of rulers/kings is difficult to establish. A few campaigns were conducted into the same regions conquered by Karib'īl the Great by his successors, revealing the difficulty Saba had in maintaining its recent conquests. In the Jawf valley, the state of Ma'in was formed in the seventh century BCE, representing a small eastern portion of Jawf, and the smallest of the South Arabian kingdoms.[144] At this time, the area had two languages. The older one was Madhabic spoken at Nashshan and Ma'in. In the reign of Karib'īl the Great, Sabaean was introduced. With the emergence of the kingdom of Ma'in and the people called Minaeans, the local Madhabic disappears, replaced by Minaic. Their capital was Qarnaw, with a second major urban center at Barāqish (modern Yathill), and they eventually became the dominant carriers of aromatics to the Mediterranean

---

144. Robin, "Sheba II," cols. 1127–29. Cf. A. F. L. Beeston, "Ma'in," *EI* 6:88.

world, establishing a vast network of colonies in the South Arabian capitals of Ḥaḍramawt (Shabwa') and Qataban (Timna'), but also throughout the Arabian Peninsula at Najran, Qaryat al-Faw, and Dedan (al-'Ulā), and the Levant.[145] The Minaeans had no *mukarribs*, issued no coinage (normally a sign of independence), and were probably under Sabaean oversight and guardianship, although with their own distinctive pantheon, institutions, and language. Nevertheless, the small kingdom produced a corpus of over a thousand texts.[146] Among the more interesting are the so-called Hierodulenlisten, or better just the "lists of foreign women," which attest to Minaean colonies or presence in the various kingdoms of South Arabia, Dedan, Egypt, Gaza, Qedar, Ammon and Moab in Transjordan, Sidon in Phoenicia, and Greece (*ywn*), primarily probably in the fourth century BCE.[147] The Minaeans are clearly the colonizers par excellence. By the late Hellenistic period, the kingdom came to an end. They appear in the Hebrew Bible in the postexilic literature as the Meunim, when they become active in the Levant.[148]

In contrast, by the sixth century BCE, the South Arabian tribal confederation of Qataban begins using the title of *mukarrib*, suggesting it had finally gained its independence, probably after the Sabaean defeat of the kingdom of Aswan.[149] Its capital was Timna' (modern Hajar Kuḥlān), and its territory included mainly the Wadi Bayḥān and the Wadi Harbīb, between Saba and Ḥaḍramawt. After the collapse of its kingdom, the Aswan tribe remained as a prominent member of the Qatabanian confederation, who were known as "the children of 'Amm," the chief deity of the confederacy. The confederation was composed of village communities called *sha'bs*, of which Qataban was the

---

145. Christian Robin ("La fin de royaume de Ma'īn," *Parfums d'Orient* [ed. Rika Gyselen] = *Res Orientales* 11 [1998]: 177–88) proposes the kingdom lasted until 20–10 BCE, a century after the traditional date.

146. The older *Iscrizione minee: Iscrizione sudarabiche*, vol. 1 (Naples, 1974) is now being updated and revised. See C. Robin, *Inventaire des inscriptions sudarabiques*, vol. 1, *Inabba', Haram, al-Kāfir, Kamna al-Ḥarāshif* (1992), and F. Bron, *Inventaire des inscriptions sudarabiques*, vol. 3, *Ma'īn* (1998), published jointly by the Académie des inscriptions et Belles-lettres in Paris and the Istituto Italiano per l'Africa e l'Oriente in Rome. For recent additions, see C. Robin, S. Antoni de Maigret, and F. Bron, "Nouvelles inscriptions de Ma'īn," *Arabia* 3 (2005–6): 273–80; and F. Bron, "Une nouvelle inscription d'un roi de Ma'īn," *AuOr* 26 (2008): 298–300.

147. Bron, *Inventaire*, 3:102–21. For the date, see A. Lemaire, "Les Minéens et la Transeuphratène à l'époque perse: Une approche," *Transeu* 13 (1997): 123–39.

148. In 1–2 Chronicles, Ezra, and Nehemiah. The LXX renders the Meunim consistently as *Minaioi*, although there are at least two peoples at stake, the Moabite Meunim (from Ma'on) and the South Arabians from Ma'īn. See Eph'al, *Ancient Arabs*, 68–71, 219–220; E. A. Knauf, "Meunim," *ABD* 4:801–2; and Lemaire, "Les Minéens," esp. 133–37.

149. A. F. L. Beeston, "Ḳatabān," *EI* 4:746–48; and Alessandra Avanzini, "The Hegemony of Qataban," in *Caravan Kingdoms: Yemen and the Frankincense Trade*, ed. Ann C. Gunter (Washington, DC: Arthur M. Sackler Gallery, Smithsonian Institution, 2005), 20–25.

dominant group. The king, who was also the *mukarrib* of the confederacy, was not an absolute monarch, as his powers were modified by a powerful council (ms^3wd) and the popular assembly of the landowners (*sha'bs*).[150] More than a thousand Qatabanic inscriptions document Qataban's activities between the seventh century BCE and the third century CE, including an important decree regulating the Timna' market, with restrictions placed on foreign traders, such as the Minaean colony residing in the Qatabanian capital.[151] Qataban's zenith is in the third century BCE, when its coinage and art also reflect Greek influence. The Qatabanians do not appear in the Hebrew Bible, probably because their emergence to prominence dates to after the postexilic period.

In contrast, the kingdom of Ḥaḍramawt, the remaining major South Arabian kingdom of the first millennium BCE, is mentioned in the Hebrew Bible as Hazarmaveth (Heb. *ḥăṣarmāwet*) (Gen. 10:26; 1 Chron. 1:20). This indicates both the antiquity of Ḥaḍramawt and its importance in the early first millennium BCE. The Wadi Ḥaḍramawt runs parallel to the southern coast of Arabia, with high cliffs rising to a plateau, separating it from the coastal plain to the south and the desert frontier to the north, which is adjacent to the Empty Quarter. The name Ḥaḍramawt refers to the whole region. The main centers of population today are Shibān and Tarim, which are built over ancient ruins. The ancient capital was Shabwa, located on the northwest perimeter, some eight days from the incense-producing region to the east (Pliny, *Natural History* 12.52). The location must be related to Ḥaḍramawt's commercial importance as the producer of frankincense, with Shabwa representing the principal entrepôt for the incense trade. The kingdom clearly was focused on its commercial monopoly of frankincense. Shabwa was also a cultic center, with strict regulations for the collecting and importing of incense. The principal deity was the moon god named Sîn, derived from Babylonia. He is commonly referred to as "Sîn of 'Irm," perhaps referring to the principal shrine of the deity. Pliny says that within its walls there were sixty temples (*Natural History* 6.155).

Shabwa was also the residence of the king (*Periplus Maris Erythraei* 27). The first reference to Ḥaḍramawt is in the old Sabaic inscription of the seventh century BCE, when, during the expansion of Saba under Karib'īl the Great,

---

150. For the social structure, see Andrey Korotayev, "A Socio-political Conflict in the Qatabanian Kingdom? (A Preliminary Re-interpretation of the Qatabanic Inscription RÉS 3566)," *PSAS* 27 (1997): 141–58.

151. Alessandra Avanzini, *Corpus of South Arabian Inscriptions*, vol. 1, pt. 3, *Qatabanic, Marginal Qatabanic, Aswamite Inscriptions* (Pisa: PLUS, 2004), esp. 205A–C (pp. 284–90) for the famous Market Code of Qataban. For recent additions to the corpus, see Romolo Loreto, "South Arabian Inscriptions from Domestic Buildings from Tamna' and the Archaeological Evidence," *AAE* 22 (2011): 59–96.

an alliance was made with Yada''il, the king of Ḥaḍramawt (*RES* 3945), after which their relations with Saba fall into obscurity until the first century CE. Most of the royal inscriptions are after 300 BCE, so a gap exists from the first mention of a king of Ḥaḍramawt and the succeeding monarchs of the fourth century. It is therefore difficult to establish a direct order of royal succession. There is now no doubt about the antiquity of Shabwa. Between 1973 and 1981, the French project directed by Jacqueline Pirenne excavated the Ḥaḍrami capital at Shabwa, exposing six levels of occupation with radiocarbon dates ranging from the nineteenth to the sixth centuries BCE, with a gap between about the seventeenth century and the beginning of the first millennium BCE.[152] The extensive ruins now embrace three modern villages. The excavations exposed the fortified walls of the ancient settlement, the tower domestic residences, and a complex fortress. By the fifth century BCE, the first buildings were erected with dedications in the monumental Sabaic script. The political and cultural zenith of Shabwa was in the second century BCE and the first century CE. During this time, the port at Qanā on the southern coast was developed, as was a distant frontier trading post at Khor Rori on the eastern coast at Dhofar (called Sumārun), which is probably to be identified with Moscha, a port involved in international commerce between India and the Mediterranean.

3. Pertinence of Arabia for Ancient Israel

In the Hebrew Bible, the early history of Arabia and the Arabs is preserved in the book of Genesis, in four genealogies probably reflecting the Arabian world of the sixth century BCE. These four genealogies are dominated by or have a substantial Arab element: Cush and his sons (10:6–7), Joktan and his sons (10:26–30), Keturah and her sons (25:1–4), and Ishmael and his sons (25:12–16). These segmented genealogies rarely involve more than several generations and represent largely artificial creations retrojected into primeval history. Any systematic and comprehensive analysis of these Genesis genealogies is difficult because of the corruption of the names and the artificial creation of the lineages.[153] A brief analysis of the Genesis genealogies reveals the prominence of Arabia and Arabs therein.

---

152. Jean-François Breton, "Quelques dates pour l'archéologie sudarabique," in Robin, *Arabia Antiqua*, 88–95; cf. L. Badre, "Le sondage stratigraphique de Shabwa, 1976–1981," in *Fouilles de Shabwa*, vol. 2, ed. Jean-François Breton (Institut Français d'Archéologie du Proche-Orient, 1991), 232–36.

153. Robert T. Wilson, *Genealogy and History in the Biblical World* (New Haven: Yale University Press, 1977), provides a general survey of genealogies in the Near East, but does not examine the "Arabian" genealogies in Genesis. The most useful analysis is by F. V. Winnett,

The sons of Cush are listed as Seba, Havilah, Sabtah, Raamah, and Sabteca, and the sons of Raamah are given as Sheba and Dedan (Gen. 10:7; 1 Chron. 1:9). Although Africa appears to be the context, locations in southwestern Arabia have also been proposed in identifying the toponyms.[154] Seba may represent the capital of Meroe in Ethiopia or Sabaean colonies in Ethiopia, and Sabtah is interpreted as the capital of Ḥaḍramawt, and Sabteca as the village of Shabaka in Ḥaḍramawt. Havilah has been more troublesome, but the famous Ḫaulān tribe of southwestern Arabia has been proposed, attested in a Sabaean text from the time of Karib'īl Watar in the seventh century BCE (*RES* 3946.3).[155] The identification of Raamah (Heb. *ra'mâ*) must be a prominent place in Arabia, and the most likely possibility is the large oasis of Najran, whose ancient name was Ragmat (RGMT), located in southwestern Saudi Arabia on the border of Yemen, between Sheba (Saba) and Dedan (Al-'Ulā), and attested in South Arabian inscriptions.[156]

The Joktan genealogy in the so-called Table of Nations lists as his thirteen sons Almodad, Sheleph, Hazarmaveth, Jerah, Hadoram, Uzal, Diklah, Obal, Abimael, Sheba, Ophir, Havilah, and Jobab (Gen. 10:26–30).[157] The eponym Joktan (Heb. *yoqṭān*) was interpreted by Arab genealogists as designating the South Arabian tribe known as Qaḥtān. The inclusion of Hazarmaveth, Hebrew for Ḥaḍramawt, and Sheba or the Sabaeans, suggests that the federation represents South Arabia. The identity of the other toponyms or ethnic terms is then sought in South Arabia. Uzal is taken as the pre-Islamic name of Ṣanʻāʼ, the modern capital of North Yemen, and Diklah as the Sabaean city of Ṣirwāḥ, near Mārib, but a confusing array of proposals has been made for Ophir (including Africa), and the others defy any convincing identification. Havilah reappears, being both the son of Cush (Gen. 10:7; 1 Chron. 1:9) and the son of Joktan (Gen. 10:29; 1 Chron. 1:23), and the name also appears in the expression "from Havilah to Shur" (i.e., from southern Palestine to western Sinai), suggesting another designation is at stake.[158]

"The Arabian Genealogies in the Book of Genesis," in *Translating and Understanding the Old Testament: Essays in Honor of Herbert Gordon May*, ed. Harry Thomas Frank and William L. Reed (Nashville: Abingdon, 1970), 171–96. Thomas Hieke, *Die Genealogien der Genesis*, HBS 39 (Freiburg: Herder, 2003) offers a reader-text form-critical approach, with an excellent bibliography.

154. Winnett, "Arabian Genealogies," 173–81, emphasizes Africa, but the entries for toponyms by W. W. Müller in *ABD* (cited by Winnett) focus on Arabia for the identifications.

155. For Seba, see J. Briend, "Sheba I. Dans la Bible," *DBSup* 12:1046; Strabo, *Geography* 16.4.8–20 [770]; cf. Josephus, *Jewish Antiquities* 2.249. For the Ḫaulān, see W. W. Müller, "Havilah," *ABD* 3:81.

156. W. W. Müller, "Raamah," *ABD* 5:597; cf. Winnett, "Arabian Genealogies," 179.

157. Hieke, *Genealogien der Genesis*, 99–114.

158. Eph'al, *Ancient Arabs*, 235.

The Keturah genealogy lists her sons as Zimran, Jokshan, Medan, Midian, Ishbak, and Shuah. Of these sons, Jokshan was the father of Sheba and Dedan, and Dedan had three sons, and Midian five (Gen. 25:1–4; cf. 1 Chron. 1:32–33). The name "Keturah" (Heb. *qəṭûrâ*; cf. *qəṭōret*, "incense") suggests that the genealogy reflects the international trade in aromatics of South Arabia and the major North Arabian caravan posts.[159] Her six sons include Midian (northwest Arabia) and Ishbak and Shuah (the Euphrates region); her son Jokshan is the father of Sheba (Saba in South Arabia) and Dedan (the LXX adds *Thaiman* = Taymā'), and the sons of Midian include the Arabian tribe Ephah known from Assyrian sources (*Hayappa*). The genealogy appears to be artificial, created to express a commercial function. This solitary reference to Keturah in Genesis, the matriarchal descent of the genealogy, and the reappearance of Sheba and Dedan (the Cushite genealogy in Gen. 10:7 has Raamah as the father), all betray its contrived nature.

In contrast, Hagar, the Egyptian handmaiden of Sarah, with whom Abraham fathered a son named Ishmael, is the legendary mother of the Ishmaelites (Gen. 16:5–16; 21:8–21), but her descendants are traced through Ishmael. The name of Hagar is well known throughout Arabia.[160] Ishmael is more specifically represented as the eponymous ancestor of a confederation of twelve Arab tribes: Nebaioth, Kedar, Adbeel, Mibsam, Mishma, Dumah, Massa, Hadad, Tema, Jetur, Naphish, and Kedemah, who dwell from Havilah to Shur—that is, Assyria to Egypt (Gen. 25:13–15, 18; 1 Chron. 1:28–31). Half of the twelve sons clearly represent Arabian tribes or places known from the Assyrian records: Nabayat (cf. Gen. 25:13, Nebaioth), Qidri (cf. 25:13, Kedar), Idibailui (cf. 25:13, Adbeel), Massa (25:14; cf. Pliny, *Natural History* 6.30), and the toponyms of Dumah and Tema.[161] Two of the other sons of Ishmael may be represented in Assyrian texts: Mishma may represent the Arab tribe *Išmmeʿ*, mentioned under Assurbanipal, and Naphish may be the Arab tribe of

---

159. Winnett, "Arabian Genealogies," 188–93, provides a penetrating analysis; cf. Eph'al, *Ancient Arabs*, 231–33.

160. "Hagar" is used for people in the area of Bahrain and northeast Arabia in the third millennium BCE, and is the name used for Arabia in the hieroglyphic subject list of the Persian king Darius I. In South Arabian, *hgr* means "town, city" (A. F. L. Beeston et al., eds., *Dictionnaire Sabéen* [Beirouth: Librarie du Liban, 1982], 56). Third-century BCE coins were issued in East Arabia with the title "king of HGR" (M. Huth and Peter G. Van Alfen, eds., *Coinage of the Caravan Kingdoms: Studies in Ancient Arabian Monetization* [New York: American Numismatic Society, 2010], 111 and 319).

161. Winnett, "Arabian Genealogies," 193–96; Eph'al, *Ancient Arabs*, 60–63, 231–40; Ernst Axel Knauf, *Ismael: Untersuchungen zur Geschichte Palästinas und Nordarabiens im 1. Jahrtausend v. Chr.* (Wiesbaden: Harrassowitz, 1985), 49–91; Hieke, *Genealogien der Genesis*, 144–50. See Tadmor, *Inscriptions of Tiglath-pileser III*, 312–13, for a list of biblical names in the Assyrian texts.

Na-pi-ša-a-a mentioned in connection with Massa in the rebellion of Qedar.[162] Of the rest, Hadad is a personal name of Edomite kings, Jetur the eponym for the Itureans in Syria, and Kedemah (Heb. *qēdəmâ*) may just refer to the "sons of the East"; Mibsam remains enigmatic.[163]

Essentially the core of Ishmael reflects the Arabian tribal confederacy that existed from Tiglath-pileser III to Assurbanipal. There has been a recent attempt to disassociate the descendants of Ishmael from the Arabs,[164] but the book of *Jubilees* (20:13), written ca. 170–140 BCE, explicitly declares that the Arabs are Ishmaelites.[165] The geographical sphere of Ishmael's sons is primarily North Arabia and the Levant, embracing the Sinai (Adbeel), Syria-Gilead (Jetur, the later Itureans), Qedar, Dumah, and Taymā' in North Arabia, and perhaps northeast Arabia (Nebaioth and Massa). Taymanitic inscriptions from the sixth/fifth century BCE at Jebel Ghunaym near the oasis mention both Masa' and Nabayat (Heb. *nəbāyōt*), and a "war against Dedan."[166] The major North Arabian oases appear in the Hebrew Bible during the same period: Taymā' (Isa. 21:14, Tema), Adumatu (Isa. 21:11, Dumah), Dedan (Isa. 21:13), and perhaps Bazu (Jer. 25:23, Buz). These allusions to the major tribes and settlements of Arabia in the eighth through the fifth centuries BCE suggest the historical context for the creation of the genealogical lists in Genesis and Chronicles.

The most controversial reference to Arabia is the legendary visit of the queen of Sheba to King Solomon in the tenth century BCE (1 Kings 10:1–13; 2 Chron. 9:1–12). The account is generally perceived as anachronistic, a later projection into the period by editors in order to embellish and enhance the reign of Solomon. The queen's camels bear "spices, and very much gold, and precious stones," and Solomon receives tribute from all the "kings of Arabia" (1 Kings 10:2, 15; 2 Chron. 9:1, 14), developments that can be documented in the eighth century BCE and later, and no queens are mentioned in the royal inscriptions of South Arabia during the first millennium BCE. A string of queens are known from North Arabia in the Assyrian period, but this

---

162. Knauf, *Ismael*, 80–81 (Naphish); and Knauf, "Mishma," *ABD* 4:871. Winnett suggests the tribe of Mishma may refer to Jebel Mishma', some 200 km. east of Taymā' ("Arab Genealogies," 194).

163. Knauf, *Ismael*, 68–81, summarized and developed further in the appropriate entries in *ABD*.

164. I. Eph'al, "Ishmael and 'Arab(s)': A Transformation of Ethnological Terms," *JNES* 35 (1976): 228–31; and Fergus Millar, "Hagar, Ishmael, Josephus and the Origins of Islam," in *Rome, the Greek World, and the East*, vol. 3, *The Greek World, the Jews and the East*, ed. H. M. Cotton and G. M. Rogers (Chapel Hill: University of North Carolina Press, 2006), 360–62.

165. For the date, see James C. VanderKam, "Jubilees, Book of," *ABD* 3:1030.

166. Winnett and Reed, *Ancient Records from North Arabia*, 100–103, nos. 13–16, 21–23.

means a shorter journey than described in the account. The legendary long journey—from South Arabia to Jerusalem is over 1,500 miles and a half-year journey by camel caravan—has rendered the account questionable. On the other hand, as we have seen, an Assyrian text mentions a camel caravan of Taymanites and Sabaeans functioning in the middle Euphrates during the mid-eighth century BCE, which has infused new life into the debate. Another Sabaean text indicates that just such a long journey took place ca. 600 BCE, when a caravan leader from Saba visited Dedan, Gaza, and "the villages of Judah."[167] Achaeological evidence supports this lengthy venture. In the excavations at the city of David, some sherds inscribed in South Arabian letters were discovered in a stratum dated to before the destruction of the temple in 586 BCE.[168] The pottery is local ware and suggests the pots were incised by residents of Jerusalem. Finally, a Sabaean text from Mārib describes a military conflict in the early third century CE in which the Sabaean king Shaʻar Awtar defeated King Ilʻazz Yaluṭ of Ḥaḍramawt in the Wadi Bayḥān, and sent a small Sabaean detachment to the royal palace in Shabwa to rescue the queen, who was a sister the Sabaean king.[169] This is the first reference to a South Arabian queen and the first evidence of matrimonial alliances in the South Arabian dynasties. That queens existed earlier in the first millennium BCE remains possible; their seeming absence might be only a reflection of the character of our sources.

There are additional signs of the South Arabian incense trade in the Levant during the eighth century BCE. At Beersheba, Stratum II, destroyed probably in the late eighth century, small cuboid limestone altars were discovered, decorated with geometric designs and camels, along with a rectangular limestone object, perhaps a large seal, that was incised on the end with three or four

---

167. Liverani, "Early Caravan Trade," 111–15; and Bron and Lemaire, "Nouvelle inscription sabéenne." See also A. Lemaire, "Solomon & Sheba, Inc.: New Inscription Confirms Trade Relations between 'Towns of Judah' and South Arabia," *BAR* 36, no. 1 (2010): 54–59. See Graf, "Arabs in Palestine from the Neo-Assyrian to the Persian Period," 292–95, for South Arabian presence in the Beersheba Valley.

168. Yigal Shiloh, "South Arabian Inscriptions from the City of David, Jerusalem," *PEQ* 119 (1987): 9–18; and Maria Höfner, "Remarks on Potsherds with Incised South Arabian Letters," in *Excavations at the City of David, 1978–1985, Directed by Yigal Shiloh*, vol. 6, ed. Donald T. Ariel (Jerusalem: Hebrew University of Jerusalem, 2000), 26–28. For earlier discussion, see Benjamin Sass, "Arabs and Greeks in Late First Temple Jerusalem," *PEQ* 122 (1990): 59–61; and the cautious appraisal by F. Bron, "Vestiges de l'écriture sud-sémitique dans le croissant fertile," in Lozachmeur, *Présence arabe*, 81–91.

169. Muṭahhar ʻAlī Al-Iryānī, *Yemen History, 34 New Inscriptions, Explanation and Interpretation* (Cairo: Centre des Études Yéménites à Ṣanʻāʼ, 1973), 74–86, no. 13 [in Arabic] (summary in J. Ryckmans, "Himyaritica [3]," *Le Muséon* 87 [1974]: 247–56); and A. F. L. Beeston, "Ḥaḍramawt," *EI* 3:336.

letters in South Arabian script, rendered as *khn* (priest).[170] In addition, at Tel 'Aroer, 22 kilometers southeast of Beersheba, two fragmentary inscriptions in South or North Arabian were incised on local pottery vessels, dating also to the eighth century BCE.[171] Further north, 22 kilometers south of Tel Dor, on the Palestinian coast, a Phoenician sanctuary some 5 kilometers inland at Eliakhin yielded inscriptions and formulae that suggest connections with Taymā' and North Arabia in the Sharon Plain of Palestine in the same period.[172] These details are not meant as an attempt to substantiate the account of Sheba and Solomon, but they do illuminate the milieu, which may have provided the basis for the creation of the legend.

In a series of interesting studies, it has been suggested that Ezekiel 27:12–25 may contain the earliest description of the commercial overland trade routes between the Levant and South Arabia. After a poetic introduction, it is proposed that the following prose section represents an extraneous archaic document providing Tyrian trade relationships inserted into the poetic oracle that the prophet delivered allegedly just before the siege of the island city by Nebuchadnezzar II between 600 and 585 BCE.[173] This prose "document" is riddled with *hapax legomena*, redundancies of names, and corrupted forms of toponyms that probably reflect its technical nature and archaic origins. The arrangement of the toponyms appears to represent a northwest to southeast trajectory, suggesting it may reflect a series of trade routes, including the Persian royal road between Sardis and Susa (27:12–15), the coastal road along the eastern Mediterranean (27:17), the Transjordanian King's Highway from Syria to Edom (27:16, 18), the incense route along the western side of the Arabian Peninsula (27:19–22), and possibly the *ḫarrān šarri*, the road between

---

170. Lily Singer-Avitz, "Beersheba—A Gateway Community in Southern Arabian Long-Distance Trade in the Eighth Century B.C.E.," *TA* 26, no. 1 (1999): 41–44 (altars) and 50–52 (seal). The inscription was deciphered by François Bron. There is a parallel of *khn* on a sherd from Yalā in North Yemen; see Garbini, "Le iscrizioni," 83 (fig. 15) and 89 (fig. 27).

171. Yifat Thareani, *Tell 'Aroer: The Iron Age II Caravan Town and the Hellenistic-Early Roman Settlement*, Nelson Glueck School of Biblical Archaeology 8 (Jerusalem: Hebrew Union College, 2011), 228 (color plates 4–5; plates 231:1; 207:1).

172. Robert Deutsch and Michael Heltzer, *Forty New Ancient West Semitic Inscriptions* (Tel Aviv-Jaffa: Archaeological Center Publication, 1994), 87; cf. André Lemaire, "Remarques sur les relations entre la Phénicie et le Nord de l'Arabie," *ErIsr* 29 (2009): 101*–2*.

173. Mario Liverani, "The Trade Network of Tyre according to Ezek. 27," in *Ah, Assyria . . . Studies in Assyrian History and Ancient Near Eastern Historiography Presented to Hayim Tadmor* (Jerusalem: Magnes Press/Hebrew University, 1991), 67–70, suggests it is an "archaic" document of the eighth century BCE; cf. Walter Zimmerli, *Ezekiel 2: A Commentary on the Book of the Prophet Ezekiel, Chapters 25–48*, trans. James D. Martin, Hermeneia (Philadelphia: Fortress, 1983), 54–55, 63. Note that Cyprus, Egypt, and the Phoenician cities of the poetic section (27:6–9) disappear in the prose section, and neither contains a reference to Babylon. Cf. Lemaire, "Remarques," 101*.

Assur and Carchemish (27:23).[174] In regard to Arabia, the reference in 27:22 to "Sheba and Raamah [Najran]" is sandwiched between references to "Dedan" (27:20) and "[North] Arabia and all the princes of Kedar" (27:21), with perhaps some Assyrian localities in 27:23.[175] Just when and how the prophetic oracle was produced remains a mystery.

As this discussion demonstrates, Arabia and Arabians never played a prominent role in biblical history, but they nevertheless penetrated the narrative in innumerable ways from the Abrahamic tradition to the postexilic period. The cultural centers of both North and South Arabia are embedded in the genealogies of Genesis as the descendants of Abraham's son Ishmael. During the Neo-Assyrian period, the burgeoning Arabian incense trade stemming from the caravan kingdoms of South Arabia is reflected in the archaeological, epigraphic, and literary tradition associated with Judah and the coastal peoples of Gaza and other ports in the eastern Mediterranean. The geopolitical movements involved in the succession of imperial powers of Mesopotamia and Iran led to a westward shift in the center of the Arab Qedarite confederacy from Jawf in north-central Arabia to southern Transjordan, Palestine, and the northwest of the Arabian Peninsula, symbolized by the presence of "Geshem the Arab" on the periphery of Judah in the time of Nehemiah. Rather than a silent spectator lurking in the shadows, the Arabian world should be seen as an active participant that interacted with ancient Israel.

---

174. Proposed by Hans Peter Rüger, "Das Tyrusorakel Ez 27" (PhD diss., University of Tübingen, 1961), summarized by Zimmerli, *Ezekiel 2*, 70–71.

175. Raamah (Ezek. 27:22) appears to represent *rgmtm*, the ancient name of Najran in the first millennium BCE. See Müller, "Raamah," 597. If *'ărām* (Aram) in 27:16 (MT) is accepted, a similar gap exists between Damascus and Dedan. The possible upper Mesopotamian toponyms in 27:23 break the northwest-southeast trajectory of the list, and it has been suggested that the text has corrupted a string of South Arabian towns, including the ports of Aden and Qānī'. See R. Dussaud, "Les Phéniciens au Negeb et Arabie d'après un texte des Ras Shamra," *Revue de l'histoire des religions* 108 (1933): 43–47; and Hermann von Wissmann, "Geographische Grundlagen und Frühzeit der Geschichte Südarabiens," *Saeculum* 4 (1953): 98–99. But the proposal of Qānī' is anachronistic, as the archaeological excavations of the settlement indicate it was not founded until the first century BCE. See J.-F. Salles and A. Sedov, *Qānī': Le port antique du Ḥaḍramawt entre la Méditerranée, l'Afrique et l'Inde* (Turnhout: Brepols, 2010), 371–74. In addition, the identification of the Mesopotamian toponyms is equally unsatisfactory; see I. M. Diakonoff, "The Naval Power and Trade of Tyre," *IEJ* 42 (1992): 188–89. The interpretation of both the MT and LXX remains problematic. In Ezek. 27:23, the MT adds "the merchants of Sheba" after "Eden"/Aden.

For Further Reading

Ali-Ghabban, Ali Ibrahim, et al., eds. *Roads of Arabia: Archaeology and History of the Kingdom of Saudi Arabia*. Paris: Somagy Art Publishers for the Musée du Louvre, 2010.

Breton, Jean-François. *Arabia Felix: From the Time of the Queen of Sheba; Eighth Century B.C. to First Century A.D.* Notre Dame, IN: University of Notre Dame Press, 1999.

Briend, Jacques. "Sheba I. Dans la Bible" (cols. 1043–46). *DBSup* 12. Edited by Jacques Briend and É. Cothenet. Paris: Letouzey et Ané, 1996.

Ephʻal, Israel. *The Ancient Arabs: Nomads on the Borders of the Fertile Crescent, 9th–5th Centuries B.C.* Jerusalem: The Hebrew University Press; Leiden: Brill, 1982.

Potts, Daniel T. *The Arabian Gulf in Antiquity*. 2 vols. Oxford: Clarendon, 1990.

Robin, Christian. "Sheba II. Dans les inscriptions d'Arabie du Sud" (cols. 1047–1254). *DBSup* 12. Edited by Jacques Briend and É. Cothenet. Paris: Letouzey et Ané, 1996.

Seipel, Wilfred, ed. *Jemen: Kunst und Archäologie im Land der Königin von Saba'*. Vienna: Das Museum; Milan: Skira, 1998.

Simpson, St John, ed. *Queen of Sheba: Treasures from Ancient Yemen*. London: British Museum Press, 2002.

Winnett, F. V., and W. L. Reed. *Ancient Records from North Arabia*. Near and Middle East Series 6. Toronto: University of Toronto Press, 1970.

See the journals *Proceedings of the Seminar for Arabian Studies* (1970–) and *Arabian Archaeology and Epigraphy* (1989–) for recent philological and archaeological work.

13

Greece and the Greeks

Walter Burkert

Greece has remained famous and influential as the origin of decisive "Western" achievements, such as demonstrative mathematics and natural science, "classical" art and literature, and the general human self-reflection called philosophy; the most important Greek idea, and loanword, is "democracy" (people's rule), with the postulate of personal freedom and equal rights in an open society. This process and success have been described and praised again and again for centuries. The usual perspective is as if Greece had grown from a felicitous seed on its own account to reach an unprecedented level of mind, art, literature, and science.

This was the consequence of the unique position of Greece as the guardian of an uninterrupted tradition through literature and artifacts, through school systems and handbooks, through translations into Latin and into Arabic. The catastrophe of the Turkish conquest (1453 CE) coincided with the reefflorescence of the studies of classical Greek in "Western" culture.

This monopoly has been broken for about two hundred years, as languages and literature of more ancient civilizations have become understandable again, while more and more careful excavations have brought to light the cultural levels and achievements of these older layers. Hence it is time to look at the Greek

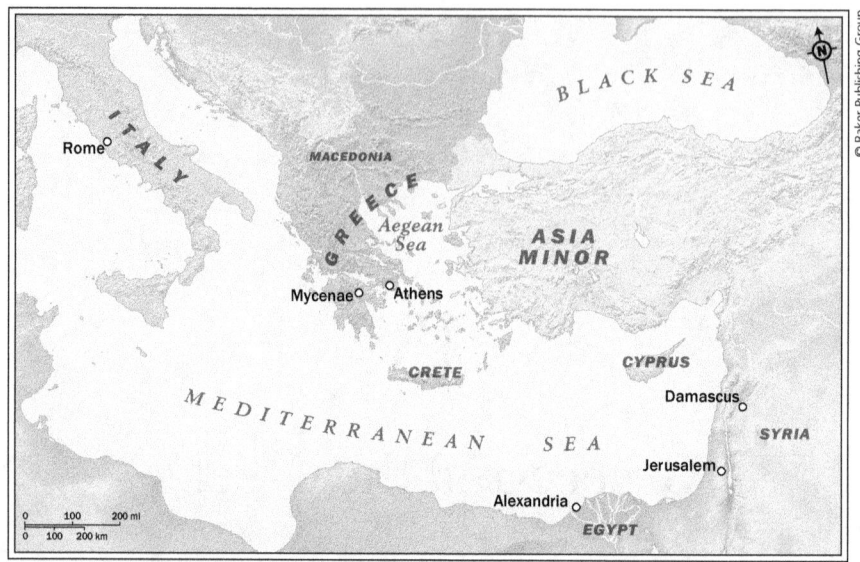

Figure 13.1. Greece

development from the viewpoint of the earlier dominant cultures, commonly called the "ancient Near East," including the very special development of Israel in Palestine. The question is how Greece, a marginal region of the great Eastern empires, rose to become the epitome of modernization and self-consciousness, acknowledged and imitated through the whole of the Mediterranean world and even farther east. There appears a unique success of craftsmanship, of language and thought, of societal interplay and intellectual sophistication, with just one sudden and transitory military flash: Alexander the Great.

1. A Late Bronze Age *Koinē*

It is writing that has the power to preserve documents with pertinent self-interpretation. This decisive invention happened in both Mesopotamia and Egypt toward the end of the fourth millennium, when cuneiform writing, on the one side, and hieroglyphs, on the other, came into use. This went together with progress in technology and in the organization of society. Writing gives a decisive push both to the economy and to the exercise of power. We find a growing use of metals and the creation of monarchic "states": there were "kings" who, while wielding power, claimed special relations to superior entities, to "gods." This makes what is commonly called the high civilizations of the Bronze Age, roughly the third and second millennia. The Late Bronze

Age (ca. 1500–1200)[1] in particular provides the background for Greece as we know it.

In that period Egypt was already looking back to more than one thousand years of pharaonic kingship, which left the pyramids (about 2600/2500) as persistent monuments of its fame. In Mesopotamia, a plurality of city-states had long developed, with some starts toward an empire by military expansion; the names of the great kings Sargon (2340–2285) and Naram-Sin (2260–2224) have remained known. There was a variegated and prolific use of literacy through schools, which also developed poetry in hymns and tales. The living language was changing from idiosyncratic Sumerian to Semitic Akkadian. In between Egypt and Mesopotamia, Syria had smaller kingdoms, dominated by cuneiform culture and threatened by conquests from the east and from the south. An important archive—Sumerian writing adapted to West Semitic—survives from Ebla, a city destroyed by Naram-Sin about 2240.[2]

In the second millennium, cultural and military interactions multiplied to make up one world of rivaling high cultures, which has been called the Bronze Age *koinē* (community), characterized by monarchs, writing, and polytheism.[3] Best known from rich documentation is Mari on the Euphrates, destroyed by Babylon about 1700. Not much later, Egypt fell prey to invaders from Palestine/Syria, called Hyksos ("shepherd-kings") by the Egyptians. When these had been expelled again, Egypt began to expand on its own toward Syria. At that time, sizable royal powers had developed in Anatolia and North Syria too: Hittites and Hurrians who adopted forms of cuneiform writing. Written documentation also comes from the cities Alalakh and Ugarit along the Mediterranean (ca. 1400–1200). The Hittite realm expanded by subduing the Hurrians and then clashed with the power of Egypt in consequence; a memorable battle between the Egyptian Ramesses II and the Hittite Muwatalli was fought at Qadesh in Northern Syria about 1280. The ensuing peace treaty is preserved both in Egyptian and in Akkadian: cuneiform Akkadian had established itself as the common diplomatic dialect.

Bronze Age civilization had its impact on Europe. It gave rise to the first European high culture, at Crete: the "Minoan" civilization.[4] It is characterized

---

1. Unless otherwise noted, dates in the following are BCE.
2. P. Matthiae, *Ebla: La città del trono* (Turin: Einaudi, 2010); Matthiae, *Gli archivi reali di Ebla* (Milan: Mondadori università, 2008).
3. A term coined by Cyrus Gordon; see N. Marinatos, *Minoan Kingship and the Solar Goddess: A Near Eastern Koine* (Champaign-Urbana: University of Illinois Press, 2010).
4. A term coined by Arthur Evans; Minos, king of Knossos, is a figure of Greek mythology, not attested in the Bronze Age.

by large palaces, evidently run by kings and adorned with wall paintings, of which Knossos remains the most impressive example. There is an unmistakable artistic style—well adapted to modern feelings—which was quite successful in its time: Minoan artists were called to Egypt and to Syria; wall paintings at Tell Dab'a in Egypt, in the post-Hyksos epoch, were evidently done by Minoan artists.[5]

An enormous eruption of the volcano of Thera/Santorini must have had catastrophic consequences in the eastern Mediterranean; some palaces in Crete were finally destroyed. The date of this event remains highly controversial: was it about 1500, or rather about 1630? Right at Thera (modern Akrotiri), a Minoan town was covered with meters of ashes and thus preserved as a kind of Pompeii; excavations are not yet completed.[6] So far no written documents have been found there.

The Minoans had developed a writing system, probably from a "modern" Syrian prototype: a pure syllabary, which contained about eighty signs. It is called "Linear A"; it remains undeciphered, which means that Minoan language is unknown so far. Minoan trade went as far as the northern Aegean. There are Minoan seals from Samothrace and a Linear A inscription from Troy.

It is in the wake of the Minoans that "Greeks" first make their appearance. Greek is a living language from Indo-European stock, one of the earliest attested and best known from this language family. Grecian territory was not tied to the modern frontiers of Greece. Already in the Bronze Age, Greeks settled beyond the Balkan Peninsula on the Aegean islands, especially Crete and Cyprus, on the coast of Asia Minor, and even in southern Italy and Sicily. Minoan Linear A is found to change to Linear B by about 1400; and in 1952 CE it was discovered that this language is Greek,[7] with expected archaisms as against later alphabetic Greek. Archives of clay tablets in Linear B were found in the palace of Knossos and also in Kydonia/Chania in Crete, but especially in palaces on the continent, in Pylos, Mycenae, Tiryns, and Thebes. There are also ceramics with Linear B characters. Modern scholarship has adopted the name "Mycenaeans" for this population, in distinction from the Minoans of Crete, taking the name from the most imposing fortified palace on the continent. There must have been some kind of Greek conquest of Crete

---

5. M. Bietak, N. Marinatos, and C. Palivou, *Taureador Scenes in Tell el-Dab'a (Avaris) and Knossos* (Vienna: Österreichische Akademie der Wissenschaften, 2007).

6. C. G. Doumas, *Thera: Pompeii of the Ancient Aegean; Excavations at Akrotiri, 1967–79* (London: Thames & Hudson, 1983); Doumas, *The Wall-Paintings of Thera* (Athens: Thera Foundation, 1991).

7. Y. Duhoux and A. Morpurgo Davies, eds., *A Companion to Linear B: Mycenaean Greek Texts and Their World*, vols. 1 and 2 (Leuven: Peeters, 2008 and 2011).

(about 1370?), which is not attested in any literary source. Later the Minoan language seems to disappear from Crete, leaving Greek in various dialects.

The most spectacular relics of Mycenaean civilization are the buildings at Mycenae: "Cyclopean walls" with the "Lion Gate" to mark the imposing palace, and the greatest and best preserved of those beehive tombs called *tholoi* by specialists, the "Treasury of Atreus" (thirteenth century); it is the most impressive building from the Bronze Age for the whole of Europe. The ancient designation as "treasury" (*thēsauros*) probably reflects the happiness of tomb robbers at the end of the Bronze Age. Remaining untouched were the "shaft graves," royal tombs behind the Lion Gate at Mycenae, where Heinrich Schliemann found the famous gold masks and other golden objects (sixteenth century). Names from later Greek mythology have been applied to the localities and monuments of Mycenae: Atreus, Agamemnon, Clytemnestra; in a similar vein, Nestor is located in Pylos—but there is no basis for this in any Bronze Age document so far.

Contacts with Egypt and Syria, as developed by the Minoans, were no less important for the Mycenaean epoch. A hieroglyphic inscription from the tomb of Amenophis III in Egypt records gifts from "Keftiu" and "Tanaia" and mentions place-names such as Amnisos, Knossos, Mukana, and Thebes.[8] "Keftiu" clearly refers to Crete, called Caphtor in the Hebrew Bible. "Tanaia," then, corresponding to *Danaoi* ("Greeks" in Homeric language), should be the Egyptian designation for Greece in the fourteenth century, including Mycenae and Thebes. Greek *Aigyptos*, in turn, seems to render "Hikuptah" (City of God Ptah), the Egyptian name for Memphis; a personal name *Aigyptios* appears in Linear B.

The Aegean coast of Anatolia was part of the Minoan-Mycenaean world. At Miletus both Linear A and Linear B inscriptions have been found in Bronze Age tombs. Tradition derived the city's name from Cretan Milatos. It seems that Anatolian Miletus was not affected by the general breakdown at about 1200; archaeologists do not find any hiatus there at that time.

Mycenaean contacts went as far as the Hittites of Asia Minor. A clearly Mycenaean sword was dedicated to the Storm God by the Hittite king Tudhaliya; it was booty from "Assuwa," as the inscription (in Akkadian) states.[9]

---

8. E. Edel, *Die Ortsnamenlisten aus dem Totentempel Amenophis III* (Bonn: Hanstein, 1966); new fragments: P. W. Haider, "War ein 'Groß-Ionien' tatsächlich um 1360 v. Chr. in Westkleinasien existent? Eine kritische Analyse zu den Lesungen und Identifizierungen der jüngst entdeckten topographischen Namenslisten aus der Regierungszeit Amenophis' III," *Klio* 90 (2008): 291–306.

9. O. Hansen, "A Mycenaean Sword from Bogazköy-Hattusa Found in 1991," *The Annual of the British School at Athens* 89 (1994): 213–16.

Assuwa (i.e., "Asia") was a region on the Aegean coast at that time. Hittite rock sculptures, with inscriptions in hieroglyphic Hittite, are found as far west as Karabel near Sardis—warrior images that Herodotus (*Histories* 2.106) saw—along with a seated figure at the rock façade of Mount Sipylos near Magnesia/Manissa, exposed to dropping water;[10] later Greeks, on account of their own mythology, called this image "Niobe," the mother whose children were all killed by gods and who turned into stone, still weeping.

A protracted controversy has developed concerning the names Achiyava and Wilusa, which appear in Hittite texts. Are these Achaia, country of Greek *Achaioi*, and Wilios/Ilios—that is, Troy? *Achaioi* is one of the names for Greeks in the Homeric epics, which narrate the "Trojan War"; a Greek tribe *Achaioi* occupied the northern Peloponnesus—the province is called Achaea still today. One Hittite text mentions a king Alaksandus from Wilusa: Is this Alexandros-Paris, the Trojan prince in Homer? The chronology does not fit: the Hittite document is from about 1300; a possible date for the historically elusive "Trojan War" would be about 1200. The geographical setting of Achiyava, in spite of growing knowledge about Hittite geography, has remained controversial and will remain so, unless new evidence should appear.[11] In Iron Age Cilicia, a new text (eighth century) mentions a country named Hia;[12] is this *Achia*, Achaia? There was a "House of Mopsos" ruling at that time in Cilician Azitawada/Karatepe, and linguists insist that Mopsos is a Greek name; myth makes Mopsos a seer emigrating to Cilicia. Is this a Bronze Age tradition?

To sum up: Greek Bronze Age contacts with Asia Minor are as clear as those with Syria and Egypt, which made meetings with Hittites nearly unavoidable. But precise details of place and time will remain controversial. The main question concerns the "Trojan War." There is that most remarkable Bronze Age citadel near the Dardanelles, called Hissarlık ("ruin-like") in Turkish, excavated first by Schliemann; it was in existence through various stages since about 2300. Was it ever attacked and destroyed by a Greek coalition, headed by the king of Mycenae? There is just one written document from the place, a not very informative seal (after 1200?).[13] Archaeological indications point

10. Inscription of Karabel: J. D. Hawkins, "Tarkondemos and the Land of Mira," *AnSt* 48 (1998): 1–31; monument: E. Akurgal and M. Hirmer, *Die Kunst der Hethiter* (Munich: Hirmer, 1961), plate 22; "Niobe": plate 23.

11. M. Gander, *Die geographischen Beziehungen der Lukka-Länder* (Heidelberg: Winter, 2010).

12. R. Tekoğlu and A. Lemaire, "La bilingue royale louvito-phénicienne de Çineköy," CRAI 144 (2000): 961–1007.

13. J. D. Hawkins and F. Easton, "A Hieroglyphic Seal from Troia," *Studia Troica* 6 (1996): 111–18.

toward a final destruction of the place somewhat after 1200—that is, later than the end of the palace at Mycenae; this would leave no place for a king of Mycenae organizing a "Trojan War." Some hundreds of years later there was a moderate Greek city in the place, called Ilion; it was identified by the Greeks with the *Ilios* or *Troie* of the Homeric epics and hence accepted as "origin," via Aeneas, even by Rome.

2. Catastrophe and Continuities

Most Bronze Age civilizations around the Aegean collapsed in a catastrophic event about 1200 BCE; it struck Greece with Pylos and Mycenae, Hittite Anatolia, Syria with Ugarit, and Palestine. Palaces, large stone architecture, and even metalwork practically disappeared for some centuries; writing systems fell out of use and were forgotten, Linear B as well as Ugaritic and cuneiform Hittite. The palace of Pylos was burnt, the palace of Mycenae was abandoned by about 1200. There follow "dark centuries," without writing, without major architecture, without centralized power. Less affected were Egypt and Mesopotamia. Catastrophes and continuities seem to interpenetrate at Cyprus. The details and reasons for these multiple breakdowns are obscured by the disappearance of literacy; only hypotheses are left—invasions or economic failure, social upset, plague, and drought have all been proposed.

As to Greeks, it seems that the system of palaces and palace economy broke down by about 1200 at Mycenae, Tiryns, Pylos, and Thebes; but people, settlements, and language, including place-names and gods' names, persisted at a more or less reduced scale. Cyprus probably had Late Mycenaean immigrants; a linear script was used there far into the Hellenistic age. The sanctuary of the goddess of Paphos remained important down to the Roman period. This goddess was locally called *wanassa* (Queen) in clearly Mycenaean language; her name became generally known as Aphrodite, but also as just Kypris ("She from Cyprus").

Egyptian texts mention attacks by "people of the sea" after 1200, of whom the "Philistines" (*Plst* in Egyptian, *Pəlištîm* in Hebrew, *Palaistinoi* in Greek) are the most tangible ones. They left their name to Palestine. Biblical tradition says they came from Crete; some think they were Greek. Their ceramic style is clearly Aegean and may be called a kind of debased Mycenaean. There is no decisive clue so far as to their "nationality" and language. They adapted to Syrian tradition and adopted a Semitic language. They settled in cities, some of which became well known and persist today, such as Gaza, Ashkelon, and Ashdod.

3. Early Iron Age: Sea Trade, Writing, and Assyria

After the wide-ranging catastrophe that marks the end of the Bronze Age, a new world gradually emerged around the eastern Mediterranean. Scholarship now speaks of the "Iron Age," according to one important detail of technological progress, which slowly took over; iron is far more difficult to produce than bronze, but steel is much more effective for weapons as well as for tools, especially for working stone. More important was the social change, the temporary retreat of imperial powers to leave space for a wide diversity of "nations," clans, and cities, with all sorts of conflicts and chances. A chief in Karkamis (Carchemish) by the Euphrates, about 800, writes in Luwian hieroglyphs that he knows twelve languages and four scripts.[14]

In this period we find Philistine townships in Palestine, often in conflict with Israel, and flourishing coastal cities such as Tyre and Sidon farther north in Syria—the Greeks spoke of "Phoenicians" (*Phoinikēs*, "reddish" people). Adjoining them there were small dynasties of Arameans and Luwians, from northern Syria to Anatolia, where Hittite tradition was still dominant, including Hittite hieroglyphic script and a Luwian language. Farther northwest a major kingdom of Phrygians (*Phryges*) was established, probably by immigrants from the west during the period of turmoil; their language is western Indo-European. Another powerful kingdom developed toward the east in what is now Armenia: Urartu. Urartian is related to Bronze Age Hurrian; the Urartians kept cuneiform writing. Farther west, from Cyprus across southwest Anatolia to the Aegean islands, Crete, and the Balkan Peninsula, there was a population of Greeks.

In the early Iron Age there were three dominant forces that, at different levels, wrought change within this world, bringing progress and crisis: the development of sea trade, the spread of alphabetic writing, and the Assyrian Empire.

Sea trade, in spite of natural dangers, proved a stunning success. It turned toward the West especially in search of metals, and held further chances for economic gain and growth. Probably it was simply the breakdown of palace economy that started private enterprise. Long-distance trade cannot be controlled by royal bureaucracy; it functions through private risk and gain of individuals or families. It was the Phoenicians, the cities of Tyre and Sidon, who took the lead, closely followed by the Greeks. It brought prosperity to the cities and encouraged representational art. Ivory carving became an international sign of wealth.

---

14. H. Çambel, ed., *Corpus of Hieroglyphic Luwian Inscriptions*, vol. 2 (Berlin: de Gruyter, 2000), 131.

In the midst of such interrelations there was the spread of an easy writing system, which took literacy from the hands of royal or temple bureaucrats and made it available to the enterprising individual. There had been several experiments in the Middle and Late Bronze Age to develop a simpler form of writing as against traditional hieroglyphs and cuneiform, those complicated systems that required lifelong practice. Syllabic "linear" scripts had been one of these simplifications. More radical was the alphabet, which apparently was invented by some Semitic speaker by the middle of the second millennium; about 1400, a priest at Ugarit developed a cuneifom modification of the alphabet, which did not spread beyond Ugarit. Alphabetic writing means to write neither word-symbols nor syllables, but rather single sounds of speech; it can do with about twenty-five signs. The inventor had the grand idea to develop a catch line for memorization, a kind of comic strip: "ox, house, stick, door . . ."; in Hebrew this is: *aleph, bet, gimel, dalet*. Greeks just repeated these sounds: *alpha, bēta, gamma, delta*. Etruscans, it seems, and Romans made further simplifications: *a, be, ce, de*. For about 3,500 years everyone has learned this sequence, including our latest computers.

In spite of the age of this invention, there are very few documents before about 1000. The dramatic expansion seems to come with the ninth century. It probably has to do with the fact that alphabetic writing invaded Assyrian bureaucracy, in spite of marked dislike from the side of the traditional "Lords of the Tablets." In some pictures we see both kinds of writers, the "writer of tablets" and the "writer of scrolls,"[15] who has to stand back; but the future was his. The alphabet was easy to learn, and it could be used for any language. Thus alphabetic writing crossed the language frontiers and went west. Greek seems to have played the role of forerunner—even if there is an argument that Phrygians, not Greeks, were the organizers of vowel writing.[16] The earliest Greek letters are dated to about 800;[17] records of the Olympic Games started in 776.

Too much has been made of the fact that Semitic script does without vowels, as Israelis and Arabs still do today; they write long vowels nevertheless, whereas Greeks developed a fixed system of vowel writing, with five, then seven, signs. It was a mixture of misunderstanding and genius. For Greeks,

15. R. Schrott, *Homers Heimat: Der Kampf um Troia und seine realen Hintergründe* (Munich: Hanser, 2008), fig. 10, and cover.

16. C. Brixhe, "Nouvelle chronologie anatolienne et date d'élaboration des alphabets grec et phrygien," CRAI 148 (2004): 271–89; Brixhe, "Zônè et Samothrace: Lueurs sur la langue thrace et nouveau chapitre de la grammaire comparée?," CRAI 150 (2006): 128.

17. SEG 48 (1998): 1266; W. Burkert, *Babylon Memphis Persepolis: Eastern Contexts of Greek Culture* (Cambridge, MA: Harvard University Press, 2004), 147n10.

alpha begins with *a* and not with a glottal stop (*aleph*). They had no *y* in their own language and thus heard *yād* (hand) as *iota*, beginning with *i*, but they consciously made two letters out of *waw*, with a slight change in form: F (digamma) and Y (upsilon); they had no need to do the same for *yād*, as the Phrygians did. From now on it was the Greek alphabet that spread from Asia Minor through Italy to Spain.

History, in traditional understanding, happens through military actions. The great onset of military power came from the East, the developing Assyrian Empire. "Lord of the Whole" and "Lord of the Four Quarters of the World" had been old titles of Mesopotamian kings; but it was the kings of Assur in Mesopotamia who gave a new and actual meaning to these. Organizing superior military power, they began to attack and to plunder their neighbors, the adjacent tribes, kingdoms, or cities, in a systematic way year after year; they took booty and enforced devastating tributes, which made their superior army self-sustaining. In full consciousness of their power, the Assyrian kings built splendid palaces to celebrate their glory: Kalhu/Nimrud (Assurnasirpal), Dur-Sharrukin/Khorsabad (Sargon II), Nineveh (Sennacherib and Assurbanipal). Their expansion had turned west, toward Syria, since the ninth century: Assurnasirpal reached the Mediterranean before 850. The climax came in the eighth and seventh centuries: Damascus was conquered about 800; the northern part of Palestine/Israel fell prey to the Assyrians in 722; Assyrians invaded Cyprus and made Greek "kings" pay their tribute to the Great King; and Sargon II (722–705) left a cuneiform stela at Kition/Larnaka (Cyprus), mentioning some Greek names of evidently Greek "kings."[18] Ionians fought a naval battle with Assyrians close to Tarsos in Cilicia about 700. Jerusalem was attacked by Sennacherib in about 700, but was saved in this instance through diplomacy or, as the Bible has it, by a plague that struck the Assyrian besiegers (2 Kings 19:35//2 Chron. 32:21//Isa. 37:36). Sidon was destroyed in 672. Egypt came under Assyrian domination from 671 to 655.

The main evidence capturing the imperial propaganda of the Assyrian "Empire" is found in the royal inscriptions. They give a devastating picture of bellicose violence: the king, almost every year, rises to make war; he conquers opposing kings and cities and takes immeasurable booty; and his grandeur seems to be based on sheer aggression, robbery, and cruelty. This leads us to overlook that there were other aspects, too: power would guarantee peace. A newly found inscription from Cilicia (dating to about 700) proclaims that the king of Assyria has become a "father" of the local king and city: "We have

---

18. D. D. Luckenbill, *Ancient Records of Assyria and Babylonia*, vol. 2, *From Sargon to the End* (Chicago: University of Chicago Press, 1927), 36 (§70).

become one people."¹⁹ In a similar vein, Sennacherib's envoys to Jerusalem praise the happiness of submission and peace, a message that the Israelite war party tries to withhold from their people (see 2 Kings 18–19). Rich and startling finds from tombs at Salamis, Cyprus, from the eighth/seventh century suggested a "Homeric" style of exuberance to the excavators; they come from the Assyrian period.

Assyrians in Syria bring forth the first clear testimony for Greeks (about 738): a cuneiform letter mentions invaders from "the country Iaunaia"—that is, "Ionia." They had plundered the Syrian coast; the Assyrian commander pursued them to the midst of the sea.²⁰ The name appearing here, Iauna, evidently corresponds to the Greek tribal name of *Iaōnes/Iōnes*. It appears as *yāwān* in the Hebrew Bible and has remained the Eastern designation for Greeks to the present day—Turkish *Iunan(lar)*; its origin and precise signification from the Greek side are problems not to be solved here.

It was in a similar context that Greeks came into possession of some beautiful bronze pieces of horse harness that, according to their Aramean inscription, had belonged to Hazael, king of Damascus (844–803).²¹ Were these gifts from high-ranking aristocrats, or just robbers' booty? The Greeks piously dedicated them to Hera at Samos and to Apollo at Eretria. We can only speculate about whether any Greek noticed the letters they bear; they are nearly identical with early Greek writing.

A direct line from Greeks to Assyria was established through the Lydians from Asia Minor: King Gyges of Lydia, with Sardis for his capital, had risen to power mainly through the discovery and production of gold in the Paktolus River close to Sardis. It was Gyges who established contact with Assurbanipal's Nineveh, as recorded in the successive editions of Assurbanipal's annals.²² Gyges's envoys thus opened up the land route from Anatolia to Iraq, which was to be called the King's Highway. This must have happened about 670. Gyges evidently was seeking allies for the defense against invading tribes, the *Kimmerioi* (Akk. *gimirru*). From the viewpoint of Nineveh it was rather a kind of vassalship. The annals disapprovingly note the treachery of Gyges, who

---

19. Inscription from Çineköy; see Tekoğlu and Lemaire, "La bilingue royale louvito-phénicienne de Çineköy."

20. H. W. Saggs, "The Nimrud Letters, 1952. Part VI: The Death of Ukinzer; and Other Letters," *Iraq* 25 (1963): 76–78; W. Burkert, *The Orientalizing Revolution: Near Eastern Influence on Greek Culture in the Early Archaic Age* (Cambridge, MA: Harvard University Press, 1992), 12.

21. H. Kyrieleis and W. Röllig, "Ein altorientalischer Pferdeschmuck aus dem Heraion von Samos," *MDAI* 103 (1988): 37–57; Burkert, *Orientalizing Revolution*, 19.

22. M. Streck, ed., *Assurbanipal und die letzten assyrischen Könige bis zum Untergange Niniveh's* (Leipzig: Hinrichs, 1916), 20–24; Luckenbill, *Ancient Records*, 326, 351–52.

took up contact with Egypt when the latter regained its independence from Assyria; Gyges thus justly fell in a battle against the Kimmerians (after 650).

Gyges had forced most of the "Ionian" cities of Asia Minor to submit to his kingdom. In spite of tensions, a close and fruitful partnership developed. Lydia was a center of riches, and it had its Oriental contacts. Lydians and Greeks used the same alphabet, but it seems the Greeks were more talkative: there survive many more Ionian inscriptions than Lydian ones. Greeks had long been steeped in international sea trade. We may imagine at least some Greeks accompanying the Lydian envoys to Nineveh. The name of Nineveh—Assyrian *Ninua*—became known to Greeks as *Ninos*. Gyges, and still more the later Lydian king Kroisos, made spectacular gifts of gold to the Greek oracle at Delphi. Thus the whole of Greece knew about "Gyges, with much gold."[23] Since the end of the eighth century, "Oriental" votive gifts are found more and more in Greek sanctuaries, at Delphi as well as at Olympia, the rising center of Greek religious cult and sports, but also in Hera's sanctuary at Samos and with Artemis of Ephesus.

What the Assyrians hardly noticed is that the center of civilization was shifting from the Near East to the Mediterranean. While the Eastern peoples and cities, be they Luwians, Arameans, Phoenicians, Egyptians, or Israelites, were suffering heavily from conquest and exploitation—the most splendid collection of Phoenician ivories ended up in Kalhu/Nimrud, palace of King Assurnasirpal (ninth century)—the Assyrian grip had its limits. Beyond it there were the Greeks, the most Eastern of Westerners. Greek settlements were immune, as far as we can see, from the military catastrophes that befell the Luwians, Arameans, Phoenicians, Palestinians, and Egyptians. They got their chance and their "miracle," including, of course, alphabetic writing.

4. Colonizing and Orientalizing

Greece, as it now emerges, is mainly a region of coexisting independent cities (*poleis*). Political activities were multifarious and unstable and still the responsibility and pride of the "citizens" (*politai*) of their respective *poleis*. A decisive fact is that kings were absent, or abolished, except for the fringe regions of Macedonia and Epirus and the special case of Lakedaimon/Sparta. There two families of "kings" coexisted—the local term was *laōagetai*, "people's leaders"—who claimed descendance from mythical Heracles. Their power

---

23. Archilochus (7th c.) Fr. 19 (M. L. West, ed., *Iambi et elegi Graeci ante Alexandrum cantati*, vol. 1, *Archilochus, Hipponax, Theognidea*, 2nd ed. [Oxford: Oxford University Press, 1989]).

was limited by a council of "elders" (*gerontia*, "senate" in Latin translation) and, since 752, by elected "overseers" (*ephoroi*); basic decisions were made by public assemblies of the "people" (*dēmos*). The other cities developed public administration without monarchies, "political" authorities with varying terms and details; normally there was a general assembly, a select "council" (*boulē*), and a set of elected magistrates.

The experience of a *polis* community in competition with neighbors found expression in the powerful evolution of sports. Sporting events became major festivals with intercity importance—most of all the Olympic Games. Olympia, the sanctuary, held the "tomb" of mythical Pelops, which gave to the country the name "Pelops's Island," *Peloponnēsos*. Running for one *stadion* (180 m.) was the leading discipline. The games were held every fourth year. The Greeks dated 776 as the year of the "first" Olympiad, but the cult was much older—776 may have to do with the advent of writing. A special happening was attributed to the fifteenth Olympiad (720): the victor lost his loincloth while running and thus was acclaimed in the nude. In consequence, male nudity became a distinctive specialty of Greek sports, in contrast to all neighboring civilizations; it made a new concept of male "beauty." On the other hand, the "nude goddess," an Eastern type imitated for some time in small idols for dedications and even in Cretan temple decoration, disappeared. Females, but for one priestess, were excluded from the Olympic Games.

After the model of and soon in competition with the Phoenicians, Greeks developed sea trade to new and prosperous dimensions. There was a trading line from Boeotia and Euboea via Cyprus to Syria by the ninth century, with permanent trade posts there, such as Al Mina.[24] And there was an increasingly flourishing line of commerce to the West, via islands such as Ithaca. Phoenicians had already founded a "New City" in the West (814), *qart hadasht* in Tunis, rendered *Karchēdōn* in Greek and *Carthago* in Latin; from there, they brought southwestern Sicily, Sardinia, and the southern part of Spain into dependence. Greeks, keeping contacts with them, took hold of islands such as Pithecussa/Ischia and founded their own "New City," Neapolis (Naples) in western Italy (about 750), while, toward the eastern side of Italy, Taras (Tarent) took a brilliant development. Still more promising was Sicily, notwithstanding impending conflicts with the Carthaginians and the antagonism between "Ionian" cities such as Catane (Catania) and "Dorian" cities. Syrakusai (Syracuse), founded about 750, was to become the most prominent of these, but also Akragas (Agrigento) and Selinous (Selinunte) on the southern coast were to flourish. *Colonia* is a Latin word; the Greek word was *apoikia*

---

24. See A. Villing, ed., *The Greeks in the East* (London: British Museum, 2005).

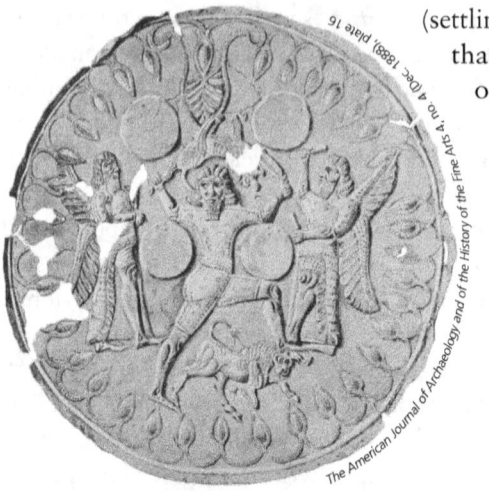

Figure 13.2. Bronze tympanon from Ida, probably Greek Zeus, Assyrian style

(settling apart). In contrast to the Carthaginians, who organized a kind of empire, Greek *apoikiai* were independent cities, keeping some relations with the "metropolis" by customs and religious ritual, but being free from any control, with chances for all kinds of conflict and even war.

Greek "colonization," in the eighth and seventh centuries, no doubt had to do with the pressure of a growing population, but also with progress in civilization, which made the Greeks in the West superior to indigenous populations. Greeks had writing, but more astounding was the rise of craftsmanship, *technē*, which came to mean "art" in a new key. Metallurgy took a fresh start, possibly stimulated by emigrating Oriental craftsmen. And there was an abundance of first-rate marble. What survives to our day is especially ceramics. It is in this field that the beginning of a new epoch can be traced already by about 1050: perfect shapes due to a quickly rotating pottery wheel with paintings black on red; this is done with finer against coarser clay, and it needs a complicated system of firing to come out. The leading place for the refined *technē* was Athens. The style is called "Proto-Geometric," developing into "Geometric" (ninth/eighth century) and then revolutionized, by the middle of the eighth century, through "Orientalizing" contacts.

At that time new iconography, getting rid of geometric patterns, brought Eastern ornaments and pictures, and more and more a full freedom of representation developed. The predilection for lion images and for fantastic beasts such as griffins, sirens, sphinxes, and chimeras is still reminiscent of the Eastern origins.[25] It was not only Phoenicia (i.e., Tyre and Sidon) that influenced Greek craftsmanship and iconography, but in particular North Syria with its Luwian-Hittite tradition. Large stone sculpture was produced there for Luwian palaces, with those fantastic beasts; Greeks were clearly influenced by these.

25. Sphinx: lion body, human head; griffin: lion body, bird's head; siren: bird's body, human head; chimera (she-goat): lion, snake tail, additional human or goat head.

Big bronze tripods, sometimes adorned with griffins' heads, were produced in North Syria. They first came to Greece as imports, to be dedicated at religious centers such as Olympia; they were then imitated by local craftsmen. It remains for specialists to distinguish imported from local pieces.

Among votive bronze shields, dated to the eighth century and dedicated in the sacred cave of Zeus at Mount Ida in Crete, there is one piece with a relief that looks absolutely Assyrian: a god standing on a bull and swinging a lion, in between two winged attendants whose garments are Assyrian, too (fig. 13.2). Some think it an imported piece, but usually it is taken for a local product, together with some other less-striking exemplars.[26] There are other traces of Eastern craftsmen who took up work in Crete, possibly fugitives from the Assyrians; they transferred their bronze techniques to Greek artisans. In the Ida cave, the Assyrian god probably represents Zeus. Elsewhere, too, in bronze work, images of Greek mythology first appear toward the end of the eighth century: Heracles fighting the multiheaded snake, the Hydra, and the Trojan horse, on wheels. Vase pictures and relief *pithoi* were to follow. Greek mythology becomes visible, growing out of Oriental stimuli.[27]

5. The Advent of Literature: "Homer"

Poetry, in all probability, is of aboriginal age, an efflorescence of human language that commands attention by sound and is easy to memorize by formal patterns. The unique case with Greece was that one form of traditional poetry, "epics," performed by traveling "singers," spread through the whole of Greece with a special dialect and then, transformed by writing, became the basis of literacy. Greek epic language is in fact an artistic construct, yet for this reason understandable beyond the local dialects. It concentrated on a few groups of tales, about the war of Troy, about the kings of Thebes, and about Heracles the son of Zeus. The most surprising event was an early breakthrough to literature, with an uncommonly well-done text: the *Iliad* of "Homer." This poem rather quickly appears to dominate the media, and soon it gets established as an absolute classic.

The *Iliad* is about the "wrath of Achilles," the quarrel of this hero with his general Agamemnon, king of Mycenae, who is leading the Greek army against Troy. Achilles withdraws from battle but allows his friend Patroclus

26. P. Blome, *Die figürliche Bildwelt Kretas in der geometrischen und frügarchaischen Periode* (Mainz: von Zabern, 1982), plate 3,3.
27. K. Schefold, *Götter- und Heldensagen der Griechen in der früh- und hocharchaischen Kunst* (Munich: Hirmer, 1993).

to fight, and he is killed by the Trojan Hector. Now Achilles must return to war to kill Hector, knowing that his own death is to follow. In the text we have, this tale is artfully expanded to comprise the totality of the Trojan War. The background or origin of the *Iliad* lies in the darkness of putative orality. We know nothing about the creation, the author, or the circumstances of producing such a large written text—in fact, a library of twenty-four leather scrolls. Unverifiable tradition names *Homēros* as author of the *Iliad*. Most controversial is the date of this achievement. The written text obviously presupposes the alphabet; hence many think of the eighth century, but there are arguments that rather point to about 660/650 for the text we read.[28] Just one similar text has survived, the *Odyssey*, with Odysseus, on his return from Troy to Ithaca, roving through far-flung parts of the sea with most astonishing wonders and monsters, and then killing the "suitors" who had assembled at Ithaca to woo his wife, Penelope. The *Odyssey* was generally attributed to "Homer," too. Tradition names the island of Chios as the home of *Homēros*; this goes together with the fact that in the sixth century *Homēridai* from Chios became prominent through public recitations of "their" poetry. At Athens, these performances were integrated into the great *polis* festival of Panathenaia, probably about 530. As writing spread further, "Homer" became the main school text, too. In consequence, Homer was known just about everywhere: we find Homer towering not only over poetry but also over the whole of the spiritual and conceptual world of the Greeks. His tales about the "Olympic" gods in particular, involved in the Trojan War, give the basis and form to Greek religious ideas. There were no sacred books; hence there was no rival to "Homer," "from the beginning, because they all have learned . . ."[29]

If we focus on the time of about 660/650 for "Homer," this is more than four generations after the advent of writing, but it is just the time when at Nineveh Assurbanipal founded his libraries and when the Lydian king Gyges sent his envoys to Nineveh. Gyges even had interest in Greek epic poetry.[30] Homer's *Iliad*, in some details, shows striking connections to the great Akkadian epics.

28. W. Burkert, *Kleine Schriften*, vol. 1, *Homerica*, ed. C. Riedweg (Göttingen: Vandenhoeck & Ruprecht, 2001), 59–71; M. L. West, *The Making of the Iliad: Disquisition and Analytical Commentary* (Oxford: Oxford University Press, 2011).

29. Xenophanes 21 B 10 (Hermann Diels, *Die Fragmente der Vorsokratiker*, 8th ed. [Hamburg: Rowohlt, 1957]).

30. Story of the poet Magnes: Nikolaos 90 F 62 (Felix Jacoby, ed., *Die Fragmente der griechischen Historiker* [Leiden: Brill, 1954–64]), probably from Xanthos the Lydian (5th cent.). For Homer's Oriental touch, see M. L. West, *The East Face of Helicon: West Asiatic Elements in Greek Poetry and Myth* (Oxford: Clarendon, 1997); Burkert, *Babylon Memphis Persepolis*, 20–48.

6. After the Fall of Assyria

The Assyrian Empire met with a sudden and violent end: a coalition of Babylonians and Medes destroyed Nineveh in 612, leaving a field of ruins that even lost its local name.[31]

It was the king of Babylon, Nebuchadnezzar (605–562), who succeeded in bringing back to Babylon an empire's power and splendor, at least for one generation. He had to fight Egypt, which had regained its independence after the Assyrian interlude. Israel was situated right in the middle of this conflict, and this time diplomacy failed: in 586, Jerusalem was conquered and destroyed, and a large part of the population was forcibly transferred to Babylon. It was the empire's policy to eliminate nations and national conflicts; similar disasters had happened to many cities and tribes already at the time of the Assyrian superpower. The unique fate of Israel was that this was not the end of the "people": a core group was adamant to cling to their own tradition and to their god, to refuse assimilation and to be ready for a new start.

Greeks were not directly touched by the Near Eastern power games. The fall of the superpower eased tensions in general. Egypt now emerged as the most attractive center, which still never sent conquering troops abroad but rather evolved as a dominant market. The elites of Cyprus in particular adopted Egyptian forms, Egyptian fashions, and Egyptian gods; Greek cities from Asia and the motherland strengthened their economic contacts with Egypt. Some time before 600, Naukratis was established by pharaonic permit as a common commercial center for Greeks, with separate sanctuaries and commercial bases for the Ionian cities in particular. Individual Greeks tried to make their fortunes as mercenaries or by business enterprise. It is through mercenaries that the name "Babylon" first appears in Greek literature: the brother of the poet Alcaeus (beginning of sixth century) had been serving Nebuchadnezzar. There is an Egyptianizing stela of a certain Pedon, citizen of Priene, with a Greek inscription; Pedon boasts that King Psamtek (probably Psamtek II, about 600) donated to him "a golden chain, and a city, on account of his 'manliness.'"[32]

No doubt there was marked progress of wealth and lifestyle in the Greek world at the time. Side by side with vase painting, stone architecture and large sculpture were now evolving, largely following Egyptian models but finding a special Greek style before long. Greek marble sculpture begins around 700. The availability of first-rate marble both in the islands and in the Greek

---

31. In 401 Xenophon crossed the ruins (*Anabasis* 3.4.10) without realizing this was Ninos, a name he should have known from Herodotus.

32. *SEG* 37 (1987): 994; *SEG* 39 (1989): 1266.

central mountains was an important prerequisite. Soon neighbors tried to imitate the Greek style, even if they had to import the marble. Egypt especially presented a model for statues of standing youths, which now became popular as dedications in sanctuaries and as memoirs at tombs. The position of their legs is clearly Egyptian, but Greeks opted for complete nudity, following the ideal of "beauty" as developed in sports (fig. 13.3). Temples—a Latin word—had adorned Egyptian sanctuaries for a long time; Greeks began to construct analogous "dwellings" (*naoi*) for gods. From small beginnings in the eighth and seventh centuries, a boom developed shortly before 600. Now the style was standardized: oblong tetragons with entrance from the small side, a heritage from Mycenaean *megara*. New was the use of tiles that made a sloping roof; columns were added, distantly following Egyptian models. Soon the "classical" Greek standards, called Dorian, Ionian, or Corinthian in later systematization, were there. Greeks never tried to rival the monumental size of Egyptian architecture; it was detailed elaboration of proportions through superior craftsmanship that counted. For bronze statues, hollow casting (lost-wax method) became common in the sixth century to produce light figures with a thin fabric, resplendent originally with a golden color; very few originals have survived.

Greek works of art came to be generally acknowledged as surpassing in brilliant style and liveliness whatever had been available before. "International" imitation began. Without central organization or conquest, Greek culture was becoming the leading culture in the Mediterranean region.

Greek success was particularly notable in Italy, with Etruscans and "Italiote" tribes, including, toward 500, the newly emerging center of *Latini*, Rome. Etruscans as well as *Veneti* on the Adriatic Sea became a booming market for Greek products, especially for painted vases; some Greek craftsmen settled right in Italy and established workshops there with outstanding production. Along with the pictures on Greek artifacts, Greek myths became popular too; they were translated into vernacular languages, with Greek names sometimes distorted: Herakles became Etruscan Hercle, Latin Hercules; Odysseus/Olytteus changed to Ulysses/Ulixes in Latin. It had been an old practice to identify gods across language barriers, as Egyptians and Hittites, Mesopotamians and Syrians had always done; thus Greek, Etruscan, and Latin pantheons came to interrelate. Only one god generally retained his Greek name: Apollo, famous for his oracular power; his cult came to Rome, via Cumae, by about 500.

The Mesopotamian connection, on the other side, continued to play its role, especially in the progress of astronomy. Days, months, and the circle of the year had been observed and counted by humans everywhere since time immemorial. But it is in cuneiform tablets from the Iron Age that more detailed observations and insights are documented. The moon completes a cycle through certain constellations every month, which makes a "path of the moon" in the sky; five stars are not fixed to constellations, but are wandering to and fro—Babylonians called them "sheep" (*bibbu*), Greeks "errant stars" (*planētēs*). An important discovery, based on protracted observation, was that these *bibbu* too are following the "path of the moon," and—more difficult to observe—that even the sun is doing the same. There is a "way" in the sky that can be marked by constellations and thus remembered and identified. The Greek transformation of such knowledge still holds today: in the Greek language this circle is marked by heavenly "animals" (*zōdia*), the constellations, and hence is called *zōdiakos kyklos*, the "zodiac." Such knowledge is found in cuneiform treatises, the most important of which is MUL.APIN.[33] Mesopotamians had assigned gods to the five wandering stars, and these in particular were translated by the Greeks: Marduk/Zeus, Ishtar/Aphrodite, Nergal/Ares, Ninurta/Hermes.[34] The fifth planet was not bound to a special god in Akkadian; to call him Kronos, the father of Zeus, may have been a Greek idea. Further translation into Latin resulted in our planets' names: Jupiter, Venus, Mars, Mercury, and Saturn. This is not to forget some further details of Akkadian usage that have survived: twelve hours to fill daytime or nighttime; division of the circle into 360 "steps" (Lat.

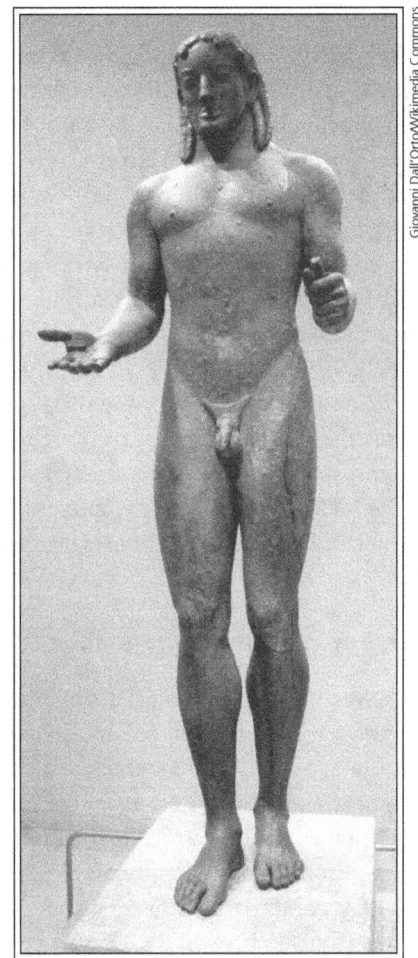

Figure 13.3. Bronze, *Piraeus Apollo*, Piraeus Museum, 6th century

---

33. R. Watson and W. Horowitz, *Writing Science before the Greeks: A Naturalistic Analysis of the Babylonian Astronomical Treatise MUL.APIN* (Leiden: Brill, 2007).
34. *RlA* 10:589–90.

gradus) according to the average "step" that the sun completes in one day; subdivision of grades and hours by the sexagesimal system (i.e., minutes and seconds), which bothers our arithmetic to the present day. The clear transfer from cuneiform to Greek cannot be precisely located and dated; it need not have been one event. Herodotus (*Histories* 2.109.3) knows about the "twelve hours" as a "Babylonian" import; Plato knows about planets and gods. The legendary prediction of a solar eclipse by Thales in 585 may at least point to a common interest in heavenly signs from East to West already at that time.

Egyptian-Greek interrelations seem to come to a climax by the first half of the sixth century. At that time we find a first-rate potter named Amasis at Athens (about 540). Was he an Egyptian, or did an Athenian family choose the name of the well-known Egyptian king Amasis (570–525)? Herodotus has the famous story of the correpondence between King Amasis and Polycrates, the tyrant of Samos, about excessive, precarious luck (*Histories* 3.40–43). Then the world suddenly changed: Persia came to the fore, Egypt succumbed, and Polycrates was murdered (522).

7. The Persian Empire and the "Persian Wars"

It was Cyrus, a warlord from Iran, who overthrew the balance of power between Egypt, Babylon, and Lydia and founded a new empire, much better organized and more stable than the Assyrian power had ever been. And in this case, Greeks no longer remained marginal observers; they were drawn right into the center of the turmoil. It is Greek historical texts that from now on become detailed and reliable.

Cyrus, starting from Persia and adopting Elamite administration and writing at Susa, answered a challenge from Lydia and marched west in 547; he overthrew the Lydian kingdom and established Persian rule at Sardis. This was also meant to subdue afresh the Greek cities of Asia Minor. Cyrus went on to conquer Babylon (539) and thus became heir to the whole political and cultural tradition and power of Mesopotamia. There is one substantial text from Cyrus that survives, a cylinder written in cuneiform Akkadian. It stresses the consent of the people of Babylon, which had been occupied without a fight; hence, somewhat excessively, the text is hailed as one of the first documents of "human rights" today.[35]

Cyrus's son Cambyses added the conquest of Egypt (525). The following king, Darius (522–486), in fact a usurper from the house of Achaemenes, was

---

35. Now housed in the British Museum; F. H. Weissbach, ed., *Die Keilinschriften der Achaemeniden* (Leipzig: Hinrichs 1911), 2–8.

the man to build up the organization of the gigantic empire, with Persepolis (a Greek name) as a political and ceremonial center; he also added India (i.e., the Indus valley) and Thrace in Europe, beyond the Bosporus. From India to Greece, from Egypt to the Black Sea, it was clear to everyone that there was a ruling "king" to guarantee order; for the Greeks, *Basileus* (King) became a kind of proper name for the Persian monarch. The local administration and power were run by the "guardian of royal power" (Persian *chshatrapata*; Gk. *satrapēs*), bound to the king by personal confidence. The Persian Empire was to last, with local revolts but without basic crises, for nearly two hundred years.

The Persian effect was quite different for Israel and for Greece. Cyrus gave up the Assyrian principle of "one people" within the empire; he was prone to allow all kinds of "national" tribes or groups to exist, with different customs and religions, provided their tribute gifts arrived properly. Hence Cyrus allowed the Jews, deported by Nebuchadnezzar in 586, to return to Jerusalem, to establish their dependent state, and to rebuild their temple. In fact this proved to be a radical group who had refused assimilation through more than fifty years in a foreign country. They were to decide what Israel should be in the future. The detailed accounts given in the biblical books of Ezra and Nehemiah are heavily reworked and sometimes contradictory, perhaps supplemented with inauthentic documents; it is thus unclear whether the temple in Jerusalem was rebuilt already at the time of Cyrus or, possibly, one hundred years later. But this much is clear: then and there came into being what Israel has been ever since—namely, a state of its own without a king, ruled by priests, worshiping one god with peculiar laws and cults based on the written law, the Torah. The Persian overlordship seems not to have presented any serious problem. Israel gratefully preserved the memory of Cyrus. The tale of how an Israelite woman, Esther, became a wife of King Artaxerxes—whichever king of that name—and decisively helped her people against an adviser who plotted Israel's extinction is probably from the Hellenistic epoch, but illustrates the unquestionable authority of the Persian king.

For the Greeks, at the western margins of the East, the Persian Empire became the great historical challenge. The "Persian Wars" have found their classical description in the account of Herodotus, the "father of history," and need not be retold here in detail. There are additional texts and documents. The conflict started some forty-seven years after Cyrus's conquest of Sardis, when things apparently had calmed down and the Persian order (*dat*) seemed to be established. The Persian satrap had completed the great marble temple of Artemis at Ephesus, which Kroisos, king of Lydia, had begun. But in 500, from complicated personal conflicts there arose a rebellion at Miletus against the king; the other Ionians took part, attacking and burning Sardis; and in retaliation Miletus was destroyed (494). Athens, which claimed to be the center and origin of the Ionians, got involved and had to face the attack of a Persian army in consequence. This army was defeated at Marathon (490)—the first and lasting military glory of Athens. The allied contingent of Sparta arrived only after the battle, in spite of the exertions of the Marathon runner.[36]

Then it was Xerxes (486–465), son and successor to Darius, who made a distinct effort to conquer the West; with a gigantic army he crossed the Dardanelles, marched south, annihilated the Spartans who tried to block the mountainous path at Thermopylae, and destroyed Athens, whose inhabitants had fled. His fleet, however, succumbed to the Athenian ships in the straits at Salamis, in front of Athens (480); the king returned to Persia, and the remaining army was defeated at Plataiai (479). The Greek victory had been unforeseeable—nay, absolutely improbable—and was experienced all the more as a decisive turn. It was the foundation of a new type of self-assurance: Greeks against Persians. This now meant *Hellēnes* against *Barbaroi*, Europe against Asia, freedom against servitude, divine ordinance against tyrannical outrage, and fighters against the weak. This was the very birth of "classical" civilization, founded on the opposition to "Asia," to the "Orient"—West against East.

Until then Sparta, with its "Peloponnesian symmachy," had been the acknowledged leader of the Greeks; but now the newly organized coalition (*symmachia*) of Greeks against Persia accepted the leadership of Athens, which reorganized the symmachy to become a form of Athenian dominance (*archē*). There followed some more victories against Persian armies; then Persia apparently gave up. Whether a formal peace was ever signed by the king (449?) is controversial. But the Greeks, including the islands of the Aegean and the Greek cities in Asia Minor, could feel "free" from Persian oppression, at least for a while.

8. The Greek Apogee

It was in these decades after the triumphal Persian Wars that Greece, with Athens for its center, rose to an unprecedented level of self-consciousness and cultural productivity. Three unique achievements had their heyday right at that time: representational art, dramatic literature, and a novel enterprise of science and reflection that was to be called philosophy. All these began to radiate through the whole of the Mediterranean world and thus came to

---

36. Pheidippides made the distance from Athens to Sparta (more than 150 mi.) in two days (Herodotus, *Histories* 6.105–6, 120). The run from Marathon to Athens (26 mi.) with the victory message is evidently a secondary invention.

characterize high civilization for a millennium; the "Greek miracle" has kept its fascination and influence even beyond antiquity.

As for art, temple building came to its climax with the grandiose temple of Zeus at Olympia (about 460) and the highly sophisticated marble temple at the acropolis of Athens, the Parthenon (438). The cult images for these were produced, in a startling and costly style, from ivory and gold. The artist, Pheidias, remained famous for centuries. At the same time, bronze sculpture and marble sculpture kept pace, with masterpieces of lasting fame and individual styles evolving from decade to decade. Masterpieces of painting with their artists are mentioned too in our records, but the works themselves are lost. What has remained is Attic red-figure vase painting, with astounding technique and unique craftsmanship. Modern scholars can distinguish and characterize hundreds of individual artists on the basis of some thirty thousand pieces.[37] Painted vases were a great success in Athenian exports, too.

Poetry found a new and expressive medium with the invention of the theater play. Theater architecture, with raised seats, evolved on the southern slope of the Acropolis. Opaque beginnings, with the name *tragōdoi* (goat-singers?) for the performers, run back to the sixth century. The oldest tragedy that survives is the *Persians* of Aeschylus, staged in 472, celebrating the battle of Salamis as the Persians' doom; the ghost of Darius rises from his tomb to testify to the glory of *Hellēnes*. The Athenian festival organization meant that three tetralogies were staged every year, each with three tragedies and *satyroi*— half-bestial companions of Dionysus—following the *tragōdoi*. The plethora of plays would bring on stage tales from the mythical repertoire, mostly known already from other genres of poetry, and add novel versions and novel plots. The one surviving trilogy, the *Oresteia* by Aeschylus, was performed in 458, with Clytemnestra murdering her husband Agamemnon, the victor of Troy, and Orestes killing his mother and finding acquittal at Athens. Particular success followed Aeschylus's younger partner Sophocles; his *Antigone* and *King Oedipus* have remained demanding masterpieces even for the modern stage. Euripides, with a trend toward innovation and experimentation, was less successful in the theater competitions of his time but left a major corpus of eighteen dramatic texts; *Medeia* and *Iphigeneia* are well-known titles from his oeuvre, and his *Bacchae* still dominates all studies and discussions about Dionysus and "the Dionysiac."

In the wake of tragedy, comedy ("revel-song") also developed in the theater of Athens; it came to life first as a form of political satire with moments of fantasy. Texts survive from Aristophanes, which were staged between 425 and

---

37. J. D. Beazley, *Attic Red-Figure Vase-Painters*, 2nd ed. (Oxford: Clarendon, 1963).

388; later, with Menander (343–291), plots focused on the circles of bourgeois society and mainly moved by eroticism gained the stage. It was this form of "comedy" that was reworked in Latin translations and transferred to Rome before 200; in this form it became the basis of Western theater in the sixteenth century, generally called "comedy" at that time.

Most important and lasting in its influence was a new movement of thought and literature that came to life in these decades. It had to do with freedom of speech as one of the permanent problems of "democracy," but was also moved by boundless curiosity about other subjects. Lively discussions obtained about all kinds of questions, about politics and politicians, about forms of civic "constitution" and rules of life, but also about the phenomena of the natural world, which found new and surprising explanations. "Wise men" (*sophoi*) had been held in high regard for a long time; now professional teachers called *sophistai* presented themselves, promising to make their pupils better, to secure a rise in rank and status beyond family or fortune through education (*paideia*). In fact, this was the invention of "higher education," since writing had ceased to be a distinction. The most prominent of the *sophistai* was Protagoras from Abdera, who came to Athens about 460. The main means to guarantee rising competence—nay, excellence—was a training in language; both rhetoric and logic have their roots in these discussions and teachings.

Deeper reflections also started at this time about language and thinking in relation to reality, called "being" with the Greek term (*onta*, *einai*): How do we match thinking and reality? The leading men were Parmenides, Anaxagoras, and Empedocles, then Democritus—all of them non-Athenians. A concept of "nature" (*physis*) was evolving; the terms "element" (*stoicheion*) and "atom" ("indivisible") were formed. No wonder there were more problems than solutions. But there was also spectacular success—for example, the explanations of the eclipses of the sun and moon and the discovery of the sphericity of the earth. Specialists developed strict mathematical proofs and built up a perfect system of geometry, which joined with astronomy to present the world as a huge and complicated but rational *kosmos* (order).

Side by side with the poets' poetry, prose writing won the day: a world of books and authors came into being, acclaimed by the reading public. Most of this has been eclipsed again by the very progress of literature, especially by evolving philosophy. For moderns, there remains a special fascination with the fragments of these original starts in thinking and formulating, the world of the pre-Socratics.

In a comedy by Aristophanes, *The Clouds* (423), the Athenian Socrates is attacked as an epitome of these modern trends, as a propagator of shrewd nonsense and immoral education. We see there was strong opposition of conservatives against the novel claims, terms, and discussions. They finally succeeded in turning "sophist" into a term of abuse; the less arrogant term "lover of wisdom," *philosophos*, had its breakthrough instead. Socrates was finally sued and condemned to death for "not believing in gods in whom the *polis* believes, and corrupting the young" by majority vote of a democratically elected court (399)—a disgrace for Athens to end a glorious century.

9. Wars and Modernization

In the midst of Hellenic "freedom" and the new intellectual brilliance evolving in these years, practical politics after the Persian Wars turned into disaster. The general ideal of *aretē*, "virtue," being better than others, led from competition to violence. Democracy, even philosophy, understood the citizens as "fighters" for the *polis*. Conflict between Athens and Sparta, the leading *poleis*, was to be expected. Economic frictions between Corinth and Athens escalated. The last battles of the Persian Wars were already interspersed with local wars. The great war, called the Peloponnesian War in retrospect, broke out in 431 and lasted nearly thirty years; Athens's main opponents were Sparta and Corinth. The worst disaster was an Athenian expedition against Syracuse (415–413), with the total destruction of an army of some thirty thousand combatants. The war ended with the total defeat of Athens (404), after Spartan diplomacy had brought the king back to the Greek scene. Persia regained its role as the dominant power of Hellas.

The system of coexisting cities proved to be self-destroying: each city was eager to conduct its own petty politics with changing alliances and wars. Sparta's victory in the Peloponnesian War was soon thwarted through Persian intervention. The king dictated "his" peace for Greece in 386, proposing "autonomy" for each city; this peace was soon broken by Sparta as well as by Boeotian Thebes. Then a splendid Theban victory (371) deprived Sparta of its prominence in Peloponnesus, but a collapse soon followed. Most of Greece was drawn into a "sacred war," which really served to plunder the accumulated riches of the oracle at Delphi, including the gold of Gyges and Kroisos (356–346). In this context a new power emerged surprisingly at the margin of Greece: Macedonia, ruled by King Philip (359–336), the most resourceful and most successful statesman of the century.

What continued to thrive nevertheless was "education," the definite spread of literacy with a rich production of books—notably, prose books for a growing reading public, a library that soon surpassed individual capacity. A literary society was in the making for the first time in cultural history. Amid political and military disasters the attraction of *paideia* was spreading in Greece and even beyond the borders of Greece.

A unique genius of thinking and writing in that epoch was Plato (428–347), who definitely inaugurated philosophy in Athens. As a prolific writer, he published "dialogues," which normally introduce Socrates as the dominant partner. He also wrote a posthumous *Apology* in the name of Socrates—a high point of world literature. Plato's theses evolve through critical dialogue, "dialectics," toward establishing higher realms of being, "ideas." His main work, *The Republic* (*Politeia*), leads from personal morality and the buildup of society toward a highest "sun" in the realm of thinking, the Good (*agathon*). The dialogue *Timaios* (*Timaeus*) seeks to derive the totality of the physical world from mathematical principles. Plato's activities took place in a locality called the *Akademia*; he had no family and left the Academy as his personal foundation for the next centuries. Plato's teachings and publications found wide resonance forthwith. Sensational, though unfortunate, were his dealings with the tyrants of Syracuse, where his friend Dion succeeded in overthrowing Dionysius (II) but was murdered before long (354). There remained Plato's works, preserved in their totality. They have their place in every pilosophical library; philosophy since has been called "a series of footnotes to Plato."[38]

Even more widespread was the influence of Aristotle (384–322), Plato's independent pupil. Aristotle was a miracle of learning and analysis; his central subject was "nature" (*physis*) in all its aspects. His copious books on zoology remained unsurpassed throughout antiquity. But Aristotle also invented formal logic. The fragmentary book on "poetics" has stirred and dominated discussions on poetry, especially since the Renaissance. His lectures were edited as a series of logic, physics, and ethics—Aristotle's terms. The lectures on what Aristotle called "first philosophy," or also "being qua being," were placed "after" (in Greek, *metá*) the lectures on "physics," and hence got the name "metaphysics." The very peak of Aristotle's influence came in Islamic philosophy and, following this, in medieval Christian theology. Aristotle's teaching had been done at a place called *Lykeion*, whence the word "lyceum" has entered many modern languages, with varying applications.

There now existed, for the next thousand years, two forms of higher education between which to choose, "philosophy" and "rhetoric." Thanks to Plato, Athens remained the center for philosophy; schools of rhetoric came to flourish in many other cities, usually through personal success. It was by

---

38. A. N. Whitehead, *Process and Reality: An Essay in Cosmology* (New York: Macmillan, 1941), 65.

these schools that Greek language, "classical" Greek language, could live on in a seemingly unchanged form down to the fall of Constantinople (1453 CE).

While this ascent was happening in Greece, the "East," in spite of the continuing concentration of power in the Persian Empire, was clearly suffering a loss of rank over against Greek innovations and Greek success. Already Darius had engaged Greek craftsmen to work on the reliefs of Persepolis. Persian kings began to rely on Greek doctors. Darius also adopted the Lydian-Greek invention of minting coins, golden *Dareikoi*, at least for the western satrapies; the king disposed of vast amounts of gold, collected from the tributes throughout his empire. More and more satrapies in the western part of the empire adopted purely Greek style in art and architecture and even in language. The Nereid monument from Xanthos, Lycia (400/370), is a highlight in the British Museum; the Mausoleum at Halicarnassus, Caria, the funerary monument for the local satrap Maussolos (died 352), was later included in the list of "world miracles"; for its inauguration, Artemisia, the widow of Maussolos, organized a literary festival at Halicarnassus, in Greek.

10. Alexander the Great and the Diadochs

The Persian Empire unexpectedly came to a sudden breakdown that changed the world. This was the work of Alexander, soon called Alexander the Great. His father, King Philip, had made Macedonia the dominant power across the whole of Greece through an ingenious mixture of diplomacy and military force; he was murdered in 336. Alexander, who had been a student of Aristotle, succeeded his father at the age of twenty, and in 334 he started the war against Persia on the flimsy pretext of revenge for Xerxes's attack some 150 years before. With his Macedonian troops he launched an unstoppable campaign through Asia Minor, Syria, and Egypt, and back toward Babylonia, Persepolis, Bactria/Afghanistan, then even farther east to India, where his troops finally rebelled and forced him to draw back. Before this world empire had found proper organization, Alexander died in Babylon at the age of thirty-two (324). He left a baby son, who was murdered before long. His generals, who were wielding the military power, acted and counteracted as "successors" (*diadochoi*), securing their own departments of "conquered land"; within twenty years they all adopted the title of "king" (*basileus*). After incessant conflict, it was three states and dynasties that were established for some time: the Ptolemies in Egypt, the Seleucids in Syria (including Iraq), and the Antigonids in Macedonia.

The Greek cities had to come to terms somehow with the new powers. Greece proper had hardly taken part in Alexander's exploits, and the Greeks never

Figure 13.4. Alexander the Great attacks the chariot of Darius of Persia (mosaic, Naples)

came to like Macedonians. There remained the conflicts and wars between various rulers, cities, and coalitions, rising and falling. In the second century the dynasty of Attalids made an impressive start in Asia Minor, with Pergamon for a capital. This was already under the aegis of the new Western power, Rome.

11. Hellenism

The lasting consequence of Alexander's campaigns was to make Greek civilization a world civilization with Greek cities, Greek books, and Greek as an international language—competing with Aramaic, the language of the Persian administration. Historians have come to call the post-Alexander epoch "Hellenistic." The explosive change of power left the old Greek cities as minor relics between conquering kings, but Alexander had also begun to found cities of a Greek type all along his campaigns, and the diadochs were following suit. Soon the whole Eastern world was interspersed with Greek cities, some of which became world metropolises, such as Alexandria in Egypt and Antioch in Syria (today Antakya, Turkey). This represented a worldwide triumph of Greek civilization, through Egypt and across Asia as far as Persia and India, without ousting native traditions and dialects. It was Greek education in particular that proved attractive throughout the "inhabited" world (*oikoumenē*). Athens, especially, succeeded in upholding the prestige of philosophy; there, in addition to Plato's Academy, other "schools" came to flourish: Aristotle's Lyceum, Epicurus's Garden, and especially the Stoa founded by Zenon and built up by Chrysippus—both of whom were immigrants from Cyprus. We know about many individuals not only from Greece and Asia Minor but also from Syria and even Carthage who came to study at Athens.

At Alexandria, the new capital of Egypt, the biggest library of Greek literature was installed by King Ptolemy I (d. 283), through royal subsidies, with a kind of Institute for Advanced Study for intellectuals called the *Mouseion* (Place of the Muses). Later Pergamon tried to follow suit. With royal sponsorship, astounding progress was achieved in mathematics, astronomy, medicine, and other forms of science, at Alexandria and elsewhere. Euclid published his *Elements* (*Stoicheia*) of geometry, which was to remain the basis of mathematical theory and school practice for the next two thousand years. Astronomers described the planetary movements by "epicycles" and discussed a heliocentric system. Eratosthenes of Alexandria made the most exact measurement of the earth's periphery. Archimedes of Syracuse, a unique genius of mathematics, worked with infinitesimals, discovered the geometric formulas for the surface ($4\pi r^2$) and volume ($[4/3]\pi r^3$) of spheres, and invented spirals in theory, and then transferred them to practical use—as pumps, winepresses, and screws. Apollonios of Perge developed the conic sections. Herophilos and Ersasistratos, doctors at Alexandria, revealed the existence and the functions of nerves through anatomy.

Then, in the course of the third century, a new power unexpectedly appeared in the West: Rome. It was Pyrrhus, king of Epirus, a relative of Alexander, who wished to enlarge his power and went west to assist Tarentum against Italiote neighbors. He attacked the Romans but ended with a grandiose failure (280–275). His disastrous victories have become proverbial; he returned to Greece and died in a local war (272). The Romans had already established their *imperium* (command) throughout Italy and went on to interfere in Sicily; this led to war with the Carthaginians, called *Poeni* in Latin, who controlled about half of Sicily. The First Punic War (264–253) ended with Sicily becoming the first *provincia* of the *imperium Romanum*, a territory administered by a Roman governor. Syracuse had sided with the Romans and thus, under Hiero, a tyrant bearing the title of "king," flourished for a final time; but in the Second Punic War (218–202), Syracuse changed sides and was conquered by the Romans (212), with the killing of Archimedes that has remained famous.

Right after their victory over Carthage, the Romans began to interfere directly in Greece, Asia Minor, and Egypt. Before long this brought about the end of Macedonia (168), organized as a *provincia* (148); in 168 the Romans also stopped the campaign of the Seleucid king Antiochus IV against Egypt, by a simple order of the Roman general. In Asia Minor the kingdom of Pergamon cultivated an alliance with Rome and thus reached its climax, documented by the grandiose Altar of Zeus; the country was donated to Rome by testament in 133 and became *Asia provincia*. The last Seleucid was deposed by Pompey in 63; Ptolemaic Egypt ended with the death of Cleopatra in 31.

The triumphal progress of the Roman Empire had a surprising consequence: Rome itself became progressively hellenized. Already by 240 Rome adopted theater, *comoedia*, with texts translated and adapted from Greek. The texts of Plautus and Terence survive. Aemilius Paulus, who conquered Macedonia in 168, was reported to have been overcome by the statue of the Pheidiasian Zeus in the temple at Olympia; he took one thousand hostages from Greece to Rome. One of these, Polybius of Megalopolis, remained in Rome and became an esteemed friend to one of the foremost Roman families, the Scipiones; he wrote the best history of his "Roman" century. In 155 Athens sent a delegation to Rome to have some local problem decided by the senate; for ambassadors the Athenians chose three philosophers, the presidents of the schools of Plato, Aristotle, and the Stoa. Carneades of Cyrene, head of the Academy, had an overwhelming success in Rome with some public lectures (in Greek no doubt), which were acclaimed by the Roman youth in search of modernism. Greece, though defeated and eclipsed, had nevertheless "caught" the victor, as Horace put it.[39]

12. Israel: Conflicts of Hellenization

The province of Yehud remained largely unnoticed within the Persian Empire, simply because there were no problems. Herodotus, with all his worldwide interests, does not once mention Israel or Jerusalem. Alexander, on his way from Syria to Egypt and back, did not stop at Jerusalem—even if later Jewish and Christian texts tried to fill the void with invented details.[40] It is with Aristotle's pupils that we find the first substantial reports in Greek literature about Jews (*Ioudaioi*), on account of their special religious rituals. Theophrastus, Aristotle's pupil and successor, was himself elaborating a fundamental criticism of animal sacrifice, in a book *On Piety*, and in this context he noted the peculiar position of the Jews.[41] Among Syrians, Theophrastus writes, the

---

39. Horace, *Epistle* 2.1.156.
40. A. Demandt, *Alexander der Grosse: Leben und Legende* (Munich: Beck, 2009), 183–87.
41. Theophrastus Fr. 584 A (W. W. Fortenbaugh et al., ed. and trans., *Theophrastus of Eresus: Sources for His Life, Writings, Thought, and Influence* [Leiden: Brill, 1992]) = Porphyry, *On*

Jews do sacrifice animals, but they do not feast on them; they burn them whole at night, while fasting and "conversing with each other about the divine; for they are a race of philosophers." They also observe the stars, and they call to God in prayers. For Greeks, animal sacrifice always meant feasting: "If someone should order us to sacrifice in the same way, we would give up this practice," Theophrastus comments. He does not mention the special taboo on pork in the text we have; probably this rule was generally known, but not too astonishing amid all kinds of local customs. Today it remains one of the foremost taboos, also having been taken up in Islam.

There was a rising emigration of Jews during the Persian period throughout the Hellenistic world, especially toward the big cities. The main recipient was Alexandria. Jews kept their identity through the strict rules of daily life, celebrating the Sabbath and abhorring pork, and having a local meeting house (Gk. *synagōgē*)—the only temple was in Jerusalem. More difficult to preserve was Hebrew, the sacred language; Alexandrians spoke Greek or Egyptian, and in the Seleucid area Aramaic had a good standing. Thus in third-century Alexandria, Greek translations of the sacred Scriptures were needed. Legend makes this an effort of seventy translators, organized by King Ptolemy II (285–246); guided by God, they arrived at one text. Reality was more complex. The Greek Bible was completed at some point, by the first century BCE certainly, and was known as the work of the "Seventy" translators, the Septuagint.[42]

Crisis, however, broke out in Yehud itself. The Seleucid king Antiochus IV (175–164) had adopted the title *Epiphanēs*, "Representing Divine Evidence," probably following his Egyptian relatives. The historian Polybius, his contemporary, commented that this king should rather have been called *Epimanēs*, "the Mad One."[43] Antiochus's idea was to homogenize his kingdom toward a common Hellenic civilization and hence to abolish the peculiar Jewish customs, which, in his view, expressed "hatred of humanity" (*misanthrōpia*).[44] Quarrels were going on in Jerusalem between traditionalists and hellenizing modernists. One stumbling block for integration was circumcision, especially vis-à-vis the practice of nude sports. Antiochus, suffering from his forced retreat from Egypt (168), transferred his energy to Jerusalem. We are told that he entered the temple, violating the Mosaic law, and made it a sanctuary of

---

Abstinence 2.26, quoted also by Eusebius, *Preparation for the Gospel* 9.2.1. For further mentions of Jews, see Clearchus Fr. 6; Demetrius of Phaleron Fr. 201 (F. Wehrli, ed., *Die Schule des Aristoteles: Texte und Kommentar*, vols. 3 [*Klearchos*] and 4 [*Demetrios von Phaleron*] [Basel: Schwabe, 1968 and 1969]).

42. *Septuaginta*, ed. A. Rahlfs (Stuttgart: Württembergische Bibelanstalt, 1935); for the legend of the "Seventy," see the *Letter of Aristeas*.

43. Polybius, *Histories* 26.1a.1; cf. Diodorus, *Library of History* 29.32; 31.16.

44. Diodorus, *Library of History* 35.1.3.

Greek Zeus—that he had a pig sacrificed on the altar in front of the temple, had the blood sprayed across the sacred books, and forced the high priest and other Jews to eat pork.[45] This started a fierce revolt, which the Seleucids proved unable to suppress. The leading family of the Jewish insurgents was the Maccabees; their history survives in Greek, incorporated into the Septuagint. The rebels conquered Jerusalem and reinstalled the Mosaic cult (165). In the following decades there were ups and downs, but the Jews finally succeeded in securing Israel/*Ioudaia* as an independent state, run by the high priest and his council. This council is called the Sanhedrin, still a Greek term (*synedrion*, "session"): Jews remained part of a Hellenistic world.

Just in the years of Antiochus, it seems, a strange book appeared, written partly in Hebrew, with its central piece in Aramaic—purportedly the story of a certain Daniel ("My judge is God") from the time of Nebuchadnezzar, but evidently reflecting the contemporary situation of about 165. The Aramaic chapters imaginatively describe the sequence of four world monarchies: a statue of four metals—gold, silver, bronze, and iron—with feet of clay, or else four animals—a lion, bear, and panther, succeeded by a monster with ten horns.[46] This evidently refers to the Assyrian, Median, Persian, and Greek Empires in succession, ending with the split power of the diadochs; they all are to be followed by an absolutely new beginning, the rule of God himself, as "the Son of Man" comes down from the clouds of heaven. Perhaps this book was a gift from Jews in Babylon for the reopening of the temple in Jerusalem (165/4); the Aramaic parts may be older. Soon afterward, once Antiochus had disappeared, it seemed suitable to skip the Medes and to find the real monster of power in the Roman Empire. The enormous impact of the book of Daniel may be seen in those instances when Jesus called himself the Son of Man; Christians, in consequence, accepted the four monarchies as the final revelation about world history, to be followed by the end of the world. Hence, the Holy Roman Empire had its fictional existence until 1806 CE.

Real history was more complicated. A man of Idumaean (i.e., Arab) origin with a Greek name, Herodes, gained power in Judea and became "king" by approbation of Rome (37–4 BCE); he successfully steered his state through the Roman revolutions and became a friend of Augustus, always acknowledging Roman supremacy. After his death, anti-Hellenic and anti-Roman attitudes spread all the more in Palestine, which finally led to rebellion, war, and the destruction of Jerusalem (70 CE). This meant the final separation of Judaism and Hellenism. Judaism survived in exile, with centers in Galilee and in Babylon.

45. Diodorus, *Library of History* 35.1.4.
46. See Daniel 2 and 7.

13. Toward the "End of Antiquity"

By the epoch of Augustus, the whole of the Greek world had become part of the Roman Empire. This was not at all the end of Greece; on the contrary, the eastern part of the empire became all the more Greek. No one would speak Latin there but soldiers and jurists. Thanks to the peace guaranteed by the empire, Greeks had in fact a much better life in their cities than in the bellicose times before. Many of them could live on their "education," since men of power as well as whole cities wished to have brilliant Greeks for company, for advice, and for show. Rhetoric thus opened careers, and science made further progress. The great comprehensive works on astronomy, geography, and music were written at Alexandria's *Mouseion* by Ptolemy (ca. 100–170 CE); and a library of medical knowledge was left by Galen (129–199 CE). These and further books were to dominate science for the next thousand years, especially in Arabic translations. In the fourth century CE the cultural revolution of Christianity took place, with Constantinople (Istanbul) as the new center. Yet Christianity had long met with Greek literature and philosophy and continued to produce a plethora of Greek books in the best style, while Eastern Christianity also gave rise to native church languages such as Syriac (a form of Aramaic), Coptic, Gothic, Armenian, and Georgian. Greek language and literature were still based on the continuing school system, bound to the seemingly immutable grammar and vocabulary of the "classical" past. Conscious of the continuity with the Roman Empire, the Greeks called themselves *Rhomaioi*; modern historians speak of the Byzantine epoch. This went on until the final Turkish conquest of Constantinople in 1453 CE. The decline and fall of the Western Roman Empire, mainly through Germanic tribes, is not the topic of this essay, nor is the Eastern onslaught of Muslims, of Arabs, and of Turks. Restored in the nineteenth century, Greece both boasts and suffers from a glorious past amid the problems of modernity.

For Further Reading

Anagnostopoulos, Georgios, ed. *A Companion to Aristotle*. Oxford: Wiley-Blackwell, 2009.

Annas, Julia, and Christopher Rowe, eds. *New Perspectives on Plato, Modern and Ancient*. Cambridge, MA: Harvard University Press, 2003.

Barnes, Jonathan. *The Presocratic Philosophers*. London: Routledge & Kegan Paul, 1979.

Boardman, John. *The Greeks Overseas: Their Early Colonies and Trade*. 4th ed. London: Thames & Hudson, 1999.

Boardman, John, Jasper Griffin, and Oswyn Murray, eds. *The Oxford History of Greece and the Hellenistic World*. Oxford: Oxford University Press, 2001.

Briant, Pierre. *From Cyrus to Alexander: A History of the Persian Empire*. Winona Lake, IN: Eisenbrauns, 2002.

Bugh, Glenn R., ed. *The Cambridge Companion to the Hellenistic World*. Cambridge: Cambridge University Press, 2006.

Cline, Eric H., ed. *The Oxford Handbook of the Bronze Age Aegean*. Oxford: Oxford University Press, 2010.

Demandt, Alexander. *Alexander der Grosse: Leben und Legende*. Munich: Beck, 2009.

Dickinson, Oliver. *The Aegean from Bronze Age to Iron Age: Continuity and Change between the Twelfth and Eighth Centuries BC*. London: Routledge, 2006.

Fraser, Peter M. *Ptolemaic Alexandria*. Oxford: Clarendon, 1972.

Gregory, Justina, ed. *A Companion to Greek Tragedy*. Oxford: Blackwell, 2009.

Hornblower, Simon. *The Greek World: 479–323 BC*. 4th ed. London: Routledge, 2011.

Kuhrt, Amélie, and Susan Sherwin-White, eds. *From Samarkand to Sardis: A New Approach to the Seleucid Empire*. Berkeley: University of California Press, 1993.

Lloyd, G. E. R. *Greek Science after Aristotle*. London: Chatto & Windus, 1973.

Meier, Christian. *A Culture of Freedom: Ancient Greece and the Origin of Europe*. Oxford: Oxford University Press, 2011.

Neugebauer, Otto. *A History of Ancient Mathematical Astronomy*. 3 vols. Berlin: Springer, 1975.

Osborne, Robin. *Greece in the Making, 1200–479 BC*. 2nd ed. London: Routledge, 2009.

Shelmerdine, Cynthia W., ed. *The Cambridge Companion to the Aegean Bronze Age*. Cambridge: Cambridge University Press, 2008.

West, Martin L. *The Making of the Iliad: Disquisition and Analytical Commentary*. Oxford: Oxford University Press, 2011.

Index of Authors

Abraham, Katherine, 133n75, 134, 134n78, 394n36
Abusch, Tzvi, 72n100
Adams, Robert McC., 438n88
Adelsberger, Katherine, 322n30
Agut-Labordère, Damien, 395n40
Ahituv, Shmuel, 342n97
Ahmed, K. M., 242n57
Aitken, Kenneth T., 159n67
Akkermans, P., 241n51
Akurgal, E., 472n10
Al-Amri, Yosha Abdel Salam, 315n9
al-Ansary, A. T., 447n117
Albà, Adelina Millet, 18n40
Albertz, Rainer, 347n115, 347n119, 348n120, 401n61
Albright, William F., 102n180, 109n4, 230n2, 277, 277n25, 295, 295n76
Al-Ghazzi, Abdulaziz Saud, 433n67
Al-Hasan, Hussein bin Ali Abu, 447n117
Al-Iryāni, Muṭahhar 'Alī, 462n169
Al-Mu'azzin, Muna, 449n122
al-Said, Said F., 444n110, 447n117, 448n120
Amigues, Suzanne, 382n10
'Amr, Abdel-Jalil, 343n103
André-Salivni, B., 428n39
Arico, Ashley Fiutko, 327n48, 344n106
Arnaud, Daniel, 144n14, 236n31
Arnold, Bill T., 96n167, 124n57, 127nn63–65, 128n66, 135n79, 256nn102–3, 258n110, 355n6, 355n8
Assaf, A. Abou, 246n70
Assmann, Jan, 169n2

Aster, Shawn Zelig, 84nn130–31, 96n166
Astour, Michael C., 267n1
Attridge, Harold W., 293n74, 295n76
Aufrecht, Walter E., 319n24, 340n90
Avanzini, Alessandra, 422n15, 424n19, 451n129, 456n149, 457n151
Avigad, Nahman, 342n95

Babaev, I., 409n82
Badre, L., 458n152
Bagg, A. M., 254n99
Baker, H. D., 253n91
Bakir, T., 405n72
Balken, Kemal, 69n89
Balla, Márta, 336n74, 338n83
Barjamovic, Gojko, 8n17
Barnett, R. D., 436n79, 438n87
Bartlett, John R., 330n55, 333n69, 334nn70–71, 337n77, 338n78, 342n100, 347n116, 347n118
Bates, Robert D., 94n159
Bawden, Garth, 434n72
Beaulieu, Paul-Alain, 28n60, 124nn57–58, 126n60, 129n70, 264n133, 442n102, 443n105, 446n114
Beazley, J. D., 489n37
Beck, Pirhiya, 344n108, 350n132
Beckerath, J. von, 288n57
Becking, Bob, 152n47
Beckman, Gary, 221n52
Bedford, Peter R., 401n61
Beeston, A. F. L., 424n18, 455n144, 456n149, 460n160, 462n169
Beit-Arieh, Itzhaq, 330n56, 347n116, 350n132

501

Ben-Ami, D., 244n64
Bennett, Crystal-M., 336n74, 337n77, 338n83
Ben-Shlomo, David, 369n47, 370n52, 371n58
Ben-Tor, A., 244n64
Ben-Yosef, Erez, 331nn59–60
Benz, Brendon C., 23n49
Benz, Frank L., 272n15
Ben-Zvi, I., 446n114
Bergamini, G., 113n12
Berger, P.-R., 128n67, 129n69
Berlejung, A., 234n22
Berman, Joshua A., 226n69
Bienkowski, Piotr, 318n22, 319n23, 320n27, 322n28, 330n58, 333n68, 336nn74–75, 337nn76–77, 338n83, 339nn84–85
Bietak, M., 470n5
Bill, Adele, 409n82
Black, Jeremy, 69n91
Blakely, Jeffery A., 49n18
Blois, François de, 420n9, 432n64
Blome, P., 481n26
Boardman, John, 55n36, 405n71
Bodi, D., 122n52
Bonatz, D., 257n106, 261n124
Bonechi, Marco, 10n23
Bordreuil, Pierre, 145n17, 150n39, 151n45, 153, 153n50, 164n75, 246n70, 342n96, 423n17
Bottéro, Jean, 25n52, 68n87, 74n110
Boucharlat, Rémy, 387nn17–18, 391n21
Bounni, A., 145n16
Bourke, Stephen, 348n121
Bowersock, G. W., 430n48
Bramlett, Kent V., 314n6
Breasted, James Henry, 213n29
Breton, Jean-François, 450n123, 453n138, 458n152
Briant, Pierre, 379nn1–2, 380nn3–5, 382nn9–10, 383n12, 384nn13–14, 387n17, 389n20, 392nn23–26, 393n29, 392nn31–32, 394nn33–34, 394n37, 395nn39–40, 397n43, 397n45, 398n46, 398n48, 399n51, 399n53, 400n56, 401nn57–59, 401n61, 402nn62–63, 403nn64–66, 403n68, 404n69, 405n71, 405n73, 407nn76–78, 408n79, 409n83, 410n84, 411nn85–86, 412nn88–89, 413nn90–91
Briend, J., 459n155
Bright, John, 3n5
Brinkman, John A., 57n44, 116nn22–23, 119, 120n38, 126n60, 252n84, 256n103, 258n108, 425n26, 428n39
Brixhe, C., 475n16

Bron, François, 423n18, 454n143, 456nn146–47, 462nn167–68, 463n170
Brown, Brian, 40n2, 73n107
Bryce, Trevor, 2n1, 197n1, 203n7, 204n8, 205n10, 207n11, 208n15, 209n16, 209n18, 211n20, 211n22, 215n35, 215n37, 218n46, 222n54, 222n56, 223n57, 225nn63–65, 227n72
Buccellati, Giorgio, 2n3, 5n8
Bunnens, G., 239nn39–40
Burkert, W., 475n17, 477nn20–21, 482n28, 482n30
Burnett, Joel S., 290n64, 343n104, 344n105, 346n113, 347n115, 348n124
Byrne, Ryan, 426n31

Calmeyer, Peter, 407
Çambel, H., 474n14
Caquot, André, 154n55, 163n74
Carpenter, Rhys, 271n12
Carr, David, 79n120
Casabonne, Olivier, 203n6, 405n71, 408n80
Cathcart, Kevin J., 143n12
Charpin, Dominique, 3n4, 9, 9n19, 11n28, 12n31, 13n32, 25n56
Chauveau, Michel, 392n24, 395n40, 405n71
Cholidis, N., 257n107
Cifola, Barbara, 364n27
Clark, Douglas R., 315n12, 320n27, 349n127
Clark, Geoffrey A., 339n87
Clarysse, Willy, 418n2
Clay, Albert T., 128n67
Clemens, David M., 161n69
Clermont-Ganneau, C., 288n55
Cogan, Mordechai, 48, 48n16, 49, 84–85, 84n134, 85nn135–36, 125n59, 249n75, 328n51, 362n21
Cohen, Chaim, 93n154, 163n73
Cohen, Mark E., 71n97
Cohen, Rudolph, 350n131
Cohn, Robert L., 355n4
Cole, S. W., 234n20
Collins, Billie Jean, 197n1, 208n15, 216n42, 218n49, 221n52, 225n62, 226nn68–70, 227nn71–72
Collins, J., 447n116
Coogan, Michael D., 154n55
Cooke, G. A., 279, 279n33
Cooley, Jeffrey L., 121n45
Cooper, Jerrold S., 19n42
Cornelius, Izak, 151n44
Cresson, Bruce, 347n116
Cribb, R. L. D., 233n17

Index of Authors

Cross, Frank Moore., 277, 277n26, 282n42, 292n73, 340n91, 444n107
Crouch, Carly, 97n169
Cunchillos, Jesús-Luis, 164n76
Curtis, J. E., 247n71, 387n17

Dalix, Anne-Sophie, 163n74
Dalley, Stephanie, 49n19, 80–81, 80n121, 83n129, 94, 94nn160–61, 239n40, 338n82, 339n86, 443n106
Dandamayev, M. A., 426n32
Darbandi, Seyed Mohammad Reza, 383n11
Da Riva, R., 127n61
Darnell, John, 277n27
Daviau, P. M. Michèle, 315n12, 319n23, 323n36, 324n39, 326n45, 327n50, 342n94, 342n99, 343n104, 345nn109–10, 346n113, 350nn130–31, 424n23
Davies, A. Morpurgo, 470n7
Day, Peggy L., 143n12
Dayton, J. E., 433n67
Dearman, J. A., 323n33, 342n97
Degen, R., 446n113
Delemen, Inci, 405n71
Demandt, A., 496n40
de Martino, Stefano, 207n12, 216n39
Demsky, Aaron, 359n11
de Odorico, Marco, 58n48, 63n62
Descat, Raymond, 393n28, 394n37, 413n91
Deutsch, Robert, 463n172
Dever, William G., 22n46
Dezső, Tamás, 52n31, 58n49
Diakonoff, I. M., 464n175
Dick, M. B., 71n95
Diels, Hermann, 482n29
Dietrich, Manfried, 148n35, 155n62, 451n126
Dietrich, Walter, 360n17
Dijk, Jacobus van, 181n10
Dincol, Ali M., 198n2, 207n12
Dincol, Belkis, 198n2, 207n12
Dion, Paul-Eugène, 27n57, 239n38, 243n61, 258n108, 316nn14–15, 317n17, 320n26, 323n36, 324n39, 342n94, 342n99, 343n104, 346n113, 424n23
Dobbs-Allsopp, F. W., 328n52
Dolan, Annlee, 350n130
Donner, Herbert, 268n2, 279, 279n34
Dörfler, Walter, 213n31
Dornemann, Rudolph H., 317n17, 318n20, 343n103
Dothan, Moshe, 355n5, 371n57

Dothan, Trude, 353n1, 355nn4–5, 365n30, 365n33, 368–69, 368n43, 369nn47–48
Doumas, C. G., 470n6
Drews, Robert, 362n23
Driver, G. R., 44n10
Duhoux, Y., 470n7
Dunand, M., 284n47, 287n53, 288n59
Durand, Jean-Marie, 8n18, 9, 9nn20–21, 10n26, 11n27, 13n32, 13n34, 25n54, 26n55
Dusinberre, Elspeth, 405n71, 410n84
Dussaud, R., 285n49, 288n57, 464n175

Easton, F., 472n13
Edel, Elmar, 209n18, 213n28, 471n8
Edelman, Diana V., 335n70, 338n79
Edwards, Ruth B., 272n14
Edzard, D., 124, 124n57
Eggler, Jürg, 345n111
Ehrlich, Carl S., 252n86, 360n18, 361n19, 364n26, 365nn33–34, 366n38, 374n67, 375n70
Eichmann, R., 440n94, 442n104
Eidem, Jesper, 41n5
Elat, Moshe, 67n81
Elayi, Josette, 411n85
Elitsur, Y., 236n28
Elkowicz, Dominik, 376n72
Eph'al, Israel, 417n1, 419nn3–4, 419nn6–7, 425n27, 426n30, 426n32, 430n51, 435n74, 436nn77–78, 436n80, 437n82, 437n84, 437n86, 438n87, 442n99, 442n102, 443n105, 451n126, 454n141, 456n148, 459n158, 460n159, 460n161, 461n164
Eshel, Esther, 439n92
Eshel, Hannah, 401n60
Eskoubi, Khalid M., 444n110
Evans, Arthur, 469n4

Fales, F. M., 59n51, 61n54, 124n57, 240n41, 253n92, 258n108, 263n131, 436n76
Farber, Walter, 75n112
Farès, Saba, 449n121
Farès-Drappeau, Saba, 448n118
Fatkin, Danielle S., 322n30
Faulkner, M., 436n79
Faust, Avraham, 49n20, 83n126, 354n3, 369n46
Feliu, Lluís, 18n39
Fink, A. S., 259n114
Finkelstein, Israel, 48n17, 115n21, 118nn31–32, 244n64, 359n14, 364n28, 369n45, 370n52
Finkelstein, J. J., 150n41
Fisher, Loren R., 154n51

Fleming, Dan, 4n7, 8n18, 9n21, 13nn34–35, 18n38, 23nn47–48, 25n52, 26n55, 27n57, 232, 232nn10–11
Fortenbaugh, W. W., 496n41
Foster, Benjamin R., 73n102, 120n40, 121n47, 122, 122n51
Fowler, M. D., 425n25
Fox, Michael V., 191n19
Frahm, Eckart, 113n15, 437n83, 451n126
Frame, Grant, 119n34, 119n36, 120nn37–38, 122n49, 257n105, 258n109, 258n112
Franken, H. J., 348n123
Freedman, David Noel, 282n42
Freu, Jacques, 147n31, 202n6
Fried, Lisbeth S., 402n62
Friedrich, Johannes, 280, 280n37, 283nn45–46
Fuchs, Andreas, 83n129, 254n98, 430n50, 436nn80–81, 451n125

Gachet-Bizollon, Jacqueline, 151n43
Gadd, C. J., 419n8, 442n103, 446n114
Gagoshidze, I., 409n82
Galil, Gershon, 67n84
Galter, Hannes D., 451nn125–26, 454n139
Gander, Max, 224n61, 472n11
Gane, Roy E., 340n90
Garbini, Giovanni, 451n129, 453n137, 454n142, 463n170
Gardiner, Alan H., 276–77, 276n23, 277n24
Garr, W. Randall, 280n41
Garrison, Mark B., 387n16
Gasche, Hermann, 110n6
Gass, Erasmus, 342n99
Gelb, I. J., 428n37
George, Andrew R., 10, 10n22, 108, 108n2, 115, 115n21, 117n28, 131n73
Gerardi, Pamela, 438n87
Ghareeb, Romel, 344n105
Gibson, John C. L., 279, 279n35
Gilibert, A., 257n107
Ginsberg, H. L., 159n66
Gitin, Seymour, 373n62, 373n65, 454n143
Gitler, Haim, 411n85
Glaser, Edmund, 451
Glass, Jonathan, 433n68
Glassner, Jean-Jacques, 90n150, 112n9, 112n11, 119n35, 122n50, 127nn64–65, 128n66, 135n79, 242n56
Glatt, D. A., 249n75
Godley, A. D., 270n10, 271nn11–12, 272n13, 306nn104–5
Goetze, Albrecht, 150n38

Goguel, Anne, 338n82, 443n106
Goldwasser, Orly, 277n28
Gonnella, J., 240n43
Gordon, Cyrus, 469n3
Goren, Y., 115n21
Görg, Manfred, 142n9
Goulart, Christine K., 340n90
Grabbe, Lester L., 4n6, 401nn60–61
Graf, David F., 425n28, 435n74, 439n92, 446n115, 462n167
Gratz, Claudia, 410n84
Grayson, A. Kirk, 27n58, 45nn13–14, 51n27, 51n29, 59n52, 61n56, 62n59, 91n151, 91n153, 93, 93n155, 100n173, 112n9, 122n50, 127nn63–65, 128n66, 135n79, 237n33, 253n93, 295n78, 299nn84–86, 300nn87–90, 417n1, 431n54
Green, Anthony, 69n91
Greenfield, J. C., 73n103
Greenstein, Edward L., 141n1
Groom, Nigel, 424n21
Gropp, Douglas M., 402n63
Gruntfest, Y., 444n110
Gur-Arieh, S., 252n86
Guzzo, Maria Giulia Amadasi, 253n89, 279, 280n36

Haas, Volkert, 204n9, 216n42
Hackett, Jo Ann, 348n123
Hadley, Judith, 152n48
Haider, P. W., 471n8
Hallo, William W., 69n90, 93n157
Hallock, R. T., 432nn62–63
Halpern, Baruch, 94n159, 360nn17–18
Hamilton, Gordon, 277, 277n27
Hansen, O., 471n9
Hardin, James W., 49n18
Harding, G. L., 424n24, 433n67
Harris, Zellig, 280, 280n37, 280n41
Harrison, Timothy, 224n59, 240n47
Hassell, Jonathan, 425n25
Hausleiter, Arnulf, 440n94, 441n96, 442n104, 444n108, 445n112
Hawkins, J. David, 198n2, 207n11, 222n55, 224n59, 225n66, 239n37, 240, 240nn44–47, 241n48, 472n10, 472n13
Hawley, Robert, 147n30, 164nn76–77, 166n81
Hayajneh, H., 424n19, 444n110
Hayes, John H., 47, 47n15, 93n158
Hays, Christopher B., 86n144
Hazenbos, Joost, 212n23
Heimpel, Wolfgang, 8n18

Heltzer, Michael, 444n110, 463n172
Henkelman, Wouter, 382n8, 382n10, 387n16, 390n20, 393n34, 403n67, 418n2, 432n65
Herdner, Andrée, 154n55
Herion, Gary A., 95n165
Herr, Larry G., 315n12, 320nn25–27, 339n87, 340n89, 349n127
Hess, C. W., 242n57
Hieke, Thomas, 459n153, 459n157, 460n161
Higham, Thomas, 331n60
Hirmer, M., 472n10
Hirsch, H. E., 428n37
Hirschberg, H., 446n114
Hitchcock, Louise A., 373n63
Hoffmeier, James K., 142n8, 189n17, 190, 190n18, 288n57, 434n70
Hoffner, Harry A., Jr., 216n40, 218n45, 226n67
Höfner, Maria, 462n168
Hoftijzer, J., 280n38
Højlund, Fleming, 428n38, 428n41
Holladay, John S., Jr., 49n21
Holloway, Steven W., 85, 85n138, 85n140, 94nn163–64
Homès-Fredericq, Denyse, 323n32
Hommel, F., 451
Honeyman, A. M., 292n72
Horn, Siegfried H., 317n19
Hornung, Erich, 169n1
Horowitz, Wayne, 83n128, 118n30, 431n54, 442n100, 485n33
Horowitz, William J., 161n68
Horst, Pieter W. van der, 103n184, 152n47
Hout, Theo van den, 202n4, 205n10, 209nn16–17, 216n41
Huehnergard J., 117n29, 147n29, 164n76
Huff, Dietrich, 387n17
Humbert, J. B., 317n17
Hunter, Manfred, 68n87
Hurowitz, Victor Avigdor, 101n174
Huth, M., 460n160

Ingraham, Michael Lloyd, 433n67
Invernizzi, Antonio, 424n22
Iren, Kaan, 405n72
Irvine, A. K, 424n18
Irvine, S. A., 255n101

Jacobs, Bruno, 411n87
Jacoby, Felix, 482n30
Jamme, Albert, 451n127
Janković, Bojana, 395n38, 398n50
Ji, Chang-Ho, 341n92, 349n128
Joannès, Francis, 133n75, 244n65, 394n36

Jones, H. L., 275n19
Jones, Sian, 17n37
Jong, Albert de, 387n16
Jong, Matthijs J. de, 88n147
Jongeling, Karel, 280, 280n38, 280n40
Jursa, Michael, 127, 127n62, 393n30, 394n36, 398n47, 399n50

Kafafi, Zeiden, 348n122
Kalimi, Isaac, 401n61
Kaptan, Deniz, 405n72, 411n85
Keel, Othmar, 192n20, 193n21, 194, 194n22, 345n111
Kelm, George L., 348n42
Kent, Roland G., 386n15
Kerr, Robert, 280, 280n40
Kertai, David, 40n2, 43, 43n9
Khanjian, John, 154n52
Khayyata, W., 240n43
Kienast, B., 428n37
Kienlin, Alexander von, 410n84
Killebrew, Ann E., 355n7, 364n29, 369n44, 370nn50–51, 376n72
King, G. M. D., 445n110
King, L. W., 121n45
King, Philip J., 293n74
Kitchen, Kenneth, 23n46, 312nn3–4, 313n5, 322nn29–30, 330n57, 450n124
Klauser, Nicole, 441n95
Klengel, Horst, 197n1, 200n3, 205n10, 213n28, 213n31
Kletter, Raz, 375n69
Klinger, Jörg, 197n1, 203n7
Knapp, A., 251n81
Knauf, Ernst Axel, 330n55, 331n61, 347nn117–18, 402n62, 424n19, 431n58, 434n69, 456n148, 460n161, 461nn162–63
Knauß, Florian S., 409n82
Knoppers, Gary N., 401nn60–61
Knutson, F. Brent 154n52
Kohlmeyer, Kay, 224n58, 240n43, 260n122
Koldewey, Robert, 113n12, 130n71, 131n72
Konuk, Koray, 411n85
Koppen, Frans van, 112nn10–11
Korotayev, Andrey, 457n150
Korpe, M., 405n74
Kottsieper, Ingo, 263n130, 402n62
Koutsoukou, Anthi, 317n17, 349n125
Kraeling, E. G. H., 234n21
Krahmalkov, Charles, 280, 280n38
Kratz, Reinhard G., 402n62
Krauss, F. R., 13n33

Kühne, Cord, 218n49
Kuhrt, Amélie, 8n16, 54n34, 230n3, 363n25, 365n34, 367n40, 382n8, 383n12, 387n17, 388n19, 389n20, 393nn29–30, 393n32, 394nn33–35, 394n37, 397n42, 397n45, 398n48, 399nn53–54, 400n56, 401n59, 402n62, 403n64, 403n68, 404n70, 405n74, 408n80
Kutter, J., 261n125
Kvanvig, Helge S., 101n175
Kyrieleis, H., 477n21

LaBianca, Øystein, 311n1, 315n13
Lagarce, E., 145n16
Lagarce, J., 145n16
Lamberg-Karlovsky, C. C., 429, 429n42
Lambert, W. G., 69, 69n90, 72n98, 120, 120n39, 120n41, 121n48, 442n102, 443n105
Landsberger, Benno, 50n24, 69n89
Lanfranchi, Giovanni B., 86n142
Langdon, Stephen H., 129n69
Langgut, D., 118nn31–32
Larson, Mogens Trolle, 8n17
Laursen, Steffen Terp, 428n41
Lehman, Gunnar, 376n72
Leichty, Erle, 52n31, 53n32, 303n97, 304nn99–101, 430nn51–52, 431n57, 437nn85–86
Lemaire, André, 133n75, 224n61, 251, 251n77, 251n81, 254n94, 401n60, 423n16, 439n91, 439n93, 443n106, 444n110, 446n113, 454n143, 456nn147–48, 462n167, 463nn172–73, 472n12, 477n19
Lemche, Niels Peter, 2n2
Lete, Gregorio del Olmo, 161n69
Levine, Louis D., 84n131
Levinson, Bernard, 84n129
Levy, Thomas E., 331nn60–64, 332nn65–66, 333n67
Lewis, Theodore J., 146n28
Lichtheim, Miriam, 296n79
Lidzbarski, Mark, 279, 279n32
Lipiński, Edward, 27n57, 234n21, 236n31, 245n66, 374n66
Lipschits, Oded, 401n61
Litt, T., 118nn31–32
Liverani, Mario, 40, 56n43, 57, 57n45, 82n125, 232n12, 431n55, 441n98, 454n140, 462n167, 463n173
Livingstone, Alasdair, 77, 77nn118–19, 441nn97–98, 442n102
Lloyd, Seton, 71n96
Lombard, P., 428n39

Lönnqvist, M. A., 234n19
Lopez-Ruiz, Carolina, 224n61
Loreto, Romolo, 453n136, 457n151
Loretz, Oswald, 155n62
Lowery, R. H., 86, 86n143
Luckenbill, D. D., 476n18, 477n22
Lundlin, A. G., 423n17
Luraghi, Nino, 60n53
Lyon, David G., 64n68

Macadam, Henry Innes, 429n43, 430n48
Macchi, Jean-Daniel, 29n61
MacDonald, Burton, 316n16, 329n54, 330n56, 336n73, 339n87
MacDonald, Michael C. A., 339n87, 411n87, 419n5, 421n12, 424n18, 449n122
MacGinnis, J. D. A., 56n42
Machinist, Peter, 56n42, 64n65, 64nn67–69, 76nn113–15, 84n131, 93n154, 102n179, 104nn186–87
Maciá, Lorena Miralles, 164n75
Mack-Fisher, Loren R., 154n53
Magnanini, Pietro, 279, 280n36
Maier, Aren M., 252n86, 358n10, 359n11, 370n52, 373n63, 374n67, 375n68, 376n72
Maigret, Alessandro de, 420n11, 452, 452n132, 453n135, 453n137
Maigret, S. Antoni de, 456n146
Malamat, Abraham, 236, 236nn29–30
Malbran-Labat, F., 215n38
Mankowksi, Paul, 84, 84n132
Mann, Michael, 58n47
Mansour, Sahar, 317n17
Maraqteen, Mohammad, 445n111
Margalit, Baruch, 160n67
Marinatos, N., 469n3, 470n5
Martin, C. J, 392n24
Martin, James D., 463n173
Martin, L., 257n107
Masetti-Rouault, M. G., 246n68
Master, Daniel M., 372n59
Matthews, Roger, 410n84
Matthiae, P., 469n2
Mayer, Walter, 148n35
Mazar, Amihai, 348n42, 370n54
Mazzoni, Stefania, 225n64
McCarter, P. Kyle, Jr., 271n12, 276n22, 280, 280n39, 317n19
McClellan, T. L., 232n14
McGeough, Kevin M., 165nn78–79
McGovern, Patrick E., 314nn6–7, 315n8, 315nn10–11, 317n18

McKenzie, Steven L., 359n14
McLaughlin, John L., 164n75
Mebert, Joachim, 110n6
Melchert, H. Craig, 197n1, 214n33
Melville, Sarah C., 56, 56n40
Mendenhall, George E., 95n165, 434n69
Michalowski, Piotr, 2n3, 5n9, 6nn11–12, 7n14, 12n29, 111n7, 135n81
Michel, Cécile, 8n17
Miles, J. C., 44n10
Millard, A. R., 89n149, 166n81, 246n70, 253nn90–91, 424n22
Miller, Fergus, 461n164
Miller, J. Maxwell, 47n15, 329n53
Miller, Jarod L., 200n3, 220n51
Momani, Ahmed, 317n17, 349n125
Mommsen, H., 115n21
Moor, Johannes C. de, 152n47
Moran, William, 24, 24n51, 96n167, 121, 121n48, 141nn5–6, 146n22, 148n36, 175n9, 268n3, 268nn5–8
Moritz, S., 426n29
Morrow, William, 83n128, 84n133, 117n28
Morton, William H., 325n42
Moscati, S., 231n4, 298, 298n82
Mousavi, Ali, 391n21
Mowinckel, Sigmund, 121, 121n43
Müller, Walter W., 424n18, 425n25, 444n110, 453n138, 459nn154–56, 464n175
Murphy, Roland E., 327n47
Musil, Alois, 431n53

Na'aman, Nadav, 48n17, 115n21, 327n49, 353n2, 368n41, 441n98
Nadali, Davide, 62n60, 65n70
Najjar, Mohammad, 317n17, 331n60
Nasshef, Khaled, 428n40
Naveh, Joseph, 278, 278n30, 340n91, 373n61, 398n49
Nebes, Norbert, 422n14, 451n125
Nehmé, Laïla, 449n122
Neiling, Jens, 405n71
Niehr, H., 259nn115–16, 262n127
Ninow, Friedbert, 323n32
Nissinen, Martti, 86n145, 102, 102nn177–78
Nöldeke, T., 419n3
Nougayrol, Jean, 213n30
Novák, M., 259n117
Novotny, Jamie R., 45n13, 51n27, 51n29, 59n52, 91n151, 91n153

O'Connor, David, 172n3
O'Connor, Michael Patrick, 160n167

Oded, Bustenay, 63, 63n61, 63nn63–64, 64, 64n65
Oden, Robert A., 293n74, 295n76
Oeming, Manfred, 401n61
Ökse, A. Tuba, 218n48
Oldfather, C. H., 272n17, 273n18
Olijdam, Eric, 428n39
Olmstead, Albert T., 40, 84, 381n6, 382n7
Oppenheim, A. Leo, 40, 40n1, 52n31, 68, 68n85, 302nn95–96, 304n102, 305n103, 338n80
Oren, Eliezer D., 362n24
Ornan, Tallay, 195n23
Oshima, Takayoshi, 83n128, 118n30
Otto, Eckart, 98, 98n170, 136
Ozan, Grégoire, 10n24

Palivou, C., 470n5
Pappi, C., 242n57
Pardee, Dennis, 141n2, 144nn14–15, 145n17, 146n28, 147n29, 148nn34–35, 150n39, 151n46, 153, 153n50, 154n55, 155n58, 155nn60–61, 156, 156n63, 156n65, 161nn68–69, 163nn72–73, 164nn75–77, 165n80, 259n113, 342n96, 423nn16–17
Parker, Bradley J., 85n140, 94n162
Parker, Heather Dana Davis, 327n48, 344n106
Parker, Simon B., 154nn55–56, 155n62, 159nn66–67, 340n88
Parpola, Simo, 50n24, 52, 52n30, 61, 61n55, 62n59, 69, 69n93, 74n110, 85n137, 86n145, 87n146, 95n165, 290n63, 419n4, 425n27, 426n31
Parr, Peter J., 433nn67–68, 434nn71–72
Pearce, Laurie E., 133n75, 134, 134n77, 401n60
Pecchioli-Daddi, Franca, 212n24
Peckham, J. Brian, 280, 280n39, 290n66
Pentiuc, Eugen, 28n59
Perrot, Jean, 389n20
Petit, Lucas, 348n122
Pfälzner, P., 241n50
Philby, H. St. John, 432, 432n66
Pirenne, Jacqueline, 451–52, 451n128, 452n131, 454n142, 458
Pitard, Wayne T., 141n2, 155n59, 156n64, 161n68, 231n8, 232n13, 233n18, 236n27, 250, 250n76, 252n90
Podany, Amanda, 28n59, 117, 117n27, 268n6
Pongratz-Leisten, B., 120n42
Porada, Edith, 287n52
Porten, Bezalel, 394n37, 399n52, 439n92
Porter, Anne, 2n3, 6nn11–13, 7, 7n15, 16, 17n36, 19, 19n42
Porter, Benjamin W., 322n30

Postgate, J. N., 21n6, 64, 64n66, 65, 65nn73–75, 66nn78–79, 67, 67n80, 67n83, 85, 85n139, 85n141, 436n76
Potts, Daniel T., 427nn33–36, 428n39, 430n48, 430n50, 431n53, 431n56, 431n59, 432n60, 432n62, 432n65, 442n101
Press, Michael D., 371n58, 375n72
Pruzsinszky, Regine, 28n59, 110n6
Puech, Émile, 447n116
Puhvel, Jaan, 204n9

Quaintance, D. Scott, 339n87

Rabinowitz, I., 439n90
Rackham, H., 275nn20–21
Radner, Karen, 45n12, 50n25, 52n31, 65, 65n72, 66nn76–77, 253n92
Rahlfs, A., 497n42
Rainey, Anson, 141n3, 150n38
Ramzjou, S., 387n17
Rawlinson, George, 391n21
Ray, John, 423n16
Reade, Julian, 428n39
Redford, Donald B., 172n4, 173n5, 189n17, 268n4, 268n8
Redmount, Carol A., 173n6
Reed, William L., 327n48, 435n73, 438n89, 444n109, 445n111, 448n119, 461n166
Rehm, Ellen, 405n71
Reiner, Erica, 40n1, 303n98
Retsö, Jan, 419n5
Reynolds, Frances, 437n86
Richardson, Seth, 74n109, 107n1
Roberts, J. J. M., 328n52
Robin, Christian, 420n11, 422n13, 423n18, 450n123, 453n135, 454n142, 455n144, 456nn145–46
Robson, E. Iliff, 307nn107–8
Rochberg, F., 136n83
Roche, Carole, 147n30
Röllig, Wolfgang, 268n2, 279, 279n34, 280, 280n37, 283nn45–46, 477n21
Rollinger, Robert, 382n8, 390n20
Rollston, Christopher A., 277nn27–28, 282n42, 285n48, 286n51, 290n62, 293n74, 298n83, 340n89, 341n92, 342n97
Ron, Hagai, 331n59
Rose, B., 405n74, 406, 406n75
Roth, Martha T., 44n10, 76n117, 113nn13–14
Rothenberg, Benno, 331n59, 433n68
Routledge, Bruce, 314n7, 315n8, 322n30, 323n31, 323n34, 323n36, 324nn37–38, 325nn40–43, 326n44, 326n46, 328n51, 338n81, 343n103, 344nn106–7, 346n114, 350n129
Routledge, Carolyn, 323n31
Rowley H. H., 94n159
Rowton, M. B., 231–32, 231n6
Rüger, Hans Peter, 464n174
Rummel, Stan, 154n51
Russell, John Malcolm, 51n28
Ruzicka, Stephen, 392n24
Ryckmans, J., 462n169

Sader, Hélène, 27n57, 232, 232n13, 292n71
Saggs, H. W. F., 45, 45n11, 54, 54n35, 58, 58n46, 61n54, 69, 69nn92–93, 71n97, 75, 75n11, 477n20
Sallaberger, Walther, 6n10, 6n12
Salles, Jean-François, 430n48, 464n175
Salvini, Mirjo, 25n53
Sandars, N. K., 362n24
Sanders, Seth, 12n29, 83n128, 166n81
Sandhaus, D., 244n64
Sass, Benjamin, 277, 277n27, 285n48, 342n95, 345n112, 370n53, 375n71, 424n19, 453n137, 462n168
Sasson, Jack, 11, 11n28, 102n181
Schaeffer, C. F. A., 143n11
Schäfer-Lichtenberger, Christa, 373n64
Schaudig, Hanspeter, 111n8, 132n74, 135nn80–81, 442n104
Schefold, K., 481n27
Schipper, Bernd U., 187n16
Schloen, J. David, 165n79, 259n114, 372n59
Schmitt, Rüdiger, 347n115, 347n119, 348n120
Schneider, Tammi J., 68n87, 71n97
Schniedewind, William M., 84n130
Schrott, R., 475n15
Schwartz, G. M., 231, 231nn7–9, 241n51
Schwemer, D., 259n118
Sedov, A. V., 452n133, 453n134, 464n175
Seeher, Jürgen, 216n39
Segert, Stanislav, 280, 280n37
Seitz, Christopher R., 50n23
Seow, C. L., 328n52, 348n123
Sevinç, N., 405n74
Shaar, Ron, 331n59
Shai, Itzhaq, 370n52
Shaked, Shaul, 398n49
Shaw, Ian, 171n2
Shea, Michael O'Dwyer, 424n22
Sherman, Charles L., 307n106
Sherratt, Andrew, 62n58

Index of Authors

Sherratt, Susan, 62n58
Shiloh, Yigal, 462n168
Sima, Alexander, 421n12
Singer, Caroline, 424n20
Singer, Itamar, 10n25, 141n4, 142n7, 143n10, 147n31, 150n40, 200n3, 207n13, 208n14, 212nn25–26, 213n30, 213n32, 214nn33–34, 215nn35–36, 217n44, 224n60, 226n67, 227n72, 375n70
Singer-Avitz, Lily, 370n53, 463n170
Slanski, Kathryn E., 117nn24–25, 121n44, 121n46, 123n54
Smith, Duane E., 154n53
Smith, George, 34–35, 40
Smith, H. S., 392n24
Smith, Mark S., 70n94, 135n82, 143n11, 147n32, 152n49, 154nn54–55, 155n57, 156n64, 163nn70–71, 163n74, 290n64
Smith, Neil G., 333n67
Smith, W. S., 83n127
Soldt, W. van, 117n29, 144n13, 145n17, 147n30, 242n57
Sommerfeld, W., 116n23, 117, 117n25, 120, 120n41
Spek, Robartus J. van der, 420n10, 429n45
Spieckermann, Hermann, 85, 85n137
Stager, Lawrence E., 293n74, 372n59
Staubli, T., 261n123
Steen, E. van der, 232–33, 233n15, 314n6, 315n8, 348n121
Stein, Peter, 422nn13–14, 423n18
Steiner, Margaret, 424n23
Steinkeller, Piotr, 110n5
Steinmann, A., 447n116
Stern, Ephraim, 55n37, 82, 82nn122–23, 91n152, 371n55
Stieglitz, Robert R., 430n49
Stolper, Matthew W., 390n20, 418n2, 432n65
Stone, Brian Jack, 369n49
Strawn, Brent A., 93n158
Streck, Maximilian, 54n34, 256n104, 477n22
Stronach, D., 104n185, 387n17
Summerer, Lâtife, 407n78, 410n84
Sun, Chloe, 159n67
Suriano, M. J., 251n81
Sweeney, Deborah, 365n31
Sweet, R. F. G., 76n116
Swinnen, Ingrid M., 323n32
Sznycer, Maurice, 154n55
Szuchman, Jeffery J., 230n1, 231n5, 233nn16–17

Tadmor, Hayim, 40, 43n7, 50n24, 62n57, 67n82, 69n88, 93n157, 97n168, 125n59, 253n90, 255n100, 301nn91–93, 302n94, 362n21, 365n36, 425n26, 435n75, 436n76, 436n78, 454n139, 460n161
Taffer, Avia, 207n12
Tallis, N., 247n71
Taracha, Piotr, 202n6, 217n43, 220nn50–51, 221nn52–53
Taraqji, A., 242n59
Tauxe, Lisa, 331nn59–60
Tavernier, Jan, 403n67
Taylor, John, 183n13, 184, 184n15
Tekoğlu, Recai, 224n61, 472n12, 477n19
Tenu, A., 242n53
Thackeray, H. St. J., 295n77, 298n81
Thareani, Yifat, 463n171
Theis, Christoffer, 142n9
Thompson, Dorothy, 418n2
Thompson, Thomas L., 4n6
Tomback, Richard, 280, 280n38
Tombul, M., 405n74
Toorn, Karel van der, 19n41, 103n184, 152n47
Tropper, Josef, 424n19
Trufaut, Susanne Müller, 101n176
Tsukimoto, Akio, 73n101, 73nn104–7, 74n108, 237n32
Tuplin, Christopher, 393n27, 393n31, 410n84
Tyson, Craig William, 349n126

Uehlinger, Christoph, 101n176, 102n179, 194, 194n22, 251n82, 345n112
Unger, Eckhard, 128n68
Ungnad, A., 432n61
Ussishkin, David, 252n86

Van Alfen, Peter G., 460n160
Van Beek, Gus, 452n130
Van De Mieroop, Marc, 50n26, 65n71
Vanderhooft, David S., 55n39, 56n41, 102nn182–83, 127n61, 129n74, 133n76, 342n100, 343nn101–2, 347n116
VanderKam, James C., 461n165
Vattioni, F., 426n30
Vaux, Roland de, 359n16
Veen, Peter van der, 142n9
Veenhof, Klaas R., 41n5
Vidal, Jordi, 62n60
Villard, P., 148n33
Villing, A., 479n24
Vittmann, Günther, 392nn23–24

Wachsmann, Shelley, 365n32
Waerzeggers, Caroline, 382n8
Wasmuth, M., 390n20
Watanabe, Kazuko, 62n59, 95n165, 290n63
Waters, Matthew, 54n33
Watson, R., 485n33
Watson, Wilfred G. E., 154n56
Wehrli, F., 497n41
Weidner, E. F., 133n75
Weigl, Michael, 342n94
Weinstein, J., 242n60
Weippert, Manfred, 363n24, 438n87
Weiss, Ehud, 49n20, 83n126
Weissbach, F. M., 486n35
West, M. L., 478n23, 482n28, 482n30
Westbrook, Raymond, 43n8, 114, 114n17, 114n19, 136
Whitaker, Richard E., 328n52
Whitehead, A. N., 492n38
Wiesehöfer, Josef, 382n8, 412n88
Wilhelm, Gernot, 198n2, 220n50
Wilson, Andrew, 322n30
Wilson, John A., 142n8
Wilson, Robert T., 458n153
Wimmer, Stefan J., 359n11
Winnett, Fred V., 327n48, 435n73, 438n89, 444n109, 445n111, 448n119, 458n153, 459n154, 459n156, 460n159, 460n161, 461n162, 461n166
Winter, Irene, 270, 270n9, 287n52
Wissmann, Hermann von, 464n175
Woods, Christopher, 12n29, 123n53, 124, 124nn55–56
Worschech, Udo, 341n93
Wossink, A., 242n57

Wright, David, 114, 115n20, 136, 160n67
Wunsch, Cornelia, 133n75

Yadin, Yigael, 244n64, 359n13
Yakar, Jak, 207n12
Yakubovich, Ilya, 224n61, 225n65
Yamada, Shigeo., 69n88, 301nn91–93, 302n94, 425n26, 436n76
Yardeni, Ada, 394n37, 399n52, 439n92
Yasur-Landau, Asaf, 365n31
Yisrael, Yigal, 350n131
Yon, Marguerite, 144n13, 145n18, 146nn19–21, 146nn23–28, 151n42
Younger, K. Lawson, 93, 93n156, 230n1, 233n17, 234n19, 234n22, 236nn27–28, 238, 238nn34–35, 239n40, 240n41, 241n48, 245n67, 248n74, 251n79, 251n81, 252n87, 253n89, 253n91, 254n99, 256n104, 259n113, 262n126, 262n129, 318n21
Younker, Randall W., 311n1, 315n13
Yoyotte, J., 400n55

Zadok, R., 241n52, 256n104, 426n32
Zarins, Juris, 428n38
Zayadine, Fawzi, 317n17, 323n34, 341n93, 443n106
Zevit, Ziony, 347n119
Ziffer, Irit, 287n52, 375n69
Zimansky, P., 252n85
Zimmerli, Walter, 463n173, 464n174
Zimmer-Vorhaus, Caroline, 218n47
Zorn, Jeffrey R., 359n15
Zournatzi, Antigoni, 383n11
Zuckerman, Alexander, 359n11
Zwickel, Wolfgang, 375n69

Index of Scripture and Other Ancient Sources

Old Testament

Genesis
1   135, 135n82
1–11   135
1:2   155
1:21   155
6–9   135
10   108, 135, 355
10:6–7   458
10:7   459, 460
10:8–10   109
10:8–12   102
10:10–12   102
10:22   234
10:26   457
10:26–30   458, 459
10:29   459
11   109, 135
11:1–9   108
11:4   129
11:28   109
11:31   3, 109
12:5   1
14:5   163
15:19   272n16
15:19–21   15
16:5–16   460
21   100
21:8–21   460
21:32–34   356
22:21   235
25:1–4   458, 460
25:1–6   434
25:4   436
25:12–16   458
25:13   460
25:13–15   436, 460
25:14   460
25:18   460
26:1   356
26:8   356
32:4   329
36:8–9   329
36:21   329
36:31–39   332
37   100
37:25–36   434
39   100
47:11   179
49:20   29

Exodus
1:11   179
2–4   434
2:1   99
2:10   99
3   2
3:8   2, 15
12:37   179
13:13–15   165
13:17   356
15:2   153
15:17   157
18   434
20:22–23:19   114
21:2–6   165
21:22   114
25–31   101
32   152
35–40   101

Leviticus
1:3   162
3:1   162
10:1–2   358
26:30   166

Numbers
6:24–26   164
8:11–15   162
8:21   162
13:29   16
14:45   330
18:11   162
21:8–9   163
21:14   90
21:29   346
21:31   16
22–24   348
23:7   235
23:22   152, 165
24:8   152, 165
24:18   329
25   434
33:3   179
33:5   179
33:42–43   331
34:3–4   330

Deuteronomy
1:6–8   16
1:44   330
2–3   16
2:4–19   97
2:10–11   163
2:24   16
3:1   16
3:8   16
4:44–27:8   97
4:47   16
7:8   165
8:9   311n2
10:1–2   97
13:2–19   97
13:6   165
18:10–11   163
18:20–22   97
23:3–4   322

511

23:8–9 337
27:15–26 97
28 136
28:1–14 97
28:15–68 97
29:21 97
30:10 97
31:4 16
31:10–13 97
31:24–29 97
31:26 97
32:1 153
32:8–9 152
32:41–42 157

Joshua

1:4 227
2:10 16
7:1 157
9:10 16
10:5 16
10:12 16
10:13 90
12 1
12:8 15
13:2–3 356
15:1–3 330
24:8 16
24:12 16

Judges

1 15
1:26 227
1:27–33 15
1:34–36 15
3:1–6 356
3:10 235
4–5 161
4:17 141
4:17–22 104
5:4 329, 346
5:6 165
5:24 141
6–8 434
6:19–24 163
8:1–2 157
10:6 235
10:6–7 356
10:8 16
11:21 16
11:24 346

13 356
13–16 356
13:1 356
13:19 163
14–15 356
15:15 356
16:1–3 356, 357
16:4–31 356, 357
20:43–46 157

1 Samuel

4:1–7:1 357
5:6 357n9
5:9 357n9
5:12 357n9
6:4–5 357n9
6:17 2
7:2–14 358
9:2 359
10:27b–11:15 317
13–14 358
17 358
17:51 104
20:29 165
20:34 165
21:11–16 360
27:1–28:2 360
28 161
28–29 358
29 360
29–31 360
31:10 162, 360

2 Samuel

1 360
1:21 160
6:9–12 361
8:1 360
8:2 325
8:3–12 243
8:9–10 243
8:13–14 333
8:15–18 165
9:11 165
9:13 165
10 235
10:1–2 317
10:1–5 317
10:1–11:1 317
10:6–19 243
12:26 317

12:26–31 317
12:29 317
12:30 317
15–20 159
15:17–22 361
17:27–29 317–18
18:2 361
18:18 159
19:29 165
20:23–26 165
21:19 359

1 Kings

2:7 165
2:39–41 361
3:5–15 159
4 165
4:29–33 77
5 192, 296
5–9 101
5:1–4 360
5:1–5 100
5:6 296
5:6–18 100
5:7 77
5:12 77
5:18 296
6 296
6:1 298
6:38 298
7:13–47 296
7:13–51 100
8:1–11 100
8:12–61 100
8:62–66 100
9:3–9 100
9:6 101
9:6–9 101
9:10–14 296
9:20 16
9:26–28 297
10:1–13 461
10:2 461
10:11 297
10:15 461
10:22 297
10:23 101
10:29 227, 235
11:1 227, 297
11:5 297, 346
11:7 346
11:15–16 333

11:23–25 243
11:33 346
11:40 184
11:41 90
14:19 90
14:21 318
14:25–26 184
14:29 90
14:31 318
15:16–22 244
15:18–20 248
15:27 361
16:15–17 361
16:29–31 298
18:42 163
20 248, 249, 250
22 248, 249, 250
22:19 152
22:19–23 156
22:20–23 156
22:48 333
22:48–49 334

2 Kings

1:2–3 362
1:6 362
4:34–35 163
7:6 227
8:2–3 361
8:7–15 249
8:16–18 298
8:20–22 334
8:28–29 251
9 251
9:14–15a 251
10:32–33 252, 318, 327, 334
12:17–18 318
12:18 361, 375
13:3 253, 318
13:22 318, 361, 375
13:24–25 253
14:7 335
14:22 335
14:25 254
14:28 254
15:19–20 47
15:27 90
15:29 319
15:37 255
16 366

Index of Scripture and Other Ancient Sources

16:5–7 335
16:5–9 48, 255
16:9 236, 256
16:10–11 86
16:17–18 85n141
17:4 48
18 64, 92
18–19 78, 90, 93, 477
18:4 163
18:13–16 91
18:17 90
18:17–19:9a 90
18:17–19:37 92
18:32 64, 65
19:7–9 93
19:9 185
19:9b–37 92
19:35 476
19:36–37 52
20 159
20:12 125
20:18 125
21:24 49n23
22–23 97
22:3 55n38
22:8 97
23:5 152
23:7 162
23:29 187
23:31–35 187
24:1–2 319, 329, 337
24:7 128
25:9 338

1 Chronicles

1:9 459
1:17 234
1:20 457
1:23 459
1:28–31 460
1:29–30 436
1:32–33 434, 460
1:33 436
7:34 235
13:12–14 361
15:24–25 361
18:1 360
18:3–11 243
19 235
19:1–20:3 317
19:6–19 243

20:2 317
20:5 359

2 Chronicles

1:17 227, 235
2–7 101
2:1–16 296
3:14 151
8:7 16
8:17–18 296
9:1 461
9:1–12 461
9:10 296
9:14 461
9:21 296
12:2–9 184
16:1–6 244
17:11 361
21:16–17 361
25:11 334
25:12 335
26:6–7 361
28:16–18 335
28:18 361
32:1–23 92
32:21 476
34:3 55n38
35:20–24 187
36:1–4 187
36:19 338
36:20 135

Ezra

1:2–4 401
2:53 347
4:2 52, 103
4:10 54, 103
6:2–5 401
6:22 103

Nehemiah

2:10 320
2:19 320, 439
6:1 439
6:2 439
6:6 439
7:55 346
9:32 103
13:1–2 322
13:23–24 322, 329

Job

1–2 159
3:8 158
6:18–19 440
7:12 158
41:1 158

Psalms

2 194
2:7 193
11:7 162
17:15 162
22 72
29 143
29:1 152, 157
38 72
42:3 162
45:7 163
48:3 143
49:15 158
58:10 157
63:2 162
68:23 157
74:13 153, 155
74:14 139, 153, 158
82 156
83:12 425
88:11 163
89:9–11 157
92:10 157
104 191
110 194
110:1 193
137 133, 136, 338
145:13 157

Proverbs

2:18 163
9:18 163
22:17–24:22 191

Song of Songs

1–8 102
8:6 164

Isaiah

1:8 51
2:5–6 362
2:5–22 96n166

5:26–30 33
5:26b–30 60–61
6 156
7:4 87
7:6 255
11:11 103
11:16 103
14:9 153, 161
14:12 152
14:18–20 50
14:21 60
15–16 327
19:23–24 49
20 49
20:2–3 87
21:11 461
21:13 461
21:14 461
22:6 236
25:8 153, 158
26:14 153
26:19 153
27:1 139, 153, 158
27:13 103
29:7 59
31:4–5 88
34:5–7 157
36–37 92
37:9 185
37:36 476
37:37–38 52
38 159
40–55 135
40:9 87
44:28 135
45:1 135
46:1–2 132
49:25–26 157
51:9–11 157
60:6 436
63:1–6 157

Jeremiah

1:8 87
2:18 103
2:36 103
5:15 109
6:14 87
8:11 87
9:20[21] 153, 158
16:5 164

19 87
25:23 461
25:23–24 431
27:1–3 337
27:1–11 319
27:3 316
35:11 235
40:7–41:18 320
40:11–12 320, 337
40:14 320, 340
47 362
48 327, 329
48:7 329
48:46 346
48:47 329
49:1–6 319
49:6 320
49:9 157
49:35 109n3
50–51 136
50:21 257

Lamentations

1:15 157
5:6 103

Ezekiel

1 101n175
1–3 156
2:6 87
4:1–15 87
14:14 139, 159
14:20 139, 159
16 100
21:23–27 320
23 103
23:23 257
25–48 463n173
25:10 329
25:12 338
27:6–9 463n173
27:12–25 463
27:16 463, 464n175
27:17 463
27:18 463
27:19–22 463
27:20 464
27:22 464
27:23 464
28:3 139, 159
29:18 305

31 103
32:22–23 103
35 337
35:5 338
35:14–15 338
39:19 157
40–48 101
43:7 166

Daniel

1–6 137
1:3–4 134
2 498n46
7 156, 498n46

Hosea

5:13 103
7:11 103
8:9 103
11:11 103

Joel

2:21–22 87
3:13 Eng. 157
4:13 Heb. 157

Amos

1:5 236
1:6–8 362
1:12 336
1:13–15 319
1:15 319
2:9–10 16
6:1 109n3
6:7 164
9:7 236, 355, 362

Obadiah

5 157
11–14 338

Jonah

1:2 104
3:3 102n181

Micah

5:5 102
7:12 103

Nahum

2:6 56
3:1 57
3:8–9 53
3:19 57, 125

Habakkuk

1:12–17 136
3:3 346
3:5 152
3:7 346

Zephaniah

1:5 152
2:8–9 319
2:11–13 103
2:13 103
2:13–15 57

Zechariah

8:13–15 87
9:1 254n95
10:10–12 103

Malachi

1:3 338

Old Testament Apocrypha

1 Esdras

4:45 338
7:15 103

Judith

1:1 104
13 161

1 Maccabees

7:41 104

2 Maccabees

3:11 322
4:26 322
5:7 322

3 Maccabees

6:5 104

4 Maccabees

13:9 103

Tobit

14:4 104
14:15 104

Old Testament Pseudepigrapha

Jubilees

4:20 139, 159
20:13 461

New Testament

Matthew

12:41 104

Mark

7:24–30 308

Luke

11:30–32 104

Revelation

14:14–20 157
17:5 136
19:15 157
21:4 158

Josephus

Against Apion

1.17–18 295n77, 297n80
1.18 298

Jewish Antiquities

2.249 459n155
10.181–82 320, 329
12.160 322

Index of Scripture and Other Ancient Sources 515

13.374   329
14.382   329

Inscriptions

Aramaic Texts

Bar-Rakib Inscription 261, 263
Bukān Inscription 263
Hadad Inscription 263
Hazael Booty Inscription 252
Katumuwa Inscription 259, 261, 262n128, 263
Kulamuwa Inscription 240, 282, 293
Melqart Stela 235, 262
Panamuwa Inscription 260, 262, 263
Proverbs of Ahiqar 263
Sefire Inscription 235n24, 254
Tel Dan Stela 250, 260, 263, 334
Tell Afis Stela 253
Tell Fekheriye Inscription 246, 261, 263, 293, 294
Zakkur Inscription 235n23, 239, 253, 254, 261

Phoenician Texts

Abda Sherd 287, 288
Abibaʻal Inscription 287, 288, 289
Ahiram Inscription 288
Azarbaʻal Inscription 284, 285
Elibaʻal Inscription 287, 288
Eshmunazar Sarcophagus 291, 292
Honeyman Inscription 292
Ittobaʻal Inscription 285, 286
Karatepe Inscription 293
Kition Bowl 293
Nora Inscription 292
Shipitbaʻal Inscription 288–90
Tabnit 291
Yehawmilk Inscription 290, 291
Yehimilk Inscription 282, 287, 288, 290

Transjordanian Texts

Amman Citadel Inscription 317, 318, 340, 346
Amman Statue Inscription 321
Amman Theater Inscription 340
Dayr ʻAlla Plaster Inscription 348
Kerak Fragment 321, 341
Marzeaḥ Papyrus 342
Mesha Inscription 321, 325–27, 341, 346, 349
Tall Siran Inscription 316, 321, 340

Other Ancient Near Eastern Sources

ANET Texts

29   343n101
202   210n19
243   149n37
260–62   363
262–63   363
281–82   334, 365n35
282   321, 335n72
286–87   328
287   302n95, 321, 328, 335n72
291   321, 328, 335
294   304n102, 318, 321, 328, 335, 343n101
297–98   328
298   321, 328
301   319
305–6   338n80
307–8   368
352–53   150n38
378   142n8
533–34   303n98
547   150n41
561   73n103

Assyrian Texts

RIMA

2:23   237n33, 242n54
2:28–31   100n172
2:37   295n78
2:59–60   242n53
2:101–3   242n58
2:172   260n119
2:261–62 (Kurkh Monolith)   45, 58, 246n69, 248, 250
3:2   417n1
3:23–24   45n14, 299n85
3:203   254n96
3:204–5   253n93

RIMB

2:11–35   119n34
2:293   258n112
2:295   258n112

SAA

1:82   419n4
1:83   419n4
2   62n59, 89n149
2:IV, 10   290n63
3   58n48
9   69n93, 86n145
9 2.3   88

10   74n110
11:162   436n76
17:4   451n26
17:5   451n26
18:143–45   437n86

Babylonian Texts

Atraḫasis 135
Code of Hammurabi 44, 112–14, 128
Enuma Elish 120, 132, 135, 156
Gilgamesh 10, 115, 117, 135, 429
The Ḫabiru Prism of King Tunip-Teššup of Tikunani 25
Ludlul bel nemeqi 121
Poem of Erra 122
Babylonian Chronicle 32, 55, 56, 90, 112n9, 119, 122, 127, 128, 132, 134–35, 242n56

COS Texts

1.41   371n55
1.77:203   209n17
1.111:390–402   120n40
1.166:535–39   111n7
1.241–83   154n55
1:309–27   263n132
1.333–56   154n55
1.361–62   163n73
1.486–92   121n47
2.4B   312
2.5   363
2.23   325
2.24   318, 340, 346
2.25   316, 340
2.26   340
2.27   348
2.39   334
2.42   373
2.107A–D   112n10
2.113A   45n14, 318n21

2.114G   365n35
2.118   366
2.118A   67n82
2.118D   67n82
2.119B   51n27, 91n151, 91n153
2.119B–D   367
2.131   114n16, 114n18
2:152–53   235n25
2:153–54   246n70
2:155   235n23
2:156–58   262n128
2:161–62   251n80, 260n120
2:162   260n121
2:213–15   235n24
2:263–64   248n73
2:270   251n78
2:271   252n83
2:272   254n96
2:273   253n93
2:273–74   253n93
2:274   253n93
2:275–76   253n90
2:279–82   258n111
2:283–84   254n97
2.336, lines i 1–49   113n14
3:xxix–xxxiv   226n68
3.40–41   142n8
3.54   368
3.87–116   164n76
3:219   263n132

Egyptian Sources

Merenptah Stela   22, 22n46, 142

El Amarna Letters

1   148
9   43
15–16   43
31   204
45   148
46–48   148
49   148
68   24n50
70   268n5
71   24n50
73   268n5
74   24n50
75   24n50
77   24n50
79   24n50
85   24n50
88   24n50
89   146, 148
92   268n5
98   141, 148, 149
101   268n8
116   24n50
117   24n50
126   148, 149
144   24n50
146   268n7
148   24n50
151   141, 146, 148, 149
185   24n50
189   24n50
213   175n9
243   24n50
244   175n9
255   175n9, 312
256   312
272   24n50
273   24n50
290   24n50
313   24n50
364   312
366   24n50

Hittite Texts

Anitta Chronicle

in toto: 197–98, 216

CTH

121   213n27
154   205n10
163   209n18
165   213n28
171   209n16
385.9   212n23

HDT

24A   43, 209n16

Hittite Law Code

in toto: 202, 218

KBo

8.14   209n18
12.23   205n10
12.38   213n27
12.58   212n23
13.162   212n23
154/s   205n10

KUB

3.34   213n28
19.20   205n10
23.102   209n16

Manapa-Tarhunda letter

in toto: 207

Tikunani Letter

in toto: 200

Lachish Ostracon

8   328

Mari Texts

A.109   11n27
A.361   12n31
A.361 II 2′–4′   13n31
A.361 III 13′–15′   13n31
A.489   13n32
A.2730   9n21
A.2760   10n23
A.2939:13–14   26
ARM VI 76   13n35
ARM XXVI 24   18n38
ARM XXVII 135   12n30
FM 3 143   10n24
FM 7 26   10n26
M.7950+   11n28

Sumerian Texts

A Hymn to Numushda for Sîn-iqisham   20, 20n44, 21, 21n45

Lamentation over the Destruction of Sumer and Ur   111
Marriage of Martu   19, 20

Ugaritic Texts

KTU

1.1   156
1.1 II   156
1.1 III   156
1.1 V–IV   156
1.1–1.3   155
1.1–1.3 II   156
1.1–1.6   146, 156
1.1–1.25   154
1.2 I   156
1.2 IV   157
1.3 I   157
1.3 II   157
1.3 III–V   157
1.3 III–1.4 VII   156, 157
1.4–1.6   155
1.4 II–III   157
1.4 IV–V   157
1.4 VI   157
1.4 VI 18–21   142
1.4 VII   157
1.4 VIII   143
1.4 VIII–1.5 I   158
1.4 VIII–1.6   156, 158
1.5 II–VI   158
1.5 VI–1.6 I   158
1.6 I   158
1.6 II   158
1.6 III–IV   158
1.6 V   158
1.6 VI   158
1.8   155
1.9   156, 166
1.10   155
1.10 II 9   143
1.11   155
1.12   155
1.13   155, 166
1.13.2–7   157
1.14–1.16   146, 155, 159
1.14 I   159
1.14 II–III   159
1.14 III   159

Index of Scripture and Other Ancient Sources 517

1.14 IV 34–36 142	1.97 163	3.5 164	5.24 166
1.14 IV–V 159	1.100 163	3.7 164	5.25 166
1.15 I–III 159	1.101 154, 155	3.8 164	6.6–6.10 166
1.15 III 4 147	1.102 162	3.9 164, 165	6.13 146, 166
1.15 III 15 147	1.103 163	3.10 165	6.14 146, 166
1.15 IV–VI 159	1.107 163	4.13 165	6.62 166
1.16 I–II 159	1.108 154, 155	4.29 165	8.1 165
1.16 III 159	1.108.2–3 143	4.31 154	9.435 163
1.16 IV 159	1.110 148	4.35 165	
1.16 V 159	1.111 148	4.36 165	Ras Shamra
1.17–1.19 146, 155, 159	1.113 148, 163	4.38 165	1.[089] 146
	1.114 160, 163	4.40 165	2.[033] 146
1.17 I 160	1.114.1–28 154, 155	4.47 165	3.367 156n65
1.17 II 160	1.114.29–31 155	4.65 165	4.427 146
1.17 III–IV 160	1.115 162	4.66 165	5.183 146
1.17 V 160	1.116 148	4.81 165	5.194 155n58
1.17 VI 160	1.119 162	4.96.6–7 141	15.91 149
1.18 I 160	1.124 163	4.99 165	16.142 149
1.18 II–III 160	1.125 148	4.102 165	16.144 149
1.18 IV 160	1.127 162, 163	4.149.14–16 163	16.278 149
1.19 II 160	1.128 148	4.169 165	16.344 149
1.19 III 160	1.131 148	4.172 165	17.132 149
1.19 IV 160	1.132 148, 162	4.182 162	17.286 149
1.20–1.22 155, 161	1.133 166	4.219 165	17.340 149
1.23 146, 163	1.140 163	4.266 165	17.349B 149
1.23.1–29 155	1.141–1.145 163	4.280 165	19.039 155n60
1.23.30–76 155	1.145 163	4.336 165	20.033 149
1.24 146, 155	1.148 162	4.338 165	20.182 + 20.181 141
1.25 156	1.155 163	4.360 165	20.212 213n30
1.27–1.176 161	1.161 147, 150, 161, 162, 163	4.623.3 141	22.225 155n61
1.40 162		4.710 143, 154	22.439 154n53
1.41 162	1.162 162	4.728 165	34.129 150, 215n38
1.61–1.63 156	1.164 162	4.752 161	34.152.9–14 150
1.63–65 154	1.168 162	4.767 143	88.2158 141
1.65 162	1.169 163	5.2 166	92.2014 163
1.67 166	2.4 164	5.3 166	92.2016 163n74
1.71 163, 166	2.10 150, 164	5.4 166	92.2440 166
1.72 163	2.13 164	5.5 166	94.2221+ 151
1.73 166	2.16 164	5.6 166	94.2518.10 148
1.74 162	2.19 165	5.7 166	94.2965 164
1.75 156	2.20 164	5.8 166	167.160 149
1.79 156, 163	2.30 164	5.9 166	
1.80 163	2.36 165	5.10 166	**Other Greek Works**
1.81 156	2.37 164	5.11 166	
1.82 163	2.39 164	5.12 166	**Arrian**
1.83 154, 155	2.42 164	5.13 166	
1.85 163	2.61 150	5.14 166	*Anabasis of Alexander*
1.86 163	2.72 162, 164	5.15 166	
1.87 162	2.82 164	5.16 166	
1.90 162	3.1 164	5.17 166	2.15 307
1.92 154, 155	3.2 164	5.18 166	2.24 307
1.93 154, 155	3.3 164	5.19–5.21 166	6.19.3–20.10 429n45
1.96 154, 155	3.4 165	5.22 166	8.41.8 432n60

Clearchus

Fragments

6 497n41

Demetrius of Phaleron

Fragments

201 497n41

Diodorus Siculus

Library of History

3.67.1 272
5.74.1 273
16.41–45 307
29.32 497n43
31.16 497n43
35.1.3 497n44
35.1.4 498n45

Eusebius of Caesarea

Preparation for the Gospel

9.2.1 497n41

Herodotus

Histories

1.1 271
2.106 472
2.109.3 486
2.141 93
3.19 306
3.40–43 486
3.89 391
3.97 393
5.57–58 271
5.58–59 272
6.105–6.120 488n36
7 59
7.96 270

Horace

Epistles

2.1.156 496n39

Pliny the Elder

Natural History

5.13.66–67 275
5.17.75–76 275
6.30 460

6.155 457
6.156 447
12.52 457

Polybius

Histories

10.28 396
26.1a.1 497n43

Porphyry of Tyre

On Abstinence

2.26 497n41

Pseudo-Aristotle

Economics

2.1.4 393
2.2.38 398
2.34a 393

Strabo

Geography

1.2.32 421
16.1.11 429n45
16.2.22–24 273–75

16.3.2–4 430n47
16.4.8–20 459n155
16.4.27 430n47

Theophrastus

Enquiry into Plants

2.5.5 429n46
4.7.7 429n46

Fr. 584 A
496n41

Xenophon

Anabasis

3.4.10 483n31

Index of Subjects

'Abda Sherd, 288–89
abecedaries, 166, 423
Abiba'al Inscription, 287–90
Abimelech, 356
Abraham, 1–3, 103, 109, 356, 434, 460
Absalom, and Kirta, 159
Achaemenes, 384
Achaemenid Empire. *See* Persia
Achaia, 472
Achilles, 481–82
Achish, 360–61
Adad-nirari I, 42–43, 208–9
Adad-nirari II, and Arameans, 244–45
Adad-nirari III, 46, 253–54, 334, 365
Adgarkidug, and Martu, 20–21
administration
  Aramean, 258–59
  Assyrian, 62, 66, 241
  Babylonian, 111, 116–17, 127
  Hittite, 221–22
  Persian, 188, 391–99
  Ugaritic, 165
Adummatu, 437–38
Aegean catastrophe, 473
Aeschylus, 489
afterlife, in Assyrian religion, 73

agriculture
  Assyrian, 37–38, 65–66
  Persian, 395–97
  Transjordanian, 311, 315–16, 323–25, 331
Agum-Kakrime, 116
Ahab
  and Assyria, 46, 248–49
  and Phoenicia, 298
Ahaz, 47, 86, 255, 335, 361
Ahaziah, 251, 362
Ahiram Sarcophagus, 285–88
Aḫlamû, and Arameans, 237–38
Ahmose, 172–73
Ahura Mazda, 386–87
Akhenaten, 175–78, 181n10
Akītu ritual/festival, 71, 120, 131–32
Akkad, 41, 102
  and Babylonia, 107–13, 116, 122
  in Genesis, 102
  and Sumer, 12
Akkadian (language)
  and Amorites, 3, 11–14, 28
  and Assyria, 34–38, 41
  and Babylonia, 111, 115–17, 134
  and Hebrew, 83–84
  and Hittites, 200–202, 216
  and Ugarit, 153–54
Aleppo, 203, 222

and Aram, 254–55, 260
and Hittites, 223–24
Alexander, 493–96
  and Arabia, 420, 429
  and Egypt, 188–89
  and Moab, 329
  and Persia, 380, 411–12
  and Phoenicia, 274, 307
Alexandria, 188–89, 494–99
alphabet
  Arabic, 423–24, 454
  Early Linear, 277–80
  Greek, 475–78
Amarna letters, 117, 148–49, 175
  and Amorites, 10, 23–26
  and Phoenicia, 268
Amaziah, and Edom, 335
Amenhotep II, 174, 192
Amenhotep III, 174–76, 193–94, 204
Amenhotep IV, 175–78, 181n10
Amman, 314–17, 322, 343, 346
Amman Citadel, 317–18, 340, 349
Ammishtamru, 148–50
Ammon
  art of, 343–44
  "children of," 316–18
  in the Iron Age, 313–22
  religion of, 346–49

519

'Ammōn, 316
Ammurapi, 150
Amorites, 1–30
 and Arameans, 231
 and Babylonia, 111–12
 and Hittites, 227
 and Shamshi-Adad I, 41
 and Ugarit, 147, 164
Amun, 176–81, 296
Amurru
 and Arameans, 239
 and Hittites, 206–9
 and Ugarit, 149
Amurru, as Amorite god, 19–21
amurrû, in the Mari archives, 7–15
Amurrum, as Amorite homeland, 7–10, 15–16, 22
amurrum, vs. mar-tu, 5n9
Anat, 152, 155–60
Anatolia, 197–200
 and Greece, 471
 and Hittites, 203–4, 215–17, 222–27
 and Philistine origins, 353–55, 359, 363, 375
Anaxagoras, 490
ancestors
 in Assyrian religion, 72–74
 Ugaritic, 162–63
Anitta Chronicle, 197–98, 216
Anshar, and Aššur, 69
Antiochus IV, 496–98
Anu, in Assyrian religion, 69–70
'apiru, and Amorites, 4, 23–26
Apology of Hattusili, 209, 226
Aqhat, 155, 159–61
Aqqi, as drawing out Sargon, 99
Arabah, 329–31, 334–36, 344–45
Arabia, 329–30, 417–65
 and Qaus/Qos, 347
Arabic, 264, 343, 417
Arabs, migration of, 231
"Aram," origin of, 234–36
Aramaic (language), 263–64, 497–98
 and Arabia, 444–46
 vs. Ammonite, 340

Arameans, 229–65
 and Amorites, 23, 27–29
 and Assyria, 44
 and Babylonia, 118–19, 122–24
 See also Chaldeans
archaeology
 of Arabia, 427–33, 440–48, 451–54, 458, 462–63
 of Aram, 240–41
 of Assyria, 31–36
 of Babylonia, 129–31
 of Greece, 470–72
 of Hittites, 222–24
 of Persia, 381–83, 387, 407–9
 of Philistia, 368–76
 of Phoenicia, 298
 of Transjordan, 311–12, 322–23, 330–32, 335–37, 340–44, 348–50
 of Ugarit, 143–45
Archimedes, 81, 495
Arinna, 211–12, 220
Aristophanes, 489, 490
Aristotle, 492–96
Ark Narrative, 357–58
Arnuwanda, 203–4
Arpad, 252–55
Arrian, 307
art
 Aramean, 257
 Assyrian, 78–82
 Greek, 480–84, 489
 Persian, 404–11
 Phoenician, 296–97
 Transjordanian, 343–45
 See also iconography
Artaxerxes II, 391
Artaxerxes III, 188, 306, 380, 390
Asa, and Aram, 244
Ashdod, 366, 370–71
Ashdod Affair, 49
Ashdod Ware, 370
Asherat, 373–74
Ashkelon, 50, 372
Asia Minor, 471–72
 and Greece, 477–78, 493–94
Assembly of the Holy Gods of Byblos, 290

Assur (city), 41, 42, 45, 74
 excavation of, 35–36
 as not in the Bible, 102
 religion in, 71–72
Aššur (deity), 38–39, 68–69
 and Assyrian kingship, 75–76
 in Genesis, 102
 in vassal states, 84–85
Assurbanipal I, 53–55, 73–74, 77
 and Ammon, 318
 and Arabia, 437–38, 460–61
 and Edom, 335
 and Greece, 476–77
 and Moab, 328
 and Phoenicia, 304–5
 and prophecy, 87–88
 and treaties, 95–96
Assurbanipal II, 74
 and Arameans, 246–47
 and art, 78–80
Assurbanipal library, 33–36, 77
Assur-dan II, 44
 and Arameans, 244–45
Assur-etel-ilāni, 54–55
Assurnasirpal II, 45, 61
 and Phoenicia, 298–99
Assur Project, 36
Assur-uballiṭ I, 42–43, 75–76
Assuwan confederacy, 203
Assyria, 31–105
 and Ammon, 316–19
 and Arabia, 417–19, 425–31, 435–42, 451, 460–61
 and Aram, 27, 235–58, 263–64
 and Babylonia, 118–22, 125–27
 citizens of, exiles as, 63–64
 civilians, in the military, 59
 collectors, Assyrians as, 81
 communication, and Assyrian influence, 82
 ecology of, 37–38
 and Edom, 334–36
 and Egypt, 174–75, 179, 185–87
 and Greece, 474–78, 481–83
 and Hittites, 197, 206–13, 226–27

Index of Subjects

and Moab, 327–28
and Philistia, 365–68
and Phoenicia, 295, 298–305
Assyrian Chronicle, 242
Assyrian King List, 90
Assyriology, 34
Astarte, 261–62
and Egypt, 179
and Philistia, 360–62
and Phoenicia, 291–92
astrology
Arabic, 445–46
Aramean, 262–63
astronomy, Greek, 136, 484–86, 495
Atargatis, 262
Aten, 176–77
Athaliah, and Phoenicia, 298
Athens, 488–91, 496
Athirat, 152, 157–59
Augustus, and Greece, 498–99
Avaris, 172–73, 179
Azarba'al Inscription, 284–85
Azariah, and Edom, 335

Baal
and Egypt, 179
and Hadad, 260
and Philistia, 362, 374–75
and Ugarit, 146, 151–60
Ba'alat of Byblos, 289–92
Baal Cycle, 146, 155–58
Ba'al of Tyre, 303–5
Baal Sapan, 145
Ba'al Shamem, 290
Baasha, and Aram, 244
Babel, in the Bible, 103, 108–9
Babylon (city), 107–13, 401
and Amorites, 8–9, 12–15
and Assyria, 104
bāb ilim, 107–8
and Cyrus II, 134–35
expansion of, 128–29
in Genesis, 102
Hittite sacking of, 201
and Jews, 498
KÁ.DINGIR.RA, 107
Babylonia, 107–37
and Ammon, 319–20
and Arabia, 426–32, 436–47
and Arameans, 256

and Assyria, 32–38, 43–44, 48–57, 62–63, 68–69, 80–83
and Edom, 337–38
and Egypt, 174–75, 187
and Greece, 483–86, 493
and Hittites, 201, 209
and Moab, 328–29
and Persia, 389, 392–95, 398–99
and Philistia, 367–68
and Phoenicia, 305
Babylonian Chronicle, 32–33, 54–56, 90
Bahrain, ancient, 428–29
Balaam son of Beor, 348
Balawat Gates, 80
Balua Stela, 322–23
Bay, 180, 190
Bāzu, 430–31
bedouin, 420–21
Beirut, 291–92
Ben-Hadad, 244, 248–50, 253
Berossus, 126
Bible
and Ammon, 317–22
Amorites in, 15–17, 22–23
and Arabia, 434–36, 439–40, 456–64
and "Aram," 234–35
and Arameans, 229–30
and Assyria, 32–33, 82–104, 476–77
and Babylonia, 108–9
and Edom, 333–38
and Egypt, 189–95
and Hittites, 226–27
and Moab, 325–29
and Persia, 401, 487
and Philistia, 354–62, 375
and Phoenicia, 296–98
and Rameses, 179
and Transjordanian deities, 346–48
and Ugaritic religion, 151–53
and Ugaritic texts, 153–66
bichrome ware, 369–70
Binu Sim'al, and Amorites, 13–14, 18, 22, 25–26
Binu Yamina, and Amorites, 9, 18, 25–26

Bishri, Mount, and Arameans, 236–38
Bīt-Adini, 239–40, 247–48
Bīt-Baḫiāni, 243–46
Bīt-Zamani, 245–46, 260
British Museum, and Assyrian archaeology, 33–34, 78
burial
Arabian, 428–29
Assyrian, 73–74
Burnaburiaš II, 43
Busayra, 336–39
Byblos, 284–91, 296

Cadmus, and Phoenicians, 271–73
Calah, 45, 71
in Genesis, 102
See also Kalah; Kalhu; Nimrud
calendar, Ugaritic and Hebrew, 161–62
Cambyses, 379–80, 384, 400, 486
and Phoenicia, 305–6
Canaan, Canaanites
vs. Amorites, 2, 15–17
and Hittites, 227
peoples of, 1–3, 15–17
and Philistines, 364, 369, 375
and Ugarit, 139–43
Canaanite (language)
and Transjordanian languages, 339–40
Caphtor, and Philistia, 355, 362
Carchemish, 319
and Arameans, 238–43
and Hittites, 205–6, 222–23, 226
Carthage, 298, 305–7, 495
and Greece, 479–80
and Phoenicia, 293
Chaldeans, 136
and Arameans, 256–58
and Babylonia, 109, 119, 124–26
See also Arameans
chariots, in the Assyrian military, 59

Chemosh, 342, 346–47
  and Moab, 325–27
chronology
  Assyrian, 39–40
  Babylonian, 110
  Egyptian, 171
  Hittite, 200–201
  Sabean, 450–52
Cilicia, 222–25, 472
cities. *See* urban centers
coins
  Greek, 493
  and Persia, 408–13
colonialism
  Greek, 478–81
  Phoenician, 275–76
commerce. *See* trade
Constantinople, 499
constellations, 485
council, divine, 152–53, 156, 290
Covenant Code and Babylonian law, 114–15, 136
Crete, 469–71, 481
culture
  Ammonite, 320
  Amorite, 17–21
  Arabian, 421–25
  Aramean, 257–59
  Assyrian, 57–82
  Babylonian, 136–37
  Hittite, 216–22
  Phoenician, 275
  Transjordanian, 339–50
  Ugaritic, 139–43, 151–53
cuneiform
  and Amorites, 5n9, 8, 12
  and Arabia, 428, 441–43
  and Assyrian prophecy, 33–35, 39, 44, 88
  in Babylonia, 133–34, 338–39, 401
  and Greece, 484–86
  Hittite, 202, 216, 225–26, 469, 473
  in the Levant, 83–84
  and Ugaritic alphabet, 143, 153–54, 278n29, 475
Cush, and Arabia, 458–59
Cyprus
  and Greece, 473, 483
  and Phoenicia, 292–93

Cyrus (II) the Great, 134–35, 387, 401
  and Egypt, 187–88
  and Greece, 486–87

Dagan/Dagon, 355–58, 362, 375
  and Amorites, 18
  and Ugarit, 146, 166
Damascus, 300–301
  and Aram, 235–36, 243–56
  and Assyria, 318
  and Edom, 334–35
Daniel
  in Babylonia, 134
  and Danil, 139, 159–60
  and Greece, 498
Danil, 139, 159–61
Darius I, 379, 384–92, 399–402, 407, 411–13
  and Greece, 486–88, 493
Darius III, 412–13
Daskyleion, 405–6
David
  and Ammon, 317
  and Arameans, 243
  as conqueror, 15–16
  and Edom, 333, 343
  and Hattusili III, 226
  and Kirta, 159
  and Moab, 325
  and Philistia, 355, 358–62
Death/Mot (deity), 153, 156, 158
Dedan, 447–49, 460–63
democracy, Greek, 490
Democritus, 490
deportation
  Assyria's use of, 62–65, 83
  Babylonian, 133–34
deuterocanonical literature, and Assyria, 104
Deuteronomy, and Assyrian vassal treaties, 55, 96–98
  love in treaty language, 96
  loyalty in treaty language, 96–97
Dhana, Wadi, 453–54
Dhu-Ghābat, 449
Dibon (Dhiban), 325–27, 349–50
Dilmun, 426–32

diplomacy
  Babylonian, 117
  Egyptian, 174–75
  Hittite, 209–10
divination
  Assyrian, 74
  Hittite, 220
  Ugaritic, 163
Diyala River, 37
Dumah, 434–39
Dumaitic inscriptions, 421–22
Dur-Sharrukin (Khorsabad), 37, 48–50
  excavation of, 33–35
  in Genesis, 102

Ebabbar temple, 123–24
economy
  Assyrian, 64–68
  Persian, 413
  Transjordanian, 311, 315–16, 319, 330–32
  See also trade
Edom
  art of, 344–45
  in the Iron Age, 329–39
  religion of, 347–50
Edomite (language), 342–43
education, Greek, 490–95, 499
Egypt, 169–96
  and the alphabet, 276–77, 423
  and Ammon, 318–19, 343
  and Amorites, 23–26
  and Arabia, 434, 441
  and Arameans, 242–43, 263–64
  and Assyria, 43, 52–54, 92, 103
  and Babylonia, 117–18, 127–28
  and Edom, 330–31
  and Greece, 471–73, 483–87, 494–96
  and Hittites, 204–10, 213–15
  and the Late Bronze Age *Koinē*, 468–69
  and Moab, 322
  and Persia, 380, 388, 392–400, 404
  and Philistia, 362–68
  and Phoenicia, 287–88, 296, 306–7

Index of Subjects   523

and Transjordan, 311–13
and Ugarit, 141–42, 148–49
Ekron, 367–68, 373–74
El
  and Ammon, 343, 346–48
  and Ugarit, 151–65
Elam, 53–54, 236
Elamites
  and Babylonia, 118–20
  and Persia, 388, 393
  and Ur, 111
Elephantine, 400–402
Eliakim, and Egypt, 187
Eliba'al Inscription, 287–90
Elisha, and Ugaritic sorcerers, 163
Empedocles, 490
Enlil, and Aššur, 69
Enuma Elish (Babylonian Epic of Creation), 120–21, 132, 135, 156
Ephesus, 487
Eratosthenes of Alexandria, 495
Erra, 122
Esagila, 118–20, 131–32
Esarhaddon, 51–54, 68, 74, 125, 263
  and Arabia, 430–31, 437
  and Edom, 335
  and Egypt, 185
  and Moab, 328
  and Phoenicia, 302–4
  and prophecy, 87–88
  and treaties, 95–98
Eshmunazar Sarcophagus inscription, 291–92
Eshnunna, and Amorites, 8–9, 12–14
Esther, 487
Etemenanki, 131
Ethbaal, 298
Etruscans, and Greece, 475, 484
Euclid, 495
Euphrates River, and Assyrian geography, 37
Euripides, 489
Eusebius of Caesarea, 294, 295
exile, as a mass deportation, 62–63

exodus, historicity of, 189–91
extispicy, in Assyrian religion, 74
Ezekiel, and the Poem of Erra, 122

families
  in Assyria, 67, 71
  and Transjordanian religion, 347–48
  Ugaritic, 161, 165
Faynan, 336–37
  and mining, 331–34
figurines, Transjordanian, 345, 349
fortifications, Assyrian, 59–60
furniture, and Assyrian art, 81

Gardiner, Alan, and the alphabet, 276–77
Gath, 374–75
Gaza, 365–66
Gedaliah, 132
Genesis
  and Arabia, 458–61
  and "Aram," 234–35
  and Assyria, 102–3
  and Babylonia, 135–36
  and Philistia, 355–56
geography
  and Arabia, 417–21
  of Assyria, 37–39
  of Babylonia, 107–10, 118, 127
  Egyptian, 169–71
  and Hittites, 197–98
  of Persia, 379–81
  and Philistia, 353–54, 357
  Transjordanian, 309–14
  and Ugarit, 139–46
German Oriental Society, and Assyrian archaeology, 35
Geshem the Arab, 439
Gilgamesh Epic, 115–17
  Amurrû in, 9–10
God. See Yahweh/Yhwh
goddesses
  in Philistine religion, 360–62, 371–75
  See also Anat; Astarte; Atargatis; Ishtar; Kubaba; Tiamat

gods
  Arabian, 438, 445, 449–50, 456
  Aramean, 259, 445
  Assyrian, 38–39, 64, 69–70, 85
  Babylonian, 120
  Greek, 273, 484
  Hittite, 204, 218–21
  Mesopotamian, 19
  Phoenician, 273, 290–91
  Transjordanian, 348
  Ugaritic, 157
  See also moon god; sun god
Goliath, 358–59
Great Hymn to the Aten, 191
Greece, 467–500
  and Ammon, 322
  and Arabia, 420, 429–30, 451, 456–57
  and Assyria, 33, 60
  and Babylonia, 126, 136
  and Egypt, 186–89
  and Hittites, 224
  and Moab, 329
  and Persia, 381–83, 391–95, 403–5, 411–13
  and Phoenicia, 270–76, 282–83, 294–95, 306–8
Gregory the Great, on art, 79
Gyges, 477–78, 482, 491

Hadad, 252–53, 259–63
Hadadezer, 243, 248–51
Hadad Statue, 259–60
Ḥaḍramawt, 455–59, 462
Hagar, and Arabia, 460
Ḥagarānu, 425
Hamath, 248–49, 253–56
Hammurabi, 112–15, 126–29, 201
  and Assyrian kingship, 76–77
Hammurabi, Code of, 44, 113–15
Hana, and Amorites, 12–14, 22–26
Hanun, 317
Hanunu, 94, 366
"Harper Letters," 36
Harran (Haran), religion of, 18

Harran Inscriptions, 442–43
Hatti
  and Babylonia, 127–28
  and Egypt, 174–75
Hattusa, 198–201, 204, 207, 211, 214–16
Hattusili I, 198–203
Hattusili III, 208–13, 226
Havilah, 459
Hazael, 249–53, 260, 300
  and Ammon, 318
  and Edom, 334
  and Greece, 477
  and Moab, 327
  and Philistia, 361, 375
Hebat, 221
Hebrew
  and Arameans, 229–30
  and Transjordanian languages, 340–43
hegemony
  Assyrian, 85–86, 114–15, 302–4, 327–28
  Babylonian, 127–28
hellenization, 494–98
  and Egypt, 188–89
herding
  in Assyria, 66
  Transjordanian, 311, 315–16, 330
  See also pastoralism
ḥerem, 157
Herihor, 182
Herodes, 498
Hezekiah
  and Assyria, 49–51, 59, 91–94
  and Babylonia, 125
  and Egypt, 185, 194
  and Kirta, 159
  and Moab, 328
  and Philistia, 366–67
hieroglyphics
  and the alphabet, 276–77
  vs. cuneiform, 225–26
Hiram, 296–98, 301
historiography
  Assyrian vs. Hebrew, 89–102
  Hittite, 216
  Phoenician, 294–95
history
  of Arabia, 421–25
  of Arameans, 243–57
  of Assyria, 31–36, 40–57
  and the Bible, 189–91
  of Egypt, 171–89
  of Persia, 379–81, 411–13
Hittites, 197–228
  vs. Amorites, 2, 15–16
  and Arameans, 238–41
  and Assyria, 42–43
  and Babylonia, 115
  and Egypt, 177–79, 182
  and famine, 213–15
  festivals, Hittite, 217–20
  and Greece, 469–72
  treaties of, 97
  and Ugarit, 149–51, 164
Homer, 481–82
  on Phoenicians, 271
Horemheb, 177–78
Hoshea, and Assyria, 48
household, divine, 152–53
Hurrians, 197–228
  and Amorites, 11
  and Ugarit, 148
Hyksos, 469–70
  and Egypt, 172–73, 179–80, 190

iconography
  Greek, 480–81
  Persian, 404–11
  See also art
Iliad, 481–82
Illuyanka, 217–19
Inab, Martu in, 20–21
incense, Arabian, 424–25, 432, 457
Incense Kingdoms, 420–21, 455
inscriptions
  Arabian, 419–25, 438–39, 442–43, 447–63
  and Aram, 235, 237–42, 246, 250–54, 259–63
  Assyrian, 34–36, 39–40, 44–54, 58–63, 73–79, 91–94, 100
  Babylonian, 117–23, 126–29
  and Greece, 470–72, 476–78
  Hittite, 211–16, 222–26
  Persian, 383–86, 399–405, 408–9
  and Philistia, 362–65, 372–73
  Phoenician, 267–68, 276–94
  Transjordanian, 312–13, 316–18, 321, 325–28, 339–43, 346–48
  Ugaritic, 166
Instruction of Amenemope, 191
irrigation, 397, 453–54
Isaac, and Philistines, 356
Isaiah
  and Assyria, 33, 49–52, 57–60, 79, 87–88, 92, 125
  and Babylonia, 125, 132
  on Cyrus II, 135
Ishmael, birth narrative of, 100
Ishmaelites, 460–61
Ishtar
  and Assyrian religion, 69–70, 86–88
  and Sargon, 99
Ishtar Gate, 129–31
Isin, and Babylonia, 111–12, 122
Israel
  and Ammon, 317–19
  and Amorites, 22
  and Aram, 248–51, 255
  and Assyria, 46–49, 53
  and Babylonia, 135–37, 483
  and Edom, 334–35, 343
  and Egypt, 189–95
  and the Enuma Elish, 120–21
  and Greece, 468, 496–98
  and Hyksos, 172–73
  and mass deportation, 63
  and Moab, 346
  origin of, 1–3
  and Philistia, 360–61, 371–72, 376
  and Phoenicia, 298
  as tribal pastoralists, 29
  and Ugarit, 139–43
ivory, in Assyrian art, 81

Jabbok, 316–17
Jael, 104, 141, 161
Jebel Bishri, as Amorite homeland, 6, 9
Jehoahaz
  and Aram, 252
  and Assyria, 249

Jehoiakim
  and Edom, 337
  and Egypt, 187
  and Moab, 328–29
Jehoram (Israel)
  and Phoenicia, 298
Jehoram/Joram (Judah)
  and Aram, 250–51
  and Philistia, 361
Jehoshaphat
  and Edom, 333
  and Philistia, 361
Jehu
  and Aram, 249–51
  and Assyria, 46
Jeremiah, and Babylonia, 109
Jeroboam I, and Egypt, 184, 189
Jeroboam II
  and Aram, 254
  and Assyria, 47
Jerusalem
  and Ammon, 319–20
  and Arabia, 461–62
  and Assyria, 51–52, 59–60, 476–77
  and Babylonia, 187, 483
  and Edom, 338
  and Greece, 496–98
  and Persia, 401–2
  and Phoenicia, 296–98
  Sennacherib's siege of, 91–95
  and Sheshonq I, 184
Jesus and the Syro-Phoenician woman, 308
Jezebel, as a Phoenician, 298
Jezireh, 235, 238, 241–46, 257–58
Joash
  and Aram, 252
  and Assyria, 300
Job, and Kirta, 159
Joktan, and Arabia, 458–59
Jonathan, and Philistia, 360
Joseph, 189–91
  birth narrative of, 100
  and Midian, 434
Joshua
  and Israel's origin, 1, 15–16
  and Philistia, 355

Josiah, 101
  and Assyria, 55
  and the Deuteronomic Code, 97
  and Egypt, 187–89
Judah
  and Ammon, 318–22
  and Arabia, 439, 461–62
  and Aram, 251–52, 255
  and Assyria, 47–55, 59, 79, 81–104
  and Babylonia, 109, 125–26, 132–37
  and Edom, 333–38, 343
  and Egypt, 184, 187–95
  and Greece, 496–98
  and Hammurabi's Laws, 114–15
  and mass deportation, 63
  and Moab, 328–29
  and Persia, 401–2
  and Philistia, 360–62, 366–67, 373, 376
  and Phoenicia, 296–98

Kadmos, vs. Cadmus, 272
Kalah, 33, 36–37
kaldū, kaldu, 124–26
Kalhu, 45–47, 56, 74. *See also* Calah; Kalah; Nimrud
Kanes(h), 8, 35–36, 197–98
Karak Plateau, 322–23
Karduniash, 107
Karib'īl Watar, 455–57
Karkamis. *See* Carchemish
kārum, 42, 49, 67, 197
Kaska, 203–7
  and Hittites, 216, 222
Kassites, 115–19
Keturah
  and Arabia, 458–60
  and Midian, 434–36
Kharga Oasis, 395–97
Khirbet en-Nahas (KEN), 332–33, 337
Kilamuwa Inscription, 293
kings
  and prophecy, 87–88
  as temple-builders, 100–101
kingship
  Assyrian, 75–82, 476–77
  Babylonian, 128–29

  Egyptian, 175–78, 193–95
  Hittite, 220–21, 224–25
  Persian, 383–87, 399–400
  Ugaritic, 151, 158–61
kinship
  Ammonite, 315–18
  Edomite, 332
  Moabite, 325–26
Kir, 236–37
Kirta, 155, 159, 162
kispu rite, 72–73
Kition Bowl, 293
Koinē, Bronze Age, 468–73
Kothar, 153, 156–57, 160
Kubaba, 261–62
kudurru, 116–17, 121–23
Kültepe. *See* Kanes(h)
Kurigalzu, 116
Kurkh Monolith, 45, 58, 248–50, 299–300, 318n21
Kurunta, 211, 222
Kuyunjik, excavation of. *See* Nineveh: excavation of

Lab'ayu, and Amorites, 23–26
Lachish, and Assyria, 51, 58, 79
Lagash, 427
Lamentation over the Destruction of Sumer and Ur, 111
language
  Ammonite, 340
  and Amorites, 3, 9–14, 27–28
  and Arameans, 263–64
  and Assyria, 38–41
  and Greece, 468–69, 493, 497–99
  and Hittites, 216, 225–26
  and Persian diversity, 381–83, 391–92, 403, 409
  Phoenician, 279–84, 293–94
  Transjordanian, 339–43
  and Ugarit, 143, 146–48, 153
Laqē, 245–46
Larsa, and Babylonia, 111–12
laws
  Assyrian, 44, 97–98
  Babylonian, 113–15, 136
  Hittite, 202, 218
Layard, Austen Henry, and Assyrian archaeology, 33

Letter of Aristeas, 497n42
Levant
  and Arameans, 242–43
  and Egypt, 23–24, 173–75, 185–86
  peoples of the, 1–3
Leviathan, 139, 153, 158
Libyans, and Egypt, 179–85
Liḥyan, 444, 447–49
līmu, lists of, 89–90
Linear A, 470, 471
Linear B, 470, 471, 473
lists
  eponym, 89–91
  king
    Assyrian, 39–41, 44, 89–90, 304
    Babylonian, 112, 144
  records, of Israel and Judah, 90–91
  Ugaritic, 144, 147–48, 163
literature
  Aramean, 263–64
  Assyrian, 83
  Babylonian, 115–22
  Greek, 481–82, 489–90, 496, 499
  Ugaritic, 153–66
lmlk seals, 194–95
Lucian, 293n74
Ludlul bel nemeqi, 121
Luli (king of Sidon), 50, 302
Luwians
  and Arameans, 239–40, 248, 253, 257–63
  and Greece, 474, 478–80
  and Hittites, 216, 220–26
  language of, 222–26
Lydia, 477–78, 486

Maccabees, 498
Macedonia, 493–94
Magnes, 482n30
Maʿin, 455–56
Makā, 419–20, 432
Manasseh, and Assyria, 52–53
Marathon, 488
Marduk
  in Assyrian religion, 68–70
  vs. Baal, 156
  and Babylonia, 118–22, 128–32
  and Cyrus II, 135

Marduk-apla-iddina II, 125
Mari
  and Amorites, 3, 7–15, 18–22, 25–28
  and Arabia, 427, 430
  and Aram, 253
  and Babylonia, 110–12
  and nomadism, 232
  and Ugarit, 148
Mārib, 453–55, 462
marriage
  diplomatic, 94, 112, 117, 149–50, 174–79, 204–5, 209–10, 222
  sacred, 98–99, 162
Marriage of Martu, 19–21
MAR.TU, 7n14, 111
Martu, as Amorite god, 19–21
Martu/mar-tu, 4, 7, 15
  vs. amurrum, 5n9
marzēaḥ, 163–65
mathematics, Greek, 495
Matiʿʿel, 254–55
Medes, and Assyria, 55–56
medicine, Ugaritic vs. Hebrew, 163
Medinet Habu, 363–65
Megiddo, 187
Megiddo Ivory, 192
Memphis, 185
Menahem, and Assyria, 47
Menander of Ephesus, 295, 297, 490
Merenptah, 179–80, 213–15
  and Philistia, 363
  and Ugarit vs. Israel, 141–42
Merenptah Stela, 142
Merodach-baladan I, 125, 436–37
Merodach-baladan II, 124
Mesha, 325–27, 346–49
Mesha (Stela) Inscription (MI), 325–27, 341, 342, 346, 349–50
Meshwesh tribe, 183
Mesopotamia, 38
  and Akkad, 41
  Amorites in, 5–7, 16, 19–21, 28–29
  and Greece, 484–85
  peoples of, 1–3
  religion in, 68

Meydancıkkale, 408
Middle Assyrian Laws, 98
Midian, and Arabia, 432–37
migration
  of Amorites, 3–4, 25
  and Arameans, 28, 230–31, 234
  in Babylonia, 118–19, 122
  and Egypt, 179–80
  and Transjordan, 311–12
Milcom, 343, 346–49
Miletus, 471, 487–88
military
  of the ʿapiru, 24–26
  Assyrian, 45–46, 57–61, 78–90
  and history, 476
Minaeans, 455–56
Minoans, 469–71
Mittani
  and Arameans, 241
  and Assyria, 42–43
  and Egypt, 174–76
  and Hittites, 177, 203–9
  and Ugarit, 148
Moab
  art of, 344
  in the Iron Age, 322–29
  religion of, 346–50
Moabite language, 341–42
monochrome ware, 369
monotheism, 69, 101
moon god
  and Amorites, 18, 21
  See also Sîn
Moses, 189
  birth account of, 99
  and Israel's origin, 1, 15
Mujib, 323–27
mukarrib, 450–51, 456–57
Mursili I, 200–201
Mursili II, 206–7
Mursili III, 43, 208–9, 212
Muwatalli I, 202–3
Muwatalli II, 179, 207–8, 221
Mycenae, 359, 470–73, 484
  and pottery, 369, 433

Nabateans, and Moab, 329
Nabātu, 425
Nabayat, 437–38, 444, 460, 461

Index of Subjects

Nabonidus, 124, 134–35
  and Arabia, 419, 432, 442–47
  and Edom, 338–39
Nabonidus Chronicle, 442–43
Nabopolassar, 55–56, 126–27
Nabû, 77, 132
  in Assyrian religion, 68–70
Nabû-apla-iddina, 123–24
Nahash, 317
names, Ugaritic vs. Hebrew, 139–41
Naram-Sin, 12, 41, 75, 469
narû. See *kudurru*
nasīku, 256–58
Nebuchadnezzar I, 119–22
  and Ammon, 319–20
  and Arabia, 419, 431, 441, 463
  and Edom, 337
  and Greece, 483
  in Judith, 104
  and Moab, 328
  and Phoenicia, 305
Nebuchadnezzar II, 57, 112, 126–30
  in the Bible, 109
  and Philistia, 367–68
Neco, Pharaoh, 127
necropolis, Bahrain, 428–29
Nefertiti, 177, 180
Negev, and Edom, 336
Nehushtan, and Ugaritic medicine, 163
Nekau II, 187–89
Neo-Assyrian Empire, 32–33, 36, 39, 44–57, 76. *See also* Assyria
Nigmaddu III, 213
Nile River, 169–71
Nimrod
  in the Bible, 102–3, 108–9
  in Judaism, Christianity, and Islam, 103
Nimrud
  art in, 78
  excavation of, 33, 36
  ziggurat in, 71
  See also Calah; Kalah; Kalhu
Nineveh, 39, 41, 45
  as Assyria's capital, 50–53
  in the Bible, 102–4, 125

  excavation of, 33–35
  fall of, 56–57
  and Greece, 477–78
  location of, 37
Nippur, 133
Niqmaddu I, 148–49
Niqmaddu III, 150
Niqmepa, 149–50
nomadism
  and Edom, 330
  models of, 230–34
  in Transjordan, 313
nomads
  Amorites as, 13–14, 22, 25
  Amorites not as, 4, 7, 26
  Arabs as, 418–21
  Arameans not as, 27–28
Nubia
  and Assyria, 53
  and Egypt, 173–74, 178, 181–82, 185–87
Numushda, and Martu, 20–21

oaths, in Assyrian treaties, 95
Odyssey, 482
Og, as an Amorite, 16
olives, and Ekron, 373
Olmstead, Albert Ten Eyck, on Persian history, 381–82
Olympic Games, 479
omens, in Assyrian religion, 74–75
Omri
  and Moab, 325
  and Phoenicia, 298
oracles, Assyrian vs. Hebrew, 86–88
Orientalizing, Greek, 478–81
origins
  of Arameans, 230–43
  of Israel, 1–3
Orontes River, and Amorites, 10
Osorkon the Elder, 183

Palace Decrees, 44
palaces
  Assyrian, 66, 78–81
  Persian, 387–91
  Ugaritic, 146, 151
Palastu, 365
Palistin, 224, 240, 375n71

Panehsy, 181
Papyrus Harris I, 363–64
parallelism, 154. *See also* poetry, biblical
Parmenides, 490
Pasargadae, 387
pastoralism
  and Amorites, 4–7, 13–22, 29
  and Arameans, 27–28, 231–33, 256–58
  Midian, 434
Pekah
  and Aram, 255
  and Assyria, 48
Peloponnesian War, 491
Pentapolis, 356, 362, 370
Persepolis, 388–90, 397, 408
Persia, 379–415
  and Ammon, 320–22
  and Arabia, 432
  and storage depots, 398–99
  diversity of, 381–83, 388–89, 403–4, 487
  and Edom, 339
  and Egypt, 187–88
  and Greece, 486–88, 491–93
  and Moab, 329
  and Phoenicia, 305–6
  residences, of Persian kings, 387–91
  and taxes, 391–95
Petra, 337
Philistia, 353–77
  and Greece, 473–74
Philistines
  Aegean origin of, 353, 359–64, 369–75
  and Arameans, 240–42
  in Canaan, 2
  and Hittites, 224, 226
Philo of Byblos, 294–95
philosophy, Greek, 490–93
Phoenicia, 267–308
  and Arabia, 429–30, 463
  and Assyria, 60, 67
  and Egypt, 192–93
  and Greece, 478–80
  and Persia, 395
Phoenician language
  alphabet, 271–73, 276–81
  vs. Aramaic, 281–82, 294

as a Canaanite language, 280–82
vs. Hebrew, 283–84
matres lectionis, as not in Phoenician, 282–83
orthography, 282–83
philology, 279–80
script, 277–78, 286–89, 293–94, 340
verbs, Phoenician, 283–84
Pithom, 191
Piy, 185
Piyamaradu, 207, 210
Plato, 486, 492, 495–96
poetry, biblical
 and Egyptian, 191
 and Ugaritic, 154–55
polis, 478–79, 491
politics
 Edomite, 332
 Moabite, 324–25
Polyaenus, 382n10
Porphyry of Tyre, 294
pottery
 Arabian, 433, 452–53, 462
 Edomite, 333, 336–39
 Philistine, 368–70, 374–75
prayer
 in Assyrian religion, 71–72
 Ugaritic, 162
priestess, as Sargon's mother, 98–99
priests
 Egyptian, 181–82
 Hittite, 218
Processional Way, 129–32
propaganda, Assyria's use of, 61–62, 76, 79, 476–77
prophecy, Assyrian, 74, 86–88
prophecy, biblical
 on Assyria, 103–4
 vs. Assyrian, 86–88
 on Babylonia, 136
Protagoras, 490
Proverbs, and Instruction of Amenemope, 191
Proverbs of Ahiqar, 263–64
Psalms
 and Assyrian prayers, 72
 and Egyptian kingship, 193–94
 and the Enuma Elish, 121

Psamtek I, 186–87
Psamtek II, 187–89
 and Greece, 483
Pseudo-Aristotle, 393
pseudoautobiography, 98
Psusennes I, 182–84
Psusennes II, 183–84
Pughat, 160–61
purulli, 217–19

Qadesh
 and Arameans, 242
 and Egypt, 178–79
 and Hittites, 206–8
Qadmos, vs. Cadmus, 272
Qataban, 451–57
Qatna, and Amorites, 9–10
Qaus/Qos, 347–50
Qedar, 434–39, 444, 461–63
queens
 Arabian, 461–62
 Qedarite, 438
Qurayya, 432–34

Raamah, 459–60, 464
Rabbah, as Amman, 317–18
rab šāqēh, 64, 90–93
rāgintu, 86
Rameses (city), 179, 191
Ramesses I, 178
Ramesses II, 178–79, 208–10, 213–15, 226
 and Edom, 330
 and Moab, 322
 and Philistia, 363
 and Shasu, 313
Ramesses III, 180–81, 215
 and Edom, 330
 and Philistia, 363–65
 and Shasu, 313
Ramesses XI, 181–82
Rassam, Hormuzd, and Assyrian archaeology, 33
Rassam Cylinder, 91
Ras Shamra, 143, 166
Re, 176. See also sun god
reliefs, Assyrian, 78
religion
 of Amorites, 17–19
 Arabian, 438, 445–49
 Aramean, 259–63
 Assyrian, 68–75, 84–85

 in Babylonia, 120, 123–24, 131–32
 Egyptian, 169, 175–78
 Greek, 473
 Hittite, 204, 211–12, 217–21
 Persian, 386–87, 400–404
 Philistine, 361–62, 371–75
 Transjordanian, 346–50
 of Ugarit, 151–53, 161–64
Rephaim, 150, 153–55, 161–63
Rezin, 255
rhetoric, Greek, 492–93, 499
Rim-Sin of Larsa, 112
rituals
 Assyrian, 71
 Hittite, 220
 Ugaritic, 161–63
Rome, and Greece, 484, 495–99
Rowton, M. B., on nomadism, 231–32
Royal Chronicle, 442–43

Saba, Sabaeans, 450–55, 459–62
Sabaic inscriptions, 422–23
Sahr, 261–63
Sais, 186–87
Samaria
 and Assyria, 48–49, 318
 and Persia, 402
Šammuramat, 46
Samsi, 435–38, 442
Samsi-Addu, and Amorites, 11
Samson, and Philistia, 356–57
Sanchuniathon, 294–95
Sapanu, Mount, 145
sarcophagus, Persian, 405–7. See also Ahiram Sarcophagus; Eshmunazar Sarcophagus inscription
Sardis, 487
Sargon (the Great), 12, 41, 200, 469
 birth account of, 98–100
Sargon II, 48–52, 58–60, 63–66, 69, 83, 94, 98, 125
 and Arabia, 419, 426, 436, 442, 451
 and Aram, 256
 and Greece, 476
 and Moab, 328
 and Philistia, 366
 and Phoenicia, 302

satrapies, Persian, 391–93
Saul
  and Ammon, 317
  and Astarte, 162
  and Philistia, 355, 358–60
scribes, 19, 59, 108, 122, 227, 231, 279, 285–87, 293
  curriculum of, 113, 133, 166, 199, 217
  and language, 8–14, 83–84, 117, 183n13
Scythians, and Persia, 407
Sea, in the Baal Cycle, 156–57
Sealand, 126n60
seals
  Assyrian, 79–80
  Persian, 405–6
  Transjordanian, 345
Sea Peoples, 118, 150
  and Arameans, 240–42
  and Egypt, 179–82
  and Greece, 473
  and Hittites, 215, 224–27
  and Philistines, 362–65, 371n55
Seir, 329–31
Seleucids, 496–98
Sennacherib, 50–51, 56, 59, 63–64, 76–77, 125
  and Arabia, 419, 436–37, 451
  and art, 78–81
  and Egypt, 185
  and Greece, 476–77
  and Phoenicia, 302
  siege of, 91–95
Septuagint, 497–98
Sethnakht, 180
Seti I, 178, 208
Shabaqo, 185
Shabwa, 457–58
Shalmaneser I, 179, 209
Shalmaneser II, 45
Shalmaneser III, 45–46, 58, 80
  and Ammon, 318n21
  and Arabia, 417, 425
  and Arameans, 239–40, 247–52
  and Phoenicia, 299–300
Shalmaneser V, 125, 366
Shamash, 261–63
  in Assyrian religion, 70
  in Babylonia, 113, 123–24
Shamshi-Adad I, 41, 75, 112
Shamshi-Adad V, 46
Shamshi-ilu, 46, 254
Shasu, 313
  and Edom, 330–31
  and Moab, 322–23
Sheba, 459–64
Shem, and Aram, 234
Sheshonq I/Shishak, 183–84, 189, 287–89
  and Ammon, 318
  and Edom, 332
Shipitba'al Inscription, 288–90
Shulgi of Ur, 110–11
  and Amorites, 6
Shuruppak (Fara), and Amorites, 6–7
Shutruk-Nahhunte, 118
Sidon, 273–75, 291–92, 297–98, 302–3
  and Assyria, 50
siege warfare, Assyrian, 58–60
Sihon, as an Amorite, 16
Sîn, 70, 261, 299, 442, 445, 457
Sinai, and Arabia, 434
"Sin of Sargon," 50
šipir maḫḫe, 87
slaves
  in Assyria, 67–68
  exiles as, 63–64
Smith, George, and Assyriology, 34–35, 40
Socrates, 490–92
solar disk, 70, 192–94, 221, 261, 291, 386, 404
soldiers, types of, 58–59
Solomon
  administration of, 77, 165
  and Amorites, 16
  and Arabia, 461–63
  and Arameans, 243
  and Kirta, 159
  and Phoenicia, 296–98
  as temple-builder, 100–101
songs, Hurrian/Hittite, 217–18
sophistai, 490
Sophocles, 489
sources
  of Assyrian history, 32–33, 39–40, 79, 92–93
  of Persian history, 381–83
  of Philistine history, 362–68
  of Phoenician history, 269–76, 294–308
  of Ugaritic history, 146–49
Sparta, 488, 491
statues
  Assurnasirpal II, 78
  in Assyrian religion, 70
  Marduk, 118–20, 132
  Nabû, 132
  Sheshonq I, 287–88
  Transjordanian, 343–45
  See also Hadad Statue
storm god, 217, 220, 246, 260–61, 471
  Adad/Hadad, 70, 259, 260, 263
  of Aleppo, 223, 240, 254, 260
  Baal, 146, 152
  near Çineköy, 224
  Storm God of Hatti, 220, 221
"Story of Wenamun," 296
Subarian, and Amorites, 11
substitute king ritual, 74, 75
Südburg inscriptions, 213–16, 222
šulmu, and šālôm, 87
Sumer, and Babylonia, 107–16, 122
Sumerians, and Amorites, 5–8, 12, 19–21
summodeism, 70
Sumu-abum, 112
sun god, 152
  in Aram, 261–63
  and Egypt, 175–78, 192–94
  Hittite (Sun God and Sun Goddess), 211–13, 220–21
  and the lmlk seals, 194–95
  See also Shamash; solar disk
Sun-God Tablet, 123–24
Suppiliuliuma I, 149, 177, 204–6, 217, 221
Suppiliuliuma II, 212–17, 222
Susa, 388–91
Suteans, and Babylonia, 122–23
Sutû, and Arameans, 237–38
symmachy, Greek, 488
Syracuse, 495

Syria, 469–70
  Amorites in, 5–9, 16, 27–29
  and Arabia, 426–28, 441
  and Arameans, 229–30, 235–41, 247–48, 262
  and Assyria, 33, 41–42, 46–47
  and Egypt, 174, 180
  and Hittites, 200, 203–6, 222–27
  and Phoenicians, 273

Table of Nations, 108, 135, 234, 355, 459
Tabnit, inscription of, 291
Taharqo, 185–86, 189, 194
Taita, 223–24, 260
  and Arameans, 240–41
Tale of the Two Brothers, 191
Tanis, 182, 363, 394
Tarhuntassa, 207, 211, 214–15
Tarut Island, 427
Taurus Mountains, 37, 45
Tausret, 180, 190
Tawilan, 338–39
Taymā', 439–47, 463
  Jews in, 446–47
Taymanitic inscriptions, 421–22, 461
technē, 480–81
Telipinu, 202
Tell Dan Stela, 250–51
Tell Fekheriye Stela inscription, 246, 261, 263, 293–94
Tell Qasile, 370–71
Temanites, 245
temple-building accounts, 77, 100–101, 296–98
temples
  Assyrian, 70–71
  Greek, 489
  Hittite, 218
  at Medinet Habu, 363–65
  Philistine, 371
  Transjordanian, 348–50
  Ugaritic, 151
Tennes, 306–7
Terqa, religion of, 18
Teshub, 217, 221
Te'umman, 54
theater, Greek, 489–90, 496
Thebes, 172–73, 176–77, 181–82, 186

Thera, 470
Thermopylae, 488
Thutmose I, 173–74, 192
Thutmose II, 174n8
Thutmose III, 174, 192
Thutmose IV, 204
Tiamat, 120, 132
  and Genesis, 135
Tiglath-pileser I, 44, 100–101, 121–22
  and Arameans, 241–42
  and Phoenicia, 295
  tablet of, 34
Tiglath-pileser III, 47–48, 61–63, 69, 76, 93–94
  and Arabia, 419, 425–26, 435, 442, 461
  and Aram, 255–56
  and Edom, 335
  and Moab, 327
  and Philistia, 365–67
  and Phoenicia, 300–302
Tigris River, and Assyrian geography, 37
Til-Barsib, 239–40, 248–49
"Tobiah the Ammonite," 320–22
trade
  Arabian, 424–27, 432, 440, 454, 457, 462–63
  Assyrian, 42, 45, 67, 83, 94
  Greek, 474–75, 478–80
  Persian, 394–95, 412–13
  Transjordanian, 314–15, 319, 328–32, 335–36
tribes
  '*apiru* not as, 25–26
  Arameans as, 27–28
  Israel as, 29
tribute
  Assyrian use of, 45–50, 62, 91–92, 246–47, 300–301, 327–28, 335
  Babylonian use of, 127
  Persian use of, 391–94
Trinity, and Assyrian religion, 69
Trojan War, 472–73, 481–82
Tudhaliya I/II, 202–4, 217
Tudhaliya IV, 210–14
Tukulti-Ninurta I, 210–12

Tukulti-Ninurti II, and Arameans, 244–46
Tutankhamun, 177–78
Tyre, 273–75, 296–97, 300–308
  and Arabia, 463

Ugarit, 139–67
  and Amorites, 10
  and Babylonia, 118
  and Egypt, 175
  and Hittites, 205–6, 213
Ugaritic (language), 143, 146–48, 153, 166
  alphabet of, 278n29, 423
  legal texts, 164–65
  letters, 164
Ur
  and Amorites, 1–9, 12–15, 21, 111–12
  and Babylonia, 110–12
Urartu, and Assyria, 45–47, 52
urban centers
  Amorites in, 19–22, 25–28
  Arameans in, 27–28
  and Midian, 434
  and tribal nomads, 231–33
Uzziah, and Philistia, 361

vassals, Assyrian, 84–86, 95–98
Vassal Treaties of Esarhaddon, 95–98

"weapon of Aššur," 70
wisdom
  and Assyrian kingship, 76–77
  See also Proverbs, and Instruction of Amenemope; songs, Hurrian/Hittite
writing
  in Egypt, 468–69
  and Greece, 474–78
  See also cuneiform

Xenophanes, 482n29
Xerxes I, 306, 488

Yahweh/Yhwh
  and Assyria, 103–4
  in the Deuteronomic treaty, 96–97

and Hebrew prophecy,
    87–88
and the siege of Sennacherib, 92
as the sun god, 195
in the temple-building account, 101
and Transjordanian deities,
    346–48
Yalā, Wadi, 453
Yamani, 49
Yamhad, and Amorites, 9–10
Yamutbal, and Amorites, 26

Yehawmilk, inscription of,
    290–91
Yehimilk Inscription, 287–90
Ytpn, 160–61

zabbu/zabbatu, 87
Zagros Mountains, 37
Zakkur, 254
Zarqa, Wadi, 316–17
Zedekiah
    and Babylonia, 187
    and Edom, 337
    and Egypt, 189

Zeus, 273, 403, 481, 485, 489,
    496–98
ziggurats
    Assyrian, 71
    in Babylon, 131
Zimri-Lim
    and Amorites, 10–14, 18,
        22–24
    and Arabia, 427
    and Babylonia, 112
    and Ugarit, 148
Zincirli, 222, 225, 257, 261, 262
Zobah, 243

www.ingramcontent.com/pod-product-compliance
Lightning Source LLC
Chambersburg PA
CBHW071133300426
44113CB00009B/957